Hellenic Studies 99

The *Iliad* and the Oral Epic Tradition

Recent Titles in the Hellenic Studies Series

Blemished Kings
Suitors in the Odyssey, Blame Poetics, and Irish Satire

Greek Media Discourse from Reconstitution of Democracy to Memorandums of Understanding
Transformations and Symbolisms

Euripides' Ino
Commentary, Reconstruction, Text and Translation

Greek Language, Italian Landscape
Griko and the Re-storying of a Linguistic Minority

Lovers of the Soul, Lovers of the Body

Audible Punctuation
Performative Pause in Homeric Prosody

Who Am I?
(Mis)Identity and the Polis in Oedipus Tyrannus

Demetrios of Scepsis and His Troikos Diakosmos
Ancient and Modern Readings of a Lost Contribution to Ancient Scholarship

Homer's Thebes
Epic Rivalries and the Appropriation of Mythical Pasts

The Cypria

Homeric Imagery and the Natural Environment

Achilles Unbound
Multiformity and Tradition in the Homeric Epics

In Her Own Words
The Life and Poetry of Aelia Eudocia

Particles in Ancient Greek Discourse
Exploring Particle Use across Genres

Agamemnon, the Pathetic Despot
Reading Characterization in Homer

Singer of Tales
Third Edition

One Man Show
The Dynamics of Performance in the Iliad and Odyssey

http://chs.harvard.edu/chs/publications

THE *ILIAD* AND THE ORAL EPIC TRADITION

BY
KAROL ZIELIŃSKI

TRANSLATED BY
ANNA ROJKOWSKA

Center for Hellenic Studies
Trustees for Harvard University
Washington, DC
Distributed by Harvard University Press
Cambridge, Massachusetts, and London, England
2023

The Iliad and the Oral Epic Tradition
by Karol Zieliński

Published by The Center for Hellenic Studies, Trustees for Harvard University, Washington, DC
Distributed by Harvard University Press, Cambridge, Massachusetts and London, England
Printed by Gasch Printing, Odenton, MD
Cover Design: Joni Godlove

NATIONAL PROGRAMME FOR THE DEVELOPMENT OF HUMANITIES

The translation of this book was financed by the Ministry of Science and Higher Education of the Republic of Poland, as part of the National Program for the Development of the Humanities No. 0105/NPRH4/H3a/83/2016.

ISBN: 978-0-674-29243-7
Library of Congress Control Number: 2023944150

To Sława

παντοδαπῶς ἤ νικᾷ φῦλα γυναικῶν

Enough and too much has been written about the Epic Cycle. Upon scanty quotations and a jejune epitome a tedious literature has been built.

T. W. Allen (1908)

... the onus is now on oralists to demonstrate that there is any significant way in which the status of the Iliad as an oral-derived text precludes or limits the application of familiar interpretative strategies

Douglas L. Cairns (2001)

Table of Contents

Acknowledgements

I WOULD LIKE to express my heartfelt thanks to everyone who contributed to this book. First of all, I would like to thank its translator, Anna Rojkowska, who took care of the smallest details and consulted with me regarding the meaning of each ambiguous phrase. It would be difficult to imagine a better translator. It even seems to me that she has become infected with a passion for the problem of the functioning of oral culture. Carolyn Higbie, copyeditor of this book, put in a tremendous amount of work to ensure its clarity and conformance with the editorial rules of the series. On more than one occasion, she firmly but subtly straightened the path of my thoughts and insisted on the precision of expression. My thanks also go to Jill Curry Robbins and Bruce King for their contribution to the editing of the book. I am grateful to the Hellenic Series editorial board for selecting my work for publication in their series.

I am also very grateful to my family and friends who supported me in my work. In the first place, I would like to thank my wife Slawa, to whom have I dedicated the book, and what I wrote in the dedication is in no way exaggerated. Moreover, I would like to thank my (now grown-up) children, Aleksandra, Fryderyk, and Danuta, because in a way the book took away a part of their childhood. I know that my colleagues who, along with me, established the Center for Interdisciplinary Research on the Relationship between Oral and Written Cultures at the University of Wrocław, kept their fingers crossed for me. I want to thank them for their support.

Preface to the English Edition

THIS BOOK WAS written in Polish in 2012 and published in 2014 by Wydawnictwo Uniwersytetu Wrocławskiego (Wrocław University Publishing House). The prospect of translating the text into English gave me a chance to update and correct it. Since 2012, many important works dealing with the composition of the *Iliad*, the circumstances of its creation, and its relation with unpreserved oral traditions have been published. Though interesting and thought-provoking, these studies have not significantly influenced the shape of the concepts presented here. The reorganization of my argument seemed superfluous, especially as it risked a broader discussion and the insertion of new paragraphs, which would have disturbed the logical shape of the book. Therefore, in many cases, especially when it was necessary to mark the difference between my ideas and the positions of other scholars, I decided to confine myself to making a reference to the relevant studies in the footnotes. More recent books are discussed in the Introduction because it was difficult to insert new extensive references without re-writing the argument of the book. Some titles were unavailable to me or reached me too late, so I was not able to refer to them here in the way they deserve. I hope their authors will forgive me this omission.

At the time when the book was being written, discussion of the oral character of the Homeric poems was largely nonexistent in Poland. That was a great handicap, though it also presented certain advantages. I could follow the discussion from a distance, slowly formulating my own standpoint. At the beginning of this century, the views of the two most important schools in Homeric research—neoanalysis and oral theory—were very polarized and attempts to combine these positions seemed to me unsatisfactory and based on faulty premises. There was something that was lacking in both approaches and by attempting to discover what that was I came to the conclusion that the issues needed to be reconsidered—and more largely, that it was necessary to boldly reconstruct the oral tradition of the *Iliad* and redefine the understanding of the oral composition of that work. All the propositions presented in this book are closely interconnected, and individual theses profit from a comprehensive approach to the subject.

The field of Homeric research is vast. Given the length and scope of this particular study, it was not possible to present and comment upon the views of all scholars; such scrupulousness would have greatly cluttered the book. Rather, I tried to refer to opinions that were—in my opinion—the most characteristic or relevant to the argument. Sometimes I permited myself to attribute certain positions to a particular school, e.g. to neoanalysis, rather than to the scholar whose position became widely disseminated. I hope that these simplifications will not detract from the value of the arguments put forward in this book.

Keeping in mind the original scope of the publication, I refrained from introducing many corrections or from expanding it. In a book dealing with such broad topics as the composition of the *Iliad*, with so many research threads and problems, changes tend to have a domino effect: if you knock over one tile, the next one falls under its weight.

Having returned to my work after a few years, I now see the issues in a much broader context. If I were writing this book today, I would put more stress on some elements and would slightly reorganize the whole. But it wouldn't make sense to re-write the entirety. I have therefore decided to amplify the original a bit by adding a few paragraphs, with sufficient arguments to make my claims understandable, although I am aware that for many readers the issues would require more extensive explanation. I hope that in the future it will be possible to come back to these issues and to develop them properly.

Despite the passage of time since the original publication, I remain convinced of the proposals that I offer. Indeed, I now find further corroboration for them, especially in the comparative material. As well, my theses—though perhaps controversial—have met with approval, although rather more among folklorists and anthropologists than classical scholars. That disparity is likely due to my taking into account the particular phenomena of oral culture and looking to those phenomena for proof of my own claims. In recent years, the search for the middle way between *imitatio* and traditional referentiality has gained momentum and seems to parallel my ideas. Such studies assume that the functioning of allusions to specific events in the mythic *fabula* is a fact that can be analyzed, whereas I try to point out how such a fact could come into existence and why it plays such a significant role in the narrative. In the context of these recent publications some of my statements may appear too cautious, and certain explanations may seem redundant, but it was not possible to introduce extensive changes to the text which would bring it fully into line with the latest state of knowledge.

One of the things that this book seeks to change is our perception of the singer *as a creative author*. The notion of creativity is usually inseparably connected with inventiveness. That is why all kinds of novelties, whether expansions typical of oral tradition (e.g. biographies of background characters) or various kinds of perceived influences (e.g. transformation of motifs from

Mesopotamian epics or "intertextual" references to other poems of the Trojan Cycle), are usually seen as the author's individual contribution to the *Iliad* and celebrated as manifestations of his need to show his originality. This way of thinking is constantly creeping into Homeric scholarship, even though oral theory makes it obvious that oral poets are not motivated by the drive to originality. However, the need to appreciate Homer's greatness is irresistible. Thus, on the one hand, the constant admiration of his innovation and, on the other, the denial of its existence. I reject both positions as too extreme; rather, I am of the opinion that what we often consider "innovative" is an inherent element of Homer's skill as a storyteller, which absolutely results from the conditions of oral performance. I do not mean that everything that we find in Homer must be a part of the already existing tradition, of which very little has been preserved to our times except the two long Homeric poems. Homer is part of this tradition, and the best evidence of its creative potential. *Any* new grain an oral poet adds must be in line with tradition; later on, it will grow or not, depending on whether it is picked up by future singers. What this claim means in practice is that Homer, far from being the culmination of tradition, is—because of circumstances beyond his control—only one frozen-in-time element taken from the flowing current of an ever-changing epic song based on the multiplication and differentiation of a certain mythic pattern. Some Homeric "added" threads were continued, others weren't. Homer is indubitably a creative poet, and this book is an attempt to show the character of his creativeness, but it is not a kind of creativeness that would put him outside tradition or in any way make him independent of it.

One thing is certain: we are only at the beginning of the path to the understanding of the specific nature of oral creation. Thanks to the research of previous generations of scholars, and especially the groundbreaking studies of Milman Parry and Albert Lord, oral tradition is no longer *terra incognita*, but still there is a lot to discover. I also have the impression that scholars have become much too entrenched in their positions, focusing too much on one problem, such as the duration of the "frozen-in-time" moment: was it the tiny moment of the dictation of the text or the scores of years needed for the dough to rise, before the *Iliad* could be baked? So I have deliberately steered clear of some important subjects, not because I disregard them but because I must first clean the foreground. Some questions have to be postponed.

Finally, to quote Catullus: *Quare habe tibi quidquid hoc libelli—qualecumque ...*

Introduction

DESPITE A VAST number of studies, many times more voluminous than Homer's poems, the basic questions remain unanswered: how and in what circumstances did the poems originate, and what essentially are they? One reason for this central mystery is that they are the only extant works of their sort to emerge from the uncertain historical circumstances that surround the beginnings of Greek civilization (most frequently dated to the eighth century BCE). There is no reason to think that this state of knowledge will be changed. Instead, what one can attempt to do is to provide plausible explanations for what the *Iliad* grew out of, what it dwells in, and what it refers to. Thanks to oral-theory studies, we know that Homer's poems grew out of the oral epic tradition, which began when the Greeks first arrived in Greece, i.e. in the early second millennium BCE, or even in the earlier times of the Proto-Indo-European period. Therefore, much can be said about Homer's basic compositional style and technique, but this does not explain the monumentality of his works. According to many scholars this monumentality, and to some also the artistry, means the introduction of a "new quality" to the epic tradition. This thesis is based on the comparison of Homer's poetry with literature that appeared later, but also with oral works created at more or less the same time or even earlier. In reference to the epic Cycle, Aristotle presented Homer's poetry as without parallels in slightly later works. According to the ancient writers, these cyclic poems were composed by authors later than Homer, called the *neoteroi* ("younger poets"). Their poetry never matched Homer's craft and never achieved such spectacularly epic proportions. Then again, in the eyes of modern scholars Homer is not seen to be at the start but at the pinnacle; from this perspective the assumption of the gradual degeneration of later epic poetry is no longer so obvious. If we accept the point of view preferred by modern scholars that the works of the cyclic poets reflect extra-Homeric or pre-Homeric poetry, their dependence on Homer is also strongly questioned. The *opinio communis* of ancient times that the Cyclic epic songs were a continuation of Homeric narratives seems absurd not only from the neo-analytical point of view, which contrasts the primary plot of the Cycle with the secondary plot of the *Iliad*, but also because one can hardly imagine information being passed on for over two hundred years by various poets, who add complementary plots to the *Iliad* as further installments in a story that is not yet fully told. Aristotle's critique of the quality of the cyclic poems is also suspect. If these were, indeed, later poems and in one way or another reliant on Homer, why did they not at least attempt—however ineptly—to emulate his style and craft? Why did they not start their narratives *in medias res*? Why do other works lack Homer's dramatization of events and the extensive use of speeches? If we accept the view of the horizontalists and assume that the *Iliad* and *Odyssey* were composed by different authors, that would be the only known example of one poet imitating the style of another, and exceedingly successfully at that. Why then did no other poets follow in a similar fashion?

The traditional view of the epic cycle should therefore be verified—though that would be very hard to do by traditional means. There are exceptionally few extant manuscript fragments, and the contribution of papyrus discoveries has hardly been impressive. The most recent edition of the epic cycle[1] provides only 5 such fragments: *Aethiopis* fr. 2 (1 line) Panyassis *Heraclea* fr. 13 (2 lines), *Minyas* fr. 7 (29 fragmentary lines), *Phoronis* fr. 6 (1 line), and the unattributed fr. 12 (1.5 lines): a total of just 34.5 lines! We cannot reasonably count on a new papyrus discovery that will in any significant way increase our knowledge. And even if we found more written texts, would it shed any light on the epic tradition out of which the *Iliad* emerged? Written texts, after all, represent a different form of creation, one that might have been influenced by the actual use of writing as much as by the poetry of Homer, which by then might have appeared in written form. Reconstructing the oral tradition might, therefore, seem impossible without the miraculous ability to travel back in time, and readers might think this book a mere collection of speculations on a subject that can never be convincingly verified.

The works of Milman Parry and Albert Bates Lord, however, have provided a comparative perspective for the study of Homer. One can even speak of applying an empirical approach (something unparalleled in classical studies) to ancient epic poetry, showing that oral poetry used similar techniques and patterns, irrespective of a given culture's geographic and chronological location. Unfortunately, globalization and universal education have drastically reduced the possibilities of conducting synchronous research into oral cultures. Nevertheless, there are still diachronic studies to refer to, for we have sufficient research tools to analyze the rich ethnographic collections and texts of various ancient and medieval civilizations. Of course, when undertaking the comparative method, one has to take into account the various differences resulting from the diverse cultural particularities of poetry in various countries and epochs.

1 West 2003a.

Extensive study of oral cultures permits definitions of the structure and shape of epic oral song, of the conditions and ways in which it was formed, of how it was performed, and of the actual performers. We have at our disposal much information on these topics.[2] In many respects the creation of epic songs evolved in ways similar to those observed in the countries of former Yugoslavia. This, in turn, raises the fundamental question as to whether or not the *Iliad* differs in significant ways from the contemporary tradition. A primary requirement is to ascertain whether what appear to be aspects of its distinctness and exceptionality are indeed not reflected in the oral tradition. If what has so far appeared to be new was, in fact, typical, the *Iliad* will be rightfully qualified as an oral song.

For indeed, the orality of the *Iliad* is far from obvious. A large number of scholars claim that the *Iliad* is markedly different from the oral tradition and that it may have originally been composed to some extent—though opinions vary as to the actual extent—with writing, which determined its shape, size, and artistry. According to some, Parry's mechanistic approach even deprives Homer of poetic ingenuity,[3] whereas Homer changes traditional formulae in a way that indicates the introduction of individual solutions. In this scenario, the influence of writing is not always mentioned; there are suggestions that individual and innovative solutions could have been present in oral culture, but Homer completely reframed it, or that the functioning of oral culture should be redefined. There are even claims that the Homeric texts should be open to contemporary literary criticism.[4] However, an important question remains: how could individualized, often one-off phrases be preserved, if it weren't for the support of writing? In oral culture, everything (from a single phrase to the

2 For instance, we know that oral transmission is not limited to poetic traditions based on speech rhythm. Tedlock (1977:507–508), a scholar of Indigenous American culture, even asserts that poetic form is exceptional and suggests it emerged in association with the appearance of writing. Tedlock's opinion is greatly exaggerated and does not take into account the presence of epic song in Eurasian oral cultures. On the formation of meter due to a stabilized pronunciation of memorized phrases, see Nagy 1974, esp. Ch. 6.

3 The first to present this view were Bowra 1952:240: "Behind him [Homer] lie centuries of oral performance, largely improvised, with all its wealth of formulae adapted to an exacting metre; these he knows and uses fully. But if he knows writing and is able to commit his poems to it, he is enabled to give a far greater precision and care to what he says than any improvising poet ever can. Since it is almost impossible to believe that the *Iliad* and *Odyssey* were ever improvised, and the richness of their poetry suggests some reliance on writing, we may see in them examples of what happens when writing comes to help the oral bard. He continues to compose in the same manner as before, but with far greater care and effectiveness," and Wade-Gery (1952:38–39), who put it more metaphorically: "As Darwin seemed to many to have removed the finger of God from the creation of the world and of man, so Milman Parry has seemed to some to remove the creative poet from the *Iliad* and *Odyssey*"; see Cairns 2001:33–56.

4 Cairns 2001:52.

entire story) can only last through repetition, and therefore any innovative approach must take a form that will enable its repetition. Moreover, repetition necessitates that both the phrase and the whole story be rearticulated in the process of performing the oral epic. How could one remember something that was invented only for one particular performance?

It is, in fact, difficult to determine whether a written work is part of oral literature. Studies of the appearance and nature of the formulae most characteristic to the oral style have brought significant results. Richard Janko has shown the fallibility of methods that simply rely on quantifying the occurrence of formulaic phrases. Less frequent appearances of formulaic phrases surely cannot be treated as evidence that the text is no longer of an oral nature. Janko therefore proposes a more systematic approach to assessing the appearance of formulae on the basis of:

1. formulaic language displaying the principles of economy and scope, as articulated by Parry;
2. the low frequency of necessary enjambment;[5] or
3. the fast selection of formulae in oral composition.

Richard Janko points out that in the comparative study of economy and scope within the works of individual authors or poetic schools both geographic and chronological factors should be considered. He notes, nonetheless, that the unity of the tradition is striking[6]; that is, in the Homeric Hymns, which themselves evidence the abundance and extensiveness of the epic tradition, there are formulae characteristic of both Homer and Hesiod alike. But even such a study cannot provide a definite result; rather, it proves that medieval texts, which were undoubtedly composed in writing, sometimes contain a considerable percentage of formulaic language.[7]

Hence, the emergence of a thesis of the existence of a transitional stage between the oral tradition and written literature. This notion undermined Lord's important observation that there is a fundamental difference between the two compositional techniques.[8] Discouraged by strong criticism, Lord

5 Janko 1990a:33: "Parry's distinction, valid for the extreme cases on which he based it [Homer vs. Apollonius and Vergil] is less useful as a negative test for oral origins in poems of a predominantly oral style."

6 Janko 1990a:26.

7 Medieval heroic epics to various degrees indicate associations with the oral tradition. Kullmann (1984:319–323) points to the specific characteristics of the epic in its transition to written poetry in the medieval period.

8 Lord 1960:129: "The two techniques are, I submit, contradictory and mutually exclusive." See Lord 1968.

gradually modified his radical statement.[9] Minna Skafte Jensen argues, nevertheless, that criticism of Lord's proposition was largely based on a misunderstanding of his oral theory and on the conviction of many scholars that Homeric poetry cannot be compared with relatively quite recent oral compositions recorded in various parts of the world, as these are rudimentary in relation to the greatness of Homer.[10] Jensen, referring to her experiences in the writing down of Greenland Inuit oral traditions argues that the transitional stage in no way marks an improvement on the oral version.[11]

The "genius" of Homer should therefore be treated in a bipolar manner: it is based either on the oral poetic technique or on the application of alphabetic writing. In the latter case, we should view the *Iliad* and *Odyssey* as transitional texts, combining both the oral and the written style. Contact with writing, even if only through slow dictation, would have allowed for the improvement of certain phrases and lines.[12] The problem, however, arises from our own concentration on the influence of writing on orality, while we meanwhile observe a rather varied effect of orality on writers in ancient and medieval cultures.[13] However, if we assume that the greatness of Homer springs from the oral poetic technique, it means that the whole of the Homeric message is conventional, even when it seems to diverge from tradition and lean toward new and unconventional forms of expression. Yet why should it be tantamount to a denial of the poet's great talent? Identifying in his poetry any schematic structures would, in the eyes of many, deprive Homer of the originality that provided a basis for the formation and development of literary works. Such fears may be considered as a "romantic obsession" that inclines people to defend the ingenuity and originality of the author.[14] Originality does not appear to be an important factor in

9 The heated polemics even took on the form of personal attacks (Lord 1968 and Amory Parry 1971). Lord's moderated stance: 1974, 1978, 1981, 1986; see Foley 1988:45–46, 51–52, 54–55.

10 Jensen (1998) criticizes the conclusions of Curschmann (1967), in particular, analyzing medieval English, French, and German poetry, as well as (Finnegan 1976 and 1977), studying the oral tradition in Sierra Leone.

11 Jensen 1998:6: "And in any case, such transitional texts are very far from what Homeric scholars envisage when they imagine that Homer had the best of two worlds and combined the traditional oral epic singer's professional art with the written intellectual's sophistication and taste for grandiose compositional effects." See Jensen 2011:185–187.

12 Teodorsson 2006:179–180. Slowing down the rhythm of song performance does not help the singer to improve the song; instead, he gets tired, irritated, and, above all, loses the enthusiasm that accompanies the ordinary performance of the song in front of the audience (for more about disadvantages of dictation theories see González 2013:Ch. 1, Ch. 2).

13 Schaefer (1997) maintains that oral culture thus left an impression on the authors of medieval written texts. In specific cases, it is therefore possible to consider the degree and type of oral structures present in emerging literary culture.

14 This is pointed out by Thalmann (1984:xv), who recommends prior familiarization with the conventions governing Homer's oral tradition.

the oral tradition and following conventions in no way diminishes the talent of the singer who gave us the version of the *Iliad* that we know—though undoubtedly it is a talent of a different sort. This is probably best assessed by William G. Thalmann:

> As for the poet, there surely was artistry on his part, artistry of a high quality though perhaps different from the way we conceive it. The poet's talent was the ability to express whatever he wanted to in the conventional forms, so that these did not limit him but were part of his language.[15]

The mechanical nature of oral transmission does not hinder or prevent creativity. Jack Goody has shown that an oral text is subject to modification with every successive rendition, to which quite new elements may be added with great ease.[16] There are two important reservations with regard to this view. Firstly, the dynamics of the oral tradition are only noticeable from the outside, whereas internally the tradition appears to be static. This means that the singer not only does not notice the introduction of changes, but even consciously tries to avoid them. Secondly, the transformation and addition of elements do not occur arbitrarily and they do not express the freedom to create fiction (the "free-floating use of the creative imagination," as Goody puts it[17]), but instead remain in the accepted tradition of structures and meanings.[18] One therefore cannot add anything that does not belong to the tradition or swap elements around at will, though with time these elements may undergo reinterpretation and revaluation.

Gregory Nagy, whose own views, as well as those of his mentor, Albert Bates Lord, have been criticized as radical, has expressed the impression that many critics cite *The Singer of Tales*, but few appear to have actually read the book.[19] That situation was even more pronounced with the publication of works from the *Parry Collection of Serbo-Croatian Heroic Songs*. The difficulty of learning Slavic poetry is, no doubt, the reason why it rather rarely appears in the bibliographies of scholars of Homer. Consequently, it was easier for scholars to ignore Lord's observations. Particular attention should be drawn to the song of the

15 Thalmann 1984:30–31.

16 Goody 1977; 1986; 2010.

17 Goody 2010:10.

18 Szyjewski 2016:207: "Despite Jack Goody's claim, myths do not change arbitrarily... The content volatility is strongly limited due to the requirements of the syntagm, as well as to dominant trends of metaphorization, and to the model of the world in the form of a cosmological system."

19 Nagy 1996a:1: "Though it [*The Singer of Tales*] is cited by many who offer various arguments about 'oral poetry,' the book is often treated only superficially, and there are even instances where those who agree or disagree with it have evidently not read it at all."

finest singer encountered by Parry and Lord, Avdo Međedović's *The Wedding of Smailagić Meho*. It is not only exceptionally long (the second longest recorded song, comparable in length to the *Odyssey*), but also one of great artistry. We know that Avdo learned it towards the end of the nineteenth century (around forty years before he performed it in 1935) from a small book that, as Lord deduced, was an 1886 edition of songs sung by Šemić.[20] Međedović altered the song in an astonishing way, adding importance and pathos to given events. A simple story became in his rendition an account of an exceptionally important and massive military undertaking. Lord points out that the skillful elaborations of the tale do not merely serve a decorative purpose, but also add an essential splendor befitting the status of the presented events.[21] Međedović uses dialogues and fills them with subtle insinuations of the protagonists' feelings. Major events are anticipated and the actions of the heroes are ironized. The plot develops according to a moral rationale, which the protagonists have to face. All these elements mean that we are dealing with a great epic tale. The exceptional circumstances in which it was created allow us to observe how the text of a song can be changed when sung by a talented singer (*guslar*). The singer himself does not even realize that in many ways he is digressing from the original and is ready to defend his interpretation as the most correct one. Analogies to Homer's treatment of subjects are very plain to see. Yet in this case we have a reference point, the source for Avdo's version, which is Šemić's song. To some extent a similar function might be played by the cyclic epics in relation to the great songs of Homer. This means it is justifiable to think of earlier versions of the *Iliad* and *Odyssey* that are very different from Homer's epics. A talented singer could tell the same story, but add so much splendor, magnificence, and tragedy to it that earlier versions fade into oblivion.

***

This book does not include any studies of Greek epic formulae, if only because they do not answer the question as to what an epic song or an epic cycle was. Instead, I will focus on the story pattern. My impression is that this aspect has been rather neglected; there have so far only been comparisons between the findings of Parry and Lord and the structure of Homer's poems. First to be undertaken is an analysis of known story patterns in ancient literature, including the repetition of certain structures and certain sequences of scenes, which may indicate the use of the same story pattern in various songs. It turns out that even epic cycles reveal distinct schema. The same elements are repeated in a number

20 Lord 1974:13.
21 Lord 1974:13–34.

of poems, which allows us to infer that epic cycles were created according to a certain pattern.

The nature of the epic cycle is the subject of my first chapter. Its elaborate structure seems to have no equivalent in other oral traditions, which is why answering the question as to how it was created and what was the place of the song in the cycle appears to be a key to understanding the whole of the Greek epic. How were the roles of particular protagonists determined and how was the entire sequence of the plot developed? How are we to understand the constant presence of certain elements that, despite all the variability, could never be changed? Demodokos's songs recount particular episodes in the perspective of the entire war. Strikingly, the same shape and perspective are revealed by the cyclic poems, which makes it possible to identify them as oral songs. In this respect, they correspond to the structure of the *Iliad*, which recounts an episode from the perspective of the story of the entire war. Therefore, another basic task is to answer the questions of how a single episode is employed in the structure of the cycle and how the inclusion of individual episodes did not disrupt the entire cycle. In other words, what were the limits of creativity in the variable oral epic? Understanding this process will allow us to locate the *Iliad* in the cyclic structure. Hence, the neoanalytic question as to whether the *Iliad* is an essential element in the cycle should instead ask whether it was possible for the *Iliad* to become part of the Trojan Cycle.

Analysis of epic cycle summaries indicates the repetition of many story elements and even sequences of events appearing in a similar context, though in a variable form. In order to discover how the *Iliad* became part of the epic cycle, it is essential to compare its storyline with similar scenes or repeated sequences in extant epic and mythological sources (Ch. 2). Basically, mythological sources should be treated as the remnants of now lost pre-Homeric epics. The same schemes are used in various ways, often losing their original meaning. The *Iliad* should, therefore, be viewed as a palimpsest, containing ancient stories and thought structures, often no longer understood or marginalized, but nevertheless respected and preserved on account of the inertial force of oral epic tradition. Thus, the singer will only make changes sanctioned by the tradition in which he persists. A comparison of the actions of various heroes in the Trojan Cycle will allow for the reconstruction of the story patterns that lie at the origins of the Cycle. Its successive protagonists are presented in a similar situation and may be treated as successive allomorphs of the same story pattern. What remains to be answered is whether all the similarities in the construction of characters and actions amount to convincing evidence of a distinct epic tradition. In other words, are the references sufficient evidence of a tradition functioning in a given song? The question then follows of the extent of the epic cycle, its actual size, and how far it goes beyond extant summaries.

A thus reconstructed pre-Homeric epic appears to be of a very different nature to the works of Homer. Chapter 3 will provide an in-depth analysis of the fantasy, fairy-tale, and magical aspects of the world of the epic cycle. These aspects are often contrasted with greater realism of the *Iliad*. Closer examination of Homer's poem leads us to conclude, however, that Homer must have been aware of the fantastical qualities of the heroes in the material on which he based his poetry. Homer reinterprets the materials he had at his disposal in accordance with what he intended to say in his song and perhaps also with the expectations of his audience. The latter factor, however, should not be overestimated, since magical and fantastical elements are hardly lacking in "contemporary" and "later" cyclic poetry. We might therefore speak of its "latent" presence also in the poetry of the *Iliad*. Homer's poems appear to be of a historical type in the Greek epic tradition, but still indicate an awareness of the fairy-tale epic stage, to use Eleazar Meletinsky's (2009) nomenclature. As an example, I will discuss the function and meaning of magic objects in both the *Iliad* and the epic cycle. Mythical figures, such as Cheiron and Memnon, are deliberately avoided by the author of the *Iliad*. Analysis of the fairy-tale dimension of the epic allows us to look at the problem of the historicity of the Trojan War. Finding similarities in the construction of many cycles also reveals how new cycles were formed in the epic tradition.

The study of the structures and forms of epic songs and entire cycles demonstrates that the *Iliad* is a typical oral epic song, developing characteristic story patterns, whereas the originality of the work appears to be reflected in the singer's freedom in presenting the epic theme. The second part of this book presents, on the other hand, an analysis of the structure of the entire *Iliad* to verify the thesis that its specific artistry differs from the remaining epics and thus implies that the author referred to a written text. If, in turn, it can be shown that Homer's exceptional artistry was derived from the oral tradition, the theory of the poem being based on a written source becomes superfluous.

The interpretative problems of the *Iliad* largely result from a failure to understand the specifics of oral performance. In Chapter 4, I first discuss Homer's audience and their awareness of allusions to episodes within the song, as well as in other songs known to them and the singer—familiarity with the cycle, that is. The possibilities of the listeners' perception of allusions need to be studied because they are the basis for assessing the singer's method and ability to influence their responses. The epic is a song of praise and therefore it is biased. The singer must adapt the narrative to the overriding goal of praising the given hero. This could be achieved, for example, at the cost of other epic heroes, which would allow for a known story to be presented in a way that was totally new and attractive to listeners. The singer adopts a specific narrative strategy appropriate for auditory reception, which is quite different from a strategy suitable for a reader's reception. A basic role here is played by allusions, which suggest what will eventually happen and which sometimes create expectations only to disappoint them. Knowledge that goes beyond the immediate song allows the listener to receive the story differently. The listener, moved by the singer, will alternately feel fear and relief and, at other times, an ironic perspective upon the hero's experiences. Here, however, questions must also be asked about both the more attentive and the average listener's perceptive abilities.

This topic is further examined in Chapter 5, but in a broader perspective. I will present several scenes from the *Iliad* in the context of how the singer affects the emotions of fear and relief, as well as a deeper sense of irony, by referring to analogous scenes from the Cycle. By suggesting similarities to known episodes or, rather, images, the singer is not only able to dramatize the action, but also, through the repetition of scenes following the same patterns, create an atmosphere of suspense, which deepens the listener's experience. Thanks to this method, the singer achieves the desired emotional tension at the death of Patroklos. This scene is not an imitation of the death of Achilles, as the neoanalysts have viewed it, nor is it an inconsequential, fairly typical scene as the oralists argue, but instead a well thought-out sequence of events foretelling the death of Achilles. And the death of Achilles is foretold in such a way that the listener, who is also aware of the tradition, experiences that death as if it was happening, although it does not actually occur in the poem.

In Chapter 6, I attempt to read Homer's text as it would have been heard by the listener. The listener would hear the text linearly, and only once, but the series of repetitions, anticipations, and, above all, the arrangement of particular passages, as well as the entire text in accordance with the criteria of ring composition, allowed him to verify what he heard and arrive at the heart of the matter, as the author intended. I analyze the conflict between Achilles and Agamemnon (Book 1), the mission to Achilles (Book 9), and the scene of Achilles' conversation with Patroklos (Book 16). This last scene shows, in particular, how Homer presents the main hero, Achilles, his character, and also his relations with other leaders. I will consider the heroes' intentions, hidden in what they say, as well as the intentions of the narrator, who makes use of the listener's knowledge of the events of the Trojan War. Furthermore, arguments will be presented against the view that Homer never expresses moral judgments.

The proper perspective for the character of Achilles, as well as the whole Homeric epic, should be viewed in comparison with other epic traditions. Homer is the "golden gate" through which we can peer into a pre-literate past. The possibilities provided by Homer's poetry in this respect are comparable to nothing else. The key to opening this gate are the findings of studies of oral tradition in diverse phases of cultural development around the world. The creation of epics and epic heroes followed an analogous course in various cultures, demonstrating a common pattern that primarily stems from the specificity of oral transmission. The conservatism of the oral tradition serves to preserve once adopted patterns. According to Claude Lévi-Strauss (1958:Ch. 12; 1969:2–9; 1981:27ff., 644-645), mythological tales are common to very broad cultural circles, expanding beyond ethnic and language boundaries. However, the structure in the understanding of Lévi-Strauss, i.e. the most basic one, will not be explored in this book; an even less important role will be played by the process of diffusion noticeable, for example, in the influence of Middle Eastern literature on Greek tradition, or even widely, on Indo-European stories in general.

Outline of Research History

I have provided below an outline of key trends in Homeric studies, so as to make it easier for the reader to follow the arguments of this book, though I have limited the presentation to an essential minimum. In addition, I provide a brief introduction to philological studies of cyclic poetry.

Neoanalysis

Analytic studies, which focused on the "Homeric Question," had been exhausted by the 1930s. Unitarian scholarship, in opposition to analytic work, was usually limited to aesthetic appraisals and failed to present a counterargument to the scientific evidence of the pluralists. Successful responses to analytic work shared its approach and applied similar research methods. These included the studies of Milman Parry as well as of neoanalytic scholars, who effectively used analytic studies and findings to disprove that same approach.

As a precursor of neoanalysis one might consider Wolfgang Schadewaldt's *Iliasstudien* (1938), which tried to show the stylistic unity of selected books of the *Iliad* (11, 8, 9, 1) as evidence disproving the pluralist arguments of dividing the books into layers. Schadewaldt expanded on his unitarian views in *Von Homers Welt und Werk. Aufsätze und Auslegungen zur Homerischen Frage* (1951). Karl Reinhardt's *Das Parisurteil* (1938), which tries to show that the Judgment of Paris scene was known to the author of the *Iliad*, may be similarly assessed.[22]

22 A precise list of the precursors of the neoanalytic approach (O. Gruppe, D. Mülder, E. Löwy), a history of neoanalytic studies, and its most important theses are presented by Kullmann (1981

Neoanalysis, as a recognizable school within Homeric studies, began with Heinrich Pestalozzi, *Die Achilleis als Quelle der Ilias* (1945) and, independently, with Johannes Th. Kakridis, *Homeric Researches* (1949). Neoanalysis opposed the prioritizing of Homer's works by demonstrating that the author of the *Iliad* and *Odyssey* was familiar with the epic cyclic tradition. According to neoanalytic studies, the *Iliad* appears to be secondary in relation to the *Aethiopis* and other Trojan Cycle works, contrary to what was previously assumed. Perhaps the most important contribution of the Neoanalytic school is to locate the *Iliad* within an extensive epic tradition.[23] Wolfgang Kullmann's *Die Quellen der Ilias. Troischer Sagenkreis* (1960) includes a detailed list of *antehomerica* and *posthomerica* found in the *Iliad*. In turn, an original way of interpreting the repetition of Homeric phrases was proposed by Georg Schoeck in *Ilias und Aithiopis. Kyklische Motive in homerischer Brechung* (1961). Unaware of Parry's theory, Schoeck argued that repetitions resulted from a cyclic pattern, which the author of the *Iliad* tried to imitate. In later years, neoanalysis generally ceased gaining many new supporters, though the idea of parallelism in some of the scenes did seem attractive. In particular, Mühlestein's argument (1972) that Euphorbos is a double of Paris was widely accepted; Roberto Nickel (2002), in turn, sees Euphorbos as replacing Achilles. Kullmann undertook efforts to adapt the results of neoanalytic studies to oral theory: it was no longer a question of literary imitation, but of crafting the *Iliad* from a better known song—the *Aethiopis*. Thus, the theory of the secondariness of the Homeric poem remained.

Neoanalysis, therefore, makes use of available knowledge about the plots of cyclic poems to show that the author of the *Iliad* consciously adapted the more important themes to compose his work. The striking similarities between the *Aethiopis* and the *Iliad* serve as evidence of imitation, though particular themes lose their importance. In the *Aethiopis*, Achilles withdraws from the fighting, most probably influenced by the prophecy of his mother, Thetis, but then returns following the death of his friend Antilochos. Antilochos had managed to save his father, Nestor, from an attack by Memnon, but paid for his heroic deed with his own life. Achilles kills Memnon, but then is himself killed (in accordance with the prophecy) by Paris, who fires at him an arrow divinely guided by Apollo. In both poems we observe the same sequence of events: the prophecy of Thetis, the withdrawal of Achilles, the intervention and death of Achilles' friend (Patroklos/Antilochos), Achilles' revenge on the killer of his friend, and consequently the death of Achilles himself—though in the *Iliad* that death is not narrated, but foretold. However, in Homer some elements of the story pattern

---

and 1984). Reinhardt's further research findings are presented in *Die Ilias und ihr Dichter* (1961).

23 Finkelberg 2015:6 is of the same opinion.

seem not to fit the story so well as in the *Aethiopis*, which can be demonstrated with the following examples. The lamentation of Thetis and the Nereids over the body of Patroklos seems to be a duplication of their lamentation over the body of Achilles, a far more closely related hero. Likewise, the organization of games in honor of the deceased Patroklos is an imitation of the games organized in honor of Achilles after his death. Achilles' *therapôn*, however, does not seem to be a hero of sufficient rank to warrant funeral games. Antilochos's sacrificing of his own life to save his father is very weakly reflected in the scene where Diomedes rescues Nestor, because, unlike the previous story pattern, Diomedes survives. The derivation of the *Iliad* from the Cycle is confirmed by the survival of all the Achaean leaders with the exception of Patroklos, who appears to have either been added to the Cycle or whose role has been elevated for him to appear alongside the most important heroes.

To sum up, neoanalysis assumes that the *Iliad* is an original work, creating a new, untraditional episode that, nevertheless, imitates other works that belong to the epic tradition. Homer's work was, therefore, created at the end of the oral epic tradition in a new, monumental form. The author made use of traditional formulae and typical scenes, but applied a new model to shape the story, where themes known from other songs were transformed and adapted to create an original story. It is possible that this model of imitation had something to do with written texts and the influence of Near Eastern cultures, where epics had been recorded in writing since the Sumerian era.[24]

Oral theory

Undoubtedly a far greater impact was achieved by oral theory, which began with the theses of Milman Parry, who argued that the repetition of Homeric phrases indicates the use of a traditional style and, inspired by Antoine Meillet, considered the traditional style as a sign of the oral performance of song. In the years 1933–1935, Parry went on to study living oral tradition in the former Yugoslavia, which resulted in the colossal *Parry Collection of Oral Literature* (1953), with subsequent volumes, including *Serbo-Croatian Heroic Songs* (M. Parry, A. B. Lord, and D. E. Bynum, eds.). Parry's work only became widely known *in extenso* when his son, Adam Parry, collected all his papers, thirty-six years after his death, in *The Making of Homeric Verse: Collected Papers of Milman Parry* (1971). Oral theory is no less indebted to *The Singer of Tales* (1960), the book by Parry's assistant in Yugoslavia, Albert Bates Lord, in which he presents the basic thesis of oral theory—namely, that the performance of the song is inextricably linked

24 Kullmann 1984:319 and 322–323. On the influence of Near Eastern cultures on Homeric poetry, see Burkert 1984:95–101.

with its creation. Lord joins the description of the song's performance, the singer's education, and the many aspects of performance circumstances with a comparative study of Slavic songs and Homer's epics. Lord points to three structural elements in the oral song: formulae, typical scenes,[25] and story patterns. Lord also considers the artistry in Homeric song as relative (to the formality of the language, to the conventionality of the song, and to the singer's inconsequence in presenting the themes), and its monumentality as an outcome dictated by the way in which songs were created and written down. Right up to his last works, Lord maintained and developed his ideas about oral theory, even more strongly advocating the need to conduct comparative, synchronic, and diachronic studies, not limited to epic poetry: *Epic Singers and Oral Tradition* (1991), and *The Singer Resumes the Tale* (1995).

Oral theory is currently used to study a vast number of cultures around the world, as well as diverse ancient and medieval transmissions. With regard to ancient Greece, it has already experienced its periods of fervent enthusiasm, conservative critique, doubts about its appropriateness, and, of course, rapid development. To this day, it is the predominant method of studying archaic Greek poetry, though it is no longer strictly limited to archaic poetry or to poetry at all. I will present here only some of the principal trends in oral theory, as they are relevant to the arguments of this book.

An important contribution to oral theory preceding Lord's book were the articles of James A. Notopoulos, in which, among other things, he illuminated Homer's paratactic style (1949), his use of ring composition, and the function of anticipation in the shaping of a paratactic compositional unity (Notopoulos 1950, 1951). He also accepted an earlier comparison of the *Iliad* with the geometric style, adapting it to Homer's paratactic style (Notopoulos 1957). Moreover, he conducted his own research into contemporary Cretan oral epics, showing analogies with Parry's reading of Homer (e.g. Notopoulos 1952). However, the unity of the *Iliad* as an oral *Ringkomposition* work and its link with the geometric style of vase painting, is primarily associated with the exceptional book of Cedric H. Whitman, *Homer and the Heroic Tradition* (1958). Whitman showed that ring composition is typical for oral poetry and serves as a model of construction on both the micro-scale—e.g. speeches—and the macro-scale, as in the construction of the entire work, which is indicated in the parallel scenes at the start and end of the poem. By trying to show the genius of Homer, Whitman points to the mutual relations between the image, the symbol, and the formula.

25 Strictly speaking, Lord used the term "themes" (as used in folklore studies), but the more generally used form is "typical scenes," as a consequence of the term *typische Szenen*, which was already functioning in Homeric studies (see Arend 1933).

A polemic stance to both Lord and Whitman is presented in Geoffrey S. Kirk's *The Songs of Homer* (1962). Kirk transforms the orality of Homer. Like Whitman, he expresses admiration for Homer's artistry, but objects to the comparison to the art of painting. While accepting the findings of Parry and Lord, Kirk makes a rather arbitrary distinction between the stages of development and degradation in oral poetry, placing Homer among the still creative singers and the Slavic *guslari* as non-creative in their rote repetitions. Homer's poems were created much earlier than they were recorded in writing, but they nevertheless retained their original form thanks to repetitions of rhapsodes.[26]

Kirk's book, though much quoted, has not had much impact on our perception of Homer's orality, and instead demonstrates an unfortunately common scholarly underappreciation of the value of Slavic epics and the parallels adduced by Parry and Lord (e.g. Dihle 1970:46). However, as Foley has argued (Foley 1990; 1995), this lack of appreciation results from a superficial understanding of this particular type of poetry and its possibilities.

Similar disbelief in the value of the cultural parallel was expressed, for example, by Albin Lesky, the first German scholar to recognize oral theory (Lesky 1963, 1967). Differences between Homer's poetry and Yugoslav songs, in his opinion, compel us to the conclusion that the *Iliad* was originally a written text and its author more similar to a literate poet than a *guslar* in a Bosnian café.

The irrationality of Kirk's depiction of the development of orality was shown by Adam Parry (1966), who argued that preserving a song in unchanged form through oral transmission for hundreds of years is simply impossible. Parry also criticized Lord's notion of the *Iliad* having been dictated, because this did not take into account the different status of writing in twentieth-century Yugoslavia in comparison with Greece in the eighth century BCE. For this reason, too, Adam Parry favored the theory that the song was written down by the author himself. Parry's evidence included the concision of the works and the economy of their artistic means of expression, free from the influence of the listeners' reactions.[27] Homer's artistry, despite the use of set phrases, is also confirmed in the language used by his characters, how they themselves are described (Parry 1956a and 1956b), and even the symbolic use of epithets and detailed elements of everyday life, as was pointed out by Anne Amory Parry (Amory Parry 1966; 1971; 1973). The oral artistry of Homer and the specificity of oral aesthetics were likewise articulated by Notopoulos (1964), Patzer (1972), and in the subsequent articles of Mark W. Edwards (1966; modality of style: 1968; the "answering" formula: 1969; speech

26 González (2013:15–70) argues that a "dichotomy between the 'creative singer/poet' and the 'reproducing rhapsode'" is "profoundly misleading."

27 A. Parry 1966:215: "... I would suggest the usefulness of writing in enabling the poet to compose a long but coherent work without immediate dependence on the vagaries of his audience."

introductions: 1970; typical scenes, catalogues: 1980b; all of which is summed up in the book, *Homer: Poet of the Iliad*, 1987).

Admiration of Homer's artistry, however, also became a reason for the renewed criticism of the oral theory. In his *Homer on Life and Death* (1980), Jasper Griffin, considering the symbolism and pathos in scenes from the lives and deaths of heroes, comes to the conclusion that their diversity contradicts the mechanical construction seemingly implied by the theses of Parry and Lord. Griffin, therefore, argues that Homer's individualistic style is more indicative of a written than an oral form. Hence, the formulaic style is used by the poet in a new type of composition. Opinions in the same spirit are expressed by other distinguished scholars, such as Albrecht Dihle (1970), Douglas L. Cairns (2001:53) and Martin L. West (2003:11), Peter Ahrensdorf (2014:5–9). Jasper Griffin maintained his criticism of the oral theory in subsequent works (e.g. Griffin 2004:167). This stance has, of course, been criticized by supporters of the theory (see Kelly 2007:1–4). John Miles Foley, in turn, has tried to strike a balance between the two opposing views, claiming that, despite certain similarities, oral cultures have distinctive differences, whereas with today's level of literacy we can speak neither of a pure oral culture nor of a pure literary culture (Foley 1997:159–165).[28]

In opposition to these views, Gregory Nagy argues that Homeric poems are indubitably a part of the oral tradition. Crucial is Nagy's early book *The Best of the Achaeans: Concepts of the Hero in Archaic Greek Poetry* (1979; rev. ed. 1999). Among its many original theses, one should especially note his presentation of the mutual and complementary dependence of cult and poetic concepts of the hero. In the Trojan Cycle, two heroes, Achilles and Odysseus, rival each other for the status of "the best of the Achaeans" and, in the story, for the status of conqueror of Troy. The typology of the poetry of praise and blame, introduced in *Best of the Achaeans*, was later discussed more widely in *Ancient Greek Epic and Praise Poetry: Some Typological Considerations* (1986). The concept of the gradual shaping of the poetic text, first in the oral tradition, next in the literary tradition, and undergoing a two-stage "crystallization" on both levels, is presented by Nagy in *Poetry as Performance: Homer and Beyond* (1996a).[29] Nagy has accentuated Lord's idea of the multiformity of the song, which includes an earlier *Iliad.*

28 The basis for forming such an opinion is provided by Rosalind Thomas, who points to the contemporariness of ancient Greek oral and literary culture (Thomas 1989 and 1992).

29 The evolutionary model of making the Homeric songs has become an alternative to the concept of dictation as a one-off event, whether the text was taken down by a scribe, by the author himself, or perhaps by his student over many years of work. This last possibility was suggested by West 2001. The arguments for the concept of dictation were also put forward by Janko 1990b and 1998. For a criticism of the concept of dictation, see González 2013:Ch. 1 and 2. Ready (2019:Chs. 3, 4, and 5) shows the scribe as a performer who affects the shape of the text being created.

The emergence of the monumental work is associated with the development of the pan-Hellenic culture (Nagy 1990b:17–81), and the adoption of the song's "canonical" form,[30] with the process of diffusion being halted when the song became part of the Peisistratid Panathenaia, which Nagy has metaphorically described as the "Panathenaic bottleneck" (2001). Nagy takes up questions of oral and written versions of Homer's text in subsequent publications: *Homeric Questions* (1996b), *Homeric Responses* (Nagy 2003a), *Homer's Text and Language* (2004), *Homer the Classic* (Nagy 2008), and *Homer the Preclassic* (Nagy 2010).

A somewhat different continuation of Lord's ideas is presented by John Miles Foley, who returns to the direct comparison of Homer's texts with Bosnian and Old English epics (Foley 1990:2002), as well as performance theory (Foley 1995, 1998). Foley has also developed a concept of metonymically linking the meaning of particular performance elements with tradition (traditional referentiality, Foley 1991; referentiality of scenes, Foley 1999a). He also advocates the idea that the *Iliad* and *Odyssey* are not fully oral works but, like early Medieval epic (*Beowulf* or *Chanson de Roland*) they should be treated as oral-derived texts (Foley 1990; 1991; 2011a). Another noteworthy comparative study is William Whallon's *Formula, Character, and Context: Studies in Homeric, Old English, and Old Testament Poetry* (1969), in which he places greater emphasis on determining the differences between oral poetries, rather than on listing the similarities.

Zlatan Čolaković (2006; 2019; see also Danek 2012) put forward an interesting thesis, namely that the "Slavic Homer," i.e. Bosnian singer Avdo Međedović, who for Parry and Lord was a point of reference showing the potential of the oral author, should be regarded as an author influenced by written tradition (a "post-traditional singer"). However, in my opinion, this concept was rightly criticized by Elmer (2010).

Neoanalysis and oral theory

From the perspective of oral theory, any similarities in the narrative are due to singers using the same, repeated structures of the oral tradition. The similarities are therefore accidental and do not add any contextual meaning to particular phrases or scenes. Hence in Anglo-Saxon countries, where the theories of Parry and Lord prevailed, neoanalysis was, for a long time, ignored. Then, in the 1980s and early 90s some influential scholars did accept some of its assumptions. In more recent years, such "concessions" have been strongly criticized and the dominant view among oral theory supporters is still that similarities in

30 In the conditions of pan-Hellenic—earlier, pan-Ionic—festivals, elements of local traditions were eliminated in favour of a universal system understandable for the diversified audiences gathering on these occasions.

particular scenes result solely from their typicality in oral poetry. Nevertheless, papers combining both methods in various degrees do appear in literature.

Neoanalytic scholars have often tried to adapt to oral theory. Kullmann has repeatedly stated that oral theory does not disqualify the findings of his method. In his opinion, the major difference between the two methods is that neoanalysis sees in Homer's epic "a comparatively high degree of individual creation,"[31] which would suggest the end of the oral age and the composition of poems with the use of writing. Among the many themes that are repeated in Homer's poems and cyclic poetry, Kullmann tries to identify those that belonged to tradition and could be used independently and those that were copied from other poems. The same themes could be applied to different characters, but a particular character is not a typical element and therefore basic themes in their "biography," above all the character's death, remained unchanged. For this reason, too, Patroklos may simultaneously play the role of Antilochos and Achilles, just as Hektor may sometimes play the role of Memnon and, at other times, that of Paris. The *Iliad* and *Aethiopis* thus show many similarities and shared themes, where the former generally seems to be the secondary work—which seems to rule out a situation where both epics shared a common source (*Ur-form*).[32] Therefore, apart from following traditional patterns, an important function was played by Homer's inventiveness in transforming themes.

Kullmann concludes that the *Iliad*'s theme of Achilles' wrath is not taken from tradition, but is instead the invention of the singer or poet, who adds the episode to the traditional canon. The main plot of the story, however, is traditional, expressing the most essential themes, such as "Achilles, the best of the Achaeans" (in reference to the work of Nagy 1999 [1979]) or "the tenth year of the Trojan War." This construct partially depends on the traditional oral style, but also makes use of themes developed in specific epics or their oral precursors. For that reason, Kullmann does not consider it right to draw direct parallels between Homer's poetry and the epics of South Slavs.

An intermediate stance is taken up by scholars also identified as oralists. Bernard Fenik, in his study of fight scenes in the *Iliad* as typical (Fenik 1968), applies a meticulous analysis similar to those of Kakridis and Kullmann. To various degrees, Alfred Heubeck (1989; 1992), Mark W. Edwards (1991) and Richard Janko (1992) have accepted the basic thesis that Homeric themes are derivative with regard to the tradition of the Cycle. On the other hand, Laura M. Slatkin in *The Power of Thetis: Allusion and Interpretation in the Iliad* (1991) shows how alive and respected by Homer the epic tradition was.

31 Kullmann 1984:311.

32 Kullmann 1984:315.

Jonathan S. Burgess, in *The Tradition of the Trojan War in Homer and the Epic Cycle* (2001), indicates that the author of the *Iliad* must, indeed, have been aware of scenes known from the Trojan Cycle. The Cycle, in turn, though open to innovation, was essentially a compact and stable story. Burgess however, does not refrain from attacking significant findings of the Neoanalytic school—for example, the presence in the *Aethiopis* of a sense of revenge driving Achilles to kill Memnon (1997).

Kenneth Dowden (1996), by contrast, embracing Neoanalytic findings almost in their entirety, has argued that, on the one hand, we should distinguish what in Homer is typical and clearly belonging to the oral tradition and, on the other, what may be understood as Homer's creative imitation of other existing epics. In the latter case, Homer proceeds like a typical author of the individual style, whose work is replete with allusions to a "canon of facts" known from tradition and other epic works, especially the *Aethiopis*. Homer often deliberately finds solutions other than the traditional ones and avoids direct references to more known events. In this respect, he differs from the much more traditional author of the *Aethiopis*.

A similar standpoint is taken by Douglas L. Cairns (2001), who treats Homeric references to traditional tales as allusions that are understandable by the listeners of the epic.[33] Cairns also notes that the familiarity with events from outside the story narrated in the *Iliad* give listeners deeper insight into the poem.[34]

A specific way of reconciling the two stances was proposed by Malcolm M. Willcock, first in his *Companion to the Iliad* (1978), and later in an article on neoanalysis, in *A New Companion to Homer* (1997): Homer may simply be referring to a song known to us as the *Aethiopis*, which was actually part of his repertoire (authorship of the *Aethiopis* is sometimes attributed to Homer). This idea has been supported by West (2003), but criticized by Kullmann (2005) in defense

33 Cairns 2001:42–43: "It may be objected that, striking though the parallel between the two sequences [the death of Patroklos and the death of Achilles] is both in detail and in broad sweep, the similarities are to be attributed not to the use of typical scenes as a standard feature of the oral poet's art; but surely even use of a type-scene in one context might remind an audience of its use in another, especially where the latter is a significant and familiar one. Where, moreover, a motif seems more appropriate in one context than another, there must be a presumption that it has been adapted from the context where it is more at home: thus, while it is true that Achilles goes to face both Hektor and Memnon with the knowledge that his own death must follow, the statement of Thetis that it will follow 'straightaway' (18.96) upon the death of Hektor is simply not as true as it would be in the case of Achilles' confrontation with Memnon."

34 Cairns 2001:44: "Though it is no doubt true that the character's orientation towards past and the future could be a significant feature even if relevant elements of past and future had been invented, this case in particular shows how the audience's knowledge of events subsequent to those narrated in the poem can lend an extra dimension to their response."

of "true" neoanalysis, and by Allan (2005), who sees it as an aberration from an oralist point of view. Criticism of Willcock's stance is more justified from Burgess's point of view, because it is important to note the coherence and consistency of the cyclic tradition.

Neoanalysis, then, noticed the problem of linking particular themes present in Homeric poems with the oral epic tradition. Nevertheless, some scholars claim that in the oral tradition there function neither allusions nor imitation in any form."

Adrian Kelly (2006; 2012) assumes that parallels in plots cannot be treated as an allusion or imitation of other texts or plots if it is possible to find a reason for their placement in a given context.[35] Similarly Jensen believes that neoanalysis strives to add meanings absent in Homeric poems.[36]

John Miles Foley and Justin Arft (2015) set four principles governing the oral tradition. Firstly, "a poetic tradition consists not of artifacts but of instances ... that were generated from a large and malleable body of narrative."[37] Secondly, there is a "difference between repetition and recurrence," of which the latter treatment is characteristic for the oral tradition and oral-derived works. The recurrence is not a reference to any specific fictional situation, but only a variant replication of a traditional pattern. Formulae, typical scenes, and story patterns are not repeated but "they idiomatically recur as the poet (re-)makes the poem-instance." Thirdly, both the particular elements of the oral technique and the whole songs are metonymically related to the multi-form tradition and meanings that tradition assigns to them.[38] Fourthly, products of the oral tradition have never created nodes allowing establishment of a "fixed and final" common plot. None of the versions of a given story plays a more special role in tradition nor is "authoritative" in relation to others.[39] Therefore, from this point of view, it is inconceivable to accept any idea of intertextual relationship or of the continuity of the plot throughout various tales.

The theory of traditional referentiality has been slightly re-formulated by Barbara Graziosi and Johannes Haubold (2005). They strongly underline the role of the audience in giving meaning to the message during a performance. To the listeners familiar with tradition some motifs and formular phrases reverberate in the repetition. This resonance either confirms what is already known to

35 Kelly 2012:255: "There is nothing inexplicable or poorly motivated here [in the *Iliad*], and nothing which would be better motivated in another text/poem/story than it is in the *Iliad*."

36 Jensen 1980:36: "The interpretations tend to read into the text what is not there."

37 Foley and Arft 2015:83.

38 Foley and Arft 2015 2015:84-85. Foley 1991.

39 Foley and Arft 2015:85.

them, in which case it endows these utterances with the authority of tradition, or—if it is new or even contrary to tradition—it attracts their attention. In the latter case the dissonance born in the confrontation with tradition suggests that here is something special, which needs particular attention of the audience.

Alongside the above-mentioned positions, there appear proposals demonstrating that it was possible for allusions to function within the oral tradition. Jonathan S. Burgess (2006; 2009; 2012) treats Homeric references to cyclic material as "motif transference"—active in effect upon the audience of such festivals as the Panathenaia and having implicit correspondence with mythic tradition (conversely to stories from outside the Trojan Cycle, which are explicit in character and fulfill a paradigmatic function in Homeric poems).

Such migrations of motifs from the Cyclic narratives to Homeric poems cannot be defined as "quotations," because they do not function in Homer as repetitions of traditional events, but every time appear in a transformed form. Burgess states that the transfer of motifs "in an allusive manner" enables us to regard Homer as "meta-Cyclic." Like Dowden, he thinks that the creative transformation of traditional motifs distinguishes Homer from the Cyclic tradition and situates his poems outside of it. Nevertheless, thanks to the intertextual allusions to the Cycle, Homeric epics become infused with a depth of meaning.[40]

Christos C. Tsagalis (2008; 2011), who shares Burgess's opinion on the functioning of intertextual references within the oral tradition, is of the opinion that research should take into account the factor of competition. The transformation of traditional motifs in the *Iliad* and the *Odyssey* is a result of performative competition, which might have provoked the desire to create the best fulfillment of tradition.[41] Hence, according to Tsagalis, Homer may be described not only as "meta-Cyclic" but also "meta-epic."[42] Unquestionably, he locates Homer outside the rest of the oral tradition, treating his poems as a separate entity of a different nature. He also believes that thanks to the intertextual allusiveness Homeric poems gained refinement securing them a special position within the epic tradition.[43]

40 Burgess 2009:71 takes into account that in the conditions of intertextuality the audience can interpret certain reflections of motifs as a significant allusion.

41 Intertextual relationships between the *Iliad* and *Odyssey* were earlier suggested by Pucci (1987).

42 This term is taken from Finkelberg (2003; 2015) who suggests that some differences between the Cyclic and Hesiodic tradition taken together and the preserved Homeric epics (where the motifs of the destruction of heroes, their immortalization, and the contribution of returning heroes to the colonization of lands outside Greece are suppressed) indicate that Homer goes beyond the oral tradition.

43 Tsagalis's article "γυναίων εἵνεκα δώρων: Interformularity and Intertraditionality in Theban and Homeric Epic," *Trends in Classics* 6:357–398, where he introduces the term "intertraditionality"to

The above-mentioned proposals show that there is an urgent need to combine the findings of these two schools. This conclusion is prompted by the reading of *Homeric Contexts. Neoanalysis and the Interpretation of Oral Poetry* (Montanari, Rengakos, and Tsagalis 2012). The collected articles by more than twenty scholars reveal not only a diversity of positions, but also a need for a multi-sided view of the issues raised by the conference.

Noting the recently growing interest in linking the position of oral theory and neoanalysis, Franco Montanari assumes that, considering the stabilization of texts in the liminal phase of the transition from orality to writing, there is a possibility that the author of the *Iliad* could make references to other epic works (Montanari, Rengakos, and Tsagalis 2012:6):

> On the one hand, we have the idea that as the oral tradition evolved over time, it little by little reached a phase of texts that were fixed and more or less stably memorized, although not yet enshrined in the unchangeable medium of the written form. Thus one can speak of gradually fixed performance traditions. On the other side stands the idea that the "sources" of the Homeric poems need not necessarily have been written poems: they may, instead, have been oral poems fixed by virtue of memorization, and therefore existing in a form that was no longer improvised and unstable, even though it was not written. ... a memorized oral text, i.e. one that is substantially stabilized, is equivalent to a written text, even though in modes and forms that do not coincide exactly with those characteristic of a totally literate civilization, and such a text can act as an individual source/model. Its earlier poetic history may have been part of totally oral poetry, rooted in the traditional practice of improvisation, and the "typical" in the forms of content and expression belongs precisely to this kind of poetry. But at a later stage, traditional improvised poetry gave way to a situation featuring fixed and individual oral texts, which also allowed for mutual relations of source-model and imitation. Typical scenes or traditional themes could thus become individual motifs belonging to a specific poetic-narrative context and endowed with particular elements peculiar to that individual poem; a scene could be entirely composed of fully traditional elements and yet constitute an individual variation of a certain motif.

illustrate the relationship of Homeric poems to rival oral traditions was unfortunately unavailable to me.

So it would no longer be "pure orality" based on improvisation but rather a slow, gradual process of transformation, with elements of imitation, well known to us from written literature.

This balanced opinion, to which many contemporary philologists subscribe, seems to me totally faulty. Firstly, it is formulated with such a degree of generality that it does not convey any idea of what could have triggered these changes or how the whole process could have happened. Secondly, Montanari goes too far in trying to combine Gregory Nagy's concept of the evolutionary development of Homeric texts with Martin West's view that in Homer's case we cannot speak of orality as understood by Parry and Lord. The aim of all his effort is to confirm scholars' expectation that even if Homer's works differ slightly from the texts produced in a written culture, they already contain germs of literary imitation, and so can safely be approached philologically from the perspective of intertextual relationships. Thirdly, Montanari assumes the need to take into account the findings of neoanalysis, since he postulates, after Kullmann, that the gradual stabilization of the entire epic tradition gave rise to a *Faktenkanon*, which the author of the *Iliad* had to respect.[44] In Chapter 1, I will try to demonstrate that such a "historical" model of understanding the past is foreign to the oral poets and no less to the author of the *Iliad*. For Kullmann, "the wrath of Achilles and his fight against Hektor are not central events of the Trojan cycle of myths."[45] In the next chapters, I will try to prove that the wrath of Achilles and his heroic deed—i.e. killing the most dangerous enemy—is absolutely central and, in a way, even *the only* event of the Trojan War depicted in this epic cycle.

An intriguing point of view and a real challenge to my ideas are Bruno Currie's hypotheses, introduced in the *Homeric Contexts* and further developed in a later monograph (2012 and 2016). Currie demonstrates an unquestionable link between some Greek epic narrations and Near Eastern poetry and suggests the need to take into account textual allusions regardless of whether we are dealing with "a purely oral" or "a mixed oral and written tradition."[46] I believe that our positions are not mutually exclusive, but since the matter needs to be considered and discussed in depth, I do not refer to Currie's arguments more extensively in this publication. In his work, Currie accepts assumptions similar to mine: "that there was abundant Greek hexameter poetry preceding the *Iliad*; that the poet of the *Iliad* and (some of) his audience knew (some of) that poetry; that we, too, may occasionally glimpse that earlier poetry, however dimly; that Homer alludes

44 Montanari 2012:9–10.

45 Kullmann 1984:317.

46 However, much more convincing is Bachvarova (2016), who suggests that the transmission of Anatolian and Mesopotamian motifs into Greek culture was made primarily by bilingual oral performers.

to; and that he does so, typically, in order to highlight differences in his own approach."[47] I also share Currie's position that the use of allusions is not exclusively a feature of the *Iliad* but that it applies to Greek tradition as a whole (the focus of my attention, however, remains more on the unpreserved oral tradition). However, according to Currie, allusions refer to individual works (although he assumes hypothetically the existence of some of them),[48] while I believe that allusions do not refer to a specific text but to particular events and situations recalled by multiverse tradition (understood not as a series of random and unrelated songs but an open set of works analogously situated in one macro-story, see Ch. 1 and 5, below). Compared to Tsagalis's concept of intertextuality, Currie does not think of the mutual interaction of the individual works of the extant epic, but of the unidirectional allusion of work A to work B.[49] Currie shows "Homer's allusive art" on the level of poetics rather than the plot of the myth (although he also repeatedly draws attention to the impact of allusions on listeners). Thus the practical methodological criterion for recognizing allusions that can be regarded as "marked and meaningful"[50] in Currie's case is different than in mine.

Egbert Bakker (2013) points out that in the mind of the singer particular formulas are linked to contexts where they have been used before. In this sense, one can speak of a scale of increasing interformularity. This is because certain phrases and even sets of formulas are linked in the singer's mind to specific contexts, to which, by repeating a given set of phrases, he directly refers.[51] The link between formulaic language and context stems from performance practice, where certain elements of speech are repeated many times. The repeti-

47 Currie 2016:2–3.

48 Currie 2016:12: "Individual poems may be fixed enough to serve as an object of allusion."

49 Currie 2016:17.

50 Currie 2016:33–34: "The condition of markedness will be met when allusion is claimed between passages which share striking and distinctive non-typical elements, or typical elements that are deployed in contextually striking and distinctive ways. Markedness limits the possibility that the connection between two (or more) contexts is due just to coincidence or to typology. The meaningfulness requirement guarantees that a claimed allusion should increase our understanding of a passage or help it to make sense in a larger interpretative framework." See Barker and Christensen's criticism (2019:Introduction).

51 Bakker 2013:159: "The more restricted an expression, the more specific the context in which it is uttered, and the higher the point at which it can be placed on the scale. (On the other hand, a high frequency of a context to which a given phrase is restricted will lower its position on the scale, since frequency diminishes specificity.) It is also important to observe that the continuum of increasing specificity is quintessentially cognitive: it is based on the judgment of the performer/poet and the audience as to the degree of similarity between two contexts: the more specific a formula and/or the more restricted its distribution, the greater the possible awareness of its recurrence and of its potential for signaling meaningful repetition. In this way the scale of interformularity does not code what is for the modern reader or scholar—the scholar of Virgil or Apollonius of Rhodes—the likelihood of allusion or quotation, but what is for the epic poet and his audience specificity of the similarity of scenes to each other."

tions are also not random but rather a self-reflexive or even conscious choice by the performers. At the low end of this scale there are expressions which are a regular response to a recurrent need (Bakker refers to this as a "verbal ritual") of introducing a hero who plays a given role, especially when he is about to speak. Higher up on this scale there are formulaic expressions which, repeated within the epic, tip the viewer off to their previous use in a different context. What is possible or appropriate in one context, ceases to be so or is so only apparently in another. Individual repetitions can act as "suggestive allomorphs" of other instances of a given theme; the replicated allomorphs reveal the range of possibilities for various uses of a given theme. At the top of the scale of interformularity is, according to Bakker, the situation "where the repetition may extend across the boundary of the work."[52] Bakker finds examples of deliberate evocation of formulas used in the *Iliad* to impress listeners who remember the Iliadic use of given formulas and can juxtapose it with the present one.[53] I discuss more deeply Bakker's views in Chapter 5.

Basing his argument on comparative studies of contemporary oral cultures, Jonathan L. Ready (2019) points to the possibility of a text becoming fixed within the oral tradition and observes the workings of the mechanisms of entextualization.[54] There can be no free transformations of the plot, and the works of the oral poets are not entirely ephemeral as they are linked with the tradition of performance rather than one-off performance. Homeric poets were able to produce during each performance utterances "capable of outliving the moment."[55] The oral poet also ties his story to other stories, taking into account past and future events, and thus creates anticipatory intertextuality. Ready also points to the importance of the scribe's role in the process of shaping the piece during dictation.

Although I refrain in my book from trying to find an answer to how the text of the *Iliad* was finally formed, I believe that Ready's position supports my understanding of the poem's text as an intentionally reconfigured plot reproduced in successive performative allomorphs of the myth.

Elton T. E. Barker and Joel P. Christensen (2019) revisit Foley's concept of traditional referentiality and Graziosi and Haubold's concept of resonance, while criticizing the search for intentional allusions and intertextual references

52 Bakker 2013:168.

53 Leodes' supplication and Odysseus's refusal (*Odyssey* 22.312) and Lycaon's supplication and Achilles' refusal (*Iliad* 21.74); see Bakker 2013:154–156, 168–169.

54 Entextualization is "the process of rendering a given instance of discourse a text, detachable from its local context" (Ready 2019:18, quoted after: Urban, G. 1996. "Entextualization, Replication, and Power." In *Natural Histories of Discourse*, eds. M. Silverstein and G. Urban, 21–44. Chicago).

55 Ready 2019:15.

in Homeric studies. Instead, to describe how references are used in the oral tradition, they refer to the rhizome theory, in which individual realizations of the tradition would exhibit ahierarchical "connectivity and potential for adaptation and change."[56] This "potential for change" is revealed in the performative competition and influences the shape of individual poems. The large number of references in Homeric poems to the theme of the Theban Wars is due to the mutual rivalry between the two epic traditions (in this sense, the rivalry is described by the scholars as "dynamic" and "multidirectional"). The reason why the Trojan epic tradition has overshadowed the Theban tradition is that the Homeric poems are better adapted under agonistic conditions to the growing needs of Panhellenism.

Fabian Horn (2021) assumes that "the narrative elements surrounding the story of the death of Achilles were reasonably well-known, stable, and specific enough for the poet or poets of the *Iliad* to be able to recognise these traditional motifs and their original context."[57] In a number of references, especially in the depiction of Patroklos's death, they are used by the author of the *Iliad* as external analepses and prolepses foreshadowing Achilles' death and symbolically alluding to the fall of Troy.[58] Horn opines that numerous similarities between the *Iliad*'s narrative and the story of Achilles as depicted in the *Aethiopis* are structural in nature and show how traditional material was deliberately and masterfully used by the author of the *Iliad*. The poet needs the transference of motifs and symbolic correspondences to bring out the heroic aspect of Achilles, who is destined to death rewarded only by eternal fame.

Thomas J. Nelson (2021; 2022) postulates that Homeric poems contain allusions to the wider epic tradition, the scale and significance of which he shows in his analysis of individual passages in the *Iliad* and *Odyssey*. Homer, trying to compete with other epic traditions, seeks to outdo alternative versions of the tradition and find the approval of the audience for his own (see Kelly 2008). In this sense, the Homeric vision of Penelope is meant to trump previous versions. This conclusion is possible due to highlighting "an ongoing intertextual rivalry within the *Odyssey* centered around the figure of Penelope."[59] Nelson's approach, seeking not so much links between one text and another text or a specific work of oral tradition, but rather finding out "how the *Odyssey* appropriates and repurposes the characters and themes of a rival oral tradition"[60] is very close to my own strategy in this book. Using this methodology, Nelson

56 Barker and Christensen 2019:Introduction.

57 Horn 2021:3.

58 Horn 2021:17.

59 Nelson 2021:29.

60 Nelson 2021:30.

interprets the entire action of Book 1 of the *Iliad* as a series of allusions to the issue of the offering of Iphigenia at the departure of the fleet from Aulis. This analepsis to the events preceding the narrative of the *Iliad* ties the *Iliad* to tradition, at the same time being an instance of its differentiation. Nelson assumes that certain elements of the myth are essential and therefore they remain stable within tradition.[61] What is of particular importance for my argument, Nelson draws attention to the sequence of mythological motifs, which, in his view, is reconfigured accordingly to the needs of the narrative.

Cyclic poetry

Studies of Greek cyclic epics are hampered for several reasons—above all, the extremely small number of extant sources, limited to modest citations and brief descriptions of content, scattered far and wide across the whole of ancient Greek literature. Most of this material is found in scholia to Homer,[62] but also in the scholia to other poets, especially Pindar and Lycophron. The contribution of papyrus discoveries to knowledge of the Cycle has been negligible. A summary of their contents is found in an extract from Proclus's *Chrestomathy* in Photius's antiquarian *Library* (ninth century CE). Of the same provenance are the summaries of the cyclic poems currently included in *Iliad* manuscripts.[63] Unfortunately, the identity of Proclus is hard to determine. Most probably he was either a grammarian under Antonine dynastic rule (second century CE) or a Neoplatonist who lived three hundred years later (and died in 485 CE).[64] The difference in dates is significant, since it is assumed that when writing these summaries, Proclus still had texts of the Cycle.[65] Still it must also be acknowledged that even in that earlier period access to such sources was already extremely rare,[66] which

61 Nelson 2022:57.

62 The poetry citations are from the scholia attributed to Aristarchus, who argued against cyclic versions and referred to them, whereas Zenodotus simply omitted whatever he felt was inappropriate to Homer.

63 Fantuzzi and Tsagalis 2015:34–40.

64 Huxley 1969:123–124; Severyns 1928:245. Currently the first option is preferred, West 2013:7–11; Fantuzzi and Tsagalis 2015:35.

65 A sentence introducing the summaries in the *Chrestomathy* states that the poems only survived to Proclus's lifetime because they supplemented the poetry of Homer. Welcker (1865) and other German scholars after him (e.g. Wilamowitz 1884:331) cast doubt over the probability of Proclus having at his disposal original cyclic poems and instead believed that he only had extracts (in accord with the then prevalent identification of Proclus as a fifth-century Neoplatonist). A defense of the *Chrestomathy* statement (τοῦ ἐπικοῦ κύκλου τὰ ποιήματα διασώθεται) was successfully undertaken by Allen (1908).

66 Severyns (1928:75–76) notes that there is evidence that cyclic epics were unknown in those times. Joannes Philoponus states that such poetry was not read in the times of Peisandros (222–235 CE) and that it had disappeared by the sixth century CE.

undoubtedly makes less certain the reliability of Proclus's summary. Apart from very brief outlines, the summary also includes information on the authorship of particular poems and the number of books. Yet the question of the extent to which all this information corresponds to the actual form and content of the poems remains, for it is certain that the purpose of this epitome was to provide readers of Homer basic insight into what preceded and also followed the events described in the *Iliad* and *Odyssey* (see the scholion to Clement of Alexandria, *Protrepticus* 2.30). At many points, ancient testimonia actually contradict Proclus or provide other versions (e.g. Apollodorus, Pausanias). Likewise, the question of the authorship of the poems is uncertain, since here, too, there are large divergences.[67] On the other hand, we know that Attic tragedies were also often based on cyclic poetry, and therefore they may be treated as a polyphony of voices recounting the same events.

The argument, supported by linguistic analysis,[68] that cyclic poetry appeared later than Homer was long persistent, though ultimately disproved by the studies of Richard Janko (who dated the *Kypria* to around 675 BCE).[69] The view that the cyclic poems were derived from Homer by later *epigones*, whose form and style were vastly inferior to Homer's masterpieces, was prevalent in the late Classical and Hellenistic periods. All information from these sources was, therefore, treated by ancient critics as substandard and unreliable. The question of Homer's dominant position, however, has in recent decades been questioned as a result of neoanalytic studies and the recurring question of the late writing-down of Homeric poetry (the Peisistratid edition). In addition to this, there is also iconographic evidence from the Archaic period that shows that on vase paintings the dominant themes came from the cyclic epics, whereas Homer's epics only started being illustrated in the second half of the sixth century BCE.[70]

While knowledge of the cyclic poems in later antiquity is sketchy, the outline of the macro-story of the Trojan War must have been fairly well known (as corroborated by the *Tabulae Iliacae*), if only from the works of mythographers and summaries of the whole Cycle, much earlier than Proclus's ones. West suggested that such a summary had already been prepared in the fourth century BCE by Phayllos.[71]

67 For example, the *Kypria* is attributed to Stasinus, but also to Homer; on another account, the *Kypria* was composed as a gift from Homer to Stasinus. For discussion of the authorship of the poems, see Davies 1989a:100n; West 2013:23; Fantuzzi and Tsagalis 2015:22–24.

68 Wackernagel 1970:178–183; Dihle 1970:148–149; Davies 1989b.

69 Janko 1990a:171–176 i 200. On dating of the cyclic poems, see West 2013:96–196; Burgess 2015:51–52.

70 See Lowenstam 1997; Burgess 2001:35–44.

71 West 2013:17–18.

Another issue is the equivocal use of the term "cycle" (*kyklos*). Sometimes it refers only to the events of the Trojan War, and other times not only to the Trojan Cycle, but also to the Theban Cycle, the Gigantomachy, etc., and sometimes even all mythological stories are presented in an epic generally called *The Cycle*.

The compilation and segregation of all sorts of diverse data from historical sources, their analysis, and their verification of value have been the main tasks of scholars engaged in the study of the epic cycle. The pioneering work, as in many other subjects concerning ancient Greek literature, was carried out by Friedrich Gottlieb Welcker in *Der epische Zyklus oder die Homerischen Geschichte* (1835).[72] Today, the most important books on the subject are Albert Severyns (1928)[73] and Malcolm Davies (1989a). All the above studies, however, are strongly influenced by the authority of ancient scholars. Therefore, they treat historical sources as dependent in content and form on the poems of Homer and share the ancient authors' negative appraisals of cyclic poetry. On the other hand, it was Welcker who first suggested that at least some of the material in cyclic poems could be traditional or even pre-Homeric.

The cyclic poems have been regarded as inferior and essentially different from the poetry of Homer. This view has been supported by Griffin (1977), who notes that unlike Homer's two monumental poems, which are essentially rationalistic, cyclic poems are replete with fairy-tale elements and miraculous events.[74]

A new perspective was added by the Neoanalysts, who removed from the Greek epic tradition the burden of Homeric supremacy—at least in the sense that Homer was not regarded as the originator of cyclic poetry plots.

In the second half of the twentieth century, cyclic poetry studies came under the increasingly stronger influence of oral theory. Hermann Fränkel (1975) claimed that cyclic poetry represents the oral epic tradition in the same way as Homer's poems. The Cycle, according to him, was a never-ending story, accessible to the *aoidoi*; where one epic song ends, another begins.

Studies undertaken at the turn of this century have given yet another insight into the subject. Ingrid E. Holmberg (1998) argued that the cyclic poems naturally stemmed from the same oral tradition as Homer's poetry, but the writing down or stabilization of the oral *Iliad* and *Odyssey* text led to the need to

72 Welcker 1865–1882. Later, the cyclic epic was analyzed only as an aspect of Homeric questions; the most distinguished of these analyses, if only on account of its impact, was Wilamowitz 1884:328–380.

73 This is just one of his several works on the subject.

74 Griffin 1977:45 also notes other distinguishing features: "In the Cycle both heroism and realism are rejected in favour of an over-heated taste for sadistically coloured scenes; more striking, even more perverse effects are once again what is desired."

record other traditional songs as prequels and sequels of the two monumental works. Holmberg rightly attributes the multiformity of the cyclic poems to their oral origins, which she also sees in the epic songs' absence of normalized form, which only came with the integrated and uniform works of Homer. Homer's works should therefore be seen as displaying a "new quality," affecting the form of the epic Cycle, as well as the development of later Western literature.

Burgess (2001), in turn, primarily stressed that cyclic stories preceded those of Homer, though he criticized many other findings of the Neoalysists, stating that neoanalytic reconstructions were often based on very tenuous evidence (1995; 1997; 2004b). Nonetheless, Burgess (1996 and 2001) also pointed out that the *Kypria*, as well as other cyclic poems, included stories that went beyond what is mentioned in Proclus's summary. The *Kypria*, *Aethiopis*, *Little Iliad*, and *Ilioupersis (The Sack of Ilium)* were not subsequent episodes of a continuous cyclic narrative but, in his opinion, an account of the entire Trojan War.[75] From Burgess's point of view, nothing stands in the way of assuming that cyclic poems were created independently of Homer's *Iliad*.

The fluidity of the boundaries of cyclic poetry was earlier pointed out by E. Christian Kopff (1983), who argued that the *Aethiopis* could have previously included a scene with Priam paying a ransom for his son's body (as dramatized in Book 24 of the *Iliad*) and, conversely, the *Iliad* could have initially contained a scene of the killing of the Amazonian queen, Penthesileia, which according to Proclus's account is linked with the *Aethiopis*.

The subject of the multiform nature of cyclic poems and its presence in Homer is also undertaken by Finkelberg (2000), Nagy (2001), and Burgess (2002).

Two monumental works on the *Cycle* have appeared recently: the commentary of Martin L. West (2013), which in addition to an analysis of the testimonia includes an attempt to reconstruct as accurately as possible the poems, and *The Greek Epic Cycle and its Ancient Reception: A Companion*, edited by Marco Fantuzzi and Christos C. Tsagalis (2015), which presents a multitude of relevant subjects and aspects.

[75] Burgess 1996:91: "The possibility is that the original *Kypria* covered the whole Trojan war."

1

Cycle and Song

The Cycle Phenomenon: Determining the Narrative and the Role of the Heroes

SCHOLARS HAVE ALWAYS realized that a work such as the *Iliad* could not have appeared out of nothing. Simultaneously or earlier, there must have existed similar poetry. Yet practically nothing is known of such poetry and, besides, from the outset it was considered vastly inferior to the poetry of Homer. The studies of the neoanalysts and, later, the oralists have revealed beyond all doubt that the Trojan Cycle is not only not derivative of the *Iliad* but is also the source of the latter's basic plot. The complexities of the relationship between the two will be discussed later. First, let us focus on the interdependence of plot. In comparison with other epic traditions, it would seem this is a phenomenon peculiar to Greek poetry.

One must assume that the *Iliad* and *Odyssey* mention events from other epic poems that were known to the listener. We can therefore speak of a certain "super-text"[1] to which the singer refers and is thus able to play a game with meanings that the listener would understand. Since the archaic and classical periods, the super-text plot was represented in the works of "*epigones*" or newer poets, recognized as the imitators and continuators of Homer. From the Hellenistic period onwards, all these works were collectively called "the cycle" (ἐπικὸς κύκλος),[2] which indicates that the plots in these works were considered to be components of a particular whole. The whole plot also encompassed the *Iliad* and *Odyssey*, although there was also always differentiation between Homer's epics and other cyclic poems on account of the exceptional literary

1 I use the term "super-text" after Dowden 1996:51 (see Ford 1992:41 "divinely superintended tale"), although it would be better to use the term "super-story," or "macro-story," which I sporadically use later.

2 Callimachus *Epigram* 28. The "Cycle" was the commonly used name in Roman times (Burgess 2005:347), which is not to say that it was not also used earlier (Aristotle *Posterior Analytics* 77b32). Some scholars, such as Nagy (1996a:75), believe that the name is very old, going back to the very start of Indo-European poetry. This problem will be more fully discussed below.

value of the former. It is possible that at least some of cyclic poems were created to some extent on account of Homer's dilogy.[3] A more probable explanation would be that the writing down of the *Iliad* and *Odyssey* provided the incentive for the writing down or "literary embellishment" of other cyclic poems.[4] This, however, does not alter the fact that the parallel themes and allusions to a super-text in Homer's epics could only be possible if cyclic poems were part of an already widespread and active tradition in Homer's lifetime. This tradition was represented by an undetermined number of songs, perhaps to some extent corresponding to cyclic epics, though they may also have appeared in a different form. What is most important here is the mutual cross-referencing by authors of various songs, whose plots thus acquired a relative consistency. This trend was sufficiently strong and long-lasting that it not only created a framework for one major event, the Trojan War, but also various cycles that were interwoven with one another so as to create an encompassing cosmology and genealogy of several generations of heroes. A symbol of this could be the posthumous marriage of Achilles with Medea and their immortal cohabitation on the Isles of the Blessed.[5]

Hence, practically everything that the ancient Greek mythographers passed on to us as mythology is the material of elaborate epic cycles, often also related to one another. The poetry of the South Slavs, which served as the basis for formulating the oral theory, does not actually reveal any connections between various songs, in particular ones that would oblige another singer to respect a certain arrangement of events or, for instance, take into account the roles

3 See, for example, such narrative elements as the association in the *Ilioupersis* of the female servant of Helen (*Iliad* 3.144) with Aithra, the mother of Theseus, or in the *Telegony* the foretelling of the death of Odysseus by the hand of his own son, Telegonus, which came ἐξ ἁλός, "from the sea" (prophecy of Teiresias, *Odyssey* 9.134–135, while in reality the phrase was supposed to mean "from beyond the sea"; the *Telegony* scene results from a misunderstanding of the *Odyssey* text). These arguments are not very convincing. For there is no certainty that the author of the *Iliad* was unaware of Aithra's specific background, and he could always have not mentioned it for some other reason. Similarly, Teiresias's prophecy can be explained in various ways (Burgess 2005:349). The problem might also lie in Proclus's summary, which links events in the *Kypria* with those in the *Iliad*, such as the abductions of Chryseis and Briseis, as well as the killing of Protesilaos by Hektor. These events might, indeed, have existed in the *Kypria* or they might have been added by Proclus.

4 This view is held by Holmberg 1998.

5 Apollodorus *Epitome* 5.5: λέγεται δὲ μετὰ θάνατον Ἀχιλλεὺς ἐν Μακάρων νήσοις Μηδείᾳ συνοικεῖν. According to other sources, Achilles posthumously married Helen or Iphigenia. In each situation, the event ends the main narrative. Achilles' marriage with Medea is in vain in the approach of Statius, who in his unfinished poem about Achilles links the story of Troy with the Argonaut expedition. In the broader perspective, the *Achilleis* story closes the entire heroic age. This perspective is different from that of the *Kypria*, for instance, which shows a common cause for the Theban War and the Trojan War. The meaning and the way in which different perspectives were outlined shall be discussed later in this chapter.

assigned to heroes. Many Yugoslav songs set their action in important historical events, such as the Battle of Kosovo or the sack of Baghdad, and yet one is disappointed to find there is no suggested continuation in the plot as in the case of the sack of Thebes or Troy.

The role of seeds that would store the power to form plots that go beyond a single song and performance may provide allusions to other plots or the names of the most important heroes recurring in various other songs.

Lord notes that while allusions to other stories are atypical for South Slavs, it does occur in Germanic epics. In *Beowulf*, we find many references to the Germanic tradition:

> ... allusions to Germanic stories and legends. Insofar as the events and personages come from tales and songs in oral tradition, these allusions are easily accepted as part of the oral traditional poem. They point to a poet who was conversant with Germanic legend and history or, put another way, a poet in a rich tradition that contained many songs and stories from the Teutonic past.[6]

As an example, Lord cites the singer singing the ballad of the sons of Finn, the Frisian king who is the hero of another epic, *The Battle of Finnsburg*. According to Lord, such references are analogous to those found in Homer, such as Kirke mentioning the Argonauts (*Odyssey* 12.66–72) or Agamemnon the birth of Herakles (*Iliad* 19.91–99). The role of allusion is noted by Lord only in a very limited way, but it does shed the first ray of light on the phenomenon of the *Iliad* in the mythological context of Greek epics.

It is with the memorization of names and toponyms that Yugoslav *guslari* begin learning their songs because this is what individualizes particular songs. The repetition of names connected with the same characters appearing in the same roles in other songs is fundamental for the continuation of the plot in a new song. In oral tradition, however, such consistency is very difficult to achieve. Known in Homer is the appearance of diverse people with the same name, sometimes even on opposing sides of the conflict. Such oversights with regard to minor characters are in oral performance nothing extraordinary. Often, we can note that the names of significant characters are repeated in various cyclic epics.[7] On the other hand, no one can mistake Theseus or Achilles with anyone else.

6 Lord 1995:109.

7 To give just one example, Kyknos, who played the role of an important enemy of both Herakles and Achilles.

Prince Marko is the hero of many Serbian songs, but one cannot expect a continuation of his story, and his other achievements are also rarely mentioned.[8] The reason for this may be, in part, the state of preservation of the song-cycle of this hero, who in the midst of the fray—fighting Musa—reminds Vila that she was supposed to support him:

> Where art thou this day, sworn sister Vila?
> Where art thou this day? Foul fall thee!
> Falsely didst thou swear,
> Thou wouldst be with me to aid me,
> If haply I should come into evil straits! (translation, D. H. Low)

Among the songs about the Prince, however, there is only mention of his battle with Vila, but not about her promise. Mentioned sometimes is the name of Marko's wife, Jela (Jelica), but the song about his wedding does not mention the name of his bride. Repeated are some of the names of his friends, especially Miloš of Pocerje and "winged" Relja of Pazar.

The application of other names seems much more fluid. In Bosnian poetry the names of both Murat and Šarac could be given to a young hero performing a heroic deed as well as to his enemy—who is usually shown in the bad light of his crimes.[9] A similar dislocation of names can also be observed in the Homeric poems.[10] However, some characters play the same or similar roles and in various

8 An exception is Marko's killing of the robber Musa in the song of *Prince Marko and Đemo Berđanin*, where Đemo seeks to avenge the death of his brother Musa.

9 In songs of return sung by Franje Vuković in Bihac (**Parry 1905**) and by Murat Žunić in Biha (**Parry 1939**), Šarac is the chief positive hero who returns from captivity. [Here and elsewhere, song numbers are denoted by bold text.] On the other hand, in songs of the same type sung at Bijelo Polje by Husein Dupljak (**Parry 6812**), Mustafa Čelebić (**Parry 12408**), Šaćir Dupljak (**Parry 12417**), and Avdo Međedović (**Parry 12465**), Šarac is the actual enemy, who tries to abduct the main hero's betrothed and is therefore killed by the hero. Of course, other names are possible for both the main hero, as well as his archenemy. It is interesting that Šarac, in Žunić's song, invents a story where he presents himself as Bećiragić Meho, the hero of a completely different song, which was sung by Mumin Vlahovljak (**Parry 12468**). This is strikingly similar to, for instance, a story invented by Odysseus in which the hero presents the son of Idomeneus as his enemy. Besides, it is surprising that the name Šarac is used at all in reference to people, since it is primarily the name of Prince Marko's remarkable horse, who accompanies the hero in all his adventures. The name comes from the color of the horse, which is more like that of cattle than a heroic steed. "His horse is not as other, / But piebald like as a cattle-beast" (translation, D. H. Low).

10 Many Trojan warriors bear clearly Greek names, to mention only Alexander and Hektor. The case of Hippothoos is more interesting. In the *Iliad*, Ἱππόθοος is the name of a son of Priam (24.251) and also of the leader of the Pelasgians, Trojan allies (2.840–843). This name also appears among the names of the Achaean leaders participating in chariot races in the depiction of the funeral games for Patroklos on the François Vase. Only one among the names of the competitors presented on the vase (Diomedes) matches the account of the race in the *Iliad*, which probably indicates a different tradition of presenting this event than that in our *Iliad* (see González 2013:64).

songs have the same personal traits. Tale of Orašac appears as a hero indispensable for the success of various adventures in quite independent songs. He is an exceptionally courageous hero with absolutely unheroic conduct and external appearance, yet his presence seems to have a magical quality because it ensures military success. Foley notes that it was only thanks to their familiarity with the heroic tradition that listeners were able to appreciate the comedy of this portrayal (in fact, it was a *condicio sine qua non* for understanding this character). Therefore, each time a metonymy of the epic tradition is evoked, there is, at once, a gibe at the conventionally heroic portrayal of the protagonist, as well as a presentation to the public of a character they probably knew from other songs.[11] Another figure that appears in various songs in a *primus inter pares* role is Mustajbeg. He is presented both on the side of the main hero (as in *The Wedding of Smailagić Meho*), and also as his enemy, "he often heads up the party of suitors vying for an imprisoned hero's wife or fiancée in a Return Song," and thus he performs a similar role to Antinoos in the *Odyssey*.[12]

In the Trojan Cycle, we have a certain established sequence of events to which are ascribed specific characters, sometimes in an arbitrary fashion. At other times, however, the same tasks are undertaken by various heroes (this most often happens when two or three people are involved). This is not a unique situation. The case is similar in the Caucasian Nart epic. Eleazar Meletinsky notes that some themes may be associated with various heroes, yet "in comparison with other epics, the Nart epic is exceptionally consistent in ascribing particular themes to specific heroes."[13] Thus a certain stabilization in linking definite people to specifically defined acts may be considered a consistent trend, though not a necessarily obligatory one in the case of every epic tradition.

In his analysis of traditional epic language, Milman Parry pointed to Homer's observable conversion of certain epithets from distinctive to generic.

11 Foley (1995:39–41) draws attention to the first of these aspects. His argument starts with Mustajbeg (*The Wedding of Smailagić Meho*, 9169–9194) explaining to other pashas assembled before the expedition the reason for the unnatural appearance and behavior of Tale of Orašac. Hence, he assumes (it would seem) that Mustajbeg's explanation addressed to the public in the song was, in actual fact, addressed to the real audience, allowing them to accept Tale as an antihero. On the other hand, one cannot but think that for the real public such information was unnecessary because Tale, with such characteristics, could well have been known to them. Indeed, this is highly probable because this particular hero appears in many songs sung by various singers. Mustajbeg's explanation may also be a conventional form of introducing a character that was quite different from other heroes. In other words, the public would have been surprised if Tale were to be presented in any other way.

12 Foley (1995:40), who adds: "Mustajbeg is also by nature a dangerous, duplicitous person, the very one who in the heat of battle closes the city gates on a countryman and permits his capture by the enemy."

13 Meletinsky 2009:163.

However, when we consider how the epic cycle was formed, we have to look back to an earlier stage when distinct epithets were linked to particular heroes, so as to determine the exact moment when a particular deed was attributed to only one hero. Around a nominal group (name + epithet), various stories were later built, taking into account the predetermined character of the hero.[14] Such an *êthopoiia*, so willingly ascribed to Homer, might, on the other hand, merely be a dramatized and deepened version of traditionally accepted characters, at least with regard to the main heroes.

In Homer we see not only the application of traditional material, but also its transformation, which certainly hinders finding the single event that was the reason for giving the hero one distinctive epithet. We should also appreciate that we can never fully trust cyclic poems that appeared after Homer. For while the *Iliad* did, indeed, rely on the oral cyclic tradition, as did the cyclic poems, those cyclic poems could also to some extent rely on the *Iliad*.

Of course, this does not mean that trying to determine why particular distinctive epithets were formed is necessarily futile. One might, for instance, be tempted to try to find the origins of the epithet "swift-footed Achilles." It is of a traditional nature,[15] but the *Iliad* provides no explanation as to why Achilles should be called "swift-footed." The narrative in other cyclic works, however, does. In the *Kypria,* Achilles runs after Priam's son Troilos, who is riding a chariot. Achilles catches up with Troilos and kills him. "Swift-footed" therefore means "able to catch up with anyone" or "from whom no one can escape." In the *Iliad,* an allusion to this feat is Achilles chasing after the fleeing Hektor, also a son of Priam. One might say that this was a duplication of the story pattern inherited from tradition. Yet the pursuit of Hektor can in no way apply to the "swift-footed" epithet. For a start, the chase is exceptionally long, which emphasizes the stamina rather than the speed of the runners, but above all Achilles does not catch up with the Trojan. Instead, Hektor himself decides that further running is pointless (thus advised by his brother Deiphobos, or rather Athena in Deiphobos's embodiment). In the *Kypria*, the chase scene fulfils the traditional requirements: Achilles is so swift that he can catch up with anyone; he is so fast as to outpace a horse. The *Iliad* scene, on the other hand, might be a refined transformation of this tradition, where the idea that "no one can escape Achilles" is veiled. It is Hektor who decides to stop. Hektor submits to

14 See Foley 1991:18–22 on South Slavic epic; 22–28, 139–150 on Homeric epic; 195–210 on Old English; the epithet is metonymic in such instances as "Tale of Orašac," "Swift-footed Achilles," and "Beowulf, the son of Ecgtheow."

15 Its traditional character is indicated by the abundance of uses and diversity of formulae with the same meaning: ποδάρκης δῖος Ἀχιλλεύς, πόδας ὠκὺς Ἀχιλλεύς, abbreviated as: ὠκὺς Ἀχιλλεύς, ποδώκης ... Ἀχιλλεύς, Ἀχιλῆα πόδας ταχύν, (πόδας) ταχὺν ἀμφ' Αχιλῆα, ποδώκεος ἄντ' Ἀχιλῆος.

fate, albeit with the conviction that he will win, and because he does not know his real fate, he decides to fight.[16] Therefore, it is not so much that the *Iliad* alters a scene from the *Kypria*, but rather that it transforms a traditional theme, whereas the *Kypria* scene more closely follows tradition. The story with the killing of Troilos may, indeed, be the reason why Achilles was called "swift-footed," but there might also be other reasons. This epithet is also consistent with the Cyclic tradition that Achilles was taught by the centaur Cheiron. In the *Iliad*, Homer mentions only that Achilles had acquired from Cheiron the ability to heal wounds, but he does not mention the more important skills of fighting and killing acquired during expeditions to hunt down dangerous wild animals. These hunting expeditions are described by Pindar (*Nemeans* 3.43–52) and included lessons in cruelty (the killing of beasts) and perhaps the eating of the raw meat of slain animals (a heroic initiation), as well as an important detail: bringing into the camp beasts which were still alive (3.47–48: σώματα δὲ παρὰ … / Κένταυρον ἀσθμαίνοντα κόμιζειν, "the still panting bodies [of animals] he would bring to the centaur"), captured thanks to the swiftness of his feet (3.51–52: κτείνοντ' ἐλάφους ἄνευ κυνῶν δολίων τ' ἑρκέων. / ποσσὶ γὰρ κράτεσκε, "killing deer without dogs or treacherous snares because his legs were better [than theirs]").[17] Ancient sources also mention Achilles' special diet, prepared according to the instructions of Cheiron, which included the innards of slaughtered animals, even predators such as lions and bears. James G. Frazer argues that in many cultures it was believed that one could acquire the strength and other characteristics of wild animals by eating their flesh and drinking their blood. Apparently, also included in Achilles' diet there was deer bone marrow which, as Frazer argues, was supposed to provide Achilles with swiftness in running.[18]

Whatever explanation we find in the narrative for the main hero of the Trojan War being given the "swift-footed" epithet, it will not explain the exact meaning and rank of an epithet that for many was of little, if any, significance

16 Scodel (2002:13–14) assumes that Homer avoided mentioning the death of Troilos because he wanted to distance himself from the traditional cruelty of Achilles, as is portrayed in his killing of Troilos. The *Iliad* suggests the nobility of Achilles' character by not mentioning his cruelty in the period preceding his outburst of rage.

17 See Robbins 1993:14–16.

18 Frazer (1921b:70–71n2) explains the special diet as sympathetic magic: "The flesh and marrows of lions, wild boars, and bears were no doubt supposed to impart to the youthful hero who partook of them the strength and courage of these animals, while the marrows of fawns or deer may have been thought to ensure the fleetness of foot for which he was afterwards so conspicuous." Apollodorus (*Library* 3.13.6) mentions the innards of lions and boars and the marrow of deer and bears. Statius (*Achilleid* 2.382–384) only mentions the flesh and marrow of lions. According to Philostratos (*Heroica* 20.2), the diet consisted of wild honeycombs and deer bone marrow, whereas *Etymologicum Magnum* (s.v. Ἀχιλλεύς) only mentions deer marrow.

when describing such a great warrior. In several ancient geographic sources we find a toponym called Ἀχιλλέως δρόμος, "Achilles' running track," sometimes identified as the Island of Leuke, where Achilles was supposed to have been taken after he died to become immortal.[19] The running track was the starting point and basis for all Greek-organized sporting events, including the Olympic Games. The competing runners were young people, both men and women. It is telling that in the *Odyssey* Odysseus boasts of being able to compete with the Phaeacian youth, and only declines to compete in the running on account of having been unable to exercise his legs during long sea voyages (8.230–233). Achilles is a young hero type, a protagonist of the oral song. In the *Odyssey*, that is the role to which Odysseus also aspires, despite his age, and hence his need to justify why he will not compete in the running. The young hero has his analogue in the cult where a young boy winning a race gains heroic status (often embodied as a deity in youthful vigor, demonstrating his strength and willingness to marry—*hieros gamos*).[20] This was possibly preserved in the original epic. Pausanias (3.12.1) mentions a Spartan myth according to which Odysseus was to win the hand of Penelope in a running contest.[21] The "swift-footed" epithet therefore not only identifies Achilles as a hero, as is indicated by Foley's referentiality concept, but more precisely as a "young hero," whose epic role is linked with cult.[22] The episode of killing Troilos by Peleides can therefore be identified as the etiological myth of the phrase "swift-footed Achilles"—a myth of this sort is by nature only one of several possible ones.

Therefore, behind a distinctive epithet there is no concrete event in the epic hero's biography but a characteristic ability, most often supernatural,

19 This island is located off the north coast of the Black Sea, to the west of Crimea (Strabo 7.3.19, Anyonymous *Periplus of the Euxine Sea* 58). Porucznik (2013:43–44) argues that the anonymous *Periplus of the Euxine Sea* (64), as well as Arrian's *Periplus* (20.1) are mistaken to associate "Achilles' running track" with Leuke Island (see also Olshausen 1991:35–37).

20 Fast running was the basis of all Greek sports agons, e.g. the length of the stadium to the altar of Zeus to initiate the Olympic Games, with the names of the winners marking the sequence in which the games were to be played.

21 Contests for the hand of a princess, a theme often appearing in the Greek epic, have Indo-European roots (*varyaśulka* in the *Mahābhārata*; see Jamison 1999): in the *Odyssey* the archery contests for the hand of Penelope (when Penelope appears before her suitors to receive gifts and expressions of admiration, 18.158–303; Telemachos presenting Penelope as a contest prize, 21.106–107; the archery trials, 21.108–423), the contests with the Phaeacian youth, as if for the hand of Nausikaa (Lattimore 1969; Garner 1992), the duel between Menelaos and Paris (*Iliad* 3.70–72), which alludes to a contest for the hand of Helen (Hesiod fr. 197 M.- W.), the killing of Hektor by Achilles entitles his son Neoptolemos to take Andromache as booty (Edwards 1987:65), the chariot race victory of Pelops to win the hand of Hippodamia, Hippomenes' defeat of Atalanta in a footrace to win her hand (Hesiod frr. 73–76 M-W), Oedipus's defeat of the Sphinx to win the hand of Jocasta, etc. This theme often appears in folk tradition and fairy tales and frequently involves elements of life-threatening danger.

22 Compare Graziosi and Haubold 2005:51–53; Barker and Christensen 2019: Introduction.

distinguishing him from ordinary people and also in a specific way from other epic heroes. Relja of Pazar is described as "winged" and sometimes demonstrates feats that are only possible thanks to the supernatural ability of flying. Similarly, in the myth of the Argonauts, the sons of the North Wind Boreas, Kalais and Zetes are able to fly and catch in the air the harpies plaguing Phineus.

The formation of a coherent interconnected plot is a consequence of it being treated as a record of the past. In oral culture, historical data are passed on by word of mouth, and therefore there has to exist a belief in their veracity. The singer has heard the song from his predecessor. He treats it as an expression of tradition and accepts that it is a true story, as everything that stems from tradition. Yugoslav singers only assessed whether a song was bad or good. That is, they assessed the quality of the story. Tradition guaranteed the authenticity, and that is why it was so important for the singer to be convinced of the need to preserve the song in an unchanged form.[23] In my opinion, the reason why the singers were convinced they could not change a single word in the song—they claimed that they repeated it word for word (*reč pro reč*)—was because they needed to control the action of the song. In reality, the *guslar* only tried to remember the sequence of events (which usually took a day), but not the actual words. The entire song he presented in his individual way, using his own formulaic language and narrative imagery. That is why what seems paradoxical to us, the assurance that the message is literal, while the diversity of oral renditions is obvious, did not seem paradoxical to the singers interviewed by Parry and Lord. Instead, they often boasted to Parry and Lord that after hearing just one rendition, they were able to repeat a song in exactly the same way or even better than before. That "better than before" of course depended on the singer's talent—that is, the gift of storytelling. The *guslar* tries to avoid the mistake of omitting an element or including one that would upset his narrative.[24] This is the decisive factor in maintaining story pattern stability in oral tradition.[25]

23 The *guslar* comments were cited by Finkelberg 1998:139; see Lord 1974:71–74.

24 We all know the situation when someone spontaneously tries to tell us about a movie, and after some time realizes that he or she has left out an important part of the plot without which rest of the story does not make sense. The singer cannot make such a mistake.

25 Czeremski (2016b) points out that the stability of the tradition (asymmetrical and more visible on the plane of transmission of meanings than in the plane of expression) is determined in the models of thinking, basic for the human mind and shaped in the process of its evolution. This stability "results from the fact that oral techniques preclude the possibility of going beyond a relatively small and relatively unchangeable set of conceptual models" (174). Czeremski (2016b:158) proposes a model of fixing semiotic constructs in the oral tradition based on four assumptions: 1. Certain forms of thinking are more natural for the human mind than others; 2. Those forms which burden the human cognitive apparatus less are more natural; 3. Writing

In the Greek tradition, truth could also be testified by a Muse.[26] Here, we have to understand some basic concepts. The Muse does not inspire the *aoidos* to sing a song. Nor, contrary to popular belief, does she provide him with poetic talent. The author of the *Iliad* sees himself as merely relaying the words of the Muse. He is her voice, the voice that is audible to everyone. For him and for the public what he was saying was the history of past events, ones that had really happened. They happened a long, long time ago, but they were witnessed and remembered by the Muse as a daughter of Mnemosyne (Memory). This is not literary fiction. The events come to life as they are recounted, and they exist each time for the listeners in the version they hear. No one verifies the version they hear, so the singer does not need to "hide behind" the Muse. No one will say that they know a different version unless the singer, in a flurry of fantasy, steps beyond a framework of the Greek epic (more about which later), by having, for instance, Odysseus die at Troy and Achilles survive. But then again, making such a "grave mistake" would actually be impossible because it would alter the story pattern.

The religious dimension, however, is much deeper. What for us is the epic's mythical and literary material, for the singer was the past—that is, the real actions of gods and people as stated by Hesiod (*Theogony* 100–101) and the *Homeric Hymn to Apollo* 158–161.[27]

The establishment of a relatively compact story cycle and saga must have been related to situating the epic hero within a web of religious beliefs. Just as deities acquired certain permanent qualities, so too the epic hero must also have to a greater or lesser extent been associated with certain characteristics. Moreover, unlike the case of Muslim and Christian Slavs in former Yugoslavia, in ancient Greece heroic myths function also as a cult-tale. The epic song myth had incredible potential for freeing itself and even multiplying quite independently of the cult. Nevertheless, in many ways the association between myth and cult is still very noticeable and tangible in Greek culture; indeed, myth and cult mutually affected each other.

This point of view is supported by Paul Kiparsky's universally accepted explanation.[28] For many years scholars have struggled with the inherent

facilitates the use of unnatural ways of thinking; 4. Oral cultures gravitate toward natural ways of thinking.

26 According to Finkelberg (1998:151), this afforded the opportunity to transform the traditional text. Finkelberg (1998:71–72) also gathered information on determining the veracity of poetry from various cultures.

27 Ford 1992:47: "This whole is what I call the poetry of the past, a presentation of ancient but ever real and valid stories about gods and early mortals. ... it is in a literary, religious, and cosmological sense that Homer's epic may be defined as poetry of the past."

28 Kiparsky 1976.

paradox of oral song. On the one hand, the discoveries of Parry and Lord point to variability as a determining feature of song. On the other hand, it seems to be the case that Homer's poetry survived basically unchanged before being widely recorded in written form. So how was it possible for Homer's poems to remain so well preserved over a period of two or three centuries? One frequent answer is that the "primitive" and "variable" Slavic songs cannot be compared with the refined epics of Homer.[29] Kiparsky's explanation is much more elucidating. This scholar has demonstrated that the stabilization of oral song text depends on the function the song serves, and texts that were used in cults and rituals were enduring. The stability of Homer's epics, according to Kiparsky, could be compared with the durability of Sanskrit poetry, which not only originally emerged as oral poetry, but has survived unchanged primarily in oral form to this day, despite also having been written down. Contemporary comparative studies see the matter much more broadly and show that in oral cultures it is the performance practice that causes utterances to set into their characteristic shape, which has great stability, going much beyond the individual performance. Ready outlines the extent to which the phenomenon of entextualization applies to Homeric poetics, and points to two main factors determining the stability of an utterance formalized according to the demands of performance circumstances.[30] The first is grounded in cognitive research. The story is a common component of the memory of the singer and his audience. The degree to which the "text" is organized determines how deeply it sinks into the memory of all participants of the performance, and that is why poets strive to make it memorizable.[31] The second factor responsible for the retention of the work is its coherence achieved in the course of the performer's interrelationship with the audience, who are able to fill in the gaps in his/her narrative because of the knowledge of other stories functioning in a given tradition.[32]

Attaching certain names and epithets to distinct epic heroes is therefore a consequence of the functioning of the story in a certain established universe connecting the performer and his audience during the performance, and also of a correlation between the epic and the cult versions. The religious aspect of the epic gives it integrity and some narrative coherence. The epic, in turn, allows the myth to acquire universal qualities and break out of the local community to the wider community, tribe, ethnic group, or nation speaking the same language.

29 See Kirk 1966.

30 Ready 2019:20.

31 Saussy (2016:157–163), following Rubin (1995:70), stresses the special role that aural stimulants like rhythm, rhyme, assonances, etc. play in the process of memorization (158): "The more densely the text is packed with pattern, the more securely it takes up residence in the prepared mind."

32 Ready 2019:21.

The second cohesive element in the creation of the cycle is the inclusion of various songs concerning the same historical reality. To use Eleazar Meletinsky's terminology, this was the stage of creating a historical epic, i.e. one that uses a certain historical context from the people's past as the underlying idea, a material and spiritual cultural background to earlier epic stories of the fairy-tale or mythological sort.[33] This historical reality is far more concrete than vague imaginings of what happened in the beginning, in the world in which the culture-hero usually acted. It does not, however, mean that the epic now referred to real history. These were also just imaginings of a bygone, often glorious past, full of blatant anachronisms, as well as the brutality and primitivism attributed to that earlier era. After all, in that bygone age everything must have been much simpler, crueler, and more primitive, lacking things that were present in the culture of the singer—for example, firearms in the times of Prince Marko, or writing in the epoch described by Homer (although there was actually no problem with the singer including such elements in the narrative). These stories thus become more plausible and more easily identified with the past, whose vestiges usually only serve as a base.

In the broader context, we should view the development of the heroic myth in connection with the phenomenon of pan-Hellenization. Gregory Nagy has created an evolutionary model for the making of Homeric poetry.[34] In this model, there are five phases of development, during which Homer's poetry gradually loses its fluidity or multiformity. What interests us, the establishment of the distinctive names and epithets, and the shaping of the story cycle, is found in Nagy's description of the first two phases:

1. "a relatively most fluid period, with no written texts, extending from the early second millennium into the middle of the eighth century in the first millennium."
2. "a more formative or 'pan-Hellenic' period, still with no written texts, from the middle of the eighth century to the middle of the sixth."[35]

33 Meletinsky 2009:417–440.

34 First proposed in Nagy 1981 and more broadly in Nagy 1995, 1996a, 1996b. The objections against this model have been collected by Currie (2016:15–16). They rather do not apply to the concept put forward in this book, as it is focused on how the *Iliad* was created rather than how it has been preserved in the form known to us, although this distinction may seem surprising to many scholars. In the course of my argument, however, I hope to show some of the issues pointed out by Currie in a slightly different light, partly changing the optics of Nagy's model, and partly deflecting some of the criticism about it.

35 Nagy 1996a:109–112 and 1996b:25. One of these dates, however, might need to be revised: the arrival of the Greeks in Greece is generally accepted to be ca. 2100 or ca. 1900 BCE. Robert Drews (1988) sensibly and analytically argues the date should be ca. 1600 BCE.

The pan-Hellenization of the epic was possible thanks to its performance at pan-Hellenic festivals, such as the Pythian Games at Delphi or the Panathenaia in Athens. Pan-Hellenic tradition countered the multiformity of local traditions. According to Nagy, "the degree of Panhellenic synthesis of content and composition corresponds to the degree to which the performance of the composition was diffused."[36] From this point of view, the *Iliad* and *Odyssey* "are more Panhellenic than Epic Cycle poetry."[37] However, the shaping of cyclic poetry also involved going beyond local tradition. When the *Iliad* and *Odyssey* came to the fore, the cyclic myths were already to a considerable extent universalized. The most important heroes had already been ascribed their roles.

The fluidity of the first period is hard to prove on account of the lack of historical sources, but we are forced to assume that the process in which the cycles developed was very long term. Therefore, the unifying of the narrative must have occurred much earlier. Perhaps in the eighth century there was suddenly a rapid pan-Hellenization, but the process must have already been present in Greek culture for some time.[38] One might also hazard the argument that if we make a distinction between the epic and the saga as a form of narration without meter, then thanks to the plasticity of its form, the epic could have compiled various narratives. And this epic form must have served to integrate the cycle plot.

Scholars concede that the *Iliad* is set in a certain mythology and cyclic plot, but this opinion is usually treated with reservation. For example, Martin Mueller writes:

> Homer's narrative is not particularly allusive or cryptic—it differs in this regard from an epic like *Beowulf*—but it assumes on the part of its readers a general knowledge of a set of stories no longer current in our culture ... . We cannot decide with certainty whether Homer did not know or did not choose to refer to the elements of the narrative tradition known to us only from post-Homeric sources, and the situation is

36 Nagy 1996b:25.

37 Nagy 1996b:25. Influenced by the book of Douglas Frame (2009, esp. Chs. 10 and 11), which suggests that Homeric poetry was originally developed during Ionian Dodecapolis festivals in Asia Minor at the turn of the seventh century BCE, Nagy (2010) modernized and intriguingly developed his own concept. The Homeric tradition, including the *Iliad* and the *Odyssey*, as well as the cyclic poems originally ascribed to Homer, was developed through successive though still mutually competing pan-Aeolian, pan-Ionian, and pan-Athenian traditions. The concentration of narratives at common religious festivals must have been conducive to the creation of an interrelated narrative.

38 Also, Tsagalis (2011) is of the opinion that the tendency towards pan-Hellenization must have started to function earlier (he uses the term "Proto-Panhellenism"), and it was then when the Trojan and Theban cycles were shaped.

> further complicated by the fact that virtually all stories include many and often significant variants.[39]

Similar statements have been made by other scholars of Homer. As in the above citation, they claim that the allusions in Homer are not sufficient to hinder the recipient from understanding the story, but they nonetheless provide enough puzzling discrepancies with the mythological tradition, as it is known from other sources. Following the findings of C. Lévi-Strauss,[40] many scholars nevertheless believe it is hard to talk about a canonical version of myths within the Greek tradition. Homer's adaptation of myths for the sake of narrative[41] would be the typical behavior of epic poets in his day. For it is natural in oral culture for a narrative to be adapted to the needs of the situation and context.[42] Tradition adopts forms appropriate to current needs. Changes in the narrative do not fundamentally change the actual story, nor need they spoil it. It is difficult to imagine Homer deliberately wishing to break with tradition. Such an approach seems quite anachronistic. Homer's ignorance also seems unlikely: the lack of references to myths that later became very popular does not necessarily mean he was unaware of them, especially as there is no shortage of allusions to lesser-known myths, some which only appear in his poetry. Instead, this may rather be evidence of Homer's great discernment in mythological and epic tradition. Indeed, his silence regarding certain myths may result from a dialogue with tradition, one that is not obvious to us, since the dialogue is primarily with a contemporary listener who would have been receptive to far more allusions than we can imagine. Nagy notes that many of the discrepancies and inconsistencies found in Homer might actually perform a fundamental role in the epic on a larger scale.[43]

It is not difficult to say why this should be so. Lord noted that although it was hard to find cross-referencing in Serbian or Bosnian songs, they do all have

39 Mueller 1984:28.

40 Lévi-Strauss 1958:Ch. 11.

41 Adapting the myth to the occasion is a well-known observation made by Willcock (1964). Willcock and many other scholars felt this meant an opportunity for the poet to break with tradition and use their own artistic inventiveness. This view has been opposed by Nagy (1996b:136), in whose opinion such changes "are a matter of selection within tradition." A similarly critical opinion is expressed by Tsagalis (2008:25–26), who notes that multiform transformations serve to make intertextual connections between various oral traditions presented in various works: "*Intertextually, autoschediasmata* are a 'surface-phenomenon', which ceases to exist when seen as the compositional *exploration*, not *invention*, of mythical diversity widely diffused by living oral epic traditions. Intertextually perceived invention is nothing more than intertextually oriented exploration."

42 Zieliński 2015b.

43 Nagy 1996b:138.

a common code of meanings. Formulae and themes are not only units organizing the song, they also transfer the entire code of meaning from tradition. In other words, the song may be properly understood only after a certain number of other songs. Epic song not only entertains, it also serves an important social purpose, in Lord's opinion. Beginning from Lord's work, Foley developed his theory of traditional referentiality, according to which understanding each and every element requires reference to the whole tradition, and hence the importance of the metonymy of elements in oral song.[44] Characteristic of oral poetry is reference to what is common in a whole set of epic texts—that is, what results from tradition. In written literature, references are made to specific works.[45] Contrary to Foley's claims, I do not think that this rules out the possibility of an oral epic referring to a specific event known in epic tradition.[46] The functioning of references to events depicted in other songs has, moreover, been confirmed in both Serbian and Bosnian traditions (Danek 1998, 2002, 2010, 2016; Čolaković and Rojc-Čolaković 2004; Čolaković 2006, 2019).[47] Some scholars (Currie 2016) declare the necessity of tracing them in Homeric poems, although, contrary to Currie, I do not believe that allusions should be understood as citing the text of another author as it is in the written tradition. The agreement as to their functioning in the oral tradition does not necessarily mean assuming that they are analogous to such that became the norm in Alexandrian literature.[48] The allusiveness of the oral tradition may be of a different kind than that to which we are accustomed in chirographic culture. I believe these allusions to be oriented not towards the evocation of individual songs or parts of songs but towards the metonymic inclusion of the macro-story[49] (present in the consciousness of the singer and his audience), in particular moments, and in the organization of the entire narrative of the *Iliad*. Characteristic features of these allusions and,

44 Foley 1991:2–37.

45 Foley 1991:8n63: "… a traditional work depends primarily on elements and strategies that were in place long before the execution of the present version or text, long before the present nominal author learned the inherited craft."

46 Foley and Arft 2015:86. Compare Currie (2016:6–7): "It is curious that a scholar who would save the 'traditional oral idiom' for 'oral derived texts' should exclude the allusive idiom from those texts." Currie (2016:8–11) is also of the opinion that the functioning of traditional referentiality does not exclude "specific allusions."

47 Danek (1998; 2002; 2016) argues that while such references cannot be found in the Muslim Bosnian tradition, they are present in the Christian Serbian tradition. However, Čolaković (2006:169) points to some internal references in the Bosnian tradition as well.

48 Currie 2016:24–29.

49 "Metonymic" because, as we shall see, the various threads of the narrative (both such as the episodes with Diomedes or Patroklos and the version of "Achilles' wrath" presented in the *Iliad*) are allomorphic recreations of the "primary" story.

above all, the manner and purpose of their use and their effect on listeners will be discussed in greater detail in Chapters 4 and 5.

Meanwhile, let us return to the forming of a network of connections between various songs in the same tradition. The first stage in this process must have been the appearance of a common denominator in the form of a favorite hero and situation around whom songs are grouped. Thus, the same hero began appearing in many songs, such as Gilgamesh, Herakles, or Theseus, and in Serbian songs, Prince Marko. Alternatively, there are "extraordinary pairs" in the myths of various cultural spheres, often represented as twins.[50] Usually, in successive songs, the task of the hero is to kill a monster. The repetition of the plot means that we are dealing with the replication of the song in variable versions. But these versions start differing from one another more and more with the result that, finally, they give the impression of being the hero's subsequent achievements. Indeed, when we look at the Prince Marko "song cycle," it is hard not to notice that the sequence of the songs there does not result from the plot of the songs, but from the intention of the scholar recording them. It is difficult to apply the term "cycle"[51] to songs that focus on the actions of just one hero, and it would be better to rather call it a quasi-cycle. It seems that the key moment to the integration of various songs came with the application of a narrative superstructure. We have, for example, the Twelve Labors of Herakles, in which the epic hero performs as penance successive achievements in the service of King Eurystheus. This submission to the ruler of Thebes contains in itself the reason why the hero's fate becomes dependent on a divine plan—the actions of the gods. Each successive accomplishment of Herakles is connected with the other ones only by one superior cause-and-effect relationship. The successive works do not result from one another. With each one, the story of Herakles is as if it is being taken up again and again. "Again" means more songs here, the number of which has been limited to the magic number of twelve. In the course of this book, we shall be discussing the cosmogonic frame of the epic, which integrated all the hero's actions and was also responsible for the more refined cyclical structure that developed in Greece.

In the next phase, the hero teams up with other heroes who support him on a mission and, with time, the mission becomes more important than the actual hero. This is evident in the common features of many Greek epic-cycle plots. Certain events are repeated following a specific pattern. This schematism seems parallel to that of oral song. The cycle usually concerns some sort of

50 Frame (2009) demonstrates how the Indo-European solar myth of divine twins is used on various levels and in relation to many pairs of heroes who are brothers.

51 Unfortunately, the term "cycle" is applied to all sorts of epics grouped around the actions of just one figure.

expedition, which requires preparations. After the expedition reaches its destination, usually auspiciously, an important role is also played by the heroes' return home, which is not always auspicious. An inseparable element of the cycle structure is the Catalogue of Heroes, be it the Trojan Cycle, the Theban Cycle, the Voyage of the Argonauts, or the hunt for the Calydonian Boar. This is not a unique feature of the Greek epic. It is interesting to note that the best Yugoslav *guslar*, Avdo Međedović, used in his various songs the same Catalogue of Heroes, often regardless of the song plot or whether a particular hero actually had played a role in it.[52] The names appear of warriors who were never even invited to participate in the given adventure. Greek cycles encompass three generations of heroes, and sometimes the heroes of one epic also appear in other epics. Although genealogical chronology is usually respected, a hero can always be replaced by his son.

The opinion of some scholars that Homer had broken with tradition primarily results from understanding the epic cycle as a collection of tales arranged in a chronological order—for example, the Trojan Cycle—from the wedding of Peleus and Thetis to the ill-fated return of the heroes from Troy. This view is not only very superficial, it also in no way reflects what can be observed in Greek epic tradition, or the oral tradition in general. Such a misunderstanding of the epic cycle probably registers an anachronistic search for a consequential development of the story and a predilection for arranging actions and events in a presupposed order.

In its broad spectrum, the Greek epic resembles the Sanskrit epic. If we search the beginning of the causal link of the plot of *Mahābhārata*, we find various stories going back ever deeper into the cosmogonic and cosmological history. Ultimately, it comes down to a conflict between the asuras and devas. We can also say that the particular episodes of the *Mahābhārata* are in some way a realization of that cosmic conflict. Let us note that an analogy can be drawn with the Trojan Cycle: the Abduction of Helen or the Judgment of Paris are at the same time the start of the whole story, as well as its subsequent elements. On the one hand, we can look back to the birth of Helen, on the other, the birth of Paris to find the beginnings of a story that, nevertheless, can also be connected with the circumstances of Achilles' birth. From this perspective, the wedding of Peleus and Thetis also has its cosmogonic dimension: Zeus and Poseidon were deterred from sexual designs on Thetis by a prophecy that her son would become greater than his father. Therefore, the decision for a cosmic mésalliance was made, one that was ominous for humankind. The goddess was to marry a mortal. This theme is at once the beginning and a subsequent element in the cycle. *Kypria*

52 Lord 1974:28–30; see Lord 1960:86.

fragment 1, presenting the start of the poem, provides us with an even deeper reason for the Trojan War: the complaints of Gaia that she is tired of bearing the burden of such a large number of people provoke the pity of Zeus, who decides to start a war to reduce the human population. A scholiast to the *Iliad* citing this fragment (Schol. D to 1.5) suggests that the marriage of a mortal with a goddess (Peleus and Thetis) and Zeus's fathering of a beautiful daughter (Helen) were proposed by the mischievous Momos, the god of mockery. Proclus's summary of the *Kypria* starts with Zeus and Themis planning the Trojan War; the second-century papyrus commentary (*Oxy.* 3829 ii 9) states more precisely that the king of the gods consults with the goddess[53] on how to end the godlessness of the generation of heroes. It is therefore hard to say where the story begins, especially when the scholiast notes that Zeus took pity on Earth by first starting the Theban War. Thus, we see that the start of the story in *Kypria* fr. 1 refers to a completely different epic cycle. Finding the start to the story is equally difficult to finding its definitive end. In a certain sense, it is the Fall of Troy, but this is, of course, followed by the story of the Returns, with their own multiple themes, which in the case of Odysseus and Agamemnon also involve the next generation. The song becomes part of the cycle, being at the same time its metonym and also its supplement. The meaning of the cycle is provided by tradition, but it can be remodeled by an individual singer in particular songs. Even the metamorphosis of a traditional song such as the fate of Beowulf put into a Christian context does not separate the song from tradition. Quite the opposite, understanding the song still requires recourse to its tradition.

The cycle is not, therefore, a "chronological" arrangement of themes. Such an arrangement of traditional stories was applied in the *Kalevala*, for example, but that reflects the modern approach to composing a tale.[54] Rather, a fitting

53 This papyrus fragment provided the premise for correcting (Heyne) the manuscript summary, which states that the goddess was Thetis, since Aristophanes of Byzantium and Aristarchus saw in this place similarities between the *Kypria* text and Book 1 of the *Iliad*, where Zeus and Thetis collude to save the honor of Achilles (Severyns 1928:247). Holmberg (1998:462), however, rightly notes it is more probable that Themis, as the goddess of law and order, would have been consulted on a plan to punish humankind for not showing the gods due respect.

54 Elias Lönnrot grouped runes about Väinämöinen to obtain a continuous storyline, not only by making selections of various versions, but also resorting to contamination (e.g. by combining Kaukomöinen, Lemminkäinen, and Ahti as one character, Lemminkäinen; Meletinsky 2009:147), putting into order various generations (e.g. linking diverse epic heroes as the sons of Kaleva; Meletinsky 2009:152), and even—as we know—supplementing the runes with his own poetry (approximately three percent). See Foley 2004:178–179. This is an example of nineteenth-century ethnographic gathering of folklore texts. Another example are the Serbian Christian epics collected by Vuk Stefanović Karadžić. A somewhat different approach, but with similar results, was undertaken to prepare a scholarly edition of the Armenian epic *David of Sassoun* (1939), creating a unified text based on fifty variants recorded in diverse Armenian dialects.

analogy to the Cycle would be the *Mahābhārata*, though in Greece a story of such colossal proportions was never created.[55] A parallel situation to the creation of the *Mahābhārata* could have occurred during the Hellenistic period. Such efforts were most probably undertaken, but by then the Cycle would have been constructed along new rules that were different from those of the ancient tradition. Evidence of this are attempts to add subsequent lines to earlier works, e.g. the first line of the *Aethiopis* was to be a direct continuation of the *Iliad* (*Aethiopis* fr. 1; schol. T *ad Iliad* 24.804a).[56] Burgess rightly notes that "no epic could begin in this way."[57] In the Hellenistic period, the past was already viewed historically and therefore the stories were artificially put together in chronological order. The demise of the traditional Greek cycle, however, was primarily due to the works of Homer, which broke away from and overshadowed the cyclic tradition, reducing it to a mere supplement to Homer's poetry.[58]

The *Mahābhārata* seemingly constitutes a complicated amalgam of diverse stories. On closer inspection, however, it turns out that despite occasional inconsistencies and incomplete confirmations, the stories are interconnected in a fairly coherent system of themes and events, thanks to which individual episodes refer to a wider plot and mythological context. Particular episodes overlap and complement each other as part of an interwoven narrative and yet individually each of them also acquires importance thanks to a metonymical connection with cosmogonic tales (one might even speak of a certain hierarchy of stories and corresponding meanings).[59] The logic of the

55 Arguments in favor of comparing the archaic Greek epic with that of Sanskrit on account of similar conditions and principles in the development of "mega-text" are presented by Nagy (1996b:26–32)—in accordance with Nagy's concepts, we can speak of Sanskrit texts being formed through "text-fixation" or "textualization" in conditions of pan-Indianization and accompanying text "diffusion" similar to the pan-Hellenic trend that began in Greece in the eighth century BCE.

56 The concept of creating a work chronologically encompassing the whole of history is apparent in the *Hellenica*, where Xenophon links his historical narrative with Thucydides' *History of the Peloponnesian War* without any introduction, but by simply starting a new paragraph with the phrase μετὰ δὲ ταῦτα ("and next ..."). The idea of continuing the narrative is therefore already present in historical literature of the fourth century BCE and was not necessarily a consequence of Xenophon's individual writing ambitions—perhaps it was rather part of a general effort to write the whole of history by continuing on from the works of predecessors; Fantuzzi and Tsagalis 2015:20.

57 Burgess 2005:348.

58 Shapiro (1989:73) points to how Peisistratos gave the *Iliad* and *Odyssey* a privileged position in the Panathenaia. The reasons for this included political ambitions, for instance by suggesting family connections between Peisistratos and the son of Nestor in the *Odyssey*.

59 My attention was drawn to this aspect of the *Mahābhārata* by the Sanskritist Artur Karp; and see Grintzer 1974, who points to the oral provenance and character of the two major Indian epics, showing how many of their themes are wrongly treated as invalid interpolations, whereas together with the repetitions and contradictions, they actually fulfill all the

Greek cycle might be much more easily understood if we see the similarities with the Sanskrit epic. Every event in the *Mahābhārata* has its place in the structure of the whole and understanding it depends on understanding the whole, but the event itself also influences understanding the whole. A similar, limited unity is present in the *Iliad*, which Finkelberg defines as even identical to the suggested unity of the *Mahābhārata*: "The poems of Homer can be characterized as complex unities in which each part possesses its own narrative function subordinated to the purposes of the whole."[60] This relationship of side stories to the main current of events in the *Iliad* seems to be expressed with more precision by Alden: "preoccupations of the primary narrative are explored and interpreted in the other narratives of the poem: none of the narratives of the *Iliad* is there by accident, and none is merely ornamental; the elements of each are related to some aspect of the main story."[61]

These independent appraisals state that unification based on the same principles is not unique or original in Homer's poetry. There is just one difference: the pan-Hellenic unification process concerned only individual songs presenting major episodes in the whole of the story, but not the entire cycle—that is, the whole of the story encompassing all the episodes of a single war. One might therefore tentatively suggest that if not for the ingenuity of the *Iliad* and *Odyssey*, in Greece there might have been conditions for the creation of a Hellenistic *Mahābhārata*: a cycle encompassing the cosmogony and history of heroes.

The *Iliad* and *Odyssey* grew out of epic tales of a mythological nature. It seems that an epic song could start at any point, describe any episode in the myth, and even quite freely shape it. This freedom generated, on the one hand, the original variability of the traditional myth and, on the other hand, the possibility of reinventing episodes or adding new ones while somehow connecting them with the main axis of events. The reasons for this could be twofold: the desire

conditions of oral development. In the multiform *Mahābhārata* and *Ramayana*, there are no inorganic elements; they all in a measurable way correspond to the framework of the whole. The degree of their relevance, however, also results from the ideological, chiefly religious and aesthetic, reinterpretations they were subjected to in later periods. For Europeans it might be difficult to recognize the harmony and interdependence of the Indian epic. Instead, when juxtaposing Greek epic cycle stories with the *Mahābhārata*, we are more likely to think as Fränkel did (1975:17–18): "None is planless and amorphous, like the *Mahābhārata*, and never is a series of unconnected stories forcibly held together by a contrivance of a purely external framework as in *The Thousand and One Nights*." What we are interested in, however, is the interdependence of themes and how they are bound together by overriding structures. Moreover, I will also be trying to show that the structure of the cyclic stories was not all that harmonious.

60 Finkelberg 1998:136.

61 Alden 2000:vii.

to present an event or minor issue in greater detail, or the desire to combine other local histories with a major course of events. Whether transforming or creating new epic tales, both methods gave the *aoidos* considerable space for invention, thus preventing the story from ossifying and dying. This trend was continued in Greek poetry in subsequent centuries, the best example of which is Attic tragedy.

The appearance of diverse versions of the same events is evidence of the existence of various versions of songs in the oral tradition.[62] According to Burgess, the diversity of iconographic paintings of *Iliad* scenes in the seventh to sixth centuries BCE also indicates the existence of various songs of the *Iliad*.[63] The same scenes may be played out by characters other than those who appear in the version known to us, or the course of events may be different. The appearance of diverse characters in given scenes is evidence of the instability of certain roles in given themes. Among the Achaean warriors we cannot find anyone who on the basis of the *Iliad* or *Odyssey* could be identified as a Trojan, but the same role could be played by various heroes—for example, contrary to the *Iliad*, Diomedes could take part in the embassy to Achilles.[64] This instability is typical for oral poetry, but it does not occur in the Yugoslav poetry studied by Parry and Lord. But I do not think that the placing of particular heroes in particular roles was entirely arbitrary. We may observe connections between certain heroes quite independently of the story as such but originating from the very old structures of oral poetry. Nevertheless, certain facts, such as the sack of Troy or the death of Achilles, remain unchanged and form an important part of the cyclic story.

The Cycle of Songs and the Cycle of Time

The above reflections allowed us to look at the epic cycle as a collection of poems that set the chronological framework of the plot of a given myth as its coherent storyline, a macro-story any place within which a particular epic song

62 See Holmberg 1998; Finkelberg 2000; Burgess 2002.

63 Burgess 2001:35–44. González (2013:46–70) demonstrates that iconography connected with the story of the *Iliad* does not corroborate the existence of a unified text fixed in writing, but rather denotes that in the seventh and sixth centuries BCE a fluid, multiform Iliadic tradition was at work.

64 This is parallel to the presentation of characters appearing at Troy at the start of the war—for example, Protesilaos or Palamedes—together with those who, like Memnon, appear towards its end (see Burgess 2001:92). It is also possible that putting in one place heroes from various stages of the narrative is an artistic device (a visual abridgement of plots of many songs). Or else, it may be evidence of the existence of songs encompassing the whole war (which I will discuss later) or of the showing of a single episode from the perspective of the entire war, which is the most probable explanation.

can begin. Various episodes were centered around a main course of mythological events, creating a so-called κύκλος, cycle or "wheel." What is uncertain, however, is how this wheel turned.

The term κύκλος

The association of the term κύκλος with the epic cycle has been explained variously, on account of the variety of contexts to which the term is referred in the sources.[65] Attempts have been made to show that the term was added later to already existing poetry or, contrariwise, that it is strictly linked with the creation of epic poetry and has its parallels in other Indo-European poetry.[66] An issue I feel has not been raised too often is the evolution of the meaning of the term during the shift from oral poetry to written poetry. What functioned in a certain way in oral culture took on a different meaning when epic poetry started being recorded in writing. Here, I would also like to draw particular attention to a largely overlooked aspect of Archaic Greek epic composition: the spatial and temporal circularity of the narrative.

Kyklos, the figure of a turning wheel or circle might also be a reflection on human life as the wheel of change, or death as a return to birth.[67] The metaphorical image of the wheel of life, though not so much expressed as in Indian culture,[68] seems to be deeply rooted in Greek culture. Herodotus has one of his characters say: κύκλος τῶν ἀνθρωπηίων ἐστὶ πραγμάτων, περιφερόμενος δὲ οὐκ ἐᾷ αἰεὶ τοὺς αὐτοὺς εὐτυχεῖν, "men's fortunes are on a wheel, which in its turning does not allow the same man to prosper forever" (1.207.2). Martin West

65 Fantuzzi and Tsagalis (2015:1–7) name five contexts which are found in the sources: "(a) an idea of uniformity and continuity; (b) a notion of 'ring form'; (c) the concept of completeness; (d) an encircling or framing function; and (e) a poetics based on manufacturing a perfected whole." I would also like to refer the reader to this important title for comparison with the views presented in this book.

66 Nagy (1996a:74–76) believes that in the Indo-European tradition, one can observe the composition of poetry being likened to a well-constructed chariot (as in *Rig-Veda* 1.130.6). In Greek poetry, this was reflected in the concept of the *kyklos* (wheel) to describe epic poetry generally focused around the Trojan War and the fact that the art of a poet was likened to that of a carpenter and joiner, whose skills were both technical and conceptual. The Mycenaean word, written in the Linear B script, for the chariot is a-mo = Greek *harmo*, which is an abstract noun ("joining") from the verb root *ar-, discernible in the Greek verb *ar-ar-iskô*. From this core word comes the name *Homêros*, meaning he who joins together (*homo-* + *ar-*), being a prototype name for a poet (similarly to *Hesi-odos*, "he who sends out a voice"). The verb *arariskê* applies to poetry, e.g. *Hymn to Apollo* 164 "How beautiful is their joined-together song," as well as in the literal meaning in reference to the work of a jointer ἤραρε τέκτων (*Iliad* 4.110, 23.712).

67 Thalmann (1984:9–10) sees a connection between the shape of the world, Achilles' shield depicting it, and ring composition (see Stanley 1993:9–13).

68 On the reincarnation cycle in Plato, see Harrison 1927:271–273.

considers this to have been a popular notion[69] and suggests that it could have been shared by Archilochus in fr. 128.6–7 W, who turns to his θυμός:

> ἀλλὰ χαρτοῖσίν τε χαῖρε καὶ κακοῖσιν ἀσχάλα
> μὴ λίην, γίνωσκε δ' οἷος ῥυσμὸς ἀνθρώπους ἔχει
>
> enjoy the joys and grieve the misfortunes
> but not too much, know (be always able to see) how ῥυθμός governs people.

Ῥυθμός (= ῥυσμός) "here means order, the order of things, something that repeats itself with a certain regularity,"[70] but the image behind this formulation (also at Archilochus fr. 13W) is not one of an alternating or pendulum movement, as was suggested by H. Fränkel.[71] West stresses that the original meaning of ῥυθμός was "shape." This shape, as West suggests, is a wheel, and the most probable origin of this word is a wheel performed in a dancing procession.[72] The times of fortune and misfortune experienced by man are not so much the whims of gods as the participation in both fortune and misfortune assigned to him from birth (by the Moirai, Hesiod *Theogony* 905–906 αἵ τε διδοῦσι / θνητοῖς ἀνθρώποισιν ἔχειν ἀγαθόν τε κακόν τε). Hektor (*Iliad* 6.487–489) presents the limits of human faith as participation in what is assigned from birth (ἐπὴν τὰ πρῶτα γένηται):

> οὐ γάρ τίς μ' ὑπὲρ αἶσαν ἀνὴρ Ἄϊδι προϊάψει·
> μοῖραν δ' οὔ τινά φημι πεφυγμένον ἔμμεναι ἀνδρῶν,
> οὐ κακὸν οὐδὲ μὲν ἐσθλόν, ἐπὴν τὰ πρῶτα γένηται.
>
> for no one will cast me into Hades contrary to what is assigned to me [*aisa*],
> for—I say—from assignment [*moira*] no man can escape,
> good or bad, as soon as his life begins.

This assignment (αἶσα and μοῖρα are equivalent)[73] cannot be changed, from which Hektor also draws an optimistic conclusion. The cyclic image of the world is not so much the changes of a turning wheel as the forming of a circle that sets out and upon completion returns to where it began. Knowledge of what inevi-

69 West 1974:131; e.g. Sophocles *Trachiniae* 129–131.
70 Bartol 1999:121.
71 Fränkel 1975:143–144.
72 West 1974:131; see Aristophanes *Thesmophoriazusae* 953–958.
73 Kirk 1990:224.

tably awaits man allows him to accept his fate (to put it more precisely: accept the misfortunes that afflict him). This, in turn, means that misfortune must also inevitably afflict the enemy, which might result in your good fortune.

Also the course of time is not perceived linearly, but as circles turning to define predetermined periods.[74] Κύκλος was applied to define such a period, as in Euripides *Alcestis* 449:

> Σπάρτᾳ κύκλος ἀνίκα Καρνείου περινίσσεται ὥρας
> μηνός
>
> In Sparta, when the turning circle returns to the time of the month
> of the Karnea

The story of the myth and the epic is not only delineated by shape but also by number, which for the ancient people marked the rebirth of the world.

Cyclic space

Epic songs—for example, those of Demodokos—presenting episodes of a greater whole known to the singer and listeners, may present various events within the cycle, regardless of leaps in time, as long as they maintain the overriding chronology. No doubt, even a totally new episode could be freely added to a well-developed cycle because the public would be well aware of all the surrounding events. This begs the fundamental question as to how, in the performance of songs, new stories could be added without disrupting the narrative so that it remained continuous, coherent, and logical.

Every episodic song could refer to the whole story. The system gave the story a timeframe and allowed episodes to be included in the course of events, while minimalizing the possibility of mistakes and the mixing up of events. For, despite many observed inconsistencies, the story cycle is a fairly coherent whole within a temporal-spatial frame. The spatial frame is set in the complementary pattern of an expedition and return where everything, like a pendulum, returns to the point of departure. Let us look at the Phoenician rendering of history (Figures 1a-b, opposite), which strikingly resembles the epic pattern.

The hero goes hunting. In the mountains, he kills a deer and skins it. To feast with the gods, he offers them a sacrifice. This is accepted, the visible sign of which is a winged deity or an eagle flying above an altar. The hero continues his trek through the mountains to experience a dangerous encounter with a

74 Nakassis (2004:215–233) points to an Archaic Greek model of cosmic geography where the sun rises and sets in one place. This transition gateway, so fundamental to Archaic Greek mythology, has been identified by him with Eliade's *axis mundi*.

Figure 1a. Gilded silver dish from the Bernardini tomb at Praeneste. Phoenician, ca. 7th century BCE.

Figure 1b. Drawing of dish, after G. Markoe, *Phoenician Bronze and Silver Bowls from Cyprus and the Mediterranean* (1985), p. 278.

giant ape-like monster, which throws rocks at him. The hero is saved by the winged deity. Under the auspicious sign of the flying eagle, the hero is able to capture the monster and triumphantly return to his castle. The way the story is told is not so much structured by the roundness of the vessel as by storytelling convention, one that is easily recognized as the epic convention.[75] The expedition assumes the necessity of a triumphant return. But the return from the hunt is endangered by the encounter with the monster. The two events occur in the mountains, which the hero overcomes twice: by setting out on the hunting expedition and by returning from it. Divine intervention saves the hero at the last moment. Avoiding death, however, is not the end of the story. Instead, it is the defeat of the monster, which is possible thanks to divine support. Not without reason, a central element in the story is the sacrifice made to the gods, which represents a good relationship with the gods.

A similar structure seems to be present in various Greek epic cycles. Certain events are repeated, creating an analogous scheme, one that is enclosed in space. This schematism seems to be parallel to the schematism of oral song. The cycle most usually involves some sort of expedition which is preceded by preparations. Once the expedition reaches its goal—usually with success—an important role is played by the hero's return. A characteristic feature of the Greek tradition is that the returns are not always successful, as is seen in the Argonaut Cycle, the Trojan Cycle, and perhaps even the Herakles Cycle.

The above-mentioned symmetry of cycles appears to be an important feature, or even an essential structural design. It is also a specific feature of individual epic songs. Many scholars have shown extensively that ring composition constitutes the characteristic skeletal structure of the *Iliad*, organizing not only individual parts of its content and main speeches, but also the entirety of the work, determining its coherent and unified character.[76] The cycle also has this characteristic coherence. As I have already mentioned, the Greek epic cycle presenting an expedition had to include two elements of no less significance than the actual expedition: the journey to the destination and the return.[77] Let us note that in the Argonaut, Theban, and Trojan Cycles the journeys there and back are far more developed aspects than the story of the expedition's actual goal. Even in the *Iliad* the fear of the Achaeans is not focused on the prospect of defeat, death, or enslavement, but on the possibility of "no return." In itself, the

75 Regardless of whether or not it concerns Gilgamesh's capture of Humbaba.

76 Very important are the observations of Cedric Whitman (1958), widely accepted by other scholars and corroborated by their own studies. More on ring composition below.

77 The basic pattern of the heroic tale as described by Joseph Campbell (1949), who refers to it as the quest (Departure–Initiation–Return), was transferred in Greek tradition from the episodic song to the Cycle—i.e. the macro-story.

Song of Return, so frequently represented in the songs collected by Parry and Lord, often includes a final theme of return to the captivity from which the hero had originally managed to escape to restore order in his home.[78] Return means a return to the original situation, a fundamental concept in the cyclic perception of time, life, and the order of nature.[79]

Cycle time

We should consider whether the way in which the narrative turns full circle, returning to its start, is dictated by a cyclic perception of time. Since the birth of cultural anthropology, it has been known that the earliest civilizations had a cyclic perception of time, but the pattern only became widely known thanks to Eliade's concept of the eternal return. The calendars of the ancient peoples were strictly associated with cults. The cycle signified the end of one world and the birth of a new world.

Time in archaic epics and related texts is usually described with repeatedly defined periods, which certainly makes it worthwhile to consider whether they had any real influence on the composition of epics both with regard to the whole cycle as well as individual songs.

First, however, let us look at how precise the chronology in oral song was. In Book 2 of his *Histories*, Herodotus refers to the abduction of Helen by Paris. In Homer's text, he finds information about Paris and Helen staying in Phoenicia, Sidon (*Odyssey* 6.289), and Egypt (*Odyssey* 4.227), and this makes Herodotus come to the following conclusion (2.117):

> These verses and this passage prove most clearly that the *Kypria* is not the work of Homer but of someone else. For the *Kypria* relates that Alexander reached Ilion with Helen in three days from Sparta, having a "fair wind and a smooth sea," but according to the *Iliad*, he wandered from his course in bringing her.[80]

78 Therefore, I have a different view of the *Odyssey's* oral structure from that of Foley (1999a:Ch. 5), who because of his scepticism about the possibility of resolving the old conflict between the pluralists and unitarians regarding whether or not the last book belongs to the work, believes listeners familiar with the tradition would accept two endings: one where the spouses unite, the other concordant with the frequent presence of the "Song of Return" in the tradition.

79 In South Slav songs, the return to enslavement is associated with the hero being magnanimously released or the oppressor being justly punished, which also means a restoration of cosmic order. This adds a new level to the hero's prediction of restoring order in his own home.

80 Ἐν τούτοισι τοῖσι ἔπεσι δηλοῖ ὅτι ἠπίστατο τὴν ἐς Αἴγυπτον Ἀλεξάνδρου πλάνην· ὁμουρέει γὰρ ἡ Συρίη Αἰγύπτῳ, οἱ δὲ Φοίνικες, τῶν ἐστι ἡ Σιδών, ἐν τῇ Συρίῃ οἰκέουσι. Κατὰ ταῦτα δὲ τὰ ἔπεα καὶ τόδε [τὸ χώριον] οὐκ ἥκιστα ἀλλὰ μάλιστα δηλοῖ ὅτι οὐκ Ὁμήρου τὰ Κύπρια ἔπεα ἐστι ἀλλ' ἄλλου τινός· ἐν μὲν γὰρ τοῖσι Κυπρίοισι εἴρηται ὡς τριταῖος ἐκ Σπάρτης Ἀλέξανδρος ἀπίκετο ἐς

The veracity of Herodotus's statement has, however, been undermined by Proclus's summary of the *Kypria*—here, the voyage of Alexander and Helen was to pass through Phoenician Sidon, which he was to occupy, and Cyprus.[81] A way to understand these discrepancies was not provided until the emergence of the oral theory. Margalit Finkelberg argued that the functioning of various versions of cyclic poems was possible evidence for the differences in the accounts of the journey provided by Herodotus and Proclus's summary of the *Kypria*. Let us first refrain from discussing her second thesis that multiformity, so typical for oral works, is not apparent in the *Iliad* or in any of its ancient testimonia.[82] Instead, we will focus on Herodotus's reasoning—which is logical reasoning, with which it is hard not to agree. But that is because we have been taught to reason the way he does. It is the reasoning of a historian. If we have two essentially differing accounts of a given fact, they cannot originate from the same person. Yet this logic does not have to apply to the oral epic poet. Depending on the circumstances and needs of the moment, he would be able to compose a song where a sea voyage could be shortened or considerably prolonged. Herodotus must have read the *Kypria*, where for some purpose the singer shortened the voyage. Why? Without the text it is impossible to give a definite answer. Perhaps there was something superfluous or unwanted in the storm an enraged Hera sent to make Paris's ship drift off course on the voyage home (χειμῶνα δὲ αὐτοῖς ἐφίστησιν Ἥρα)?[83] The text Herodotus read seems to diverge from the "norm" even more, since the very title, *Kypria*, may link the narrative with the island visited by Alexander, an island where Proclus indicates that Alexander "spent a long time," πολὺν διέτριβε χρόνον ἐν Φοινίκηι καὶ Κύπρωι (the links with Cyprus seem also to be indicated by extant fragments of a song describing the bathing and dressing of Aphrodite, frr. 5, 6, and 7 W).[84] Moreover, the structure of the cycle might—in my opinion—have a symmetric form, like that of the *Iliad*. If that is the case, the return voyage of Menelaos and Helen, partly presented in the *Odyssey*, may be the reverse of the voyage to Troy. This could be so especially because, thanks to comparative studies, we know that the version that tells that Helen

---

τὸ Ἴλιον ἄγων Ἑλένην, εὐαέϊ τε χρησάμενος καὶ θαλάσσῃ λείῃ· ἐν δὲ Ἰλιάδι λέγει ὡς ἐπλάζετο ἄγων αὐτήν.

81 The mention of Cyprus, not present in the *Iliad*, indicates that here Proclus was referring to a cyclic poem and not making a compilation as a supplement to the *Iliad*.

82 This thesis was met with a sharp retort from Nagy (2001).

83 Similarly damaging for the *Odyssey* is the wrath of Athena pursuing the Achaeans as they return from Troy (Proclus's *Chrestomathy* and *Nostoi*).

84 Scholars associate the intriguing title of the work with Cyprus as the place where it was created or with Aphrodite, the goddess of Cyprus, on account of her role in the story (Huxley 1969: 128–129; Davies 1989a:33). See my discussion of Demodokos's second song below.

never actually arrived in Troy, but was only represented there as an εἴδωλον ('specter') while she remained in Egypt, need not have been reliant on the abduction of Helen as depicted in the *Iliad*.[85] All this, however, is of secondary importance to the observation that the voyage to Troy undertaken by Paris and Helen could have taken different courses, depending not only on the version of a particular poet, but even the particular song or performance of the same *aoidos*. For someone examining the source as a historian it would be impossible, but to the singer of epics both versions could be equally true, as both versions have the same authorizations of truth in epic poetry. I draw attention to this because what the epic poet would have felt had happened and his sense of time was by nature very different from our imagination of the event, trained as we are to think historically. These differences in reasoning also have to do with the specifics of oral culture—logic and analysis are the products of literary culture.[86]

Achilles declares (*Iliad* 9.363) that his return voyage to Phthia, if nothing stands in the way, will last three days. That is the same number of days, according to Herodotus's version of the *Kypria*, that Paris, having abducted Helen, was to sail unhindered from Sparta to Troy. The period of three days therefore has a symbolic—perhaps even magical—meaning. Three days means a short, unhindered time. This statement somewhat conflicts with Achilles' appraisal that the distance between Phthia and Troy is vast (*Iliad* 9.156–157).[87]

Therefore, we cannot speak of chronology in epic poetry with historical accuracy. Let us note that numbers in reference to the duration of time had a symbolic or even magical meaning.

We know that up to the fourth century BCE in Greece, time was measured according to *octaeteris*, which had been devised by the Minoans in the Middle Bronze Age. This was an eight-year sun-and-moon cycle, which made the solar and lunar calendars virtually commensurable. Eight solar years, each of 365 days, are in total 2,920 days. In that time, there are 99 months of 29½ days, giving a total of 2920½ days. The difference between the two calendars in that period is

85 Edmunds 1997:422–423, compare Austin 1994:1–20.

86 See Ong (2002:29) who takes Jack Goody's (1977) stance into account. This does not, of course, mean that people within an oral culture do not think logically. Levy-Bruhl's theory about the illogicality of the primitive mind was rightly refuted by Evans-Pritchard (1976), who demonstrated that primitive cultures use logic in the same way as civilized cultures do—the only difference is the system of reference. The key statement for Aristotelian logic that *a* does not equal -*a* may not function in oral culture, not because the difference is not perceived, but because oral culture does not verify the truthfulness of stories by juxtaposing them, as Herodotus did.

87 Of course, these differences in distance could be connected with Achilles' emotional state, but it also could be a valorization of convention.

only half a day.[88] To make the lunar and solar years match, an additional thirty-day month was introduced after two, four, and eight years.[89] Thus, in addition to the *octaeteris*, there was also a *trieteris* and *penteteris*.

In these mathematical calculations only one tiny thing is overlooked: human imagination. After all, in nature half a day cannot form a caesura. While the Greeks used the term ἔτος to define a time cycle lasting from a month to "nine" years or even longer, they used the term ἐνιαυτός for the "point" where one cycle ends and a new one begins.[90]

The Trojan War—as is generally known—lasted ten years. In *Iliad* 2.329, Odysseus cites the seer Kalchas's interpretation of a sign sent to the Achaeans in Aulis before the expedition, stating that on the tenth year Troy will fall. But not so many lines earlier, at 2.295, he says that the ninth year of their stay at Troy is about to run its course ἡμῖν δ' εἴνατός ἐστι περιτροπέων ἐνιαυτός; literally, "the year ends its cycle." We cannot accept this information to mean that ahead of them is another whole year of war, for regardless of what developments followed in the cycle narrative, the situation would be presented that the conquest of Troy was about to happen, as if it were "five to twelve" (*Iliad* 18.95–96).

88 Henriksson and Blomberg 1996:100–101: "[I]n eight solar years, each of 365 days, there are 2,920 days. During the same period, there are 99 lunations, each of 29 ½ days, giving a total of 2,920 ½ days—an apparent difference of only a half day between the solar and lunar calendars. By the fourth century BCE, the solar year was accepted as 365 ¼ days, which over eight years gave a total 2,922 days, making the *octaeteris* less accurate than had been thought. Indications that the *octaeteris* was known in Greece over such a long period imply a continuity of learning from the Minoan era to post-Homeric Greece." Interesting in this respect are the observations of Michael Ovenden (1965:1–18). Aratus's *Phaenomena* present an image of the sky as seen between 3000 and 1800 BCE from a latitude of the 34 ½° to 37 ½° N, i.e. from the Mediterranean region. Ovenden concludes: "The tradition of the constellations must have been handed down by word of mouth for two millennia."

89 Hannah 2015:1565–1567. See Jones 2015:1583–1588 for more on Greek mathematical astronomy.

90 Harrison 1927:183. This is consistent with the definition of the year ἐνιαυτός as "the day when the year runs its course." The generally accepted distinctions of ἐνιαυτός and ἔτος, where "ἐνιαυτός is the space of the year; ἔτος is a year as one in a series of years, which make up time or any given period of time" (Merry and Riddell 1886) was questioned by Emlyn-Jones (1967:156–161), who stated that these were interchangeable terms. However, a more detailed historical analysis of the formulae containing these definitions of the year carried out by Beekes (1969:138–143) confirms the earlier opinion. In formulae identified as "old," ἔτος is found in the forms of the accusative and dative singular with a numeral, whereas ἐνιαυτός is found in the accusative, singular and plural, and in the genitive plural and is linked with the adjective τελεσφόρος, as well as the participles περι-τελλ-/-πλ- derived from the same pre-Indo-European core word *kuel- meaning 'turn away, turn back' (cf. τέλος, τέλσον). Therefore, ἐνιαυτός together with epithets means "the turning point in the year-cycle." Thus, similarly to the τέλσον performed by a ploughman, at this point turning the oxen (*Iliad* 13.707, 18.544, 18.547), ἐνιαυτός means the point in time, or rather day, when one year ends and another begins.

Apollodorus tries to rationalize the perception of the length of the Trojan War, which is why he refers to the expedition to Teuthrania as an explanation for why the war lasted twenty years, showing that the first expedition lasted two years and was followed by an eight-year break (*Epitome* 3.18). He also indicates that events following the suicide of Ajax took place in the tenth year of the war (*Epitome* 5.8)! But this is precisely the reasoning of a quasi-historian to try to find measurable time for a multitude of events.

The symbolic and magical significance of the *octaeteris* period is linked with its cult and mythic function, but it is understood in various ways. Frazer postulates a link between the eight-year cycle and the limiting of royal authority. At the end of this cycle, the king had to give way to the new king (originally, he would be killed) or at least renew his magical powers. The renewal of the powers of the sorcerer-king was associated with the renewal of the world through the Sacred Marriage of the Sun and the Moon, when solar and lunar calendars converge. Thus is explained, for instance, the Homeric description of the Cretan king Minos as a ἐννέωρος, "nine-year-old" (*Odyssey* 19.178–179). The royal couple became the embodiments of the Sun and the Moon and married each other or renewed their marriage. At eight-year intervals, specific holidays were celebrated in Delphi and Thebes, including the Pythian games, which linked the eight-year period with Apollo's penance for killing the water dragon.[91] Not only Frazer accepted K. O. Müller's assumption (in *Die Dorrier*, 2.483) that the Olympic Games were also originally held at eight-year intervals, as in the case of the Pythian Games; accurate calculations confirming this hypothesis are also presented by F. M. Cornford.[92] The Olympic Games interval lasted alternately fifty months and forty-nine months. Thus, the Games were always held sometime around the end of August and start of September, but the basis for the calculations was the winter solstice. Cornford

91 Frazer 1912:80. Testimonia concerning the Pythian Games, originally taking place every eight years: scholia to Pindar; Censorinus *De die natali* 18.6; Eustathius *ad Odyssey* 3.267. Frazer (1921a, 1:218–219n1) describes *octaeteris* as a period of penance and expiation ("the eight years' period of expiation") present in many myths: the twelve labors of Herakles, in penance for killing his own children, according to Apollodorus (*Library* 2.5.11) lasted eight years and one month; Kadmos served Ares for eight years as penance for killing a dragon, the descendent of Ares (Apollodorus 3.4.2); Apollo was to serve Admetos for a year for killing the Cyclopes (Apollodorus 3.10.4), but according to Servius (*ad* Vergil *Aeneid* 7.761) this was a period of nine years; the eating of human flesh in the ritual of Lykaion Zeus allegedly caused a nine-year transformation into a wolf, which is reflected in the myth of Lykaon (Pausanias *Description of Greece* 8.2; Pliny *Natural History* 8.81; Augustine *De civitate Dei* 18.17); banishment of the gods for a broken promise (Hesiod *Theogony* 793–804). According to Frazer, in all these cases we are dealing with a period called the "great year," after which the sun, moon, and planets took up the same positions as at the start. Compare Henriksson and Blomberg 1993.

92 Cornford 1927:225.

also confirmed that such an orientation of the cycle had no association with pastoral or agricultural life, but with the observed movements of the Sun and the Moon and the cult of the marriage of these gods.

Such solar-lunar weddings renew the waning forces of nature in a magic ritual. The point in time where such changes are possible was treated with great effort, care, and attention, for the fulfillment of the event was essential to further existence. Harrison links the turning point that ends and at the same time starts a period with a "rite of passage," signifying Closing and Opening, Falling Asleep and Reawakening, Death and Resurrection.[93]

Frazer presents various periods as *octaeteris*. Meanwhile, if we look closely at Homer's phrasing, it is evident that we are dealing with a specific period that can be defined algebraically as 9 + 1. Nine is the number for the duration of the period, whereas ten is its end. The duration of the Trojan War is repeatedly stated in epics as lasting ten years, but it is always the formula 9 + 1. This is a magic number, and it implies a whole multitude of events. According to Hesiod, for example, nine years is how long the punishment lasts for a god who breaks an oath, and in the tenth year he rejoins the other gods (*Theogony* 803):

> ἐννέα πάντ' ἔτεα· δεκάτῳ δ' ἐπιμίσγεται αὖτις
>
> all of nine years, and in the tenth he joins them again

This entire period Hesiod calls εἰνάετες, i.e. nine years and not what we would calculate as eight years. This is because the Greeks counted time including the present moment. For instance, when we say in two days' time in reference to the day after tomorrow, the ancient Greeks would say in three days' time because they would include the present day.[94] However, when we include the data in the calendar, we notice that the period must have lasted eight years, whereas the ninth year must have been a coda to this period. Let us take a closer look at the sign that served in the prophecy of Kalchas at *Iliad* 2.326–329:

> ὡς οὗτος κατὰ τέκνα φάγε στρουθοῖο καὶ αὐτὴν
> ὀκτώ, ἀτὰρ μήτηρ ἐνάτη ἦν ἣ τέκε τέκνα,

93 Harrison 1927.

94 Frazer (1912:59) points out that this method of counting was used not only by the Greeks but also the Romans. A. Schmidt (*Handbuch der griechischen Chronologie*, Jena, 1888:95ff.; after Frazer 1912:59), states that this method of counting did not apply to numbers higher than nine. As we shall later see, the number 20 (as in the case of the number of years Odysseus was absent from home) was also understood algebraically as 2 × (9 + 1).

ὣς ἡμεῖς τοσσαῦτ' ἔτεα πτολεμίξομεν αὖθι,
τῷ δεκάτῳ δὲ πόλιν αἱρήσομεν εὐρυάγυιαν.

as he [the snake] ate the chicks and their mother,
eight of them in all, and the ninth was the one that gave birth to
them,
so too we shall fight for as many years,
and on the tenth we shall take the city of wide streets.[95]

In this passage we basically find the significant problem of time in all its perplexity. The war should have actually lasted eight years, and the eating of the mother bird would mean the capture of the city in the ninth year. The ninth year should therefore mark the end of the war. The metaphor is clear: the children of Troy will die first and then the one who gave birth to them, Troy. But the numbers are 9 + 1 and the tenth is the last. The way we calculate time, these numbers do not match.

In the *Iliad*, the question of how long the Trojan War lasted seems even more complicated because in *Iliad* 24.765–766 Helen says:

ἤδη γὰρ νῦν μοι τόδε εἰκοστὸν ἔτος ἐστὶν
ἐξ οὗ κεῖθεν ἔβην καὶ ἐμῆς ἀπελήλυθα πάτρης·

twenty years have now passed
since I arrived here and left my homeland.

This statement causes further confusion: how could Helen speak of twenty years if the war lasted ten years? Homer must therefore assume ten years passed from the abduction of Helen before the expedition to Troy even began. Therefore, he may have been aware of the events mentioned in the *Kypria* and the aforementioned stay of the fugitive couple in Sidon. According to the *Kypria*, the Achaeans spent ten years building up forces, first organizing a failed expedition against Teuthrania, and only then organizing a second expedition (against Troy), the most important element of which is the sacrifice of Iphigenia. If that is the case, how can the author of the *Odyssey* (2.175) say that Odysseus returns home after a twenty-year absence?

Gilbert Murray ingeniously linked the duration of Odysseus's absence from home with cyclic time.[96] He noted that the eight-year cycle had a discrepancy of one and half days, which was not eliminated until the mathematician Meton

95 The prophecy is also presented in this way by Apollodorus *Epitome* 3.15.
96 Murray 1907:210–212.

introduced a nineteen-year system. The last day of the nineteen-year period, which at the same time was the first day of the next twenty-year period, was a time during the winter solstice when the paths of the new Moon and the reborn Sun crossed. This day was called Σύνοδος Ἡλίου καὶ Σελήνης, "conjunction of the Sun and the Moon." Murray concludes that Odysseus was united with Penelope on a strictly defined day (*Odyssey* 13.93) when the nineteenth year is completed with the first day of the twentieth year (22.102; 1.170; 17.327; 2.175). This is the same year the Athenians called the "old-new" day, ἕνη καὶ νέα (serving as a turning point in the calculation of time—ἐνιαυτός). Odysseus takes revenge and restores his authority and marries exactly on the day when the nineteen-year cycle is completed. Murray points to Odysseus's clear association with the path of the Sun, whereby Odysseus was a Year-King, the embodiment of the magical force of the Sun.

Murray was completely wrong to assume that the *Odyssey* was the product of many centuries of tradition, ultimately supported by the calculations of Meton from around 430 BCE! The precision of the Athenian mathematician's calculations might actually reflect the far older cyclic tradition that combines two *ennaeteris*.[97] Murray's suggested precision in determining time might have only a symbolic significance, and I would venture to say that rather than Meton's Great Cycle it might actually be a reference to the doubling of the *octaeteris* or *ennaeteris* cycle. It might be associated with understanding the *ennaeteris* as a combination of two four-year periods, called the *penteteris* (five-year periods). The combination of two Olympiads according to ancient Greek calculations was not eight years but nine, but if we add two five-year periods, we get a ten-year period. However, it could also mean that a period of sixteen years was called a twenty-year period. The doubling of a two-Olympiad period could mean not sixteen years, but in the minds of archaic Greeks, twenty years. Several reasons might be behind this assumption. It might correspond better to the matter of Telemachos's immaturity. It is difficult to believe that a twenty-year-old youth (in classical Athens he would have already finished his service in the *ephebeia)* had still not acquired full maturity rights. In Rome at the age of sixteen one could become a senator and wear the *toga praetexta*. This took place during the Liberalia, on March 17. Harrison considers the start of spring to be the most suitable time for initiation ceremonies.[98]

97 The nineteen-year cycle was in use in Mesopotamia at least from the second half of the sixth century BCE (Ossendrijver 2015:1867). The alignment of solar and lunar calendars in twenty-year cycles was also noticed in China (where the calendar was accordingly changed in the sixth century BCE) and in Mayan culture: Zawielski 1981:18, 24.

98 Ovid *Fasti* 3.771. See Harrison 1927:196-198 on the participation of the Curetes and Salii in the spring New Year cult.

Either way, if the author of the *Odyssey* was as aware of events preceding the Trojan War as the author of the *Iliad*, he would know that Odysseus would have been absent from home for thirty years, not twenty! Nevertheless, I believe that here too we cannot impose our logic in measuring time. Here, we are dealing with numbers of magical significance. The period expressed algebraically as $2 \times (9 + 1)$ may represent the finite time for the existence of the universe. Once this period ends, the world has to be reborn to live again. The formula $2 \times (9 + 1)$ is therefore a number closing the entire epic narrative. And so, it contains the whole voyage there and back. It means a return to the starting point, the place of birth. Odysseus not only regains his wife and crown, but also returns to the land of the living: he is resurrected.[99] The expansion of the epic cycle meant that maintaining absolute continuity of events in this period became impossible. This was not so much due to the abundance of introduced episodes, but to the accepted perspective from which a story could be told: a different perspective applied to the sack of Troy and a different one to the return from Troy. One may therefore propose the hypothesis that for both songs, and perhaps for every epic song, a twenty-year perspective was essential.[100]

Cyclic time constitutes overlapping and complementary circles. The last year automatically becomes the first year of the next period and the first year the last year of the preceding period. One can therefore perhaps surmise that the tenth year was the day that remained when the lunar calendar was superimposed on the solar calendar. It is actually half a day that remains, but a day cannot be divided, so it is at once the last day of the old year that passes and the first of the new year that has arrived.

We should also note that this system of measuring time, as well as epic periods, surely had much older precedents outside of Greek culture.[101] The acceptance of similar meanings in other cultures, including most certainly the Minoan culture, could have led to confusions with Greek definitions that were difficult to explain, and this was why the supplement to the *octaeteris* was the tenth year and not the ninth. This might also mean that the original Greek

99 See Breed 1999.

100 Not by accident, in my opinion, Helen makes this statement almost at the end of the poem. The judgment of Paris is also mentioned in the last book (*Iliad* 24.28–30). Tsagalis (2008:137–149) proposes, in my opinion unconvincingly, an alternative solution. According to Tsagalis, the *Iliad* adopts the timeframe of the *Odyssey* in Helen's deliberately deceptive statement, by which she aims to win the sympathy of the Trojans. Helen likens herself to Odysseus, who is widely recognized as a hero absent from home for twenty years (149): "This is a polemical gesture against the *Iliad*, intending to subordinate it to the extended timeframe of the *Odyssey*. ... The awkwardness of this number ... presupposes the *Odyssey*'s pan-Hellenic impact and diffusion."

101 The ideas proposed by Frazer, Cornford, and Murray are incorrect insofar as they assume the strict chronology was based on developed astronomy, which did not happen until later. For a contrary approach, see Henriksson and Blomberg 1993, 1996, 2015.

calendar resembled the original Roman calendar, with ten months and a winter period of sixty-one unnumbered days.

Presented in the Hittite theogonic epic about Kumarbi, there are four generations of gods who successively ruled as kings: Alalu, Anu, Kumarbi, and Teshup. The first two eons are introduced with the same phrase, suggesting the same formula:

> For nine years Alalu was the king of the heaven. But in the ninth year Anu turned in battle against Alalu and defeated him, (the god) Alalu.
>
> For nine years Anu was the king of the heaven. [But] in the ninth year Anu turned in battle against Kumarbi, [and] Kumarbi, a descendant of Alalu, turned in battle against Anu.[102]

The ninth year is the year of completion; there is no mention of a tenth year! The next fragment of the Hittite song maintains the same convention. It mentions the successive months of the pregnancy of Earth, who was fertilized by the semen of Anu, which Kumarbi had spat out: "... and Ea, the master of wisdom, examines [her], counting [the months]. The first month, the second [month, the third month passed]. The fourth month, fifth month, sixth month passed. [The seventh month,] eighth month, ninth month passed. The tenth month begins. In the tenth month the Earth began to cry out. The Earth cried out ... the children were born ...."[103] Let us notice that the counting of the successive nine months is contained in a formulation composed of three lines, each including three months.

Ten lunar months equals 295 days.[104] A woman's pregnancy usually lasts 266 days. Therefore, if nine lunar months are 265 and a half days, Earth, like a woman, gave birth on the first day of the tenth month. The image of a pregnancy completed in the tenth month, an image undoubtedly not rare in the catalogues of theogonic poetry (if not older, certainly not younger than epics of the heroic type),[105] influenced the author of the *Iliad* to apply the number ten to close the

102 Popko 1971:465, on whose translations of cuneiform script I rely here (KUB t. XXXIII 120 + 119 + t. XXXVI 31; copy B: KUB XXXVI 1 [= A III 26 ff.]). Teshup's takeover of power from Kumarbi is being described, though in a fragmentary way, which is why it is hard to say whether the same formula also appears in this place. Scholars have no doubt that Hesiod's *Theogony* was clearly influenced by this and other Middle Eastern poems (see, e.g. Penglase 1994; West 1997). Likewise, many themes in the *Iliad* have their sources in the Eastern traditions.

103 The translation is based on Popko 1971:466–467.

104 Provided that the duration of the lunar month is taken (after Henriksson and Blomberg 1996) as 29½ days, due to the alternation of 29- and 30-day months. Nowadays, pregnancy calculations assume 28 days as the length of the menstrual cycle, which in effect makes the length of pregnancy equal to 9½ lunar months.

105 The ten-month pregnancy of Smyrna before she gave birth to Adonis (Apollodorus *Library* 3.14.4 δεκαμηνιαίῳ ... χρόνῳ). Hannah 2015:1564: "The phases of the moon provide a means for timing

cycle of years. In the Hittite poem, the number nine closes the sequence of years, which seems more reasonable in face of the eight-year cycle of heavenly bodies. The formula of 9 + 1 months could have been used as a magic number to present other periods where something matures and eventually "is born." Hence, the talk of periods of years and days subordinated to the expression 9 + 1.[106] The perspective of eight years being completed by the ninth year, as the closing year for the whole period, may actually be just one month closing one period and opening the next, as attested by the precise guidelines provided by Apollodorus regarding the duration of the penance of Herakles, who performed his twelve labors for eight years and one month (*Library* 2.5.11).[107]

Cycles of the *Iliad*

The above considerations should help us to understand how the author of the *Iliad* perceived time in his song's plot. Time and space in the *Iliad* are rarely considered other than from the point of view of the functions they performed in the narrative.[108] Also, the specificity of expressing time in oral culture has been relatively rarely studied. For it is either seen as the mechanical repetition of traditional formulae, to which the singer attaches no importance and which remain unconnected and have no influence on other events, or alternatively, the scholars' understanding of time relations makes such a profound impression on their opinions that they search for chronological consequences and conditions of the described event. For example, Andrew Dalby begins his (valuable) considerations on locating the oral tradition narrative in time with a statement that there is a lack of precise dating in oral culture, as evidenced by the fact that Homer does not state when the Trojan War actually took place.[109] This seemingly innocuous statement assumes a certain model of thought, where we try to place information about events on a chronological axis.[110] Meanwhile, the author of the *Iliad* proceeds in

Odysseus's return to Ithaca (*Odyssey* 19.307), and the whole months are used to count the length of a pregnancy (*Iliad* 19.117, compare the *Homeric Hymn to Hermes* line 11), but overall the year in these sources was a seasonal and agricultural one, and therefore solar rather than lunar."

106 Lord (1960:296n15) notes that the numbers "nine," "twelve," and "twenty" are commonly found in Yugoslav songs about returns or the capture of cities. This is evidence of the remarkable durability of the concept, which must also have been based on an understanding of time as a cycle enclosed in these magical numbers.

107 Singor (1991:34) believes that the significance of the number twelve was adopted from the Middle East, where it universally appears in rituals and myths, whereas the number nine has a more Indo-European provenance.

108 Here, of seminal importance is the work of Hellwig 1964.

109 Dalby 2006:21–27.

110 There can be various methods of dating the Trojan War. Attempts to confront Homeric narratives with astronomical optics do not seem unreasonable, especially because unusual astronomical phenomena, such as full solar eclipses, may have focused narratives about the past

exactly the opposite direction: he tries to place described events within the tradition of the Trojan War—that is, the Trojan War is the actual reference point of the whole story. The war itself is certainly real for him, but its placement in time is quite amorphous and unimportant and only relatively correlated with other oral stories. Discussing all the aspects of this issue would require a separate book; here, let us only look at a few selected examples to further support the argument.

Counting the number of days in the *Iliad* might seem a simple, straightforward task, yet the reason for and method of delimiting a particular timeframe for the described actions and events remain a mystery. At the same time, the time references that the poet does give are largely surprising.

The study of the chronology of the *Iliad* shows that the distribution of events maintains a clear symmetry. Friedrich Stählin stated that the content of the work is laid out in a linear fashion. This linearity, however, is considerably systematized, thanks to applying a rhythm to the succession of events and symmetry through the application of chiasmus. This system of interdependence between various passages in Homer's epic he likened to the geometric style of vase paintings. The association of Homer's poetry with a geometric style was also explored by other scholars, but the most influential ideas were those of Whitman, who connected this symmetry with oral theory.[111] An important construction design in oral song was—according to Whitman—ring composition, which integrated particular passages in the work—for example, speech—bound together by the entirety of the work. The work is so subordinate to the system that not only do individual events and scenes from the beginning and end correspond symmetrically, but also divisions of time counted in days. From the chronological point of view, the symmetry is slightly inaccurate. Moreover, it does not explain the specific distribution of the days.

Linking style in the visual arts with the construction of a literary work was later criticized, chiefly by G. S. Kirk and Oliver Taplin. This rather unconvincing criticism denies the very possibility that visual art might influence the structure of literary work (the application of symmetry in poetry does not have to correspond exactly with symmetry in the visual arts)[112] and points to a certain inadequacy of the Geometric style as too static and too schematically repetitive in comparison with the *Iliad*.[113] Kirk also casts doubt on the symmetric interde-

(Henriksson 2012:67: "Six solar eclipses have been used to determine an absolute chronology for the pharaohs from the 18th, 19th and 20th dynasties in Egypt, and two solar eclipses date the exodus from Egypt by the people of Israel"). Henriksson 2012 suggests that the description of sudden darkness appearing on the battlefield (*Iliad* 17.366–377) can be linked to a total solar eclipse in the vicinity of Troy falling on June 11, 1312 BCE at 12:36 PM.

111 Stählin 1923; Whitman 1958:249–284.

112 Kirk 1962:263–265.

113 Taplin 1992:18n16. Nagy (2010:273–310), though in a different context, nevertheless successfully shows the relationship between iconography from the Geometric period and Homeric epic poetry.

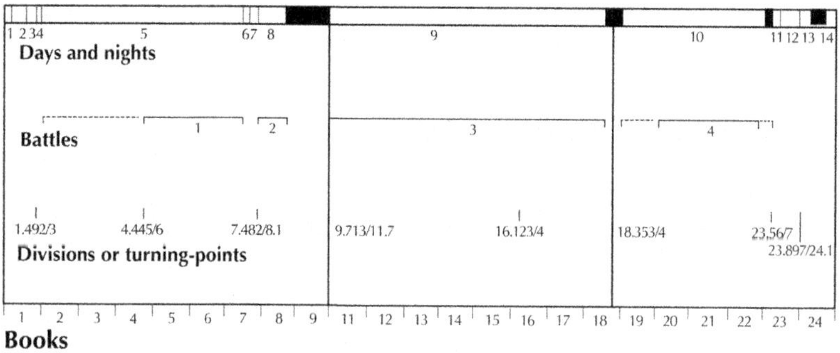

Table 1. The Calendar of the *Iliad*, according to Taplin.

pendence of parallel twelve-day periods: in Book 1, when the gods stay with the Ethiopians, and in Book 24, when Hektor's body is maltreated for twelve days and Achilles promises Priam a twelve-day truce. He argues that in the last book:

> These intervals, both closely concerned with the treatment of Hektor's body, might be deliberately similar; that reduces, if anything, the likelihood of an intentional connection between this eleven-days divine absence in book 1 and one particular member of the pair of interrelated intervals of book 24.[114]

Kirk stresses that Homer's use of time-interval expressions are of a formulaic nature—the time-periods are of eleven, ten, and twelve days[115]—and therefore suggests the singer used the period expressions randomly. Taplin (Table 1), arguing that the *Iliad* is divided into three parts, completely disregards the interdependence of time intervals and instead considers as significant the *Iliad's* fourteen-day calendar, which only counts the days when action occurs. I consider both these stances to be wrong and shall answer them in reverse order. The suggestion to count those days on which action takes place seems useful, but it is hard to understand why, in his calculations, Taplin omits the last two days, which are clearly marked in the narrative with a rising sun, *Iliad* 24.785 and 24.788.[116] Not including these two days indeed upsets the chronological symmetry in the *Iliad*. This is illustrated in Table 2 (below, p. 73), which shows a

114 Kirk 1985:105; Kirk 1962:261–263.

115 Kirk (1985:105): "Different intervals are also possible ... sometimes with similar wording based on ἐνδεκάτη, δεκάτη in place of δυωδεκάτη."

116 Taplin only makes the evasive statement (1992:18): "Day 14: Priam is awoken by Hermes before the dawn which rises at 24.695. This day includes the laments for Hektor and closes with Priam's instructions for the eleven days of funeral (24.777 ff.)." Whereas these verses clearly state the arrival of Dawn, i.e. subsequent days of action. 24.785: "When on the tenth day Eos brought light to mortals,

chronological record of the *Iliad* based on the findings of Peters and Stählin with all the days when action took place marked.[117]

Although the division of the epic poem into books happened later, the initial and final events contained in the first and last book are linked with information regarding time intervals. In the first and last books, these events last four days (days in which action takes place), while the rest of the book presents the constant development of events, which lasts eight successive days. The succession of all the eventful days, therefore, follows the pattern 4 + 8 + 4, which appears to be quite symmetrical, contrary to Taplin's calculations.

By summing up the number of days in which action takes place and whose passing is mentioned (hereafter called narrative days), we get the number 50 in accordance with, in my opinion, the most reliable calculations of Peters and Stählin. The ninth day of definite action is at the same time as the twenty-fifth day of the whole *Iliad* calendar, including the longest narrative sequence, accounting for one third of the work. In his interpretation, Stählin not only designates the axis of symmetry, but also includes a sort of passage between two of Achilles' periods of μῆνις (*mênis*, 'anger'), one directed against Agamemnon to the detriment of the Achaeans and the other against Hektor

they carried brave Hektor, and, in tears, laid his body on the summit of the pyre"; 24.788: "But as soon as early Eos, the rosy-fingered, appeared, then gathered the folk about the pyre of glorious Hektor."

117 I do not find more recent calculations of the number of days in the *Iliad* convincing. Hellwig (1964:40), who follows E. Balensiefen (*Die Zeitgestaltung in Homers Ilias* [Diss. Tübingen, 1955]), supports the number 50, while Latacz (2004:193), who follows M. Stoevesandt (*Der Mythos vom Troianischen Krieg im Spiegel der* "Ilias" in *Troja. Traum und Wirklichkeit* [2001], 92), supports 51 days. The difference between the calculations of Peters and Stählin concerns whether Thetis went to Zeus on the twentieth or the twenty-first day of action—that is, if the twelfth day is the last day of the gods' stay with the Ethiopians, before their return to Olympus, or the one before the last. Stählin (1923:298) assumes that the return was on the last day: "Die 12 Tage sind nach Morgenröten gezählt, mit Anbruch der ersten geben die Götter weg, mit Anbruch der zwölften kommen sie zurück." The *Iliad* text in this place (9.493–494) is not entirely clear. A significant difference emerges in interpretations regarding which day of action is the longest day, the third day of the battle, including the *aristeia* and death of Patroklos. According to Stählin, it is day 25, taking up a central position in the symmetrical structure of the epic. If it is day 26, the symmetry is lost. In the calculations of Latacz, the increase in the number of days by one results from a different interpretation of when and for how long the body of Hektor was defiled. Stoevesandt and Latacz completely abandon the Homeric perception of time as periods and adopt a purely linear chronology, where the defilement of Hektor's corpse lasts sometime between the thirtieth and fortieth days of action. This refers to the twelve-day period, but as I have shown in the table, it necessitates synchronization with the nine-day quarrel of the gods. This historical method of reasoning, assuming a chronological sequence of events distorts, in my opinion, the concept of a work based on the cyclic perception of time characteristic of oral culture.

to the detriment of the Trojans.[118] In Stählin's diagram, Books 9 and 22 are the culminations of Achilles' wrath.[119]

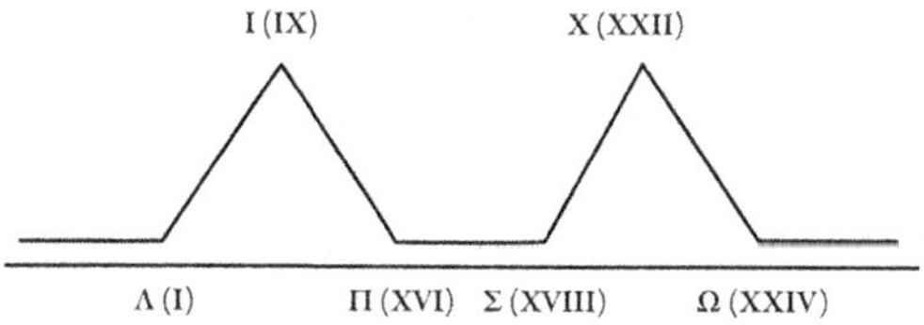

The number of fifty days in the *Iliad* is acquired by including specified interludes in between the days of action. Kirk treats these interludes as if the poet used them haphazardly. Yet their inclusion must have originally had a meaning, the defining of time between nine and twelve days. Moreover, there is no reason to assume that Homer had absolutely no knowledge or understanding of the magical significance of numbers.

A nine-day period never functions on its own, but it always has to be followed by the tenth day, as at *Iliad* 1.53–54:

> ἐννῆμαρ μὲν ἀνὰ στρατὸν ᾤχετο κῆλα θεοῖο,
> τῇ δεκάτῃ δ' ἀγορὴν δὲ καλέσσατο λαὸν Ἀχιλλεύς
>
> for nine days the soldiers were shot by the god's arrows,
> on the tenth day Achilles summoned the army to assemble.

The arrival of the tenth day might be emphasized with a formula describing dawn, as at *Iliad* 6.174–175:

> ἐννῆμαρ ξείνισσε καὶ ἐννέα βοῦς ἱέρευσεν.
> ἀλλ' ὅτε δὴ δεκάτη ἐφάνη ῥοδοδάκτυλος Ἠώς
>
> for nine days' space he showed him entertainment, and slew nine oxen,
> Howbeit when on the tenth, rosy-fingered Dawn appeared ...

[118] The anger of Achilles at the Trojans, however, is never defined as *mênis* (Kim 2000:156).

[119] Stählin 1923:295. Of course, Stählin interprets the *Iliad* as a product of literary culture, and therefore tries to perceive the action as leading to a climax and then declining as the story is resolved. According to Ong (2002:141–146), however, Freytag's Pyramid has no application in oral creativity and has no application to Homer. See further, Ch. 4, below.

The magical significance of the number of days 9 + 1 is also seen in a passus from Hesiod's *Theogony* 722–723,[120] describing the distance between heaven and earth (and then again in 724–725, the distance between earth and Tartarus):[121]

> ἐννέα γὰρ νύκτας τε καὶ ἤματα χάλκεος ἄκμων
> οὐρανόθεν κατιών, δεκάτῃ κ' ἐς γαῖαν ἵκοιτο
>
> for nine nights and days the bronze anvil
> from heaven falling, on the tenth would reach earth.

It is highly probable that the number 9 + 1 began to play an independent role in the epic narrative and that the period of 9 + 1 days served a similar function as 9 + 1 years. The magic number 9 + 1, present in nine-year and nine-day periods, is not unique to the poetry of Homer and Hesiod. As well, in Apollodorus's account of the Trojan War, there are suggestions that this method of counting was firmly established in the Trojan Cycle tradition. Hermione is nine when her mother, Helen, abandons her, and Achilles is nine when his mother Thetis tries to hide him so that he will not go to war.[122] After nine years, the allies of the Trojans arrive at Troy.[123] Moreover, it seemed important for Apollodorus to note that Paris was hosted by Menelaos for nine days, and on the tenth day, the Spartan king had to sail to Crete.[124]

The 9 + 1 period in reference to the *Iliad* narrative is twice stated *expressis verbis*: 1) days 1–10, for the arrival of the angry Apollo and the spreading of the plague among the Achaeans, 2) days 29–38, for the dispute of the gods and the fate of the maltreated body of Hektor; although here, the tenth day is not literally stated, but rather there is reference to the nine-day period as most probably having been completed (*Iliad* 24.107 ἐννῆμαρ δὴ νεῖκος ἐν ἀθανάτοισιν <u>ὄρωρεν</u>).[125] They do not correspond to each other in the symmetry of the work, but they are probably not the only 9 + 1 periods serving a function in its construction.

120 Frazer (1912:70) qualifies this *passus* as being connected with the *octaeteris*, the eight-, or rather nine-year period of penance.

121 Homer generally defines this distance as being the same (*Iliad* 8.16).

122 Apollodorus *Epitome* 3.3: ἡ δὲ ἐνναέτη Ἑρμιόνην καταλιποῦσα, ... , ἀνάγεται τῆς νυκτὸς σὺν αὐτῷ; *Library* 3.13.8: Ὡς δὲ ἐγένετο ἐνναετὴς Ἀχιλλεύς, Κάλχαντος λέγοντος οὐ δύνασθαι χωρὶς αὐτοῦ Τροίαν αἱρεθῆναι, Θέτις προειδυῖα ὅτι δεῖ στρατευόμενον αὐτὸν ἀπολέσθαι, κρύψασα ἐσθῆτι γυναικείᾳ ὡς παρθένον Λυκομήδει παρέθετο.

123 Apollodorus *Epitome* 3.34: Ἐνναετοῦς δὲ χρόνου διελθόντος παραγίνονται τοῖς Τρωσὶ σύμμαχοι· ἐκ τῶν περιοίκων πόλεων Αἰνείας Ἀγχίσου καὶ σὺν αὐτῷ Ἀρχέλοχος καὶ Ἀκάμας Ἀντήνορος καὶ Θεανοῦς, Δαρδανίων ἡγούμενοι, Θρακῶν Ἀκάμας Εὐσώρου, Κικόνων Εὔφημος Τροιζήνου, Παιόνων Πυραίχμης, Παφλαγόνων κτλ.

124 *Epitome* 3.3: (Paris) ἐφ' ἡμήρας δ' ἐννέα ξενισθεὶς παρὰ Μενελάῳ, τῇ δεκάτῃ πορευθέντος εἰς Κρήτην..., πείθει τὴν Ἑλένην ἀπαγαγεῖν σὺν ἑαυτῷ. ἡ δὲ ἐνναέτη Ἑρμιόνην καταλιποῦσα... , ἀνάγεται τῆς νυκτὸς σὺν αὐτῷ.

125 Stählin 1923:299.

A																				B do Ψ								Ω																					
20																				8								22																					
1	2	3	4	5	6	7	8	9	10	11	12	13	14	15	16	17	18	19	20	21	22	23	24	25	26	27	28	29	30	31	32	33	34	35	36	37	38	39	40	41	42	43	44	45	46	47	48	49	50
1									2	3									4	5	6	7	8	9	10	11	12										13	14									15	16	
1	2	3	4	5	6	7	8	9																				1	2	3	4	5	6	7	8	9		1	2	3	4	5	6	7	8	9			
								1	2	3	4	5	6	7	8	9	10	11	12							1	2	3	4	5	6	7	8	9	10	11	12	1	2	3	4	5	6	7	8	9	10	11	12

Table 2. The Calendar of the *Iliad*, according to Peters and Stählin.

Days in the *Iliad* when action took place (second row, corresponding days of action in the *Iliad* marked grey):

1. The Chryses episode (1.12–52).
2. Achilles summons an assembly on the tenth day of the plague (1.54–476).
3. Ships return from Chryse (1.477–478).
4. Thetis sets out to see Zeus after the gods return from a twelve-day stay with the Ethiopians. The last day before the battle (1.493–611).
5. The first day of the battle—the fighting ends unresolved (2.48–7.57).
6. The gathering and cremation of the bodies of the fallen.
7. Burial of the warriors' ashes. Construction of the wall and moat.
8. The second day of the battle (8.1–848). Defeat of the Achaeans. Includes the night during which the emissaries go to Achilles (Book 9) and possibly the expedition of Odysseus and Diomedes (Book 10).
9. The third day of the battle. The day of Hektor's triumph: the Trojans reach the ships, Patroklos's counterattack, fighting for the body of Patroklos, retreat of the Achaeans. The longest continuous narrative: 11.1–18.242. Includes the night 18.243–617.
10. The fourth day of the battle. Achilles defeats the Trojans and kills Hektor (19.1–23.61).
11. Patroklos placed on the pyre. Cremation of his body.
12. Burial of Patroklos's ashes. Games held in his honor (23.266–897).
13. Apollo speaks, after twelve days, of the maltreatment of Hektor's corpse by Achilles (24.31). Zeus speaks about the nine-day dispute of the gods (24.107). Achilles informed about the decision of the gods.
14. The return of Priam with the body of Hektor. Priam orders the gathering of wood for the funeral pyre (24.777). He informs about the twelve-day truce.
15. The day after the nine-day gathering of wood. Hektor's body placed on the pyre. Cremation of the body (24.785).
16. Burial of Hektor's ashes. A wake in his honor (24.788).

Periods marked *expressis verbis* in Homer (*third and fourth rows*):

17. Nine days of plague cast on the Achaeans by Apollo (1.53), probably continuing from the first day of narration, as there is no statement that it started the next day.
18. Twelve-day absence of the gods from Troy. On the tenth day, Thetis says that the gods have been with the Ethiopians since the previous day (1.423). Thetis plans to ask Zeus on the twelfth day—the day of return (1.425). Therefore, this period should probably be counted from the ninth day of the narration.
19. On the thirteenth day—i.e. the thirty-eighth day of narration according to Stählin—Apollo gives a speech after twelve days of Achilles' maltreatment of Hektor's body, and that is therefore counted from the twenty-seventh day—i.e. the day Patroklos's body was placed on the pyre. It also seems possible to count this twelve-day period from Hektor's death—i.e. the twenty-sixth day—when the defilement of his body is described for the first time. This period, nevertheless, needs to be synchronized with the next one.
20. That same day, Zeus says that the dispute over condemning Achilles lasted nine days (24.107). Zeus is, therefore, clearly speaking of the next day—the tenth, which is the thirty-eighth day of narration.
21. The twelve-day truce begins on the thirty-ninth day, which must clearly end on the fiftieth day after the arrival of Chryses at the Achaean camp.
22. That same day, in accordance with Priam's order, the Trojans begin a nine-day period of gathering wood (24.784).

If we look at the days mentioned in the *Iliad* as arranged in Table 1, we will notice a relationship between the 9 + 1 periods and the twelve-day periods. The last period of days (39–50) is the twelve-day truce, which includes a nine-day period of gathering wood for Hektor's pyre, one day (48 = 15), when Hektor's body is placed on the pyre, and one day (49 = 16), when Hektor's ashes and bones are buried. This gives us 9 + 1 + 1 = 11, the next day, the twelfth, completes the phase, and is only counted this way in twelve-day periods.[126]

[126] One could venture the hypothesis that after the nine-day hosting of Paris (as mentioned by Apollodorus), on the tenth day Menelaos has to leave. The next day (or night), the lovers Paris and Helen are united and decide to elope, which happens the next day, which must be the twelfth day.

Let us compare: after 1–9 days of the plague, one day follows in which the assembly decides to placate the anger of the deity; the Achaeans sail to Chryse where they return to Chryses, the priest of Apollo, his daughter, and Chryses prays to Apollo to sooth his anger; sacrifices are offered to the deity (10 = 2); then for one day the ships return from their mission (11 = 3)—in all, 9 + 1 + 1 = 11. The next day, the plague ends and the army returns to health, completing the number 12, but this day is not mentioned. These two periods of 1–12 days and 39–50 days correspond with each other in the symmetry of the *Iliad*. The conceptual significance is no doubt associated with the role played by Apollo in the story of the Trojan War. At the start, the god's anger at the insult to his priest is placated, and at the end the remains of Hektor are buried, the mistreatment of which Apollo, the god protecting the Trojans, had disapproved and for which he will take the life of Achilles, most probably on the fiftieth and final day, thus completing the cycle and the whole story.

We can therefore say, contrary to the views of Kirk, that the start of the *Iliad* and the period at its end mutually correspond, though they are not named *expressis verbis*. In accordance with the ring composition principle, scenes correspond with each other in rings of successively smaller radius. In this case, we can speak of an outer ring binding together the action. The two twelve-day periods of the inner ring also correspond, though here too it must be deduced: 1) 9–20 days for the stay of the gods with the Ethiopians, which prohibits Thetis from immediately submitting her request to Zeus; and 2) 27–39 days when Apollo speaks of the twelve days of the maltreatment of Hektor's body. Multiple similarities link the two periods. For one, both initially interlock with the preceding period. By synchronizing the statement of Apollo (24.31) with that of Zeus (24.107) concerning the nine-day dispute of the gods on whether or not to react to Achilles' behavior, we notice that because both periods (9 + 1 and 12) end on the same day (38), they must have started on different days. The twelve-day period of the maltreatment of Hektor's body must start earlier, during the funeral of Patroklos: day 27 = 11 and day 28 = 12. These days belong to the central part of the song's continuous narrative. The stay of the gods with the Ethiopians, temporarily delaying the consequences of Achilles' withdrawal from the fighting, must begin on the ninth day because on the tenth day Thetis says the gods had left for Ethiopia the day before. In other words, the first two days of this period occur on the ninth and tenth days of the preceding period. If in accordance with the strict perception of linearity, Thetis, meeting her son on the tenth day of the narrative, tells him she will meet Zeus the next day (similarly to how in the final phase Achilles decides the truce is to begin the next day), the next period would begin the next day, and thus we would be dealing with the ideal symmetry of twenty-two days in both the first book and the last book. This, however, is impossible on account of the narrative: Thetis would have no reason to postpone her visit to Zeus if he was still on Olympus. The maltreatment of Hektor's body symmetrically corresponds to this period because that is also probably when the gods stayed with the Ethiopians. On day 27 = 11, Iris visits the winds Boreas and Zephyr, urging them to hear Achilles' prayer and help burn the body of Patroklos. Iris, however, refuses to sit beside them, saying she must fly to the land of the Ethiopians to partake in the sacred feast of the gods (23.205–207). Zeus dispatches Iris to Thetis with a message to urge her son to give back the corpse of Hektor on the twelfth day; that is clearly the day the gods are to return from Ethiopia. Therefore, the meeting with Thetis takes place at an identical moment and in the same circumstances as the first time. And, therefore, the inner ring is the sojourn of the gods in the land of the Ethiopians. This, in turn, provides an answer to the question of why Homer introduced a twelve-day period of grace between Thetis's hearing Achilles' complaint and Thetis passing the complaint on to Zeus, which is in no way justified by any reasons of narrative. The absence of the gods means in every culture the possibility of people experiencing evil and misfortune.[127] The absence of the gods means that Achilles is able to defile Hektor's corpse.[128] Yet here the author faces a moral problem: can the gods allow for such a shameful treatment of, by the poet's own description, such a noble prince of Troy? The narrator presents an impassioned argument between the gods, ended with a decision to stop Achilles from committing evil and to return dignity to Hektor by having his body returned to his father. The gods therefore return and put right the wrongs committed in their absence. Likewise, in Book 1 Achilles suffers an undeserved wrong when, as it turns out, the gods are absent. Here, the return of the gods is associated with the decision of Zeus to put right the wrong encountered by Achilles.[129]

[127] Likewise, in the imagination of the Greeks. In one of the letters by Alciphron (*Epistle* 3.35), the protagonist complains about a drought that cannot be prevented by any of the sacrifices the inhabitants offer to Zeus, Who Sends Down Rain (Ὑέτιος). The narrator explains this by the absence of gods: ἔοικε γὰρ πρὸς ἑτέροις ἔθνεσιν ὁ Ζεύς ὢν τῶν τῇδε ἀμελεῖν, "it seems Zeus is staying with other nations and cannot look after us." The durability of such convictions is evidenced by a Polish song from the Second World War: "The enemy has invaded Poland ... and precisely because Lord Jesus is asleep" (*Wróg napadł na Polskę... a właśnie dlatego że Pan Jezus drzemie*); compare *Iliad* 14.352–15.28.

[128] Hellwig (1964:24–28) notes that the gods take up positions around the human domain, from where they observe and intervene (28): "In fünf Etappen nähern sich also die Götter dem Geschehen: Äthiopien—Olymp—Ida und Samothrake—Grabmal des Herakles und "Kallikolone"—Schlachtfeld."

[129] This theme is presented in the *Odyssey*: the sojourn of the gods in the land of the Ethiopians allows Poseidon to inflict suffering on Odysseus.

At the same time, we cannot forget that periods here serve a conventional function, and we cannot apply strict logic to all the information provided by Homer, as in Book 1, where Achilles sits next to the ships while the fighting rages (1.488–492):

> αὐτὰρ ὃ μήνιε νηυσὶ παρήμενος ὠκυπόροισι
> διογενὴς Πηλῆος υἱὸς πόδας ὠκὺς Ἀχιλλεύς·
> οὔτε ποτ' εἰς ἀγορὴν πωλέσκετο κυδιάνειραν
> οὔτε ποτ' ἐς πόλεμον, ἀλλὰ φθινύθεσκε φίλον κῆρ
> αὖθι μένων, ποθέεσκε δ' ἀϋτήν τε πτόλεμόν τε.
>
> He in turn felt anger [*mênis*], sitting next to fast ships,
> from a divine family, son of Peleus, swift-footed Achilles.
> And not once did he appear in the agora, which brings men glory,
> or on the battlefield, but with dear heart pining
> staying put, yearning for the battle clamor and combat.

Although the battle, which starts on day 21 = 5, is presented as if it were the first battle since Achilles' withdrawal from the fighting, this is a space of time that exists and at once does not exist. Similarly, for twelve days Achilles maltreated the corpse of Hektor, but nothing happens to it because the deities Aphrodite (23.183–187) and Apollo (23.188–191, 24.18–21) in a magical way protect it from Achilles' actions and decay. The situation is identical—as if time did not pass at all.

The collecting of wood for Hektor's funeral pyre lasts nine days, whereas the funeral of Patroklos has no designated time at all. Therefore, the singer uses periods of time fairly loosely, in accord with the needs of the narrative. Nevertheless, they are essential to maintaining the right symmetry and rhythm in the work.

The middle part of the *Iliad*, forming its core, consists of eight days interlocking on one side with the 9 + 1 + 1 day period of Achilles' withdrawal from battle, and on the other with the twelve-day maltreatment of Hektor's body.

Homer, insofar as he is the author of this construction of the song, intended a narrative of fifty days. The symmetrical axis, as we have noticed, is day 25 = 9. The fiftieth day, in turn, is only foretold as the day (after Hektor's funeral) when the battle will be resumed. There is much reason to assume the day of the resumption of battle will also be the day of Achilles' death because its imminence is repeatedly foretold (18.95–96, 19.408–409, 22.359–360, 23.81, 24.131–132).[130] A signal for

[130] Compare West 2003b:6: "The death of Achilles, after all, was a theme very much on the *Iliad* poet's mind. He is constantly looking forward to it, and indeed creates the expectation that it will occur before the end of the poem."

the listener that the death of Achilles will occur on the fiftieth day is also given, I would suggest, in the scene of Patroklos's funeral, (23.138–153):

> οἳ δ' ὅτε χῶρον ἵκανον ὅθί σφισι πέφραδ' Ἀχιλλεὺς
> κάτθεσαν, αἶψα δέ οἱ μενοεικέα νήεον ὕλην.
> ἔνθ' αὖτ' ἄλλ' ἐνόησε ποδάρκης δῖος Ἀχιλλεὺς
> στὰς ἀπάνευθε πυρῆς ξανθὴν ἀπεκείρατο χαίτην,
> τήν ῥα Σπερχειῷ ποταμῷ τρέφε τηλεθόωσαν·
> ὀχθήσας δ' ἄρα εἶπεν ἰδὼν ἐπὶ οἴνοπα πόντον·
> Σπερχεί' ἄλλως σοί γε πατὴρ ἠρήσατο Πηλεὺς
> κεῖσέ με νοστήσαντα φίλην ἐς πατρίδα γαῖαν
> σοί τε κόμην κερέειν ῥέξειν θ' ἱερὴν ἑκατόμβην,
> πεντήκοντα δ' ἔνορχα παρ' αὐτόθι μῆλ' ἱερεύσειν
> ἐς πηγάς, ὅθι τοι τέμενος βωμός τε θυήεις.
> ὣς ἠρᾶθ' ὃ γέρων, σὺ δέ οἱ νόον οὐκ ἐτέλεσσας.
> νῦν δ' ἐπεὶ οὐ νέομαί γε φίλην ἐς πατρίδα γαῖαν
> Πατρόκλῳ ἥρωϊ κόμην ὀπάσαιμι φέρεσθαι.
> ὣς εἰπὼν ἐν χερσὶ κόμην ἑτάροιο φίλοιο
> θῆκεν, τοῖσι δὲ πᾶσιν ὑφ' ἵμερον ὦρσε γόοιο.

> But when they came to the place that Achilles had appointed,
> they set down the body, and quickly built a high pyre of wood.
> Then swift-footed, godly Achilles had another thought:
> moving away from the pyre he started to cut his blond hair,
> the hair that he had been growing for the river god Spercheios;
> and then his face became gloomy and he spoke, looking over the
> wine-faced sea:
> "Spercheios, in vain did my father Peleus conjure you
> [and vowed] that if I came home to my dear native land,
> I would cut my hair to you and offer a holy hecatomb,
> and on the self-same spot I would sacrifice fifty rams
> into your springs, where are your temenos and altar smelling of
> incense.
> So prayed that old man, but you did not fulfil his desire.[131]
> So now, since I will not return to my dear native land,

131 " ... but you did not fulfil his desire": Achilles does not express this gesture as being of his own volition. He suggests that the god broke the promise. Achilles does not relieve the god from the agreement—as one might have expected—but puts the onus on the deity for breaking a promise. This is probably because he wants to avoid the curse for breaking an agreement, even though the hero has already accepted imminent death. Let us note that the hero's death is also described as an inability to return home.

> I will offer my hair to the hero Patroklos."
> So he spoke and put his hair in the hands of his dear comrade
> and in all of them was aroused the desire to lament.

By cutting off a lock of his hair, Achilles accepts that he will die on the battlefield. Achilles voluntarily forsakes his return to his dear native land. In face of the prophecy allowing him to decide his fate, the loss of his friend makes him decide that he, too, will die. From Homer's perspective, behind this decision to accept an early death, posthumous fame was of secondary importance. This decision leaves unfulfilled the promise made to the river god Spercheios of sacrificing fifty rams. The fifty rams signifying life and a return home are replaced by the fifty days fulfilling the decision and circumstances of Achilles' own death. The fifty days are the hecatomb of the self-sacrifice offered by Achilles, and self-sacrifice is an important condition (if not *sine qua non*) of attaining hero status. Similarly, in the *Odyssey* the 360 pigs devoured by the suitors: one was eaten every day, and in Murray's view this signified the passing of days until Odysseus's return.[132]

The number fifty does not seem accidental, and it also concerns the fifty months of the *penteteris* period. Harrison and Cornford find analogies with fifty daughters of Endymion and Selene, and the fifty daughters of Danaos. These myths function within a complex of beliefs concerning solar-lunar marriages and rites of passage.

One of the characteristic features of Homer's style is the doubling of characters and scenes. These doubles are never identical but are subjected to modal transformations, often involving a game of similarities and opposites. The construction of these scenes frequently involves dividing a scene or a group of scenes into two equal parts. *Exempli gratia*, the result of the scene of Achilles gathering the Achaeans together is the hero's withdrawal from battle and Agamemnon's bellicose claim that they will manage to fight without him. One might then expect that this scene would be followed by one in which Agamemnon leads the Achaeans into battle. Homer, however, preferred to add another scene of the Achaeans gathering together, and this time Agamemnon raises the morale of the troops. Again, one might think that this scene is completely redundant and at odds with Achilles' position near the ships, abstaining from the war council and the fighting. For the listener, it gives the impression that during that time there had been no fighting at all. On the other hand, the scene is justified because it reveals to the listener a psychological consequence in accord with the author's intention. Instead

132 Murray 1907:212.

of directly showing the discouragement of the troops and apprehension or even disappointment with Agamemnon's stance, which resulted in Achilles' withdrawal, the singer presents a separate scene of the army gathered in a bad mood, which is rapidly transformed into general optimism when the fleeing soldiers are turned back by Odysseus. Moreover, the singer aligns the second assembly scene with an episode showing Achilles' anger in the perspective of the whole war. Thus, the author is also able to hold back the unsuccessful initial battles of the Achaeans in expectation of the return of the gods from the land of the Ethiopians, when Achilles' request can be submitted to Zeus. Yet from the point of view of the continuity of narrative, this expectation is also unnecessary.

In my opinion, the arrangement of the time episodes performs a more important function than the arrangement of the content of the monumental version of the song. Three days of fighting are not required for Achilles' request to be fulfilled, but they are necessary to build up a mounting sense of menace, which reaches its climax when Hektor approaches the line of Achaean ships and sets fire to the first one. Instead of Achilles, Patroklos engages in battle. That scene delays Achilles' return to battle, but at the same time it plays an important role in anticipating Achilles' death, which, in accordance with Homer's intentions, is the only means by which it is communicated in the poem. As well, the outcome of the first day of fighting, before the defeat of the Achaeans, remains unresolved. The first day of battle performs two important functions, both of which present the episode in the perspective of the whole war: it documents the moral right of the Achaeans to victory (the duel between Paris and Menelaos, and Pandaros's treacherous shot),[133] and it proclaims their advantage and victory in the whole war. It also performs an extremely important role in presenting the subject of the song: the *aristeia* of Diomedes, on the one hand, contrasts with the behavior of Achilles, implying the heroism that can be achieved by a young warrior in combat and, on the other, provides a model version of the anticipated deaths of Patroklos and Achilles.[134] The first and second days of battle serve as a retardant of action by duplicating scenes of Achaean defeat and the death of Patroklos, who like Diomedes serves as a substitute for Achilles.

The arrangement of content is subordinated to the periodic structure. Days 22 = 6, "collecting of the fallen warriors and the cremation of their bodies," and 23 = 7, "burying of the ashes of cremated warriors; building of wall and moat,"

[133] Schein 1984:24; Schein 1997:353–354.

[134] See Ch. 5, below.

are the typical consequences of a battle scene that ends with the death of a hero. This conclusion is prompted by the following comparison:

Days after the death of Patroklos

27 = 11 “placing of Patroklos on the pyre; cremation of his body”

28 = 12 “burial of Patroklos’s ashes; games in his honor”

Days after the delivery of the body of Hektor and nine days of cutting down trees

48 = 15 “placing of Hektor on the pyre; cremation of his body”

49 = 16 “burial of Hektor’s ashes; wake”

One can observe that one element shows greater modality than the rest: in the first case, after burying the ashes, we have the building of a wall and moat, in the second case, games in honor of the hero are held, and in the third a wake is held in the hero’s honor. Nevertheless, all these items are essential; the singer cannot mention these days without the additional element. Likewise, he cannot present the death of a hero on the battlefield without a subsequent two days for the cremation and the burial of the ashes.

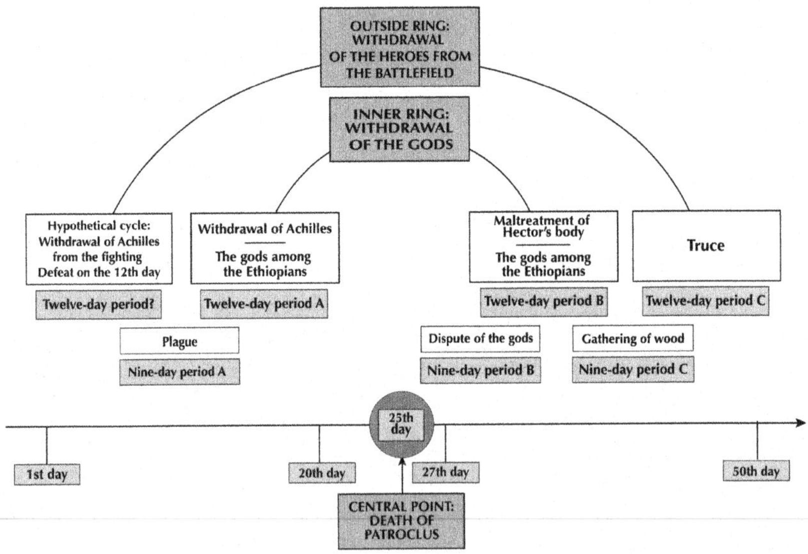

Figure 2. Layout of periods in the ring composition of the *Iliad*.

If we take a closer look at the layout of the periods of time within the composition of the *Iliad* (see Figure 2, above), we will notice that they play a more important role in relation to the organization of the plot. Two twelve-day periods in the second part of the work meet in the same point as corresponding periods of 9 + 1 days, at the convergence of narrative days 38 –39. We can see that the overlapping of two kinds of periods allows for the simultaneous presentation of events in the world of the gods and in the world of the mortals. Since the absence of gods leads to the harming of Achilles, a periodic analogy also appears in the first part of the work, though it is not so clearly marked. More importantly, the periods are arranged in accordance with the principles of ring composition. In the inner ring, we have parallel twelve-day periods in which the gods withdraw to visit the happy Ethiopians. This primarily means that the gods do not intervene in the war, which leads to a heinous crime. In turn, the external ring concentrates on the mortals refraining from the fight. The truce declared by Achilles in the last part of the work corresponds to the period of the plague and Achilles' decision to withdraw from the fighting. The middle section of the composition concerns Achilles and his substitutes (Diomedes and Patroklos) fighting, while the central point concerns Patroklos's fight and death. The overlapping of two periods in the first part provides space in the central part of the work (the second twelve-day period begins on the ninth day of the first one) for the days of fighting. The sum of four twelve-day periods is forty-eight days. If the analogy to the fifty-month Olympiad period is correct, the number forty-eight could refer to the forty-eight daughters of Danaos. who were presented, according to Pindar *Pythian* 9.112–125, as a prize for suitors competing in a race. Scholia to Pindar explain that the number of daughters presented as prizes was smaller because Hypermnestra and Amymone were already married. Cornford believes that the two missing daughters signify the first and last months of the *penteteris* because they were both married to the Sun.[135] The number twelve is associated with the solar cycle. Pindar testifies that the tethrippon race comprised twelve laps, which may be associated with the twelve-month journey of the sun (*Olympian* 3.33–34 δωδεκάγναμπτον περὶ τέρμα δρόμου / ἵππων, "in their course the horses circled twelve times around the post"; cf. *Olympian* 6.75 and 2.50).[136]

This association of time, as it functions in the epic, with the cyclic solar and lunar calendars does not necessarily mean epic heroes had solar-lunar origins, as was once hypothesized in the early stages of cultural anthropology. Solar and lunar myths, though present in Greek epic only in a residual form, nevertheless

[135] Cornford 1927:232. Cornford, however, suggests that the number 48 is the sum of three sixteens and therefore an analogy to the sixteen women in the Heraean Games at Olympia.

[136] Cornford 1927:228.

affected the construction of proto-epic plots.[137] These early plots gave the hero's actions a cosmic dimension, allowing him to bind together the cosmic structure of time.

The symmetrical and linear arrangement

The opinion that the *Iliad*'s symmetry was intended for a monumental poem therefore seems unfounded. Here a fairly simple cyclic arrangement is disrupted by the fragmentation of themes and the expansion of narrative. The very idea of symmetry in song, however, seems much older than the Geometric period of geometry of Greek painting. Perhaps it had functioned in Greek epic song from its earliest stages of development.

It should be noted that while an exact symmetry would seem to be disrupted by two twelve-day periods overlapping at the start, unlike in the coda, where they appear one after the other, this is not actually the case because symmetry is maintained by other means. The three-part linear arrangement does not collide with the circularity of the composition but harmonizes with it. In the linear arrangement, we are dealing with a threefold repetition of a heroic story in which the hero's *aristeia* leads to an encounter with the god Apollo and consequently the hero's death.[138] In the *aristeias* of Diomedes, Patroklos, and Achilles, the *Iliad* three times repeats the same model (basic for epic songs), known to the singer and his listeners alike. And yet only in the second case is the hero eventually killed. This is an image in anticipation of the death of Achilles, being at the same time an allomorph of that death. It occurs in the middle of the middle day of the described events (*Iliad* 16.778–781),[139] whose presentation is disproportionately long in comparison with the rest. The death of Patroklos is preceded by his heroic struggle, and later by a description of the fighting for his body. For Stählin, as we have seen, this central point was only a moment of transition between the two wraths of Achilles. For such a secondary reason, that is an extremely momentous scene. Later on (in Chapter 5), our discussion will show

[137] The presence and influence of the solar myth in the shaping of the Greek epic tradition is indicated by Frame 2005 and Tsagalis 2008, particularly in his Ch. 4. The herds of Helios on Thrinacia, which Frame (2005:42–43) associates with the solar myth, comprise seven herds of cattle and seven herds of sheep, with fifty animals in both (*Odyssey* 12.127–130), from which we can connect the number fifty with the solar myth. We can also double the solar number when we count the number of cities conquered by Achilles: twelve conquered with ships and twelve conquered on land, though the last, Troy, he did not actually capture. On the similarities with three-, seven- and twelve-day intervals in Near Eastern poetry and the possible influences of that literature on Homer, see West 1997:250–251.

[138] This will be discussed in greater detail in Ch. 5, below.

[139] In the *Iliad*, midday always means a critical moment in the battle, and the repeated formulae on this occasion announce a change for the benefit of the other side.

that the hero-protagonist's death is a key moment of anticipation, retardation, and reconstruction that is typical of the oral tradition.

The arrangement adopted in Homer's *Iliad* seems to lose its original structure in favor of the multiplication of the content and drama of events. The fifty-day period of the *Iliad* is straddled by two events: the insulting of a priest of Apollo, Chryses, on the first day, and the prophecy of the death of Achilles on the last, fiftieth day. The events of the first day only indirectly lead to what is to be resolved on the last day. A more important reason is the offending of Achilles, mentioned in the invocation, but it is not found at the start of the narrative. The death of Achilles is separated from the period pattern and transferred to the end of the narrative, as an objective to which the narrative is heading. The death of his friend not only makes Achilles return to the fight, but it also results in the hero's own death. The pattern, as we can see, shows a flexibility that is similar to the flexibility of formulae and typical scenes.

An Episode from the Perspective of the Whole

The idea of symmetry pervades the *Iliad* and is not in the least limited to balancing the periods of action. This subject has already been well researched, so here I shall only summarize the most important findings.

The symmetry of the work is primarily determined by the balance between the scenes in the first three and last three books.[140]

1. Book 1: Agamemnon rejects the plea and the ransom of Chryses and does not return his daughter; 24: Achilles accepts the plea and ransom of Priam and returns to him the body of his son. In both cases the mover of events is Apollo: in 1.43–52 he hears the prayer of Chryses, steps down from Olympus, and spreads the plague in the Greek camp; in 24.33–54 Apollo censures the other gods for supporting Achilles in his disgraceful treatment of Hektor's body and starts a discussion that ends with Zeus deciding that the ransom for Hektor's body should be received.
2. Scenes on Olympus at the start of Book 24 and the end of Book 1. In both books, Zeus and Thetis meet and the subject of the discussion is also the same: Achilles.
3. Books 2 and 23: the descriptions of the Greek army; the Catalogue of Ships introduces the chief commanders, while the games in honor of Patroklos in Book 23 seem to mark their farewell.

140 See Schein 1997:345–348.

4. Books 3 and 22: the duels of Paris and Menelaos and of Hektor and Achilles. The first signals the start of the war, the second its end.

The parallelism of scenes is based not only on similarities, but also on the reversal of situations and meanings. *Exempli gratia*, Thetis's two visits to Zeus on Olympus contrast with each other. The first time the goddess arrives alone, surreptitiously, with a request to the ruler of Olympus on behalf of her son, and her visit is received by Hera with irritation, leading to an argument between the spouses. The second time, Thetis is invited to Olympus, not at her request but at that of Zeus, who wants her to intervene with her son on his behalf; when she enters the palace she is warmly greeted by Hera, acting in accordance with her spouse's will. While in Book 1 Thetis sends Achilles' request to Zeus, in Book 24 she brings her son a request from this god.

Many of these elements of the ring composition are a collection of instantly recognizable allusions to the start (Books 2–4) and end of the war (chiefly in the final books). These allusions are numerous and vary in character, but we shall first deal with the most significant ones.

The system of allusions allows the author to place the *Iliad* in the cycle as a digression to the story of the entire war. The allusions take on various forms: brief hints in the speeches of heroes or telling characteristics in comparisons.[141] They include entire scenes, suggesting how events will turn out at the start of the war. The Catalogue of Ships at 2.494–760 probably corresponds to the traditional description of the Greek fleet in Aulis. The duel between Menelaos and Paris in Book 3 (meaningful, if it were placed in the initial phase of the war) is supported by such passages as Antenor's recollections of the embassy of Odysseus and Menelaos to Troy before the war. Helen's *teichoscopia* seems ridiculous when, in the ninth year of the war, she first recognizes the leaders of the Trojan army that had invaded the country.[142] Helen is even surprised that on the battlefield she does not see her brothers Kastor and Polydeukes. The *teichoscopia* of the main heroine, who recognizes the leaders of the army that has come to win her back after her abduction turns out to be typical of Indo-European epics. Jamison has indeed found an undoubted parallel in the *teichoscopia* of Draupadī observing the arrival of the Pandava brothers, who have come to rescue her.[143]

141 See Kullmann 1968.

142 A reasonable attempt at explaining the presence of this "absurdity" in the plot of the *Iliad* was made by Roisman (2005b), who suggests that Priam's questions about the Achaean leaders are prompted by the old man's desire to make contact with a dazzlingly beautiful woman; at first, Helen answers with due politeness, but as time passes, she becomes tired of talking to old men and excuses herself from giving further answers.

143 Jamison 1994.

In accordance with the suggestions of the neoanalysts, all the above-mentioned scenes not only apply to other places in the cycle, but also seem to have been extracted from them and inserted into the song narrative of the wrath of Achilles. Thus, we return to the matter of adding "new" elements to oral tradition. The oral epic, according to Lord's findings, is a collection of subjects arranged in an appropriate order, in total creating a certain dramatic whole.[144] The omission of a theme or an even more significant element is, in the eyes of singers, a mistake, which can ruin the whole song. The same opinion confronts the singer when he adds something new to the song. Hence the constant assurances of singers that their performance of the song is faithful to the original, word for word, which does not alter the fact that they do make alterations, whether deliberate or inadvertent; this is the very flexibility and multiformity of oral poetry.

What exactly does it mean that the above scenes were taken from other places in the cycle? Certainly, we cannot follow the neoanalysts, who argued that particular scenes were based on parallel scenes in the *Kypria* and *Aethiopis*. These scenes were no doubt the topics of many songs about the start of the Trojan War.

We do not know whether or not the transference of these scenes to the song describing the end of the war was typical of Greek oral song.[145] Nevertheless, this device fulfils a role similar to that of an allusion, and like many other allusions, positions a work in the cycle of space and time. The insertion of these scenes, justified by the concept of symmetry, might seem artificial from a contemporary point of view. And yet, it is in precisely such a way that the unity of the work is defined and became the norm for other literary works.

We can ask: if there had been other versions of the *Iliad* as an oral song, would our extant version—with those scenes placed where they are—be a secondary work? There appear to be borrowed elements used to complete the work, but would not the *Iliad* as an oral song, insofar as such a version existed, have had to be devoid of such themes? The organization of text in the *Iliad*, with regard to the maintaining of symmetrical balance, has turned out to be primary, not secondary. Therefore, in trying to find an original version, we must assume its symmetry because the initial and final scenes forming the symmetry are so well matched to the content. If, for example, the presentation of the leaders (in the Catalogue of Ships and the *teichoscopia*) in the first part of the book corresponds to their "farewell" (according to Kullmann's expression) in Patroklos's

144 Lord 1960:99–101.

145 Dowden (1996:55–58) believes that the employment of allusions to other epic works in an attempt to present the picture of the entire war is a feature of a non-traditional style. Therefore, the way allusions are used in the *Iliad* represents, in his opinion, a break with oral tradition.

funeral and games, where the performance of the heroes foretells their fate in the story cycle, then the use of these allusions extending beyond the work are in this case far more coherent with the narrative of the whole. This is because there is no reason to assume that the funeral of Patroklos was not a traditional theme in songs about the wrath of Achilles, present in various lost versions of the *Iliad*. The funeral is a consequence of Patroklos' death, and in the epic narrative the games are the most significant part of it. The spectacular funeral of this hero and the games in his honor are probably a reference to the traditional image of the funeral and to games in honor of Achilles, but they also must be related to the motif of Patroklos, since he plays the role of Peleides' substitute, who dies on his behalf.

These scenes, as we have seen, "extend" the action of the *Iliad*, giving the recipient an awareness of the beginning and end of the war. It can therefore be argued that the reason why these alien scenes were included in the *Iliad* was the desire to present the whole war from the perspective of a single episode. If the symmetrical structure containing information about the start and end of the war was traditional, then the telling of a story in a song required it to be presented from the perspective of the whole war.[146]

The most frequently used story pattern in oral epic song is the Song of Return—that is, the story of the husband freed from captivity, who returns home, takes revenge on rival suitors for his woman, and is eventually reunited with his woman. Normally, the initial presentation of the hero's sufferings in captivity is followed by an explanation of how he had been captured, on which quest, with whom and against whom, and with what outcome. This is, of course, information essential for the listener, who wants to learn about a concrete hero and situation, rather than an anonymous person and timeless situation. We also find out whom the hero left at home and in what circumstances. All this information delineates the time-space frame of the work. Yet it can also be the case that the hero is already a figure known from other songs—to such an extent, perhaps, that they know his character or typical character traits and thus recognize his distinctive and conventional epithets. Such a song is, then, one of the episodes associated with that particular hero. In the *Odyssey*, information on Odysseus's participation in the Trojan War is dispersed throughout and only of an allusive nature, supporting the main narrative by drawing parallels between what Odysseus achieved during the war and what he is to achieve on Ithaca. It is the singer's assumption that the listeners have knowledge of what happened

146 Lord (1960:187) sees the *Iliad* as a construction including events that belong to the start of the war but have been extended to apply to the long period pattern. If we accept this point of view, presentation from the perspective of the entire war would be obligatory.

in the war and the role played there by their hero. This information probably belonged not solely to those who also knew the *Iliad* (of course, the theme of captivity in the *Odyssey* is separated from the war theme, since Odysseus is held captive not by the enemy but by the nymph Calypso). The extent to which the story pattern is used in the cycle tradition is also demonstrated by the clear marking of where the song begins (in the song of Demodokos [*Odyssey* 8.499-500]: "and he began when ..."; in the invocation to the *Iliad* [1.6–7]: "from the moment Agamemnon and Achilles quarreled with each other ..."). In the structure of the invocation, these words signal the start of the narrative.

There arises the problem of determining how a highly complementary cyclic structure within which individual songs could function actually emerged. Arguments that it was either created on the basis of Homer's songs (assuming epigone cyclic poetry) or was preceded by another author's work on the entire Trojan War to which the *Iliad* then alludes (Schmidt and Stählin) have been proven wrong.[147] First we must assume that there were many songs comprising the cycle before the emergence of the *Iliad*. Of course, at the very root of the cycle there must have been the first song, presenting the abduction of Helen and the Achaean expedition against Troy (let us call it the basic song), but such a state of development certainly did not directly precede the *Iliad*.[148]

The songs on this subject must have had an episode in the context of the whole war. The process by which the cycle emerged as a phenomenon in itself might even have been a more significant development in literature than that of the monumental work. The cycle developed in two ways: on the one hand, added episodes created new songs not directly linked to the main song about the war and, on the other hand, many songs, based on the same pattern, repeated the Trojan War theme to effectively "extend" the war, though "in real time" it did not last longer than the one described in the basic song. The *Iliad* may, for instance, speak of the imminent death of Achilles, which is most probably due to happen the day after the funeral wake in honor of Hektor—that is, after the *Iliad* ends, whereas in the *Aethiopis* his death is preceded by many other events, also probably extended in time. The tale of the Trojan prince Paris returning to the court from exile on Mount Ida might be the subject of a separate song, though most probably it was a mere digression

147 If it were true, we would be dealing with references to a known literary work, whereas we are actually dealing with a series of ad hoc allusions to a collection of events rooted in tradition. Thus, tradition was not contained in any particular work, but was brought to life every time a song based on it was performed.

148 It would be also unreasonable to assume that at the beginning of the tradition there was a song that included all the important events contained in the Trojan War Cycle, which would later be distributed into particular songs.

in another song. But the course of the actual war always follows the same pattern: Achilles performs a heroic act to save the Achaeans. The figure of Achilles might be replaced, for example, by Patroklos (whose demise foretells the death of the former) or, after Achilles' death, by his son Neoptolemos. The duplicated story pattern was also always subject to flexibility, which is why stories could diverge from the original pattern but could not, for all the constant transformations, reshape it completely.

What set of songs made up the cycle?

First, let us return to the comparison of the cycle with other collections of oral songs. The difficulties of constructing a coherent story is clearly evident in the case of the *Kalevala*, which is based on oral transmissions and which tries to extract a consistent narrative sequence from this incongruous content. The poems of the Trojan Cycle, like the *Mahābhārata*, were subordinated to narrative continuity and a coherent storyline in a completely different way. This is not the continuity expressed in Proclus's summary of the Cycle because this views cyclic poems as a supplement to the *Iliad* and *Odyssey* and also has a historical approach to the chronology of events. Instead, the similarities with the *Mahābhārata* show that the tendency to group epics in a cycle was not a unique phenomenon of ancient Greek culture.

Jonathan Burgess has drawn attention to the difference between a saga and an epic myth cycle:

> Many conceive of the Troy story as a saga with a detailed commemoration of deeds worthy of notice because they are heroic and noble. If that were so, there could be many different versions of the battles fought in the period of a few weeks in the tenth year of the war. But I view the Troy story as being a series of major actions spread over ten years, each of importance for the overall narrative.[149]

Systems of allusions in the poems of Homer do not refer to a general vision of mythological events associated with certain characters, but to a complexly arranged mythological story passed on to us through cyclic poems. Therefore, the freedom of poetic creativity is very limited. A song may develop one of the cyclic themes which, like a faraway sign, the singer can never lose sight of. For the singer, the theme is like a historical fact that cannot be altered. In the fluid oral tradition, there is a certain constant, independent of what was later recorded in writing, which can be called the epic cycle story phenomenon. For

[149] Burgess 2001:60.

the singer, it is the σήματα (*sêmata*) signs, which set the course of the song, and in epic code they symbolize the glow of glory. In oral culture, these signs have an almost material dimension. As Walter J. Ong has noted, particular objects are associated with particular stories. For example, the sword might symbolize the awarding of a privilege and be treated as evidence in law court proceedings.[150] This story of this item was part of family lore. The history of its origins determines the value of the object in rituals of reciprocity.[151] The story tells us about something more than the object; it tells us about relations between people and their positions. For the story linked with an object manifests the respect bestowed on its owner or his progenitor.

In oral culture, these objects, like iconography, serve not so much to illustrate the myth as—in my opinion—to inspire the telling of the story.[152] The story in oral culture is also linked with landscape elements: rocks, rivers, trees, etc. The same elements can take on various meanings in the multiform myth and epic versions, but they are so inextricably bound to stories that the myth cannot be told without them.[153] It is only with the advent of writing that, firstly, the story could be separated from the landscape elements and, secondly, places were imagined in the cartographic sense. Hektor, assuming victory over Achilles, imagines his own tomb and that one day passing sailors will see "from afar a visible sign" where lies the one who defeated Achilles in battle. According to Nagy, the tomb was a σῆμα (*sêma*), a sign for future generations, passed on by word of mouth—that is, through epic song.[154] One could specify that σήματα meant facts, or perhaps rather images engrained in tradition, even taking on real form. They are known in the cycle to which the allusions in the song refer and thus allow the song to become part of the cyclic tradition.[155]

Due to the scarcity of sources, it is hard to say which particular events or even gestures are σήματα for the singer and his listeners. Nevertheless, we

150 Ong 2002:95.

151 On the significance of ritual reciprocity, see Seaford 1994.

152 This function is primarily performed, in my opinion, by artifacts such as the Ramsund stone or the Bayeux tapestry (even if some texts appear on the latter). An excellent example of this is Achilles' shield, the images of which serve the purpose of starting a narrative. A similar role is played by the images of the Trojan War on the purple robe woven by Helen (*Iliad* 3.125–128). By looking at the images, the storyteller's memory is activated, so that he is able to start and carry on his story. Compare Ready 2019:21.

153 Szyjewski (2014) shows that elements of the Australian landscape, thanks to strict repetition in mythology, provide a sense of identity for the oral community.

154 Nagy 1999:340–342.

155 Yates (1966, esp. Ch. 3) shows how memorizing in rhetorical art involved using specific places and representations in the construction of speech, e.g. the carvings on sacred buildings. This technique of linking mnemonics with creativity has its origins, in my opinion, in the oral tradition.

know the signs concern matters that are important for the whole story. In our appraisals, on the other hand, we may be mistaken as to the value of specific "signs," overrating some and underrating others. We may also assume that the importance of certain signs changed with the development of epic songs; some matters became more important than others that had been very important in earlier tradition. From the perspective of the *Iliad*, of basic importance are "the death of Achilles" and the "fall of Troy," but for the singer no less important could be certain incidents leading up to these main events. That various details we would naturally ignore might have been of key importance to the singer may be illustrated by an analogy between Balkan songs of return and the *Odyssey*. The singer might modify elements in the story structure, but he cannot ignore any of them. For example, in Balkan songs an important feature is the recognition of the hero by his horse. In the *Odyssey*, the horses Odysseus takes on the expedition or captures on the way, e.g. the horses of Rhesus, are passed over in silence (this is somewhat rationalized when Telemachos turns down the offer of chariot horses from Menelaos, explaining that they would be of little use on Ithaca). Nonetheless, there must be a scene where a faithful animal recognizes his master, and so it is, when Odysseus is recognized by his faithful dog.[156]

From the studies of the neoanalysts one should excerpt the main thought (remodeling it significantly) that in the *Iliad* Homer presents many situations and events in a way that require the listener to know, as he did, other epic songs presenting parallel "facts," or rather images persisting in memory,[157] from the story of the Trojan War. In his "innovativeness," the author of the extant version of the *Iliad* applies the familiar emphasis to the tragic sense of the story and tragic irony. This is apparent, for example, in Homer's surprising results from the games held in honor of Patroklos (a neo-analytic argument greatly emphasized by Kullmann). In the more typical version of the *Aethiopis*, in the games held in honor of Achilles, the winners are the best Greeks in their given fields. Yet in the *Iliad* the best each time encounter failure, which seems to be associated with the prophecy of fatal events occurring later on in the Cycle (e.g. the case of Ajax, the son of Oileus, Teucer, or the peculiar victory of Antilochos). The game played with the listener, who knew the normal course of events and the most important "facts," was probably typical not only of Homer, but also of every other talented singer.

156 The image of a dog guarding the house is also a better match for the narrative. Reece (1993: 168–170) discusses the use of this motif in the *Odyssey* and points out that sometimes even Odysseus himself is pictured as a watchdog (see also Rose 1979).

157 On images embedded in the singer's and his audience's memory, see pp. 412, 439, and 486–504.

Trojan Cycle poems present the main events and moments of the Trojan War. Burgess argues that while the *Iliad* and *Odyssey* were mere branches, the Cycle poems were the tree trunk.[158] This suggests that cyclic poems consist of traditional songs, perhaps of not great poetic inventiveness. Therefore, we cannot speak of the full authorship of, for instance, Arctinus. This is not only traditional material, but also the traditional framework of contents, which could be subjected to the need of flexibility predominating in oral poetry.

The discrepancies in summaries of the Cycle and extant fragments, especially those concerning the beginnings and the endings of works, may be evidence that traditional versions encompassing the subject as broadly as suggested in the summaries did not exist or, alternatively, that there existed various versions, still only in oral form. Hellenistic scholars not only desired to determine the one original text from various versions, just as in the case of the *Iliad* and *Odyssey*, but also to unify all these texts into a consistent story. And they, too, encountered problems in finding the beginnings and endings. It is not merely a matter of manipulating the beginnings and endings of books, as Burgess suggests.[159] Traditional oral song, as we shall soon see, had very characteristic beginnings and endings, although during transmission they may have adopted a fluid form. The boundaries of an oral song are, therefore, of a different nature than the definite boundaries in written literature. The transposing of songs for the purposes of publishing, which had emerged in the Hellenistic period, could thus have led to misunderstandings and distortions. The idea of shaping a story was based on the poems of Homer, which to some extent influenced all categories of Greek literature, both poetry and prose. Then again, up until the advent of normative rhetoric, the arrangement of all stories was not entirely free from the oral tradition, as is evidenced, for instance, in the structure of Greek drama or Herodotus's *Histories*. Cyclic poems had, therefore, first to adopt a literary form, and second, their forms relied on their coexistence—that is, that they all together transmitted the story of the entire Trojan War. Even with earlier written forms, diverse traditions probably still resulted in very diversely shaped works. Such a multiform undertaking must have posed many problems. Hence, no doubt, the unfavorable view of cyclic poetry held by the Alexandrian community (e.g. Callimachus and Aristarchus). The first comparisons of this sort might have already appeared in fourth-century Athens, where these unfavorable opinions about the cyclic tradition were already formed (Aristotle *Poetics* 1451a23–30, 1459a30–b7). This attitude probably emerged after the rhapsodic tradition (Aristotle represents nascent philological interests), but the impulse

[158] Burgess 2001:1.

[159] Burgess 2001:135–143.

to compare and contrast might already have been present. We should keep in mind that we have only summaries of the works and that these cannot be entirely reliable because they do not reveal the content so much as simply the sequence of stories in the Cycle. Nor can it be ruled out that it was the tastes of the Hellenistic period that ultimately influenced the shape of these works. Hellenistic publishers could have endeavored to end the stories in a literary style, which might also have dictated a consistent plot sequence. The existence of many versions might also have inclined Hellenistic publishers to do the same. Therefore, even if the works had been created quite independently of the *Iliad*, in the written version they would, nevertheless, be treated as if they relied on the *Iliad*, not only in content but also in form.

The negative opinion of Aristotle and later critics regarding the literary value of cyclic poetry was, however, based on a misunderstanding. Aristotle compares available texts and decides that the structure of the *Iliad* is more highly organized because it is comparable to the structure of the Greek tragedy, which was what principally interested him. Then again, many themes could be "cut out" from the cyclic poems to write a tragedy (1459a30–b7; there is no reason to doubt the authenticity of this passage in the *Poetics*, *pace* Burgess). In this sense, the *Iliad* concentrates on one theme, the wrath of Achilles, and gives it a dramatic, even tragic, perspective. Cyclic epics lack appropriate drama and that tragic perspective, but instead they have many themes. From the point of view of developing literary aesthetics of the time, this would be seen as a fault. What Aristotle and other ancient scholars failed to take into account, however, was the fact that the dramatic or even tragic perspective of a work depended not on the genius of the author but on the talent of the song performer, the *aoidos*, who altered and elaborated on the song as he saw fit, but who remained loyal to the traditional story in terms of the selection of scenes and themes. The same song could be elaborate and refined or take on a form that was crude and simple—so too, the cyclic poems and the *Iliad*. We may assume that the ancients had at their disposal various means for elaborating traditional songs, including cyclic poems, as well as Homer's poems.

So how can we determine what cyclic poems really looked like?

Firstly, in order to find the essence of the cyclic poem, we should try to recreate its form from when it was still an oral song. Here, the immanent structures of the song should be extracted, taking into account the possibility that over generations certain elements changed. In this sense, in antiquity the shape of the cyclic poem in written form did not necessarily reflect the shape of oral song. Ancient scholars could have exposed certain elements of the plot that in the oral song tradition did not have greater meaning but were instead very important for the aesthetics of a literary work. The fluidity and multiformity of traditional song was essentially unnoticed, or actually considered damaging. And yet the song could have undergone a fundamental metamorphosis in the rendition of a talented *aoidos*. In oral tradition a song did not exist as something completed and finite. That is, however, how it was perceived in the nascent theory of literature. From the point of view of oral tradition, the failings of a song resulted not from the song itself, but from its performance. Conversely, from the point of view of an aesthetic appraisal of a literary work, the extent to which a poem differed from the definitive poetry of Homer was considered its fundamental failing.[160] Cyclic songs could even have the same goals as the *Iliad* in presenting a single episode in the context of the whole Trojan War (that might well have been the case with the *Kypria* and *Aethiopis*). It has also been suggested that the written versions of the *Kypria* and *Little Iliad* encompassed the entire Trojan War.[161] Such a thesis would render the *Kypria* and the *Aethiopis* typical in their presentation of information in catalogue style.[162] I find it difficult to agree with this view, for the accumulation of events in the summaries of these works will remain unintelligible to us until we decipher their interrelationships on the basis of a reconstruction that takes into account how the story pattern of an oral epic song developed.

Every great song was, therefore, also a *sui generis* "cycle" (*kyklos*), telling the whole story from beginning to end. The *kyklos* includes successive traditional themes, which the *aoidos* might appropriately invoke. Cyclic poems do not reveal that they were written down *in statu nascendi*, but rather that they had a potential to develop a cycle, which was not, however, the objective of the performing singer. After all, he could not perform the whole cycle in one performance, and even a series of performances for a whole cycle would be unrealistic. The performance itself could not deviate significantly from what is presented in the *Odyssey* 8. If we assume that the songs of Demodokos are short

160 The probable narrative style of cyclic poems is often contrasted with the style of Homeric songs, which abound in speeches. However, the descriptive style might well reflect the taste of its recipients.

161 Aristotle (*Poetics* 1459a30–b7, cited above) criticizes most of the poets for creating as the object of their narrative a single figure or a section of time forming one action (πρᾶξις) made up of many episodes. As examples of the latter, he cites the *Kypria* and *Little Iliad*. Burgess (1996:91–96), analyzing this unclear passage, concludes that these works, nevertheless, present the whole Trojan War. It would, however, be simpler to assume that, in accordance with the functioning of song in oral culture, each of these songs presented its events in the context of the entire war, setting its plot in a universally known sequence of events.

162 Burgess 1996:95: "It may well have achieved the charm of catalogue poetry which manages to present in allusive fashion a large amount of information, yet expand at times to present a vivid encapsulation of some episode." The separation of one episode as an elaborate digression is, indeed, typical in catalogue poetry, as we can see in the works of Hesiod. In this sense, Homer's style would in a way mean pausing on just one episode and fitting it into the catalogue whole solely through the use of allusions and functions.

episodes concerning a single theme, it is important to note that these themes are presented in a specific order: the first song refers to the start of the war and the third its end. We would, therefore, have a chronology of a "higher order." The "Cycle" might mean not so much the development of the song, but rather an ordered way of presenting subjects on a macro scale. In this sense, the *kyklos*-song could have been deposited in a community of *aoidoi*, as the ancient tradition maintains, or it was actually created within such a community, as we are more inclined to assume. Thus any changes of subject or occasional gaps could be concealed by making the contents more uniform. Such a *kyklos*-poem could not be perceived as something new (or worse still, divergent from tradition!), for in every song there was an episode potentially referring to the whole. When, for instance, Demodokos is encouraged to sing a song about the Trojan Horse, he does not sing the entire story and all its known aspects. Instead, he refers to just one theme, appropriate to the occasion because the whole story is already known to the public as much as it is to him.

Secondly, we should also take into account the structural differences between a literary work and a traditional oral song. The structural cues for the beginning and end of a song might be difficult to identify.[163] Similarly difficult is the end of the *Iliad* for ancient and modern scholars alike (e.g. Wilamowitz, representing the analyst school, argues that there must have been a missing final scene presenting the death of the Achilles[164]). These differences influenced the division of one theme between two works: the dispute over Achilles' armor ends the *Aethiopis* and begins the *Little Iliad*, regardless of whether such boundaries between the songs actually existed, or were present only in the summaries. From the point of view of a literary work, this is conceivable, especially if organized from the perspective of the whole story of the Trojan War. Despite some inconvenience, the linking together of overlapping themes is overcome at no greater cost. In oral songs, on the other hand, the division of themes makes no sense and is practically impossible. The subject of the dispute is of key importance to the structure of Greek epic song and in a certain sense is the basis of its existence.[165]

163 We can observe a "lack of ending" in Hesiod's *Theogony*, supposedly continued by the *Catalogue of Women*. The *Theogony* starts repeatedly with the praise of the Muses, as if a poet, having exhausted a theme, must again and again begin anew. The catalogues, with their chain-like construction, are linked with one another. This construction method questions the sense of why the poem should be believed as finished in this or that place.

164 Wilamowitz 1916:77–79, 513.

165 Burgess (2004c:6) presents a fundamentally different view. He believes that the beginnings and endings of cyclic works in Proclus's summary may reflect "performance units" in the practice of rhapsodes. He gives an example of dividing the scene of the dispute over Achilles' armor between the relevant epics: "The early, independent manifestations of these poems would have not had such abrupt starts and stops, but rhapsodes performing these portions of each poem together may well have effected such a transition." Burgess's position is based on the conviction that

Thirdly and most importantly, Proclus's summary is addressed to readers of Homer, who—in that time—must have had specially prepared knowledge of the Trojan War, otherwise it would have been largely unintelligible. The summary, moreover, presents the events in historical sequence, a perspective that must first have been applied by mythographers. If we take into account the sheer vastness and multitude of oral poetry, applying chronological order to the events seems like an exceptionally difficult task. Epic poetry applied such order only on the basis of genealogy. If the work of Apollodorus can give us an idea of what the work of the first mythographers like Pherecydes looked like, we would notice attempts to chronologically order the mythological material, with frequent marking of the multiformity of the myth. The existence of many versions is often identified by divergences in genealogies. The greatest problem, however, is that mythical tales ordered according to genealogies are not synchronized, often to a great degree. For the oral poet this was never a major issue. Of course, it only becomes a problem when we try to order myths chronologically, from a historical perspective.

When we consider that myths are the framework for—or at least an element of—digression in epic songs, and oral songs are self-contained and integral works, then we will see that applying a historical sequence to the narrative, as the mythographers had done, violates the song structure. It may also violate possible relationships between songs—for example, in a cycle. A historical, "chronological" narrative will present the myth in a one-sided, or perhaps even superficial, manner. It only satisfies the need to order events in a sequence, which might well be unrealizable in the mythological narrative. For a simple comparison, let us just think of how the narrative is presented in the *Iliad* and *Odyssey*. Between such works and the methods of the mythographers there exists a void. Any attempt to put into order the events of the Trojan War on the basis of the *Iliad* will inevitably fail. Therefore, without the summaries serving as our guides, we would quite lose our bearings. On the other hand, I believe thinking of the *Iliad* as something separate from tradition is also a major

---

subsequent cyclic pieces would be performed in succession as a continuous stream of epic (6): "One rhapsode might have ended his performance from a poem with a particular scene that the next rhapsode, performing from a second poem, chose to repeat as an entry point." If I understand it correctly, the next rhapsode would decide to continue the story sung just before, maybe trying to improve the scene with which his predecessor ended his performance. Unfortunately, Burgess does not elaborate this point. The question arises, how could a performer end his "performance unit" with a dispute? Undoubtedly, Burgess's proposal stems from the perception of the "chronological" continuity of the cyclic story. Even if we accept Burgess's proposition, it cannot, in my opinion, refer to the period preceding by many generations the time of the writing down of the poems, but at the latest to the classical period, when cyclic works already functioned in circulation as fixed "texts" and could be performed by rhapsodes analogically to Homeric epics.

misunderstanding. The style of allowing the listener to understand an event through allusions to events that already existed in the listener's consciousness must have been traditional; such a story-telling technique allows the audience to see the story in the broader context of their own knowledge.

Proclus selected from the available cyclic songs information that concerned events preceding or following the *Iliad*. He was not interested in relating the full content of those songs, but only such information as would help the reader of Homer's poetry. Proclus's reader was used to viewing everything from a historical perspective and wished to locate the poetry in the abundance of events related in stories from the Trojan Cycle. There is no reason to assume that the presentation of an episode in the perspective of the whole war was unique to the *Iliad*. The other epic composition from that period, the *Odyssey*, also presents an episode, the return of Odysseus, from the perspective of the return of all remaining heroes from Troy. Of course, this work is also attributed to Homer, but there are very few concrete arguments to support that he was the author of both works and, moreover, it in no way indicates that this particular way of telling a story was an innovative break with tradition. Burgess has identified discrepancies between the meaning of certain fragments and the point in time allocated to them in Proclus's summary.[166] This is strong evidence that cyclic songs, as also the *Iliad*, described the whole of the Trojan War without applying historical and chronological criteria.[167] I would go further to say that songs belonging to the epic cycle presented an episode or a collection of episodes from the cycle in the perspective of the entire war—that is, in a way similar to the *Iliad*. And I would add that this by no means meant that such songs took on monumental proportions.

The structure of an epic song

The integrity of an oral epic song is, in my opinion, an exceptionally important component of the cycle structure, and one that is virtually unnoticed in discussions on the subject. The general scholarly consensus has been that oral songs do not adopt a distinctive form. According to Ford, stability of the theme in oral poetry was a far more important priority than the stability of

[166] *Exempli gratia*: *Little Iliad* fr. 4 W depicts the landing of Achilles on Skyros already after the wounding of Telephos, which in the arrangement of the Cycle, according to Proclus, occurs in the *Kypria*; *Kypria* fr. 31 W in turn states: νήπιος, ὃς πατέρα κτείνας παῖδας καταλείπει, "foolish is he who having killed the father leaves the son alive," which, according to scholars, could be a reference to the judgment of Astyanax, the son of Hektor, after the fall of Troy, and yet in Proclus's summary it is ascribed to the actual Fall of Ilion (see too Fantuzzi and Tsagalis 2015:32–33).

[167] This point argues against the opinion of Dowden (1996, mentioned above) that presenting the whole war in the *Iliad* was Homer's departure from the oral poetry of the Cycle.

form.[168] Notopoulos assumes that the overriding principle of epic composition was the paratactic connection of themes.[169] The view of this scholar can be easily illustrated by the example of catalogue poetry, such as Hesiod's *Theogony*. Paratactic structures resulted in a continuous song, which is sustained by successive additions and basically never ends in any clear way.[170] Ford similarly perceives the shaping of all epic poetry, including the works of Homer. For while, in his opinion, we are dealing with clear designators at the beginning, there are no such designators at the end of these works, and the reservations of the analysts as to the authenticity of the endings of the *Iliad* and *Odyssey* are in this respect a significant argument. A different appraisal of the structure of Homer's poems is held by Finkelberg who, like Heubeck, sees the *Iliad* as a consistent and complete form.[171] Nevertheless, with regard to cyclic poetry, Finkelberg, like Ford, shares the view of Thalmann that the cycle was created through the paratactic linking of songs, similarly to Hesiod's *Theogony* because these epic stories were told *ab ovo*.[172] Therefore, Finkelberg sees the complete unity of the *Iliad* as an exception, signifying a new quality. An important role in her appraisal is played by the scene of the recovery of Hektor's body, which in an extraordinary way completes the portrayal of Achilles and is "the first study of character in European literature."[173] Yet one could argue that the depth of this scene is due to its ring composition. Achilles' handing over of Hektor's body to old Priam is contrasted with Agamemnon's refusal to return to Chryses his daughter. The entirety is enclosed in an even more important, yet generally unnoticed, frame. The next scene, that of Hektor's funeral, is a prelude to the death of Achilles, which returns to the invocation and its prophecy that misfortune and death will be brought forth by the hero's wrath, as well as to the traditional conflict between Achilles and Apollo, the victim of which will be the hero. This ring composition is a structure inextricably associated with oral poetry.[174] It allows the listener to understand the whole message when the

168 Ford 1992:33.

169 Notopoulos 1964:46.

170 Ford 1992:83: "Open-endedness is the law of the genre."

171 Heubeck 1978:14; Finkelberg (1998:131–134) believes that unity and variety of poetic narratives indicate that Homer was not limited to maintaining the sequence of events by means of point-by-point composition, and instead applied the "poetics of truth," sanctioned in his creativity by the Muses.

172 Thalmann 1984:75–77; Finkelberg 1998:137–139; Ford 1992:44–46.

173 Finkelberg (1998:133, 135–136) also rejects the view of Austin (1966:295–312) that the digressive nature of Homer's narrative destroys the unity of the story.

174 Minchin (2001:181–202) points out that what we call ring composition is, in fact, the natural way of oral storytelling in Western culture (Labov's model). Hence, she concludes that Homer did not use any special compositional technique as a strategy that is different from ours. She, however, does not see this strategy being used to construct the whole epic (the great ring linking

singer returns in reverse order to themes and thoughts and, most importantly of all, when the ring of the largest radius returns from the very beginning to the end of the situation. Thus, the listener of oral poetry, familiar with this organization of material, acquires an understanding of the most important aspect of the message.[175] The message of this scene will be discussed in detail in the last chapter of this book. Here, I shall only stress that ring composition is the determining factor of integration in oral song.[176] Ring composition restrains the narrative parataxis, but also imposes its external structure, ensuring unity in oral song.[177]

The structure of the epic song from the perspective of the epic cycle has not yet been sufficiently studied. I do not wish to conduct such a study here, but I will instead share a few observations that might add new perspectives to this area of research. The generally known Song of Return scheme was worked out by Lord. It comprises constant elements, called themes, that appear in a set order: the song always starts with the hero's Absence (A), which means Devastation (D) for him in

---

the beginning with the end of the *Iliad*) or the reversal of meanings in repeated themes, and yet there is reason to believe these were elements of a poetic technique, without doubt an oral one. See also Cook 2014; Arft 2017.

175 The function of ring composition in epic expression is noticed by Thalmann (1984:16): "By the end of the passage, when the same ideas are recapitulated, they are understood more fully, in all their implications because the development in the middle part has shed a new light upon them. ... A proposition is stated, reasons are given for it, and it is repeated at the end—but with all the weight of the intervening argument behind it." The application of ring composition has, however, been variously explained, for example, as an adornment or loose form; so Van Groningen 1935. Stanley (1993:7), conversely, describes it as a "form consistent with its origin in an accretive parataxis," thus emphasizing the association between the structure and the paratactic style of oral poetry. Stanley also offers a typology of ring composition (6–9), as well as a subject bibliography (307–308, 21). Thalmann (1984:7) similarly tries to define the meaning of *hysteron proteron*, as if it were a prototype of ring composition: "... it makes possible a short preview of all the forthcoming topics, it allows the poet to get his ideas in order before he proceeds to detailed treatment of each, and it lets the audience know what is to come, so that they never lose sight of the overall plan." Thalmann points to ring composition as a method of expressing subtle and hidden meanings (12–16).

176 According to van Otterlo (1948:43), this is not so much about repeating at the end what was said at the beginning, as actually anticipating the end at the beginning. More on ring composition in Ch. 6.

177 In addition to ring composition, there may be other ways of marking the end of a narrative in the oral tradition. Kelly (2007b:382–384) argues that the ending of the *Iliad* reveals the compositional principle of "decreasing doublets" in order to suggest to listeners that the singer has already exhausted the theme, and to discourage them from the possible expectation of continuing the narrative. Hektor's funeral is depicted on a significantly smaller scale than that of Patroklos: "The audience are summoning the earlier scene as they experience the final one. ... the audience is being directed back into the text not in order to magnify the current scene but to set it in a larger context" (Kelly 2007b:383). Similarly, Kelly (2007b:384–387) sees the ending of the *Odyssey*, i.e. the scene of Odysseus's skirmish with the suitors' families, as a smaller-scale representation of his battle with the suitors.

captivity and for his loved one left at home; after negotiations, the hero gains the right to Return (R), on returning, he exacts Retribution (Rt) against his rivals or opponents, after which, there is a Wedding (W) or Re-wedding with his loved one. Retribution is often preceded by many Recognition scenes, whereas the Wedding is not usually the end of the story, but is instead followed by a return to captivity, for instance, to keep a promise the hero gave to his captor at the start of the story.

The basic pattern is:

A > D > R > Rt > W

Put in greater detail, it should be:

prison > devastation > return > recognition >
retribution > wedding or re-wedding > return to prison

As we can see, this pattern is sufficiently flexible for variations to be freely added. For instance, heroes can be doubled or substituted, there may be a son, complications on the return journey, a whole range of relationships between the hero and rival suitors and also various tests of loyalty.

Lord showed, without great difficulty, that the pattern can be applied to the *Odyssey*.[178] But let us look at the pattern from a different angle. The *Odyssey* has been perceived by many scholars as an exceptionally refined story, even more so than the *Iliad*. The *Telemachy* interferes with the return of Odysseus. The listeners, together with Odysseus's son, Telemachos, learn of the hero's achievements at Troy from what is reported by the hero's friends. The hero's actual return is later related by Odysseus himself in the second quarter of the work. The author's use of all these measures in no way alters the pattern of the Song of Return. The narrative can start in no other place than when Odysseus is on the island of Calypso because that is where he is held prisoner. Thus, even if the singer had constructed a strictly linear storyline, this story still could not start at any other point—for example, sailing off from Troy.[179]

178 There exist hundreds of versions of the Song of Return, not only in Yugoslavia, but also in other cultures widely scattered over time and space, such as medieval England, nineteenth-century Russia, Albania, Bulgaria, Turkey, and Kyrgyzstan, among others.

179 Hölscher (1978:55–61) considers this beginning to be unnatural and copied from the *Iliad* in the way it concentrates on the last several days of the war. He believes a typical start to a "Return of the Hero" epic would be the moment of sailing out from Troy. Intriguingly, however, concealed in the epic he sees a "simple" folk tale. Going off to war, the husband tells his wife that if he should not return before their new-born son grows a beard, she should leave the house and find another husband. A trace of this tale is present in the *Odyssey*: when the time nears, Penelope will declare that she has almost finished weaving the shroud and is ready to marry one of her suitors. This simple story is altered by the creator of the epic, who gives it a different meaning.

The singer, in accordance with the objectives of his story, may modify certain elements. The author of the *Odyssey* presents a situation where the mother of Odysseus is no longer alive when he returns to the island of Ithaca. This absence clearly departs from the typical Song of Return, where the mother usually plays a leading role at home in the recognition scene. It shows the conviction that the mother is always the most faithful person to her son. Normally, she is the one who waits, yearning for the hero's return, the first to recognize him, and to pass on the most crucial information as to who had or had not remained faithful. Normally, it is only after passing on this information that the mother dies, devastated by the longing for her son. Homer alters this straightforward situation but does not abandon it. Odysseus meets his mother before he returns to Ithaca in the Land of the Dead, where it turns out that she had died of longing for her son. Nonetheless, she passes on to him key information concerning his wife, son, and father. A figure representing the mother also has to be found on Ithaca. This role is played by Odysseus's wet-nurse Eurykleia, who spectacularly recognizes Odysseus by identifying his childhood scar. She, moreover, informs him about the fidelity of individual people and also provides other help. In the scenes of Odysseus's recognition, there also has to be a death. Instead of his mother, now his most faithful dog dies, who was the first on Ithaca to recognize him (as we have seen, Argos recognizing his master is similar to the faithful horse recognizing his master in Balkan poetry). Therefore, the mother still performs the same functions, only the place in the narrative where the hero encounters her is altered. Of course, one cannot omit this significant element in the story, so there are equivalents of the mother's recognition (Eurykleia) and the mother's death (Argos) in the places where these events normally occur. Thus, despite the transference of Odysseus's meeting with his mother to the Land of the Dead,[180] every detail of this part of the story pattern remains unaltered.

The last element of the Song of Return—the hero's return to prison—is usually the most variable, and sometimes omitted. Such a return might spoil the listener's optimistic mood, raised as it was not only by the hero's retribution against rival suitors for his wife or loved one, but also, more often than not, by a subsequent wedding. After keeping his word and returning to captivity, the hero's punishment may be annulled or he might kill his captor, either covertly or in open battle, assisted by old friends who come to his rescue.[181] The end of the *Odyssey* also involves a re-wedding after the killing of rival suitors, though it includes yet another ending, different in nature to those of Yugoslav songs—that

[180] In fact, here we have to do only with a changed order of the story: "mother passes information and dies" is transformed into "mother dies and then (or in spite of it) passes information."

[181] Lord 1991:219.

is, a conflict with the suitors' families. According to the prophecy of Teiresias, however, Odysseus should leave his home once he has restored order to it. The very existence of the "return to prison" theme, as I see it, is an essential part of the original story pattern of this song because it means that the song has turned full circle. The hero returns to the starting point one way or another; there might or might not be a reward for his achievements, but it is not the act of freeing his house from intruders that constitutes the end of the story.[182]

Thus, a song is also a cycle—the action returns to the starting point. In analyzing the *Odyssey* as a Song of Return, we come to the same conclusion as in the analysis of the *Iliad*, where successive ending scenes refer to scenes at the start of the work in reverse order.

It is readily apparent then, that Homer applies to his songs a traditional shape. If the listeners had not had a deep-rooted understanding of the ring composition structure, they would not have understood the poetry of Homer. Hence, there is no reason to assume that other oral songs were not structured in the same way, thereby attaining integrity, or "organic unity," to use Aristotle's language.[183] The idea of the cycle may be understood as a story encompassing a certain completeness of events, where the narrative returns to the starting point after achieving its goal, and this may be applied to a single song, as well as to the main cycle narrative to which the song refers.

The First Song of Demodokos and the Invocations to the *Iliad* and *Odyssey*

If we are to speak of the Greek epic as a genre, the first issue to determine is the shape of pre-Homeric epic song. This is a question of whether or not, and if so, to what extent, it can be recovered and whether it is of a different quality

182 See Lord 1960:182–183. An element of this return to the start may be the prophecy of Odysseus's death, if we read the expression ἐξ ἁλός as "from the sea," and not as is currently accepted "beyond the sea," in accordance with Teiresias's prophecy, which could be taken to mean that Odysseus was to travel to a people who do not know how to sail. Associating the cause of death with the sea might seem paradoxical if the task awaiting the hero is deep inland, but exactly such paradoxes may characterize prophecies (for comparison, in Demodokos's first song, Agamemnon is pleased that his best warriors quarrel). Of course, this does not have to support the *Telegony* tradition, in which Odysseus is killed by Telegonos, his own son by Kirke. This is rather a vague reference to Odysseus's sea wanderings, whose starting point is the desolate island of Kalypso and the wrath of Poseidon, which pursues him; once the latter has been realized, Odysseus can achieve hero status, just as Apollo grants Achilles hero status by destroying him (a theme that I will discuss below).

183 This is why I find it hard to agree with the view of Scodel (2002:48–49, and passim) that individual episodes in the *Iliad* and *Odyssey* could be treated as separate songs (e.g. the *Doloneia* or the funeral of Patroklos in the *Iliad* and the Kyklopes and Kirke episodes in the *Odyssey*).

when compared with the *Iliad* and *Odyssey*. Today's comparative studies allow us to say that here and there in various oral traditions certain common features may be found, but each time there appear clear differences. It is highly unlikely that all the qualities of an epic can be encapsulated in a single definition.[184] The greatest number of Homeric features are found in the epics of the South Slavs, and in the Bosnian Muslim tradition in particular. This particularly applies to the "morphology" of the poetics, the similar formulaic structures, typical scenes, and story patterns: the Return, the Abduction of the Bride, and the Besieged City. Bosnian songs stand out in terms of length and craftsmanship: they can include several hundred to several thousand verses. It has quite often been argued that we should not draw these parallels with the poems of Homer and, at most, similarities may be found in the songs sung by Demodokos in the *Odyssey*, interpreted as brief evocations of single episodes. In other traditions, however, the song may take on Homeric proportions, such as the *Siri Epic* recorded by Finnish and Indian scholars in 1990, including 15,683 verses, which makes it almost as long as the *Iliad*. In the case of epics of the Turkic peoples, concentrating on the heroes Gesar and Janggar, (and including Mongol and Tibetan epics), we might have hundreds of thousands of verses—ten times longer than Homer's poems. Taking into account that other epics are shorter—the early medieval epic *Beowulf*, for instance, has only 3,182 verses—we can say the *Iliad* and *Odyssey* are epics of more or less average size.[185] In the broader world of epics, there are other similarities with the Greek tradition. Here we shall only concentrate on the most significant examples. The *Siri Epic* begins with an elaborate series of invocations, perhaps similar to the *Homeric Hymns*, serving as *prooimia* to epic performances. Serbian and Bosnian songs, on the other hand, begin with a prologue, often appealing for providence, called *pripjevi*, and resembling invocations.[186] We can find many analogies to catalogues and comparisons, though none are as elaborate as the Homeric comparisons.[187] Sometimes the epic is associated with other poetic genres, and that is also noticeable in the Greek tradition, where the same myths are presented in various types of poetry. Interesting for our discussion is the

184 Taking into account the various differences, most appropriate seems to be the definition of Lauri Honko: "Epics are great narratives about exemplars, originally performed by specialised singers as superstories which excel in length, power of expression and significance of content over other narratives and function as a source of identity representations in the traditional community or group receiving the epic" (cited from Foley 2004:181).

185 Foley 2004:173–181. Radlov's collection of Kyrgyz epic songs, concerning the hero Manas, is sung by two singers, and has around 250,000 verses (Chadwick and Zhirmunsky 1969:279–280, 304–306).

186 Foley 2004:183.

187 Foley 2004:184.

surprise of a singer of songs about Mwindo, Condi Rureke, when he was asked by Daniel Biebuyck to sing the entire Mwindo epic as he knew it. The problem is that only one part or parts of the epic are ever sung.[188]

The best starting point for our appraisal of the Greek epic form and the position of particular songs in the epic tradition should be the places where Homer presents the performance and content of songs. Of these the most important are the songs performed at the court of the Phaeacian king, Alkinoos, by the singer Demodokos because here Homer's narrative tells us something about their content.

The first and third of these songs relate to each other, as well as to episodes in the Trojan War.[189] They are both sung indoors, for a limited audience of invited guests, unlike the second song, which is sung in the square for the Phaeacian public.

The theme of the first song is chosen by the singer (inspired by the Muse), while the subject of the third song is requested by Odysseus. Assuming that the latter epic scene holds some truth about performance, Odysseus's request receives a twofold explanation. For Heubeck, scenes of Demodokos performing songs are typical of the oral epic tradition. Odysseus's request for a song about the wooden horse is, thus, a reference to the typical talent of oral poets, who were able to sing a song on any subject, even if it had not previously been in their repertoire. Ford, in turn, thinks the scene might refer to frequent situations where the public requests that the singer sing a song about their favorite theme.[190] However, neither of these considerations corresponds exactly to the situation presented in the *Odyssey*.

The popularity of songs about the Trojan War is perhaps testified by the formula applied in Demodokos's first song: it belongs to the *oimê*, "whose fame then reached the heaven" (8.74). The themes of both the first and the third song refer to the same group of events, so it is hard to speak of song themes being perfectly random. This does not mean, however, that Odysseus's request was necessarily in line with tastes of the Phaeacian public. For we should note that the *Odyssey* presents a specific situation, which—from our point of view—is quite unreal. How could Demodokos know of the Trojan War, if the Phaeacian island is described as a magical place inaccessible to others (7.30–33, 7.201–205, 13.180–181) and Odysseus appears to be the first (and the last) person from the

188 Biebuyck and Mateéne 1969:14. Foley (2004:177) comments as follows: "The African narratives teach us that 'the epic' lives beyond the boundaries of any single performance or text, although it idiomatically informs each one of them. Audiences are crucial partners in the transaction of epic."

189 Odysseus, turning to Demodokos after the break in the sports contest, during which the second song is sung, praises him for the performance of the first song, whereas the second song he does not seem to notice, or it has no meaning for him (*Odyssey* 8.489–491).

190 Heubeck 1978:15–16, 1988:10; Ford 1992:18–23, 1997:401–402.

outside to have reached it? In oral culture, a singer learns new songs by listening to other singers and stories are passed on by word of mouth. In the *Odyssey*, the way in which *aoidoi* learn stories is falsified. The singers are presented as being permanently bound to one place, and they owe their knowledge solely to the Muse. Therefore, they sing as if through divine inspiration, which is supposed to mean that what they sing is the truth. This illusion is especially strongly accentuated in the case of the poet singer Phemios (describing himself as *autodidaktos*, "the one who taught himself [to sing?] songs" and learned tales from the Muse, 22.347–348), who sings at Odysseus's house on Ithaca, where there was, after all, the possibility of hearing tales from travelers and newcomers. The illusion is to make the words sung by the singer more credible, though it could be argued that the actual singer was unaware of this illusion and instead was convinced of the truth of the tale because it was told thanks to the Muse (8.479–481). The preceding is connected with Homer's conviction that stories of the Trojan War were as popular in Odysseus's time as they were in his own day.[191] When Demodokos chooses as his theme a quarrel between Odysseus and Achilles, one might expect that Odysseus would be surprised that this story was already known at the Phaeacian court. Of course, no surprise is expressed, but rather an explanation in the formula, "the fame [of these events] then [already] reached heaven" (*Odyssey* 8.74). Either way, after listening to this song, Odysseus may assume that the singer knows other songs about that particular war, and therefore asks him to sing about the wooden horse. We do not need to assume that the *aoidos* knows any particular song, but he knows the story of the fall of Troy. Demodokos's song might mean improvisation on the given theme, but the

191 See Zieliński (2015a), who suggests that ensuring credibility via the authority of the Muse distinguishes a song sung by an *aoidos* from other, possibly false tales. The fictitious identities of Odysseus serve only to deceive other characters in the work and not the audience because they do not conform to tradition. They only pretend to conform. This is because multiformity in tradition cannot change the essence of the song. Hence, we cannot assume, for example, that Phemios will sing an alternative story of the fate of Odysseus, in which the hero perishes somewhere on the way because tradition presents him as a hero who returns home. That is the shape of the Song of Return. Once at home, there are many alternative solutions (for example, to the matter of Penelope's loyalty), but return Odysseus must. By comparison, a passage in *Beowulf* (867–882) also shows that it was typical in that oral culture for a situation where the singer assumes that if the story was well-known in his day, it was also that way at the time when the related events took place. An unnamed vassal of King Hrothgar, "mindful of rhythms, / who ancient traditions treasured in memory" (translation, J. L. Hall), during Beowulf's return from the pursuit of the wounded Grendel, improvises a song praising the achievements of Beowulf by comparing them to the achievements of Sigemund. The singer thus introduces his patron to the epic tradition. The author of *Beowulf*, therefore, believes the story is true, and thanks to the song he must have become well known immediately after he had performed his heroic feat. Returning to his homeland, Beowulf does not boast to his king about what he achieved in Denmark, but rather assumes that his deeds are already generally known. For more on truth and lie in the *Odyssey* (see H. Parry 1994).

actual events in the song are not of the poet's invention nor based solely on what is suggested by Odysseus. Demodokos's song includes names (for example, Menelaos and Deiphobos) and events not mentioned by Odysseus at all. For Odysseus, as a participant of the events described by Demodokos, the criterion of the truth seems significant. He praises the singer for presenting in the first song the event "as if you had seen it yourself or heard about it from someone who was there."[192] Demodokos seems to know an abundance of actions leading up to the capture of Troy, from which he can make selections. The improvisation, therefore, occurs from within the whole perspective of events that he already knows.

The epic song has no title but is distinguished by the subject that Odysseus suggests: the wooden horse. The subject could equally well have been the Wrath of Achilles or Odysseus's Return. There is no reason to speak of a difference between Demodokos's songs and Homer's poetry.

Demodokos's two songs discussed above are only reported, unlike his second song, which can be called a "song within a song." The content of the first and third song are, nevertheless, described, albeit in a completely different way.

Over half a century ago, it was noticed that the first song of Demodokos is similar to the *Iliad* invocation.[193] Unfortunately, this observation has only been used in attempts to ascertain whether this story is Homer's innovation or an element of tradition.[194] Similarities to the *Iliad* invocation do not necessarily mean the song was based on the *Iliad*. Similarities have frequently been shown between the invocations in both of Homer's works as well as in the *Kypria*. These similarities are, then, more probably a result of the author or authors following a pattern that was applied to particular songs.[195] Let us look at Demodokos's first song (8.73–82) from the perspective of its similarities to extant invocations in ancient Greek epics:

> Μοῦσ' ἄρ' ἀοιδὸν ἀνῆκεν ἀειδέμεναι κλέα ἀνδρῶν,
> οἴμης, τῆς τότ' ἄρα κλέος οὐρανὸν εὐρὺν ἵκανε,
> νεῖκος Ὀδυσσῆος καὶ Πηλεΐδεω Ἀχιλῆος,
> ὥς ποτε δηρίσαντο θεῶν ἐν δαιτὶ θαλείῃ

192 8.491. It is not necessarily the kind of confirmation of truth, in which the events are verified against what Odysseus remembers. Such understanding may be deceptive because Odysseus's recognition of the "truth" of the story may be influenced by his approval of the way in which his role in these events is presented.

193 Marg 1956:16–29.

194 Innovation: von der Mühll 1940:718, 45–48; Marg 1956; Braswell 1982:130; Finkelberg 1987:128–132; tradition: Nagy 1999:15–65.

195 Notopoulos 1964:33; Finkelberg 1987:128: "Resemblances of this kind, which are common enough in epic poetry, usually indicate that what is being dealt with are typical epic subjects based on a common pattern."

> ἐκπάγλοισ' ἐπέεσσιν, ἄναξ δ' ἀνδρῶν Ἀγαμέμνων
> χαῖρε νόῳ, ὅ τ' ἄριστοι Ἀχαιῶν δηριόωντο.
> ὣς γάρ οἱ χρείων μυθήσατο Φοῖβος Ἀπόλλων
> Πυθοῖ ἐν ἠγαθέῃ, ὅθ' ὑπέρβη λάϊνον οὐδὸν
> χρησόμενος. τότε γάρ ῥα κυλίνδετο πήματος ἀρχὴ
> Τρωσί τε καὶ Δαναοῖσι Διὸς μεγάλου διὰ βουλάς.

> The Muse allowed the *aoidos* to sing of the glory of men,
> from a song [*oimê*] whose glory then reached the vast heavens,
> of the quarrel between Odysseus and Achilles the son of Peleus,
> how at an opulent feast of the gods they once clashed
> using terrible words, but the ruler of men, Agamemnon,
> rejoiced in his heart that the best of Achaeans were fighting each other.
> Thus had the oracular Phoibos Apollo prophesied to him
> at holy Pytho [Delphi], where he crossed the stone threshold
> to ask the oracle. For it was then that began the misfortunes
> for the Trojans and Danaans in agreement with the plan of the great Zeus.

The first line of the invocation to the *Iliad* and *Odyssey* contains a word marking the subject of the song with a characteristic definition and an apostrophe to the Muse with the verb in the imperative. In the *Iliad* the subject is "wrath," μῆνις (*mênis*), defined distinctively by the term "whose?"—"Achilles, the son of Peleus," Πηληϊάδεω Ἀχιλῆος. The nature and rank of this wrath is given by the epithet οὐλομένην 'cursed, baneful'. Similarly, in the *Odyssey* "man" ἀνήρ is defined with the characterizing epithet πολύτροπος 'using deceits'. The reference to the Muse μῆνιν ἄειδε θεά 'sing of wrath, goddess' in the *Iliad* corresponds to ἄνδρα μοι ἔννεπε Μοῦσα 'tell me, Muse, of the man' in the *Odyssey*. The singer, thus, creates the illusion that the words the listeners will hear in a moment will be actually the words of the Muse. Demodokos's song is related to us in the third person, but the narrator of the *Odyssey* does not omit a single detail from the start of the song pattern. The phrase "the Muse allowed the *aoidos* to sing κλέα ἀνδρῶν"—that is, the epic song[196]—does not mean anything other than that Demodokos had asked the Muse to sing a song on the requested subject, which of course was understood as a request for the Muse to allow the

[196] Ford (1992:57) believes that κλέα ἀνδρῶν is a term for a story about the general past (the genitive ἀνδρῶν indicates a story about heroes/ancestors as opposed to a story about gods). In his opinion, the *sensu stricto* term for epic story is ἀοιδή (*aoidê*). Nonetheless, here we are dealing with a song sanctioned in its truth by the Muse.

aoidos to sing the song. The subject of the song is the dispute, νεῖκος (*neikos*), distinctively defined as analogous to the *Iliad*'s question "whose?"—"Odysseus and Achilles the son of Peleus."

Of the more important similarities between the invocations in Homer's two poems, let us mention, following Samuel E. Bassett:[197] a) syntax: in the *Iliad* the subject is specified with the four-syllable adjective οὐλομένην, which corresponds with the four-syllable epithet πολύτροπον in the *Odyssey*,[198] and next further characterized by relative clauses (ἣ μυρί' Ἀχαιοῖς ἄλγε' ἔθηκεν and ὃς μάλα πολλὰ πλάγχθη), followed by two paratactically added sentences with δέ (πολλὰς δ', αὐτοὺς δέ and πολλῶν δ', πολλὰ δ'); b) both *prooimia* emphasize the accumulation of events and refer to a vast diversity of subjects (μυρί' and μάλα πολλά; πολλὰς δ' and πολλῶν δ', πολλὰ δ'); c) marking suffering as a subject of the work (ἄλγε' ἔθηκεν and πάθεν ἄλγεα); d) a return at the end of the invocation to its start; e) significant divergence of subject from what is presented in the songs; f) arbitrariness as to the moment when the narrative starts (ἄειδε ... ἐξ οὗ δὴ τὰ πρῶτα διαστήτην ἐρίσαντε, "begin the song from the moment when they [Achilles and Agamemnon] stood back because they had quarreled" and τῶν ἁμόθεν γε ... εἰπέ, "begin with those [voyages] anywhere").

We see that the syntax in Demodokos's song is different, but this should not surprise us, since it is presented in a third-person narrative.

Apart from that, Demodokos's song has many common themes with other invocations. The subject of the quarrel *neikos* (νεῖκος) is parallel to the wrath of Achilles, which is a consequence of his *neikos* with Agamemnon. Both the *Iliad* (1.5) and the *Kypria* (fr. 1.7) include the expression Διὸς δ' ἐτελείετο βουλή, "and realized was the plan of Zeus."[199] Demodokos's song contains a similar expression Διὸς μεγάλου διὰ βουλάς, which is used in the same context: the suffering experienced by the people was part of the far-reaching plan of Zeus.[200] The fragment containing the invocation to the *Kypria* is perhaps too short to include a subsequent conjugated element. In the *Iliad*, immediately after the lines considered to be the narrator's invocation,

197 Bassett 1923.

198 I believe that in the *Odyssey* πολύτροπον serves both purposes.

199 Towards the end of Proclus's *Kypria* summary there is another mention of Zeus's plan: καὶ Διὸς βουλὴ ὅπως ἐπικουφίσῃ τοὺς Τρῶας Ἀχιλλέα τῆς συμμαχίας τῆς Ἑλλήνων ἀποστήσας, "[appears] also the plan of Zeus to help the Trojans [by making] Achilles stop supporting the Greeks." However, we do not know what exactly this plan involved. Perhaps this was another version of the Wrath of Achilles (see Burgess 1996:82 and 92). Allan (2008) argues that the use of this phrase on the one hand, links the presented narration with the macro-story, while on the other it enables the presentation of a different version of the heroic and divine myth.

200 *Catalogue of Women* fr. 204.95–103 also seems to suggest that Zeus's plan was the cause of the war, in order to definitively separate gods from people.

the narrator points to Apollo as the cause of the misfortunes. This might be related to Apollo's role in traditional songs about Achilles. According to Nagy, the conflict between the god and the hero was the reason that the latter achieved hero status on an epic scale.[201] Achilles' conflict with Apollo results in his death, which is a prerequisite for this hero's apotheosis. Demodokos's song presents the dual actions of the gods: the plan of Zeus and the direct action of Apollo. The quarrel of the heroes, recognized by Agamemnon as a sign of the prophecy being fulfilled, is greeted by him with joy—but is he not in some way deceived? Misinterpretation of prophecies by mortals is a topos in Greek tradition. In the *Odyssey*, the main hero's conflict with Poseidon is mentioned sometime after the invocation (1.20).[202] Two gods appear, and their role is similar: Helios's wrath pursues Odysseus's comrades and reaches them,[203] while Odysseus himself is pursued by the wrath of Poseidon. Corresponding to Zeus's plan in the *Iliad* is Athena's plan of leading Odysseus back to Ithaca in the *Odyssey* (νημερτέα βούλην, "the plan that assuredly will come to fruition," 1.86).[204] But the goddess herself does not reveal this plan until the meeting of the gods (1.88–95).

In comparing Homer's invocation with Demodokos's song, we notice that in both, there appears the theme of a feast. The quarrel between Achilles and Odysseus occurs during a feast of the gods ἐν δαιτὶ θαλείῃ. In the *Iliad*, dying Achaeans become the prey, ἑλώρια, for dogs and a feast, δαΐς, for scavenging birds (1.4–5),[205] whereas in the *Odyssey* invocation, Odysseus's comrades pay with their lives for eating, ἤσθιον, the oxen of Helios (1.8–9). In each case, the theme appears in the context of misfortune: the feast is either the cause or the

201 Nagy 1999:67–210.

202 Significantly, Odysseus in this case is called ἀντιθέος, which could originally mean "he who stands to fight the gods." See below, Ch. 6, for conflict of heroes with gods.

203 The wrath of Helios most probably lies in a deep layer of the epic, which was originally largely influenced by the solar myth. See Frame (2005:20–81), who further develops the idea of Denys Page (1955b:2).

204 See Bassett 1923:345–347.

205 The word δαῖτα is used in place of πᾶσι present in the vulgate. It appears in the version of Zenodotus, who, nevertheless, athetized verses 4–5. Aristarchus criticizes this interpretation, using the false argument that Homer does not apply this word in reference to the food of animals, whereas it does actually appear in *Iliad* 24.43 (see Kirk 1985:53 *ad* 1.4–5). I would even see it as a reference in the final part of the book to its start, where the word is used to describe Achilles' destructive conduct as contrary to the laws of the people and gods. The counterargument that the audience would find it hard to identify the allusion in such a vast text seems inadequate, insofar as the allusion could be a typical element in reference to the destructive wrath of Achilles. Redfield (1979:104–105) defends the version with δαῖτα, demonstrating a deliberate crossing of mental barriers—a surprising collocation "a feast of animals, as a reversal of the natural order, would have been a kind of culture shock for the Greek receiver. In the poem men become bestial; in the proem the carrion-eating beasts do a manlike thing."

result of death. This is because the "feast of the gods" theme—that is, the feast of gods with mortals—inherently contains the theme of dispute, which cannot turn out well for mortals. In the Trojan War myth this archetypical meaning is given to the wedding of Peleus and Thetis, where gods and mortals feast and the first quarrel is begun by none other than the goddess Eris, the personification of strife and discord.[206]

Assuming that the quarrel between Odysseus and Achilles was a traditional element, Gregory Nagy situates the feast on Lemnos, where the heroes stop over on their way to Troy. This feast is mentioned in Proclus's summary and the *Iliad*.[207] Proclus's summary of the *Kypria* is as follows:

> καὶ εὐωχουμένων αὐτῶν Φιλοκτήτης ὑφ' ὕδρου πληγεὶς διὰ τὴν δυσοσμίαν ἐν Λήμνῳ κατελείφθη. καὶ Ἀχιλλεὺς ὕστερος κληθεὶς διαφέρεται πρὸς Ἀγαμέμνονα. τελούντων δὲ αὐτῶν Ἀπόλλονι θυσίαν, ἐκ τοῦ βωμοῦ προσελθὼν ὕδρος δάκνει Φιλοκτήτην
>
> During their feast, Philoktetes is bitten by a water snake and on account of the bad smell of the wound is left behind on Lemnos. Achilles quarrels with Agamemnon because he was invited to the feast too late. When they lay sacrifices to Apollo, the water snake crawls from the altar and bites Philoktetes.

The feast theme is connected with the theme of laying offerings to a god[208] and of quarrelling, νεῖκος. In the *Iliad*, Agamemnon returns to the feast on Lemnos, berating his warriors (8.228–234):

> αἰδώς, Ἀργεῖοι, κάκ' ἐλέγχεα, εἶδος ἀγητοί,
> πῇ ἔβαν εὐχωλαί, ὅτε δὴ φάμεν εἶναι ἄριστοι,
> ἃς ὁπότ' ἐν Λήμνῳ κενεαυχέες ἠγοράασθε,

[206] Proclus's summary: παραγενομένη δὲ Ἔρις εὐωχουμένων τῶν θεῶν ἐν τοῖς Πηλέως γάμοις νεῖκος περὶ κάλλους ἐνίστησιν Ἀθηνᾷ, Ἥρᾳ καὶ Ἀφροδίτῃ, "when the gods feast at the wedding of Peleus, Eris arrives and starts a dispute (νεῖκος) over the beauty of Athena, Hera, and Aphrodite."

[207] It remains unclear as to whether the feast took place on Lemnos. That location is suggested by scholia to Homer and Eustathius *ad Iliad* 2.721–725 (Homer speaks of Philoktetes, who is left by the Greeks on Lemnos, suffering from a stinking snakebite). Apollodorus and most probably Proclus situate the feast on Tenedos, but also say that Philoktetes had to remain on Lemnos. On the other hand, in Sophocles' *Philoktetes* (263–270, 1326–1328), the feast and the leaving of Philoktetes take place on the small island of Chryse, not far from Lemnos; see Frazer 1921b:194–197. The diversity of locations results from the diversity of versions, which in my opinion indicates that the story belongs to tradition.

[208] The feast is mentioned by Homer and Proclus, whereas according to Apollodorus the incident with Philoktetes took place during the laying of sacrifices to Apollo, *Epitome* 3.27 τελούντων δὲ αὐτῶν Ἀπόλλωνι θυσίαν. We can safely associate these sacrifices with the feast; see Frazer 1921b:195 ("the feast mentioned by Proclus may have been sacrificial").

ἔσθοντες κρέα πολλὰ βοῶν ὀρθοκραιράων,
πίνοντες κρητῆρας ἐπιστεφέας οἴνοιο,
Τρώων ἄνθ' ἑκατόν τε διηκοσίων τε ἕκαστος
στήσεσθ' ἐν πολέμῳ;

shame, Argives, disgrace, admirable in outward form,
where are your boasts (we say we are the best)[209]
which once on Lemnos you eagerly declared,
eating abundantly the flesh of straight-horned oxen,
drinking brimming kraters of wine,[210]
that each one of you would match in battle one or two hundred
Trojans?

Nagy suggests that during the boasting, discord might have broken out among the leaders as to who would capture Troy, and it was against this background that the story of the quarrel between Achilles and Odysseus in Demodokos's song is based. Nagy bases this hypothesis on the traditional, in his opinion, theme of the rivalry between Achilles and Odysseus entitled "the best of the Achaeans." Proclus's summary mentions a quarrel between Agamemnon and Achilles, which is not so much evidence of mutual imitation, as that the feast on Lemnos could be the starting point of more than one epic song—the start, that is, of a whole series of events.

The situation presented in Demodokos's song is also the "start of misfortunes," πήματος ἀρχή. In the *Iliad*, the expression πῆμα means misery and suffering caused by war. When one side achieves νίκη 'victory' and κῦδος 'glory', the other side suffers πῆμα (*pêma*).[211] Thus the word is usually linked with the perpetrator of the misery: Paris (3.50, 6.282), Helen (3.160), Poseidon (15.42), Achaean ships (15.721), Achilles for the Trojans (22.288, 22.421, 24.781),[212] and Achilles for the Achaeans (9.229), Hektor (11.347) for Diomedes

[209] Anacoluthon: Homer's phraseology sometimes strongly reflects the character of spoken language; for a different appraisal, see Kirk 1990:318.

[210] Agamemnon's seemingly gauche expression (Greeks did not drink from kraters) perfectly reflects the atmosphere of that feast. It can be compared with the drunkenness of soldiers described by Xenophon (*Anabasis* 4.5.32) and the elegies of Archilochus (frr. 2 and 4 W). Agamemnon might be mockingly suggesting that the boasting of the warriors resulted from the madness brought about by excessive eating and drinking (compare the madness that overcame the suitors during their feast). Therefore, I cannot agree with Kirk's opinion (1990:318) that drinking from kraters makes no sense and must result from carelessness or a rhapsode's alteration.

[211] See, for example, *Iliad* 8.176. On the meaning of πῆμα and ἄλγεα as "suffering" in epic diction, see Nagy 1999:74–81.

[212] Diomedes is the cause of πῆμα also for Ares (*Iliad* 8.886).

and Odysseus, and Dolon (10.453) and Zeus (17.688) for the Achaeans. Nagy rightly notes that Achilles is perceived as a cause of misery for the Achaeans when he withdraws from the fighting and for the Trojans when he joins the fight.[213] It was also typical to present Helen as a cause of misery for both sides, as is indicated by the scene of Helen weaving a picture of the war (3.125–128):

> ἣ δὲ μέγαν ἱστὸν ὕφαινε
> δίπλακα πορφυρέην, πολέας δ' ἐνέπασσεν ἀέθλους
> Τρώων θ' ἱπποδάμων καὶ Ἀχαιῶν χαλκοχιτώνων,
> οὓς ἕθεν εἵνεκ' ἔπασχον ὑπ' Ἄρηος παλαμάων
>
> and she wove a great purple robe
> double fold, with images of many duels,
> Trojans taming horses and Achaeans clad in bronze,
> who on her account suffered under the hand of Ares.

In the epic tradition, it is very important to stress the ambivalent, magic way of acting of the heroine, who brings destruction to both parties, and to show the point which started an avalanche of calamities. Demodokos's first song is set at the start of the Trojan War. The Achaeans have not yet landed near Troy, but that moment is very close. It is not exactly known whether the phrase πήματος ἀρχή refers to the moment of the feast, the quarrel of the leaders (βασιλεῖς), or an earlier situation when Agamemnon asks the oracle of Apollo at Delphi. The verb κυλίνδετο suggests that from that very moment, as if inevitably, further events started "to unfold." We thus return to the question of when the Trojan War actually began. Reference to Zeus's plan, as we have seen, sets the start in a cosmogonic and cosmological primordial dimension. The designation ἀρχή (*archê*) places it in an "earthly" scenery of events, as the moment when the divine plan begins to be realized. We see that the song can set the start at any moment, and not only the story in the song, but the whole Trojan War. In the *Iliad*, the "start" is marked twice. In Book 3, when Achaeans and Trojans seem to clash for the first time, Menelaos speaks (3.98–100):

> φρονέω δὲ διακρινθήμεναι ἤδη
> Ἀργείους καὶ Τρῶας, ἐπεὶ κακὰ πολλὰ πέπασθε
> εἵνεκ' ἐμῆς ἔριδος καὶ Ἀλεξάνδρου ἕνεκ' ἀρχῆς [214]

[213] Nagy 1999:69–83.

[214] The lection ἀρχῆς, "beginning," appears in the manuscript authorized by Aristarchus; whereas Zenodotus in this place read ἄτης, "blinding," which is supported by Kirk 1985:277.

> I think it is time to settle the dispute
> between the Argives and Trojans, for you have suffered much misery
> because of my quarrel [*eris*] and because of Alexander's beginning [*archê*].

This ineffectively literal translation brings out the "unnaturalness" of Menelaos's language. This is because it is subordinated to the formal announcement of the start of the war. Included here are all the required elements: the common suffering of Achaeans and Trojans, the quarrel theme (ἔρις [*eris*], quite surprisingly described by Menelaos as "my," because the quarrel of individual leaders results in misery for everyone), and the theme of the beginning ascribed to the actions of Paris. The start of the war, and its cause, from the perspective of the *Iliad* is the abduction of Helen by Paris.[215] This information is specified by Hektor in an internal monologue (22.114–117), where he speaks of returning to the Achaeans Helen and the treasures brought to Troy by Paris, ἥ τ' ἔπλετο νείκεος ἀρχή, "and she [Helen] became the beginning/cause [*archê*] of the quarrel [*neikos*]."[216] As the *Odyssey* (11.436–439) confirms, Helen is traditionally perceived as the start of hardships.[217] Homer again uses the noun ἀρχή, thus marking the beginning of the unhappy fate of Patroklos, *Iliad* 11.604: κακοῦ δ' ἄρα οἱ πέλεν ἀρχή, that was the beginning of his misfortune." This is an exceptional use of the standard presentation of the start of the Trojan War as a misfortune that foretells future events.[218]

Demodokos's song is only reported to us and, therefore, it is difficult to say whether or not this is a ring composition similar to the *Iliad* and *Odyssey*. On the other hand, the next characteristic feature of the invocation, the striking omissions in predicting events described in the song, probably plays a more important role than has been acknowledged. Whoever summarized the *Iliad* would not be able to omit Hektor or Patroklos. After all, they are linked with the most

215 Menelaos calls attention to this, pointing out that the quarrel arose not from his, but Paris's fault.

216 In light of Bakker's research into syntactic compounds, I am inclined to disagree with the interpretation of Richardson that ἥ opening that part of the statement refers to "the whole of what precedes, i.e. the rape of Helen, and is attracted to the case of ἀρχή (1993:119 *ad Iliad* 22.115–116). The pronoun refers to Helen and might be a trace of the traditional ascribing of guilt to her, as well as to Paris.

217 In the *Odyssey*, the start of the war is referred to by Odysseus (9.436–439): ὢ πόποι, ἦ μάλα δὴ γόνον Ἀτρέος εὐρύοπα Ζεὺς / ἐκπλάγως ἤχθηρε γυναικείας διὰ βουλὰς / ἐξ ἀρχῆς· Ἑλένης μὲν ἀπωλόμεθ' εἵνεκα πολλοί / σοὶ δὲ Κλυταιμνήστρη δόλον ἤρτυε τηλόθ' ἐόντι ("Heavens, indeed, the family of Atreus did Zeus of sweeping countenance / so much hate due to feminine counsel / that from the start; for Helen's sake [*archê*] many died / and for you [Agamemnon] Klytaimestra prepared a snare when you were far from home").

218 Moreover, in the *Odyssey*, there is talk of "the beginning of contests and slaughter" (21.4, 24.169); likewise, the *Iliad* also mentions the beginning of the destruction of Patroklos and the beginning of a friendship already made in the previous generation (1.188, 2.254, 17.69, 21.35).

important events in the work. There is also no mention of the aim of the plot: the death of Achilles. Similarly, in the *Odyssey*, the invocation mentions only the return of Odysseus, whereas it is silent about the song's most important subject: the revenge on the suitors, as well as Odysseus's recovery of his wife, son, and authority. Just as in the case of the *Iliad*, unmentioned is the aim of the song's plot.[219] Bassett argues that Homer slowly builds up the action in his works. But the problem probably lies elsewhere. If in both cases there are such omissions, we should accept that the invocation did not serve as a summary at all. It was rather an introduction to encourage the audience to listen to the song patiently. No small role must have been played by exaggeration, for example, by stressing how vast and terrible was the misery and suffering. This is the frequent purpose of the adjective πολύς, "many, a lot of," as well as expressions such as μυρία.[220] In the *Iliad*, there is mention of the bodies of Achaeans being devoured by scavengers, whereas later on in the story no such events take place. In view of these significant omissions in the invocations to the *Iliad* and *Odyssey*, it is hard to agree with opinions that Demodokos's song relates just a brief episode and nothing more; rather, this invocation only introduces the subject, but does not serve as even a cursory summary.

One could say that the invocation does not summarize the song plot but presents its formal frame. It consists of a few elements that, one way or another, should appear. As is evident from the beginning of the *Odyssey*, not all the elements can be mentioned in the few lines of the invocation. It seems, nevertheless, that it is a principle of oral poetry that all the elements must appear in the story, no matter how. If that is the case, let us note that even a minor detail, such as the irrational joy of Agamemnon at the quarrel of the leading warriors, might be a traditional element. In the *Iliad*, the invocation is followed by a description of the quarrel between Achilles and Agamemnon. When the quarrel between the two leaders does arise, Nestor speaks out and his first words are that the quarrel will bring joy to Priam, his sons, and all Trojans (1.255–256):

> ἦ κεν γηθήσαι Πρίαμος Πριάμοιό τε παῖδες,
> ἄλλοί τε Τρῶες μέγα κεν κεχαροίατο θυμῷ

[219] By the aim of the song I mean a set of diverse allusions and predictions focused around a single event, at which point the story ends.

[220] The adjective μυρία generally means "very numerous, countless," but it is related to μύρια, which means "ten thousand," the largest number in the Greek language (probably considered as the highest, countless, infinite because on your hands you could only count up to 9,999). Using such a phrase is typical in colloquial language for exaggeration. It is similar to when we speak of millions to express a large number with obvious exaggeration.

truly would Priam and the sons of Priam rejoice
and the rest of the Trojans would be most glad at heart.

Most important in our analysis is the arbitrariness of the moment where the narrative can begin. The formulation οἴμης, τῆς τότ' ἄρα κλέος οὐρανὸν εὐρὺν ἵκανε, "from the song [*oimê*] whose fame then reached the vast heavens" might mean that the singer knows many songs and that he has selected one of them. Homer presents Demodokos as a singer familiar with the theme of the Trojan War, which in his opinion was already widely known. Yet the matter is presented in such a way as if οἴμη (*oimê*) was a story sequence known to the singer, and one that he could start at any moment he chose. The meaning of *oimê* was difficult to determine, and the uncertain etymology allowed it to be considered as a metaphoric way of saying "paths" or "threads."[221]

In order to assess what *oimê* really meant, let us return to the aforementioned question as to whether Demodokos's first song was the poet's innovation or whether it was an element of a now-lost tradition.

Von der Mühll, in his influential article for *Real Encyclopädie*, stated that it was the poet's own invention unsupported by tradition (αὐτοσχηδίασμα) and although he changed his opinion a few years later, accepting the possibility that it is based on a story in the *Kypria*,[222] the idea that it was the author's invention gained successive advocates. Marg found structural parallels between Demodokos's first song and the invocation to the *Iliad* and considered the song to be the invention of the author of the *Odyssey* based on that invocation. The innovation concept assumes that the poet was being creative and that the similarities are the result of conscious imitation. This is, therefore, creation of an individual style, and the research method typical of "classical" philology. The question, however, remains as to what purpose this creative imitation could possibly serve.

The judgments of subsequent scholars have taken into account the principles of oral poetry. Braswell argued that Demodokos's story was invented to anticipate the quarrel between Odysseus and Euryalus (*Odyssey* 8.159–255). Finkelberg rightly criticized this view, stating that Homer could have found a traditionally better-known theme of Odysseus's quarrelling, for example, with

221 The etymology of *oimê* as "path, road" is accepted in the etymological dictionaries of Frisk and Chantraine s.v.; also Schadewaldt 1951:74–75; Svenbro 1976:36; and Ford 1992:42. "Song path" is, moreover, recognized as an Indo-European metaphor, Durante 1958, 1976:176–177. Another accepted etymology is "thread": Pagliaro 1951:25–30; Lanata 1963:11–12; Nagy 1996a:63–64.

222 Von der Mühll 1940 and 1954. The thought of Von der Mühll that the quarrel between Odysseus and Achilles should be associated with the *Kypria* is supported by the neoanalysts; see Kullmann 1960:100 and 272.

Aias over Achilles' armor.[223] The similarities of the song with the invocations in the *Iliad*, *Odyssey*, and *Kypria* allow us to conclude that this was a traditional pattern for introducing songs. Finkelberg believes that Demodokos's first and third songs serve to anticipate the scene in which the Phaeacians recognize Odysseus. While the song about the wooden horse depicts the end of the Trojan War, the first song is about its beginning, from the perspective of Odysseus's glory. Finkelberg surmises that, on account of the lack of a story in the Trojan Cycle that announces any glorious role played by Odysseus towards the end of the war (the *Kypria* provides only some rather inglorious episodes of the hero's earlier achievements: Odysseus pretending to be insane to avoid going on the expedition and murdering Palamedes, as revenge for the latter's uncovering of his ploy), Homer invents a story that meets the requirements of glory for Odysseus and tells it in a schematic way, typical of the oral style.

Broeniman agreed with Marg that the quarrel between Odysseus and Achilles was based on the invocation to the *Iliad*, but also said that this was a "twisted" version of the *Iliad* for the uninitiated Phaeacians (as if they did not know that Achilles had "in reality" quarreled with Agamemnon). This argument is based on the assumption that the Phaeacians are presented as a people of quite different mentality and customs than the Achaeans. Odysseus must first teach them the principles of hospitality and instruct the singer how to correctly present in the third song his role in the capture of Troy.[224] Broeniman therefore, like Finkelberg, believes Demodokos's first and third songs are connected with each other, but unfoundedly also assumes that the first song shows Odysseus in a bad light.[225] Quite strange also is his view of an allusion to the *Iliad* with which the hero of the epic cannot agree, for this makes us wonder how Homer's public would have received it. Of course, this concept assumes the priority of the *Iliad* with little regard for the typical elements in Demodokos's rendition.

Hence, the fundamental question: is there really a dividing line between tradition and innovation? The relativity of this distinction is well described by Ruth Scodel:

> Much of what some scholars call "invented" might better be called "contextually bound." Homer may very well have invented a given detail in a subordinate narrative that serves the rhetorical purpose of

223 Marg 1956; Braswell 1982:130; Finkelberg 1987.

224 Broeniman (1996), who in this respect develops the view of Rose (1969a). Broeniman's justification for the paradoxical situation is not very satisfying. All his arguments are based on two false claims: 1) that the "aberrations" of the Phaeacians can be read against an idea of "normality" in the Homeric world; 2) that the Greek epic tradition is limited to the tradition of the *Iliad*.

225 Broeniman (1996:12) believes that in the conflict with Achilles, Odysseus plays an inglorious role of Agamemnon.

> its immediate context, but so may his teacher, his teacher's teacher, or another bard from whom he adapted this section. Someone invented it. However, what matters more is that its transmission is bound to its context, without which it has no function and makes little sense.[226]

If the "road" or "thread" were a major song from which the singer could arbitrarily select an episode, then Demodokos's performance could be treated as a fragment of that song. Nothing, however, suggests that.[227] The Homeric description of Demodokos's song mentions only an invocation, but the song might continue and contain far more content than the quarrel of two warriors at a feast and the joy of a third who looks on. Demodokos's song was probably not short: Odysseus discreetly wiped a tear from his eye, "every time the singer stopped his performance" (8.87 ἦ τοι ὅτε λήξειεν θεῖος ἀοιδός), whereas the intrigued Phaeacians urged him to continue the story. The only rational reason for these breaks could be the singer's tiredness due to the long narrative. If we only know the introduction to the song as in the *Iliad*, why cannot we expect that the quarrel between Achilles and Odysseus was as developed as that between Achilles and Agamemnon? From Alkinoos's reaction, it is hard to determine whether or not the singer managed to end his song. One might accept that Alkinoos's politeness[228] means that he had patiently waited until the end, before proposing another form of entertainment for the guest, whose negative reaction seems to suggest that the song for some reason displeased him. One might also assume that the song was actually interrupted, and the audience did not know the outcome of Achilles' dispute with Odysseus. The Phaeacians would then be left unaware, as would the audience of the *Odyssey* as well, who would have to make do with the invocation. This understatement would mean that for the author of the *Odyssey* the consequences of the quarrel are not that important and that, instead, he is concentrating on the impression he wants to give his external audience. In the first song of Demodokos, the author of the *Odyssey* wants to pose the problem, so that it can be resolved in the third song, where the audience can finally learn who really conquered the city and, therefore, also who is the ultimate winner in the quarrel.

Demodokos's selection of the subject of his story from *oimê* is evidence of the great variety of subjects in the cycle. The singer is also oriented with great proficiency in the super-story, since not only does he know a number of

226 Scodel 2002:29; see Nagy 1996b:81–106.

227 Judging by the way it is related, Demodokos's song would be limited to an invocation. But an invocation is an introduction to a song, a presentation of its subject matter, and the starting point for the action, and not the recitation of its fragment.

228 Alkinoos says ἤδη μὲν δαιτὸς κεκορήμεθα θυμὸν ἐσής / φόρμιγγος ("we have already satisfied the soul with feasting and the phorminx").

"episodes" that he might select from, but he is also ready to start the narrative at whatever point the public requests. We have seen that marking the place where the narrative begins is an important element of the invocation and helps to orient the listeners in the sequence of events known to them. The author of the *Odyssey* literally boasts of his abilities in this respect, since he tells the Muse to begin the story where she will (1.10 ἁμόθεν, "starting from any point of events, anywhere"). It is as if it was all the same to him because he is so well oriented in the voluminous story of Odysseus and is able to start his song at any point of narrative and carry it on to the designated end. The author of the *Odyssey* therefore gives the impression that the story of Odysseus was one great *oimê*. In turn, the singer Phemios, begging for Odysseus to spare his life, declares that he knows many *oimai* (pl. of *oimê*).[229] This means that he is able to start recounting from any point in such a "great story" as that of the Trojan War or the Voyage of the Argonauts, which is mentioned in the *Odyssey*; he might also sing of the fortunes of Herakles, to which both the *Iliad* and the *Odyssey* refer on multiple occasions, or of Theseus, whose mother is mentioned in the *Iliad*, or the Hunting of the Kalydonian Boar, since Homer remembers Meleagros, or the fate of Oedipus and his descendants. The Muse instructs Demodokos to sing of the glory of heroes, which suggests that he might select a song of a different sort, though not wedding or funeral song, as this was not the occasion, but most probably a song praising the gods—one example of which is the singer's second song on the romance between Ares and Aphrodite. But this is just one episode from many *oimai*, of which the most famous were no doubt songs about the births of successive generations of gods and the fights between them (including the Titanomachy, the Gigantomachy, and revolt of the Olympian gods mentioned in the *Iliad*).[230] That is hundreds of thousands of lines! The talents and knowledge of these singers are comparable to the abilities of Kirgiz and Turkic epic singers in northern Asia.

The story thus told is always understood as a part of something much lengthier. Ford believes its entirety is held in the memory of the past, which is

[229] See *Odyssey* 22.347–348: "The goddess inculcated in my heart *oimai* of various sorts"; 8.479–481: "Among all the people on earth the singers are respected because the Muse taught them *oimai* and fell in love with the singers' fraternity."

[230] The extant fragment of Proclus's *Chrestomathia* (Photius B 21) suggests that the cycle begins with the joining of Heaven and Earth, out of which were born three Hekatoncheires and three Kyklopes, through the history of the gods, right up to Odysseus's landing on Ithaca, where he was to perish, unrecognized, killed by his son, Telegonos (ἄρχεται μὲν ἐκ τῆς Οὐρανοῦ καὶ Γῆς μυθολογουμένης μίξεως, ἐξ ἧς αὐτῷ καὶ τρεῖς παῖδας ἑκατόγχειρας καὶ τρεῖς γεννῶσι Κύκλωπας, διαπορεύεται δὲ τά τε ἄλλως περὶ θεῶν τοῖς Ἕλλησι μυθολογούμενα ... καὶ περατοῦται ὁ ἐπικὸς κύκλος ... μέχρι τῆς ἀποβάσεως Ὀδυσσέως τῆς εἰς Ἰθάκην, ἐν ᾗ καὶ ὑπὸ τοῦ παιδὸς Τηλεγόνου ἀγνοοῦντος κτείνεται).

possessed by the Muse, who, nevertheless, helps the singer make the selection. In the past this was known as an enormous number of individual stories united by their stability and continuity.[231] Ford treats *oimê* as a technical term referring to an individual story in the heroic repertoire. All *oimai* comprise an image of the entire world in the past. Undertaking the next rendition of a song, the singer turns (μεταβαίνειν) to the subsequent *aoidê*[232] or *oimê*. An individual *aoidê* song presents the world of the past and at the same time seems to activate an *oimê*. Thus, the song seems ephemeral in relation to the permanent *oimai* stored in the common memory. Such "roads" or "threads" are, therefore, nothing other than cycles presenting all the epic stories animated in performance.[233]

In the Slavic tradition, the *guslar* has at his disposal only a limited set of songs, which he could only expand on by learning new ones. We may speak of the ability to improvise, evidence of which are the songs of Salih Ugljanin and Milovan Vojičić praising Milman Parry. But this innovation was not so apparent in the actual performance of the songs—that is, it did not appear that the singer was actually improvising a new song.[234] If *oimai* means the singer knowing an epic story, there are two ways of looking at it.

On the one hand, it might mean knowing a set of songs. But then it would be essential to know enough songs to cover the whole cycle story, including all the key moments. This would be a definite number (mathematically speaking, a "closed interval"). A situation like that, however, would be an ideal state where the singer knows a canon of songs and communicates with the audience, who know the same canon of songs. This looks implausible and does not seem to correspond to the Homeric image of Demodokos performing songs. Even the

231 Ford 1992:41–43.

232 Ford (1992:43–44) treats this verb also as a technical term, see *Odyssey* 8.492. Finkelberg (1998:51–53) referring to the dichotomies "knowledge: lack of knowledge" and "teaching: giving," makes the significant distinction that the Muse teaches *oimê* and gives *aoidê*. The first, therefore, is a derivative of the singer's ability and, in the second case, the Muse's role is to convey a stimulus for the singing to start at a specific point—that is, to select the material.

233 Rubin (1995:62) argues that in oral traditions imagery is basically spatial and this is the reason why "Homeric epic refers to itself as *oimê* (path)." Rubin states (61–62): "It may be no accident that epic heroes are always on the move; invoking a highly developed spatial-memory system increases memorability. ... individual images are better for spatial relations than for sequencing, but by using a series of images tied to a path that passes through a known sequence of places, the order of events can be made more stable. ... Because such spatial layout typically follows a known path, order information can be preserved."

234 This, however, might be a misleading impression because in oral performance, repeated structural elements are constantly subjected to transformations (of expansion and compression, in Nagy's terminology). Soliński (2019) notes that during the performance of East Slavic *bylinas*, the singer does not use a predetermined formula, but always remodels it even at the cost of metrical "correctness" (a view based on the research by Putilov 2001). This observation undermines the dominant conviction that mechanical repetition is necessary to facilitate the flow of narrative.

song about the wooden horse, if we accept that it corresponds to a song known to the singer and his audience alike, is a theme in traditional material from which the singer selects scenes. On the other hand, if we agree with Finkelberg that in the case of Demodokos's first song, Homer creates the story, we may assume that it is not so much the singer having at his disposal a set of specific songs as the singer knowing the epic plot, which allows him to activate or perhaps create episodes in the basic course of events (mathematically speaking, an "open interval").

The story itself must still present the traditionally established order of the most important events. The singer, nevertheless, can creatively transform it—for example, through improvisation. Even if not all *aoidoi* had such abilities, there must have been some who did, evidence of which is the portrayal of Demodokos in the *Odyssey*. This requires us to take a closer look at the second possibility. For knowledge of a set of songs cannot explain how a coherent plot—here, the cycle—was formed. Above all, we notice a certain precedence of the cycle in relation to individual songs. We see a situation where a singer, knowing the basic arrangement of events in a cycle, is able to adapt his song to current needs and create a new episode within the generally known story and the context of the whole war. Therefore, we cannot speak of innovation based on imitation, or of repeating ready-made and already known songs. As examples of episodes added to the main story cycle, we may, after all, also consider the *Iliad* and *Odyssey*.[235]

Contrary to the boasts of the author of the *Odyssey*, the song cannot be started at any point. The previously presented comparison between the arrangement of the *Odyssey* and that of the Song of Return allows us to conclude that, in such a form, the plot of the song cannot start anywhere else other than Odysseus's imprisonment on the island of Ogygia.[236] In the case of the *Iliad*, a plot of this form could probably only begin with the story of the Wrath of Achilles caused by the quarrel.[237] This, however, raises the question as to whether those are the only places where the songs can start—that is, whether there could exist quite different versions of the Wrath of Achilles and Return of Odysseus. It seems to me that in both cases, the course of events contains certain flaws, indicating that other versions of these songs might have existed. In both works, there is a problem of situating within the plot the theme of the conflict of the hero with the gods, which is fundamental to the Greek epic tradition.[238] In the

235 Ford (1992:109–111) understands Telemachos's praise of a "new song" to be in reference to the return of Odysseus as the last of the Songs of Return of Heroes from the Trojan War. However, it is only in the heroic age that this epic song could be considered "new," because normally it is a part of tradition.

236 Alternatively, other places of the hero's imprisonment are also possible.

237 Bassett 1923:341: "In the *Iliad* the natural and obvious starting-point is the quarrel."

238 About the role of the conflict in the structure of Greek epic tradition, see Nagy 1999:289–295.

Odyssey, Poseidon in anger pursues Odysseus, but the reason for this anger does not really fit into the chronology of events. Poseidon wants to avenge his son, the Kyklops Polyphemus, but Odysseus does not reach the island of the Kyklopes until after the middle of his voyages. In the remaining *nostoi*, it is the anger of Athena that prevents the Achaeans from safely returning to their homes. It is Athena who raises the storm that stands in the way of the heroes returning from Troy.[239] This inconsistency of motives is present in the *Odyssey* itself, for the reason for Athena's wrath is included in Hermes' speech to the nymph Kalypso (5.105–111):

> φησί τοι ἄνδρα παρεῖναι ὀιζυρώτατον ἄλλων,
> τῶν ἀνδρῶν, οἳ ἄστυ πέρι Πριάμοιο μάχοντο
> εἰνάετες, δεκάτῳ δὲ πόλιν πέρσαντες ἔβησαν
> οἴκαδ'· ἀτὰρ ἐν νόστῳ Ἀθηναίην ἀλίτοντο,
> ἥ σφιν ἐπῶρσ' ἄνεμόν τε κακὸν καὶ κύματα μακρά.
> ἔνθ' ἄλλοι μὲν πάντες ἀπέφθιθεν ἐσθλοὶ ἑταῖροι,
> τὸν δ' ἄρα δεῦρ' ἄνεμός τε φέρων καὶ κῦμα πέλασσεν.

> They say that here with you is the most wretched of the "remaining,"
> men who had fought over the city of Priam
> for nine years, conquered the city in the tenth and returned
> home, but on the way back they wronged Athena,
> who sent against them an evil wind and great waves.
> Then all the other noble comrades perished,
> and this one the wind and waves brought here.[240]

239 *Odyssey* 5.108–110. Proclus, summary *Nostoi*: (1) Ἀθηνᾶ Ἀγαμέμνονα καὶ Μενέλαον εἰς ἔριν καθίστησι περὶ τοῦ ἔκπλου. Ἀγαμέμνων μὲν οὖν τὸν τῆς Ἀθηνᾶς ἐξιλασόμενος χόλον ἐπιμένει· Διομήδης δὲ καὶ Νέστωρ ἀναχθέντες εἰς τὴν οἰκείαν διασώιζονται. μεθ' οὓς ἐκπλεύσας ὁ Μενέλαος, <χειμῶνι περιπεσών, Ap.> μετὰ πέντε νεῶν εἰς Αἴγυπτον παραγίνεται. τῶν λοιπῶν διαφθαρεισῶν νεῶν ἐν τῶι πελάγει ("Athena causes a quarrel between Agamemnon and Menelaos over the homeward voyage. Agamemnon stays so as to appease Athena's wrath. Diomedes and Nestor, however, set sail and arrive home safely. Next, Menelaos sets sail, but is attacked by a storm, only five ships reach Egypt, and the remaining ships are sunk at sea"). This account is very incomplete. We do not known why Athena causes a quarrel between the fraternal-leaders, or how they realized that the goddess was angry at them. Perhaps it is about unfavorable winds, as in the case of the wrath of Artemis stopping the fleet sailing out from Aulis, but why then were Diomedes and Nestor able to sail out and safely reach home? (An answer is given by Frame 2009, esp. Ch. 6, who interprets the role of Nestor as "the homebringer"). Nevertheless, we see that the combined themes of quarrelling between heroes and the wrath of deities serve to initiate the plot of the whole song.

240 These verses posed problems for ancient and modern scholars, hence they were often athetized. According to Clay (1983), Odysseus was originally the victim of Athena. Scodel (2002:115–116) notes that since Zeus has to explain the exact reasons for Poseidon's wrath (1.68–75), the anger of this god was not necessarily known to the listeners. The wrath of three deities moves the plot

Here, the fate of individual heroes is, in my opinion, a variation of the story. It must have been deeply rooted in pre-Homeric mentality. Athena supports the Achaeans very actively, often in collaboration with Hera because Paris's choice had insulted both of them (according to *Iliad* 24.29, he had offended both of the goddesses, which diminished their esteem in the eyes of others). The anger of Athena at Aias, the son of Oileus, in the *Ilioupersis* is motivated by his disgracing of Kassandra at the statue of Athena. For this sole reason, however, the goddess' wrath then turns on all the Achaeans. Proclus's summary of Ἰλίου πέρσις (*Ilioupersis*) shows Achaean fear that divine anger will fall on all of them because they spared Aias's life: ἐφ' ᾧ παροξυνθέντες οἱ Ἕλληνες καταλεῦσαι βουλεύονται τὸν Αἴαντα· ὁ δὲ ἐπὶ τὸν τῆς Ἀθηνᾶς βωμὸν καταφεύγει, καὶ διασῴζεται ἐκ τοῦ ἐπικειμένου κινδύνου· ἐπεὶ δὲ ἀποπλέουσιν οἱ Ἕλληνες, φθορὰν αὐτοῖς ἡ Ἀθηνᾶ κατὰ τὸ πέλαγος μηχανᾶται, "The Greeks outraged by this [action], decide to stone Aias to death. He escapes to the altar of Athena and thus escapes the danger, but when the Greeks sail away, Athena plans to destroy them at sea."[241] The author of the *Odyssey*, however, does not perceive Odysseus's wanderings from the perspective of the wrath of Athena, but rather she is the hero's protector and guardian.[242]

in the *Odyssey*: Athena, Poseidon, and Helios, though the wrath of the goddess is not emphasized. The large number of possible solutions seems to result from the many possible versions in the oral tradition.

241 The version of the codices φθορὰν αὐτοῖς 'their loss', was wrongly replaced by West's correction of φθορὰν αὐτῷ 'his loss'. For offending deities there is collective responsibility. Similarly, Agamemnon's offense results in the plague that affects all the Achaeans. Also, the Achaeans decide to punish Aias in a way that is typical for a *pharmakos*, one selected to be sacrificed for the general good.

242 The justification for the wrath of Athena pursuing the returning Achaeans could have been independent of the crimes against Kassandra. Athena is the guardian and protector of the city of Troy. During the war, she does not hear the prayers of the Trojans, as is stated in the *Iliad* (6.311–312). The Trojans must have attributed their defeat to the wrath of the goddess, who normally protected them (as the Hebrews saw their defeats as a consequence of their offending Yahweh). After the war, Athena is again able to defend her city and punish the invaders; and an immediate reason for their punishment was their inappropriate behavior during the taking of the city, especially the offense by the deity. The act of Aias, son of Oileus, might just be an exemplification of the reason for anger, just as Achilles' killing of Troilos might be just one of the possible mythological aetiologies explaining Apollo's wrath against Achilles. Nestor in the *Odyssey* (3.137–158) presents a dispute between the Atreidai as leading to a disruption in the army: those who sail away immediately with Menelaos are guaranteed a return, whereas those who remain with Agamemnon suffer the wrath of the goddess. The author of the *Odyssey* lifts the responsibility from Agamemnon, only blaming him for the stupidity of not knowing that the sacrifices could not appease the goddess. In the Trojan tradition, when Agamemnon is a party to the dispute, it usually means he is at fault: the crisis at Aulis and the one depicted in the *Iliad* are the result of an offense against a deity by Agamemnon. In the *Odyssey*, we have a paradox: Agamemnon incurs the wrath of the goddess, even though he tries to propitiate her with a hecatomb (which implies that the crime that brings the divine wrath must have already been

In the *Iliad*, the conflict between Apollo and Achilles also appears to be veiled; not until the last day of battle does Achilles express awareness of his imminent death on account of Apollo (21.275–277). Meanwhile, the listeners are reminded of Apollo's role in Achilles' death through allusions to the battlefield encounters of that god with Diomedes and Patroklos. In this context, the wrath of Apollo on the Achaeans, upon whom he sends the plague for the offense of his priest, seems a rather artificial addition of secondary importance to the rest of the plot. Taking into account Achilles' statement, his conflict with Apollo is associated with the prophecy the young hero learns from his mother, Thetis. Therefore, we probably have a situation analogous to the role of Apollo in Demodokos's song, where the god is presented as an oracle appearing to Agamemnon. The oracle could have played a much larger role in the epic tradition than is indicated by Homer's poetry. After all, this theme is directly linked with the ever-present theme of "Zeus's plan," preceding the action and providing a cosmogonic and cosmological dimension to the plot.

The conflict between the hero and the deity plays a fundamental role in mythology and epic. It is essential for the principal character to acquire hero status in the eschatological dimension. The conflict ends with the hero's death, with which his fate is completed. The *Odyssey* in this respect contains the important piece of information that Odysseus will eventually encounter death from the sea, which could be understood as the fulfillment of Poseidon's wrath. In the *Iliad*, Achilles' conflict with Apollo is not so prominent, but the scholia have preserved an alternative invocation to the *Iliad*, which speaks of the coexistence of the wrath of the hero and that of the god. This is evidence not only of differences between the texts, but also of the possible existence of an alternative version of the *Iliad*:

> ἔσπετε νῦν μοι, Μοῦσαι, Ὀλύμπια δώματ' ἔχουσαι
> ὅππως δὴ μῆνίς τε χόλος θ' ἕλε Πηλείωνα
> Λητοῦς τ' ἀγλαὸν υἱόν· ὁ γὰρ βασιλῆϊ χολωθείς
>
> tell me now Muses, having a palace on Olympus,
> how did wrath and rage overcome the son of Peleus
> and the wonderful son of Leto: for he was angered at the king.[243]

committed). Frame (2009:179–180) explains this situation by the fact that the Atreidai reenact the twin myth, in which the twin who represents restraint is not destined to return to his home, which also means he is not destined to return to life. Clay (1983:50–51) suggests there is a tradition in which Odysseus was also guilty of the goddess' wrath.

243 Aristoxenus claimed that some of the texts may have had such a *prooimion*. According to Nicanor and Crates, cited in the *Anecdotum Romanum*, the bibliophile Apellicon possessed the text with a single-line invocation: Μούσας ἀείδω καὶ Απόλλωνα κλυτότοξον ("The Muses I praise, and Apollo with his famous bow"). See Erbse 1969:I.3.

Homer's poems, therefore. look like "deformed" compositions of the Return of Odysseus and the Wrath of Achilles. They, nevertheless, retain the mechanical structure of an oral song and show the potential modality of the oral technique. Homer does not abandon the fundamental theme of the hero's conflict with the deity—as an oral poet he is unable to—but he does reconstruct and adapt it to his needs.

Knowledge of the *oimê*, therefore, means knowledge of a whole series of events, from which the singer selects the start of his song. The selection of a starting point means selecting an episode, but selecting where in the episode the song should start is no longer so arbitrary because the oral epic song is governed by the mechanics of its construction. Likewise, selecting a place for the episode is not entirely arbitrary. It might seem that along the entire storyline, one can arbitrarily select specific events. This, however, is not the case because episodes as the subject of the song are only grouped in certain places.

The song had to mark the beginning of the story—the cause of the presented events—as well as the end—the point of the whole story.[244] In other words, it had to show the consequences of the narrated events, as well as their original cause. In this way, the song tells the listener about an episode in the context of the whole Trojan War. It also relates a certain course of events from the *oimê*, which may be used as allusions in various parts of the song to make the listener aware of the consequences and importance of particular events in the story structure of the whole cycle.

The Third Song of Demodokos

What motivates the singer in the selection of songs and how he makes use of the traditional material is apparent in the third song of Demodokos.

The subject of Demodokos's third song is suggested by the public. Odysseus's identity is not yet revealed, so no one knows who he really is. Therefore, when he asks for a song about the wooden horse, only he knows it will be about him. For everyone else it is a story about the Trojan War, so well known that Odysseus assumes Demodokos must know it. Thus, he turns to the *aoidos* (8.486–498):

> δὴ τότε Δημόδοκον προσέφη πολύμητις Ὀδυσσεύς·
> Δημόδοκ', ἔξοχα δή σε βροτῶν αἰνίζομ' ἁπάντων·
> ἢ σέ γε Μοῦσ' ἐδίδαξε, Διὸς πάϊς, ἢ σέ γ' Ἀπόλλων·
> λίην γὰρ κατὰ κόσμον Ἀχαιῶν οἶτον ἀείδεις,

244 In the invocation to the *Iliad* (1.6) that beginning is marked as a quarrel between Achilles and Agamemnon. West 2011:80 states: "But τὰ πρῶτα indicates that it is the beginning of a story rather than a point in the middle of a continuous saga."

> ὅσσ' ἔρξαν τ' ἔπαθόν τε καὶ ὅσσ' ἐμόγησαν Ἀχαιοί,
> ὥς τέ που ἢ αὐτὸς παρεὼν ἢ ἄλλου ἀκούσας.
> ἀλλ' ἄγε δὴ μετάβηθι καὶ ἵππου κόσμον ἄεισον
> δουρατέου, τὸν Ἐπειὸς ἐποίησεν σὺν Ἀθήνῃ,
> ὅν ποτ' ἐς ἀκρόπολιν δόλῳ ἤγαγε δῖος Ὀδυσσεὺς
> ἀνδρῶν ἐμπλήσας, οἳ Ἴλιον ἐξαλάπαξαν.
> αἴ κεν δή μοι ταῦτα κατὰ μοῖραν καταλέξῃς,
> αὐτίκα καὶ πᾶσιν μυθήσομαι ἀνθρώποισιν,
> ὡς ἄρα τοι πρόφρων θεὸς ὤπασε θέσπιν ἀοιδήν."

> Then spoke to Demodokos wily Odysseus:
> "Demodokos, above all mortals I praise you.
> Either the Muse, the daughter of Zeus, or Apollo himself taught you,
> for having regard for order, you sing of the fate of the Achaeans:
> how much they achieved, and how much they toiled and suffered,
> as if you had been there yourself, or heard it from someone [who was].
> But change your theme, and sing a song about the wooden horse,
> which was built by Epeios with Athena's help,
> and then through guile it was brought to the acropolis by divine Odysseus,
> having first been filled with warriors, who sacked Ilion.
> If you sing for me properly this tale,
> I will immediately to all people declare,
> how the kind god had endowed you with inspired song."

Odysseus not only gives the singer the subject, "a song about the wooden horse," but also the outline of the plot: it was built by Epeios "together with" Athena, guilefully brought into the acropolis by Odysseus, having first been filled with warriors, who then took the city. Therefore, Odysseus not only indicates the theme, but also its most important points, which he should take into account. Not only the content of the song is important, but also how it is presented. Odysseus sets a condition, to present everything κατὰ μοῖραν (*kata moiran*), as previously he praised Demodokos for performing the earlier song κατὰ κόσμον (*kata kosmon*). Both Ford and Finkelberg understand these synonymous terms to mean maintaining the presented scenes in the paratactic order of events. Ford only tries to specify that κατὰ μοῖραν suggests taking into account the small details of the story.[245] Nagy's semantic analysis of the noun μοῖρα indicates that

245 Ford 1992:122–124; Finkelberg 1998:124–126.

moira, "ration, share, part," works as a synonym of αἶσα (*aisa*) 'destiny, fate', and also of the expressions κατὰ μοῖραν / κατ' αἶσαν 'in accordance with destiny', and also probably may preserve its original meaning as 'a piece of meat', which refers to someone's due share in the community's division of a sacrificial animal.[246] The expression κατὰ μοῖραν, therefore. means "in accordance with what befalls" or "in accordance with what is due." This inclines me to conclude that Demodokos's task is to take into account the given figure's rank and role played in the story. Odysseus, appearing incognito, has the immodest desire to have his role in the capture of Troy emphasized. That is why he is ready to praise far and wide the singer for his song, but not his talent.[247] Let us note that the listener's request imposes specific conditions to be fulfilled: only by stressing the achievements of the hero of the song can he be guaranteed appropriate amount of glory. The story, even if it is known, has to be modified. The singer or the listener makes a choice not only of the theme, but also as to which of the epic heroes becomes the object of praise. In view of the large number of epic heroes, it turns out to be important to indicate which one is most worthy of *kleos*.

Demodokos's third song is presented differently from the first. We are informed of the whole order of events, of which some are emphasized. Thus, it is no longer reminiscent of an invocation, but rather of a summary,[248] from which it transpires that Demodokos knows more events leading to the capture of Ilion than what Odysseus mentions (8.499–520):

> ὣς φάθ', ὁ δ' ὁρμηθεὶς θεοῦ ἤρχετο, φαῖνε δ' ἀοιδήν,
> ἔνθεν ἑλών, ὡς οἱ μὲν ἐϋσσέλμων ἐπὶ νηῶν
> βάντες ἀπέπλειον, πῦρ ἐν κλισίῃσι βαλόντες,
> Ἀργεῖοι, τοὶ δ' ἤδη ἀγακλυτὸν ἀμφ' Ὀδυσῆα
> εἵατ' ἐνὶ Τρώων ἀγορῇ κεκαλυμμένοι ἵππῳ·

246 Nagy 1999:134–135.

247 The translation of the last line depends on the understanding of the context of what is said. The predominant opinion is that Odysseus will not praise Demodokos for that one song that a "god had endowed," but for his ability in singing such songs. Of course, the skill of interesting storytelling is important, but that cannot be emphasized by Odysseus, for whom, as for the rest of the audience, skill in storytelling entails an enhanced visualization and emotional experience of events, which serves to confirm their veracity. Nor can he praise the singer for his knowledge of many *oimai*, though that too could be a reason for pride. He can only praise the *aoidos* for the song that he requested. As further analysis will show, Odysseus wants to praise the *aoidos* for this particular song.

248 Minchin (2001:197) connects the shape of the story with a typical Odysseyean presentation of a response to someone demanding information on a subject; that is why the story lacks any introduction (an abstract), which could be referred to in the conclusion (a resolution) or coda (the sequence, that is, of entrance talk, abstract, resolution, coda). That is how Minchin also explains why Demodokos's song is not a ring composition.

αὐτοὶ γάρ μιν Τρῶες ἐς ἀκρόπολιν ἐρύσαντο.
ὣς ὁ μὲν ἑστήκει, τοὶ δ' ἄκριτα πόλλ' ἀγόρευον
ἥμενοι ἀμφ' αὐτόν· τρίχα δέ σφισιν ἥνδανε βουλή,
ἠὲ διατμῆξαι κοῖλον δόρυ νηλέϊ χαλκῷ,
ἢ κατὰ πετράων βαλέειν ἐρύσαντας ἐπ' ἄκρης,
ἢ ἐάαν μέγ' ἄγαλμα θεῶν θελκτήριον εἶναι,
τῇ περ δὴ καὶ ἔπειτα τελευτήσεσθαι ἔμελλεν·
αἶσα γὰρ ἦν ἀπολέσθαι, ἐπὴν πόλις ἀμφικαλύψῃ
δουράτεον μέγαν ἵππον, ὅθ' εἵατο πάντες ἄριστοι
Ἀργεῖοι Τρώεσσι φόνον καὶ κῆρα φέροντες.
ἤειδεν δ' ὡς ἄστυ διέπραθον υἷες Ἀχαιῶν
ἱππόθεν ἐκχύμενοι, κοῖλον λόχον ἐκπρολιπόντες.
ἄλλον δ' ἄλλῃ ἄειδε πόλιν κεραϊζέμεν αἰπήν,
αὐτὰρ Ὀδυσσῆα προτὶ δώματα Δηϊφόβοιο
βήμεναι, ἠΰτ' Ἄρηα, σὺν ἀντιθέῳ Μενελάῳ.
κεῖθι δὴ αἰνότατον πόλεμον φάτο τολμήσαντα
νικῆσαι καὶ ἔπειτα διὰ μεγάθυμον Ἀθήνην.

so he spoke. Then he began, stimulated[249] by the god, and "wove" the song,
taking up the story when they embarked on well-built ships
and sailed away, having first set fire to the tents,
the Argives, and around glorious Odysseus
they were already pulled, hidden in the horse, to the Trojan agora;
for the Trojans themselves pulled it [the Horse] up to the acropolis.
As it [the Horse] stood, they [the Trojans] sat around it
and, gathered together, they discussed, unable to take a decision.
Three counsels seemed good:
either cleave[250] the hollow wood with pitiless bronze,[251]
or drag it up the scarp and cast it down onto the rocks,
or leave it as a great gift to make amends with the gods[252]

249 Stimulation might mean falling into a trance. Such a situation often appears in shamanic songs. The singer gradually comes to, brought about by the sound of instruments, and trying his voice, often pronouncing disjointed words and syllables, without any association and quite uncoordinated, before he begins to sing the actual song (see Eliade 2001).

250 Perhaps διαπλῆξαι, "pierce."

251 This counsel is absent in the Proclus version, where the Trojans consider whether or not to push the horse over a precipice, burn it, or sacrifice it to Athena. This diversity is evidence of the existence of many versions and independent narratives of the *Odyssey*.

252 The horse serves the purpose of a memento or votive offering as a θελκτήριον for the gods—a magical way, that is, of attracting the gods to this place and/or appeasing their wrath.

and thus it was that they would proceed,
for it was their fate to perish, once the city enshrouds[253]
the great wooden horse, where sat the best
Argives, bringing the Trojans death and destruction.
He sang how the sons of Achaeans destroyed the city
pouring out of the horse, abandoning the hollowed-out trap.
He sang of others, how in other places they sacked the lofty city,
and of Odysseus, who went to the palace of Deiphobos,
like Ares, with equally godlike Menelaos.
He described how they engaged in the most terrible fighting,
and finally triumphed with the aid of great-hearted Athena.

The improvisations of the singer are subjected to a framework of content and a hierarchy of people and actions. For a start, the *aoidos* preserves the traditional order of scenes known to him—that is, not strictly what is requested by Odysseus, but what is generally known in tradition, where the order of events is already established. Secondly, the singer makes a selection from the traditional sequence of events. The reason why he has to make a selection is to meet the expectations of the requester. Odysseus wants to be presented as the real conqueror of Troy and, regardless of what was sung in Demodokos's first song, as the victor in the dispute with Achilles over the title "the best of the Achaeans."

In the song, Demodokos omits events already known from other stories told by Menelaos (*Odyssey* 4.265–289) and Helen (*Odyssey* 4.235–264). The latter's relation of Odysseus's sneaking into Troy is an anticipation of his guileful feat in having the Horse brought into the city. The selection of themes is not in order to economize on narrative and avoid repeating what the audience of the *Odyssey* already knows (by comparison, the author of the *Iliad* often repeats facts). The selection is made, rather, to emphasize certain events in the episode of the epic and ignore others, which to us might seem more important or much better known. This serves a functional purpose. In his relation of the song, the narrator invokes a sequence of events in the story of the capture of Troy, which the singer has selected to appropriately present the achievements of Odysseus. The narrator's summary of Demodokos's song only hints at the feats of others, ἄλλον δ' ἄλλῃ, while foregrounding those of Odysseus. The slaying of Deiphobos "in the most terrible fighting" means slaying the leader of the Trojans, for after the deaths of Hektor and Paris, it was Deiphobos who held this position. This feat is, therefore, equivalent to

253 It is possible that use of the word ἀμφικαλύψῃ 'cast over, covered' is not only a synonym of "conceal," but also gives the original play of words typical for an oracle.

Achilles' slaying of Hektor in the *Iliad*.[254] The heroic image of Odysseus as the conqueror of Troy, who captures the city not only through deception, but also by valor in fighting, is thus realized.[255]

Indeed, in the *Odyssey*, Odysseus's achievements are not limited to artful trickery. For the author of the *Odyssey*, it is essential that, like other heroes, he should manifest his heroism in fighting. The slaying of the suitors and earlier his duel with the beggar Iros reveal Odysseus's βίη (*biê*), "strength." Thus does Odysseus make his claim to the title of "best of the Achaeans."[256] Braswell has pointed out that Demodokos's second song corresponds to a situation that occurs during the Phaeacian sports *agôn*. Euryalos, the son of Alkinoos, mocks Odysseus, provoking him to take part in the contest. In the song the slow Hephaistos defeats the handsome and fast but unintelligent Ares with deception. As Braswell notes, this corresponds to the image of Odysseus and Euryalos, who is good looking but thoughtless (Euryalos scornfully notes that the guest does not look like an athlete; Odysseus in turn says he cannot run in the race because his legs were weakened after a long sea voyage). Alkinoos tries to stop the dispute from escalating and calls for entertainment. The singer seems to react to the situation by presenting a story that reflects the problem resulting from the dispute, but now transferred to the world of the gods. The intention of this story is to transform anger into laughter. Euryalos draws a conclusion from this story and offers Odysseus a reward analogous to the one offered to Hephaistos in compensation for the insult he suffered.[257] With Braswell's observation, we see that all three of Demodokos's songs fit the context of this situation, and Euryalos's reaction shows that epic narratives are read by the participants of the performance as communications with a hidden message, just like Aesop's fables, which often functioned as a warning.[258] But that is only part of the truth. For the author of the *Odyssey*, Odysseus's triumph over Euryalos serves to achieve more far-reaching goals. Demodokos's first song presents Odysseus's dispute with Achilles, with unknown result. Finkelberg rightly sees the dispute resolved in the third song, where, thanks to his ingenuity, Odysseus becomes the real conqueror of Troy. In the epic tradition, Achilles is presented in the same

254 Here, Hektor might even be ignored because the status of Deiphobos is determined by his marriage with Helen after the death of Paris.

255 H. Parry (1994:13–15) suggests that even the many lies of Odysseus in the *Odyssey* are almost every time justified and have a certain quality of nobility, since they do not stem from any low motives of the hero who resorts to them.

256 Nagy (1999) only notes in accordance with the scholia that Odysseus, who had craft (δόλος), was in conflict with Achilles, who had greater βίη 'strength', for the title of 'best of the Achaeans', ἄριστος Ἀχαιῶν.

257 Braswell 1982.

258 See p. 490, below.

way as Euryalos and Ares—as young, handsome, and swift-footed. Demodokos's second song suggests Odysseus's superiority over Achilles, whose heroic image proves worthless in the face of the former's guile and intellect. The dispute with Euryalos, therefore, also serves to mark this advantage of the protagonist of the *Odyssey* over the protagonist of the *Iliad* or, more probably, over Achilles as the principal character of other songs of the Trojan War—of the whole tradition, that is, of the Trojan Cycle. For the author of the poem, the success achieved through guile, so typical for Odysseus, was insufficient. That is why it is essential for Odysseus to win the discus-throwing contest, so as to prove he is more powerful than all the rest. And that is why the third of Demodokos's songs is necessary. It reveals that this hero combines in his action both skills: craftiness and bravery.

Thus, in the epic code, the slaying of Deiphobos means the slaying of a son of Priam, which should have been reserved for Achilles. The aspect selected to be emphasized even concerns the same scene. Proclus's summary of the *Ilioupersis* adds that Deiphobos not only took over command after Hektor, but also married Helen after the death of Paris. Moreover, the poem recounts that the beauty of the naked Helen prevents her first husband from killing her. The pluralists argued that Demodokos's songs were later additions of poets relying on "real" Homer, and that the only significance of this scene was the slaying of the enemy leader. But the significance is more complex: it is Homer who selects from the traditional sequence of scenes only those that reveal the heroism of Odysseus.[259] The participation of Odysseus in the duel between Menelaos and Deiphobos indicates that in the adaptation of traditional material to the needs of a performance there is room not only for the performer's selection, but also for invention.

Demodokos's song is biased,[260] but then so is the whole of the *Odyssey*. In Trojan Cycle epics, the image of Odysseus is far from glorious.[261] The aim of the singer in the *Odyssey* is to praise this hero, for the epic song, in accordance with Aristotle's testimony, as well as of Indo-European comparative studies, should

[259] Aristotle (*Poetics* 1451a23–30) notes that Homer is selective about episodes from the life of Odysseus. He points out that Homer omitted those details considered unessential or improbable in relation to the *Odyssey* story. Therefore, Homer was guided by what he considered to be the "organic whole" of the work.

[260] Compare Scodel 2002:83: "Demodokos's song of the Trojan horse certainly is performed in response to Odysseus's request and serves to prepare the audience for Odysseus's own narrative. It can serve Odysseus's needs precisely because Demodokos is not singing with the purpose of praising a known patron. Demodokos has no axe to grind; his praise of Odysseus therefore rings true."

[261] This is apparent, as was previously noted by Finkelberg, in cyclic poem scenes involving Odysseus, as well as later poetry, especially tragedies.

be defined as a song of praise.[262] The singer will not refrain from altering traditional material, from selecting scenes, or altering semantic accents to expose the virtues of his hero.[263] Likewise, the author of the *Iliad* has a biased approach and even alters Achilles' past, so as to accentuate the changes in the hero's character, and consequently the tragedy of his fate.[264]

The songs of Odysseus's return and the wrath of Achilles may, therefore, be diversely presented, and the portrayal of the same scenes might be very different from the ones we know. The same song theme can be presented in various ways, without altering the basic course of events. In this sense, the factor of creativity in the making of oral songs was always bound by the restrictions of tradition. On the other hand, provided it adopted the established traditional pattern, an epic song could be created spontaneously, freely selecting its starting point in the story cycle. This is a system allowing for the creation of new songs that in no way lose their traditional nature. Every song grows out of a cycle as an integral part and, at the same time, as an autonomous element. The creation of songs at such moments is desired but also unnoticed. A new song is, from the start, a traditional song. A new song does not go beyond the cycle, instead it accentuates episodes that might have been previously seen and presented in a different way.[265] The singer's, as well as his audience's, knowledge of the cycle allows the song to be placed as an element in context and in reference to other events.[266]

262 Nagy 1999:293–295. Ford (1992:200–201), like many prior scholars, assumes that epic, as a poetry of praise, "changed its goal" and stopped praising the ruler; it was originally panegyric. However, I believe that this evolutionary model is too simple: the praise of the patron was formulated in such a way that he came to be perceived as a hero of the past and was, thus, subject to heroization (see Zieliński 2006:134–137, 145). Again, we should refer to the aforementioned passage in *Beowulf* (lines 867–882), illustrating the mechanism of introducing a contemporary figure to the epic tradition (Zieliński 2015a:46–47). In praising Beowulf, the vassal "changes the words" of the song—that is, he praised Beowulf's feat in terms of the song already known to him of Sigemund.

263 Kelly (2008:177–182) argues that obvious changes in the representations of some events in the utterances of epic characters in relation to what happens in the narrative of the epic disclose the characters' bias resulting from persuasive needs. The listeners thus get two versions of events and, in view of the clear bias of the epic heroes (Achilles *Iliad* 1.384–386, Odysseus *Odyssey* 23.310–343, Persephone *Hymn to Demeter* 413), they recognize the truth of the version previously told *in extenso*. This indicates, according to Kelly, the freedom and bias in the presentation in the performance practice of the *aoidoi*.

264 See Ch. 6, below.

265 According to Scodel (2002:53–54), the words of Telemachos (1.351–352) refer to a new song in the singer's repertoire. According to Ford (see above, n235), they refer to a new theme.

266 Scodel (2002:34) cites an interesting parallel with the *wayang kulit* shadow puppet theatre of Java: "*Dhalangs* [puppeteers] regularly invent stories, using the traditional characters and story types in slightly new arrangements. Their terminology distinguishes "trunk" stories from "branch" stories, and although their definitions of these terms differ, they recognize a canonical structure that is not changeable, as well as considerable room for invention. Moreover, the stories from the earlier parts of the epic tradition have fallen out of the repertory." The puppeteers meet the

The cycle therefore appears to us as an established and widely known sequence of events. The theme of a song evokes in listeners many associations with other themes in a given cycle. But the singer never needs to repeat every theme; it was enough that for the singer and the audience to know about them. He could emphasize some scenes at the cost of others, and he could even slightly alter their contents and meaning so as to reveal to the listeners new aspects of already known events. Nonetheless, he is not allowed to change the basic events or their meaning. But even slight modifications can change the role played by a given character in the macro-story and turn antiheroic Odysseus into a hero protagonist. The limits to which a good singer is subjected are signaled by Odysseus. The singer is to present the song "in order," κατὰ κόσμον (8.489). He, therefore, expects a certain order of events—that is, the traditional scenes of the story. The song itself is called by Odysseus κόσμος (ἵππου κόσμον ἄεισον δουρατέου, "sing for me the order [i.e. the song] of the wooden horse").[267] The traditional sequence of events, in turn, obliges the singer to also duly honor specific deeds as κατὰ μοῖραν (8.496). The song is, therefore, constantly an element of tradition, and the singer needs to make it praise a given hero.

The presentation of an epic assumes two important premises, which will be further specified in subsequent chapters. The first is that there exists a certain sequence of scenes in the cycle—the "super-text" or, rather, "super-story" to which the singer refers. The second is a clear sequence of events, with a beginning and end. The singer could, however, select the beginning and end of a series of events. It depended on what kind of perspective the song should have. The author of the *Odyssey* presents Demodokos's first and third song fairly tersely, but clearly enough to tell us that both took the perspective of the whole war. Their beginnings and endings for the perspective of the whole war are, however, different from those of the "super-text" in the *Iliad*. This was probably typical of every cyclic epic song performance: individual singers saw the beginning and end in various places, though traditionally there were a limited number of places in the epic story with which the events of the Trojan War were linked.

Demodokos's Second Song

Demodokos's first song presents the cause of events from the perspective of Odysseus's involvement in the Trojan War. The quarrel between Achilles and Odysseus, which occurs during the "feast of the gods," must result from the rivalry of the heroes which was essential to the conquest of Troy—though in

expectations of their patrons: "The *dhalang* was able to generate a 'new' story that satisfied the patron" (36).

267 Finkelberg (1998:126) interprets κόσμος as a synonym of "song."

epic language it would rather be said: "which of them will take Troy." We have already noted that despite the length of the song, the external public does not recognize the contents, having at their disposal only predictions similar to the invocations of other Homeric poems. Limiting the report to the invocation no doubt results from the supposition that the whole song would reveal the outcome of such a dispute and, therefore, the actual winner and loser. Noticing Odysseus's sadness, Alkinoos finally interrupts the song, which might suggest that the listener does not receive an answer to the result of the dispute. The matter remains unresolved, and it is Odysseus who eventually asks the singer to present the capture of Troy in such a way so as to expose the role of none other than Odysseus. To Menelaos's and Helen's earlier stories about Odysseus's guiles during the capture of the city, the third song adds another element: the fight with Deiphobos. This feat raises the status of the hero's achievements, making them equal to those of Achilles.[268] We may assume that traditionally, the fight was only between the two husbands of Helen. Odysseus was added to the fight in Demodokos's song. This does not alter the tradition in any essential way, but it does transform it somewhat. Thus, the author of the *Odyssey* presents Odysseus as the real conqueror of the city and the victor of the initial dispute. It may also mean that the perception of Odysseus as the conqueror of Troy may not necessarily be traditional. It is only the *Odyssey* that emphasizes that Odysseus's idea of introducing the wooden horse to Troy enabled the capture the city. Ergo, if the later post-Homeric tradition depicted Odysseus as the conqueror of Troy, it could only be due to the version preserved by the *Odyssey*.

For scholars, Demodokos's second song seemed so unconnected with the other two that one way or another its differences were defined on the level of function and form. It was assumed to be a hymn-like *prooimion* to an actual epic (though here it would precede a dancing or athletic *agôn*), or an interlude, or even a lyrical song on account of the dancing. Unlike the other two songs, Demodokos performed it to the general public gathered in the agora. For many analysts, this, together with the whole passage about the contests in the agora, was a novella by a younger poet, artificially added in between the songs sung at the court of King Alkinoos. After all, Odysseus praises the *aoidos* for the first song but seems not to notice the second song at all. Moreover, the song is described in a completely different way from the others, giving the impression of a precise citation. However, let us note that all three songs are described differently, and this might indicate an intentional strategy of the author of the *Odyssey*. Let us infer that the second song is an integral part of the plot. It has

[268] Here, also we may find an analogy to the aforementioned *Beowulf* passage where the actions of the main protagonist are compared with the heroism of Sigemund.

been observed that the story of Hephaistos ensnaring Ares is also an anticipation of what will occur on Ithaca, and this is another piece of evidence that this passage is an integral part of the work.[269] While the Muse influences the singer to sing in the first song about heroes—*klea andrôn*, that is—in the second song, the singer himself decides that now the theme should be about gods—*klea theôn*.

In our analysis we shall concentrate only on the start or introduction of the song, 8.268–269:

> ὡς τὰ πρῶτα μίγησαν ἐν Ἡφαίστοιο δόμοισι
> λάθρῃ
>
> how at first they united in the house of Hephaistos
> secretly

Nagy notes that the syntax of the statement is appropriate for introducing the main theme of the performance and includes the concept of "a beginning," *ta prôta*, "that has cosmogonic implications."[270] This observation leads to the conclusion that this is not the two lovers' first encounter, but the marking of the beginning of a story, and it is a story that goes beyond the love affair between Ares and Aphrodite.[271]

Marked is the beginning of the divine plan. But what is the significance of this beginning and what end does it correspond to? Let us start by saying it is comparable to marking the beginning of the war in the divine plan, which we have called the cosmogonic and cosmological frame. The beginning of the divine plan, which includes Gaia complaining to Zeus, Zeus consulting Themis, and the marriage of Peleus and Thetis, corresponds to the human plan: the Judgment of Paris and abduction of Helen. In the *Iliad*, the referents of the beginning are connected with Paris's fault in violating the rules of hospitality, as well as the collective fault of the Trojans—their collective responsibility results from the fact that they stood on the side of the one breaking moral law, but in the story it is shown as Pandaros's breaking of the truce, guaranteed by sacrifices and oaths, which is a transgression calling for the vengeance of the gods. At the same time, Helen is absolved (by Priam), though in tradition there certainly

269 Rose 1969b:172–178; Andersen 1977:13; Alden 2000:2–3, and 2017:329–340. Burkert (1960) also found analogies with the myths and rituals of the Middle East, which, according to Nagy, contradicts scholarly suggestions of interpolation and points, rather, toward an archaism (Nagy 2010:88–89).

270 Nagy 2010:87.

271 Compare *Iliad* 1.6.

were also versions where she was still burdened with guilt.[272] The fault of the Trojans brings about disaster, the fall of Troy.

Demodokos's second song is about marital infidelity, a violation of moral law. Grave violation of moral law is a constant element in the structure of myth. By comparing tragedies with epic poems, Richard Seaford has concluded that Homer's epics avoided or toned down themes of incest, family murder, or other drastic moral transgressions.[273] In this song, the whole situation is also underplayed by treating it with humor. The victim gets his revenge, but it is bloodless and devoid of cruelty. Hephaistos is satisfied to receive material compensation, promised to him by Poseidon, who is a relative of the unfaithful wife. By accepting the ransom, Hephaistos refrains from bloody revenge (*Odyssey* 8.344–359). A similar situation occurs in the *Iliad*: Aias provides an excuse for Achilles by saying that even the family of a murder victim accepts a ransom and refrains from taking revenge (*Iliad* 9.632–636). By refusing the ransom offer, Achilles proceeds cruelly. He does not help the Achaeans, which results in their defeat and the shedding of blood. Then, after Patroklos's death, Achilles again refuses a ransom and instead takes bloody revenge. Similarly, Odysseus remains insensitive to any pleas or attempts of mediation from the suitors and is compelled to retaliate in a gory manner. It is the task of heroes like Odysseus or Achilles to take revenge, and it must be brutal and bloody. In none of these situations, however, is the hero forced to make a difficult moral decision; no moral norm is transgressed in such a way that could bring him shame. Achilles' grave transgression is the overlong maltreatment of the corpse of his defeated enemy. How was that to blemish his character? The hero's "sin" was carefully chosen.

Though the story of the love affair between Ares and Aphrodite is an anticipation of what occurs on Ithaca, or even an alternative version in which the hero encounters at home an unfaithful wife, the listener must establish the parallels between the events. In this regard, the similarities between the god Hephaistos and the returning hero are suggestive. Nagy notes that the theme

272 Hence, the ambiguity regarding Helen's culpability, which poses such a problem for scholars (Ryan 1965; Groten 1968; Collins 1988; Austin 1994; Graver 1995; Mayer 1996; Ebbott 1999; Roisman 2006; Blondell 2010, Zieliński 2021b). It is difficult to reconcile Helen's self-accusation with Priam's judgment. The ambivalence about Helen's fault persists in lyric poetry: some blame her, others exonerate her.

273 Seaford 1994:11–13. This probably concerns a Panathenaic tradition or, more specifically, the *Iliad* and *Odyssey*. In other poems, crimes are very dramatically described. For example, although the *Iliad* and *Odyssey* often describe abductions, they never mention rapes, whereas cyclic poetry does tell us of Aias, the son of Oileus, raping Kassandra. The poems of Homer do not directly state the sacrifice of Iphigenia, the murder of Agamemnon by his wife Klytaimestra, the need for Orestes to kill his mother, the incest and patricide committed by Oedipus, etc.

of the lameness of the blacksmith god is repeated in Odysseus's complaint that his legs are weakened by long sea voyages.[274] Odysseus uses this as an excuse to refrain from the race during the athletics competition on Scheria. One should add that this quality contrasts with Achilles' swift-footedness, which is not only his distinctive feature but also belongs to any young hero who is a protagonist in the oral epic tradition. Lacking this quality, Odysseus appears as an antihero, which is consistent with his traditional image as a trickster using deception (originally probably also magic),[275] and not heroic strength. Someone strong/young/swift being defeated by someone who is weaker/older/slower has the pattern of many of Aesop's fables, where the wronged individual, seemingly unable to get his own back, has a specific quality, or the help of an extraordinary friend, or ultimately the support of Zeus, as the guarantor of *dikê*, which enables him to take revenge. This is a form of wisdom typical of an oral culture, where the narrative performs the function of applying to the situation and context a warning in the form of a puzzle for the culprit. Such situations also have their comical aspect, which is used by Homer.[276] The strong similarity between Hephaistos and Odysseus continues when the latter is exposed to ridicule. Hephaistos's trap evokes laughter among the gods, who are amused by Hephaistos's surprising means of revenge. Thus, this lame deity eased the tension at the feast of the gods by playing the role of an absurd cupbearer (*Iliad* 1.584–600). Similarly, Odysseus becomes the object of ridicule when he engages in a boxing duel with the beggar Iros or when he reaches for a bow, as if he were just clowning about.

The reason why Odysseus as a vagabond and later a beggar should be likened to Hephaistos is explained in Demodokos's second song. The humiliated and unappreciated god is able to get his revenge by preparing a trap. In a similar way, Odysseus achieves victory over the suitors. If the story in the song is the beginning, its end must be the events on Ithaca after Odysseus's return home. Here, however, arises the difficulty of seeing how the love affair between

274 Nagy 2010:90.

275 Zieliński 2020:187–200.

276 Exposing Ares and Aphrodite to ridicule is consistent with the model of using the power of laughter in iambic blame poetry. Blame excludes an individual from the community because having their fault named tarnishes their reputation and exposes the community to danger: an individual's misdeed might provoke the punishment of the gods, which will affect the whole community. The laughter of the group makes it impossible for the individual who has been blamed to seek its support and makes it difficult to exact revenge on his accuser. However, attacking others with words has such serious consequences that the accuser is also in danger. In order to avoid the shamed person's retaliation, various safeguards are applied to the behavior of both the individual and the community. One of these is playing the jester, wherein the attacker expresses self-depreciation and thus removes the motive of the other side to seek revenge (see Zieliński 2004:211–212; Zieliński 2010:199–200).

Ares and Aphrodite can lead to Odysseus's recovery of his wife. How would the unfaithfulness of Aphrodite move the course of events to Odysseus's purging the suitors from his house? Searching for such logical and direct consequences of events is not usual in oral culture. What is typical, however, is for the deities to set the course of events in which mortals are later involved, and this becomes the epic theme. Marking in a tale, that is in a particular song, the place where the macro-story begins, helps listeners to place that song in a broader course of events. But the episode of the beginning (here in the form of a digression) serves simultaneously as an anticipation of the end of both the story and the macro-story. Therefore, a mention of the beginning is also an allusion to the image of the end. Between both images there is a relation of causality: what will happen is caused by what did happen at the beginning. It introduces tension into the story, which rouses the interests and expectations of the listeners. After all, the story of mortal heroes, once entered into the cosmogonic frame, becomes a part of cosmic events.

If *a* denotes the story of Odysseus's role in the Trojan War, and *b* the story of the cunning husband exacting revenge for the stealing of his wife, we obtain the following pattern of events:

a1—b1—a2—b2

The number one denotes the start of the macro-story, and two denotes its end. The end is the solution to the problem that arises at the beginning.

The song referring to the start of the Trojan War—Demodokos's first song, marked here as *a1*—includes a reference to the cosmogonic framework in the citation of Zeus's plan. This is similar to other songs of the cycle, the *Kypria* and *Iliad*, where references are also made to Zeus's plan as the original cause of the events. Zeus's plan, in one way or another, involves the total or partial obliteration of humanity. This decision results from a disruption in the order of things. Order was built on moral principles, even if these had not yet been normatively formulated as they would later be in literary culture. The tone of some Greek myths has led many scholars to question whether such moral principles were applied in Greek religion at all. Such a conclusion is irrational because Greek gods, and especially Zeus, from the beginning were seen as the guarantors of the existence of world order.[277] Reasons for the Trojan War are always associated with disorder in the world, and in particular with moral disorder. Earth complains about the noise made by people and, on account of their multitude, their crushing weight. Zeus therefore plans to start wars over Thebes and Troy. In another version, Momos gives Zeus insidious advice to arrange a

[277] Lloyd-Jones 1971.

marriage between a mortal and a goddess and thus bring misery to humanity. The marriage of Peleus with Thetis disrupts the order of things and the fateful consequence for the world is the birth of Achilles. The suffering and death of people is a way to restore the correct order of things.[278]

The almost innocent playfulness of the gods, therefore, had to result in the death of many people so as to restore moral order. Odysseus restores world order by taking revenge and restoring order to his home, where the moral order had been violated many times: attempts to seduce his wife, attempts to deprive his son and heir of his property and even his life, and violation of hospitality rules (described as the "devouring" of property).[279] Such an adding up of wrongs is characteristic in oral poetry. Behind Odysseus's revenge stands the categorical imperative to protect home and family. It is not by chance that Aphrodite meets Ares nowhere else than in the home, in the bed she should share only with Hephaistos. Demodokos's second song shows a scene that may be described as the first case of adultery. Aphrodite's infidelity is, therefore, the original reason for misfortunes threatening the family. To us it might seem strange that this original sin should be committed by a goddess and not a mortal, but in the broader perspective of comparative mythology comparanda emerge. The bathing of Aphrodite and the Charites dressing her in new clothes in her sanctuary in Cyprus, to which the goddess returned (*Odyssey* 8.62–366), also suggest ritual cleansing.[280] But the cleansing of a single goddess does not cleanse the whole world, where adultery remains forever. This is not so much a story with a universal message as an association, in a way typical of oral culture, of a traditional image with a concrete example. The wisdom of the tale is not of a universal nature, but it is used for a specific situation where it can apply.[281]

Therefore, if we look at the composition of the *Odyssey*, we will notice that this particular song, seemingly unconnected with anything else, is a key

278 But only Hesiod speaks of the transgressions of successive generations of mortals (heroes) directly (*Works and Days* 109–201).

279 For the association of avarice with "devouring," see Nagy 1999:222–232; Zieliński 2010:206–208.

280 A similar description of the bathing of Aphrodite attended by the Charites is found in *Kypria* fr. 5 W. Scholars usually associate this description with preparing her to compete in the Judgment of Paris. Similarities in the two descriptions are not so much imitation as a traditional epic image. However, the oral poet did not use this image by chance, for it was always associated with a specific significance. Linking the bathing of Aphrodite with the Judgment of Paris might mean this goddess was perceived as the initiator of the misery in the epic macro-story. The actions of Kypris set in motion the course of events in the Trojan War similar to the way in which the chain of events is set in the return of Odysseus. Perhaps this justifies the title of the poem *Kypria*, "Cypriot Tales." The appropriateness of this title is a subject of discussion—scholars have argued for the possible link of the author with the work's Cyprian content; see also Currie 2016:202: "Cyprus would also be a plausible place to locate the early receptions of Dumuzi-Inanna songs and *Gilgamesh* into Greek hexameter poetry."

281 See Zieliński 2015b:295–302.

reference point to the significance of the whole poem. The whole *Odyssey* plot is its consequence and fulfillment.

Differences between Homer and the Cycle

Let us now follow the basic arguments pointing to differences between cyclic songs and the poems of Homer. In the analysis of the songs of Demodokos, while it is hard to find ontological differences, teleological ones might exist to such an extent that we might argue that these songs are basically dissimilar.

Finkelberg has endeavored to list the most significant characteristics of Homer's poems:[282]

1. structural unity, achieved by transforming a traditional saga in accordance with the requirements of an organic composition,
2. narrative diversity, achieved through a very large number of digressions as part of the main plot,
3. introduction of new episodes of the poet's own invention, thanks to the intensive use of the "imitation" strategy,
4. the Homeric style, which unlike cyclic poetry is characterized by the plentiful use of various speeches and the individualization of figures, as indicated in the testimony of Aristotle (*Poetics* 24).

With regard to the first characteristic, I have already mentioned that Finkelberg does not take into account the integrity of oral song and only notices parataxis as the principle of creation. In accordance with the ring composition rule, scenes returning to the start of the song serve as referents to its end, and thus allow the listeners to encompass the basic ideas expressed in the work. The bracket thus closed by the ring composition is not, however, identical with the attaining of the goal of the story (in the case of the *Iliad*, it is the death of Achilles). The Homeric "organic whole" is also based on the selection and processing of events contained in the cyclic tradition. The choice depends on how the main hero needs to be praised, though it is possible to make even radical changes to his traditional image. Transforming the myth—characteristically for Homer—serves not only the immediate context, but often also foretells the outcome of the plot. The events on Ithaca in the *Odyssey* are predicted by, for example, the tales of Menelaos and Helen about the exploits of Odysseus, the song of Demodokos about the romance between Ares and Aphrodite, and the tale of Odysseus escaping from Polyphemus's cave.[283] All of these present

282 Finkelberg 1998:155.

283 See Ch. 2, pp. 245–246, below.

the pattern of a stronger opponent being defeated by an emphatically weaker one. They constantly prepare for the final showdown, i.e. the killing of the suitors. Therefore, the singer basically intends to introduce an episode implying praise of the hero. But it might be preceded by actions that introduce the listener to what will follow. All references are to the main episode. Organic unity results from what the performance requires.

As far as digressiveness is concerned, even Proclus's cursory summary of the *Kypria* (3–4) allows us to notice the presence of even elaborate digressions: Nestor tells Menelaos about how Epopeus seduced the daughter of Lykurgos and besieged the city, the story of Oedipus, the madness of Herakles, and Theseus and Ariadne. And all of this is told in one sitting. The typicality of digressions is also confirmed in the poetry of Hesiod. It even seems to be immanently associated with the paratactic style, which allows for the development of diverse subjects or themes in the linked catalogue chain. The catalogues in the *Theogony* are, however, subordinated to the main idea of praising world-ordering Zeus, which affects the selection, organization, and transformation of traditional material.

Properly understood, the rules of imitation also do not seem to be a distinguishing feature of Homer. As has already been shown, this was a rather general practice among singers, allowing them to emphasize particular episodes in the cycle and also to include new ones.

Aristotle's testimony regarding the large number of speeches is relevant, but not in every case, as it only applies to other written cyclic poems. The development of speeches and the individualization of characters was actually typical of a broader tradition. How else could so many of the formulae that are used in the speeches be developed? In a minimal way, we might assume that this is a specifically Homeric style in certain circles, such as the singers' "guild"—the Homeridai or Kreophyleoi. It is also difficult to discern an essential difference in this regard, since the performance of epics in Homer's day was based on rivalry and singing contests. Would just one singer show off with the abundance of speeches and the individualization of characters and all other singers limit themselves to the "meager" possibilities offered by tradition?[284]

As evidence of the "colorless" style of cyclic poems, a passage from the *Little Iliad* is often presented (Tzetzes in Lycophron 1268):

> αὐτὰρ Ἀχιλλῆος μεγαθύμου φαίδιμος υἱὸς
> Ἑκτορέην ἄλοχον κάταγεν κοίλας ἐπὶ νῆας
> παῖδα δ' ἑλὼν ἐκ κόλπου ἐϋπλοκάμοιο τιθήνης

[284] Of course, it is difficult to say whether Demodokos was a typical *aoidos* or rather an ideal representation of how Homer imagined an *aoidos*. Demodokos's second song, however, contains expressions in the *oratio recta* form.

> ῥῖψε ποδὸς τεταγὼν ἀπὸ πύργου, τὸν δὲ πεσόντα
> ἔλλαβε πορφύρεος θάνατος καὶ μοῖρα κραταιή
>
> Then the wonderful son of the great Achilles
> led the wife of Hektor to the hollow ships,
> but her son he snatched from the nurse of beautiful plaited hair
> and holding his feet, cast him from the tower, who when he fell,
> was caught by purple death and cruel Moira.

It has been claimed these lines lack the pomp and pathos of Homer's style. Hainsworth directly asks: "Could not Neoptolemos speak, one wonders. Had Andromache no feelings? Had the poet no feelings?"[285] Finkelberg describes this style as impersonal.[286] In Homer's poetry we also find a mixture of elaborate and abbreviated styles. On the other hand, of course not every singer could simultaneously master both styles as well as Homer evidently did.

Is it at all satisfactory to contrast all other epics with the *Iliad* and *Odyssey*? Other epics, including the cyclic *Kypria*, have also been ascribed to Homer. Would the *Kypria* be traditional poetry and the *Iliad* a completely new, revolutionary narrative concept? If we assume such a qualitative difference in intensifying emotional impact, then most probably that would be the style of other works attributed to Homer, such as the *Thebaid* and the *Sack of Oichalia*. Burkert notes similarities in the presentation of the tragic fates of Achilles in the *Iliad* and Herakles in the *Sack of Oichalia*.[287] We may, therefore, speak of a certain trend in the epic style, appreciated more in later antiquity and connected with the authority of Homer. Jacoby's theory that the *Odyssey* was created by a poet from the school of Homer, the author of the *Iliad*, adopting the structural ideas of that great epic, would be easier to accept when viewed more broadly as a trend of development, in accord with Burkert's suggestion of Homeridai and Kreophyleoi.[288]

We assume that every cyclic song concentrates on just one episode but also conveys an image of the whole Trojan War. The *Iliad*, also concentrating on a single episode, alludes to what happened at Troy, the cause of the war, and its result. That the *Iliad* does not directly recount the whole war does not distinguish it from the rest of tradition. We cannot say for certain whether other cyclic poems directly told the whole story of the war, as is suggested by Aristotle with regard to the *Kypria* and the *Little Iliad*. The differences between Proclus's summary and the extant fragments indicate that these cyclic works

285 Hainsworth 1970:97.

286 Finkelberg 1998:156.

287 Burkert 1972:82–85.

288 Burkert 1972; see Graziosi 2002:208–217.

are characterized by allusions to events preceding and following on from the main narrative—that is, to the causes and consequences of the war. Like the *Iliad*, they refer to the macro-story present in the minds of the performers and their listeners, and this awareness to which poets refer allows them to freely create new details.

Such a poem is not a catalogue because—as shall be shown in subsequent chapters—the poet refers to the listeners' knowledge of all the main events of the war, including those related in the song, as well as to the fate of individual heroes. The poet can, then, play a game with the listeners, affecting their emotions and leaving them to some extent uncertain how the story will turn out, whether or not it will happen in accordance with the listeners' knowledge and expectations. The effectiveness of this game, which is determined by the poet's ability to create atmospheres of fear and relief, pathos and irony, depends on the talent of the song's performer, who is also at the same time the author. Therefore, despite the seeming canonicity of the main events, listeners have the feeling that they are experiencing something at once new and at the same time close to their heart; something that is easy for them to imagine and judge, which preserves the charm of the extraordinary, in all its color, splendor and mystery. In this respect, the *Iliad* is no different from other cyclic poems or from other songs about Achilles' wrath against Agamemnon. The difference may only be the degree of perfection in using allusions to evoke feelings in the listener—that is, the ability to conduct a dialogue with the listener.

The Place of the *Iliad* in the Cycle Story

One of the first confirmations of the above interpretation of the Cycle and cyclic song is the question of the place of the *Iliad* within the Cycle. The use of allusions indicates to the listener not only to which macro-story the song belongs, but also where it is situated within the framework. Serving the latter purpose is Odysseus's mention of the prophecy of Kalchas that the suffering at Troy was drawing to an end and soon the city would be taken. A similar effect is produced by a reference to Philoktetes in the Catalogue of Ships, at a time when he was absent from Troy (*Iliad* 2.721–725):

> ἀλλ' ὃ μὲν ἐν νήσῳ κεῖτο κρατέρ' ἄλγεα πάσχων
> Λήμνῳ ἐν ἠγαθέῃ, ὅθι μιν λίπον υἷες Ἀχαιῶν
> ἕλκεϊ μοχθίζοντα κακῷ ὀλοόφρονος ὕδρου·
> ἔνθ' ὅ γε κεῖτ' ἀχέων· τάχα δὲ μνήσεσθαι ἔμελλον
> Ἀργεῖοι παρὰ νηυσὶ Φιλοκτήταο ἄνακτος.

> but he lay on the island, suffering terrible pain,
> on most sacred Lemnos, where the sons of the Achaeans left him,
> tormented by the vile wound [inflicted by] a water-snake intending
> his destruction,
> there he lay groaning; but soon were to be reminded
> the Argives by the ships of the king Philoktetes.

This allusion characteristically evokes what has already happened and what is to come. The listener is not only informed of the whereabouts of Philoktetes, who is not present at Troy, but there is also a suggestion that he will soon come to Troy. Without assuming that the story of Philoktetes was known to the listeners, this reference is pointless and, in the opinion of many scholars, quite dispensable. If, on the other hand, we assume the story was known, these references would have allowed the listeners to precisely locate the story in the cycle. We might even conclude that the allusion suggests that the story of Philoktetes was even more familiar to the listener than that of the wrath of Achilles. What has happened to Philoktetes is less important here than the mention that it had all happened before his arrival on the Trojan battlefield. The singer presents his story as follows: it happened when this had already occurred and that was soon to follow. The story of the arrival of Philoktetes on the battlefield was a readable signal for the audience that the war was soon to end. For the average listener the obstacle to overcome before the fall of Troy was Paris, not Hektor, as suggested by Homer; and further, it was Paris's death that marked the moment indicating the fall of Troy.

Proclus's summary presents the situation differently: it includes the story of the *Iliad* in the story of the Cycle, in between the *Kypria* and the *Aethiopis*. Proclus, therefore, presents the Trojan War sequentially, event after event, as if one were a logical consequence of the other. In general, this creates the illusion that cyclic poems explained the earlier and later fates of the heroes at Troy. Proclus presents specific poems as if they were successive episodes in the history of the Trojan War. My scepticism toward Proclus's approach might seem surprising, which is why I shall now try to explain it in detail.

In the *Iliad*, the death of Achilles is imminent, which is why the *Iliad* had to be placed before the *Aethiopis* in Proclus's chain of events, which actually presents Achilles' death. Yet by doing so the death of Achilles happens much later than is predicted in the *Iliad* because prior to Achilles' death, the *Aethiopis* describes a whole series of significant events: the arrival at Troy of the Amazons and the *aristeia* of queen Penthesileia before being killed by Achilles, the revolt of Achaean soldiers following Thersites' death, Odysseus's clearing Achilles of the crime, the arrival of the Ethiopian contingent at Troy, Achilles' withdrawal from battle, the death of Antilochos, Achilles rejoining the battle, and the killing of Memnon. The Neoanalysts have ruled out the possibility of the *Aethiopis* relying on the *Iliad*. However, the next conclusion is that Homer could not have known the *Aethiopis*. He would not have been able to build up so dramatically the events if he knew so much more would happen to Achilles before his death. And it certainly would have been almost impossible to evoke empathy if the listeners knew how much more would happen before the death so insistently foretold in the *Iliad*. This also rules out the possibility that the *Iliad* relies on the *Aethiopis*. Such conclusions, nevertheless, assume that Homer and his contemporaries viewed events from historical perspective. According to the plan presented above, the death of Achilles is to occur after the last day in the *Iliad*—that is, the day after the renewed fighting following the truce for the funeral of Hektor, which is the fiftieth day of action in the *Iliad*. I am, therefore, fully convinced that awareness of the events mentioned in the *Aethiopis* in no way hindered the singer from expressing a drama that could be appreciated by the listeners because such a historical perception of time in epics does not exist. In the oral tradition, the story takes on its shape in accord with its performance. In other words, tradition adopts the form of the performance.

It seems that Proclus tried to match the cycle story to the *Iliad*. In the *Kypria* summary, there is mention of Hektor, Briseis, and Chryseis, significant characters in the *Iliad* who are, nevertheless, not mentioned anywhere else.

Proclus attributes to Hektor the killing of Protesilaos, the first of the Achaeans to land on Trojan soil. Protesilaos is known in the *Iliad*, and memory of him plays an exceptionally important role. His ship stands on the edge of the right wing of the Achaean camp and it is the first one Hektor manages to set fire to at the height of the successful Trojan attack (15.705–747, 16.112–124; cf. 13.679–684, 15.592–617, 690–695). Why doesn't Homer make a clear allusion at this point? An ironic articulation of the coincidence of events would be quite typical of his art. We might especially expect such a narration, as Hektor again reaches the very same ship at a moment of great hope that the Achaeans might be driven out or even destroyed. Yet the *Iliad* records the killing of Protesilaos rather enigmatically (2.701–702):

> τὸν δ' ἔκτανε Δάρδανος ἀνὴρ
> νηὸς ἀποθρῴσκοντα πολὺ πρώτιστον Ἀχαιῶν.
>
> But a Dardanian man killed him [Protesilaos],
> the first of the Achaeans to jump off the ship.

Not naming Hektor performing such a significant deed is all the more intriguing because the *Iliad* does not mention any earlier achievement of this very important hero.[289] However, I first and foremost think that Homer would not have called Hektor Δάρδανος ἀνήρ.[290] The name of the Dardanian people does not seem to be synonymous with that of the Trojans. Nor are they allies of the Trojans, such as the Lycians, Phrygians, Thracians, etc.[291] The Dardanians are probably a people closely related to the Trojans and a part of the Trojan army on special terms. Their commander Aeneas (2.819–820) is the counterpart of the Trojan commander—Hektor. Their fathers are cousins, the fifth-generation descendants of Dardanos, begotten by Zeus (20.215–240). Aeneas presents his whole genealogy to Achilles so as to show that his status is equivalent to Hektor, though he is under his command. The killing of Aeneas turns out to be impossible because it would be contrary to his destiny: as the only descendent of Dardanos, he is to live and his descendants are to rule over the Troad (20.301–308).[292] Achilles cannot kill "the last of the Dardanians," though some lines later, symbolically, he kills a certain Dardanos, albeit one who is the son of Bias (20.460). Priam is also regularly called a descendant of Dardanos,[293] but Hektor never is. An identical formula, which indicates the killer of Protesilaos, is also used to describe Euphorbos, who gives the first blow when Patroklos is stunned by the god (16.806–807):

> ὄπιθεν δὲ μετάφρενον ὀξέϊ δουρί
> ὤμων μεσσηγὺς σχεδόθεν βάλε Δάρδανος ἀνήρ

> struck him in the back, casting a sharp spear,
> in between the shoulder blades, a Dardanian man.

289 Admittedly, the earlier achievements of Patroklos and Aias receive no mention. On the other hand, we are informed of the earlier exploits of Achilles, Odysseus, Menelaos, and Paris. See the *antehomerica* and *posthomerica* lists in Kullmann 1960:227–357.

290 This is accepted by Jachmann 1958:119–122; Kullmann (1960:185) considers it unlikely. He takes into account the argument that it is atypical for a famous hero to be killed by someone who is unknown, but suggests that the statement might be part of a prophecy Homer had adopted, whereby the first of the Achaeans to land on the Trojan shore was to be killed by an unknown man or, more specifically, a "Dardanian man."

291 The formulae specify the Trojans, the Dardanians, and allies: κέκλυτε μευ Τρῶες καὶ Δάρδανοι ἠδ' ἐπίκουροι (3.456, 7.348, 7.368, 8.497); Τρῶες καὶ Δαρδανίωνες (7.414, 8.154); Τρῶες και Λύκιοι καὶ Δάρδανοι ἀγχιμαχηταί (8.173, 11.286, 13.150, 15.425, 15.486, 17.184); similarly, the women καί τινα Τρωϊάδων καὶ Δαρδανίδων βαθυκόλπων (18.122); ἀμφὶ δὲ σὲ Τρωιαὶ καὶ Δαρδανίδες βαθύκολποι (18.339).

292 The hypothesis that the account of the descendants of Aeneas ruling the Troad was an attempt to please current rulers, who were probably recipients of Homer's poetry and indeed descendants of Aeneas, is flawed. Why then does the singer not make use of the opportunity and mention the genealogy of Aeneas's descendants? He does not even mention his son. For other arguments explaining the inadequacy of the account of Aeneas's lineage, see Smith 1981. Nagy (2010) associates the remark with the tradition that the Aeolians had Trojan heritage.

293 3.303, 5.159, 7.366, 13.376, 21.34, 22.352, 24.171, 24.354, 24.629, 24.631; as was Priam's grandfather Ilos, whose tomb is a σῆμα on the battlefield (11.166, 11.372).

The deaths of both Protesilaos and Patroklos (who defends the former's burnt ship against the Trojans) have to be connected with each other, even if Euphorbos does not strike the fatal blow. Homer likely preserves here a somewhat obscure construct,[294] but one thing seems certain: if it was Hektor who killed Protesilaos as a "Dardanian man," it would be unnecessary for the "Dardanian man" Euphorbos to appear in the scene in which Patroklos is killed. In both situations, the "Dardanian man" is necessary to kill a Greek hero, and in the second instance it clearly could not be Hektor.

In Proclus's summary, there are also references to Achilles' capture of Lykaon and the abduction of the maidens Briseis and Chryseis. In the first case, the presence of the story in the *Kypria* seems sanctioned by reference to events mentioned in the *Iliad*, whereas in the case of the maidens, there is reason to presume that their presence in the Cycle is quite independent of Homer's work. There is a fairly significant discrepancy between the texts because in the *Kypria* Briseis is abducted when Achilles captures Pedasos, whereas in the *Iliad* (2.690) the captured city is Lyrnessos. Scholia to the *Iliad*, in turn, provide an explanation to the short reference at *Iliad* 1.366 as to why Chryseis was taken captive in Hypoplakian Thebe and not Chryse, the destination of the Achaean suppliant mission to Chryses and Apollo: she was to appear in this city in honor of the Artemis festival. Burgess notes that the author of the *Kypria* could not explain Homer's brief mention of Chryseis and ignore the *Iliad* version concerning Briseis. Behind these inconsistencies stands the story's traditional message, and the differences simply confirm its oral nature.[295] The frequency of references in the *Iliad* to the sieges of Eëtion's Thebe and other Troad cities also seems to suggest the tradition of this theme.[296] Yet another significant divergence between the ending of the *Kypria* summary and the *Iliad* leads us to doubt the

294 Both Protesilaos and Antilochos, and in a sense Patroklos too, die as substitutes for Achilles, who is held back from the fighting by a prophecy.

295 Burgess 1996:82–84. Conversely, see West (2013:57–58), who trivializes the discrepancy in place names by suggesting that they are often even confused by scholars of Homer. He wrongly reduces the issue to the ability to memorize toponyms, which is much greater, in his opinion, in scholars, who frequently scrutinize various historical records, than for the author of a given work or summary. However, in oral culture, toponyms are far more deeply set in mythical tales than one might imagine. These are not empty names that can easily be replaced. Regardless of the fact that these places are associated with various versions of a myth, information regarding a given place is permanently set in the fabric of the oral tradition. For example, a geological formation might accept various mythological aetiologies, but it is associated only with a myth of which it is an integral part. The matter deserves a separate study and discussion. Here, I shall only point out the problem by referring to a study of the relationship between myth and landscape in Aboriginal culture: Szyjewski 2014.

296 Redfield 1994:14; Burgess 1996:83. According to Willcock (1978 *ad loc.*) and De Jong (1987a:265n103), the definite article before the name of Chryses (*Iliad* 1.11 τὸν Χρύσην) also indicates that the character is traditional.

interdependence of these two works. At the end of the *Kypria*, Zeus's plan is mentioned a second time, and in it the Trojans are helped by Achilles' withdrawal from the fighting. This is not a prediction of what happens in the *Iliad* because there Zeus helps the Trojans at the request of Thetis and after Achilles' withdrawal from the fighting. Therefore, the two plans of Zeus are not the same.[297] We do not know how the two abducted women could be involved in these events. Whatever role was played by the maidens Briseis and Chryseis, the reader of Proclus's summary has the impression their abductions are linked to the *Iliad* plot.

With the exception of these problematic details, there is practically no place for the *Iliad* in Proclus's chronology. The *Iliad* does not contribute any relevant element to the system that would affect the further course of events. This fact, often stressed by the neoanalysts, is not insignificant, but it requires a different interpretation. The suggestion of the neoanalysts that the *Iliad* was a secondary work is a misunderstanding. The *Iliad* is linked to the cycle story in a manner identical to that of Demodokos's first song. Just as Demodokos sets his story at an unspecified moment, at the start of the war, the *Iliad* is set at an unspecified moment, at the end of the war. These are not, however, accidental moments. The *Iliad* does not tell us about a random sequence of fifty days in the final phase of the war, but about *these* days in which time is fulfilled. Cyclic thinking is required: the selected moment is very significant within the *Iliad*'s own treatment of time. That is why, in the *Iliad,* Homer does not include the sequence of events that precede Achilles' death in the *Aethiopis*, though he does allude to them in scenes of his own creation. Demodokos and Homer, respecting the relevant events of the cycle, include their songs in its structure. Thus, one can create a new song that is neither entirely new nor entirely independent. All the important moments in the cycle have appeared before or beyond it. These moments belong to tradition. The singer can compose a song using already existing story patterns at various points in the story cycle, though usually it is either near the beginning or near the end of the war.

The *Iliad* shows the same story pattern as the *Aethiopis*. The sequence of the most important events is very similar, as is the doubling of themes and scenes used for dramatic effect. The *Aethiopis* starts with the arrival of Trojan allies at Troy, which enables the Trojans to confront the Achaeans on the battlefield,

297 Kullmann (1960:109, 212–214, 225–226, 358–359) surmised from this that the plan introduces the events described in the *Aethiopis* (though he later accepted the possibility that it might apply to the *Iliad* in Kullmann 1991:438). The discrepancy is also noticed by Davies (1989a:50), though he assumes a conscious or unconscious inaccuracy in the message. Burgess (1996:84–85), on the other hand, believes that the best explanation for the discrepancy is to accept that the theme of the quarrel between Achilles and Agamemnon is traditional, although it could lead to a different course of events than those we know from Homer.

outside the city walls. This theme is doubled: first to appear on the battlefield are the Amazons, next to appear are the Ethiopians. In both cases, Achilles kills the leaders of these Trojan allies, though the consequences are different. Achilles desists from taking part in the second battle, but then joins in to avenge the death of his friend. One might assume that he was driven by wrath which, on the one hand, helps him kill Memnon, and, on the other hand, leads to his annihilation, killed by Paris with Apollo's guidance. Thus, Achilles' conflict with Apollo, whose wrath annihilates the hero but also allows for his posthumous apotheosis, is shown. The story ends with the funeral of Achilles and games held in his honor, as well as Thetis taking Achilles from the funeral pyre to the island of Leuke.

We can, therefore, say that the *Aethiopis* is also a song about the Wrath of Achilles.[298] In this sort of song, the hero's anger mounts—and the listener's sense of suspense mounts when the hero withdraws from the fighting. The wrath then erupts suddenly when his friend is killed. And, in effect, the wrath leads to his own death. But while the song on the theme of the Wrath of Achilles can take on many very different forms, it must always include specific elements. Therefore, we also cannot say that the *Iliad* precedes the *Aethiopis*. The two songs are virtually synonymous. Presenting a period at the end of the war, both concentrate on the epic's main hero, Achilles. In the Cycle, both perform the same function. The death of the greatest Achaean warrior is an essential price to pay for the fall of Troy. Both the *Iliad* and the *Aethiopis* are songs about the death of Achilles; in both, his wrath is essential to revealing his heroism.

The adequacy of the *Iliad* title

In our discussion, we have considered that every song in the oral tradition is an integral creation and described the mechanism according to which particular episodes can be included in the macro-story structure. These songs should not be considered solely as components of the Cycle because they always present particular episodes in the context of the wider story, such as the Trojan War, and every time they represent the whole of the Cycle. In other words, with every performance, the Cycle is repeated. The songs of Demodokos show how the story framework of all the events can be marked in particular episodes, which are received as the beginning and end of all those same events. One story is the cause, the other the consequence. The arrangement of events is still the same, but within the same framework the cause of events can be different yet lead to the same consequences.

298 For a critique of Burgess's view that the *Aethiopis* did not include the wrath of Achilles, see Ch. 6, pp. 434–440, below.

All three of Demodokos's songs adopt a perspective where Odysseus's heroic killing of the suitors, being the essential part of the plot of the *Odyssey*, marks the denouement. It is presented as the end of the macro-story. It therefore seems reasonable to conclude that presenting a song in a specific order and taking into account its connections to all the events that we call the cycle must correspond to the performance practice of the *aoidoi*. It would be similar to the performance practice of the rhapsodes as recorded in the sources.[299] Songs performed one after the other give the impression of an entire story being told in succession.[300] In the *Iliad*, we observed similarly defined beginnings and endings, though not in the form of individual stories, but through allusions. An episode that includes allusions effectively tells the story of the entire Trojan War. In other words, such a song does not *refer* to tradition; it evokes and at the same time embodies tradition. The successive performance of songs must surely have taken on an agonistic form,[301] in two possible ways: either the singer started a story and challenged his rival to finish it, or like Demodokos, one singer would present his own image of the whole, trying to make it better than what his rivals offered. Therefore, the Cycle cannot be viewed as the sum of a certain number of songs. The definition of its beginning and end in each performance gave the Cycle a new dimension and probably also a new meaning, while at the same time it remained unchanged.

299 Nagy (2010:65–69) believes the rules of succession were introduced to the Panathenaia by the Peisistratids, but that it concerned the performance of Homer's epics (understood as cyclic epics) by alleged descendants of Homer on Chios. Earlier this rule was also known in Ionian Dodecapolis, the pan-Ionian festival preceding the Panathenaia. Nagy interprets *ek diadokhes* 'in succession, by relay', as meaning both passing on from one generation to the next, as well as alternately performing. See also Collins 2004:169–175, 192–199.

300 Already in his previous work, Nagy (1990b:202, 1996a:72–73, 2013:245–247) recognized that the same principle of *rhapsodic sequencing* at the Panathenaia goes far back in the past and is represented in the *Iliad* scene where Achilles sings *klea andrôn* and Patroklos is getting ready for his turn to continue the story. Cook (1999) believes that such is also the case with Demodokos, who continues the narrative of the first song in the third one. Pellicia (2003:113n35) expresses the reservation that the narration of the third song is not a direct continuation of the plot of the first song, and therefore there is a huge gap between the two narratives. However, Burgess (2004c:18) sees this "gap" as a confirmation of his theory that certain episodes were left out in performance ("the technique of discontinuous performance"). On Burgess's account, the whole Cycle is told through the presentation of its successive fragments; the poet need only follow the order of the plot. However, the assumed chronological order of the plot of the Cycle is, in my opinion, illusory, and the relations between the plots of songs presented in a sequence are much deeper. This issue will be discussed in more detail in the following chapters.

301 Kelly (2008:199) argues that in the *Odyssey* and Hesiod's *Works and Days*, both the awareness of the existence of alternative versions of traditional stories with which the poet competes and the degree it was possible to create them become apparent. To gain credibility, the poet boosts his authority in order to ultimately win the public's favor for his own version of events.

These arguments lead us to a seemingly minor issue: the controversy surrounding the title of the *Iliad*. Martin Mueller asks: "Why did Greeks call this poem about Achilles the *Iliad* even though Troy is not even mentioned in the poet's announcement of his theme? The traditional title points to the dual nature of the poem, which is indeed an account of the anger of Achilles, but moves beyond its own limits to include the larger event of which it is a part."[302] Mueller believes the second part of the work focuses on Hektor, who represents Troy (here, the meaning of Hektor's name is significant—"the one who holds the city," that is, the city's defender or ruler), and this shifts the hierarchy of importance to the fall of Troy, symbolized by the death of Hektor, the sole defender of Troy (6.403): "This identification of the death of Hektor with the fall of Troy is the reason why the *Iliad* avoids any references to the particular circumstances of the city's end." Mueller goes on to argue that the incompatibility of versions regarding the fall of Troy result from every version giving a different reason: the death of Hektor (*Iliad*), the Trojan Horse (*Odyssey*—even though Zeus's prophecy at *Iliad* 15.71 clearly states that Troy will fall "through Athena's cunning"), and Philoktetes' bow (*Little Iliad*): "That tradition (Philoktetes) is incompatible with both the *Iliad* and the *Odyssey* and is consequently ignored, except for a brief reference in the Catalogue of Ships (2.724)." But this brief reference is perfectly sufficient to assume that Homer knew that the fall of Troy was dependent on the presence of Philoktetes. The notion of incompatibility is inadequate with regard to the themes of cyclic songs. All three of them, and in fact there are more, represent the starting point to the fall of Troy; they are simultaneous and do not mutually exclude each other. In the next chapter, we shall see that the obstacle to capturing the city, and the overcoming of this obstacle, are the essence of the cyclic song. And on the same story pattern diverse songs were composed, which did not mean that the authors were unaware of other versions.

The question of whether the *Iliad* title is appropriate, therefore, needs to be examined from a different angle. The dual nature of the *Iliad* (as noted by Mueller) is also present in the *Odyssey*, whose invocation also refers only to the hero's homeward journey and does not mention the events on Ithaca. We have already observed that the invocation most probably never served as a summary and the lack of reference to the work's contents are a characteristic feature.

Songs in oral culture are independent units, albeit integrated with tradition. Such integration imposes certain restrictions, similar to those that occur when using the same story pattern to present various stories. Every successive performance of a song also changes it, though not enough to change its distinctiveness. It has to have individual solutions for the singer to distinguish his song

302 Mueller 1984:30.

from others. These individual features, however, involve switching elements already determined in the traditional matrix. Singers select for their repertoire the solutions they most prefer. However, they cannot be too different from the accepted model because such songs would be simply too difficult to memorize. The singer's knowledge of tradition is always only partial: he knows certain solutions and is unaware of or has forgotten others. A known song is one that the singer associates with a traditional story. Relevant here is a very instructive dialogue between Nikola Vujnović and one of the best singers encountered by Parry and Lord, Salih Ugljanin.[303]

> Nikola: What's the song which you sang just now?
>
> Salih: That's the song about when the two pashas spent the winter [the first line of the song].
>
> N: Where?
>
> S: At Temišvar.
>
> N: All right. If anyone were to say to you: "Sing me such and such a song." What would he say to you? Or, if you were to say to someone: "I sang such and such a song," meaning the one you sang just now? What is it called? What name shall we put on it? ... all right, "two pashas spent the winter," but–
>
> S: In Sement. "Sing me the song about Temišvar." That's it, the song of Temišvar ... that's what people say to me ...
>
> N: What happened at Temišvar?
>
> S: What happened? You've already heard what happened. When the pashas spent the winter and all seven kings surrounded them.
>
> N: I know, but there are many songs about Temišvar ... Have you ever heard that there are more songs about Temišvar than just that one?
>
> S: I haven't heard any songs about Temišvar except this one.
>
> N: Well, I've heard that there are other songs about Temišvar.
>
> S: Well, what isn't there in the world? Every singer has his own songs.

303 Lord 1960:286n2.

N: Then what shall we put that song down as? What's its name?

S: Its name is "At Muhač."

Here, we see how strongly a song is identified with its toponym. It is through toponyms that the singer associates his narrative with tradition. The second thing, no less important, is that there are many songs about Temišvar, but this particular singer knows only this one. It can also suggest that at pan-Ionian or pan-Athenaian festivals various songs about the same matters might have been confronted with each other. On these particular occasions, songs on the same theme could have even been expected. The singers' rivalry might have concerned not singing on any theme but one particular theme—for example, the Song of Troy.

Our *Iliad* is about a certain episode in the perspective of the entire war, and in this form it becomes part of the Trojan War cycle. In fact, every work thus finding itself in the Cycle structure could be called the *Iliad*. It is not by chance that another work about the capture of Troy is called the *Little Iliad*, and here "little" is only added to distinguish it from Homer's *Iliad*. The singer could sing about the dispute between Achilles and Agamemnon or Achilles and Odysseus, etc., and all these songs could be called the *Iliad*, rather than the song about Achilles.[304] Songs sharing a common toponymical name are frequent in Greek tradition. The *Thebaid*, also ascribed to Homer in antiquity, is not so much "a song from the Theban Cycle," as a song representing the whole cycle, the whole macro-story of the Theban War. Similarly, the *Iliad* would be a song of the entire Trojan expedition, even though it seems to describe only a brief episode.

When Demodokos sings the song about the wooden horse, the song presents at once an episode that makes sense and can be understood by those who know the Trojan War tradition, but it also defines the whole of that tradition to make it understandable and explains its meaning. Its partial quality is an illusion. We should note that, within short intervals, Demodokos sings three seemingly different songs, whereas in fact together they create an image of the entire war and the role Odysseus played in it, and at the same time an anticipation of what the hero will achieve in the final scenes of the composition.

[304] In the *Little Iliad*, the main themes are the quarrel between Aias and Odysseus over Achilles' armor and the arrival of Philoktetes in Troy. Perhaps the link between the two themes is Odysseus, who plays a significant role in bringing back the stranded hero. Subsequent tradition presents Odysseus in both cases in a negative light, which is probably linked with the *Little Iliad* tradition. Such an attitude towards Odysseus is alien to Homer, who in both his poems treats the hero with sympathy. The *Little Iliad* themes appear to be older than Homer's poetry. Therefore, Homer is clearly obliged to take into account the older tradition when situating his *Iliad* in time, but it is inconvenient for him to refer to this tradition more fully so as not to tarnish the image of his Odysseus.

We can say confidently that Demodokos's songs encompass the whole Trojan Cycle, showing its beginning and end in the context of the role played in it by Odysseus. However, a comparison with other songs of the Cycle shows that Odysseus did not necessarily deserve all the splendor for the capture of Troy. Therefore, the *Odyssey* is in praise of Odysseus in the same way as the *Iliad* is in praise of Achilles.

Oral transmission of songs

We can now try to explain the problem of how the *Iliad* might have been preserved in oral transmission. In oral tradition, many songs on the same theme may coexist and, for a singer like Salih Ugljanin, it is enough to know only one of them (in fact, he does not even know that other songs on this theme exist). He is not bothered by various versions of the song. So too, in ancient Greece. However, the situation must have changed dramatically when on a special occasion several singers were meeting at one place. They were expected to tell the stories traditionally connected with a given festival. We can assume two ways in which songs were presented and transformed on such occasions.

First, let's suppose that they had to sing about a given subject—for example, the Trojan War (let's assume that our hypothetical situation took place at the pan-Aeolian festival; in G. Nagy's "evolutionary model," this is the first stage of the creation the Trojan War tradition[305]). At the festival, each singer had to sing his version of the story. Naturally, he wanted to come out better than the others. It was in his interest to make the story absorbing for the audience. Probably at first, the singer simply improved a known story. But improving means that at every moment he had to choose a solution from a number of traditional possibilities. However, once he had made a choice, he had to take into account its consequences. For instance, let's imagine than the singer chooses the option that, at a given moment of his narrative, the main hero, instead of being killed according to tradition, survives a mortal danger. His death is only postponed, but at this moment his survival entails certain consequences. And these consequences might lead to further consequences, etc. However, it is still the same story, which the singer cannot ruin: the hero must die. The singer, instead of going straight to the point, chooses a roundabout route. His story, elastic by nature, can be conveniently stretched. Retardation is a standard principle when recounting a story—by delaying the inevitable, one can arouse the curiosity of the listeners. They are expecting certain developments, the tension is growing,

305 Nagy 2010:232–233, 241–253. Based on the formulaic and linguistic remains, Nagy also distinguishes an earlier Mycenaean period in the process of formation of the epic tradition, but it is hard to assume that the Trojan story in the form we know was already created in this period.

and meanwhile the singer postpones the crucial moment by telling stories, which lead to the expected events, but which are so interesting in themselves that they attract the attention of the audience. At some moment in this process of improvement, the song must have been perceived as possessing enough distinctive features to qualify it as new. It could have been recognized as a new independent episode within a broader narrative context—an episode perhaps in the form of an individual and integral song, although based on the same story pattern as in other songs. This new episode did not change the meaning of the original (basic) song; also unchanged was the placement of the performance of the song within the ritual activities of the festival, which accomplished the task of integrating each Greek tribe (each next episode performed the same function of communicating the myth relevant for the occasion). It was still the same story but dressed in a new plot. Then successive episodes serve as substitutes of the original one.

The second possibility is that there was no established subject at the festive *agôn*, but when one singer introduced the subject of the Trojan War, then the next one would have been expected to respond with a song or songs on the same subject. When one depicted the beginning of the events, the task of the next would be to present their end, taking special care to link the plot of his story with the plot of the previous one. Somehow, the second song would have shown the consequences of the events of the previous song. The linking of the first and third song of Demodokos is not a simple continuation of the plot. They are actually two different, autonomous stories. However, the second one seems to answer the issues raised in the first one, the first one revolving around *archê*—that is, the beginning of the whole super-story. We don't know what solution to the problem of the quarrel of heroes Demodokos intended in the first song, but it could have been at least partially different from the one given in the third one. Not wholly different, as Odysseus's praise suggests that he considers his role to have been properly highlighted. In the *Odyssey*, the impulse to show the consequences of events related the first song comes from the outside—from Odysseus himself, expecting proper appreciation. So, here we can observe an example of the active participation of the audience in giving the performance its proper shape and meaning. Sometimes, the audience might also have influenced the way in which one song evaluated the consequences of the story introduced in the preceding song, which means that there might be various consequences of the plot of the first song. In this case, the singer Demodokos follows the suggestion put forward by one of the listeners. Another listener or Demodokos himself might have found a different cause-and-effect relationship, the suggested relationships not being explicitly necessary.

In the situation when there was only one singer, there must have been opportunities for him to plan his performance in such a way that he could add an appropriate ending to the first song, introducing the subject. Perhaps even the intended ending could have affected the shape of the whole song about the beginning of events.[306] Thus, it would have been a similar process to the construction of the plot of the tragic trilogy in the early period (separate stories presenting one myth and arranged not so much according to chronology but with the aim of showing the consequences of the presented events, as in Aeschylus's trilogies). The presentation of such original epic dilogies could have involved a competition of singers. The dilogy might have been a re-enactment of the whole super-story—the whole Cycle, that is. The singers' *agôn* would have been a factor motivating the performers to a better presentation of the combined story. In such a case, the palm of preference would have been given to the best performer of a cycle—for example, the Trojan one. From this stage, it is only one step to building one song containing both the beginning and end of the macro-story—that is, an episode within the perspective of the whole Trojan War. Such circumstances would provide a perfect opportunity for the creation of monumental works.[307]

306 As in the *Iliad*, where the choice of the initial scenes must have been subordinated to the intended ending. The meaning of a story is determined by its denouement, which is its final part; in this case, it is Achilles' conduct towards Priam. However, to enable the understanding of Achilles' conduct (which must have been a kind of shock for the primary audience, see Zieliński 2021a:81–82), it was necessary to prepare the listeners for the proper reception, which the singer consistently did throughout the story. To understand the intentions of the author of the *Iliad*, it is necessary to take into account the contrasting behavior of heroes, emphasized by the ring composition. The aim of the storyteller is to gain the listeners' approval for his story. Or rather, not approval for the story itself, but for its message. In other words, the singer, using ring construction, tries to impose on his audience the intended understanding of the story. For more on meaning and ring construction in the *Iliad*, see Ch. 5 and Ch. 6, below.

307 Due to the limited time available to the rhapsodes during the Panathenaia (according to Neils [1992] only the first day of the eight-day festival was accorded to their performances), Burgess (2004c) concludes that the performance of the Homeric poems as well as other poems of the Trojan cycle must have been selective—that is, the subsequent rhapsodes kept the storyline, but omitted whole sections of the plot, "when moving from one episode to another." The Panathenaic rule that can be inferred from testimonia (i.e. turn-taking in presenting epic) would not mean, according to Burgess, that one rhapsode took over exactly where the predecessor ended, but rather that the singers sang key episodes that would together convey "the totality of the story" (9). This, of course, implies that the listeners would be familiar with the mythological superstructure, and as a confirmation of this hypothesis, Burgess cites Foley's concept of performance as metonymy of tradition (Foley 1991:42: "A representative section or episode that implies the unsung entirety of the poetic tradition"). However, the question remains as to on what occasion the audience, and en masse, could have become acquainted with the whole of such a work as the *Iliad*, if there were no written copies of the text. Of course, the problem does not exist if we look at the construction of the *Iliad* as a paratactic collection of a number of episodes arranged "chronologically." However, the *Iliad*, with its symmetrical and concentric

Songs like the *Iliad* might have been remembered for two reasons. First, since the performance of songs was connected with festive ceremonies, it follows that their content must, to some extent, have also played a sacral role. Therefore, the sacred story, which preserved the sacred myth about a hero who saved his people, must have been repeated at various religious festivals. All versions of the song about the Wrath of Achilles and, of course, every new episode showing the hero's anger, were expected re-enactments of the sacred myth. According to Kiparsky's concept, mentioned above, these sacral conditions influenced the durability of the form and content of the tale.

The hypothesis above answers the question of why such kinds of stories were preserved in oral tradition. We could say that this is exactly why an *Iliad* was saved. But it still does not answer the question of why the *Iliad* was preserved.

Another reason for remembering this particular episode of the sacred story (that is, Achilles' vengeance for killing Patroklos) is its artistic quality.[308] The agonistic aspect seems fundamental for the appearance of large-format and elaborate Homeric and Hesiodic epic,[309] though it is only a fragment of a broader picture. In oral culture, the agonistic aspect plays a crucial role in a public discourse. Derek Collins brilliantly describes the rules of competition in the *skolion* game.[310] At a symposion, every participant in the game tried to

composition, is a message as a whole. The understanding of the meaning given to the song by Homer is possible only due to the juxtaposition of the opening and closing scenes, which correspond to each other in ring composition. If the time devoted to the performance of Homeric epic at the Panathenaic festival was really too short to allow the singing of the whole of the *Iliad*, it might indeed have been necessary to confine the presentation of the song to key episodes only. Even so, Burgess's hypothesis seems doubtful. However, Burgess rightly concludes that the Panathenaic tradition of performance in relay must have been a longstanding technique before it came to be applied to Homeric poems. According to Burgess, the *Iliad* and *Odyssey* ousted cyclic poems at the Panathenaia. Again, one should ask, what could have caused some songs to be ousted by others, if the audience had a chance to hear only their fragments? In what way would one song be better than another? Clearly, Burgess does not mark any significant difference between the macro-story of the Cycle, which obviously is always somehow present in the mind of the audience, and an elaborately composed song like the *Iliad*, which always presents only an episode. In my opinion, Burgess's proposition concerning the way of presenting Homeric poems at the Panathenaia cannot be ruled out, but it seems that the technique of performing only portions of songs does not explain the creation of the *Iliad* and other epic poems.

308 Watkins 1995:68: "The art of the Indo-European poet is to say something wholly traditional in a new and interesting, but therefore *more effective* way. It is verbal activity, artistically elaborated, but directed toward a more or less immediate, concrete goal." See Ready 2019:15–74.

309 Nelson 2021:25–30.

310 Collins 2004:84–98. *Skolion* is only one of the forms of verbal competition in Greek oral culture. Martin (1989) analyzes the rivalry between characters in the *Iliad* as expressed by *mythoi*—i.e. complete acts of speaking—which are, in fact, performances. Martin concludes that the best speaker among the characters is Achilles—his speeches are characterized by the greatest creativity in the use of traditional formulaic material. As "Achilles is the poet's voice and his emblem, a heroic speaker who outdoes others in style" (p. 238), so his *mythoi* reflect the abilities

express himself better than others. Everyone wanted his opinion to obtain the greatest appreciation. This happened when a theme of conversation was chosen (for example, what is best or worst for a man). But surely songs and rhythmic utterances were more often used as a way of conducting a conversation, whether gently and with respect or provocatively and with an intention to suppress the opponent. In such a discourse, one had to be skilled to improvise. However, improvisation was based on traditional patterns of songs and utterances, which certainly helped the singers to react quickly and appropriately. In such situations, it must have come in handy to know responses that had already gained appreciation, which means that in the past they helped to win a similar rivalry. By remembering and using such responses appropriately, one could win again. No wonder then that the best response was the one that was best remembered. Among extant fragments of lyric and elegiac poetry we can find such "citations," that is, references to what Homer or other well-known poets said about this or that matter. What is a lyric poet if not a well-known author of the best responses? A recognized master of such utterances?[311] That is the main reason, in my opinion, why such poems are remembered relatively accurately in oral culture.[312]

The *Iliad* might have been regarded as the best embodiment of the sacred story. Hence, it might have been introduced in place of other songs preserving the tradition of the Trojan War. The time when it happened is only guesswork, though I think that most probably it was connected with the transfer of the pan-Ionian festivals to Athens by the Peisistratids. The song might have been composed much earlier and preserved by the guild of Homeridai. At that time, it might have seemed profitable to decide on using this song and no other song. The performance of one song only, the same at every festival, might have been a deal with the Homeridai, I suppose, done at the expense of other guilds, like the

and skill of Homer himself who—in Martin's eyes—is the best speaker, competing with other singers.

311 Thus, in the archaic period the authorship of particular poetic statements is attributed to poets known as masters in a given genre (or rather in a given mode of poetic discourse, in a statement on certain topics or of a certain character). Nagy (1985), Ford (1985), and Edmunds (1997b) note that the name of the poet Theognis, whether he was or wasn't a historical figure, fulfills the function of an authority—that is, someone with whom tradition associates poems of a certain character.

312 Nelson 2021:29: "Archaic Greek poems were not just ephemeral events but enduring artifacts that envisaged their future fame beyond the present. Poets were aware of this later reception and thus competed not only in a one-off contest with immediate rivals in the present but also against an entire canon of tradition to which they aspired to belong. Within such a broader perspective, an agonistic aspect to archaic epic's engagement with tradition is natural, even expected."

Kreophyleoi, who had other "best songs" at their disposal for such occasions.[313] Why did these guilds preserve such long songs? The only answer is that it must have been profitable. If a singer has in his repertoire a song that no other song can defeat, he takes care of it, probably also improving it again and again at successive performances. A long song cannot be easy to be remember after one hearing; moreover, it is much more than a short song burdened with the risk of corruption due to the introduction of changes. So, it is quite probable that a small society of skilled performers worked out methods of memorization analogous to those used by the Brahmins in India, which include bodily exercises during repeated recitations of texts. In this way, there might arise conditions conducive to remembering unconventional, individual solutions that contemporary researchers are inclined to associate with an individual style.

The song preserved by the Homeridai might have been performed for more than two hundred years on various occasions—mostly at pan-Ionian festivals. The transfer of pan-Ionian festivals to Athens might have been an element of policy toward achieving hegemony over other Ionian *poleis*.[314] Nagy persuades that the Homeric tradition was not the only poetic tradition at those times, and during the tyranny in Athens there were also other traditions, linked with the authority of mythical Orpheus and Musaios.[315] Homeric poetry, however, better corresponded with the democratic changes in the *polis*. The *Iliad* and the *Odyssey*, unsurpassed by any other work, finally eliminated all of them. That is why we should see them not as two incomparable poems rising high above the sea of mediocrity but as the cream of the cream—whose dominant position was sustained by the existence of certain performative conditions.

313 Both guilds were linked with the Homeric tradition, which may mean that they possessed works of identical character and similar content, which were intended for the same agonistic occasions.

314 Nagy (2010, esp. Chs. 1, 3, 6, and 8), defines what it meant to appropriate epic tradition: to gain a dominant position through taking control over Homeric poems. It might have been achieved thanks to securing the right to the organization of pan-Ionian festivals, since then called Panathenaian.

315 Nagy 2010:340–352. Martin 2001.

2

The Song and the Tradition

A Pattern of the Epic Tale

Greek Epic Story Patterns against the Background of South Slavic Songs

THE PREVIOUS CHAPTER presented the *Iliad* as a song created like other epics of the Trojan Cycle. It is one of typical episodes located in the place characteristic of epic narrative strategy—the end of a war. Each episode is perceived from the perspective of the entire campaign. The general arrangement of the content of this song is so similar to that of the *Aethiopis* that it is possible to see it as another version of the same subject. However, my point is not that one song was modeled upon the other, but that both songs are based on the same pattern and that both are songs of Achilles' wrath leading to his death. The events in one plot cannot be treated as "earlier" or "later" than the other—both take place at the same time, when the war is about to end, but before Philoktetes has been brought to Troy. Both songs occupy the same place in the structure of the entire cycle. Individual songs present only a part of a larger whole, but this whole is not understood or performed as a chronological chain of events. The song, recalling one episode, redefines the entire cycle.

These observations are only the first step in our reflection on the typicality and the originality of the *Iliad*. Before we proceed any further, it is necessary to know what patterns the song followed and what patterns were used in the construction of other songs in the cycle. Oral literature is based on schematic structures, so we should ask what schematic structures can be found in the construction of the plot. The possibilities for answering this question are limited, but perhaps it will be possible to find some ways. Before we venture to evaluate the originality of this song, we must get to know—as far as possible—the tradition in which it was born, and therefore try to determine what story patterns from the times preceding Homer can be recreated on the basis of extant fragments and how far we can go back in this respect.

We need to refer to Parry and Lord's comparative studies and to various ancient testimonia about cyclic poetry. To begin with, let's look at the primary determinant of the originality of Homer's *Iliad*—the beginning of the narrative as if in the midst of events, *in medias res*, in Horace's words (*Ars Poetica* 148). The Roman poet, drawing attention to the difference in the construction of Homer's work and cyclic poems, expresses the opinion of the ancients, who preferred this narrative technique to the linear presentation of the story from beginning to end. The aesthetic evaluation of this kind of narrative is crucial: what is told from the beginning to the end is worse than a dramatic entry directly into the middle of events.

Serbian poetry provides comparative material. The song about Prince Marko and his enemy called Nina (*Marko and Nina of Kostur*), in the extended version of Halil Bajgorić,[1] presents the story in a linear fashion: Marko, summoned by the Sultan, went to war, and during the expedition learned about the occupation of his castle by Nina. Petar Vidić, a second-rate singer, presents this song differently:[2] Marko gets a letter from the Sultan and is worried because he knows that during his absence Nina will plunder his castle and capture his wife (in another version, also his sister). Vidić starts with wine—or rakia-drinking by Marko—which can be identified as a sign in the epic code of both a misfortune and an initiation into self-sacrifice.[3] Marko, the main character, acquires knowledge about future events, which lends drama, or even tragic dimension, to his life, as the protagonist knows his fate: he goes to war, knowing what the result will be. The epic hero's tragic awareness of the fate that awaits, as in the case of Achilles, may therefore result from the general knowledge of a hero's story or his destiny. The story can be told either linearly or not, and either method is equally acceptable and, I believe, equally good. In epic oral tradition, the presentation of the hero's fate in a way that to our taste seems more tragic is neither unusual, nor, it seems, valued higher. In this Slavic example, the better singer sang a more elaborate song, while maintaining a linear narrative, whereas the inferior one started the plot *in medias res*, as does Homer.

This example permits us to draw conclusions for the entire Greek epic tradition. The tragic dimension of the *Iliad* needn't have been a novelty in an epic song. Similarly, the technique of starting the narrative *in medias res* needn't

1 Lord 1960:115–117. The song was recorded twice many years apart: the first time during the first expedition in 1935 (**Parry 6695**), the second time in 1950 (**Lord 84**).

2 The song was recorded six times in the rendition of Vidić (**Parry 6, 803a, 803b, 804, 805, 846**). The first version was written down by Kutuzov in 1933, the other ones were registered variously by Parry and his assistants in 1934 (Lord 1960:72–76).

3 Lord (1960:66) suggests that the motif of wine drinking originally signified a transition to another world, perhaps even the awareness of death.

have been new or exceptional.[4] If this kind of technique had been considered superior, maybe at least some of the cyclic poems would have applied it, instead of using linear composition. If Homer had been such a model for *epigones*, as has usually been accepted, he would have found his imitators, and not just stubborn "developers" of his minor details into extensive plots. It seems that in epic oral tradition the use of one or the other method is equally acceptable.

The search for patterns common to the whole epic tradition must be based on some assumptions. The two most basic principles should be the ones founded on Lord's research. One is the principle of multiformity, postulated by Lord and confirmed by studies of many other scholars, according to which not only do different songs fulfill the same pattern, but also the same song can take various shapes.[5] The other principle, which can be conveniently called the principle of following the pattern (mentioned in Chapter 1), was not formulated by Lord but can be deduced from his research. According to this principle, the singer can change his song, provided he leaves basic elements of the plot and certain sequences of events in their original form. The events themselves can be modified but they can't be omitted.[6] This rule makes the pattern very stable. The singer must follow it, even when he decides to deviate from the form of the song as he has previously learned or performed it. In 1950, when Sulejman Fortić performed the song about the taking of Bagdad, he deliberately omitted religious scenes as a topic then unacceptable in communist Yugoslavia—and so, dangerous to the singer. The messenger, who in the previously recorded performance first looked for the protagonist, Alija, at his home, then in the mosque garden, and finally in front of the mosque, in the later performance looks for him first at his home, then at Mujo's place, and finally at Halil's. The singer cannot break the pattern, in which the messenger finds Alija only in the third place.[7]

The reasons for changing the structure of the song can be various. The singer, for example, prefers to employ his own story forms. If he includes in his repertoire a song that follows forms used by some other singer, difficulties might follow. A significant example of this phenomenon is Avdo Međedović's

4 It is said that the plot of *Beowulf* also starts *in medias res*, for although the poem begins with the arrival of Beowulf to King Hroðgar, Grendel's assaults are already under way.

5 Lord 1960:100.

6 The necessity of plot structures being stable is clear to anyone who undertakes comparative research. Gresseth (1979:73), presenting close links between the plot of the *Odyssey* and the *Nalopākhyāna* episode in the *Mahābhārata*, points out "a compositional practice of Homer to shift and reemploy a theme rather than throw anything away." Though Gresseth notes Homer's tendency to modify instead of to reject, he has not realized that it is a composition method typical of oral tradition.

7 See Lord 1960:118.

adaptation of the epic tale of *Bećiragić Meho* (**Parry 12471**), which he heard from Mumin Vlahovljak (**Parry 12468**). The singer tried hard—even by duplicating scenes—to adapt the song to his own form. However, despite the changes he made, Mumin Vlahovljak's song remained traditional for Međedović, which means that he was deeply convinced that it could not be changed.[8] This is evident in the way he approached his adaptation: in Vlahovljak's version of the epic, the main task of capturing someone falls to a person acting in disguise, while according to the tradition known to Avdo Međedović, disguise is necessary in expeditions for rescue, not for capture.

Capture or rescue in disguise must be preceded by a scene of recognition—by a birthmark or by the hero's disclosure of his identity. In both versions of the song, Meho is a close friend of Jela, the tavern maid. In an episode involving Jela, both singers need a musical instrument; in one version, it is in Meho's hands, in the other, in the hands of the woman. A comparison with Homer shows that this seemingly inconspicuous artifact may be a very important element of recognition scenes. After returning to Ithaka, Odysseus acts in disguise. The performance of his main task is preceded by several recognition scenes, but all this is preceded by the first recognition scene, which takes place during his journey home, at the court of the Phaeacian king. Here, too, the hero appears incognito, but he becomes known to everyone, and finally recognized, thanks to a song. The singer Demodokos tells of Odysseus's exploits at Troy (*Odyssey* 8.74–82, 500–520), thus making him close to the hearts of the Phaeacians. Now the hero can let himself be recognized (by disclosing his name, 9.19–20) and can continue the tale of his fate, started by Demodokos, and thus obtain help from the Phaeacians. As we can see, Homer follows a pattern characteristic of the epic plot. The sophisticated style of the author of *Odyssey* turns out to be typical of oral epic. If we consider plots of *Bećiragić Meho* and the *Odyssey* to be replications of a pattern common to oral poetics, we'll get a clear picture of how typical motifs and constructs are transformed into elaborate Homeric motifs.

Comparative studies have identified more patterns indispensable to the structure of the epic song. In the *Song of Bagdad*, the hero meets magic birds which advise him to go to Bagdad as a beggar, swapping clothes with a real beggar he will meet on his way. Lord describes the pattern:[9]

> In this disguise he meets a queen of Bagdad in the castle garden, there is a recognition scene, and this is followed by the combat, and finally by the abduction of the queen and the capture of the city. Characteristic of the group of songs concerned with the capture of a city is the fact that

[8] Lord 1960:102–106.

[9] Lord 1960:122.

> the siege has been going on unsuccessfully for a long period of time. ... It would seem, then, that all these groups, return, rescue, wedding, capture of city are the same song in respect to the pattern of captivity and freedom ...

This story is vividly reminiscent of Helen's tale from Book 4 of the *Odyssey*, in which Odysseus disguised as a beggar sneaks into the city, is received by Helen in her palace, is recognized by her only, and on his way back to the ships kills many Trojans.[10] The pattern in the *Odyssey* parallels that in the Bosnian song, with one significant change—Odysseus does not abduct Helen, occasioned by the plot of the Trojan Cycle.[11] In Proclus's summary, the story of Odysseus's spying expedition is linked with the story of stealing the Palladion from Troy. One might presume that both stories were merged into one because of their similarity. However, the Bosnian song's exhibition of a similar pattern suggests the fragmentation of a simple pattern in an extended epic narrative. Since the stealing of the queen, which would enable the conquest of the city, is impossible, two events are introduced, as if in counterbalance: the *Odyssey* presents Helen conferring with Odysseus about ways to conquer the city and helping to introduce the wooden horse into Troy; and Odysseus is indeed shown as stealing something, but not the queen—the statue of Athena. The tale of Odysseus's spying expedition is not, then, just any story from Odysseus's past, anticipating at most the events in Ithaca, but a typical element of the structure of epic songs. Something that was used as a digression is actually an important narrative pattern of another song.

The same parts of a given song may not only appear in a flexible form, with only one of its elements altered, but can also be reinterpreted or endowed with a new meaning. Lord cites the scene of hosting the protagonist and his companion in *The Wedding of Smailagić Meho*, tremendously expanded by Avdo Međedović, in comparison to the book version known to the scholar, which embraces only verses 194–204 (Mostar 1925).[12] The eponymous character, Meho, and his standard-bearer Osman are going from Kanije to Buda and on their way

10 *Odyssey* 4.240–264. This type of story seems to be traditional. Even if Homer had never heard this story, he built it parallel to the way it might have functioned in songs dealing with another theme. Here we have a transformation of a traditional element in order to fit it in a new context; see S. West 1988:209: "The prominence of Helen in this adventure is surely an ad hoc invention; it is hard to imagine that earlier poetry offered ready-made an episode so exactly suited to the purpose of directly involving Helen in the conversation and illustrating Odysseus's characteristic qualities in a light so favorable to her." However, Helen's favoring of Odysseus may be a traditional element of the Trojan War.

11 A similar story pattern can be also discerned in Herodotus's story about Zopyros conquering Babylon for Darius (*Histories* 3.152–158).

12 Lord 1960:107–108.

they make two stops, first at Vukašin's, and then Vujadin's, who give them a warm welcome.

In South Slavic epic, each stage of a journey deserves elaborate descriptions of the hospitality extended to the heroes at noblemen's dwellings. The reader of the *Odyssey* will easily spot many similarities in the scenes of the reception of Telemachos by Nestor (3.12–68, 345–493), and then by Menelaos (4.20–305, 582–624; 15.56–215), as well as the reception of Odysseus by Alkinoos (7.153–229, 334–347; 8.57–103, 400–586; 13.3–75). Telemachos journeys with his coeval and friend, Peisistratos, son of Nestor. The recognition of the strangers' nobility from their appearance, providing them with a bath, the admiration of their appearance (and, in return, the travelers' admiration for the wealth of their host), invitations for them to stay longer, caring for their horses, the travelers' decline of further hospitality, and their departure—all these elements are not only a reflection of a similar mentality, typical of a traditional society, in which hospitality is highly valued, but also the outcome of the use of the same theme.

Lord, demonstrating analogues to Telemachos's journey, points out that such scenes are emphasized

> neither because they are realistic pictures of heroic life nor because they are artistically useful in showing passage of time, but because the archetypal journey was of a ceremonial nature and its stages were marked by significant events and meaningful encounters.[13]

Telemachos takes to the road to get news about his father. However, he does not get any clues as to what is happening to Odysseus, only what he is like as a man and a warrior. The picture he gets confirms his earlier opinion of his father. But no less important for the *Odyssey* is to show the maturation of Telemachos, who turns out to be a son worthy of his father.[14] He sets out in order to oppose the insolence of the suitors. His journey gains a special meaning. Telemachos in his travels is treated with respect by the best—he deserves their friendship. He

[13] Lord 1960:109.

[14] Thalmann (1984:37–38) shows that Telemachos's visit to Menelaos and Odysseus's to Alkinoos are built on the same structure. The similarity, however, does not involve a mechanical repetition of type-scenes; the uses of the pattern are functional and entail a change of meaning. This repetition must have been noticeable to the audience, who could draw appropriate conclusions. This issue is elaborated in depth by Reece (1993), who demonstrates that the *Odyssey* consists of a series of successive hospitality scenes. Subsequent variations of the basic scene illustrate characteristics of the host and the guest. As a result, the audience receives an essentially binary message: a good/bad host, a good/bad guest. Since the ritual of receiving guests is extremely important in this culture, by showing the heroes' behavior in this perspective, Homer is able to suggest that his audience should give the heroes' conduct a moral evaluation. A comparison with *Nalopākhyāna* (Gresseth 1979) indicates that the story itself could be told in a different way—it was possible to omit the hosting scene, which imposes moral evaluation.

gets accepted by his social class. This bond compensates for the rejection and humiliation that he encounters in his own country. Since Telemachos turns out to be a worthy member of the heroic community, he needn't try to find help in order to fight his enemies.[15] From this passage in the *Odyssey*, we can infer that by obtaining the acceptance of the heroes, his father's friends, the young man proves to be a good warrior, ready to fight his foes himself.

Let's look at just one element of this specific characterization: a hero's ability to carry on a conversation.[16] In Međedović's singing, Meho, son of Smail, behaves extremely politely towards both of his hosts, even though they are of very different status: his first host Vukašin is a man of clearly lower status—one can note the element of subordination; his second host Vujadin has a much higher status, though he also seems to hold an inferior position to that of alaybey in Meho's house. The hero treats his hosts and members of their families with utmost respect, and he is delicate and generous towards women.

Smailagić's hosts know from the very beginning who they are dealing with. The appearance and the behavior of Meho and Osman arouse their constant admiration. As if that were not enough to make the audience realize the magnificence of the protagonist, Međedović relates Vujadin's conversation with the heroic Mehmed:[17]

> When the two imperial dragons entered, Vujadin bade them be seated, filled their glass, and did honor to his guests. "I am indeed pleased, imperial lords, that you have come to my dwelling." "Thank you, Vujadin, we have found you and rejoice that we had a friend to visit." "Thank you. You are welcome, Turks. I greeted you below in the courtyard, and now again in this chamber. How are you, Meho, son of the hadji, noble

15 I am intrigued by the question of why, when addressing his father's friends, Telemachos does not ask for armed assistance to deal with his foes or why none of them proposes it himself, even if Telemachos were to reject it. The scholia also pose such questions (*ad* 4.163, 167; see Pontani 2010:II.230 and 232), but the answers, based on the speeches in the text, are rather naive: Telemachos could have guessed that the information of Odysseus's impending return comes from Athena, so he was interested only where his father is at the present moment; Odysseus's companions, Nestor and Menelaos, do not want to force their help if it is not asked for, and moreover, since they know Odysseus is alive, they do not want to deprive him of his chance for revenge. Reece (1993:87) indicates that Peisistratos's words addressed to Menelaos: ἔπος ... ἔργον 'word ... deed' (4.163) suggest that Telemachos hopes to be provided with military help. Of course, Telemachos does not organize an expedition against the suitors, but the pattern of gathering warriors for an expedition by a young man, for whom a fight will be an initiation into adulthood, is common in oral epic. The *Telemachy* is such a song inserted into the structure of the Song of Return. However, as in the spying trip of Odysseus to Troy, it is deprived of a typical ending.

16 I stress this element because it was not noticed by Reece (1993).

17 Lord 1974:116–117.

> offspring of the illustrious father? It seems to me as I look upon you in my old age that you will not be much different from your father. No, you will not be any less noble than he. God bless you, my noble son! Do not disappoint your father!" Then he greeted Osman. "Welcome, lordly plume! Pride of the Border!" "May all good things be yours, o Vujadin!" "Now Mehmed, how is your father and your uncle Cifrić Hasanaga?" They are both well, thank you." "How are things on the Austrian border and how are the lords of the Border? Do you still lead your raiding bands over the mountains, your raiding bands and your large armies? Do you march as far as the Austrian empire, broadening the borders of Sulejman's kingdom? Have the young men become better than the old? How does it seem to you, Mehmed? Are the old men better than the young?" And Mehmed answered Vujadin: "Opinions are divided, but mine shall ever be that the old men are better than the young." "Bravo! My dear son. If God grants you will be an honor to us." Then he sat beside them on a chair and filled a three-liter glass. Aged Vujadin filled all three glasses and glowed with satisfaction.

In the *Odyssey*, Telemachos's similarity to his father is noticed by Helen, while Menelaos scolds himself for not noticing it (4.136–154). This physical similarity is immediately identified with the spiritual similarity of the young man to his father. In Avdo's song, the physical similarity of the young hero to his father immediately arouses Vujadin's conviction that he will equal his father in nobility. This statement certainly aims to flatter, but Vujadin, being an old man, admonishes the hero: "Do not disappoint your father." After a conventional inquiry about the health of the elders of the family, there is a series of questions, ostensibly also conventional, but they comprise a kind of test for the young man.

The young hero answers only the last question; its importance can be inferred from its duplication—a typical means of stressing significance in oral performance. The host, without commenting upon the omission, spontaneously expresses approval for Meho's opinion. Answers to previous questions could have confirmed the young hero's merits as a knight.[18] It is no problem for a singer to come up with such a story about the youthful exploits of his protagonist. Avdo, however, foregoes such an exposition. The first three questions Meho leaves unanswered; he only expresses the view that young people are not as good as older ones. This piece of gnomic wisdom, characteristic of oral culture, is of

[18] For example, Beowulf, provoked to self-praise, tells of his achievements in a deal with Breca (529–606).

great importance in the epic code.[19] The hero, despite the glory that surrounds him, does not fall into pride, but is modest. For Avdo, it is an essential feature of the heroic ethos. Telemachos comes to Menelaos as a stranger. His appearance is not described with such an accumulation of praise as in the case of Smail Agha's son, but it unequivocally qualifies him as a hero or at least a youth of an aristocratic family, if there is a distinction between the two.[20] Together with his companion, Peisistratos, he is invited to join the wedding feast. The hero remains unrecognized.[21] The host in this case does not start a conversation (the feast is not given on the arrival of the guests), so the guest feels obliged to speak first (*Odyssey* 4.69–81):

> δὴ τότε Τηλέμαχος προσεφώνεε Νέστορος υἱόν,
> ἄγχι σχὼν κεφαλήν, ἵνα μὴ πευθοίαθ' οἱ ἄλλοι·
> "φράζεο, Νεστορίδη, τῷ ἐμῷ κεχαρισμένε θυμῷ,
> χαλκοῦ τε στεροπὴν κατὰ δώματα ἠχήεντα
> χρυσοῦ τ' ἠλέκτρου τε καὶ ἀργύρου ἠδ' ἐλέφαντος.
> Ζηνός που τοιήδε γ' Ὀλυμπίου ἔνδοθεν αὐλή,
> ὅσσα τάδ' ἄσπετα πόλλα· σέβας μ' ἔχει εἰσορόωντα."
> τοῦ δ' ἀγορεύοντος ξύνετο ξανθὸς Μενέλαος,
> καί σφεας φωνήσας ἔπεα πτερόεντα προσηύδα·
> "τέκνα φίλ', ἦ τοι Ζηνὶ βροτῶν οὐκ ἄν τις ἐρίζοι·
> ἀθάνατοι γὰρ τοῦ γε δόμοι καὶ κτήματ' ἔασιν·
> ἀνδρῶν δ' ἤ κέν τίς μοι ἐρίσσεται, ἠὲ καὶ οὐκί,
> κτήμασιν. ἦ γὰρ πολλὰ παθὼν καὶ πόλλ' ἐπαληθεὶς
>
> And then Telemachos said to Nestor's son,
> leaning his head close, so that others would not hear:
> "Look, Nestor's son, joy of my heart,

19 Lord (1974:5) notes that the respect of a son for his father, or generally of the young for older men, was personally important for Međedović, who complained of having a disobedient son. Lord mentions that the son had squandered everything, but Sulejmana Zatrić's documentary *Avdo Međedovic: Balkanski Homer* from 2011 shows that Avdo's son, Zaim, and his children still live on the same farm. Avdo considered it a great injustice because he himself was absolutely obedient to his father, or at least he had always thought so. Obedience is here a synonym for respect for parents.

20 At the gate they are spotted by Menelaos's doorkeeper, who informs his master that two unknown men have arrived (*Odyssey* 4.27): γενεῇ δὲ Διὸς μεγάλοιο ἐίκτον, "come of the line of great Zeus."

21 Reece (1993:26) mentions that refraining from asking about the visitor's name in the *Odyssey* until after he is given food is a sign of respect. Having relatives from the former Polish eastern borderlands (now in Ukraine), I can confirm from my own experience the existence of such customs in traditional communities. A guest is not asked any questions, and is not even encouraged to talk, until after he/she has eaten.

> at the sheen of bronze echoing through this house,[22]
> of gold, electrum, silver, and ivory,
> such a room [must be] in Zeus's Olympian mansion,
> untold many things as these; godly fear grips me when I look at
> all this."
> What he said fair-haired Menelaos overheard
> and uttered winged words to them:
> "My dear child, no mortal man could compete with Zeus,
> as his mansion and riches are everlasting.
> Of people, perhaps there is someone who could rival me in the
> amount of possessions,
> or not. Because much suffering and roaming the world ..."

Telemachos's admiration for the riches of his host was kindly received by Menelaos. It is true that Menelaos does not allow him to equate his palace to that of Zeus, but the comparison is flattering, nevertheless. More important is the way that Odysseus's son conveys this flattery: he does not address Menelaos directly, but speaks to his companion, in an undertone, as if in a private conversation. But it is only a pretense: the host hears the words because he is supposed to hear them. Telemachos, who is much younger, should not address his host directly in an attempt to start a conversation. He behaves with modesty and respect for older people. Menelaos, whose curiosity about the guests is piqued, stresses the difference in their ages, addressing Telemachos[23] in a way that to us may seem a bit condescending. He says (4.78): τέκνα φίλ', 'my/dear child'.[24] Here, the young hero does not wait to be asked. He finds a way to show his good points by addressing a compliment ostensibly to his companion and, in reality, to the host. He manifests intelligence and courtly manners. By uttering these words, which are not empty admiration for riches, the young man just entering the path of heroic glory passes a test confirming that he belongs to a circle of heroes. Telemachos does it in a really Odyssean way, as is shown by Menelaos's self-reproach that he should have known that he is related to Odysseus (4.148–154).

In subsequent scenes, Telemachos shows his worth and proves again and again by his hospitality that he belongs in the heroic world. Before his journey, he receives Mentes (who is, in fact, Athena).[25] After he returns to Ithaca, he receives two more people—the prophet Theoklymenos, exiled from his country, and

22 An epithet stressing the size of the room.

23 Reece (1993:79) points out that the wedding loses its importance.

24 Vujadin similarly praises Meho's answer: "Bravo! My dear son."

25 See Race (1993:80–83), who demonstrates that Telemachos displays proper behavior already when he is first introduced into the narration. Race observes rightly that "the treatment of a guest or suppliant is the touchstone of every character's ἦθος in the *Odyssey*."

Odysseus, disguised as a beggar, in the shepherd's cottage, and in the palace, where Telemachos's conduct towards guests contrasts with that of the suitors. Telemachos knows how to behave properly as a guest and as a host. The suitors don't possess this ability, which excludes them from the heroic world: though they are not welcome, they impose themselves basely upon the household, they do not know how to be hospitable, and their behavior is insulting both to their hosts and guests.

Treating the modification of plot-patterns as a manifestation of the fallibility of singers' memory distorts the picture of how the song functioned in oral culture. Modifications are introduced deliberately, though the changes are never for their own sake. They reveal the singer's intentions about how he wants to tell his story. Scholars usually perceive such changes as innovations, as tales invented ad hoc. Meanwhile, the process is always one of giving a new shape to traditional material, which is carried out through contextual adjustment. Repetition, a strategy characteristic of oral tradition, takes a flexible form.[26] Moreover, new meanings are also obtained due to the inversion and conversion of elements that make up the traditional pattern.

The search for primary narrative patterns is limited by the scarcity of sources. That is why first attempts, even the ones based on comparative studies and taking into account other epic traditions and folk tales, tried to reduce the number of plots (to match Propp's model). Albert Lord reduced the composition of both Homeric epics to the pattern *withdrawal-devastation-return.*[27] Withdrawal is the absence or loss of a person/persons; devastation is usually understood as death, calamity, defeat; finally, return—of the absent person or someone who was lost—solves the problems of the plot. Such is the plot of the *Odyssey*: Odysseus's absence leads to a disastrous situation at home; his property, son, and wife suffer. Odysseus's return brings the punishment of those who were responsible for the devastation and restores order at home. The *Iliad* is based on the same essential pattern. Achilles' withdrawal from battle brings about the Achaean defeat, the deaths of many warriors, and danger for the whole expedition. His return, accompanied by the restoration of Briseis, leads to revenge upon the perpetrators of misfortunes and the restoration of Achaean power (instead of being besieged, they are again besiegers). This paradigm is repeated in the withdrawal of Meleagros in Phoinix's story and the stealing of Helen as a cause of the war.[28]

[26] Nagy (1996b:76–77) demonstrates the working of this flexibility in the compression or expansion of type-scenes.

[27] Lord 1960:186; compare Nagler 1974:Ch. 5.

[28] Edwards 1987:62–63. Enumerating "Agamemnon's loss of Chryseis that leads to the plague" as an additional cause must be a mistake because it was the refusal to return Chryseis to her father that was the cause of the plague.

Lord notes that in both Homeric poems this essential pattern is accompanied by the same motifs:

> The loss of someone near and dear to the hero (Patroclus and Odysseus's companions); both contain the element of disguise (the armor in the *Iliad* [and Odysseus's camouflage as a beggar]); in both the return is associated with contests or games and followed by remarriage (Achilles with Briseis, Odysseus with Penelope).[29]

Lord also suggests that "a long period of time is supposed to elapse, or have elapsed"[30] before the proper action of the song. It seems to me that his analysis of the *Iliad*, in which he finds the multiplication and overlapping of several story patterns, is unsatisfactory—the singer seems to juggle these patterns in a chaotic manner, changing the roles played by his characters.[31] But undoubtedly very valuable are Lord's remarks on the similarities between the two Homeric poems: in both, the protagonist must be recognized before the fight; he possesses special weapons (Odysseus's bow and Achilles' spear, which Patroklos could not use); Achilles' fight against the god of the river, in which Hephaistos lends him support at a critical moment, corresponds to the rescue of Odysseus from death in the sea, thanks to the intervention of the goddess Leukothea.[32] Lord also points out that the origin of the story patterns is twofold: the patterns may be mythic, so the hero takes over functions reserved earlier for a god, as when the hero kills a dragon/monster; or they may be secular, as in the pattern of wrath.[33]

I would like to propose a slightly different way of identifying the original patterns of epic. On the assumption that Homer's poems spring from the same source as all other epic songs and mythic tales, I will try to demonstrate that the frequent repetition of motifs and sets of motifs bears witness to the existence of a certain schematism, which then allows us to recognize the integrity of epic song in oral transmission. Tracking such similarities in the construction

29 Lord 1960:186.

30 Lord (1960:186) does not notice the conventionality of the time calculated as a complete cycle (see Ch. 1, above) because he writes: "I believe that it was the element of the length of the Trojan War, itself apparently a historical fact, which drew the story of the bride-stealing theme. Once this was sanctified, the war became the setting for tales of absence and return, and mythic death and resurrection, associated with fertility myth and ritual."

31 E.g. Lord 1960:190: "Achilles' return to battle should mean the end of the Trojan War according to the pattern of the story of wrath. But the wrath is introductory. The withdrawal of Achilles is the key; for by it we can modulate from the wrath pattern to a pattern of death and return, which in turn evokes the complex of death by substitute."

32 Lord 1960:195–197. Also very valuable are the parallels that Lord finds with European epic of the Middle Ages and the epic of *Gilgamesh*.

33 Lord 1995:11–13.

of song narration is, of course, burdened with the risk of arbitrariness. Note, however, that in comparing patterns, we deal with a sequence of reappearing elements, and so we can apply the method used by Georges Dumézil in religious studies:[34] certain facts resurface in different configurations at a different place and time, but if they function in conjunction with one another, we cannot treat that as a coincidence.

Similarities of Cyclic Events as a Trace of Traditional Patterns

Combinations of type-scenes

If we take into account the principles of durability of epic narrative patterns and non-coincidental repetition of scenes, we can find traces of traditional patterns followed by the *aoidoi* in entering their songs into the macro-story of the Trojan Cycle. Below, I will present a handful of patterns used in the *Iliad*, which were, I believe, inherited from epic tradition, sometimes probably a very distant one.

The arrival of allies

When looking for the starting point of the *Iliad*, one has to ask why the Greeks are fighting the Trojans in the field instead of laying a regular siege to the city. The answer is far from obvious and has sometimes led researchers to strange conclusions.[35] It is an effect of treating the plot of cyclic songs as a sequence of events arranged in a chronological order: there had to be a failed assault on the city, then nothing happened for a long time, and at the end of the war there were several spectacular encounters on the plain at Troy. But the Achaean victory in individual encounters did not facilitate the capture of the city. From this point of view, the *Iliad* may simply present the most dangerous situation for the Greeks, because their ships are threatened. As I have argued in the previous chapter, such "historicism" in the analysis of the plot of an epic cycle is erroneous and anachronistic. Even if we recognize military encounters at Troy as historical, this does not mean that the epic reconstructs exactly the events associated with the capture of the city.

The sequence of activities suggested by the epics of the cycle, including the *Iliad*, is a result of certain patterns adopted by singers in the construction of their songs. In an attempt to clarify the matter from a military point of

34 Dumézil and Eribon 1996:106–108, 124–125.

35 Karkowski (2007:36–38) concludes that the war lasted so long because the Greeks—much less numerous than the Catalogue of Ships suggests—were concerned first of all about the safety of their vessels.

view, Albracht states that fights had been initiated by the besieged, who had been trying to get rid of the uncomfortable company of the besiegers.[36] The Achaeans did not so much pose a real threat to Troy, because they had no means of capturing a fortified city, as they hampered its normal functioning by plundering the neighboring area. The situation of the Trojans was further complicated by the necessity of provisioning their allies. If nobody initiated fighting, both parties behaved passively.

Perhaps these inquiries correctly reproduce the hypothetical reality of combat, but they are meaningless to the construction of an epic story. The singer knows nothing about methods of reconstruction such as Albracht used, and he can only impose his own ideas on a situation from the distant past. Creating the song, the *aiodos* has in his mind some images, which he tries to keep in the construction of the story. Its plot must, of course, be consistent with the listeners' sense of reality.

What situation occurs to the singer who intends to compose a song about the conquest of the holy city of Troy? One fact is certain: an extended and tiresome siege. It does not have to result from any particular tactics or shortage of troops attacking the city. The singer does not sing about any war; he sings about *the* war, about the war "whose fame then reached the skies." The long siege, lasting a magical period of 9 + 1 years, expresses the extent of this war and its uniqueness, which ensured its survival in song.[37]

In a similar fashion, the Bosnian *Song of Bagdad* starts in the twentieth year of Sulejman's siege of the city.[38] The song opens with the scene of a council, which has to solve the problem of the prolonged siege. As usual in such songs, there is bad and good advice: the bad advice is criticized, the good—to call reinforcements from Bosnia—is accepted.[39] The *Iliad* also starts with the scene of an assembly, at which bad advice—to sail home—is offered, and which has to address the question of how to avert the calamity threatening the army. Such scenes of an assembly, with contrasted bad and good advice (good advice leads to the capture of Troy), appear several times in a basically the same, though variable shape. The calling of reinforcements from Bosnia is similar to the

36 Albracht 2005 (1895/1896[1]):124–125.

37 West (1997:288) believes that an epic poet focuses on the final events of the war, those which determine its result. Here West notes a poetic convention, but he does not see that its long duration is a matter of convention too. He simply treats an epic poem as a record of historical reality. The *Aethiopis*, *Little Iliad*, and *Ilioupersis* depict the final phase of the Trojan War, just like the *Iliad*. According to Hesiod, the Titanomachy also lasted ten years, but the poet shows only the events of the final day (that is, as we already know, the closing day of the 9 + 1 period).

38 This number is of magical and symbolic character, though the capture of Bagdad is a historical fact.

39 Lord 1960:68.

arrival of Trojan allies at Troy. The fact that the reinforcements appear at the moment when the siege is ending reminds us of the paradoxical situation in the songs of the Trojan Cycle. The *Song of Bagdad* presents an obstacle arising at the end of the war; to overcome this obstacle it is necessary to gather and bring troops from a distant country. Such an assumption in the plot reveals ahistorical thinking, which is typical of epic. If the *Song of Bagdad* had evolved into a cycle, there could have appeared various obstacles preventing the capture of the city and various methods of dealing with this problem, e.g. bringing more contingents. The capture of the city is not presented from the point of view of Turks, but Bosnians, who can appear in the war only as an episode, even if the episode leads to the denouement. It means that the Bosnian song lacks the broad pan-Hellenic perspective of Greek epic.

A comparison of the beginning of the *Iliad* with the evidence from other cyclic poems indicates that the starting point for all Greek epic songs is a crisis. The crisis may manifest itself in various ways, but its primary reason—despite the efforts made by the Achaeans—is the failure to take Troy. The crisis requires special measures: on the road to the conquest of Troy there appear new obstacles—Hektor, Memnon, the Palladion, etc.—which must be eliminated (we will deal with this later in this chapter).

In the structure of the song, the crisis is linked with the motif of dispute between Achaean warriors, which, as we saw in the previous chapter, is the basic element for constructing epic songs. The solution to the crisis does not lead directly to the capture of Troy, rather it fulfills the condition which is essential for the Greek victory. In this way, within the cycle there is room for this and other epic songs.

The main task of the singer is to present the heroic aspect of the distant reality. He can exaggerate the extent of the war, the strength of the parties engaged, and the length of unresolved struggle, and give a heroic picture of combat. Such combat gains its heroic dimension in individual duels carried out in the open, often without the participation of third parties. Such a picture of heroism can be found not only at the siege of Troy, but also during the expedition of the Seven against Thebes, during which Theban warriors leave the city, rushing in chariots to meet their opponents from the Peloponnese. From each of the city's seven gates there rides out a commander to fight a duel with one of the enemy leaders, so the forces are perfectly balanced. The task of the singer is therefore to draw out Trojan warriors from the city.

In the case of the *Iliad*, it is not easy, because Trojan forces are, according to Agamemnon, ten times less numerous than the forces of the Achaeans (2.119–133). This should be regarded as an element of the tradition, because a one-to-one fight during the Theban expedition shows that it was possible to present a war between equal forces. Moreover, the comparison with the Theban Cycle reveals an important fact, that fighting is initiated by the besieged. Why? The answer is simple: a story of a regular siege would be non-heroic and pointless from the point of view of the narrative.

If something is needed to encourage the besieged to act, the arrival of allies provides an obvious impulse, given the imbalance in the forces on both sides. It also gives a natural starting point for an epic song about conquering a city. Later songs can speak about the arrival of the subsequent contingents of allies.

According to Proclus's summary, this is exactly the situation in the *Aethiopis*. The arrival of Amazons headed by Penthesileia leads to a fight between the Greeks and Trojans. Then the fight is renewed after Memnon arrives with the Ethiopians. In the *Iliad*, in the context of Agamemnon's quarrel with Achilles, the motif of sending troops to the battlefield is prompted by a lying dream which Zeus sends to Agamemnon. The Achaean leader wakes up certain that it is the day on which he will conquer Troy (*Iliad* 2.56–76). The author of the *Iliad*, like any other oral poet, cannot leave out significant elements for the construction of the song and therefore, he cannot pass over the role of allied leaders. Like in the *Aethiopis*, and probably other songs, they are destined to die by the hand of "the best of the Achaeans." In both the *Aethiopis* and the *Iliad*, their recent arrival is stressed, although for the construction of the *Iliad*, this is not so important because it is not the cause for the renewal of fighting. However, although we know how Agamemnon managed to prompt the Achaean warriors to start fighting, we do not know what inspired the Trojan troops to go into battle, especially since Achilles' presence dampens their eagerness to leave the fortified city. Later, only loyalty to the ethos of the hero prompts Hektor to face the Achaeans in the open field, since the position near the defensive walls is much safer for Trojans. With the army hiding behind the city walls, there is no fighting. On this day, Achilles is actually absent in the Achaean ranks, but the Trojans can only find that out during the battle.[40]

No wonder, then, that the *Iliad* emphasizes the role of the allies: Sarpedon in his speech to the fleeing Hektor stresses his own value, stating that only allies

40 There might have been a version of the *Iliad* in which the Trojans learned about Achilles' withdrawal from fighting, since it was Hera who prompted Achilles to summon the assembly in Book 1. The narrator explains it by noting the goddess' concern for the Achaeans, her favorites, who were being decimated by the plague. Ancient commentators noticed the illogicality of her intervention; during the assembly, Achilles quarrels with Agamemnon and withdraws from combat, which causes the destruction of the Achaeans on the battlefield. It has also been suggested that Hera acts in this way in order to bring about a fight in the open field, which should enable a quick and decisive victory over the Trojans (according to scholia bT; see Kirk 1985:59 *ad* 1.55–56). It is difficult to determine whether this is a deduction made from the *Iliad* or an echo of a different version of the work.

have the courage to fight against the Achaeans (5.471–488). From among all the tribes listed in the catalogue of Trojan allies, only the Lycians led by Sarpedon and Glaukos play a special role in the battle described in the *Iliad*. The actions of these two leaders are important for the course of fighting, and moreover the whole tribe itself is mentioned several times. Sarpedon is the first one to break the Achaean wall (12.395–397; 16.558);[41] only Hektor performs a greater deed, setting the first ship on fire (15.717–727).[42]

Just as the *Aethiopis* doubles the scene of the arrival of allies—Amazons and Ethiopians—at Troy, so too does the preserved version of the *Iliad*: the role of the Lycians is similar to that of the Thracians under Rhesos. Although Book 10 is widely regarded as inauthentic, there are reasons to believe that the events depicted there are an immanent part of the *Iliad*.[43] Regardless of whether the *Doloneia* was originally a part of the *Iliad* or not, it might have been a schematic nucleus of a song, which could have functioned independently, whereas in the Homeric poem it plays the role of a digression.

The possibility of the independence of the *Doloneia* from the *Iliad* is indicated by the version attributed to Pindar (Arn/A and bT *ad* 10.435). According to this version, Rhesos fought in battle only one day and was so successful that Athena and Hera, worried about the fate of the Achaeans, induced Diomedes and Odysseus to kill him when he was sleeping. Another version of the story, from the pseudo-Euripidean tragedy *Rhesos*, mentions an oracle that if Rhesos and his horses drink from the Skamandros, he will be invincible, so at night Diomedes and Odysseus kill Rhesos, who has just arrived that evening. Both the Pindar and pseudo-Euripides versions are much more logical, because in the *Iliad*, Odysseus and Diomedes learn about the arrival of the Thracians accidentally from Dolon when he is interrogated (10.421–442). The act of killing of Rhesos and twelve Thracians, and stealing their horses constitutes a benefit in itself, since it multiplies the success of the spying mission (10.484–515, 559–564).

Divine inspiration, or the knowledge of the oracle which prompts the Achaean heroes to act, is not only more sensible than the Homeric version, but also constitute a more coherent element of the narration, being directly related to the time of Rhesos's arrival at Troy. And here the time of his arrival

41 See Hainsworth 1993:359; Janko 1992:386.

42 See Janko 1992:306.

43 Fenik (1964:123–125) believes that the *Doloneia* manifests awareness and adaptation of the tradition in which killing Rhesos enables the capture of Troy. The opinion that the *Doloneia* is an integral part of the *Iliad* is shared by Mueller (1984:176), Dué and Ebbott (2010), and Bierl (2012); compare Haft (1990:52). Danek (1988:29) believes that Book 10 is formular in the same degree (around 56%) as the rest of the *Iliad*. He also demonstrates (Danek 1988:230–234) the affinity between the formulaic language of the *Doloneia* and the Homeric poems, but in his view Book 10 is a work of another *aoidos* and not much later than the main body of the *Iliad*.

is, I believe, of utmost importance. In the versions mentioned above, Rhesos arrives with the Thracians on the previous day. In the *Iliad,* these Thracians are described as νεήλυδες 'newcomers, recently arrived' (10.434), a general term, but clearly indicating that the author of this passage was aware of an earlier version of this story.[44] This is a third confirmation of the fact that the newly arrived contingent of allies not only provides support for the Trojans, but also creates an obstacle for the Greeks, for whom the need to overcome it becomes a priority. The invulnerability of Rhesos means nothing more than the fact that if he is not killed at once, Troy will remain unconquered. The killing of this hero is therefore one of the conditions necessary for capturing the city. The uniqueness of Rhesos is confirmed by the description of his unusual horses and weapons, suggesting their magical meaning.[45]

The *Iliad* does not specify when Sarpedon arrived at Troy with the Lycians, but we can infer that it happened a short while before.[46] Many scholars are surprised that the Lycians appear last[47] in the Trojan catalogue, considering how important a role they play in the poem, which may indicate that they arrived recently, maybe even on the day before the battle described in the song. This means that in this song, the most important task falls to the Lycians, and so the killing of their leader becomes a priority for the Achaeans.[48]

The coming of Trojan allies, the Lycians under Sarpedon and Thracians under Rhesos, gives a reason for battle. The duplication of the theme of the arrival of allied contingents in the *Aethiopis* and *Iliad* must be meaningful. Maybe its duplication lies at the heart of the formation of a monumental poem? The arrival of the allies bringing rescue to the besieged appears to be a typical pattern for constructing an epic song about the Trojan War or, more generally, of a song

44 This term is used in relation to horses stolen from the Thracians (10.558), which clearly corroborates our idea, since horses fulfill an important function in the oracle.

45 See Ch. 3, p. 290, below.

46 Diomedes, meeting Glaukos, one of Lycian leaders, expresses his astonishment because until that moment he has not seen him in the battlefield (6.124).

47 Kirk (1985:262) states that although it looks as if Homer had suddenly remembered them, their placement at the end can be justified: "It is remarkable that the Lukioi, Lycians, who are the most important allies in the rest of the poem, are confined to these two closing verses, which sound almost like an afterthought. Yet their position is logical enough, depending on their being at the end (as 877 τηλόθεν confirms) of this final chain of allies."

48 Time expressions used in reference to other Trojan allies confirm that the length of the allies' stay at Troy is a matter of convention. Lykaon dies on the twelfth day after returning to Troy (*Iliad* 21.46–47); right after that (21.156), Asteropaios, the leader of Paeonians, says that it is his eleventh day at Troy (perhaps it is a foreshadowing of his death on the next day)—building the time frame of the work by means of twelve-day periods is evident. In the *Doloneia*, Diomedes kills twelve Thracian warriors, which may indicate the closure of a period linked with the number twelve (Aias kills twelve Trojans, single-handedly defending Protesilaos's ship set on fire, 15.747).

about conquering a city. According to Apollodorus, all Trojan allies arrive at the end of the ninth year of the war (*Epitome* 3.34): ἐνναεοῦς δὲ χρόνου διελθόντος παραγίνονται τοῖς Τρωσὶ σύμμαχοι ("after a period of nine years, allies came to join the Trojans"). And right after that he repeats the whole Homeric Trojan catalogue. A rationalizing interpretation explaining that only now the Trojans managed to gather allied forces is absurd and distorts the essence of things. From the point of view of an epic, what happens between the beginning and the end of the war is irrelevant. All songs in this cycle begin, as we have seen in the previous chapter, at the beginning or end of the macro-story of the cycle. Evidently, if it starts at the end, it is connected to the motif of allies, who always come at the last moment, because their defeat opens the way to conquering the city. Allies are the first obstacle which must be overcome to enable the success of the Achaeans. Although there is a long list of the allies, they play practically no role in the song except for only one contingent (two, if the motif is doubled,[49] but they always act independently). The function of Trojan catalogues in the *Iliad* and *Kypria* is to show the balance of forces in the exaggerated dimension of the heroic battle (recall Agamemnon's words about the predominance of the Achaeans): the enormous power of Greek troops requires a suitably powerful opponent.[50] I don't think that the number of tribes listed in the catalogue of Trojan allies corresponds to the number of songs based on the same pattern, although it may indicate a potential for such songs. Just as surrounding an epic hero with a circle of heroes/comrades elevates his exploits, so too the value of support is increased if there are many allies, though only some of them play a significant role in the story.

49 Lycians and Thracians in the *Iliad*, Amazons and Ethiopians in the *Aethiopis*.

50 Therefore, the opinion put forward by Huxley (1969:140–141) should be regarded as erroneous and resulting from his acceptance of historicism. He claims that the location of the Trojan catalogue at the end of Proclus's summary of the *Kypria* resulted from the situation of the population of the Troad after Achilles in several expeditions had conquered twenty-three cities. According to Huxley, people deprived of the protection of city walls took refuge in Troy. This interpretation is backed by Burgess (1996:85), who suggests that from this point of view, the location of the Trojan catalogue in this place is much more logical than after the Catalogue of Ships, as it is in the *Iliad*. However, the rationality of this explanation is illusory. It would not be possible for Troy to absorb a tenfold increase in population (although the singer might not have been aware of the fact), and, moreover, the Trojan allies do not come from the regions close to Troy (I really do not know how we can count Lycians or Cilicians as Trojan neighbors). Even if we assume that there is some historical reality behind the story in the epic, it is certainly not this kind of reality (see Ch. 3, below). The macro-story of the cycle is not so coherent and consistent as to allow the presentation of the Trojan catalogue in one place in its structure only (such is the opinion of West 1966:402, against which Burgess [1996:86–90] rightly argues, maintaining that the catalogue has an equal status in both works). In my opinion, the thing must be treated more broadly: the Trojan catalogue is a typical element of an oral song and could be used in various songs based on the pattern of the conquest of the city, providing a reason for both armies to fight in the open field.

Killing a leader of the allies and killing Priam's son

The arrival of Trojan allies gives an opportunity for presenting combat in the open field and depicting the heroic valor of warriors, especially the commanders of allied armies. Penthesileia's and Memnon's deeds are described as an *aristeia*: the queen of the Amazons slays the warrior/physician Machaon, and the Ethiopian king kills Antilochos. The pseudo-Euripidean Rhesos is also shown as having an *aristeia* on the day of his arrival. Sarpedon repeatedly distinguishes himself in the battle, the greatest of his deeds being the killing of Tlepolemos (5.657–659) and breaching the Achaean wall (12.395–397).

These successes of the Trojan allies require a reaction from the Achaeans. And each time the reaction involves the death of an allied leader. This is the case with the most mysterious character, Kyknos. Mythographic sources identify him as the first significant victim on the Trojan side, however, very little is known about him. In Greek mythology, there are several people of that name. Sometimes they are differentiated by mythographers, sometimes not, and the lives of many of them are combined into the life of one. The Kyknos who dies at the outset of the Trojan War is sometimes identified with the Kyknos of Kolonai, a city in the vicinity of Troy, the father of Tenes (of whom more later). We know that this first Kyknos was a son of Poseidon and a Trojan ally (though sources do not associate him with any tribe), and that he arrived at Troy in ships.[51] Like other allied leaders, he has a unique quality: he is immune to wounds inflicted by weapons. He dies by Achilles' hand, strangled with thongs of his helmet or hit by a stone. He is usually distinguished from Kyknos, a son of Ares, killed by Herakles, but his immunity to metal weapons makes him similar to the monsters whom the hero defeats.[52]

Kyknos is slain by Achilles, but his role is much greater than one of Achilles' victims. Linking him, as Pindar does (*Olympian* 2.147), with Hektor and Memnon, other victims of Achilles, does not quite do him justice. He should not be grouped together with Priam's sons, but only with other commanders of Trojan allies. Plot structure requires both the death of an allied leader and one of Priam's sons. The killing of the leader always appears first, and the killing of Priam's son follows later. Of five similar situations, in three the killer is Achilles, who puts

51 *Scholia in Pindarum Olympian* 2.147: δὲ Ποσειδῶνος Ἀχιλλεὺς στρατευσάμενον καὶ συμμαχοῦντα τοῖς Τρωσίν "Kyknos, son of Poseidon, who went there on expedition as a Trojan ally, [was killed] by Achilles"; *Scholia et glossae in Olympian* 2.147 ὁ δὲ Ποσειδῶνος, ναῦς ἔχων καὶ συμμαχῶν τοῖς Τρωσίν, ἱσταμένος ἐν στενῷ τῆς ἐκεῖ θαλάσσης καὶ οὐκ ἐῶν τοὺς Ἕλληνας ἀποβῆναι, ὃν Ἀχιλλεὺς ἀπέκτεινεν "[Kyknos], this son of Poseidon [arrived] on ships and was a Trojan ally; he stopped in the sea strait and did not allow the Greeks to land. This one was killed by Achilles."

52 Antaios, for example, drew strength from his mother Earth, which is why Herakles choked him, raising him in the air.

an end to the feats of Kyknos, Penthesileia, and Memnon. Sarpedon is killed by Patroklos (16.480–504), but the hero, fighting in Achilles' armor, stands in for him on the battlefield (16.278–864).[53] In this epic pattern, Rhesos's death signifies a departure from the norm, because he is killed by a joint action of Diomedes and Odysseus. Working in co-operation, they perform another deed: they steal the Palladion, which protects Troy and is one of the obstacles standing in the way of capturing the city.

We could talk about the variations of a type-scene, in which an Achaean hero kills a leader of the allies, if it weren't for the fact that it is always accompanied by the motif of killing a son of Priam, and here the actor is, again, Achilles. The flexibility of the pattern does not make it unrecognizable, as is apparent from these four instances:

1. Achilles kills Kyknos, a Trojan ally, the Trojans withdraw to the city, Achilles kills Troilos, son of Priam;
2. Achilles forces Aeneas, the Dardanian leader, to run away, and kills Mestor, son of Priam;
3. Patroklos (Achilles' substitute) kills Sarpedon, the Lycian leader, the Trojans run away to the city, and Achilles kills Hektor, son of Priam;
4. Achilles kills Penthesileia, the leader of Amazons, and Memnon, the leader of Ethiopians, and then he is killed by Paris, son of Priam, at the Scaean Gate, which suggests that the Trojans must have sought shelter behind the city walls.

The killing of Achilles by Paris, son of Priam, is a significant coda to this pattern within the cycle: the killer of Priam's sons dies at the hand of one of them, the most important one, we would say, if the action of the *Iliad* didn't favor Hektor. Before this happens, the potential for the multiplication of this pattern seems unlimited. The singer can always bring new allies to Troy, and Priam is known to have a large number of children and many wives.[54] Naturally, as in the case

[53] The identification of Patroklos with Achilles is greatly determined also by his death, which substitutes for the death of Achilles. See Ch. 5, below.

[54] Apollodorus *Library* 3.12.5 enumerates the names of all forty-eight sons Priam had with various women, whereas Homer speaks generally about fifty sons and twelve daughters. The number of children is ingeniously sneaked into the text, when Homer mentions fifty chambers in the Priam's palace for his sons and twelve for his daughters, where they live with their husbands (*Iliad* 6.242–250). Homer thus avoids saying how many sons Priam has because some of them are already dead. Priam himself tells Achilles (24.495–500) that he had fifty sons (nineteen by one wife—Hekabe), but many (he does not say how many) of them are dead. Fifty and twelve are magical and symbolic numbers. Perhaps, in accordance with the interpretation proposed in the previous chapter, it is related to the fifty days of the *Iliad* and fifty last days of Achilles; similarly, the number of daughters corresponds to the number of months in a solar year.

of the Trojan catalogue, the motif of killing two enemies of this kind is rather a potentiality that does not have to be absolutely put to work.[55]

Achilles withdraws from battle and the prophecy of his death

The awareness of imminent death hangs over Achilles like the sword of Damocles. In the same way, it pervades the entire structure of the *Iliad*. His death is the unattainable goal of the song's action, since Homer attempts to present Achilles' acceptance of his premature death. In the narrative, it becomes clear that Achilles knows his fate, because it was disclosed to him by his mother, the goddess Thetis. This prediction is given again in quite dramatic circumstances,[56] when Achilles refuses to accept gifts from Agamemnon, and the embassy of Odysseus and Aias returns without having achieved its aim (*Iliad* 9.410–416):

> μήτηρ γάρ τέ μέ φησι θεὰ Θέτις ἀργυρόπεζα
> διχθαδίας κῆρας φερέμεν θανάτοιο τέλος δέ.
> εἰ μέν κ' αὖθι μένων Τρώων πόλιν ἀμφιμάχωμαι,
> ὤλετο μέν μοι νόστος, ἀτὰρ κλέος ἄφθιτον ἔσται·
> εἰ δέ κεν οἴκαδ' ἵκωμι φίλην ἐς πατρίδα γαῖαν,
> ὤλετο μοι κλέος ἐσθλόν, ἐπὶ δηρὸν δέ μοι αἰὼν
> ἔσσεται, οὐδέ κέ μ' ὦκα τέλος θανάτοιο κιχείη.

> Because my mother, the silver-footed goddess Thetis,
> told me that in one of two directions will *kêrai* carry me to the end,
>   which is death:
> If I stay here, fighting for the city of the Trojans,
>
> my return will be lost, but I will gain indestructible fame,
> and if I go back home, to my dear native land,
> the glorious fame will be lost, but my life will be long
> and I will not reach the end, which is death, soon.

In this way, the singer introduces the famous alternative, which Achilles seems to consider, but he finally decides to stay and fight against the Trojans, thus condemning himself to death there. However, this is a misleading idea. Achilles

55 Another example of this pattern is the introduction of Neoptolemos, son of Achilles, to the plot. Brought from Skyros, like his father, he takes his place on the battlefield. Neoptolemos kills Eurypylos, the leader of the newly arrived contingent of Mysians. Eurypylos is the son of Telephos, wounded by Achilles during the Teuthranian expedition. Then, during the capture of Troy, Neoptolemos kills Priam. The pattern gets a new symbolic ending.

56 The first time, Achilles mentions it very briefly, telling his mother that she bore him for a short life (*Iliad* 1.352).

dissociates himself from such thinking, when he replies to Patroklos, who asks his friend to return to the battlefield or send him alone with support for the endangered Achaeans. Patroklos speaks very cautiously, endeavoring not to irritate Achilles (*Iliad* 16.36–39):

> εἰ δέ τινα φρεσὶ σῇσι θεοπροπίην ἀλεείνεις
> καί τινά τοι πὰρ Ζηνὸς ἐπέφραδε πότνια μήτηρ,
> ἀλλ' ἐμέ περ πρόες ὦχ', ἅμα δ' ἄλλον λαὸν ὄπασσον
> Μυρμιδόνων, ἤν πού τι φόως Δαναοῖσι γένωμαι.
>
> But if you are trying to shun a divine prophecy
> and your lady mother relayed to you some words of Zeus,
> send me now speedily and give me the rest
> of the troops of the Myrmidons, so maybe I will prove to be light to
> the Danaans.

In the whole of Patroklos's speech, this one element irritates Achilles, and he refers to it immediately at the beginning of his reply, explaining his point of view (16.49–59):

> ὤ μοι διογενὲς Πατρόκλεες οἷον ἔειπες·
> οὔτε θεοπροπίης ἐμπάζομαι ἥν τινα οἶδα,
> οὔτέ τί μοι πὰρ Ζηνὸς ἐπέφραδε πότνια μήτηρ·
> ἀλλὰ τόδ' αἰνὸν ἄχος κραδίην καὶ θυμὸν ἱκάνει,
> ὁππότε δὴ τὸν ὁμοῖον ἀνὴρ ἐθέλῃσιν ἀμέρσαι
> καὶ γέρας ἂψ ἀφελέσθαι, ὅ τε κράτεϊ προβεβήκῃ·
> αἰνὸν ἄχος τό μοί ἐστιν, ἐπεὶ πάθον ἄλγεα θυμῷ.
> κούρην ἣν ἄρα μοι γέρας ἔξελον υἷες Ἀχαιῶν,
> δουρὶ δ' ἐμῷ κτεάτισσα πόλιν εὐτείχεα πέρσας,
> τὴν ἂψ ἐκ χειρῶν ἕλετο κρείων Ἀγαμέμνων
> Ἀτρεΐδης ὡς εἴ τιν' ἀτίμητον μετανάστην.
>
> Ah, what a thing you said, divine Patroklos!
> I do not care about any prophecy, even if I know one,
> Nor about what my lady mother relayed to me from Zeus.
> But this terrible grief grips my heart and soul,
> whenever a man wants to oppress his equal
> and take away a given portion of the spoil, because he surpasses him
> in power:
> I have a terrible grudge, because I suffered in my heart.
> The girl whom the sons of the Achaeans gave me as my share

> —and who was won with spears, when I destroyed her fortified city—
> this one the ruler Agamemnon, son of Atreus, took away, snatching
> her out of my arms,
> as if I were an exile who is not respected.

As we can see, he repeats the reasons for his withdrawal from combat given in the embassy scene and puts the blame upon Agamemnon.

Achilles' answer used to present problems to scholars. Why does he have to repeat his reasons to Patroklos, since he was in the tent earlier and could hear the reply given to Agamemnon's ambassadors? And why is there in the *Iliad* a double motivation for Achilles' withdrawal from fighting? I start with the view which influences the general understanding of this issue. Christopher Wilson supplied the following comment to verses 9.411–416:

> Critics have sometimes felt uneasy about this, especially in connection with XVI 36–51, where replying to a question from Patroklos Akhilleus flatly denies that it is some warning from his mother that is now holding him back from fighting himself. Akhilleus' denial there could be explained by what he then goes to say—that it is still Agamemnon's insult that holds him back, the effect of which would be diminished if he were to add that his mother's prophecy is doing so too. A more serious difficulty that the passage in XVI presents is over why Patroklos, who is present here as Akhilleus addresses the ambassadors, should already know the answer to it. Willcock makes the suggestion that the alternative fates here may have been invented for the purposes of the present passage.[57] This would be then one example—among several—of some apparent faultiness in the editing of IX in relation to the rest of poem; the passage in XVI has not been brought into line with the invention that has been introduced into IX.[58]

Indeed, analysts have often concluded that the whole of Book 9, with the embassy to Achilles, is a later addition. Among contemporary scholars, there are also voices (e.g. D. Page, W. Sale[59]) suggesting that Achilles' speeches from Books 11 and 16, in which he expresses his expectation that the Achaeans will beg him and give him gifts as an apology—as if he forgot about the gifts offered to him

57 Willcock 1978:278 *ad* 410–416: "Although these lines have always been thought very significant for the character of Achilleus in the *Iliad*, they are probably an invention for the present passage. Achilleus' fateful choice is never referred to again; and in XVI 50–51 he explicitly denies that he has had any warning from his mother."

58 Wilson 1996:236.

59 Page 1959:305; Sale 1964:86–100.

by Agamemnon and the pleas of his friends in Book 9—irrevocably testify to the incompatibility of these books; thus, the embassy scene must be secondary. I believe that such an inference is uncertain, or even faulty. We will return to this issue in Chapter 6; now let us focus on the double motivation for Achilles' withdrawal from combat.

The idea that the alternative fates presented to the hero by his mother is an innovation rests upon the acknowledgement of the priority of the *Iliad* to the rest of the cyclic poems. The motif of Achilles' withdrawal from battle is several times repeated in the macro-story of the cycle as it has come down to us. The withdrawal is always prompted by the hero's desire to avoid the threat of death. In each case, Achilles is aware of the fate that awaits him because of the prophecy communicated to him by his divine mother. An introduction to this pattern is already in the motif preceding the expedition, when Achilles avoids going to Troy, hidden by his mother among girls on the island of Skyros. During the war, the avoidance of fighting always happens according to the following pattern:

> Though warned by Thetis that he should not kill Tenes when the expedition lands on Tenedos, Achilles probably tries to keep away from a skirmish, but finally kills him in a fight. Thetis predicts Apollo's part in her son's death.[60]
>
> Thetis communicates to Achilles the prophecy that the first Achaean warrior to step on the Trojan shore will die first, and so Achilles refrains from landing. The first one to land is, therefore, Protesilaos, who is slain after a series of successes. Achilles goes ashore with the Myrmidons as the second one and kills Kyknos.[61] The

60 Apollodorus *Epitome* 3.26: Προσπλέοντας οὖν Τενέδῳ τοὺς Ἕλληνας ὁρῶν Τένης ἀπεῖργε βάλλων πέτρους, καὶ ὑπὸ Ἀχιλλέως ξίφει πληγεὶς κατὰ τὸ στῆθος θνήσκει, καίτοι Θέτιδος προειπούσης Ἀχιλλεῖ μὴ κτεῖναι Τένην· τεθνήξεσθαι γὰρ ὑπὸ Ἀπόλλωνος αὐτόν, ἐὰν κτεῖνῃ Τένην. "Having noticed the Greeks putting in at Tenedos, Tenes attacked them by throwing stones. Then he was killed by Achilles, hit with a sword in the breast, though Thetis had warned Achilles not to kill Tenes, because he himself would die by the hand of Apollo if he slew Tenes." Plutarch *Questiones Graecae* 28 relays this story with significant additions: Thetis instructs one of Achilles' servants to remind him of the prophecy, which is meant as a warning, but Achilles pursues Tenes' sister and slays Tenes in the ensuing quarrel; having discovered who the murdered man was, Achilles slays the servant, who did not warn him in time; finally, he buries Tenes in a place where later a shrine devoted to this hero was erected. This story shows traces of a later development of the motif.

61 Apollodorus *Epitome* 3.29–32: Ἀχιλλεῖ δὲ ἐπιστέλλει Θέτις πρῶτον μὴ ἀποβῆναι τῶν νεῶν· τὸν γὰρ ἀποβάντα πρῶτον πρῶτον μέλλειν τελευτήσειν. [...] τῶν δὲ Ἑλλήνων πρῶτος ἀπέβη τῆς νεὼς Πρωτεσίλαος, καὶ κτείνας οὐκ ὀλίγους τῶν βαρβάρων ὑφ' Ἕκτορος θνήσκει. [...] Πρωτεσιλάου δὲ τελευτήσαντος, ἐκβαίνει μετὰ Μυρμιδόνων Ἀχιλλεὺς καὶ λίθον βαλὼν εἰς τὴν κεφαλὴν Κύκνου κτείνει. ὡς δὲ τοῦτον νεκρὸν εἶδον οἱ βάρβαροι, φεύγουσιν εἰς τὴν πόλιν [...] μὴ θαρρούντων δὲ

> Trojans retreat to the city. Achilles kills Troilos in the temple of Apollo.[62]
>
> Memnon arrives at Troy; Thetis warns her son not to fight him and he withdraws from battle. Antilochos dies by Memnon's hand, which brings Achilles back to combat. Achilles slays Memnon and is slain by Paris and Apollo.[63]

The pattern consists of several recurring elements: there appears a dangerous opponent, not a Trojan, but usually a Trojan ally; Achilles withdraws from fighting because of a prophecy from his divine mother that killing this man will result in his own death; Achilles' wrath is awakened by the death of a companion or by some other reason; Achilles slays the enemy, thus provoking or precipitating his own death. The *Iliad* shares this construction pattern: Sarpedon and Hektor harass the Achaeans; having slain Sarpedon, Patroklos, Achilles' companion, dies by Hektor's hand; after Patroklos's death, Achilles, who has withdrawn from combat, returns to the battlefield and kills Hektor, which precipitates his own death.

The choice between a long life in the homeland and death on the battlefield in the prime of life, then eternal fame is a version of the maternal warning that holds Achilles back from fighting. Such is also the prophecy he hears from Hektor as he dies: by killing him, Achilles brings about his own death. We can see that Willcock erroneously reverses the situation: it was not Achilles' choice of one of two fates that was invented by Homer, but his motivation for refraining from combat because of Agamemnon's offensive behavior. In the

---

τῶν βαρβάρων, Ἀχιλλεὺς ἐνεδρεύσας Τρωίλον ἐν τῷ τοῦ Θυμβραίου Ἀπόλλωνος ἱερῷ φονεύει... "Thetis orders Achilles not to leave the ships because the first to land would be the first to die. ... Of the Greeks the first to land was Protesilaos, and having killed a good number of barbarians, he dies by the hand of Hektor. ... After the death of Protesilaos, Achilles lands with the Myrmidons, and kills Kyknos by throwing a stone at his head. When the barbarians see that [Kyknos] is dead, they flee back to the city. ... When the barbarians do not dare to [fight], Achilles lies in ambush and kills Troilos in the sanctuary of Thymbraean Apollo." Naturally, this is only one of several versions of Troilos's death.

62 This is according to Apollodorus; Proclus places the slaughter of Troilos after the driving off Aeneas's cattle and sacking Lyrnessos and Pedasos.

63 Proclus *Aethiopis* 2: Μέμνων δὲ [...] παραγίνεται τοῖς Τρωσὶ βοηθήσων· καὶ Θέτις τῷ παιδὶ τὰ κατὰ τὸν Μέμνονα προλέγει. καὶ συμβολῆς γενομένης Ἀντίλοχος ὑπὸ Μέμνονος ἀναιρεῖται, ἔπειτα Ἀχιλλεὺς Μέμνονα κτείνει· [...] τρεψάμενος δ' Ἀχιλλεὺς τοὺς Τρῶας καὶ εἰς τὴν πόλιν συνεισπέσων ὑπὸ Πάριδος ἀναιρεῖται καὶ Ἀπόλλωνος. "Memnon ... comes to the aid of the Trojans, and Thetis tells her son about Memnon. Then a battle occurs in which Antilochos is killed by Memnon, and then Memnon by Achilles. ... Achilles routs the Trojans, and, pursuing them into the city, is killed by Paris and Apollo." As we can see, Proclus's text is extremely enigmatic here. The interpretation that the death of Antilochos brings about the death of Achilles was proposed by the neoanalysts.

song, the motif of Achilles' drawing back from fighting as a result of a prophecy of his death, probably associated also with the alternative fates to be chosen, was traditional. Homer does not mention Thetis's warning about killing Hektor, lest it overshadow his new idea for the motivation of the hero's withdrawal. Achilles is aware of his inevitable death but accepts his fate under the influence of Patroklos's death.

In this regard, the *Iliad* repeats the pattern of the *Aethiopis*. Both works concentrate on the tragedy of Achilles, but they do it slightly differently. In the *Aethiopis*, what keeps Achilles in the camp is most probably the knowledge that he should not kill Memnon, while in the *Iliad*, Achilles denies that he refrains from fighting because of the prophecy of his death, stressing that the reason is the deprivation of honor by Agamemnon. However, Achilles' conversation with Patroklos (quoted above) indicates that this traditional motivation of Achilles' inactivity was familiar both to the author and probably also to the audience, whom the singer tries to dissuade from assessing the behavior of Thetis's son from this point of view.

As we have seen, the pattern shows both great potential for variability and stability in its traditional shape. In the *Iliad*, contrary to the traditional approach, Achilles refrains from fighting not only with a single opponent, Sarpedon or Hektor, but with all the Trojans, in order to punish the Achaeans. Achilles does so not from a lack of courage, as the song makes it evident that the hero could easily fight either of those two heroes.[64]

Mueller assumes that the essence of Homeric narration as well as the beginning of the plot is Achilles' withdrawal from combat so that he can meet Hektor in a duel outside the safety of the city walls.[65] Despite his incisive analysis, his conclusion—that the embassy cannot be successful because Achilles' absence must continue—is not inevitable. The acceptance of gifts would only render the *Patrokleis* unnecessary. But Achilles could still meet Hektor on the battlefield, because the Trojan hero was outside the walls of Troy. As we have already observed, the traditional reason why the Trojans are outside the walls is the arrival of new allies, which evens out the forces of the opponents. And as far as Achilles' inactivity is concerned, it is not the beginning of the plot. The beginning is the appearance of an extraordinary opponent. It is related to the starting point of the song—the crisis in the Achaean camp. In the *Iliad*, these elements have been reordered, but the singer does not disclose the reason why the Trojans have appeared on the plain in front of the city, creating the illusion that this is the first clash of the armies.

64 The song repeatedly stresses that Hektor's successes are possible only due to Achilles' absence on the battlefield.

65 Mueller 1984:44.

The scene of the embassy to Achilles strengthens the listener's understanding of and appreciation for the new reasons he refuses to fight the enemy: the conflict with Agamemnon and Achilles' wrath replace Achilles' fear for his life. The rejection of gifts is necessary, because Achilles must justify his anger, and, consequently, the reason for his withdrawal, which must not be less important than the withdrawal because of the oracle. The narrator implies that this new reason is not only much more important, but also much more tragic: the hero is concerned not about his own life, but about his honor. When Achilles retreated because of the oracle, he probably considered his alternative fate as revealed in another oracle; when he decided to act, he did so on impulse or by mistake, as happened with Tenes. In the answer given to Odysseus, Achilles plays with the image of a peaceful life after his return to his native Phthia. Achilles teases the envoys, just as the singer teases his audience, who know the traditional motivation for the hero's withdrawal from battle. Achilles emphasizes the value of life, so that his later decision to sacrifice it is even more tragic. However, the strength of Achilles' traditional motivation could make his declarations seem unconvincing. That is why Nestor and Patroklos keep coming back to this topic, giving Achilles an opportunity to reject these allegations and to "break with tradition." The long history of the misunderstanding of Achilles' refusal to accept gifts, which began in antiquity, indicates how difficult this task must have been for the singer.

From the perspective of the entire tradition, the fact of Achilles' death is certain, and on this one fact various stories can be built. The logic of the epic song requires that destiny be postponed. Thetis's prophecy stops Achilles from action and for a short time staves off his death, but something always happens which makes him return to battle and embrace his destiny. The prophecy stopping Achilles from fighting is coupled with another prophecy, giving him a choice of fates. The second prophecy is usually uttered at the time of Achilles' departure for the war and paves the way for the motif of his reluctance to fight (as is also true for Odysseus). It gives a tragic dimension to the hero, who withdraws from combat and in solitude weighs two possible fates.

Necessary conditions for the capture of Troy

The motif of the postponement of fate lies at the root of the basic theme of the Trojan Cycle—the capture of a city. In chronological terms, the sequence of events in the cycle is ridiculous: Hektor was killed in the *Iliad*, Achilles in the *Aethiopis*, and Troy still cannot be captured. If we look at the Trojan War from the perspective of the model structure of an epic song, we note that this is the initial situation in all epic songs of this cycle which start in the final period of the war. The expression "the final period of the war" should not be understood chronologically, however, because all these events actually take place at the same "time." It is the time when the twenty-year great cycle is about to be completed, the time of the last days of Troy, so—to use a colloquial expression—it is always "at the eleventh hour."

The time has reached its fullness, yet the Achaeans still cannot take the sacred city of Troy. They become frustrated and want to return home, then a new obstacle stands in the way of destiny. Such is always the starting point of cyclic epics: a crisis.[66] Overcoming it opens the way to conquering the city, but this does not exclude the possibility that in another song there will appear another obstacle, and its removal will be a condition essential for the success of the expedition.

A long list of such obstacles can be found in Proclus's summary of the *Little Iliad* (2–4):

> μετὰ ταῦτα Ὀδυσσεὺς λοχήσας Ἕλενον λαμβάνει, καὶ χρήσαντος περὶ τῆς ἁλώσεως τούτου Διομήδης ἐκ Λήμνου Φιλοκτήτην ἀνάγει. ἰαθεὶς δὲ οὗτος ὑπὸ Μαχάονος καὶ μονομαχήσας Ἀλεξάνδρῳ κτείνει· [...] καὶ Νεοπτόλεμον Ὀδυσσεὺς ἐκ Σκύρου ἀγαγὼν τὰ ὅπλα δίδωσι τὰ τοῦ πατρός· καὶ Ἀχιλλεὺς αὐτῷ φαντάζεται. Εὐρύπυλος δὲ ὁ Τηλέφου ἐπίκουρος τοῖς Τρωσὶ παραγίνεται, καὶ ἀριστεύοντα αὐτὸν ἀποκτείνει Νεοπτόλεμος. καὶ οἱ Τρῶες πολιορκοῦνται. καὶ Ἐπειὸς κατ' Ἀθηνᾶς προαίρεσιν τὸν δούρειον ἵππον κατασκευάζει. Ὀδυσσεύς τε αἰκισάμενος ἑαυτὸν κατάσκοπος εἰς Ἴλιον παραγίνεται· καὶ ἀναγνωρισθεὶς ὑφ' Ἑλένης περὶ τῆς ἁλώσεως τῆς πόλεως συντίθεται, κτείνας τέ τινας τῶν Τρώων ἐπὶ τὰς ναῦς ἀφικνεῖται. καὶ μετὰ ταῦτα σὺν Διομήδει τὸ Παλλάδιον ἐκκομίζει ἐκ τῆς Ἰλίου.
>
> Next Odysseus waits in an ambush and catches Helenos, and as a result of Helenos's prophecy about the capture [of the city], Diomedes fetches Philoktetes from Lemnos. Philoktetes is healed by Machaon; he fights in single combat with Alexander and kills him. ... Odysseus brings Neoptolemos from Skyros, gives him his father's armor, and then Achilles appears as a ghost [to Neoptolemos]. Eurypylos the son of Telephos arrives as a Trojan ally, and after many military successes Neoptolemos kills him. The Trojans are now closed within city walls. Then Epeios, under Athena's direction, builds the wooden horse. Odysseus disguises himself and goes into Ilion as a spy. Recognized by

66 Hölscher (1978:58) points out that a crisis is the starting point in the *Odyssey*. Odysseus is released from captivity because of the situation of his wife and son on Ithaca. That is why the *Telemachy* is the first part of the epic.

Helen, he plots with her for the capture of the city; then, having killed several Trojans, he returns to the ships. And after this he and Diomedes carry the Palladion out of Ilion.

More discourse on these events may be found in Apollodorus *Epitome* 5.8–13:

Ἤδη δὲ ὄντος τοῦ πολέμου δεκαετοῦς ἀθυμοῦσι τοῖς Ἕλλησι Κάλχας θεσπίζει, οὐκ ἄλλως ἁλῶναι δύνασθαι Τροίαν, ἂν μὴ τὰ Ἡρακλέους ἔχωσι τόξα συμμαχοῦντα. τοῦτο ἀκούσας Ὀδυσσεὺς μετὰ Διομήδους εἰς Λῆμνον ἀφικνεῖται πρὸς Φιλοκτήτην, καὶ δόλῳ ἐγκρατὴς γενόμενος τῶν τόξων πείθει πλεῖν αὐτὸν ἐπὶ Τροίαν. ὁ δὲ παραγενόμενος καὶ θεραπευθεὶς ὑπὸ Ποδαλειρίου Ἀλέξανδρον τοξεύει. τούτου δὲ ἀποθανόντος εἰς ἔριν ἔρχονται Ἕλενος καὶ Δηίφοβος ὑπὲρ τῶν Ἑλένης γάμων· προκριθέντος δὲ τοῦ Δηιφόβου Ἕλενος ἀπολιπὼν Τροίαν ἐν Ἴδῃ διετέλει. εἰπόντος δὲ Κάλχαντος Ἕλενον εἰδέναι τοὺς ῥυομένους τὴν πόλιν χρησμούς, ἐνεδρεύσας αὐτὸν Ὀδυσσεὺς καὶ χειρωσάμενος ἐπὶ τὸ στρατόπεδον ἤγαγε· καὶ ἀναγκαζόμενος ὁ Ἕλενος λέγει πῶς ἂν αἱρεθείη ἡ Ἴλιος, πρῶτον μὲν εἰ τὰ Πέλοπος ὀστᾶ κομισθείη παρ' αὐτούς, ἔπειτα εἰ Νεοπτόλεμος συμμαχοίη, τρίτον εἰ τὸ διιπετὲς παλλάδιον ἐκκλαπείη· τούτου γὰρ ἔνδον ὄντος οὐ δύνασθαι τὴν πόλιν ἁλῶναι.

Ταῦτα ἀκούσαντες Ἕλληνες τὰ μὲν Πέλοπος ὀστᾶ μετακομίζουσιν, Ὀδυσσέα δὲ καὶ Φοίνικα πρὸς Λυκομήδην πέμπουσιν εἰς Σκῦρον, οἱ δὲ πείθουσι αὐτὸν Νεοπτόλεμον προέσθαι. παραγενόμενος δὲ οὗτος εἰς τὸ στρατόπεδον καὶ λαβὼν παρ' ἑκόντος Ὀδυσσέως τὴν τοῦ πατρὸς πανοπλίαν πολλοὺς τῶν Τρώων ἀναιρεῖ. ἀφικνεῖται δὲ ὕστερον Τρωσὶ σύμμαχος Εὐρύπυλος ὁ Τηλέφου πολλὴν Μυσῶν δύναμιν ἄγων· τοῦτον ἀριστεύσαντα Νεοπτόλεμος ἀπέκτεινεν. Ὀδυσσεὺς δὲ μετὰ Διομήδους παραγενόμενος νύκτωρ εἰς τὴν πόλιν Διομήδην μὲν αὐτοῦ μένειν εἴα, αὐτὸς δὲ ἑαυτὸν αἰκισάμενος καὶ πενιχρὰν στολὴν ἐνδυσάμενος ἀγνώστως εἰς τὴν πόλιν εἰσέρχεται ὡς ἐπαίτης· γνωρισθεὶς δὲ ὑπὸ Ἑλένης δι' ἐκείνης τὸ παλλάδιον ἔκλεψε καὶ πολλοὺς κτείνας τῶν φυλασσόντων ἐπὶ τὰς ναῦς μετὰ Διομήδους κομίζει.

When the tenth year of war comes, the Greeks lose heart. So Kalchas prophesies to them they won't take Troy unless they have the aid of Herakles' bow. On hearing that, Odysseus goes with Diomedes to Philoktetes in Lemnos, and getting the possession of the bow by

> subterfuge, he persuades him to sail to Troy. Having come to Troy and being cured by Podaleirios, Philoktetes kills Alexander with his bow. When that one is dead, there is a quarrel between Helenos and Deiphobos concerning marriage with Helen. And since the decision is made in favor of Deiphobos, Helenos leaves Troy and retreats to [Mount] Ida. When Kalchas announces that Helenos knows the oracles that protect the city, Odysseus waylays and defeats him and brings him to the camp. Under duress, Helenos tells how the city can be taken. First, if the bones of Pelops are brought to them; second, if Neoptolemos fights on their side; and third, if the Palladion, which has fallen from heaven, is stolen, because as long as it is within the walls, the city cannot be taken.
>
> On hearing that, the Greeks fetch the bones of Pelops, and send Odysseus and Phoinix to Lycomedes at Scyros. They convince him to let Neoptolemos go. Arriving at the camp, he receives his father's armor from Odysseus, who gives it to him willingly. [Then] Neoptolemos kills many Trojans. Afterwards, Eurypylos, son of Telephos, comes to the aid of the Trojans, bringing a great army of Mysians. After many military successes, he is slain by Neoptolemos. Odysseus and Diomedes by night come up to [the walls of] Troy, and there Odysseus leaves Diomedes [to wait for him]. Having disfigured himself, he puts on wretched clothes and enters unrecognized into the city as a beggar. And being recognized by Helen, he with her help steals away the Palladion. After killing many guards, he takes it to the ships together with Diomedes.

These texts give an idea of the differences in the arrangement of scenes. Apollodorus's text should not be perceived only as providing details to the plots summarized by Proclus. In Proclus, the stealing of the Palladion takes place after the construction of the wooden horse. In Apollodorus, it is the other way round: Odysseus's spying trip to Troy comes first. It seems to be an unimportant instance of moving stories, but it endows these traditional themes with a different meaning—we are dealing with a different logic of events. In Proclus's version, the spying trip is a consequence of the construction of the horse by Epeios, which means that it is an element of Odysseus's preparations for bringing the horse into the city. The logic of events is similar to that in the *Odyssey*, where the story of this trip, told by Helen, constitutes a part of the story of Odysseus's contribution to the capture of Ilion. The theft of the Palladion took place later. In Apollodorus's version, Odysseus's disguise as a beggar serves the purpose of stealing the Palladion and has nothing to do with bringing the wooden horse into the city. It is simply the fulfillment of the last condition mentioned by Helenos.

In Proclus, the captive Helenos discloses the conditions under which the Achaeans will take Troy: they need to bring Philoktetes and Neoptolemos, and to steal the Palladion. In Apollodorus, Kalchas reveals that they need to bring Herakles' bow, now belonging to Philoktetes, and Kalchas also tells the Greeks that Helenos knows other oracles that protect the city. According to these oracles, there are three conditions necessary for the capture of Troy: to bring the bones of Pelops, replace Achilles with his son Neoptolemos, and steal the Palladion. We have two versions of the *Little Iliad*, or rather two different arrangements of the traditional scenes. Characteristic of the *Little Iliad* is the fact that all these conditions for the taking of Troy are accumulated in one song. This may point to the way in which cyclic songs, which later were written down, were created, grouping many traditional strands in one place.[67]

With the requirement to bring Neoptolemos, we notice a revival of the same pattern used to depict his father in the war. Neoptolemos's feats are a repetition of Achilles', but the pattern lacks an essential element: Neoptolemos is not destined to die on the battlefield, so he does not face Achilles' dilemma of choosing his fate and he does not withdraw from fighting. Therefore, although Neoptolemos echoes his father's success, he does not fulfill his basic function on the battlefield: Achilles was indispensable in the *Iliad*, not because he was the best butcher who would eliminate the toughest enemies, but because his heroic self-sacrifice was a necessary price for a spectacular victory. Nevertheless, in the life of Neoptolemos there returns the theme of a conflict with Apollo, which leads to this hero's death and cult.[68]

Other necessary conditions, as we will see in the next chapter, have magical significance. Each of them contains material for a separate song. They also seem to be independent of one another; the only possible connection seems to exist between the bones of Pelops, brought to be a talisman protecting the Achaeans, and the Palladion, stolen to deprive the Trojans of its magical protection. Bringing Philoktetes and killing Paris bear the mark of a separate plot, maybe connected with the quarrel between Odysseus and Aias, after Odysseus deceitfully obtains possession of Achilles' armor and Philoktetes' bow.[69]

67 Severyns (1928:333) holds a different view. According to him, Lesches, the reputed author of the *Little Iliad*, instead of concentrating upon one episode, drew too extensively from the mythic tradition: "La *Petite Iliade* montre le genre épique en pleine décadence, épuisé d'avoir déjà fourni une trop longue carrière."

68 Pindar *Nemean* 7.40–47, *Paean* 6.117–120. Nagy 1999:118–141.

69 In both sources, Helenos gives the three conditions necessary for the Achaean success. It is possible that the number of conditions—three—is constant, while the conditions themselves

The despair of the Achaeans unable to take Troy is revealed in repeated proposals to return home, which is a traditional motif. In the *Iliad*, these proposals are made during assemblies. Three times they are suggested by Agamemnon (2.140–141, 9.27–28, 14.75–81), once by Thersites (2.236), and once by Achilles (1.59–60). Achilles mentions it as a step that may turn out to be necessary, because he is anxious to put an end to the plague decimating the Achaeans. Agamemnon at the second assembly makes a false proposal of return, which, however, hits fertile ground, because the army is tired of the siege. Thersites reveals the fears of the army, referring to Achilles' withdrawal from combat. These three suggestions of return are made before the first battle, so the presentation of the crisis is the starting point of the action. A similar situation happens in Book 9, but this time Agamemnon's proposal is serious. After a defeat, the Achaeans are in a difficult position, and something must be done. In Book 14, Agamemnon is desperate, crying before he addresses the leaders. It follows that presenting a proposal of flight is a traditional way of showing a crisis in the army.[70]

The frequency of this motif in the cycle can be corroborated by the story in the *Kypria*, that the flight of the Achaean army was checked after Achilles' meeting with Helen: εἶτα ἀπονοστεῖν ὁρμημένους τοὺς Ἀχαίους Ἀχιλλεὺς κατέχει "Achilles stops the Achaeans who want to go home" (Proclus *Kypria* 11). Then the hero goes up Mount Ida and drives off a herd of cattle guarded by Aeneas. The prevention of the Achaeans's flight occurs after the Trojans shut themselves up in the city, and Achilles' sacking of nearby cities apparently has not improved the situation; perhaps Achilles is trying to provide food for the starving army and thus stop the Achaeans from flight. What's more important is that Achilles' action is analogous to that of Odysseus, who halts the Achaean flight in *Iliad* Book 2.

Contrary to expectations, the Achaean ventures in the *Little Iliad* do not end in the capture of Troy, though they certainly bring it closer. It is necessary to undertake another attempt, which turns out to be the construction of the wooden horse, and to find a way to bring it into the city. This is exactly the point at which the action of another cyclic poem, the *Ilioupersis*, begins, but its summary does not mention any Greek considerations of the problem of the horse. Either there wasn't any need to mention it in the summary,

may vary. This may explain why the bringing of Philoktetes was included among the conditions in Proclus's version.

70 In the simplest pattern, found in the Bosnian *Song of Bagdad*, in such circumstances there are always two pieces of advice given—first a bad one, and then a good one, which is taken to save the enterprise (Lord 1960:86). The proposal of return is bad advice, which must be followed by good advice, which will help to achieve the aim, to capture the city. The character and meaning of *euboulia* 'giving good advice' in the *Iliad* are explained by Schofield 1986:246–258.

because the subterfuge had already been outlined in the *Little Iliad*, or this song deviates from tradition, showing the problem of the horse from the Trojan, not the Achaean, perspective. The latter eventuality, however, does not seem very probable.

It seems that a crisis caused by finding a new obstacle to the capture of the city and the dejection caused by a prolonged siege are traditional motifs. It becomes necessary to eliminate the obstacle, which gives a chance for the Achaeans to demonstrate courage and resourcefulness. This pattern enables the multiplication of content, and the pattern could have been used in other songs as well. Proclus and Apollodorus might not have seen the need to mention such a conventional motif in their short summaries. If the motif of a crisis is linked with that of a dispute, as it is in the *Iliad*, it could also have been present in the *Aethiopis* where, after the death of Penthesileia, there was a scene of a gathering, which led to the conflict between Achilles and Thersites, and then to a split in the army.[71] A crisis means a moment of danger to the Achaean community, and a dispute, in turn, is an indispensable element of collective decision-making in the epic world. There may be various reasons for the danger, such as the prophecy that Rhesos, who has just arrived at Troy, may be impossible to defeat. A new problem needs to be resolved, so the crisis, which is the starting point for the story, entails a solution, which never ends in achieving the goal of the expedition, but brings it closer.

The *Little Iliad* has a distinctive feature, a long list of tasks that have to be performed in order to capture Troy. Aristotle *Poetics* 23 says that, in comparison with the *Iliad* and *Odyssey*, the work lacks compositional unity. It seems to me that his opinion might have been motivated by the accumulation of heroic deeds necessary to take Troy. The author of the epic used a simple (in his eyes perhaps sophisticated) strategy dictated by the need to exaggerate the matter, and to pique the listener's curiosity. The need to exaggerate, common in epic, is also responsible for the construction of large-scale poems. In the *Little Iliad*, the plot is not developed by a modified duplication of scenes and motifs, as in

[71] Haft (1992) juxtaposes similarities in the construction of the scenes of the assembly in Book 2 of the *Iliad* and Book 2 of the *Odyssey*. The number of similarities she finds is, I believe, slightly too high, and her conclusions are a bit too broad. However, we can quite safely say that the expanded scene of the assembly contains certain typical elements recurring in various epic songs. Haft also stresses the sorrow and despair of the speaker opening the assembly (Agamemnon, Telemachos), but she does not see that it is a method of revealing a crisis and its function in the schema of epic. An important role in the assembly scene initiating the action is played by the mention that the prophecy is just being fulfilled, which suggests that the crisis is under control (Odysseus, Halitherses). But I cannot agree with Haft's contention that in the epics all "assemblies in which these recollections of prophecies are embedded resemble each other" (224), which would suggest imitation. I rather think that in this respect variability goes quite far.

Homer or in the *Aethiopis*, but by the simple addition of heroic deeds aimed at one goal. This method of demonstrating the greatness of the song by the accumulation of events is linked with oral tradition: three tasks imposed by a seer is a typical folk-tale motif.

The Specific Character of the Trojan Cycle Patterns

Achilles and Odysseus

Gregory Nagy has pointed out that Achilles and Odysseus play a different role than the other Achaean heroes: both compete for the title of "the best of the Achaeans." They are so much above the other heroes that only they can contend for the title of the actual captors of Troy. According to Nagy, the plot of the epic songs is organized around these two characters.[72] Although it appears that Philoktetes and Neoptolemos, who eliminate major obstacles on the way to the final victory, could also play a similar role, Achilles and Odysseus possess very special qualities which set them apart from the other heroes in the cycle; moreover, from the point of view of models used in the construction of epic songs, it is possible to note many themes in which both heroes appear.

In the basic structure of an epic song, the protagonist is always a young hero. In Greek epic, both Achilles and Odysseus possess the characteristics of a young hero, but each of them also has his own distinctive, individual features. Following Nagy, we can contrast the heroes briefly by noting their way of acting: the attribute of Achilles is force, violence—βίη (*biê*), while Odysseus's is trickery, deception—δόλος (*dolos*) and artifice—μῆτις (*mêtis*).[73] This difference affects the way they are characterized: Achilles is shown as straightforward, honest, and somewhat naive; Odysseus, conversely, is cunning, ingenious, and prudent. However, one cannot attach too much importance to these character traits, because their choice depends on the singer's interpretation of the traditional theme.

Both heroes initially shirk the expedition. Odysseus explicitly expresses his reluctance and pretends madness.[74] Palamedes exposes his trick by endangering

72 Nagy (1999:42–58) builds his concept on the image from the *Odyssey* in Demodokos's first song (8.73–82). However, the transfer of this image onto that which emerges from the *Iliad* seems problematic. The *Iliad* emphasizes the rivalry between Achilles and Agamemnon for the title of "the best of the Achaeans."

73 Nagy 1999:42–58. In the conflict with Agamemnon, the opposition is between courage (*alkê*) and power (*kratos*).

74 Many sources report Odysseus's trick: Proclus *Kypria* 2; Apollodorus *Epitome* 3.6–7; Lucian *De domo* 30; Philostratos *Heroica* 11.2; Tzetzes *Scholia in Lycophronem* 818; Cicero *De officiis* 3.26.97;

the life of the hero's son, Telemachos. Odysseus's attempt to avoid participation in the expedition distinguishes him from other warriors, as described in Apollodorus: ὄντων δὲ πολλῶν προθύμων στρατεύεσθαι, παραγίνονται καὶ πρὸς Ὀδυσσέα εἰς Ἰθάκην. ὁ δὲ οὐ βουλόμενος στρατεύεσθαι προσποιεῖται μανίαν ("while many [warriors] eagerly joined the expedition, they [the Greeks] come to Odysseus in Ithaca, but he, not wishing to take part in the expedition, pretends madness").[75] Achilles does not shirk the expedition of his own will, but Thetis wants to prevent his going, conscious of the prophecy of his death in the war. She hides him, disguised as a girl among the daughters of Lykomedes on Skyros.[76] However, like in the case of Odysseus, the Greeks also reveal the deception by using a trick, and convince the hero to join them.[77]

The theme of recruiting these heroes for the expedition also combines other elements of an oral song. The heroes' indispensability for the success of the expedition is emphasized, especially in the case of Achilles, which Kalchas expresses in his prophecy (see n75 below). Usually in oral epics, the young hero fights in his own cause (e.g. Jason), whereas here he has to appear in someone else's interest. To give one's strength and even one's life for one's community is a typically epic ideal.[78] The theme of the heroes' indispensability on the battlefield is frequently used—they perform the most important deeds that cause the

Hyginus *Fabulae* 95; Servius *Commentary on Vergil Aeneid* 2.81; Lactantius Placidus *Commentary on Statius Achilleid* 1.93; *Scriptores Rerum Mythicarum Latini*, ed. G. H. Bode, vol. 1., 12.140–142 (*Primus Mythographus. Vaticanus* 35, *Secundus Mythographus Vaticanus* 200).

75 Apollodorus *Epitome* 3.6–7. Compare Proclus *Chrestomathia*, *Kypria* 5.

76 Apollodorus *Library* 3.13.8: ὡς δὲ ἐγένετο ἐνναετὴς Ἀχιλλεύς, Κάλχαντος λέγοντος οὐ δύνασθαι χωρὶς αὐτοῦ Τροίαν αἱρεθῆναι, Θέτις προειδυῖα ὅτι δεῖ στρατευόμενον αὐτὸν ἀπολέσθαι, κρύψασα ἐσθῆτι γυναικείᾳ ὡς παρθένον Λυκομήδει παρέθετο ("When Achilles was nine years old, Kalchas predicted that they wouldn't take Troy without him. Thetis, knowing this earlier, that if he took part in the expedition, he would be killed, hid him away at the court of Lykomedes, dressed as a girl and pretending to be a girl"). The motif of Achilles in female disguise concealed at the court of Lykomedes is mentioned also by other ancient sources: Bion 2.5–32; Philostratos the Younger *Imagines* 1; *Scholia in Homerum Iliad* 9.668; Hyginus *Fabulae* 96; Statius *Achilleid* 1.207–211. The same topic is also in Euripides *Men of Scyros* (Σκύριοι frr. 682–686) and perhaps also in Sophocles' play of the same title (frr. 553–561). In Proclus, this story is not mentioned, but there is the motif of Achilles' landing on Skyros after the failed Teuthranian expedition, because the traditional union of Achilles and a daughter of Lykomedes could not be omitted, as its fruit was Neoptolemos.

77 Odysseus's trick appears in several slightly different versions: Apollodorus *Library* 3.13.8; Hyginus *Fabulae* 96; Philostratos the Younger *Imagines* 1; *Scholia in Homerum Iliad* 19.326; Ovid *Metamorphoses* 13.162–170.

78 For Meletinsky (2009:181) the transition from the hero fighting in his own cause to the hero fighting for the community marks the evolution of a story towards an epic. Analyzing the Caucasian heroic stories of the Narts, he states: "The figure of Sosruko undergoes heroization in accordance with epic ideals. The hero is no longer the epitome of tribal strength, but he devotes his strength to defend tribal interests of the community."

fall of Troy. In the case of Achilles, in some enterprises, other heroes, such as Patroklos or Neoptolemos, substitute for him.

Achilles' female disguise connects him with Odysseus, who dons beggar's clothing in Ithaca, when he is preparing to take revenge on the suitors, and at Troy, when he sneaks into the city on a spying mission.[79] This parallel could be open to doubt if it weren't for the fact that all the following elements—avoiding participation in the expedition, the hero's indispensability for the success of the expedition, and a very unheroic disguise—can be found in Tale of Orašac, the unique figure of Bosnian epic. Such a fake denial of the protagonist's heroism, which undoubtedly had a magical dimension, could play an important role in shaping the structure of epic poems.[80]

The reason behind such a selection of traits is difficult to explain, but it is probably associated with the concept of sacrificing the hero in the interests of the community (the role of the scapegoat). There are other surprising elements common to the image of these heroes. Both Achilles and Odysseus kill a fellow countryman (i.e. one of the Achaeans) during the war. No other Achaean warrior does anything like this; the very *attempt* to kill a countryman drives Aias to a suicide.

Odysseus takes revenge upon Palamedes for discovering that his madness was pretended.[81] Sources give various versions of his death. One group of sources depicts a cruel trick of Odysseus, who falsely accused Palamedes of betrayal. Apollodorus *Epitome* 3.8 writes that Odysseus forced a Phrygian prisoner to write a letter ostensibly from Priam to Palamedes, and himself buried gold in Palamedes' quarters to provide evidence of treason; Agamemnon,

79 In Proclus's summary of the *Kypria*, it is reported that Achilles sneaked to Troy at night and captured Lykaon.

80 According to Apollodorus *Library* 3.4.3, Dionysos was disguised as a girl in order to conceal him from the anger of Hera. Other heroes, e.g. Herakles, appear dressed as women. Probably it is a reflection of initiation rituals, in which boys temporarily change sex. Frazer, who interprets this as a reminiscence of the habit of dressing boys as girls in order to avert the evil eye (Frazer 1893:292–310), was not familiar yet with the rites of passage and the specific nature of the post-liminal phase. The motif of denial of the hero's heroism often appears in epic songs of many peoples.

81 The defeat of Palamedes by Odysseus is reminiscent of many epic tales, in which the hero resorts to a trick to defeat a more powerful opponent, one who is a magician and master of deception; he manages to do that by outwitting the enemy (contrary to the story of the Kyklops Polyphemos, this story is about defeating a wise giant). Palamedes' prototype could have been his antithetic rival, who was a trickster or a comic character. De Vries (1933) presents Loki as a negative variant of the culture hero, in opposition to Odin; a similar function is fulfilled by Syrdon and Sosruko/Soslan in the Nart epic—see Dumézil 1948 and Meletinsky 2009:171–182; the latter juxtaposes Syrdon not only with the Scandinavian Loki but also with the Irish Bricriu and the Homeric Thersites. Foley (1995:39–41) ascribes magical meaning to the unusual, unheroic, and comic figure of Tale of Orašac, a compulsory participant in many heroic expeditions in Bosnian epic songs.

after reading the letter and finding the gold, "delivered him [Palamedes] to his allies to be stoned as a traitor" (τοῖς συμμάχοις αὐτὸν ὡς προδότην παρέδωκε καταλεῦσαι).[82] According to another version, Palamedes was killed by Odysseus in cooperation with Diomedes. Fundamental here is the evidence of Pausanias, who refers to the text of the *Kypria* (10.31.2): Παλαμήδην δὲ ἀποπνιγῆναι προελθόντα ἐπὶ ἰχθύων θήραν, Διομήδην δὲ τὸν ἀποκτείναντα εἶναι καὶ Ὀδυσσέα, ἐπιλεξάμενος ἐν ἔπεσιν οἶδα τοῖς Κυπρίοις ("I know from [reading?] the *Kypria*, that Palamedes was drowned while fishing, and his killers were Diomedes and Odysseus"). The cooperation of these two in Palamedes' murder is presented also by Dictys Cretensis (*Bellum Trojanum* 2.15), but in his version, they trick Palamedes into descending a well, and then they throw stones, burying him there.

Usually, scholars see the letter playing a fundamental role in the first version as a proof of the lateness of this story in relation to Homer. The sophistication of the intrigue seems to be another corroboration of its being a much later innovation; the killing of Palamedes by Odysseus personally carries the hallmark of a primitive shaping of action. There is another unclear moment. Apollodorus's statement, that Agamemnon gave Palamedes to his allies (τοῖς συμμάχοις), so that they would kill him, is not entirely clear. Does it mean that Agamemnon handed Palamedes over to the army, so that the warriors would execute him, excluding him from their ranks? Or perhaps Apollodorus means unspecified non-Greeks, who would carry out the killing so that the Achaeans would not be guilty of bloodshed?

The murder of Palamedes is enigmatically placed by Proclus at the end of his summary of the *Kypria*, after Lykaon is sold into slavery and Briseis is assigned to Achilles and Chryseis to Agamemnon as their prizes; the summary then mentions Zeus's decision to relieve the Trojans, and the catalogue of Trojan allies follows. All this information gives the impression of references to the *Iliad*[83] and it is highly improbable that they were a part of the traditional material. Odysseus's murder of Palamedes stands isolated from all other events. Its place in the structure of the song can only be explained by analogy to Achilles' comparable deed.

The murder done by Achilles is also known only from indirect sources. However, the fact that both killings are found in the cyclic material proves that they are extra-Homeric and independent of Homer. In the summary of the *Aethiopis*, Achilles defeats the queen of the Amazons, and the Trojans bury her body. Then the hero kills Thersites, who abused him for his ἐπὶ τῇ

82 For further details of this story see Gantz 1993:605–606.

83 Except for Zeus's plan, which is linked with a different story of Achilles' withdrawal from fighting.

Πενθεσιλείᾳ λεγόμενον ἔρωτα 'supposed love for Penthesileia', but this deed entails consequences: καὶ ἐκ τούτου στάσις γίνεται τοῖς Ἀχαιοῖς περὶ τοῦ Θερσίτου φόνου. μετὰ δὲ ταῦτα Ἀχιλλεὺς εἰς Λέσβον πλεῖ, καὶ θύσας Ἀπόλλωνι καὶ Ἀρτέμιδι καὶ Λητοῖ καθαίρεται τοῦ φόνου ὑπ' Ὀδυσσέως ("As a result there is a split in the Achaean army over the killing of Thersites. Then Achilles sails to Lesbos and after making sacrifices to Apollo, Artemis, and Leto, is purified from murder by Odysseus").[84] A comparison with Thersites' appearance before the assembly in the *Iliad* (2.211–270) suggests that his killing must have taken place at one of the Achaean meetings, so Achilles kills a Greek in front of other Greeks. It is unlike Odysseus's deed, who kills in secret. Achilles' deed causes a split in the army.

Kullmann suggests that Diomedes, a close relative of Thersites, must have been the first to turn against Achilles.[85] Though the murder in itself is a sufficient reason for everyone to shun him, its importance lies not so much in the person killed as in the deed. Killing is a crime that defiles the entire community and brings divine punishment on all its members. For this crime, Achilles should be stoned. He avoids this fate, but he needs to be purified, and from the summary we can infer that it does happen. Evidently, it could not take place in the Achaean camp, so he had to sail to nearby Lesbos—as if a foreign land. Again, there is a significant difference between Achilles and Odysseus—we know nothing about the latter undergoing any cleansing ritual.

Achilles' deed is a reaction to an offense, similar perhaps to the taking away of his honor by Agamemnon. In the *Iliad*, only Athena's intervention keeps the hero from killing the king (1.188–218), so it is a deed done on the spur of the moment. Odysseus is driven by the desire to revenge himself for being forced to go to the war. He does not act immediately, but waits until an auspicious moment; the murder takes place at the end of the war. Instead of pointless psychologizing (e.g. speculating whether only now he started to grieve for the years wasted at Troy), let's look at the song construction. Its cause is at the beginning of the war, its solution at the end—so again this is a schematic sequence of events typical of epic songs in this cycle.

[84] Proclus *Chrestomathia*, *Aethiopis* fr. 1.

[85] Kullmann 1960:102–103, 146–149. Diomedes could have taken over command of his troops. The Thersites of the cycle seems to be the same commander as in the other *aristoi*. The image of a hateful cripple without ancestry is probably Homer's innovation and probably results from the character of Thersites' speech; see Zieliński 2004:213–216. The one who reproaches is perceived as a dangerous person, especially if he is a master of this kind of speech and is apt to use it frequently, like e.g. an iambic poet. The caricature he draws of his victim reflects also on him—as he himself becomes a caricature of a hero.

Because of the scarcity of sources, it is difficult to see the link between Achilles' crime and his mother's attempt at keeping him from taking part in the expedition. Nevertheless, from the perspective of the macro-story of the cycle, these two deeds, despite being opposites, should be considered related to each other. I think here we can talk about contrasting parallel motifs.

The *Iliad* juxtaposes Achilles and Odysseus only once, when the narrator says that Thersites was loathed by both heroes. Thersites is described as quarrelsome and confrontational, which is why he is hateful to everyone, especially Odysseus and Achilles (2.220): ἔχθιστος δ' Ἀχιλῆϊ μάλιστ' ἦν ἠδ' Ὀδυσῆϊ ("particularly loathed by Achilles and Odysseus"). This information appears in verses introducing Thersites' speech, which ends with his being beaten by Odysseus with his staff and ridiculed by the army (2.225–242, 265–278). This situation is a modification of that described in the *Aethiopis*. In the *Iliad*, a person ready to start a quarrel is always described as hateful to all. This expression is not confined to Thersites; it is what Agamemnon says about Achilles (1.176–177), Idomeneus about Aias, son of Oileus (23.483), and Zeus about Ares (5.890–891).[86] It is difficult to explain the particular hatred between Thersites on the one hand and Achilles and Odysseus on the other. The explanation that hatred is here a synonym of the two greatest heroes' contempt for the dastardly Thersites seems inadequate. It is puzzling why Thersites should be hateful to Achilles, whose cause he supports in the assembly, whose arguments used in the quarrel with Agamemnon he repeats and even bolsters, and whom he calls a much better man than Agamemnon (Achilles himself only says that he is not worse than Agamemnon). The school of Neoanalysis suggests a solution to this problem by referring to the epic tradition known from the *Aethiopis*, in which there is conflict between these two characters.[87]

The conflict between Achilles and Thersites, in which Achilles, after he has been rebuked, kills his adversary, finds its parallel not only in the conflict between Odysseus and Thersites in Book 2 of the *Iliad*, in which Odysseus beats Thersites with his staff for the latter's verbal assault on Agamemnon, but also in the *Odyssey*, when Odysseus enters into an altercation with the beggar Iros, which ends in a boxing duel. In the generally accepted version of

86 The nature of disputes is so violent that the adversaries easily go over the top and hurl strong accusations; see Van Wees 1992:89–91, 122–125.

87 If we treat Thersites as a rival of the epic hero, with character traits opposite to those demanded by the heroic ethos, like Sirdon or Loki (compare n81 above), then the hostile attitudes of epic protagonists (Achilles, Odysseus) may result from the very concept of this character, his typical form in the epic tradition.

the *Aethiopis*, Achilles kills Thersites with a fist punch.[88] By analogy, Odysseus defeats Iros with one blow. He does not kill him, but a moment earlier he plays with the idea of landing a fatal blow (*Odyssey* 18.90–94). The *Iliad* and the *Odyssey* are, in turn, linked by the description of the adversary who starts the quarrel. Thersites' ugliness is analogous to that of Iros—these are the two most extensive descriptions of physical appearances in Homer, and both use the iambic convention.[89] The repetition of these elements, albeit in a different order, is not due to imitation, but rather to a pattern; although the singer is free to modify traditional material, he cannot omit the traditional element of the narrative.

The content and cause of Thersites' rebuke will also remain a mystery. From Proclus's summary (*Aethiopis* 1), we know that Thersites blamed Achilles for maintaining love relations with Penthesileia, the queen of the Amazons, recently arrived as an allxy of the Trojans and killed by Achilles. Quintus of Smyrna in his late adaptation of the story of the Trojan War (*Posthomerica* 1.538–830) presents a romantic tale of how Achilles fell in love with the Amazon he was killing.

The *Aethiopis* version may contain an element of the romantic story found in Quintus of Smyrna; it is not impossible—in the *Iliad*, Agamemnon and Achilles declare a kind of emotional attachment to Chryseis and Briseis, although the feelings might not have been very romantic. Achilles' love for Penthesileia is mentioned also in Apollodorus (*Epitome* 5.1): ὅστις μετὰ θάνατον ἐρασθεὶς τῆς Ἀμαζόνος κτείνει Θερσίτην λοιδοροῦντα αὐτόν ("after [her] death, having fallen

88 *Scholia in Lycophronem* 999: ἀνεῖλεν αὐτὸν πλήξας κονδύλῳ· οἱ δὲ τῷ δόρατι ("killed him with a punch, according to another version with a spear stroke"). The scholiast to the *Iliad* opts for a punch: κατ' ἐμὲ δὲ καὶ τοὺς λοιποὺς κονδύλῳ ("in my opinion and that of others, with a punch").

89 Scholia give two versions of the accident which resulted in Thersites' disability. In both cases, it took place during the hunt for the Calydonian boar: ΣcT *Iliad* 2.212, citing Pherecydes, inform us that driven by fear, he tried to dodge the hunt, as a result of which Meleagros threw him over a rock. ΣA on the same passage, on the authority of Euphorion, speak about Thersites leaving the appointed position for a safer one; when Meleagros, angered, ran after him, Thersites fell from a cliff. It is doubtful whether the Thersites of the Aetolian saga and the one of the Trojan Cycle are the same person (Gantz 1993:333). The reasons for his disability look like an attempt at matching a character of the same name to the Homeric image of Thersites the cripple. In my article on Thersites (Zieliński 2004), I expressed the view that if we can identify the Thersites of the *Iliad* and *Aethiopis* with the hero of the Aetolian saga, his disfigurement results from the subordination of his image to the function he performs in the scene of the assembly—that of the iambic poet, rebuke-giver, whose appearance is associated with the character of his words, which bring disgrace. Now I am more inclined to think that Thersites' lameness may be an element of tradition and Homer could have matched his appearance to his role in the assembly, taking away his heroic past. Homer regularly keeps silent about important events in the lives of less important characters, like the myth of Niobe, the end of Bellerophon, or the participation of Ankaios in the Calydonian boar hunt (perhaps this is also an instance of contamination with an Arcadian hero of the same name; see Gantz 1993:332).

in love with the Amazon, [Achilles] kills Thersites, who rebuked him). More details are given in the *Scholia in Lycophronem* 999: μετὰ θάνατον Πενθεσιλείας ἠράσθη αὐτῆς ὁ Ἀχιλλεύς, ὁ δὲ Θερσίτης λαθὼν ἐξώρυξε τοὺς ὀφθαλμοὺς αὐτῆς, ὁ δὲ νεανίας ὀργισθεὶς ἀνεῖλεν αὐτόν ("After Penthesileia's death Achilles fell in love with her, and Thersites stealthily gouged out her eyes. The youth fell into a rage and killed him").

The same scholia (*Scholia in Lycophronem* 999) also give another puzzling piece of information, that Achilles' anger overtook Thersites

> μηδὲ διὰ ἐξορύξαι τοὺς οφθαλμοὺς ἀλλ' ὅτι αἰσχροὺς λόγους κατ' Ἀχιλέως ἀπέρριπτεν ὡς δῆθεν ἐρῶντος συγγενέσθαι νέκρᾳ τῇ Πενθεσιλείᾳ. ἀντιμηχάμενος γὰρ Ἀχιλλεὺς ἐκείνῃ καὶ πολλάκις ὑφ' αὐτῆς ἡττηθεὶς, μόλις δέ ποτε περιγενόμενος καὶ ἀνελὼν αὐτὴν θαυμάζων τὴν ῥώμην ἐκείνης ὁμοῦ καὶ τὸ κάλλος καὶ νεαρὸν τῆς ἡλικίας ἐδάκρυε καὶ τοὺς Ἕλληνας παρεκάλει ταφῆς ἀξιοῦν τὴν νεάνιδα. ὑφ' οἷς Θερσίτης συμπλάττων καὶ λέγων μίξεις ἀθέσμους καὶ ἔρωτας γρόνθῳ ὑφ' αὐτοῦ πλήγεις ἀναιρεῖται. Διομήδης δὲ ἀνεψιαδὸς ὑπάρχων Θερσίτου, χολωθεὶς ἕνεκα τούτου ἐκ τοῦ ποδὸς ἑλκύσας τὴν Πενθεσίλειαν εἰς τὸν Σκάμανδρον ἔρριψεν.

> not because he gouged out his eyes, but because he spoke offensively about Achilles, who purportedly enamored [driven by lust], had intercourse with the corpse of Penthesileia. When Achilles was dueling with her, she gained advantage [?] several times, though finally he narrowly prevailed and killed her. Admiring her strength/valiance, and her youthful beauty, he cried and called the Greeks to honor the young woman with a funeral. At this [ceremony?], Thersites invents and talks about vicious sexual relations and lust, but he is hit by his [Achilles'] fist and killed. This, in turn, angers Diomedes, who is Thersites' nephew, and so he drags Penthesileia by her leg and throws her into the Scamander.

The version cited by the scholiast differs from the one found in Proclus, where the funeral was to be performed by the Trojans. In Proclus, Thersites must have hurled insults against Achilles at an assembly, because in that community such accusations could be made only in public. Plucking out the Amazon's eyes in the *Scholia in Lycophronem* version "stealthily" (λαθών) destroys the public context of this story. This version, however, shows traces of very early ideas and, perhaps, of an early shape of this, or a similar, myth. The allegation of necrophilia is not so absurd, if we consider the cultural context of the myths about the Amazons. In fact, all stories about heroes' encounters with the Amazons end in a deadly fight, in which the Amazon queen dies. Defeating the Amazon could be associated with disgracing her corpse by rape. If we assume such a background to the story of Achilles' physical contact with the slain Penthesileia, we can say that Achilles behaves in a manner typical of a hero killing the Amazon queen.[90] The epic tale, however, "spices up" Achilles' behavior, adding the motif of his enchantment with the woman's beauty.

Having explained the motif of love, we still have not come closer to understanding the reason for Thersites' rebuke (*psogos*). If we accept the version of his plucking out Penthesileia's eyes, then Thersites would join in the act of dishonoring the corpse, or he alone would take the shame for doing it. Such an explanation would make sense, provided that Achilles did not perform a ritual rape on the Amazon and was opposed to disgracing her body because of some emotional or moral reasons. This interpretation would, however, require a moment of reflection from Achilles, who in the *Iliad* is shown as someone who cannot restrain himself from defiling the body of Hektor (22.395–405, 23.24–26, 182–183, 24.15–16).

If, however, we accept the version in which Thersites uses only the iambic attack against Achilles (this weapon is also presented in the *Iliad*), then behind the attack must have been his critical attitude towards Achilles' deed. The purpose of iambic mockery is to brand someone who acts to the detriment of the community. Thus, Achilles' deed must have been regarded by Thersites as morally reprehensible. The Amazon is an enemy, so one should not fall in love with her, but why should he criticize ritual rape or rather make rape the reason for a rebuke? Perhaps here we have to do with a myth attesting to the rejection of ancient customs and rituals, just like the story from the Theban Cycle about Athena's revulsion when Tydeus devoured the brain of a dead enemy, or like those showing the departure from the customs of making human sacrifices as a

[90] In the known versions of myth, this takes the form (suppressing the original brutality) of capturing the belt of the queen of the Amazons. This motif appears in the myths of Herakles and Theseus (Gantz 1993:282–285, 397–400). The removal by a man of the belt ζώνη or ζωστήρ girding a woman's waist and supporting her dress is a metonymy of performing a sexual act with her (*Odyssey* 11.245). Even though only once attested, the phrase can be evaluated as formular; compare *Lyricorum Alexandrinorum Adespota* 11.18, and *Anthologia Palatina* 7.324. The term ζωστήρ in Homer is applied only to the belt worn by men, whereas in later literature to a woman's belt (see Pausanias 1.31.1), including that of the Amazons, e.g. Pindar fr. 172, Pausanias 5.10.9, and Diodorus Siculus 4.16.1. It is possible that the name Andromache—referring in the tradition to one of the Amazons, who fought with Herakles (Gantz 1993:397)—in the *Iliad* is transferred to Hektor's wife (Tsagalis 2008:14–15). In Homer, Eëtion's daughter, in her speech to Hektor, instructs him in military matters (*Iliad* 6.433–439), but is called to order by her husband (6.490-493) and in subsequent scenes she already presents a purely feminine nature, defenseless and dependent on her husband (see Graziosi and Haubold 2010:44–46, 202–203, 222).

propitiative offering, an example of which is the myth of Iphigenia.[91] The killing of Thersites is, then, more than unjustified, as his attack upon Achilles was made in the interest of the entire army. The rebellion of the army is, therefore, not only caused by the unacceptable killing of a compatriot, and Diomedes' action does not only reflect his respect for blood ties.

Having brought together the elements which link all these situations relating to the actions of Achilles and Odysseus, we can draw a preliminary conclusion that in the epic tradition of the Trojan Cycle an important place is taken by a fratricide committed by a young hero on one of the Achaeans. The victim, as the hero's antagonist, is presented in an unfavorable light: either as a liar/conceited man, as in the cases of Thersites of the *Iliad* and Iros, or as a slanderer, someone whose criticism demonstrates the hero's lack of heroism, e.g. Thersites of the *Aethiopis* and Palamedes. The murder happens when conflict is started by the man soon to be the victim of fratricide. The placement of the fratricide theme on the timeline of the epic plot requires, however, a more thorough analysis of the problem of rebuke.

Curse and prophecy in relation to rebuke

In all the allomorphs of the Achilles story, prophecies play an important role. There are two interrelated prophecies: one of alternative fates, which is given to him before he sets out on an expedition, and a multi-form oracle warning him against killing an unusual enemy; the latter is connected with the end of the war, as it always predicts Achilles' imminent death. These prophecies usually remove the hero from fighting and deepen his psychology. They give the singer an opportunity to heighten the dramatic effect of events, because in this simple structure (a super-enemy appears—the enemy is killed), the postponement of the decisive meeting makes it possible to extend the action.

Other prophecies fulfill an important function as a framework for constructing the epic narrative, because they provide a starting point for the logic of events. In the first song of Demodokos (*Odyssey* 8.79–82), the oracle is linked with the motif of dispute initiating the song: Agamemnon is pleased with the quarrel between his leaders, because he knows Apollo's prophecy, in which a quarrel announces the capture of Troy. Thus, the dispute between the leaders is one of the conditions for conquering the city.

This kind of prophecy is akin to the prophecy of a conditional fate. Such a prophecy, concerning Odysseus, is given in the *Odyssey* (5.288–289) by Poseidon. The god notices the hero sailing on a raft and says that a prophecy that Odysseus will escape a series of accidents when he reaches the island of the Phaeacians is

91 Zieliński 2010:193–196.

being fulfilled. Similarly, one version of the Rhesos episode assumes that if he and his horses drink from the Skamandros, he will be invincible. In this case, the condition is not fulfilled, and Rhesos meets his death earlier. The prophecy, however, triggers the action in this version of the story—it makes it necessary for the Achaeans to kill Rhesos.

In the entire cycle, the most important role falls to the prophecy about the inevitability of the fall of Troy. Demodokos's song suggests that it was not necessarily only Kalchas's prophecy given to the Achaeans in Aulis which communicated the fall of Troy and which specified the length of the war.[92] Kalchas's prophecy is mentioned in the *Iliad* at the second assembly, when it is cited by Odysseus, who tries to control the warriors, arrested in their flight, and to raise their morale before the battle (2.300–330). The prophecy, recalled just before the combat, gives the listeners a vision of a final success, no matter what happens now. It should be remembered that these prophecies are just a revelation of Διὸς βουλή 'the will of Zeus'.[93]

When we compare the abundance of prophecies in the works of the tragedians or Herodotus, they are much less significant in Homer than we would expect, because their function is suppressed. In the *Iliad*, oracles as a reason for Achilles' withdrawal from fighting are altogether eliminated. In the *Odyssey*, the oracle mentioned by Poseidon seems to be a reference to the tradition, in which it could have played a more prominent structural role; it is mentioned just when the hardships of the hero's return are nearly at an end and from the remark at the beginning of the song we know that he will reach his homeland (1.21). It seems that, contrary to popular opinion, in oral epic contemporaneous with Homer, and perhaps even at an earlier stage in its development, the role of prophecy was greater and it was used more widely.

To understand the system in which predictions are arranged, we must first analyze the function of blame (ψόγος, *psogos*) in Greek epic. Although epic is defined by Aristotle as a kind of praise poetry (ἔπαινος, *epainos*), blame—which constitutes a necessary structural element—naturally has a significant

92 According to Homer, Kalchas also led Achaean ships to Troy (*Iliad* 1.71–72). It may mean a reading of omens, which would allow the journey to continue, or only the role he played in Aulis. In the latter case, Homer refers to multiform tradition, in which Kalchas delivers the prophecy of the birds being devoured by a snake and plays a role in the sacrifice of Iphigenia.

93 On several occasions, Agamemnon mentions Zeus's promises and assurances that he will take Troy, but he never discloses when/how they were made (*Iliad* 2.112–113, 9.19–21). Twice this information appears before he proposes a disgraceful return. However, when Agamemnon makes the proposal for the third time, there is a modification: he mentions Hektor's threat, made at the Trojan assembly, that he will destroy the Achaeans and their ships (*Iliad* 14.44–48; how does Agamemnon know about it?!), and he assumes that Zeus has already ceased to support the Achaeans (14.69–73).

function.[94] Greek epic does not seem to be an exception in this respect, because blame is used also in Sanskrit epic. Just as in the *Iliad*, a fight is preceded by an exchange of rebukes. Provoking opponents is perfectly justified in a real fight, e.g. in a duel, because it may lead to an error on the part of the opponent, who might lean out from behind a shield. Sometimes warriors sneer at the defeated enemy; the most spectacular instance is Patroklos's mocking of the corpse of Kebriones (*Iliad* 16.746–751).[95] The language of blame may also be used after a struggle, when a duel ends inconclusively, and insults take the place of fighting. In the Indian epic, blame appears in an inconclusive fight of Bhima, one of the Pandavas, with Karna, one of the Kaurava brothers; an example from the *Iliad* is Hektor's insults towards Diomedes, who is running away from the battlefield (8.160–166).

In the *Mahābhārata*, an exchange of insults may also fulfill a special function. Particularly noteworthy is the scene when the two most important Pandava brothers, Yudhishthira and Arjuna, fling insults at each other.[96] In Book 8 of the poem, Arjuna, before his decisive duel with Karna, goes to his brother's tent, fearing for his life and health. Yudhishthira, who initially thinks that the struggle predicted by a prophecy is already over, learns that it is not so. Disappointed, he hurls abuse at his brother. Yudhishthira accuses Arjuna of cowardice, and even demands that he forfeit his miraculous bow, Gandiva, with which he was expected kill Karna, and give it to someone more deserving. Arjuna is in a quandary, because he swore to kill anyone who would even suggest his giving up the bow, but he does not want to kill his brother. Following Krishna's advice, he decides to fling insults at Yudhishthira, because Krishna maintained that offensive words would have the same value as killing him. Arjuna accuses his brother of cowardice, lounging in the marital bed, and an unhealthy love of gambling. According to the ethos embraced in the epic, after having uttered such foul words, Arjuna faces only one way out: suicide. Again, Krishna averts a disaster and Arjuna, obedient to his advice, praises himself. He says he is the best archer of all and has defeated half of the enemy's army (let us leave aside his cosmic bragging that he has conquered the world and that he could destroy the whole universe). After this act of boasting, he begs Yudhishthira's forgiveness and reconciliation of the brothers occurs.

Joanna Sachse believes that this exchange of insults between the brothers is introduced as a "comment" on a similar exchange between Karna (who is getting ready for a fight with Arjuna) and his charioteer Shalya. Shalya, obliged to take up this function by the law of reciprocating a kindness, accuses him of all possible cowardly deeds. According to Sachse, "Karna is bragging beyond

94 Aristotle *Poetics* Ch. 4, 1448b32–34, see Nagy 1999:253–254.

95 Griffin (1980:113–120) notes the use of the sneer in building the pathos of Homeric discourse.

96 Sachse 2004:219–222. However, this subject is still little researched.

measure, assuring that he will easily defeat Arjuna, Krishna and the whole army of the Pandavas."[97] Having compared these two scenes, Sachse concludes that Shalia, by uttering reproaches, symbolically "kills" Karna, whereas Karna, countering reproach with self-praise, commits a kind of suicide. Putting him in the wrong deprives Karna of any chance of winning, foretelling his defeat in the duel and death.

At the risk of a certain desecration of the Sanskrit text and ignoring its Hindu religious interpretation, let's look at the construction of the scenes themselves and compare them with the Greek epic. The charges that Arjuna hurls at Yudhishthira have much in common with Achilles' accusations against Agamemnon. In the Greek poem, despite the sophistication of Achilles' language, the accusations are typical of iambic poetry. In both poems, Achilles and Arjuna charge their adversary with cowardice, understood not as a flight from the battlefield, but remaining in the camp, because both Achilles and Arjuna deride their opponent for staying in their tent. Yudhishthira is condemned for excess in physical love, reproached for his lounging in bed. The basic reproach in Greek blame poetry is that of greediness (metaphorically described as gluttony), which makes people take what is not theirs or what they do not deserve: here we have Agamemnon's drunkenness and taking other warriors' captive women; its parallel in the *Mahābhārata* is the charge against Arjuna of having a bow that he does not deserve.[98]

In both cases, fratricide is stopped by divine intervention, although Krishna, acting as Arjuna's charioteer, is present physically, whereas Athena appears at the last moment and is visible only to Achilles (*Iliad* 1.198). But Krishna is also a god. In the *Mahābhārata*, as in the *Iliad*, the heroes hesitate, yet finally follow the advice of the deity. Both, instead of killing the opponent, decide to insult him to his face and both succumb to the temptation to brag. However, there is a significant difference here: in the Homeric epic, there is nothing wrong with self-praise, whereas in the Indian epic, in one instance (Arjuna) it is right, and in another (Karna) it is unacceptable. The fundamental structural difference is that the Pandava brothers are reconciled and forgive each other, and Arjuna goes to the decisive fight with Karna; whereas Achilles withdraws from combat, and as a result the reconciliation with Agamemnon, which will enable his return and a crucial duel with Hektor, requires new circumstances. Hektor, hesitating whether to duel with Achilles, fears a taunt from Poulydamas (*Iliad* 22.99–103), in front of whom he bragged earlier and whose advice he did not

97 Sachse 2004:221.

98 The typology of iambic blame: Zieliński 2004:203–213 and 2010:198–205, where, drawing on Nagy 1999:211–264, I make certain generalizations.

take (18.285–309), and so exposed the army to defeat. This is, to a certain extent, a parallel to Karna's being dispraised by Shalya.

The matter of Arjuna's miraculous bow Gandiva refers to even deeper layers of the Trojan Cycle. In the cyclic tradition, only Herakles' miraculous bow can defeat Paris. The bow is in the hands of Philoktetes, whose role in the preserved poems of the cycle does not correspond to the role of Arjuna in the *Mahābhārata*. However, the bow, taken away from Philoktetes for a brief span of time, returns to him as he is the only man who can use it.

In the *Iliad*, reproach serves as a device propelling action. It triggers a sequence of events, when action reaches a dead end. Typically, before *psogos* is used in the human world, it is used in the world of gods. In Book 4 of the *Iliad*, Agamemnon runs along the Achaean ranks, shouting encouragement and scolding those who shirk combat (4.231–249). Then, when the army is in the battlefield, he turns with both praise and reproach to his commanders. He praises Idomeneus (4.257–264), the two Aiases (4.285–291), and Nestor (4.313–316), and reprimands Menestheus and Odysseus (4.338–348), and Diomedes (4.370–400). In the structure of the poem, these reproaches are preceded by that which Zeus addresses to Hera and Athena (4.7–19). Zeus's words induce the goddesses to stir up a fight between people. Agamemnon, by means of his reproach, makes his leaders launch an attack on the enemy, so *psogos* forces gods and heroes to act.

As far as the character of these rebukes in the *Iliad* is concerned, in the world of gods they are courtly taunts and in the human world they are usually modest reprimands, combined with respect for both one's own people and enemies. More violent forms of reproach are rare. Reproaching one's own people can lead to a quarrel and conflict, so it is avoided. That is why only one conflict is stressed: that between Achilles and Agamemnon, in which rebuke is used without restriction. It would be possible to propose a thesis that in the evolution of epic, the blade of *psogos* was blunted, because in earlier, pre-Homeric times, rebuke took on a more violent dimension.

The moderation of the sphere of *psogos* is visible even in the *Iliad*. Dispute does not lead to murder—Achilles is in two minds whether to kill Agamemnon or not, but Athena stops him. The victim of his anger is, therefore, not Agamemnon but the whole army. This happens indirectly, through the actions of Zeus and the Trojans. In the *Iliad*, the punishment of Thersites has only temporary significance, as it does not affect the course of events. The scene of Thersites' aggressive taunting in the *Aethiopis* is replaced by buffoonery in the *Iliad*. Both scenes end unluckily for their protagonist. In the *Iliad*, his attempt to pretend to be better than he is does not protect Thersites; on the contrary—his behavior becomes a motive for contempt. In both cases, Thersites does not avoid punishment, although his death in the *Aethiopis* is replaced by the beating with a staff in the *Iliad.*

Evidently, in epic structure, a violent reaction to *psogos* is obligatory. In the *Iliad*, the initial scene of the gathering, in which the crisis manifests itself and counter-measures are taken, is in a way doubled, because the withdrawal of Achilles from the council and battle, makes it necessary to call another gathering to get the soldiers into battle and to push the action forward (1.54–305, 2.99–398). In both cases, it includes a verbal attack upon Agamemnon. The charges that fall from Thersites' lips are basically the same as the accusations made by Achilles, but only Thersites is punished. Recalling the analogous confrontation scene between Arjuna and Yudhishthira, we expect that someone who utters such harsh words will be punished. Perhaps Thersites doubles Achilles in his accusations against the chief leader (Yudhishthira holds a similar position as Agamemnon) only in order to be punished instead of the hero.

Christopher Brown convincingly argues that the term ἴαμβος (*iambos*, iamb), corresponding to blame poetry, originally referred to a curse.[99] The "evil word" hurts a man, excluding him from the community. It resembles a civil death; it is not easy to be purified from a curse, just as it is not easy to be purified from a crime. The rebuke is used in publicly and its victim loses his honor in the community. The motif of a curse appears several times in archaic epic and in the epics of other peoples (e.g. the curse of the ring of the Nibelungs).[100] Originally, in Greek epic it probably had the most important function in the structure of the song, but it seems that in the course of time it was replaced by a prophecy.

In Book 9 of the *Iliad*, Phoinix tells the story of Meleagros in order to convince Achilles to accept Agamemnon's gifts and return to battle. Researchers have quite easily grasped the parallel between Achilles' situation and Meleagros's fate as presented by Phoinix: Meleagros, offended, refuses to participate in fighting.[101] Homer presents a version of the myth uncorroborated by other sources, probably his "innovation," but knowing the myth of Meleagros, he stops the tale at the point where the parallel ends.

The most important link between the fates of Achilles and Meleagros is their death from the god Apollo. As the testimonia of the myth of Meleagros are scattered and very fragmentary, Gantz wrongly concludes that there were two

99 Brown 1997:30.

100 In Celtic epic, the curse which is at the disposal of the poet/sage, *fili*, is used either as a punishment for unworthy conduct or to blackmail knights and rulers—e.g. Cridenbél demanding from Dagdae the best portions of his meals or Nede demanding from King Caier a knife, which he was bound by taboo (*geas*) never to give away—see Nagy 1999:231, Compton 2006:198–199, and Chadwick and Chadwick 1932:97.

101 See Alden 2000:229–290.

independent versions of his death: one linking it with Apollo[102] and the other with the actions of Meleagros's mother Althaea.[103] These two versions do not necessarily exclude each other, since Althaea's deed could have brought about his death, which, however, was inflicted upon him by Apollo. The preserved sources only mention the fact that the god kills Meleagros, because he favors the other party in the conflict between the Aetolians and the Curetes. Apollo's inflicting death on a man, which ultimately leads to his heroization, may be a topos rooted in Greek epic deeper than its allomorphs in the Trojan Cycle (Achilles, Patroklos, Neoptolemos) would indicate. Achilles dies at the hand of Apollo, not only because this god favors the Trojans—this is only one piece of the puzzle. It is very likely that Meleagros does not meet Apollo face to face on the battlefield, but that this god supports one of his opponents. When Achilles mentions the prophecy of his death, he also says that it will be caused by Apollo, strictly speaking by an arrow of Apollo (*Iliad* 21.278). The weakness of Gantz's distinction also lies in the fact that against this version of events he sets together the testimonia of the *Iliad* and Bacchylides *Ode* 5. While both sources point, albeit differently, to Althaea's initiative in bringing about the death of Meleagros, Phoinix's story in the *Iliad* connects it with the Aetolian war with the Curetes. The fact that Phoinix does not mention the hero's death and seems not to refer to it at all only points out the omission of this motif, which would be inappropriate for the exemplum aiming to convince Achilles to act. Despite the omission, the end of the story may be present in the minds of the listeners, who may feel the irony of applying it to Achilles and so distance themselves from Phoinix's arguments, showing more sympathy for the stubbornness of the young hero.[104]

102 Hesiod fr. 25.1–13 M-W; *Greek Epic Fragments, Minyas* 5 M-W = Pausanias 10.31.3; Hesiod fr. 280.1–2 M-W.

103 Gantz 1993:331; similarly Alden 2000:239.

104 Gantz (1993:329) takes a different standpoint: "Pausanias assumed, as have others, that the Erinys destroyed him ([Pausanias] 10.31.3; so too Apollodorus [*Bibliotheca*] 1.8.3), but if he is irrevocably doomed his intransigence will become all too reasonable, and the loss of the proffered gifts scarcely of any consequence. Perhaps this point is simply to be overlooked for the sake of the story, but more likely (I think) we are meant to understand that when Althaia appeals to her son she recalls her curse (as she surely can); otherwise her appeal will have little point. If that is the situation, then Phoinix envisions a long-lived but giftless hero as an appropriate object lesson for Achilleus." It is not obvious if Althaea could recall her curse, and even if in Homer, she does, trying to induce the hero to return to battle, it does not necessarily follow that Homer assumes the hero will survive the war. Homer leaves open many possibilities for various ends of this story, but he cannot change the essence of the myth—in his eyes, the hero's destiny. Though he is free to modify various episodes from Achilles' life, and even to invent new ones, he cannot change his fate: Achilles must die at Troy. Meleagros does not face alternative fates like Achilles, but his life is linked to the survival of an object.

Much more difficult to reconcile are two versions of the behavior of Meleagros's mother Althaea. According to the *Iliad*, she curses her son for killing her brothers (9.566–572), although everything indicates that it was not murder, but an encounter on the battlefield; in other sources, at the news of her brothers' death, Althaea, enraged, burns the log upon which her son's fate was dependent. When he was still a child, she learned that he would die as soon as one of the logs in the fire burnt completely. Althaea pulled the log from the fire, put it out, and hid the log in a trunk, from which she took it out again at the critical moment. Probably Homer replaces the motif of the log with a curse, as the log does not parallel Achilles' circumstances and is not suitable for epic.[105] Gantz states that the curse is necessary to provoke her son's anger, not to bring about his death.[106] Indeed, the curse does not serve the aim of killing Meleagros but stops him from joining in the fighting. Thus, its function corresponds to that of prophecy in the pattern of Achilles' withdrawal from combat. Nevertheless, Althaea's curse does produce Meleagros's death (*Iliad* 9.565–572):

> τῇ ὅ γε παρκατέλεκτο χόλον θυμαλγέα πέσσων,
> ἐξ ἀρέων μητρὸς κεχολωμένος, ἥ ῥα θεοῖσι
> πόλλ' ἀχέουσ' ἠρᾶτο κασιγνήτοιο φόνοιο,
> πόλλα δὲ καὶ γαῖαν πολυφόρβην χερσὶν ἀλοία
> κικλήσκουσ' Ἀίδην καὶ ἐπαινὴν Περσεφόνειαν,
> πρόχνυ καθεζομένη, δεύοντο δὲ δάκρυσι κόλποι,
> παιδὶ δόμεν θάνατον· τῆς δ' ἠεροφοῖτις ἐρινὺς
> ἔκλυεν ἐξ Ἐρέβεσφιν ἀμείλιχον ἦτορ ἔχουσα

> Lying by his wife's side, nursing his painful anger,
> embittered because of his mother's curse—for she sent many prayers
> to the gods, grieving for her slain brother,[107]

105 Hansen (1997:452–453, 459–462) believes that the curse replaces extraordinary and miraculous elements of the folktale, which epic adapts for its own ends. Another example corroborating his opinion, in addition to Meleagros's log (Aarne and Thompson 1187), is the motif of the ring from the folk-tale type called *The Ogre Blinded* (Aarne and Thompson 1137); in the tale, the giant throws a ring to the one who blinded him, and the imprudent man puts it on his finger, unaware that once the ring is on the finger, it says: "Here I am," and it can be got rid of it only by cutting off the finger. In the *Odyssey*, the ring corresponds to the curse cast upon Odysseus by Polyphemos upon learning the name of the man who had blinded him (Hansen 1997:449–450).

106 Gantz 1993:330.

107 In all other ancient sources, it is mentioned that Meleagros killed Althaea's brothers, hence the translation of the attributive form κασιγνήτοιο as 'due to fraternal death'. However, in Homer there is no confirmation of such a construction, which can be found only in classical texts, so it is possible that Homer knows another version of this story, in which only one of Althaea's brothers was killed.

> and many times beat her hands upon the earth, the nurturer of
> many creatures,
> calling upon Hades and dreadful Persephone,
> sitting back on her heels [in supplicating position], many tears fell to
> her bosom,
> [she asked] for her son's death, and the Erinys roaming in the mist,
> the one with an unappeasable heart, heard her from Erebus.

The casting of the curse by Althaea is an extensive ritual. It is not simply a careless word that has just slipped from her tongue; no, her actions indicate the formal character of the curse. Such a word cannot be undone, which is stressed by the description of the Erinys who hears her. Homer indirectly suggests Meleagros's death—a direct reference would render Phoinix's argument absurd, because it would point out to Achilles that his return to fighting would bring about his death.

For us, it is more important that in the structural model of this story the curse is replaced with prophecy. The curse cast by the mother, expressing her wish of death for her son, corresponds to the prophecy of death delivered to the son by his mother. The curse is more often used in Greek epic tradition in the construction of a story. For example, in the Theban Cycle, it stimulates action several times, e.g. the paternal curse cast by Oedipus upon his sons. The curse, like the prophecy, hangs over the development of events and implies their tragic course. Since *iambos* originally, by nature and the role it played, was a curse, we can assume that in an earlier stage of epic, a reproach, which was used as an action-stimulating device, also took the form of a curse. Perhaps in the course of time, the curse was replaced by a prophecy. In the construction pattern we observe a similar sequence of themes: reproach-fratricide-curse-heroic death (the *Thebaid*, song of Meleagros) and reproach-fratricide-prophecy-heroic death (the *Aethiopis*, *Iliad*).[108]

In the *Aethiopis*, the cause of conflict is the death of Thersites (fratricide), which should bring a curse upon Achilles as the murderer. Here the story departs from the pattern: Achilles is cleansed of the crime, and riots in the army are stopped. Achilles dies heroically on the battlefield, but his death no longer relates to his crime. This relationship, however, is still vivid in the story of

[108] The motif of fratricide also undergoes evolution. Originally, it was a murder within the family. That the killings of Palamedes and Thersites were also perceived as fratricides suggests the existence of strong family-like ties within a broader social group, e.g. warriors fighting for a common cause. This may be related to the formation of proto-polis mentality, in which family ties are limited for the sake of social ties connecting the whole community. I have already pointed out that Seaford (1994:11–13) suggests that the themes of crime within the family were eliminated from epic in the process of polis development.

Meleagros, since he is killed on the battlefield as a result of his mother's curse. A maternal curse appears to be an epic equivalent of burning a log which magically embodies Meleagros's fate.

The parallel of the fates of Achilles and Meleagros is not limited to their deaths caused by Apollo. Meleagros, like Achilles, is invulnerable and is killed only by the god's arrow. If, as I have argued, the *Iliad* assumes the knowledge of Meleagros's death, the death itself is not presented in the story which Phoinix calls κλέα ἀνδρῶν 'the fame of heroes', as the death of Achilles is not shown in the *Iliad*. Just like the *Iliad*, the story of Meleagros stops just exactly a moment before the hero's death.[109]

In the fates of these heroes, the relationship between their birth and death is evident. Their life span hinges upon actions of their mothers.[110] In the case of Achilles, his death—predicted by his mother—depends on the circumstances of his birth: he was born as a mortal because of Zeus's subterfuge, who had learned the prophecy that Thetis's son would be greater than his father.[111] Achilles' mortality was therefore from the very beginning written in his fate. Epic versions of this story depict a posthumous heroic apotheosis of Achilles; it is possible that Meleagros's story ended similarly.[112] Achilles' birth causes a kind of a global crisis, a disruption of the order of the world; in fact, the disruption is already visible in the marriage of a mortal man to a goddess. It is, therefore, the first cause of the war in which he is destined to die. The war itself is also depicted in the *Kypria* on a global scale—the release of the Earth from the excess of people, wicked advice of Momos to marry a goddess to a man. These elements do not appear in the Aetolian Cycle yet.

In the *Iliad*, the prophecy that prevents Achilles from combat that will end in his death takes on a new dimension: that of an alternative of a long life and no fame, or a short one but crowned with fame. The choice made by Achilles determines his position not only as a hero,[113] but also as an epic hero, whose ἄφθιτον κλέος 'eternal fame' is guaranteed. In this basic dimension, we can notice a similarity to Odysseus in the *Odyssey*. His stay on Kalypso's island gives him security, but also plunges him into obscurity; Odysseus chooses the danger of a return journey, which, however, brings him *kleos*. The nymph offers him

109 Gantz (1993:13–14) also assumes the possibility of such an interpretation: "Meleagros suffers nothing like the death Althaia prayed for (unless we are to understand that this happens subsequently)."

110 Watkins (1995:248) explains a Hittite phrase "day of your mother" = "your death day, dying day."

111 Slatkin (1991:69–85) demonstrates that this story is respected in the *Iliad* and that it played a huge role in the structure of the macro-story.

112 The only mythical references that we have place Meleagros in Hades, but in the *Odyssey*, Achilles is also there (11.467–540, 24.15).

113 Here the shortness of life is an important distinguishing feature; Sinos 1975:27–37.

immortality, but it is equivalent to an anonymous death, which "conceals" (her name means "the one who conceals," she who brings death and obscurity), that is, in Dimock's words, "an immortality of oblivion, of no *kleos*."[114] Afraid of an anonymous death in the sea, Odysseus wishes he had died at Troy, which would give him *kleos* (*Odyssey* 5.306–310). He balances between inactivity, pleasurable but sentencing him to be "nobody," and exposing himself to danger, but gaining fame. His choice gives him back his identity and a metaphorical rebirth or resurrection, later depicted as his return from the world of the dead, leaving the caves of Kalypso and Polyphemos.[115] Both Odysseus and Achilles choose the path of action and fame, though their ways are different.

We can assume that events linked with certain heroes in preserved testimonia appear as elements of epic songs in which they play a specific role. Reproach always has the function of initiating and stimulating events. It leads to a quarrel, and in effect to fratricide—the crime committed by the hero. Originally, this crime must have inevitably led to revenge and to the death of the hero—naturally, after he had performed a heroic deed. This necessary connection between the crime and punishment was sometimes blurred, but the inevitability of death as a result of a curse, and later of a prophecy, remained. The replacement of a curse with a prophecy, which gives an alternative of the hero's destiny, may misleadingly suggest that his death can be avoided. Nevertheless, the alternative is never taken. The loosening of the cause-and-effect relationship is a consequence of dynamic transformations taking place within oral epic—transformations which in turn must have been caused by the retardation of action and a new understanding of the role and ethos of the hero. All this combined to change the causes of events, but did not bring about the deconstruction of the epic plot.

Memnon, first entrance

To check the concept outlined above, let us make a kind of test and follow the motif of Memnon, which, according to Proclus, constitutes a part of the *Aethiopis*. The sequence of events connected with the stay of this hero at Troy reflects closely the traditional model of construction in the songs of the end of the war in the Trojan Cycle, which I have sketched earlier:

1. the arrival of allies: Memnon and the Ethiopians arrive at Troy;
2. the *aristeia* of their leader: his exploits are mentioned in the sources only summarily, which means that what is important is the quan-

[114] Dimock 1956:57–58.

[115] Dimock 1956:57–58; see also Breed 1999; Newton 1984. Compare Austin 1983.

tity of defeated heroes, not their quality—he does not kill anyone important for the macro-story of the cycle;

3. a crisis: the difficulties for the Achaeans, because the Ethiopians with Memnon have joined the battle, are worsened by Achilles' withdrawal from combat under the influence of a prophecy;
4. the heroic death of an important Greek warrior slain by Memnon: Antilochos, Achilles' friend, is killed;
5. Achilles' return to battle: this means the death of Memnon;
6. the funeral of the defeated enemy: Memnon's funeral and his apotheosis—his mother, the goddess Eos, snatches him from the funeral pyre and carries him to the land of the Ethiopians, giving him immortality.

The aim of narration appears in the series of events which give us a foretaste of the death of Achilles, killed by Paris and Apollo.

The narrative begins with the presentation of the splendor of the enemy leader. With his appearance and successes, the feeling of dread intensifies, until finally listeners are depressed by the Achaeans' hopeless situation. Depression turns into a presentiment of tragedy when Achilles' decision brings about the death of Antilochos. But it is also a turning point in the action, because it makes Achilles return to the battlefield. Now the listeners start fearing for the life of the best of the Achaeans. Achilles' fight with Memnon constitutes the climax of the action. However, tension is created not by the increase in dramatic events, but by the accumulating manifestations of the uniqueness of the heroes facing each other in the duel, particularly: the string of successes of both heroes, who thanks to magical protection seem to be invincible; their miraculous (i.e. of divine origin) armor, magic weapons, and horses; and the support given to the heroes by their divine mothers, Thetis and Eos. Forces are therefore well-matched, but also magnified to the limit. Neoanalysts believe that at this point there is a scene, in which Zeus puts the fates of the heroes on the scales. They claim so because the *Psychostasia*, an unpreserved tragedy by Aeschylus, depicted the scene of weighing the souls of Achilles and Memnon.[116] In agreement with tradition, the pan with Memnon's fate goes down, so he must die.[117]

[116] Kullmann 1960:316.

[117] Pestalozzi 1945:11–15; Schadewaldt 1951:160–166; Kullmann 1960:32–34, 316–320; about Aeschylus's tragedy and its links with the *Aethiopis*, see West 2000:343–347. This picture is counterintuitive, because we tend to think that if something is heavier, it prevails. Here it is the other way round, probably because if one pan of the scale drops, it means that it is attracted by the earth, which is a place of burial and where lies the land of the dead.

This primitive type of dueling dramaturgy appears quite often in epic narratives and requires a closer treatment before we proceed any further. The main aim of the epic singer is to focus the listeners' attention on his performance, which he can do by giving them an incomparable story, something that is beyond anything they have ever heard. We return to the frequently discussed issue of exaggeration. In epic songs, the pivotal scene is that of the hero's duel with his main adversary. The singer prepares for it by presenting the uniqueness of both opponents: he stresses their extraordinary valor and strength and describes their miraculous attributes.[118] The forces are so well-matched that the duel cannot be resolved. At the crucial moment, usually when the life of the hero is endangered, the support of a deity tips the scales. The support may be in the form of indirect help in military action, advice, or deception practiced on the opponent.

To illustrate this point, let us examine the Serbian song about Prince Marko and the outlaw Musa. Musa is a renegade who terrorizes seaside towns and villages. The Sultan cannot cope with him: the highwayman defeats the vizier's army of three thousand men and all brave knights who dared face him. The only thing that remains is to appeal for help to Marko, but Marko, having spent a long time in prison, is weak and emaciated. While staying at an inn, he regains his strength, which is proved by a miraculous show of his power: he grips a piece of dry cornel wood with his hand and squeezes a few drops of juice. Then he visits Novak the smith, where he buys a saber which can hew an anvil in half. Earlier, however, that same smith forged an even better saber for Musa. Finally, comes the time for Marko's encounter with Musa. In the ensuing fight, the heroes break spears, maces, and sabers. When there are no more weapons, they wrestle man to man. But:

> For hero met hero in very sooth!
> When Deli Musa met Kraljević Marko!
> Nor might Musa overthrow Marko,
> Nor by Marko be overthrown. (translation, D. H. Low)

Finally, when Musa kneels on Marko's breast, it seems that the victory will be his. But then Marko turns to Vila who lives in the skies, and he complains that she

[118] Such an opponent of the epic hero is himself a hero-warrior. Originally, however, it was a monster: a dragon, giant, or ogre, who by nature possessed magical power giving him an advantage over the hero. The hero defeats him thanks to a wonderful artifact, an act of extraordinary courage, or even a trick that the monster does not expect from someone who is inferior to him in stature and strength.

promised to help him should he ever be in a tight spot.[119] Vila advises Marko to use his knife, and he rips the robber's belly open. Divine support never discredits the epic hero; it is seen as a justification of his actions, usually taken in the community's interest, and the epic hero is always shown as a favorite of the gods.

Memnon's story contains all elements of the pattern outlined in the above paragraphs. My conclusions are based on the results of Neoanalytic research showing the relationship of Homeric scenes with the *Aethiopis*. I have already mentioned that they have met with broad criticism, which, however, means that we need to look more closely at "Memnon's case." In the Introduction, I presented the polemics between the position of Neoanalysis and oral theory. Martin West argued, based on his analysis of this issue, against both points of view.[120] Let this serve as a reference point for my position. In brief, West disagrees that the plot of the third part of the *Iliad* was based on the fragment of the *Aethiopis* usually called the *Memnois*. According to the Neoanalysts, Achilles' duel with Memnon, which took place after the death of Antilochos, is a model for Achilles' fight with Hektor after Patroklos's death, as well as Patroklos's fight with Sarpedon.

The death of Patroklos at the Scaean Gate is also analogous to Achilles' death as presented in the *Aethiopis*. West argues that the weakness of the original concept of the *Memnois* is the character of Memnon himself. Memnon is not mentioned in the *Iliad* at all, and the Neoanalysts' explanations of this omission are, in his opinion, quite naive. According to Pestalozzi, Homer's anticipations are confined only to the death of Achilles and the fall of Troy.[121] But the number of *posthomerica* found by Kullmann in the *Iliad* argue against his opinion.[122] Schoek, in turn, states that for the characters of the *Iliad* Memnon does not exist, because he has not arrived at Troy yet.[123] "But why," West asks, "has the poet not brought him to Troy, if he is to play such a major role in the story before Achilles' death? The Lycian contingent is there from the beginning: why not the Aethiopians?"[124] In the *Iliad*, there is no mention of the Ethiopian army, West explains, because for the poet, the Ethiopians are a people living at the edge of the world, on the banks of the Okeanos, a people with whom sometimes the gods feast. They have no contact with the rest of human beings.

119 "Where art thou this day, sworn sister Vila? / Where art thou this day? Foul fall thee! / Falsely didst thou swear, / Thou wouldst be with me to aid me, / If haply I should come into evil straits!" (translation, D. H. Low). However, in the preserved songs of Marko Kraljević there are no stories in which Vila promises help to the hero.

120 West 2003b:5–11.

121 Pestalozzi 1945:8.

122 Kullmann 1960:303–358.

123 Schoeck 1961:22.

124 West 2003b:6.

West says: "The idea that a troop of them [Ethiopians] should turn up for the closing phases of the Trojan War is, on the *Iliad*'s terms, as fantastic as would be the arrival of a legion of Phaeacians or Hyperboreans."[125] West draws a simple conclusion: the composer of the *Iliad* knows the story of Achilles' death at the Scaean Gate and further events presented in the *Aethiopis*, but he knows neither Memnon nor the episode associated with him.

West's opinion is largely influenced by his belief in the secondary nature of the fantastic world in the cyclic epics—a faulty belief, which I will try to demonstrate in the next chapter. Homer's rationalism and the difference in this respect between him and cyclic poets require a much broader discussion, which is why some arguments must be presented in a different context. I refer here to the presence of supernatural beings in the epic tradition and to the immortalization of Memnon (and then of Achilles) presented in the summary of the *Aethiopis*. This explains why the *Iliad* does not mention the hero. At this point, I will limit myself to other aspects of Memnon's presence at Troy.

Another of West's objections is that Memnon is the leader of the Ethiopians, a mythical people having nothing to do with the events at Troy, except for the occasional visits of gods lured to Ethiopia by the hecatombs offered to them. As I have pointed out in Chapter 1, the visits of the gods to the Ethiopians are an extremely important element of the construction of the *Iliad*, connected not only with the principle of ring composition, but also with the cyclical perception of time, to which both the construction of a particular epic song such as the *Iliad* and the structure of the whole epic macro-story are subordinated. Twelve-day periods, during which the gods stay in Ethiopia, are important elements of the time frame encircling the proper action of the song. It seems to me that the arrangement of the oral song is subordinated to the determinants of periods of time, only partially understandable to us and perhaps already not quite clear to Homer himself.

In the feasts of the gods and the Ethiopians, one should not see isolated instances of verbal padding added for the symmetry of the work. The roles of the gods and the Ethiopians, however, are ambiguous. I have already mentioned that the absence of the gods is associated with conflicts and disaster. The reason for the presence of the Olympians in Ethiopia is probably to mark the disjuncture between the human and divine worlds. The land of the Ethiopians is synonymous with happiness—so where else could the gods stay, when they are not engaged in human affairs? The point of view of the *Iliad* is quite different than that of the *Aethiopis*. While in the former song, the Ethiopians, associated with a happy existence, emphasize the misery of the human condition inseparable from

125 West 2003b:6–7.

unhappiness and death, in the latter, the gods' involvement in the Achaean/Trojan conflict creates a completely different perspective. The character of the war changes: it is a war on a cosmic scale, in which even the "happy" Ethiopians, living on the edge of the world, take part. Such a difference in the dramatic plan of the oral songs seems to be absolutely justified, since the *Aethiopis* presents the typical and older construction of a plot. The perspective adopted in the *Iliad* is consistent with the image of Achilles, who in the Homeric song loses much of his heroic character in favor of a deeper understanding of his mortality. The *Aethiopis* is similarly consistent in the interpretation of this motif, but here the involvement of the distant Ethiopians serves the purpose of accumulating conditions for an extraordinary duel determining the outcome of the war. The mention of the Ethiopians in the *Iliad* may also be seen as a foreshadowing of the fate of Achilles. His victorious encounter with Hektor, despite the prediction of imminent death, parallels his encounter with Memnon, whereas Patroklos's death, brought about by the cooperation of Apollo and one of Priam's sons, parallels Achilles' death inflicted by Apollo and another of Priam's sons. The allusion to the arrival of the Ethiopian contingent and to the monumental duel with their king, Memnon, which is crucial for Achilles, emphasizes the inevitability of Achilles' fate.

As for the absence of the Ethiopians from the Trojan catalogue in the *Iliad*, Kullmann suggests that when the situation becomes critical, one reaches for the deepest reserves, in this case for the friends who have been "neutral" so far.[126] The Trojans' summoning of the Amazons and Ethiopians is comparable to the Achaeans' fetching of Neoptolemos and Philoktetes. But it seems to me that such realistic thinking is a misunderstanding. The Lycians are not at Troy from the very beginning, contrary to West's opinion, nor does the arrival of the Ethiopians signify the exhaustion of the Trojan forces. The arrival of a contingent of allies is a way of "renewing" the plot, of initiating a song, always starting at the same moment as far as the development of events at Troy is concerned.

West, in a spirit similar to Kullmann's, remarks that the Ethiopians living on the shores of the Okeanos do not communicate with other tribes, so who would bring them to help the Trojans? As the son of the goddess of the Dawn, Eos, and a mortal man, Tithonos (Hesiod *Theogony* 985; compare *Odyssey* 5.1 and the *Homeric Hymn to Aphrodite* 218–238), Memnon comes of the royal Trojan house of Dardanos: Tithonos was a son of Laomedon, a brother of Priam. In one version, clearly seeking to rationalize the plot, Memnon is brought by Teutamos from Assyria (Ktesias *apud* Diodorus Siculus 2.22.1; compare Plato *Leges* 685c). I

126 Kullmann 2005:12–13.

suspect, however, that the information about who brought Memnon might have been missing even in the remnants of the *Aethiopis* known to Apollodorus or Proclus. Perhaps the mention was not necessary at all; the *Iliad* does not specify who brought the Lycians. However, if we need a justification for the presence of the Ethiopians, who are related to the Trojans, on the plain of Ilion, we can assume that the Ethiopians might have been induced to come in aid by gods or at least a god. Perhaps Homer alludes to it, mentioning the feasts of the Olympians with the Ethiopians.[127] In the *Odyssey*, Memnon is mentioned twice. Described as the son of Eos, he is identified as the killer of Antilochos (4.188). Later Odysseus tells Achilles in Hades that Memnon's exceptional beauty was his only advantage over Neoptolemos (11.522).[128]

Achilles is three times the main character in Pindar's mythological exempla. Each time there is a list of his most important achievements. In *Isthmian* 5.44–47, Pindar enumerates the killings of Kyknos, Hektor, then "the fearless commander of the Ethiopians, Memnon clad in bronze armor" (καὶ στράταρχον Αἰθιόπων ἄφοβον / Μέμνονα χαλκοάραν), and the wounding of Telephos. In *Olympian* 2.81–83, Achilles kills Hektor, "the invincible, unbending pillar of Troy" (Ἕκτορα σφᾶλε Τροίας / ἄμαχον ἀστραβῆ κίονα) and Kyknos, and he also "gave to death Memnon the Ethiopian, son of the Dawn" (θανάτῳ πόρεν / Ἀοῦς τε παῖδ' Αἰθίοπα). According to *Nemean* 3.60–63, Achilles "patiently waited at Troy for the spear-bristling war-cry alala of the Lycians, Phrygians, and Dardanians, and putting his hands into the crowd of spear-bearing Ethiopians, he pounded them into the *phrenes*, so that never more might come home their ruler, a cousin of mighty Helenos, Memnon" (ὑπὸ Τροΐαν δορίκτυπον ἀλαλὰν Λυκίων / τε προσμένοι καὶ Φρυγῶν / Δαρδάνων τε καὶ ἐγχεσφόροις ἐπιμείξαις / Αἰθιόπεσσι χεῖρας ἐν φρασὶ πά- / ξαιθ' ὅπως σφίσι μὴ κοίρανος ὀπίσω / πάλιν οἴκαδ' ἀνεψιὸς ζαμενὴς Ἑλένοιο Μέμνων μόλοι).[129] All these passages indicate the equal status of cyclic stories and the *Iliad*. The killing of Memnon is always presented last with a description of varying lengths. According to Pindar, this is the most important of Achilles' achievements, and although it is

127 *Iliad* 1.423–424, 23.206–207; see Ch. 1, pp. 76–77, above.

128 Scholia comment very naively: how, then, could he be black? Compare Vergil *Aeneid* 1.489 *nigri Memnonis*. The *Homeric Hymn to Aphrodite* 225 and Tyrtaeus fr. 12.5 W connect his beauty with that of his father, Tithonos. If we assume his kinship with the Trojan royal house, then it is undeniably beauty that comes to the fore in such of its members as Ganymedes, Anchises, Paris, and Kassandra. Memnon is depicted in later poetry: Simonides devoted a dithyramb to him, fr. 539 *Poetae Melici Graeci*, Aeschylus a trilogy (frr. 127–130, 279–280 *Tragicorum Graecorum Fragmenta*), Pindar several times mentions this hero (*Isthmian* 5.40–41, *Olympian* 2.83, *Pythian* 45, *Nemean* 3.61–63).

129 The connection of Helenos with the story of Memnon remains unclear. He could have taken part in bringing the Ethiopian king to Troy. His role in the songs of the Trojan Cycle could have been more important than we can infer from testimonia. We cannot forget that in one of the versions of the *Little Iliad*, after the death of Paris, he competes with Deiphobos for Helen.

possible to reverse the order of the deaths of Kyknos and Hektor, Memnon's position is unshakeable, because his death immediately precedes that of Achilles.

If we exclude Hektor, who is an important character only in the *Iliad* and as the only son of Priam in this group belongs to a different type of victim, there remains Kyknos, the first significant victim of Achilles on the battlefield at Troy,[130] and Memnon, his last victim. Kyknos is magically invulnerable to weapons of bronze or iron, but there is also another feature that contrasts him with Memnon. Hellanikos reports (Σ 4F148) that Kyknos had been white. The scholiast, who quotes him, suggests that Kyknos's skin was white from his birth, but in another place, the same scholiast writes that his head was white (Hesiod 237 M-W). Gantz ponders the question whether he was an albino or a gray-haired man. Undoubtedly, his whiteness is related to the meaning of the name *kyknos* 'swan'; the myth of a metamorphosis into this bird appears many times in connection with characters bearing the name of Kyknos. Such a surprising combination of such special characteristics of the leaders of Trojan allies cannot be a coincidence. It seems that the juxtaposition of "white" Kyknos and "black" Memnon must have fulfilled an important function in the construction of the macro-story of the cycle.[131] In *Nemean* 3, Pindar places Memnon against the background of tribal names involved in the war on the Trojan side. The Dardanians certainly represent the Trojans themselves, whereas the Lycians and Phrygians, unlike the Ethiopians, appear in the *Iliad*. This mention of Trojan contingents is not merely Pindar's poetic device but a reference to a significant role played by allied troops in the cycle.[132] *Pythian* 6 confirms the story described in the *Aethiopis*, of Memnon's killing Antilochos,

130 In the case of Kyknos, there is a great variety of mythical versions, undoubtedly reflecting an early stage of the formation of this episode in epic oral tradition, characterized by a great degree of fluidity and freedom. Scholars erroneously distinguish between two men with this name, one associated with the landing of the Achaeans on the island of Tenedos, the other with the beginning of fighting on the continent (Gantz 1993:594). Both were supposed to be Poseidon's sons.

131 It seems appropriate to link the characteristics of these heroes with the Indo-European "black and white myth." Petrosyan (2002:49–158) demonstrates the fundamental role it played in shaping the mythic onomastics and topography of Anatolia. For Watkins (1995:62), the Trojan myth represents the war of the "white" Atreidai with the "black" Trojans (for the symbolism of these colors, see Vidal-Naquet 1998:122) and is an adaptation of the Luvian epic about the war of Arzawa with Taruiša. Petrosyan's research provides many examples of the fact that the color division did not function in the dichotomy we/they or familiar/foreign and could exist within one culture. On the opposition of "black" and "white" heroes in the Greek tradition, see also Fontenrose 1960:233–337, 254–256.

132 The Trojan catalogue is discussed in detail in Kullmann 1960:167–188. In his opinion, it must have relied on an earlier catalogue of this type, which, however, did not take the form of a separate song, such as the Catalogue of Ships. Kullmann assumes that it was part of a larger epic. The Trojan catalogue can be found at the conclusion of Proclus's summary of the *Kypria*: καὶ κατάλογος τῶν τοῖς Τρωσὶ συμμαχησάντων 'and next the catalogue of Trojan allies [is presented]'.

who dies defending his father Nestor and whose death becomes the reason for Achilles' fight against Memnon.[133]

The scene of Achilles dueling Memnon was very often a subject of vase painting. As Jonathan Burgess argues in his article "Early Images of Achilles and Memnon,"[134] the depiction of the duel, popular in the sixth century BCE, can also be found in two much earlier paintings: on a Melian amphora from the seventh century and on an Attic bowl stand from the beginning of the same century. On the amphora, each fighting figure is clearly contrasted with the other. In the warrior on the right, with a bright shield and helmet, Burgess recognizes Memnon. His skin is not darker than Achilles', but elements of his armor certainly suggest their extraordinary character. Proclus's summary mentions that Memnon's armor and weapons were made by Hephaistos: ἔχων ἡφαιστότευκτον πανοπλίαν. For Hesiod (*Theogony* 984), the most important article was his bronze helmet—Μέμνονα χαλκοκορυστήν,[135] whereas for Pindar (*Isthmian* 5.41)—the bronze armor Μέμνονα χαλκοάραν. The bright color of Memnon's armor in the painting points out that it was made from different material—from gold. West calls into question that Memnon's armor was made by Hephaistos, because only one warrior could have such armor.[136] West ignores the early testimony of Hesiod, but I think the main counterargument against his opinion is that the uniqueness of the hero regularly extends to his opponent. Immunity to weapons or invincibility is typical not only of Achilles, but also of his adversaries. They also have extraordinary divine horses, miraculous armor, and weapons. The function of these attributes will be discussed in detail in the next chapter. Now I want to stress only that nowhere is the use of magic objects reserved for one hero only, such as Achilles, and in an epic song there is never only one miraculous object, such as armor. The transition from fairy-tale epic or mythological epic to historical epic is marked by the tendency of the opponents to resemble the hero.[137]

133 A discussion on the possibility of relating Pindar's narrative (*Pythian* 6.29-39) to the scene from the *Aethiopis* will be presented in Ch. 5.

134 Burgess 2004a:33–51.

135 It is obviously a traditional formula. In a parallel scene of the *Iliad*, when Zeus ponders the fate of Patroklos, he decides that the Trojans and Ἕκτορα χαλκοκορυστήν 'Hektor in a bronze helmet' (16.654) should be driven back to the city. This scene resembles the *psychostasia* in the *Memnois*, where Zeus's scales deciding the fate of the heroes are mentioned.

136 Kullmann (2005:15–16) claims that the allegedly secondary nature of Memnon's armor made by Hephaistos can be viewed in two ways: even if Memnon's armor is modeled on Achilles', it does not mean that the *Iliad's* author did not know Memnon; and Memnon's armor is primary to Achilles', but it belongs to the episode formed in a younger version of the saga. The most important one, therefore, is the armor which is immune to weapons given to Achilles by Peleus.

137 For more on this topic, see Zieliński 2016a.

Even in the *Iliad,* Achilles has two sets of divine armor, both forged by Hephaistos.[138] The magical power of the armor Achilles gave to Patroklos is confirmed by numerous testimonia as well as the death of Patroklos, then that of Hektor, who had put on this armor, after he ripped it from Achilles' friend. The singer cannot ignore the traditional motif of Achilles' miraculous armor and highlights its role through an extensive description of Hephaistos forging a new set for the hero (18.468–615), who was deprived of the old one (18.82–85, 130–137).

That which in the *Iliad* is only a reference to the traditional value of these sets of armor in Achilles' duel with Hektor, in the *Aethiopis* retains its full meaning. Achilles' duel with Memnon has a cosmic and religious dimension. For such an extraordinary encounter, both heroes must have magic armor—it is one of the elements of the duel (sketched at the beginning of the previous sub-chapter), which—as the only one of its kind—is unique in many ways. It is this cosmic-cum-religious dimension of the "clash of the titans" that the second image on the Attic bowl stand analyzed by Burgess seems to emphasize. The scene of a real fight seems to be only a prelude to a scene of the rivalry between the souls of warriors supported by goddesses. The outcome of the fight is determined by Cheiron (probably correctly identified by Burgess)—whose figure is a reference to the lessons of hunting and killing which he gave to Achilles, and to Achilles' spear, decisive for the fight, which was also made by the centaur. A visible sign of this reading is game hanging from the stick held over Cheiron's shoulder. Burgess corroborates this interpretation by comparing this scene with a fresco scene from the "Cult Center" at Mycenae, where two goddesses seem to be deciding the fate of two miniature naked males. Burgess mentions the possibility (without insisting on it) that it may be a prototype of the duel between Achilles and Memnon and a scene of divine judgment, perhaps a *psychostasia*. The *psychostasia* marks the pinnacle of enhancing the uniqueness of the epic duel. Both warriors possess unusual parallel attributes that make them unbeatable. Their chances are so equal that the contest must be settled independently of the heroes. Even Zeus, on his own, is not able to pronounce who should win. The audience is tensely awaiting the sentence of the scales of fate.

West's main argument for Homer's ignorance of the Memnon episode, and hence his failure to use it in the *Iliad,* is the prophecy which Thetis delivers to her son after the death of Patroklos—you will now revenge yourself on Hektor, but you will die right after that. According to West, if Homer had known the sequence of events that, as suggested by the *Aethiopis,* happened between

[138] More in Ch. 3, below.

Hektor's death and Achilles' death, he would not have declared so strongly and clearly that Achilles' death would happen very soon, almost the day after Hektor's funeral. These scenes include Penthesileia, Thersites' scorn, his death, *stasis* in the Achaean camp, Achilles' purification, his return to Troy, and then the encounter with Memnon ending in the latter's death. To explain the fulfillment of the prophecy of Achilles' instantaneous death after Hektor, West assumes the existence of an earlier narrative plan, in which Achilles does not return to the ships after killing Hektor, so there are no funeral games for Patroklos, nor the ransoming of Hektor's body.[139] Such hypotheses were usually proposed by the Analysts and West in fact refers to the conception of Wilamowitz, who believed that originally the *Iliad* had also included the death of Achilles.[140]

To perceive the epic plot as if it pertained to real time, is not only unnecessary[141]—it is absolutely erroneous. The perspective of the epic song always contains the notion of the imminent death of Achilles, which is accelerated by his heroic deeds. The inevitability of certain events is an immanent part of the structure of the oral epic. The events towards which the song is heading are known to both the singer and the public. The singer makes use of this fact, feeding the audience with allusions which strengthen their awareness of what is going to happen and at the same time misleading them into thinking that perhaps it will not.[142] The inevitability of the fall of Troy and Achilles' death demarcate the time frame of the *Iliad*. In the macro-story of the cycle there are many events which must come to pass in order to make the capture of Troy possible. None of them is less important than any other and each is equally significant. They all function as the retardation of the final denouement. But it is so only from our point of view, when we look from a distance at the outline of the whole cycle. An *aoidos* never recounts the story of the whole war at one performance. He always presents only a larger or smaller fragment. At the beginning of the war, nobody calls to mind all the conditions necessary for the capture of Troy. They are revealed one by one, only when the need arises. In this way, the epic poet can multiply obstacles, always mentioning the inevitability of Achilles' death after a given condition has been fulfilled.

Quite surprisingly, West not only distances himself from oral theory,[143] but also praises the findings of the Analysts, introducing, however, one significant readjustment in their assumptions concerning the authorship of the *Iliad*.

139 West 2003b:8.

140 West 2003b:6, 12.

141 Kullmann (2005:13–14) believes that the prediction of Achilles' immediate death after slaying Hektor does not preclude the *Memnois*.

142 This method of the singer's playing with the audience will be discussed in Chs. 4 and 5.

143 West 2003b:11: "The *Iliad*, the *Odyssey*, and Cyclic poems, were not oral poems—at any rate, not in the same sense as the oral poems that Parry and Lord described—but written texts."

According to him, its subsequent strata do not indicate the contribution of many authors, but are the work of one poet, composing and elaborating his song all his life. In his view, Homer reworked the *Iliad* until it was perfect, after which it was written up. However, this perfect song is still open to various interpolations.

In 2005, there appeared two articles opposed to West's interpretation: Kullmann argues from the perspective of neoanalysis, and W. Allan attacks West from the position of oral poetry theory. Kullmann shows that West's theses are completely unconvincing, because many other, sometimes much more likely methods of imitation and adaptation can be proposed. He presents neoanalytic arguments in favor of Homer's acquaintance with the Memnon episode. Allan similarly, though more cautiously, challenges the two most important of West's theses, saying that they do not support the meaning that the scholar assigns to them.

Both critics reject West's concept of the *Iliad* as a song written up in a different shape than its previous forms, and perhaps extended over the years, even after it started functioning as a fixed text.[144] West's interpretation is a consequence of his previous findings, which were presented in his 1995 article "The Date of the *Iliad*,"[145] in which the scholar does not deny the oral character of cyclic poems, but claims that the *Iliad* is later, created as late as 670–640 BCE, or more precisely 660–650 BCE, composed with the intention of competing with Hesiod, under the obvious influence of Babylonian and Assyrian poetry, and fixed in writing. Therefore, in his calculations, West determines the moment of the appearance of Memnon in the consciousness of Greeks at around 630 or 620 BCE.[146] However, a vast majority of scholars assume that the Homeric poems came into being in the eighth century. In light of the model of the construction of epic songs, the arguments for the "rejuvenation" of the *Iliad* dependent on reading certain passages as traces of historical events (e.g. the destruction of the Achaean wall by a violent flood as a reminiscence of flooding Babylon by the Assyrians in 689 BCE) cannot be considered relevant.

The technique of an adaptation of a traditional theme allows the author of the *Iliad* to refer in various ways and in various configurations to the same scene known from tradition. In the song pattern associated with Achilles, the main task of this hero is to slay the leader of the Trojan allies. The Achilles and Memnon duel is deliberately constructed in such a way that their forces are equal, and the fate of the heroes is uncertain until the end. Everything depends

144 Allan (2005:14), referring to West's claims, uses the word "extreme," which is an understatement.

145 West 1995:203–219.

146 Kullmann (2005:15) asks why the depiction of the Ethiopians as a fantastic people should be based on a historical event and appear in a rather short period of twenty to thirty years after the *Iliad*, and before the *Odyssey*.

on Zeus's scales. I presume that here the principle of exaggerating unusual features of ethnically foreign heroes might be at play, so that their chances in the encounter with Achilles are equal.

The clash of Aeneas and Achilles, mentioned in *Iliad* 20.103–346, may be seen as a reminiscence of the technique used in Memnon's encounter with Achilles. In a fight with Achilles, it is essential to make the chances of victory equal, as Aeneas explains to Apollo, who in the form of Lykaon, a son of Priam, persuaded him to fight. According to Aeneas, he cannot fight Achilles, because Achilles always gets divine support, but if a god would make their chances equal, Achilles would not be able to defeat Aeneas easily (*Iliad* 20.97–102):

> τὼ οὐκ ἔστ' Ἀχιλῆος ἐναντίον ἄνδρα μάχεσθαι,
> αἰεὶ γὰρ πάρα εἷς γε θεῶν ὃς λοιγὸν ἀμύνει.
> καὶ δ' ἄλλως τοῦ γ' ἰθὺ βέλος πέτετ', οὐδ' ἀπολήγει
> πρὶν χροὸς ἀνδρομέοιο διελθέμεν. εἰ δὲ θεός περ
> ἶσον τείνειεν πολέμου τέλος, οὐ κε μάλα ῥέα
> νικήσει', οὐδ' εἰ παγχάλκεος εὔχεται εἶναι
>
> it is not possible to fight Achilles face to face,
> for at his side there is always one of the gods, who protects him from destruction,
> and his missile flies differently, in a straight line, and it does not stop,
> until it pierces a warrior's body. But if a god
> gave [me] equal luck in fighting, he would not
> beat me easily, even if he boasts that he is all of bronze.

Apollo inspires Aeneas with courage, reminding him that his mother is also a goddess, and a more powerful one than Thetis.[147] This issue is raised again by Aeneas himself, when he confronts Achilles (*Iliad* 20.203–209). This scene is one of several in the *Iliad* which may point to the tradition of the heroes boasting of their divine origin.[148] Mark Edwards believes that "perhaps there was something

[147] Boedeker (1974:67–69) argues that in many aspects the goddess Aphrodite took over the features of the goddess Dawn, of Indo-European origin (Greek Eos and Indo-Iranian Ušas). See also Nagy 1973; Slatkin 1991:28–31, 42, 78–79.

[148] Fenik (1968:67) notes that it is possible to deduce a rule—the more powerful the parent, the more powerful the son: Achilles boasts that the offspring of Zeus are more powerful than the children of rivers and then he kills Asteropaios (*Iliad* 21.184–191); Sarpedon, a son of Zeus, kills Tlepolemos, a son of Herakles and a grandson of Zeus (*Iliad* 5.655–667); Hera discusses the unequal status of Achilles and Hektor, because the former is of divine lineage (*Iliad* 24.56). The duel of Achilles and Aeneas is unusual in this respect because, despite the heroes' origin, the son of the mightier goddess is defeated.

similar in a scene of Akhilleus' combat with Eos' son Memnon."[149] Achilles' weapon, also of "divine origin," turns out to be superior, when Aeneas's spear cannot penetrate a layer of gold in Achilles' shield. The narrator, with characteristic irony, emphasizes the immunity of divine gifts to human efforts (20.264–266).[150] By stressing the basic difference between gods and mortals, the poet exposes his inconsistency: until the last moment, the struggle is presented as close and the winner is not known (20.288–290), but its result is determined from the outset, which is revealed in the conversation of the gods, who are preparing to intervene (20.293–295). The combination of both attitudes prolongs the atmosphere of dread.

The leader of the Trojan allies, who fuctions as the enemy of the protagonist, possesses a team of unusual horses. In this respect, Aeneas is linked both with Memnon and Rhesos, because his horses are descendants of the ones, which were given by the gods to Tros, a forefather of the Trojans (5.265–272). They were stolen by Diomedes on the first day of the battle in the *Iliad* (5.319–327). Diomedes uses them later in the *Iliad*, and thanks to them becomes an unexpected winner in the funeral games in honor of Patroklos (23.290–292, 507–510).

Aeneas escapes death because the god Poseidon rescues him from the battlefield. This intervention is a variation of the scene when Aeneas is carried from the battlefield by Aphrodite, just as he was about to be killed by Diomedes (*Iliad* 5.312–318). It is obvious that here the author of the *Iliad* makes two scenes out of one, using a chiastic order: in the first, Aeneas is rescued by his own mother, the goddess Aphrodite, from death at the hands of Diomedes, who functions in the *Iliad* as Achilles' double;[151] in the second, the danger is from the real Achilles, and the rescue is by another god, Poseidon, who substitutes for his mother. In the encounter with Diomedes, Aphrodite's support is ineffective, and Apollo has to carry Aeneas from the battlefield. This version of events clashes with Apollo's later exhortations, in which he encourages Aeneas to duel with Achilles since he has support of his mother Aphrodite, a far greater goddess than Achilles' mother. This circumstance, however, does not help Aeneas; from the powerlessness of the goddess of love we can infer that the poet uses the Memnon pattern, in which maternal support was also ineffective.

Standing face to face with Achilles, Aeneas mentions that they had an earlier encounter, on Mount Ida (this scene also appears in Proclus's summary

149 Edwards 1991:304.

150 The narrator calls Achilles a fool since he does not realize the power of divine gifts which are in his possession (20.264–267).

151 Diomedes is Achilles' double, like Patroklos, but unlike Patroklos, he is a symbol of the conduct which Achilles should choose (see Ch. 5, below).

of the *Kypria*). In comparison with the Memnon pattern, here there is a significant difference, because Aeneas says that he was saved then by Zeus (ἐμὲ Ζεὺς / εἰρύσαθ'). We have three versions of the rescues of Aeneas: by Zeus, Aphrodite-Apollo, and Poseidon. It is evidence of the stabilization of the pattern of divine intervention saving the hero from the death by the hand of Achilles—probably necessary because in the traditional pattern the encounter with Achilles must have always ended in death.

Bernard Fenik believes that these similarities result from the use of traditional patterns, which help the singer to add new episodes. In his view, however, Rhesos, Memnon, and Eurypylos have similar characteristics to Achilles only because the poet builds such heroic types according to one pattern.[152] He notes four features common to Achilles and Memnon—each is a son of a lesser goddess, both have armor made by Hephaistos, both own miraculous horses, and both are given special compensation after death due to their mother's efforts.[153] Fenik's observation should be further elaborated: the leaders of Trojan allies, Achilles' most important rivals, are brought up to his level. The magnification of heroes' forces, often to fabulous proportions, is typical of epic in general. In Greek epic, in which wars are led by heroes, their opponents lose their monstrous features and shapes.[154] Having been transformed from monsters to warriors, they need to retain greatness and uniqueness in order to attract listeners' attention. The easiest way to magnify their power, so that they are equal to their noble adversary, is to take over his traits. Old epic structure increases the interest of the listeners in the event that is just about to happen by infusing it with a sense of the incredible.[155]

Such exaggeration organizes the dramatic tension of epic songs about the conflict between Achilles and Memnon, but it no longer dominates the dramatic organization of the *Iliad*. Nevertheless, the technique of accumulation is noticeable in the poem. Walter Leaf[156] believes that the review of troops in *Iliad* 4.223–421 delays the beginning of the battle too long and slows down the action where it should be fast-paced. The presentation of the countless armies about to clash with each other (as the extensive catalogues of Achaean ships and Trojan allies indicate) seems to resemble the magnification of the

152 Fenik 1968:150.

153 Fenik 1968:149.

154 In Ch. 6, p. 573 (below), analogies of this phenomenon in other epics are pointed out.

155 The same can be observed in contemporary action films: characters played by Arnold Schwarzenegger, Sylvester Stallone, or Clint Eastwood always use enormous weapons. Often, their adversaries also have at their disposal similarly impressive weapons. Preparations for a final fight are as important in these films as the fight itself.

156 Leaf 1900–1902 *ad* 4.221.

power of Achilles and Memnon when they are facing each other and ready to fight.[157]

From the Depth of Tradition

The arming of the warrior

It seems to me that this approach, which takes into account a varied and adaptively transformed multiform epic message, and which sees in the actions of individual characters the fulfilment of traditional roles of protagonists and their antagonists, should enable us to reach into the history of Greek epic much deeper than it has been possible so far. We know that singers use repetitive formulae, scenes, and narrative patterns, and, moreover, that they always observe a certain regularity, in which these elements succeed one another, relying on a certain pattern that ensures an appropriate amount of dramatic tension and enables the preservation of important cultural content. Such a particular shape of the plot is based on ritual foundations; however, now it is difficult to ascertain the meaning of images derived from rites.

In this sub-chapter, we will look again at the two most important characters of the Trojan Cycle, Achilles and Odysseus, and try to find out how they evolved as epic developed. Both represent the type of a young hero—regardless of how many years of war elapse and, in the case of Odysseus, also the years of the journey home. The epic narrative does not calculate the passage of time in this way, as is evident in the case of Odysseus: sometimes the song indicates that time has left its mark upon the hero, and at other times he is miraculously rejuvenated, as in the competitions with the suitors and the renewal of the marriage.

In the epic song, the young hero is the focus of action. He is the only one who can succeed where other, experienced knights have failed. Often, he draws on their experience and uses their help, but his most important deeds must be performed single-handed. The crucial fight that is in store for him is an initiation into adult life. This fight introduces him to the world of men and experienced knights, although it may also lead to his destruction. His fight with the dragon, which can either take the form of a monster or a monstrous warrior,

157 The lofty stillness of this scene is probably connected with what Richardson (1990:13–17) calls "action summary." In certain important moments of the fight, the action "freezes," depending on a suggestive image, often a simile. Richardson 1990:17: "In the battles Homer is interested not so much in the movements and skirmishes on a large scale as in individual combats, deaths, and acts of valor. If the action is worth telling, it seems, it is worth telling in full. Even his occasional exceptions do not so much serve the purpose of expeditious narration of a sequence of events, the usual function of the action summary, as they offer a descriptive picture of the action."

is the climax of the song. This fundamental epic scene is always preceded by a scene of the hero donning armor. In the *Iliad*, this scene fulfills a double function: it prepares for and at the same time delays the fight, heightening the atmosphere of dread and expectation; but, by the skillful use or omission of typical elements, it suggests the victory or defeat of the hero.[158]

The Homeric description of donning armor may take an extended form or be reduced to a short mention that such an action took place. Lord observes a parallel in Slavic songs, in which the singer may devote only a short remark to this theme or elaborate it to astounding lengths. Lord notes that the elaboration or its lack is not neutral and the singer makes a deliberate choice, because "the longer version seems to be reserved for the main protagonist when he is preparing himself to go forth on a special mission."[159] He is probably right in his conjecture that it is a "survival from rites of initiation or dedication."[160]

In Homer's *Iliad*, an extended scene of arming appears four times in connection with as many heroes: Paris (3.330–338), Agamemnon (11.17–45), Patroklos (16.131–139), and Achilles (19.369–374). This should be assessed as a diffusion of the topic, which originally appeared in the story only once. It can be multiplied without losing its unique character and importance to the role of the young hero.[161] Moreover, it also shows the potentiality of cyclic epic songs, in which various characters can play the role of the young hero, and the song can organize the plot around their exploits.

Extended descriptions of the arming of heroes precede their *aristeia*.[162] A characteristic, and yet unnoticed feature of all four scenes of donning armor in the *Iliad* is that the heroes in question put on breastplates which are not their own.[163] In the case of Achilles, the hero dons new armor, made for him by Hephaistos, after the loss of his old one. Although it is not his first armor, Achilles represents the type of a young hero who needs equipment to be able to fight but hasn't any of his own. Earlier he had armor, also made by Hephaistos,

158 Compare Armstrong 1958:348–352.

159 Lord 1960:88.

160 Lord 1960:88.

161 Armstrong (1958:341–342) takes a different point of view. He assumes that the typical character of this scene makes it essential before each important fight and is astonished that there are so few scenes of the arming of heroes, and especially that there is not any description of the arming of Hektor.

162 For the *aristeia* pattern, see Krischer 1971. Of the warriors who attain *aristeia*, i.e. have a streak of victories in a series of duels, only Diomedes' arming is not described, but perhaps the passage emphasizing the glow of his armor kindled by Athena (*Iliad* 5.1–8), whose divine intervention somehow activates the warrior, is its substitute (Edwards 1987:79).

163 The traditionality of this motif is upheld two centuries later by pseudo-Hesiod's *Shield*, in which Herakles puts on Athena's armor (*Shield* 125–127). See also the preparations before the nocturnal spying expedition by Diomedes (*Iliad* 10.255–259) and Odysseus (10.260–262).

which was given him by his father and which Patroklos wore in his final battle. It belonged to "Aiakos's swift-footed grandson" (ποδώκεος Αἰακίδαο)—Achilles. The young warrior gets armor from an older warrior, often from someone in his family, because he does not yet possess his own. In the *Iliad*, this would be illogical, because Patroklos has been at Troy for nine years, so here there is another justification: Patroklos takes the place of Achilles in combat. Dressing Patroklos in Achilles' armor does not really serve the purpose of deceiving enemies,[164] but strengthens his identification with Achilles at the moment of their death.[165]

The theme a young hero setting forth to fight in borrowed armor or, more generally, armor not his own is also common in the oral tradition of the South Slavs. In the song *Bećiragić Meho* sung by Mumin Vlahovljak (**Parry 12468**),[166] the protagonist, Meho, is a young man who is so poor that Muslim heroes do not accept him in their circle. But when they learn of his tragic and heroic story, they are moved and help him to win the hand of his beloved woman. Ahmo, Halil, and the son of Mustajbey, Bećir, in turn offer him their horses, clothes, and weapons, so that he can go to the land of Christians and, unashamed by poverty, compete for the hand of the ban of Janok's daughter, Anđelija. Ahmo, Meho's uncle, gives him a string of coral[167] and tells him to exchange them for Ahmo's own horse and weapons. Halil offers him his watch,[168] telling him to address his sister, who will give him a horse, weapons, money, and festive garments (those which Halil wears only once a year). Bećir wants to borrow a horse from his father and give it to Meho, and then follow him to Janok. Finally, Meho goes to Halil's sister, who gives him all he needs for the journey, and goes to take his girl from Đuro of Radane, who is about to marry her. The hero's lack of horse and weapons, which disables

164 Hektor and the Trojans quickly recognize that it is Patroklos dressed as Achilles. This complication is a result of the author's intent to stress Patroklos's heroism; Patroklos's death is also a re-enactment of Achilles' death (more about this in Ch. 5, below).

165 Paris also wears a breastplate which is not his own but borrowed from his brother Lykaon (*Iliad* 3.333). Even Agamemnon puts on a breastplate given him by Kinyras, the king of Cyprus (11.20). This element of tradition is so important that Homer must use it, even if a figure like Agamemnon is not the type of a young hero. But this is the moment when Agamemnon goes into battle and reaches the walls of Troy—like Patroklos and Achilles, whose deeds he perhaps anticipates. What is significant about his *aristeia* is perhaps the fact that it reveals his inability to capture Troy—so he wrongly takes the title of "the best of the Achaeans"; that is, he tries to usurp the role of a hero. He does not achieve what Patroklos and Achilles do: they could take Troy, if it were not for the god Apollo standing in their way.

166 Another version of song was prompted by Parry (**Parry 12471**). He realized that Avdo Međedović, with whom he had worked for several weeks, did not know this song. Parry let him hear Mumin sing it and then Avdo sang the same song in a much longer version (the original was 158 verses long, Avdo's 558 verses), expanding it with new descriptions and comparisons, giving the characters psychological depth, and adding his own understanding of heroic conduct.

167 In Avdo's version, a golden kerchief.

168 In Avdo's version, a kerchief.

him from fighting, receives additional motivation: Meho is poor.[169] But the fact of Meho's poverty does not obliterate the basic, typically epic motivation: the hero does not have a horse, weapons, or armor, because he is too young.[170]

An additional motivation can also be found in Homer. When in the *Doloneia*, Diomedes and Odysseus are getting ready for a night excursion to spy on the Trojans, both put on someone else's armor and don't take their own weapons (*Iliad* 10.255–262):

> Τυδεΐδῃ μὲν δῶκε μενεπτόλεμος Θρασυμήδης
> φάσγανον ἄμφηκες· τὸ δ' ἑὸν παρὰ νηῒ λέλειπτο·
> καὶ σάκος· ἀμφὶ δέ οἱ κυνέην κεφαλῆφιν ἔθηκε
> ταυρείην, ἄφαλόν τε καὶ ἄλλοφον, ἥ τε καταῖτυξ
> κέκληται, ῥύεται δὲ κάρη θαλερῶν αἰζηῶν.
> Μηριόνης δ' Ὀδυσῆϊ δίδου βιὸν ἠδὲ φαρέτρην
> καὶ ξίφος, ἀμφὶ δέ οἱ κυνέην κεφαλῆφιν ἔθηκε
> ῥινοῦ ποιητήν·
>
> To Tydeides fierce in battle Thrasymedes gave
> a double-edged sword, because this one [Tydeides] had left his own
> by the ship,
> and a shield. Then on his head he placed a helmet
> of bull's hide, without a peak or crest; it is known as a
> *kataitux* [leather helmet], because it protects the head of brave young
> men.
> Meanwhile Meriones gave Odysseus a bow, quiver,
> and sword, and on his head he placed a leather helmet[171]
> made of oxen hide.

The helmet belonged to Autolykos, Odysseus's grandfather, and having been passed from hand to hand, it returns to its rightful owner (10.262–271). Putting on someone else's armor is here sanctioned by the fact that hero left his own in his tent. Homer had to invent the whole chain of transmission before Odysseus could put the helmet on his head.

169 The story of Meho's past is borrowed from another type of song, in which the protagonist is imprisoned, e.g. the Song of Return.

170 In South Slavic songs, rich clothes, which a youth puts on, are often taken out of a chest and given to him by his mother, an old servant, or nurse (Lord 1960:86–88), which is a clear indication of the fact that he has reached maturity.

171 Both epithets mean the same: helmets without horse tail. Their use here is dictated by phonetic similarity (ἄφαλόν τε καὶ ἄλλοφον), which facilitated composition.

In the song *The Wedding of Smailagić Meho*, there is still another version of this motif: already in the first scene of the assembly the young hero is wearing armor and rich clothes, but all this is the Sultan's gift to his father, Smail, and himself on the occasion of his birthday. The gifts include also a horse with a miraculous harness and a wonderful sword. Meho, kitted up with all this, is impatient for an opportunity to do mighty deeds. For Lord, there is a striking similarity between his accoutrements and those of Achilles: "They are the gifts of a supreme power to a specially chosen hero, honoring both, and blessed by the gods."[172]

Again we can see how permanent elements of oral epic are. They can be modified and multiplied, but they cannot be omitted. The hero's possession of someone else's armor and weapons may also be of magical significance. In our times, there is a superstition that wearing or possessing someone else's things protects against failure when performing an important task. In epic songs, however, the donning of someone else's armor is explained primarily by the age of the hero, who is still too young to possess his own. Usually when the hero is getting ready for action, he gets or finds the weapon, armor, and horse which used to belong to his father. Often, they are waiting for him, who is their rightful owner (like Excalibur for Arthur), but quite often he must prove that he deserves them.[173] In Homer, Achilles has got his father's armor, but, as we have seen, in the climax of the story, his grandfather Aiakos is mentioned. Similarly, the helmet placed on Odysseus's head belonged to his grandfather Autolykos. Perhaps, then, in Greek epic, inheriting from one's grandfather is of special importance. Forging new armor is a variation of putting on someone else's—this motif brings the Achilles of the *Iliad* close to Siegfried, who—because of various reasons, including the change of social status in his childhood—possesses neither armor nor weapons, so, setting forth for battle, he forges himself a sword from a meteorite.[174]

Thus, Achilles appears to be a typical epic hero whose fate is to defeat a monster. His enemy is a hero-knight, but as a leader of Trojan allies, and often of fairy-tale ancestry, he retains monstrous features. These are counterbalanced by the extraordinary invulnerability, divine horses, and weapons of Achilles, son

172 Lord 1974:16.

173 For example, in the Armenian epic of David, the hero is rebuked by an old woman for stupidly getting ready for fighting without armor, sword, or a horse, and is told to go to his uncle for his father's weapons. Both the uncle and the horse (endowed with a human voice), play a verbal *agôn* with David, before finally succumbing to him.

174 In the quasi-cycle of Marko Krajlević, we find both variants of arming the hero. Once, preparing to fight the outlaw Musa, he orders the blacksmith Novak to forge a suitable saber. Another time, he meets a Turk, who has appropriated his father's saber. Marko kills him for wickedness and for showing no mercy to his father, after which he takes the weapon. Both sabers are described as miraculous, but they do not play any role in other songs.

of a goddess. Such "monstrous" enemies are primarily "white" Kyknos, "black" Memnon, and the Amazon Penthesileia. The "monster" is multiplied, in accordance with the principles of epic cycle formation. Each time, Achilles squares up to him in the same way, as if it were his only task. Killing the "monster" brings about his own death (similar to Siegfried, Beowulf, and others), but it enables the Achaeans to capture Troy. Thanks to the prophecy given to him by his mother, Achilles knows what is going to happen. That is why he refrains from fighting each time the duel entails dangerous consequences. I think that the depression which Achilles experiences before the fight can be compared to the sadness of the young hero, frequently encountered in the Slavic epics collected by Parry and Lord. Bećiragić Meho in Mumin Vlahovljak's song is sad, as is the protagonist of the greatest song performed by Avdo Međedović—Smailagić Meho. Sadness and worries are the reasons why Marko Kraljević drinks at the beginning of the popular song *Marko and Nina of Kostur* (**Parry 6, 803, 804, 805, 846**).[175] This mood of depression accompanying or preceding the investiture of the young hero may point to his awareness or a presentiment of his own death. No wonder, since he starts on the path of self-sacrifice that rescues the community from evil. The ritual patterns of this situation are the initiation rites and the scapegoat rite.

The quarrel of the lion and the boar

The analysis of the arming scene has shown that many heroes from Troy could have been placed in the center of an epic song of the cycle. The theme of insulting the hero and his withdrawal from fighting (Meleagros, Paris, Aeneas), recurrent in the *Iliad*, displays a similar potentiality. But important roles in this theme are played only by Achilles and Odysseus. In fact, in all the plot material of the cycle, it is difficult to find a slot where one could place an epic song with the protagonist other than Achilles or Odysseus. This is confirmed by linking both heroes with the motif of conflict/dispute—*neikos*, which plays a role in the structure of the epic narrative. *Neikos* stimulates the development of action. It results from a reaction to a crisis and leads to the overcoming of difficulties.

In the Trojan Cycle, Achilles starts a dispute with Agamemnon at least twice, once with Thersites, and once with Odysseus in Demodokos's first song (*Odyssey* 8.73–82).[176] Odysseus quarrels also with Aias about Achilles' armor; in

175 Lord 1960:71–73.

176 In the Theban Cycle, there appears a dispute equal in significance and meaning, when the blinded Oedipus curses his sons, Polyneikes and Eteokles, for sending him the wrong piece of meat (the *Thebaid*).

the cycle, he brings on himself the hatred of many heroes.[177] A whole gallery of Odysseus's enemies was depicted in Polygnotos's painting showing Odysseus's visit to Hades (*Nekyia*).[178]

Demodokos's reference to Odysseus's struggle with Achilles, which sets them apart as the two most important Achaean warriors at Troy, does not only serve the purpose of highlighting Odysseus's heroic aspect. Achilles appears two more times in the *Odyssey* and both times he is a witness to the most important of Odysseus's feats. In the *Nekyia* (*Odyssey* 11.473–476), Achilles wonders at Odysseus's ingenuity which enabled him to sneak into Hades while he is alive. Odysseus replies, stressing Achilles' extraordinary role (11.483–486), perhaps connected with cult, "You mightily rule the dead." Achilles then downplays his position there and asks about his father and son. He also expresses his regret that he cannot help his father in a difficult situation, as if he were aware that someone is inflicting violence on the old man and depriving him of honor (11.488–503). The situation he depicts is parallel to that which awaits Odysseus at home, and which this hero is capable of dealing with.

Achilles' second appearance in the *Odyssey* is in Book 24, in a conversation with Agamemnon. Agamemnon praises the extraordinary splendor of the funeral that the Achaeans gave to Achilles, attended even by the Muses and Nereids (24.35–94). In the cycle, this scene prepares for the immortality of Achilles, his exaltation above other Achaean heroes. In the *Odyssey*, it is juxtaposed with the lamentation for the souls of the suitors murdered by Odysseus, his most important deed, the last one in the song (24.98–204). In Demodokos's song, the conflict between the heroes foreshadows their most significant war deeds. In the *Iliad*, the poet cannot paint the portrait of Achilles as the most important warrior at Troy without putting in the picture of its actual conqueror, Odysseus;[179] likewise, in the *Odyssey*, he cannot present the greatest exploits of the protagonist without showing Achilles' deeds in the background. This is not

177 *Odyssey* 3.136 mentions Agamemnon's dispute with Menelaos over the departure from Troy. It seems symptomatic that the quarrel between the brothers commanding the expedition takes place only after the capture of Troy, a situation diametrically opposed to all other quarrels, which are supposed to lead to a solution enabling the conquer of Ilion. Sammons (2014) points to the *Odyssey's* compatibility with the cyclic tradition of the *Nostoi* and the Attic tragedy, which was under its influence. At the same time, the *Nostoi* tradition is irreconcilable with the *Iliad's* depiction of Menelaos, although some phrases provoke Sammons to infer that the allusions in the *Iliad* testify to the fact that it was familiar to the Cyclic tradition.

178 Pausanias 10.31.1–3 claims that the enemies of Odysseus are gathered together and enumerates the following: Aias son of Telamon, Palamedes, Thersites, Aias son of Oileus, Meleagros son of Oineus. It is absolutely unclear why Meleagros was placed among Odysseus's enemies and why Aias son of Oileus was observing him.

179 Both heroes are given the epithet πτολιπόρθος 'city conqueror' in the *Iliad:* Achilles 8.372, 15.77, 21.550, 24.108; Odysseus 2.278, 10.363. Compare n194 below.

evidence of the complementary character of those two works of Homer, but of a typical way in which the deeds of these heroes are transmitted in epic. At this stage of the formation of the cycle, it was probably impossible to show only one hero, without mentioning the other. This co-existence of the two heroes, who are bound by rivalry, but also co-operation and perhaps even friendship (though this last is uncertain, considering Nagy's interpretation of the embassy to Achilles),[180] is in all likelihood a remnant of the primitive pattern of epic songs. In order to prove it, I will rely on the evidence provided by comparison of the Trojan and Theban cycles.

There is no doubt about the priority of the Theban Cycle. Homer several times refers to facts known from the cycle, and two Epigonoi (see below, p. 325) participate in the Trojan expedition: Diomedes, son of Tydeus, and Sthenelos, son of Kapeneus. There are many similarities in the construction of both cycles, but I would like to point to the doubling of the expeditions, which is necessary for success. There are two attempts to take Thebes: the first expedition, known as the Seven against Thebes, fails, and only the second one, when sons follow the steps of their fathers, ends successfully. In the Trojan Cycle, there are also two expeditions, which start in Aulis: the first destroys Teuthrania by mistake, but the second ends in the capture of Troy. Of all the Achaean participants in the first expedition, Achilles plays the most important role, when he injures Telephos, but his greatest exploits are connected to the second expedition. The need for Achilles' son, Neoptolemos, to fight at Troy after the death of his father is another analogy to the Theban Cycle: Troy is finally taken by the second generation. The games organized in honor of Archemoros (later called the Nemean Games) can be seen as a proof of the priority of the Theban Cycle. At these games, the main characters of the expedition are winners in various competitions. In the Trojan Cycle, their counterparts are the games after Achilles' death (*Aethiopis*) and in the *Iliad*, the games at the funeral for Patroklos, in which, however, the favorites lose.

Let us have a close look at one theme of the Theban Cycle connected with the organization of the first expedition against Thebes, depicted in Euripides' tragedy *The Suppliants* 131–161. Adrastos, king of Argos, receives two heroes who have been exiled from their homes and who seek refuge with him. Polyneikes has quarreled with his brother Eteokles and seeks help in regaining his inheritance from Oedipus. Tydeus, in a struggle for the Aetolian throne, has killed a male relative.[181] Polyneikes, who arrived first in Argos, lay down to rest, but

[180] Nagy 1999:49–58.

[181] Sources are not in agreement here. According to one version, he killed Alkathoos, his father's Oineus brother, according to another version, he killed the sons of Melas, another brother of Oineus, and still another version has it that he killed his own brother, Olenias (Gantz 1993:168).

when Tydeus appears, the two quarrel about a place to sleep. Adrastos is awakened and decides that their argument is the fulfillment of an oracle from Apollo: he should marry his daughters to a boar and a lion. It is unclear how he arrives at the conclusion that this is what these men are, perhaps by observing their behavior or way of fighting, though later sources suggest the men had the appropriate images on their shields or were dressed in the expected pelts.[182] Adrastos fulfills the demands of the oracle and makes them his sons-in-law: Polyneikes marries Argea, while Tydeus marries Deipyle. In Euripides, Adrastos does not understand the oracle properly, which was the reason for the final disaster—the defeat of the expedition against Thebes. It would seem that it is a turn of events typical of tragedy.

Gantz wrongly concludes that later versions of Adrastos's identification of the two heroes according to the oracle are only attempts at correcting the unclear version of Euripides.[183] But I believe it is quite probable that they rely on older epic versions of this story, even if the knowledge about them was taken from secondary sources. The motif of the reconciliation of a lion and a boar in connection with the royal wedding is recurrent in mythology. Pelias, choosing a husband for his youngest daughter, Alkestis, declares that he will give her to the man who will ride a chariot drawn by a lion and a boar. Only Admetos is able to fulfill the condition and he takes Alkestis as his wife.[184] It seems that behind both stories there is a common narrative structure, whose traces are discernible in the Trojan Cycle.

The subject of Demodokos's first song is the quarrel of Achilles and Odysseus (*Odyssey* 8.73–82). Agamemnon is glad to see his leaders at loggerheads, because according to Apollo's oracle it is a sign foreshadowing the success of the expedition. The king's reaction is an important constructive element of the song, but we don't know if Agamemnon was or wasn't deceived in his reading of the oracle. We must remember that the Trojan War really ended successfully and the song of Demodokos, which introduces this theme, concentrates on Odysseus's contribution to the capture of the city.

The myth presented above and connected with the beginning of the expedition against Thebes vividly reminds us of the pattern for constructing Demodokos's song. The central point of the Theban story is Polyneikes' argument with Tydeus. As we have seen, Achilles is frequently a party to a *neikos*

[182] Euripides suggests their fighting. Later sources give two methods of recognizing them: Apollodorus *Library* 3.6.11 and Σ *Phoinissai* 409 claim that on the heroes' shields were painted the likenesses of the heads of a lion (Polyneikes) and a boar (Tydeus), while Σ A *Iliad* 4.376, Statius *Thebaid* 1.390–497, and Hyginus *Fabulae* 69 maintain that they were dressed in the skins of these animals.

[183] Gantz 1993:510.

[184] Apollodorus *Library* 1.9.15, Hyginus *Fabulae* 50, 51; see Gantz 1993:195.

'quarrel' in the Trojan Cycle. A similar trait is suggested by Polyneikes' name: *Poly-neikes*, '[entering] many quarrels'. This man is associated with the quarrels with his father Oedipus, his brother Eteokles, and Tydeus. Nagy regards the rivalry between Achilles and Odysseus as a stock theme of Greek epic tradition.[185] It is not only marked in the *Odyssey*, but in his opinion, it is also discernible in the embassy scene, in which Achilles very forcefully rejects Odysseus's mission, saying that he hates people who think one thing and say another—criticizing Odysseus's real intentions and character (*Iliad* 9.313–314).[186] According to Nagy, in Achilles' famous greeting of the emissaries, when he uses dual verb forms, he excludes Odysseus as a disliked rival.[187] Nagy's interpretation may go too far, but his suggestion that the two heroes' rivalry over their status among the Achaeans reflects their leading roles in the Trojan Cycle, seems legitimate.

In the Theban myth, what is important is the reaction of Adrastos, the leader of the expedition, who in the heroes' dispute sees the fulfillment of a prophecy. Since this is just before the expedition against Thebes, we may understand it as parallel to Agamemnon's behavior and assume that the oracle in each case gave an answer to the question about the success of the expedition. Both events are placed at the beginning of cyclic plots. It could even be assumed that if the dispute depicted by Demodokos is one of possible "beginnings" of the Trojan Cycle, i.e. that it is one of the places where it is possible to insert a new song describing the beginning of the war, then the violent altercation of Polyneikes and Tydeus is a possible "beginning" of the Theban War. The difference between these two instances is that the fulfillment of the prophecy in the Trojan Cycle is favorable, according to Agamemnon's expectations, whereas in the Theban Cycle, it is unfavorable, considering the failure of the expedition.

The similarities in the application of the same pattern in these stories prompt a further question: does the Trojan Cycle use a parallel pattern of the *neikos* between two principal characters, ignoring their identification with the lion and the boar? If we discount fairy-tale creatures, the boar and the lion are typical monsters/animals vanquished by heroes. They are in conflict by nature, which is why their cooperation, an absolutely improbable, and thus a miraculous event, can bring remarkable results. In the *Iliad*, the boar and the lion are brought together in two formulae (5.783, 7.257; 11.293) and two similes (12.42, 17.21).

In the *Iliad*, Achilles is frequently compared to the lion because of his βίη (*biê* 'might') and unrestrained θυμός (*thymos* 'spirit, heart', 24.39–44):

185 Nagy 1999:42–58.

186 This sentence can be also viewed as a criticism of Agamemnon.

187 Nagy 1999:52–53.

ἀλλ' ὀλοῷ Ἀχιλῆϊ θεοὶ βούλεσθ' ἐπαρήγειν,
ᾧ οὔτ' ἂρ φρένες εἰσὶν ἐναίσιμοι οὔτε νόημα
γναμπτὸν ἐνὶ στήθεσσι, λέων δ' ὣς ἄγρια οἶδεν,
ὅς τ' ἐπεὶ ἂρ μεγάλῃ τε βίῃ καὶ ἀγήνορι θυμῷ
εἴξας εἶσ' ἐπὶ μῆλα βροτῶν ἵνα δαῖτα λάβῃσιν·
ὣς Αχιλεὺς ἔλεον μὲν ἀπώλεσεν, οὐδέ οἱ αἰδώς

but you, gods, want to help Achilles, the bringer of destruction,
the one who has neither righteous thoughts, nor mind
which can be bent in his breast, but like a lion he knows only
wildness,
[like the lion] who, yielding to his immense power and proud heart,
attacks flocks of sheep belonging to men, to catch a "feast,"
that's how Achilles has lost his sense of pity and has no respect for
what is decent.

Like Herakles (5.639), Achilles is also called θυμολέων 'the one who has the *thymos* of the lion' (7.228),[188] and Hekabe calls him ὠμηστής 'devourer of raw meat' (24.207). Nagy[189] notes that when Hesiod gives the fight for Oedipus's flock of sheep as a reason for the Theban War, it is related to the principle which is fundamental to epic tradition—the division of meat (here μοῖρα refers to a due share of meat).[190] Sheep belonging to people become a meal for a lion. The character of the lion thus connects the figures of Polyneikes and Achilles even more strongly than Nagy suggests. Lions destroy human property and human wealth, which is synonymous with sheep. Terrifying in their courage and audacity, they are alien to human considerations and do not share their system of values. Before the fight with Hektor, Achilles calls himself a lion, and rejects any pact with the Trojan, saying that "there are no covenants between people and lions" (*Iliad* 22.262). The hero, who becomes a lion, is no longer a man. He personifies the wildness already inaccessible to people. As is expected of him, he plays the role of a heroic warrior, but he is terrifying and criticized in Homer.[191]

188 The juxtaposition of Achilles and Herakles must mean the identification of the former as a hero. The fact that this is a purposeful strategy is evidenced by its analogical use in the *Odyssey*. This epithet, in a conventional formula, is applied to Herakles (11.267), but also to Odysseus by Penelope, in a periphrasis stressing his greatness and fame (4.814). In both poems, only these heroes are referred to in this way.

189 Nagy (1999:135–137) analyzes many passages in the *Iliad* referring to this image (19.303–321, 11.780, 22.346–347, 20.171–174).

190 Nagy 1999:130.

191 The lion metaphor may reflect the dangers of internal strife and bloodshed that a quarrel (*neikos*) brings.

If the Achilles of the *Iliad* can be connected with the lion, then I believe that the Homeric Odysseus can be linked to the boar. In the *Odyssey*, Eurykleia, Odysseus's wet-nurse, recognizes him by a scar on his leg which he got from a boar when he was hunting with Autolykos, his maternal grandfather. Despite the wound, Odysseus killed the boar (19.452–453). As Emmet Robbins notes, it is typical of Greek epic that the maternal grandfather instructs the boy in the ways of hunting, which initiates him into the life of the warrior.[192] Achilles, naturally, cannot be sent to Nereus (Thetis's father, a Titan) in the sea, so he learns to hunt with his grandmother's father, the centaur Cheiron. According to Pindar (*Nemean* 3.43–52), Achilles dragged dying lions and boars to his mentor; this training gave him courage.

The *Iliad* never shows co-operation between Odysseus and Achilles, because it would be at odds with the discreet, but present, rivalry apparent to their audience.[193] Adele Haft notes that after Books 1 and 9, which show Achilles as withdrawing from battle in order to save his undermined τιμή 'prestige', Books 2 and 10 present—both allusively and directly—Odysseus as the one who will be the real captor of Troy, without downgrading the image of Achilles.[194] Books 1 and 9 mark the beginning of the first and second parts of the tripartite oral structure of the *Iliad*. The poet, having presented the theme of Achilles as the most

192 Robbins 1993:11–12. The scholar does not notice, however, that this is a proof of the priority of Cheiron in relation to Phoinix. Among Indo-European peoples there was a widespread custom for boys of noble families to be brought up by another family, most often by the men of their mother's family, in which case the maternal grandfather acted as a foster father (see Benveniste 1973:368–370). Achilles' stay with Cheiron and Odysseus's with Autolykos are remnants of this custom. Perhaps such foster fathers had the prerogative of naming the child—traces of this can be found in the fact that these two heroes were named by, respectively, Cheiron and Autolykos.

193 A number of references in the *Iliad* and the *Odyssey*, as well as in indirect sources of the epic tradition, indicate both cooperation and rivalry between Odysseus and the Aetolian hero Thoas. According to Marx (2003), this fact reflects the existence of conscious referencing in the Homeric poems representing the pan-Hellenic (in Nagy's [1990b:70] terms canonical) tradition to the non-canonical and epichoric tradition, in which the return of Odysseus was without either miraculous elements or an ending providing a final solution based on a divine decree. The *Odyssey*, presenting a picture of antagonistic relationship between Odysseus and Thoas, suggests to primary audiences—who may have been acquainted with this 'Aetolian' tradition—the 'true' version of events, undermining the value and veracity of the 'Aetolian' one (Marks 2003:219–224).

194 Haft (1990:38–39, 51) also believes that the *Doloneia* is an integral part of the *Iliad*. This opinion is shared by Mueller 1984:176. However, I would suggest that we should change our perception of Odysseus as the sole conqueror of Troy and instead see him as a co-conqueror of the city. The *Odyssey* imposes its point of view, in which Odysseus should be considered the true conqueror of Troy, which was not necessarily reflected in tradition (see Ch. 1, p. 134, above). About possible allusions at the close of the *Iliad* to the wooden horse see Franco 2005/2006. Tsagalis (2008) suggests the existence of intertextual links between both Homeric poems. In my opinion, the *Iliad* draws from both versions functioning in tradition: the main roles in the tradition of the Trojan War are played by Achilles and Odysseus, though earlier probably by Philoktetes.

important warrior at Troy, feels obliged to balance it by recounting the feats of another traditional captor of Troy—Odysseus.

The "co-operation" of warriors is a fairly frequent motif in Greek mythology, as can be seen at Troy.[195] Nonetheless, Achilles fights alone, whereas Odysseus in the *Iliad* joins forces with Diomedes. In their concerted action on the battlefield, they are compared to two boars (11.324–326):

> τὼ δ' ἀν' ὅμιλον ἰόντε κυδοίμεον, ὡς ὅτε κάπρω
> ἐν κυσὶ θηρευτῇσι μέγα φρονέοντε πέσητον·
> ὣς ὄλεκον Τρῶας πάλιν ὀρμένω
>
> The two of them ranged, spreading confusion in the crowd, as when two boars
> zealously fall upon hunting hounds,
> even so did they kill retreating Trojans

Several dozen verses later Odysseus is compared again to a boar (11.414). Earlier, Diomedes and his companions are compared to lions or, alternatively, boars (5.782–783): λείουσιν ἐοικότες ὠμοφάγοισιν / ἢ συσὶ κάπροισιν, τῶν τε σθένος οὐκ ἀλαπαδνόν ("like lions devouring raw meat / or wild boars of inexhaustible strength"). The image of the wild boar which arises from these comparisons is that of an animal capable of attacking its persecutors, very dangerous and extremely resilient in fighting.

In the *Doloneia,* Diomedes, going on a night raid, wears a lion skin (*Iliad* 10.177). His companion in this mission is Odysseus, who puts on a leather skullcap with a row of boar tusks (10.261–265):

> ...ἀμφὶ δέ οἱ κυνέην κεφαλῆφιν ἔθηκε
> ῥινοῦ ποιητήν· πολέσιν δ' ἔντοσθεν ἱμᾶσιν
> ἐντέτατο στερεῶς· ἔκτοσθε δὲ λευκοὶ ὀδόντες
> ἀγριόδοντος ὑός θαμέες ἔχον ἔνθα καὶ ἔνθα
> εὖ καὶ ἐπισταμένως· μέσσῃ δ' ἐνὶ πῖλος ἀρήρει.
>
> He [Meriones] put on his [Odysseus's] head a helmet
> made of bull's hide; inside there were many straps
> tightly stretched, and on the outside white teeth
> of the boar of glossy tusks were stuck in rows, thickly,
> firmly and with skill; inside it was lined with felt.

195 Merkelbach 1960. See, for example, the dual form Αἴαντε 'the two Aiases'—according to Jakob Wackernagel (1969:538–546) and Denys Page (1959:235–238, 272–273) it does not refer to two people of that name in the *Iliad,* but to Aias and Teukros, sons of Telamon, who co-operate with each other.

Bryan Hainsworth notes that since Diomedes wears the lion skin and Dolon, the Trojan spy who is coming towards the Greek camp, wears the wolf skin (10.334–335), then the helmet with boar tusks must also symbolize the spirit of this animal.[196] The story of the helmet, as given by Homer, is really intriguing (10.266–271):

> τὴν ῥά ποτ' ἐξ Ἐλεῶνος Ἀμύντορος Ὀρμενίδαο
> ἐξέλετ' Αὐτόλυκος πυκινὸν δόμον ἀντιτορήσας,
> Σκάνδειαν δ' ἄρα δῶκε Κυθηρίῳ Αμφιδάμαντι·
> Ἀμφιδάμας δὲ Μόλῳ δῶκε ξεινήϊον εἶναι,
> αὐτὰρ ὃ Μηριόνῃ δῶκεν ᾧ παιδὶ φορῆναι
> δὴ τότ' Ὀδυσσῆος πύκασεν κάρη ἀμφιτεθεῖσα.
>
> this [helmet] Autolykos stole[197] from Eleon
> when he plundered the rich house of Amyntor, son of Ormenos,
> and then gave it to Amphidamas of Kythera in Scandea,
> and Amphidamas gave it as a guest-gift to Molos,
> and he finally gave it to his son Meriones to wear.
> Now the tightly covered helmet sat on Odysseus's head.

Amyntor was the father of Phoinix, Achilles' teacher according to the *Iliad*, so he really could be a contemporary of Autolykos.[198] Autolykos's theft of the helmet is not astonishing, but quite in line with his character, as presented in the *Odyssey* (19.395–397):

> μητρὸς ἑῆς πατέρ' ἐσθλόν, ὃς ἀνθρώπους ἐκέκαστο
> κλεπτοσύνῃ θ' ὅρκῳ τε· θεὸς οἱ αὐτὸς ἔδωκεν
> Ἑρμείας.
>
> his mother's noble father [Autolykos], who excelled all people
> in the thievish craft [knavery?] and in [breaking] oaths: the god
> Hermes himself
> gave him [this skill].

Hainsworth notes that this information does not fit well here,[199] but to me, the story itself is much more astonishing. Why didn't Odysseus simply get the

196 Hainsworth 1993:180.

197 Another possible reading of the text is that Autolykos "selected [this helmet] from the spoils."

198 Such helmets were worn in the fifteenth and fourteenth centuries BCE, therefore the mythical dating of its origin two generations back fits surprisingly well here.

199 Hainsworth 1993:181.

helmet from his grandfather? It would very nicely link the boar helmet with the story of the boar hunt related in the *Odyssey*. The arming of the hero takes place at a gathering of the sentinels, in exceptional circumstances, but the question is, why mention his grandfather at all?

The first hint is, I believe, the wordplay on the adjective πυκινός 'thick' and a related verb πυκάζω 'cover thickly, screen', which is used at the junction of colons in two key verses: Αὐτόλυκος | πυκινὸν δόμον ἀντιτορήσας "when Autolykos broke into the house where there were many objects" (*Iliad* 10.267) and Ὀδυσσῆος | πύκασεν "tightly covered Odysseus" (*Iliad* 10.271). In the *Odyssey* (11.525) and *Iliad* (24.779), the Trojan horse, the subterfuge linked with Odysseus, which brought about the fall of Troy, is called πυκινὸν λόχον 'a tricky trap'.[200] In this way, the singer can perhaps convey to his audience the similarity of characters of the grandfather and the grandson, both of whom use deceit and are not averse to theft. After all, Odysseus steals Rhesos's horses during the night raid.

In the tradition of the cycle, Odysseus joins with Diomedes to undertake three enterprises, which, according to various sources, show Odysseus in a rather unheroic light: the two men kill Palamedes, against whom Odysseus vowed revenge for forcing him to take part in the expedition; they bring Philoktetes to Troy, and Odysseus undertakes to shamefully steal his bow;[201] they steal the Palladion from Ilion. In some versions, on the way back to the camp Odysseus even tries to kill Diomedes secretly to be able to take all the credit for himself.[202]

The juxtaposition of these stories illustrates how collaboration can turn into conflict. The collaborations of the two heroes are very difficult; they are like a lion and a boar, dangerous and easily roused to mutual aggression. The boar helmet is the only thing Odysseus uses which has its own history[203] and which connects him to one of his ancestors. Achilles is similar: his armor and spear have their own tradition within his family.[204] The magical function of these objects is passed on by the right of inheritance. The theft of the helmet from Achilles' teacher by Odysseus's teacher highlights the conflict between the two heroes and anticipates the outcome of the war: Achilles will pay the highest price, that of his life, performing deeds necessary for the defeat of the Trojans and their allies, while Odysseus will steal from him the honor of capturing the city.

200 Haft 1990:55. When applied to the noun φρένες (*phrenes*), πυκινός refers to a man's intellectual powers, tantamount to cunning and shrewdness.

201 Apollodorus *Epitome* 5.8, Euripides *Philoktetes*, Quintus Smyrnaeus *Posthomerica* 9.325–479, Hyginus *Fabulae* 103.

202 Conon, *Narrations* 34.

203 The story of Odysseus's bow is related in the *Odyssey* 21.13–41.

204 See Ch. 3, p. 283–291, below.

The identification of Odysseus with the wild boar is, perhaps, carried out against his character, which would be more aptly likened to another animal, a fox or perhaps a wolf—as the name of his maternal grandfather Autolykos seems to indicate;[205] moreover it is Autolykos who gives Odysseus his name in the *Odyssey*, in this way making him similar to himself, or imposing his own fate upon the boy (19.407–409).[206] However, in the mythical code of epic, only the boar can be the rival and partner of the lion.

A considerable modification of the original pattern can only be evidence of its very early introduction into the Trojan Cycle. Odysseus, just like Tydeus, is Athena's favorite, and even closer to her in character, which may indicate that the pattern was already worked out. Another of her favorites is Diomedes, Tydeus's son, but in the new pattern he does not play the role of the boar, like his father, but that of the lion, and so he cooperates with the boar, i.e. Odysseus. Diomedes is a lion because in this cycle, the lion—Achilles—quarrels with Odysseus and cannot cooperate with him on the battlefield. Nonetheless, apparently there is a need for a joint action of warriors perceived as a lion and a boar. In the *Iliad*, Diomedes undertakes this collaboration, playing the role of Achilles' substitute. The *Odyssey*, referring to the picture of Odysseus-Boar, does not really draw from the *Iliad*; it takes a theme known from tradition. When both heroes appear in the song of Demodokos (*Odyssey* 8.75–77), Homer does not change the pattern of action to enable their collaboration, but introduces the motif of a quarrel, which reveals the heroes' characters, though he passes over the animal symbolism in silence.

The linking of an epic hero with the animal whose skin he wears, is most likely a very old poetic device.[207] Paris, appearing on the battlefield in *Iliad* 3.16

205 Αὐτόλυκος Auto-lykos: the second member of the word is λύκος 'wolf', hence, the name may mean 'wolf himself'.

206 This derivation of Odysseus's name from *lykos* 'wolf' was proposed by Bolling 1906:65–68; it is corroborated by the fact that the form with δ is found only in epic and other literary genres. In inscriptions, there are forms with λ: Ὀλυσ(σ)εύς, Ὀλυτ(τ)εύς, Ὀλισεύς, Οὐλιξεύς, from which Latin Ulixes. Bolling's etymology is, however, perceived as very doubtful (see Frisk 1960–1970, s.v.).

207 Goody (2010:84–94) notes that in the stories of African societies, the characters LoDagaa and Gonja fall into three categories: gods, animals, and humans (like in Aesop's fables). Sometimes they undergo transformations and change roles. Homeric epic excludes animals from the narrative—they cease to play the role of agents. The ability to change one's nature is reserved exclusively for gods, who can transform themselves into animals or humans (on the ritual-mythic transformation of a human being into an animal, the traces of which are visible in the custom of wearing animal skins by warriors, see Bierl 2012:151–155). While in the *Odyssey*, there are still transformations of a deity into an animal, in the *Iliad* gods change nearly exclusively into humans. Kirk (1990:239–241) enumerates all instances of the metamorphoses of gods and goddesses into birds in Homer and concludes that although in some cases we are dealing only with similes (*Odyssey* 1.320; 5.337; *Iliad* 15.237), in others, there are depictions of a real change

wears a leopard skin (παρδαλέην). Both ancient and modern scholars agree that he is bizarrely dressed and strangely armed, with a bow and two spears.[208] Instead of athetizing verses, we had better recognize that the representation of Paris in the leopard skin is traditional. It is true that such an anachronistic outfit is not very suitable for a duel with Menelaos. However, cutting verses is not a way out, because either we would cut out of Homer what is truly Homeric, or else we would reject the traditional epic image of Paris, inherited by the author of the *Iliad*.

Finkelberg notes that in the *Kypria*, Odysseus's role is limited to pretending madness and murdering Palamedes.[209] Let us not, however, confuse Proclus's summary with the contents of the *Kypria* or, generally, epic depicting the beginning of the Trojan War. Already significant is Odysseus's participation in the competition for Helen's hand, then his later role in bringing Iphigenia as a supposed fiancée to Achilles.[210] I think we should not take lightly the version that Odysseus brought Achilles to Troy from Skyros, where he had been concealed. Later their lives are also often linked, either directly, or indirectly. Like Achilles, Odysseus meets Helen secretly—both men do it in a way characteristic of them. On Lesbos, Odysseus purifies Achilles of the killing of Thersites. He gets Achilles' armor, which he later hands over to Achilles' son Neoptolemos, whom he brings to Troy. The connection between the heroes is even revealed in surprising details, such as the statement in the *Iliad* that Thersites hated both Odysseus and Achilles (*Iliad* 3.220–221).

Two of these stories merit close examination. There is a parallel between Achilles and Odysseus in the Trojan Cycle, though not much stressed by scholars: Odysseus's spying mission to Troy and his meeting with Helen, attested in Proclus's summary of the *Little Iliad* and in Helen's story in *Odyssey* Book 4, corresponds to Achilles' secret meeting with Helen, in Proclus's summary of the *Kypria*. Because of the popularity of the *Odyssey*, the story of Odysseus is more familiar. Odysseus sneaks into a palace disguised as a beggar, is recognized when he is being washed by a woman (in Troy by Helen, on Ithaca by Eurykleia); he reveals his plan (in the first case to Helen, in the second to Telemachos

into a bird (*Odyssey* 3.372; 22.240; *Iliad* 14.286–291). However, in the *Iliad*, there are also other passages which originally might have included the transformation of a deity into an animal, e.g. in the case of Athena's conversation with Apollo under an oak tree (7.17–53) overheard by Helenos, who is sometimes described as a bird diviner, which might indicate the ability to understand the speech of birds.

208 But compare Nickel (1997:Ch. 3) who argues that the arming scene always serves to glorify the hero who is its subject, so the Paris/Alexander arming scene in the *Iliad* confirms Paris's heroic role in epic tradition.

209 Finkelberg 1987:130.

210 Courtship of Helen: Kullmann 1960:147 n2, 154–155; the bringing of Iphigenia is less certain but see Nelson 2022:66–68.

and Eumaios, but also, in part, to Eurykleia). Then he slips away, killing many Trojans in their city and, on Ithaca, a large number of suitors. Øivind Andersen shows in detail how these and other elements of Odysseus's undercover trip to Troy foreshadow events that will take place in Ithaca.[211] According to Andersen, the same function is fulfilled by Menelaos's story about how Helen came up to the wooden horse and called the heroes hidden inside, imitating their wives' voices.[212] Menelaos's story puts Helen in a bad light, because she tries to subvert the Achaean plans. According to Kakridis, the contradiction between Helen's actions and what she says about herself occurs because these two stories come from two traditions and are artificially linked by the author of the *Odyssey*.[213] Andersen argues that both stories are Homer's innovation inserted for the sake of announcing details of later events.[214]

In an oral culture, two different versions do not indicate two traditions, and their coexistence within one work does not mean contamination, but the poet uses different variants because in his eyes all stories are rightfully part of the tradition. This happens even if he emphasizes only one of the variants. In this context, we also should not think about innovations but about using the existing

211 Andersen 1977:8–9. Helen reveals Odysseus's name after the Trojans have discovered the corpses; his self-revelation in the *Odyssey* follows the same pattern. Odysseus is the type of the hero who comes out of hiding—he first acts in disguise and only then reveals his name, as with Polyphemos or the suitors.

212 Andersen 1977:10–11. Kakridis (1971:47) assumes that Helen speaks in various Greek dialects. This rational explanation is approved by Tsagalis 2008:129. Interpretations of this kind only reveal the fact that scholars instinctively seek to rationalize Homeric epic. Helen's mimetic abilities are sanctioned by the magical and miraculous that underlie epic stories (more about it in the next chapter). The audience listening to the performance of the epic would not have asked themselves how it was possible for Helen to know the voices of the Achaean warriors' wives. The function of Helen's imitation of voices is only to emphasize the difficulty of the test to which the heroes are exposed at this critical moment. This event is related by Menelaos, whose wife Helen does not have to imitate. Menelaos does not mention whether his wife called to him or what he felt hearing her voice. The reliance on the miraculous goes hand in hand with the reliance on a pattern in presenting the story. From each story, the singer chooses the elements which he finds important and useful.

213 Kakridis 1971:40–43.

214 Andersen 1977:12–13. Olson (1989) highlights the differences between the image of Odysseus in the stories of Helen and Menelaos and later events on Ithaca, which correspond, in his opinion, to the ideological intent of the *Odyssey* to show the difference in marital relations (faithful/unfaithful wife, naive/not naive husband); see Alden 2000:5–6. We can note, however, that certain peculiarities in Helen's story, such as the Queen's questioning of the recognized beggar-Odysseus, closely refer to what will happen later in Ithaca, when Penelope questions the (nevertheless) unrecognized beggar-Odysseus. This is an example of adapting traditional tales to the needs of the narrative, analogous to how the story of Meleagros is made similar to the situation of Achilles in Phoinix's story (*Iliad* 9.524–599, see Ch. 4, pp. 409-412, below). The discrepancy between Helen's and Menelaos's stories has been widely commented on (Reece 1993:85 has bibliography). In Reece's opinion, Helen notices the failure of her trick because Odysseus has outwitted her.

tradition, according to contextual needs. Such an adjustment to context can significantly modify a story, at least according to our understanding, but it does not change its basic structure.

The notion that Homer intends to suggest Helen's duplicity does not seem right. The ambiguity concerning her behavior stems only from Menelaos's introductory remark about Helen (*Odyssey* 4.274–275): "Some δαίμων must have taken you there." However, it only points to the fact that Menelaos does not know the reason for Helen's conduct. After all, if Helen had wanted to betray the Achaeans, she could have chosen a much simpler way. As it is, she puts the Achaeans to the test. She comes to the wooden horse most probably at the crucial moment, when the Trojans are trying to decide whether to destroy it or bring it to the city, and it is probably Helen's test that determines the issue and the horse is taken into the fortress. This situation can relate to various types of tests which heroes must undergo before they perform heroic deeds. Not infrequently, it is a woman who stands in the path of the hero doing a mighty deed (in the *Odyssey*, Kirke, Kalypso, and Nausikaa appear in this role, and so does the Lady of the castle in *Sir Gawain and the Green Knight*).

Both our sources, the summary of the *Little Iliad* and Helen's words in the *Odyssey*, state that Helen was privy to Odysseus's plan for the capture of Troy. Calling the names of heroes is not inconsistent with this information (it does not necessarily imply the feminine flightiness of Helen, who a bit earlier declared her desire to go back home); conversely, it might be part of the plan. For the plan to succeed, it was absolutely necessary to convince the Trojans to bring the horse into the city, and Helen was the only one who could do it and help the Achaeans. Helen's performance convinced Deiphobos, the leader of the Trojans and her husband after the death of Paris. The elaborate plan devised by Odysseus would have been ruined if Antiklos, carried away by emotion, had responded to Helen's calls. Menelaos clearly remarks that Helen's behavior had impressed neither himself, nor Diomedes. It is quite probable that here we deal with a reverse motif of testing the hero: the test is fake, though presented as real. Odysseus also withstands this test, which takes the form of erotic temptation.

There remains the question why Menelaos was not informed about the role of Helen in Odysseus's plan.[215] It is guesswork, but I will risk a hypothesis. The account of events given to Telemachos by the king of Sparta indicates the ruler's

[215] Tsagalis (2008:122–124) sees the connection between Helen and Achilles in the *Iliad*. Both are exiles—μετανάσται—from their homeland. In the case of Helen's relationship with Odysseus, it is supposed to involve a kind of rivalry (Tsagalis 2008:128–134). Tsagalis characterizes both as worthy enemies, wise and eloquent. The laconic description of Odysseus (*Iliad* 3.200–202), confined to conventional formulae, made by Helen in the *teichoscopia* is interpreted by Tsagalis as an expression of her conviction that she cannot match Odysseus's eloquence.

ignorance in this matter. It is confirmed by the story of his attempt to kill his wife during the fall of the city, when Helen saves herself by resorting again to a trick and revealing her beautiful breasts. Why, then, does Odysseus not share the details of his plan with his companions? It seems that the reason can be inferred from the parallel situation, Achilles' meeting with Helen, which was organized by Thetis and Aphrodite. Simply, it could be a love tryst. If the author of the *Odyssey* knew a version of the story in which the meeting of Odysseus and Helen had a similar character, then her husband's ignorance as to her role in Odysseus's subterfuge becomes understandable. It is not by accident that in the third song of Demodokos (*Odyssey* 8.517–520), Odysseus stays at Menelaos's side during the slaughter of the Trojans.[216]

The guarantee of glory

In the cycle, only Achilles and Odysseus refrain from participating in the expedition. Their reluctance is connected with the remarkable role which they will play in the war: Achilles as the best warrior, and Odysseus as the captor of the city. For both Odysseus and Achilles, the restraining factor is their knowledge—fundamental for the pattern of the epic cycle[217]—that glory in war is inseparable from suffering, and, for Achilles, also death. Various ways in which they realize this fact result from the difference in their age and character. In the cycle, Achilles must choose the path of his life before each important fight. He chooses glory, for which he pays with his life—the *Iliad* is, therefore, a poem about Achilles' maturation. The same problem of staying at home and living peacefully, but without glory until old age, or going to Troy, capturing the city and suffering, but gaining glory—was faced by Odysseus. Both heroes have a choice between inactivity, associated with a peaceful and pleasurable life at home, and performing deeds which can give them fame. They basically choose between glory and oblivion.

For the first time in their heroic biography, they face the choice at the moment when they are setting out on the expedition. Achilles immediately chooses glory and does not want to stay home. Odysseus, conversely, prefers to stay home, but his decision is overridden, and he is made to travel the path

216 Demodokos intends to praise the role of Odysseus in the most important encounter leading to the defeat of the Trojan chief commander (*Odyssey* 8.517–520). However, the author of the *Odyssey* might have intended to suggest that Odysseus not only helps in the defeat of Deiphobos but also tries to shield Helen from her husband's revenge. The fight between two husbands for Helen is certainly a traditional motif, as shown by Menelaos's duel with Paris in the *Iliad*.

217 There is an analogy to Amphiaraos's reluctance to take part in the venture against Thebes, which is broken by Polyneikes' bribe. This deed leads to the Theban War and a whole series of misfortunes resulting from revenge for the death of Amphiaraos.

of glory. In the *Odyssey*, the problem is that the hero did not die at Troy. Death there would have given him immortal fame, of which the funeral is an inseparable element, perhaps because it is always accompanied by a song about the dead hero. Considering the absence of information about Odysseus, his previous achievements seem to be irrelevant. What is important to the strategy of the story is that Odysseus's role in the capture of Troy is discovered far from the human world—in the land of the Phaeacians. Telemachos gets only hints about his cunningness, but nobody unfolds before him the fullness of his father's fame, the glory of the captor of Troy. Very symptomatic is the fact that Telemachos stops the tale about his father, told by Menelaos and Helen, because he wants to go to sleep (4.294–295). Only in the killing of the suitors, in which Telemachos will play his own part, will the son see the full heroism of his father Odysseus.

William B. Stanford in his book on ambiguities in Greek literature notes Homer's comprehensive use of significant names or names which somehow relate to the semantic environment in which they were used.[218] Endowing characters with significant names is connected with the custom of giving the child a name reflecting the status of a given person or else his/her relatives (e.g. Telemachos, Megapenthes, and Eurysakes). Many signifying names were inherited from epic tradition, where they often refer to valor in battle (like Alexander, Menelaos, Sthenelos) or to the hero's function (Agamemnon, Thersites). According to Stanford, "In the *Odyssey* the use of the ambiguity of significant names is noticeably subtler and more highly stylized."[219] Nonetheless, such frequent and varied use of the meaning of proper names to demonstrate the contextual function of characters is obviously the poet's individual contribution, which is both enabled and sanctioned by epic tradition. The juxtaposition of the names of certain characters allows the listeners to assess their role in the narrative strategy of the return of Odysseus. The very name of Odysseus is provided in the poem with an etymology indicating the dual nature of the hero, who both sows hatred and reaps its effects.[220]

G. E. Dimock Jr. proposes the translation of the hero's name as "Trouble," because he brings troubles to others, and himself runs into them. Dimock demonstrates that whenever Odysseus refrains from acting, he brings upon

218 Stanford 1939:97–114.

219 Stanford 1939:101.

220 Homeric etymologizing, typical of Greek epic and generally of oral tradition, in this case is obviously wrong. The name "Odysseus" is certainly non-Greek. Attempts to identify its roots are too diverse to be reliable; most frequently the Aegean or Anatolian substrate is indicated: Frisk (1960–1970: s.v.) enumerates various hypotheses. Initially, scholars preferred the active meaning of the word *ody(ss)omai*, identifying Odysseus as the one who spreads hatred, bringing revenge on the suitors. Stanford (1952:211–213) demonstrates that the passive meaning is equally justified: "the man doomed to odium." For other etymological observations, see Austin 1972:2–3.

himself suffering and a threat of oblivion, while when he decides to act, he brings pain to others, but secures immortal fame for himself.[221] A clear example of this is the name of the king of the Laestrygonians, who murder Odysseus's comrades, whom the hero does not try to save: he is Antiphates, 'Against-fame', while the Kyklops defeated by Odysseus is Polyphemos, 'Much-fame'. Similarly, after the dissolution of the assembly on Ithaca, Antinoos, 'Against-wits', stops Telemachos, grasping his hand and insincerely proposing peace (2.301–321); his name gains the right overtone[222] by contrasting him with a man named Noemon, son of Phronios, 'Reason, son of Mind', who supplies Odysseus's son with a ship (2.386). The listener is prepared for the significance of these names by Athena's twice referring to Telemachos as οὐδ' ἀνοήμων, 'not witless' (2.270, 278), and the suitors as οὔ τι νοήμονες 'witless' (2.282).[223]

Certainly meaningful is the name of Odysseus's mother Ἀντίκλεια, literally 'Against-fame' (Anti-kleia). Dimock notes that it is contrasted with the name of his nurse, Eurykleia, 'Far-fame' (Eury-kleia), as the one who can properly recognize the hero.[224] Dimock's very incisive observation has not been properly elaborated. The figure of Odysseus's mother, in fact, combines two functions. His mother stops the hero from acting, wishing to keep him alive,[225] but, in songs of return, the mother always plays the most important function of recognizing the hero. I believe that this is why the mother figure here is split into two persons. It could be argued that, like in the case of Achilles, staying with the mother would mean the rejection of immortal fame (*kleos*). The mother, then, is someone who supports the young hero, but she is also an obstacle to his desire of achieving glory. Eurykleia is necessary for the recognition scene, which opens the way for performing the heroic deed and thus ensures his fame. In the *Odyssey*, many characters are duplicated: Melanthios and Melantho, Mentes and Mentor, Demodokos and Phemios, Kirke and

221 Dimock 1956:64. Austin (1972) develops this idea, indicating that not only Odysseus, but also his relatives recognize the duality of his nature; first and foremost, Penelope, Telemachos, and Eumaios, who avoid using the name of Odysseus during his absence, because its very sound could have sinister effects, even for the hero himself.

222 The name Anti-noos would mean "preventing against reason." but according to Frame (2009), who connects the noun *nóos* with the root *nes- meaning "return" (with the reservation that *nóos* does not mean "return," pp. 54–55), it would mean "the one who prevents the need of his [Telemachos's] father's return."

223 Austin 1972:1.

224 This is an adaptation of the pattern of Achilles. Dimock 1956:67–68: "Antikleia ('Opposed-to-fame'), in her recognition of her son in the underworld, did not seem to understand the scar's full meaning, but it is easy for Eurykleia ('Far-fame') to accept it."

225 Thetis tries to keep her son alive, concealing him on Skyros—but this is only one of many versions of the relationships between the mother and son. In the *Iliad,* she does not even try to stop Achilles from fighting, and he no longer takes heed of her predictions. A mother's lament over her living son can be seen as the beginning of spreading his posthumous glory.

Kalypso, Eumaeos and Philoitios, Amphinomos and Leodes, Antinoos and Eurymachos, Kyklopes and the Laestrygonians. Eurykleia and Eurynome are another pair performing the same function,[226] but the first one appears in a double role, since she also acts as Odysseus's mother. This situation is analogical to that in the *Iliad*, where Diomedes and Patroklos appear as doublets of two other heroes, Antilochos and Achilles.

A similar function to Antikleia is fulfilled by Antiklos (*Odyssey* 4.286), who almost reveals the trick of the Trojan horse. Ἄντικλος is a male equivalent of Odysseus's mother's name.[227] Odysseus grabs the throat of the warrior, when he wants to respond to Helen's imitation of his wife's voice. The capture of Troy by means of the wooden horse is the source of Odysseus's *kleos*. Antiklos's answer would endanger the life of the best Achaean warriors hidden in the trap and condemn the whole enterprise—both the subterfuge and the expedition itself—to failure,[228] but in the epic code it would mean robbing Odysseus of his *kleos*. The hero takes measures against depriving him of his fame as "the one who took Troy by artifice." Hence, then, the epithet ὁ πτολίπορθος is emphatically stressed by the proclitic pronoun—"this capturer of the city."[229]

The use of the same epithet for Achilles is not caused—as it is generally believed—only by the fact of his conquering many cities in the Troad and on the islands. Although Achilles is not the proper conqueror of Troy, he is the one without whom the victory would be impossible. He and Odysseus are the two principal heroes; others only provide the background. Agamemnon and Menelaos cannot achieve the aim of the expedition by themselves. Achilles *is* also a conqueror of Troy, because his sacrifice is necessary in order to take the city.[230] Probably it could be captured only as a consequence of the rivalry

226 Fenik 1974:174–180.

227 This character appears only in the *Odyssey* and is not attested anywhere else. The name of Odysseus's mother is also known only from the *Odyssey* (11.85), but here we may be dealing with a situation parallel to that when Phoinix in the *Iliad* uses a different name for Meleagros's wife: Kleopatra instead of Alkyone (9.556–558). This name, parallel to the name "Patroklos," fulfills a special function in the epic code. Kleopatra induces Meleagros to join the combat, just as Patroklos through his death induces Achilles to do the same, which results in the latter's gaining ἄφθιτον κλέος, that is joining glory of the ancestors, which was subject of earlier epic songs (Kleo-patra/Patro-klos); see Ch. 4, p. 410, below.

228 *Odyssey* 4.288: σάωσε δὲ πάντας Ἀχαίους "saved all the Achaeans"—this is how Menelaos described Odysseus's action, and this is how he perceived it. Saving a community is a deed reserved for the hero and defines him as one.

229 See Haft (1990:45–50), for whom the use of ὁ notes the particularization of the meaning of the epithet, indicating that Odysseus is the conqueror of only one city—Troy.

230 Compare Horn (2021:20) who believes that "by killing Hektor Achilles symbolically becomes the conqueror of Troy," and since the killing of Hektor is equivalent to Achilles' suicide (21): "Achilles' victory over Hektor is both tantamount to the sack of Troy and to his own death, even though he remains undefeated at the end of the *Iliad*."

between Achilles and Odysseus. It seems that the poet uses the original epic-mythical pattern, which allows Agamemnon to get Troy provided he has in his army a lion and a boar, who are in dispute. With the development of the cycle, the clarity of this pattern had been heavily blurred, but neither the author of the *Iliad* nor of the *Odyssey* could completely disregard it.

The Use of Patterns in the Trojan Cycle

The conservative character of oral composition lets us reach deeply into the darkness of the mythical and poetic imagination of Greek peoples. We can descend further and further into the depth devoid of any historical perspective. It seems to me that this kind of study, which focuses on the discovery of old narrative strata underneath the plot, is undertaken too rarely. Such attempts as are undertaken, are usually restricted to tracing a possible folk-tale background of the stories presented in the *Odyssey*.[231]

Uvo Hölscher sought to demonstrate how the requirements of epic style entailed changes in a simple folk tale.[232] Rhys Carpenter tried to find common points between the *Odyssey* and the master pattern devised by Friedrich Panzer on the basis of numerous Eurasian versions of the widespread folk tale called *The Bearson*.[233] This comparison is especially fruitful for Odysseus's adventures during his return journey to Ithaca. But the attempt to prove that the whole story of Odysseus's recapture of the throne in Ithaca is based on this tale seems far-fetched. Carpenter does not seem to be acquainted with the pattern of the oral Song of Return. I admit that the *odyssey* itself, the long journey back home, may have its roots there—some motifs appear to be quite close to the vicissitudes of life experienced by the Bearson.[234] I have already mentioned Gerald

231 The recognition of the tale of the Swan Maiden as the foundation of the myth of Achilles is presented in Ch. 6. Grintzer (1974:280–296), for example, uses Propp's model to explore the roots of Sanskrit poems (type nos. 400, 425, 301, 313, 500, 511 in Aarne and Thompson 1961). I choose not to discuss here the attempts to reconstruct Indo-European patterns of mythic and epic stories based on Dumézil's tripartite model (see Scott 1970; Baldick 1994), because the subject deserves a broader discussion. Similarly, analysis of the traces of the Indo-European black and white myth has to be postponed for another occasion.

232 Hölscher 1978. I have already mentioned how this scholar reconstructed the original form of this folk tale. From among his other findings worth mentioning here is his analysis of the scene of Telemachos's sending away of Penelope and excluding her from witnessing the contest for her hand. Penelope goes up to her room and sleeps while all that happens downstairs. When she wakes up, she sees her husband, who has returned and already dealt with the wicked suitors. This rather astonishing interruption of the action is, in Hölscher's opinion, a result of its adaptation to the ethos of epic narration (pp. 64–67).

233 Carpenter 1974:112–156.

234 Carpenter's book was first published in 1946. Undoubtedly, this issue needs to be brought up to date by including findings of more recent studies.

Gresseth's search for the common roots of the *Odyssey* and the *Nalopākhyāna* episode of the *Mahābhārata*.[235] The only fault I find with these studies is that their authors draw a very clear division between epic and folk tales. In oral culture, such boundaries are blurred and unrecognized. It is only the expansion of writing that pushes oral tradition into the niche of folk tradition.

Finding the common construction patterns of the Trojan Cycle may make it possible to understand how the cycle itself and the monumental epic song were created. That we can observe various manifestations of the same pattern proves that it was widely used to multiply songs. The only changes, and slight at that, are limited to the modification of its elements. The multiplication of the pattern is not astonishing in oral poetics, since repetition constitutes the very basis of its existence. The repetitiveness of the pattern enables the singer to learn and to re-create a song which he has heard for the first time. It also allows him to create a new song by pouring new content into traditional patterns.

This repetitiveness is related to the potentiality for creating new songs within the cycle—potentiality which has nothing in common with creative liberty. The *Iliad* mentions the wrath of Trojan heroes, Paris and Aeneas, because of which they refrain from fighting.[236] In both cases, the reasons for their wrath are unexplained. Hektor addresses his brother, who is in his palace, carried there by Aphrodite, after she had saved him from death at Menelaos's hands (*Iliad* 6.325): δαιμόνι' οὐ μὲν καλὰ χόλον τόνδ' ἔνθεο θυμῷ ("Crazy man! It is not good that you nurse this anger in your heart"). Neither the anger, nor its reasons have been mentioned before.[237] Similarly Deiphobos, unable to defeat Idomeneus on his own, goes to fetch Aeneas, standing in the back (13.459–461):

> ...τὸν δ' ὕστατον εὗρεν ὁμίλου
> ἑσταότ'· αἰεὶ γὰρ Πριάμῳ ἐπεμήνιε δίῳ
> οὕνεκ' ἄρ ἐσθλὸν ἐόντα μετ' ἀνδράσιν οὐ τι τίεσκεν.
>
> ...This one he found standing at the rear;
> since he was still angry with godly Priam
> for showing him little honor, though he excelled among the warriors.

What's astonishing is that both heroes immediately answer the call to fight and without much ado go to battle. Not only do they abandon their anger, they also do not try to explain it in any way. Its irrelevance, therefore, becomes

[235] See n6 and n14 above.

[236] The 'wrath' theme as traditional see Lord 1960:186–197; Nagler 1974:131–166; Kelly 2007a:97–98.

[237] Kirk (1990:203) assumes that Paris's wrath could have been his reaction to the inimical attitude of the Trojans after his duel with Menelaos.

even more mysterious. We can infer that the motif of anger resulting in withdrawal from fighting and then a return to it, analogical to the anger of Achilles and Meleagros from Phoinix's story, belongs to topoi.[238] Like Achilles, Aeneas returns to fighting when his φίλος 'comrade' dies.[239] However, nobody has been able to answer the question whether the repetition of this pattern supports the possibility of songs with Paris or Aeneas as their protagonist. Certain evidence in favor of this theory can be drawn from Homer's enigmatic mentions of certain facts, which would indicate that Paris and Aeneas might have been fairly well known from other songs in the cycle. They both return to battle, too eagerly forgetting their anger to leave an impression of its importance on the listeners.

It can be assumed that in other songs of the cyclic plot, their anger could have taken on larger dimensions, similar to that of Achilles or Meleagros, because wrath makes sense only when there is a serious threat to the community. One could find other places in the cycle for the wrath of Paris, which would cause him to refrain from fighting. The most appropriate moment seems to be before he kills Achilles. Paris's wrath in the *Iliad* has much in common with the Homeric story of Meleagros. Hektor, who mentions soldiers dying under the walls of Troy, then appeals to his brother to return to battle, before fire sweeps the city (6.331): μὴ τάχα ἄστυ πυρὸς δηΐοιο θέρηται ("so it won't soon burn in a consuming fire"). Answering him, Paris says that his wife has already tried to persuade him to go back to combat (6.337–338). We deal with a similar sequence of events, when Meleagros is unmoved in his anger, until the Kuretes have scaled the towers and started a fire (9.589): καὶ ἐνέπρηθον μέγα ἄστυ ("and set fire to the great city"). Finally, his wife convinces him to return to battle (9.590–595).

Paris is even closer than Achilles to the paradigm of Meleagros. Phoinix, trying to adapt this story to the situation of his foster son, says (9.550–552):

> ὄφρα μὲν οὖν Μελέαγρος Ἄρηι φίλος πολέμιζε
> τόφρα δὲ Κουρήτεσσι κακῶς ἦν, οὐδὲ δύναντο
> τείχεος ἔκτοσθεν μίμνειν πολέες περ ἐόντες
>
> as long as Meleagros, dear to Ares, fought,
> the Kuretes fared badly and they could not
> stay outside the walls, though they were numerous

[238] It also resurfaces in Poseidon's supposition that the Greeks are reluctant to fight because they are angry with Agamemnon (*Iliad* 13.108): οἳ κείνῳ ἐρίσαντες ἀμυνέμεν οὐκ ἐθέλουσι ("these ones were in conflict with him and did not want to defend [their ships]").

[239] Janko 1992:106.

It turns out that it was the Aetolians who were besieged by the Kuretes, which seems more logical, since the latter were seeking revenge upon Meleagros, who had killed his uncle(s?). Paris, besieged in Troy, could have followed his wife's (i.e. Helen's!) advice, returned to combat, and killed Achilles, who was a threat to all Trojans. Over Paris there may have hovered a specter of death, because he died at the hands of Philoktetes soon after having performed his deed. Another common point with Phoinix's Meleagros is the attitude of the hero's mother, who under the influence of her dream left her newborn baby on Mount Ida.[240] Or Paris may have refrained from fighting because of his mother's curse. Similarly, Aeneas's anger with Priam can be linked with his later making possible the continuation of Troy by saving the regalia and many Trojans.[241] It seems that the combination of the motifs of wrath and withdrawal from battle can also be found in the theme of Philoktetes, who—in Sophocles' and Euripides' tragedies—refrains from fighting and persists in his anger. There is also a motif of an unsuccessful (at least initially) attempt at persuasion by his *philoi*. The result of Philoktetes' return to battle is analogical to the return of Achilles and Meleagros: by killing Paris he removes the main obstacle to the sack of Troy.

This picture of a heroic Paris is at odds with the Homeric picture. In the *Iliad*, he is shown as a man guilty of starting the war, a coward given to a life of pleasure and lechery. His situation resembles the situation of the suitors in the *Odyssey*, because he took "something" that he did not deserve. Menelaos defeats him in a duel. He is reproached by many of those closest to him: by his brother, Hektor, for avoiding combat (*Iliad* 3.38–57; 13.769–773); by his wife, who very nearly curses him for making her life miserable (3.428–436); by Diomedes for fighting like a coward, shooting arrows from a safe place and being afraid of an open spear fight (11.385–395); and finally by his father, who condemns him, together with his other sons, after the death of Hektor (24.239–244). Paris's role in the *Iliad* is not the same as in the tradition of the cycle.[242] There, he is the chief Trojan warrior, and though he brought disaster to his homeland, he also killed Achilles, who was the main threat to the city, and his death deprives Troy of the magical protection of Apollo's bow, which was in his possession. Even in the *Iliad*, one can find traces of his valor: Hektor

[240] Hekabe's dream (when she was pregnant with Paris) that she will give birth to a fiery torch, which will set fire to the city, is mentioned in many sources: Euripides *The Trojan Women* 919–922; Vergil *Aeneid* 7.319–320; Pindar fr. 52 Maehler; Apollodorus *Library* 3.12.5; *Scholia in Homerum Iliad* 3.325; Tzetzes, *Scholia in Lycophronem* 86, 224; Cicero *De Divinatione* 1.21.42; Hyginus *Fabulae* 91; *Scriptores rerum mythicarum Latini* (*Vaticanus Mythographus Secundus* 197).

[241] The *Iliad* mentions that Aeneas's descendants will later rule over the Troad (20.306–308). In the *Aeneid*, the hero gives the crown and scepter of the Trojan rulers to Dido (*Aeneid* 1.653–655).

[242] Nickel 1997:passim.

admits that his brother is not lacking in fighting spirit, that he is ἄλκιμος—'brave, valiant' (6.521–525).

We should ponder the question what dictated this change in the image of Paris in Homer's work. Certainly, the decisive factor was the moral interpretation of the guilt of Paris, who by indulging his desires brought about the war. It is the motivation of "indulging in lust" that seems to be an innovation.

The non-combative character of Paris is indicated by two features given in Hektor's reproach (*Iliad* 3.52–55):

> οὐκ ἂν δὴ μείνειας ἀρηΐφιλον Μενέλαον;
> γνοίης χ' οἵου φωτὸς ἔχεις θαλερὴν παράκοιτιν·
> οὐκ ἄν τοι χραίσμῃ κίθαρις τά τε δῶρ' Ἀφροδίτης
> ἥ τε κόμη τό τε εἶδος ὅτ' ἐν κονίῃσι μιγείης.
>
> Cannot you stand up to Menelaos, dear to Ares?
> Then you would know what kind of man he is whose young wife you have.
> Neither your kithara, nor the gifts of Aphrodite,
> your hair or looks, will help you when they welter in dust.

Playing the kithara and having the gifts of Aphrodite, i.e. beauty, are implicitly contrasted with Menelaos's strength and valor. This contrast also ironically anticipates the death of Paris.[243] The image of the dead warrior, whose head and body lie in dust, when he falls dead on the battlefield, is typical. Hektor, however, uses an equivocal word: μιγείης, 'mix up', which is also used in reference to sexual intercourse. Hektor's diction of blame is akin to That of Archilochus: the qualities ridiculed are beauty, as unnecessary for fighting (Archilochus fr. 114 W), and excessive sexuality (Archilochus frr. 35, 41, or 196a W).

A less conventional charge is the ironic reference to playing the kithara. Aristarchus even claims that the word κίθαρις should be replaced with κίδαρις "kind of a hat," because Paris is nowhere shown as playing the lyre. The alteration is not justified. In Homer's moral criticism, this charge seems akin to Priam's calling his sons ὀρχησταί τε χοροιτυπίῃσιν ἄριστοι "most skilled dancers in dancing choirs" (*Iliad* 24.261). Putting Homer's moral interpretation aside, the fact of playing an instrument doesn't carry pejorative

243 Calling Paris's good looks a gift of Aphrodite is not necessarily a metaphor. In the cycle, it may have been said that it was a real gift of the goddess in return for Paris granting her victory. Beauty made him madly attractive even to the most beautiful woman in the world, who leaves everything for him—this version is given by Sappho, fr. 16 L-P.

connotations. Achilles himself plays the phorminx (*Iliad* 9.185–190), sitting in his tent and singing (ἄειδε) an epic song (κλέα ἀνδρῶν). Patroklos waits listening and continues from the place where Achilles stops (δέγμενος... ὅποτε λήξειεν).[244] This is the moment when the embassy sent by Agamemnon arrives. Achilles, not being able to join the combat, sings the exploits of warriors of old. There is nothing exceptional in this. He indulges in the pleasures which are typical of warriors who do not participate in fighting. For him, it was as if the war had ended.

Gilbert Murray suggested that warriors had been forbidden some forms of behavior, e.g. sleeping with women, under a common oath, which Achilles now breaks, though Troy has not been taken yet.[245] This opinion may go too far, but perhaps really the image of Achilles' pleasures presents some elements of the life of the warrior who is not engaged in combat, especially the warrior who has withdrawn from battle. Achilles does the things that are typical of peacetime—the Phaeacians listen to songs of war together with Odysseus, who also tells his own story. Sex with women may be another element contrasted with the engagement in fighting. When Aphrodite carries Paris away from battle, she leaves him in his bedroom, where he proceeds to make love to his wife, Helen (3.380–447). Meleagros, after he withdraws from fighting, also sleeps in his bedroom with his wife (9.556). Achilles, sending back the embassy emptyhanded, goes to bed with Diomede, abducted from Lesbos, and Patroklos with Iphis, a captive woman from Skyros (9.663–668). Meanwhile, other βασιλεῖς cannot give in to pleasures: they do not sleep and Achilles' rival, Odysseus, on the very same night makes a spying trip (10.138–580). Paris's lack of combativeness may, then, result from the traditional image of a hero who has withdrawn from combat and is indulging in pleasures unavailable to others—the pleasures of peacetime, here represented by sex and music. In the case of Paris, this image has acquired a negative meaning and is used in the *Iliad* to create the character of an effeminate loser.

I do not mean to suggest that the image of Paris's anger is traditional. It is not very probable for an epic song to put a hero from the enemy's side in the center of things. Despite Homer's compassion and admiration for Hektor, Aeneas, and the Trojans, it is almost certain that traditional epic songs present the point of view of the Achaeans.[246] In the Indian epic, only the Pandavas are

244 Nagy 1990b:202; 1996a:72–73; 2013:245–247.

245 Murray 1907:123–124.

246 Sale (1987 and 1989) found a relatively small number of phrases for "in (to, from) Troy" and concludes: "This means that when Homer was composing the *Iliad* there were few or no formulae available to him meaning 'in Troy-city'" (1987:35). Similarly, the rarity of formulae relating to the Trojans in the nominative implies that the Trojans traditionally were described by hostile epithets (such as suitors in the *Odyssey*), and the poets shared the Achaean point of

in the focus of attention, though the Kauravas' nobility of character is often underlined.[247]

The problem remains whether any epic song could refer to the actions of Achaean heroes other than Achilles and Odysseus. The scholiast on Lykophron (580) informs us that when the Greeks suffered hunger, Palamedes sailed to Delos to fetch the daughters of Anios. The women came to Rhoiteion and fed them, thanks to their wonderful abilities to multiply food. The scholiast refers to the authority of Kallimachos. A little earlier (570), referring to the authority of Pherecydes and the *Kypria*, he tells about the women's miraculous abilities and recalls the story of how Anios, knowing the prophecy that the war will last ten years, insisted that the Greeks stay with him for nine years and sail to Troy only in the tenth year,[248] which, as we can guess, would save them suffering and losses.[249]

This story of Anios conforms to the pattern I have proposed:

1. the crisis—hunger in the army—is comparable to that in the beginning of the *Iliad*, when many heroes die because of the plague;
2. Palamedes' expedition to fetch Anios's daughters reminds us not only of Odysseus's trip to Chryse in order to return the priest's daughter to her father and to appease the anger of Achilles, but also Odysseus's other journeys to fetch Philoktetes and Neoptolemos. It appears, then, that Palamedes competes with Odysseus; he not only

view in the war. Homer does not use them because his attitude to the Trojans is much more favorable. Homer's innovation is conscious, based on semantic and aesthetic changes (i.e. he uses the change of epithets to emphasize the situational context of the entire poem!), e.g. Thetis is repeatedly called "weeping" instead of "silver-footed" and Telemachus does not use the traditional formula πολύτλας Ὀδυσσεῦ "much-enduring Odysseus," but "my father, noble Odysseus."

247 In the *Battle of the Goths and Huns* and in other Germanic epics, the Huns are not treated as non-Germanic people. Chadwick and Chadwick (1932:81–83) believe that this is the result of the Huns' teutonization in the times in which this story is set. It seems more likely to me that it is an epic device of a cultural and even linguistic assimilation of the enemies to the heroes. The epic bears a strong analogy to the *Iliad*, in which the Trojans do not differ culturally from the Achaeans, and even speak the same language.

248 At first glance, such detailed knowledge about the future and the replacement of the sufferings of the Achaeans known from other songs with a stay in a safe place seems to be not only secondary, but also very late. And yet, the awareness of what is going to happen is typical of the oral song. The idea of avoiding dangers by staying in a safe place may be traditional, as is indicated by the version of the Trojan War, which we cannot treat as late or secondary and in which Helen's *eidôlon* gets to Troy instead of her herself.

249 Anios's daughters are also mentioned by Callimachus in the *Aetia*. Because Proclus's summary places Palamedes' death in the plot of the *Kypria*, Martin West regards both stories as fragments of this work. See West 2003a:102–104 (fr. 26) and 2013:123–125.

possesses a keen intellect, but also in the later part of the cyclic plot undertakes the same kind of task as Odysseus;

3. the bringing of Anios's daughters puts an end to the crisis.

In the face of the scarcity of sources we can only speculate, but since Palamedes is mentioned only once, and the mention is made in connection with his death brought about by Diomedes and Odysseus, we can infer that it was a direct consequence of his fetching Anios's daughters. If so, Palamedes would pay for his deed with his own death. This situation would, then, be analogical to Achilles', when putting an end to the crisis results in his death, or at least brings him closer to death. There is no reason to assume that Palamedes had to embark on the expedition in the chronologically "initial" phase of the war. The situation depicted is typical of the end of the war, when the dominant problem is the impossibility of capturing Troy.

Could there, then, exist a song based on the framework presented above? I would be rather inclined to doubt it. I would suspect that this episode could only appear as a digression in another song. The digressive character of the *Iliad* is typical of oral tradition. However, the digression is shaped according to the same pattern as the main plot of song. Behind Paris's and Aeneas's anger there is the same reason. Most probably, these two motifs do not belong to tradition, but they follow the traditional pattern. The proliferation of heroes and their opponents as well as themes is the result of increasing similarity of heroes and their enemies. One could even say that, like in the case of a monster, which is transformed into a reflection of the hero who kills it in historical epic, here too the opponents of the hero (already in the form of warriors) take up his history and conduct: Paris resembles Achilles in his anger, withdrawal from fighting, and even in the way he spends his idle time.

Repeating the pattern

This similarity of plots is the rule which enables the creation of larger epic organisms, because the multiplication of identical fragments of the plot helps to advance the action by the retardation of its denouement. We can state that in the tradition of the Trojan Cycle we regularly find the following sequence of events: Achilles, as the most important Achaean hero at Troy, always defeats the half-divine leader of the allies. It is a part of his *aristeia*. Another certain point is the death of Achilles at the hands of Paris, the most important of Priam's sons, because he is the cause of the whole conflict. It seems that the killing of another of Priam's sons, Troilos, may be an early extension of Achilles' *aristeia*. The death of Troilos may be perceived as a harbinger of the fate of Troy—it is

Achilles' contribution to its capture, which, however, takes place after his death. The multiplication of Trojan allies seems to be an equally early element. It is a fairly easy method of extending the plot, as the appearance of new contingents does not have to be mentioned at the beginning of the war. They may be also independent of the Trojan catalogue, which is based on the pattern of the Achaean catalogue. It seems that the author of the *Iliad*, intending to highlight the tragic aspect of Achilles' story, splits the hero's deeds and shares them with two people.[250] His *therapôn*, Patroklos, kills the leader of the allies, and he himself kills a son of Priam—and will die at the hands of another of his sons, as the poem does not fail to mention. For the author of the *Iliad*, the killing of a Trojan prince seems much more important than the killing of a miraculous and fairy-tale warrior, who comes in aid of Troy. This is consistent with the rationalism of Homer's works. The killing of a son of Priam may be seen as Achilles' revenge for his own death at the hands of Priam's son.[251] The *Iliad* is, thus, a song contemplating the death of Achilles, who can both experience it (in the death of Patroklos) and take revenge for it (by killing Hektor).

From the perspective of the whole cycle, therefore, the following elements of the plot pattern are subject to multiplication: the situation of crisis, when the Achaean warriors are decimated; the motive of a young warrior's withdrawal from battle and return to it (including his persistence in anger and his friends' ineffective efforts to persuade him to return to combat); killing "monstrous" leaders of the Trojan allies by Achilles or his substitutes; killing other sons of Priam by Achilles or his substitutes. The aim of all these repetitions of narrative sequences is to retard what will inevitably happen. Before the Achaeans arrived at Troy, they had to gather their fleet in Aulis twice. The entire Teuthranian expedition, dooming the Achaeans to pointless struggle and wandering over the sea, is introduced in order to show how difficult the task of capturing Troy must be, if even reaching the city is a challenge. The creation of the "double" of the expedition to Troy helps to amplify the magnitude of the war and to accumulate the problems encountered by the warriors. The principle of exaggeration is the basic method of creating dramatic tension in oral epic songs. The exaggeration is used to attract the listeners' attention, because they prefer the unique and the extraordinary.

250 The splitting of a character or event from the original pattern into two parallel ones in the *Iliad* is typical of Homeric technique (I return to it many times in the book). This is also recognized by Nelson (2022:88), who argues that Homer reworks the traditional myth of Iphigenia's sacrifice, which is the model for Book 1 of the *Iliad*, splitting the role of Agamemnon from the myth of Iphigenia and dividing it between two figures: Agamemnon and Chryses, and similarly splitting Iphigenia into a doublet: Chryseis and Briseis.

251 The revenge of Achilles' death in the cycle (*Ilioupersis*) is shown by the killing of Priam by Neoptolemos, i.e. killing the killer's father by the victim's son (another reversal of roles).

The same principle of repeating the pattern is used to create a monumental work. The duplication of patterns in the *Kypria* indicates that a tendency to create a monumental work preceded the creation of the *Iliad*, since the *Iliad* was its crowning achievement. Current scholarly opinion identifies a tripartite structure in its composition. Taplin argues that there is an immanent connection of this structure with the performance of the entire work in three sessions, probably during three-day religious ceremonies. Though I agree in general with the idea of the tripartite division of the *Iliad*, I disagree with the borders delineated by Taplin.[252] Such a division should be based on plot patterns underlying the development of the story.

The starting point of the pattern is a crisis discussed at assemblies of the Achaean army. In the *Iliad*, there are four such assemblies. They begin, almost invariably, with an unacceptable proposal to retreat, prompted by the Achaeans' hopeless situation. The councils opening Books 1 and 2 are in fact one council, which for the demands of the plot the poet has to split into two. In other words, since he cannot present all the elements shaping the action at the first assembly, he has to insert another assembly, which happened right after the first. Assemblies in Books 1/2, 9 (the council of leaders fulfills the same function), and 19 show very clearly the precarious situation of the Achaeans[253]—and finding a remedy is one of the aims of those gatherings.[254] The victory over Hektor (who throughout the poem is presented as the greatest, or even the only, threat from the Trojan side) takes place as late as the third sequence of events. The councils in Books 1/2, 9, and 19 "renew" the action of the song. Each time the singer begins as if from the same starting point, which allows him to build suspense in a familiar, traditional way. The monumentality of the *Iliad* is based on a threefold modified repetition of the same pattern.[255] Its variability in the use of

[252] Taplin 1992:11–31.

[253] 1/2: the plague decimates the Achaeans / fear of waging war without Achilles; 9: defeat on the second day of battle—the Achaeans withdraw behind their wall / anxiety about a possible serious threat to Achaean ships; 19: the situation after the death of Patroklos, who has improved the Achaean circumstances by driving the Trojans away from the ships and killing the leader of the allies. Agamemnon's proposal of launching ships is made in 14.75–81 at the council of wounded leaders. This is also a reaction to the crisis, which—though not directly—will result in Patroklos's going into battle. This scene of council displays the whole dramatic force which the council in Book 19 lacks. Achilles does not return to battle though the Achaeans are in dire need, so perhaps here we are also dealing with a split scene of council like at the beginning (Books 1 and 2).

[254] 1/2: returning Chryseis; propitiative sacrifices to Apollo / raising the morale of the troops; 9/10: embassy to Achilles / spying trip of Odysseus and Diomedes; 19: Achilles' return to combat.

[255] Thalmann (1984:52–53) explains how the doubling of the scene of the gods' conference on Olympus functions in the *Odyssey* and how this device is linked with the structure of the whole poem: both sections of the two-part structure of the work are further divided into three

the pattern lies primarily in the fact that in the second sequence of events, there is the death of Sarpedon, the leader of the Trojan allies, and in the third, the death of Priam's son Hektor.

It seems, then, that originally all songs followed one pattern, which led from despair to the prevention of the threat, the price of prevention being the death of the hero. Each time the Achaean success is paid for with suffering and a severe loss. The multiplication of the pattern allows the song to grow, like the plot of the cycle, and achieve huge dimensions. A comparison with summaries of cyclic poems lets us conclude that the creation of a monumental poem is not a phenomenon limited to Homer's works, but a tendency noticeable in the whole epic tradition. The methods of expanding the plot of a story based on a simple pattern, in which there is the problem of removing an obstacle which prevents the capture of Troy, are quite simple. Due to the duplication of motifs, typical of oral poetry, the *Aethiopis* doubles the motif of the arrival of successive leaders of Trojan allies: first comes Penthesileia, then Memnon; naturally, the poet applies the principle of variability (the Queen of the Amazons is in many respects different from the King of Ethiopia). The plot of the *Iliad* is expanded by the same method, for example by doubling the scene of the assembly. Another strategy is used in the construction of the plot of the *Little Iliad*: there, obstacles on the way to capturing Troy are accumulated—and all three obstacles require different remedies. Such a development of the epic song pattern can be also found in the *Iliad*, which undertakes to solve only one problem—the killing of Hektor, son of Priam. This is done at the expense of downplaying another motif, traditionally connected with this one, the killing of the leader of Trojan allies. It proves that the *Little Iliad* does not imitate the *Iliad*; the poem meets the expectations of its audience and presents a "lengthened" epic plot, by accumulating traditional motifs, which very probably used to be presented separately, e.g. the bringing of Philoktetes or Neoptolemos, or the theft of the Palladion.

sub-sections (each comprising four books); the council of gods precedes the sequence of Books 1–4 introducing the situation of Odysseus and the journey of Telemachos, whereas the council preceding the sequence Books 5–8 introduces Odysseus's journey.

3

Fantastic Elements of the Cycle and the Rationalism of Homer

The Fantastic and the Magical

The presence of the fantastic and magical in the Cycle and in the Homeric poems

IN POPULAR OPINION, the fantastic, magical, and romantic are foreign and secondary to the *Iliad*. The *Iliad* is perceived as rationalistic in its conception, with elements of the fairy-tale and magical suppressed. The *Iliad* is in this respect contrasted with the Cycle, in which these elements are ubiquitous.[1] The problem is that Cyclic poems are regarded as derivative and certainly later than the *Iliad*, and so their fantastic and magical layer is considered a secondary product of Greek epic. The fantastic and miraculous element is generally ascribed to folk or oriental influences, therefore it is regarded as later or secondary in relation to Greek epic[2]—as if courtly or aristocratic culture were devoid of it! Another controversial claim is that epic is a product of an aristocratic milieu. This issue is inseparable from the question of the creation of epic. We can argue that epic was neither limited to the aristocratic milieu, nor did it derive from panegyric praise poetry.[3]

1 Still very important in this respect is Griffin 1977, which I discuss later in this chapter.

2 Burkert 1972:84; also Burkert 1984.

3 The blame for prioritizing rationalism falls, in my opinion, on the historical school, and especially on the influential works of H. M. and N. K. Chadwick (Chadwick and Chadwick 1932; 1936; 1940); and C. M. Bowra (Bowra 1952). Belief in the emergence of epic from panegyrics and funeral laments presupposes a certain historical reality as a basis for epic. Fairy-tale elements were, according to these scholars, added only for the purpose of blurring this original rational image—for dramatizing action, as Bowra has it. A response was the attempt to derive myth and epic from ritual and ceremony. In the so-called neomythologism, historical references in epic songs were only an added value, serving as a backdrop to plot structures (Levy 1953). These studies were often connected with the search for a ritual and mythological archetype (De Vries 1954). Simultaneously, by applying methods typical of psychoanalysis, some scholars sought to derive epic from psychological complexes (Baudouin 1952). However, even if some of these

Neither is epic an expression of the singer's individuality, rather, it is a way for members of a tribe and later a nation to show its vitality and place in the world. The findings of the Soviet, or perhaps it is better to say, Russian historical-typological comparative method should be the starting point for any reflection on this subject, provided we abandon the once obligatory, but now outdated element of Marxist ideology. Eleazar Meletinsky was able to demonstrate that epic is a product of a community at a particular stage of development; and the living conditions of this community influence the development of epic, so it is therefore important whether it is a foraging, fishing, pastoral, or farming community.[4] Epic emerges when communal and patriarchal structures disintegrate, although such structures play a huge role in epic (it can be argued that their relaxation leads to a conflict that determines the shape of epic). In Propp's terms, the essential feature of epic is not historicity, but heroism understood as a struggle in the name of a community's ideals. In Meletinsky's view, the essence of epic lies in the figure of the hero-protagonist, and I believe that his belief reflects the crux of the matter.

Meletinsky points out that the development of epic is accompanied by a constant decrease of magical and irrational elements. The origins of epic are in the heroic tale, in which the main role is played by a man, a member of a tribe, who tries to ensure the favor of the host spirit. Sometimes he does not have to seek this favor, because he already enjoys it due to family or love relationships,

findings should be considered valuable—like the relationship between epic story patterns and initiation rites (Levy 1953) or the primacy of the cosmogonic myth, which presents the defeat of the forces of chaos by the forces of order synonymous with tribal tradition—they did not offer a comprehensive vision of the development of the epic form in its variety and cultural diversity. In this state of affairs, a revitalizing change was wrought by the Russian school. V. Zhirmunsky and V. Propp revolutionized the whole principle of conducting research by introducing studies of primitive cultures and comparing their mythic/epic narratives with the narratives of other primitive cultures in order to extract typical features of their oral literature. An equally essential breakthrough in anthropology was made by Bronisław Malinowski, who pointed out the need to include cultural context in the interpretation of ethnographic data. Using this method, the Russian School tried to recreate the original shape of the Kyrgyz and Russian epics, comparing them with the epics of the Turkish-Mongol peoples of Siberia. Newer approaches include the work of R. Bertolin Cebrian (Cebrian 2006), who proposed a model for the evolution of epic from funeral laments as a result of their separation from the original ritual context. This process is supposed to be associated with Ionian migration and the resulting separation from the tombs of ancestors. In Cebrian's opinion, mourning songs praising the deeds of the dead, performed by men, were transformed into epic, whereas the laments performed by women preserved their connection with funeral ritual. This controversial thesis is based on the view shared by many scholars that epic poetry of the Homeric type is a relatively late product of Greek culture. On the origin and definition of this genre, see Martin 2005.

4 Meletinsky 2009. This book was written in the 1940s, but for political reasons it was published as late as 1963.

his observance of taboo and other magical requirements,[5] making proper sacrifices, etc. Very quickly he is replaced by the culture hero, perceived as a creator of man or at least a giver of cultural goods. The culture hero uses magic, is cunning and often deceitful, and even resorts to theft, which is not perceived as reprehensible. A typical example of such a hero is Väinämöinen from the Finnish-Karelian epic, who uses magic and steals the Sampo, a mythical mill ensuring prosperity for people. A negative variant of the culture hero is the trickster. In Greek epic, Prometheus is a typical culture hero, possessing both his good and bad traits: the creator and benefactor of people, and at the same time a malicious fraud and thief, always in conflict with gods. Fairy-tale-cum-mythological epic, which precede historical epic, relies less on magic, typical of the culture hero, generally replacing it with the strength and courage of the epic hero. The protagonist of fairy-tale and mythological epic already evinces traces of heroic idealization and though he primarily fights to achieve his personal aims (to win a "distant bride," take revenge on his father's murderers), he also serves the community: he may defeat a monster which embodies various threats to the community and this death symbolizes the victory of cosmic order over chaos.

Heroic epic in its classical stage of development shows "a close relationship with the process of ethnic consolidation at the dawn of political history of nations."[6] The essence of this epic, however, lies not in its historicity but in the character of the epic hero. He is a warrior of extraordinary, but not unlimited strength and valor, which "pushes him to face all opponents and does not allow him to deviate from the ideal of heroic conduct."[7] His enemies, in turn, lose their monstrous features and assume the appearance of human enemies. The archaic stage of epic becomes "a glorious historical past of the nation, preceding its national history."[8] Fairy-tale and mythological motifs become marginalized in favor of the imitation of the reality purported to be historical.

In this evolutionary model of the birth of epic, we observe a significant change in relation to the concept of the historical school. According to the Chadwicks, the first epic was probably created in Mesopotamia, from where it spread throughout Eurasia. The historical-typological comparative method has shown that there are cultures in which we can observe even more archaic forms of epic. In Meletinsky's opinion, *Gilgamesh* exhibits similarities to primitive tales of North American Indians about the exploits of twins, one of whom is brought up in a village and symbolizes civilization, whereas the other is "savage,"

5 A remnant of this in Greek myth is the eating of a pomegranate seed, which makes it impossible to leave Hades, so in this case we are dealing with a negative variant.

6 Meletinsky 2009:422.

7 Meletinsky 2009:425.

8 Meletinsky 2009:428.

brought up outside the village. Together, they perform such deeds as killing monsters.[9] In the Mesopotamian epic, Enkidu displays the features of the primitive man, the savage, while Gilgamesh represents the culture hero, the founder of a city and builder of a temple. At the same time, however, both are a version of fairy-tale heroes, whose mission is to clear the earth of monsters.

Owing to a long process of the development of epic, old features can coexist with new ones and various kinds of heroes can join in one epic tradition. For example, beside typical culture heroes, like Väinämöinen from the Karelian-Finnish epic, or Sosruko from the Ossetian epic of the Narts, there may appear typical epic heroes, like Lemminkäinen and Batraz, respectively. Or the heroes may possess various traits which bear witness to the modification of their image: for example, in the figures of Herakles, Theseus, and Perseus the function of the culture hero gives way to their most important task of clearing the earth of monsters, as is characteristic of the heroes of fairy-tale epic.

Study of the epics of these non-Greek cultures does not demonstrate that rationalism is primary, so why should we assume that Greek epic was any different in this respect? It would be unique on a global scale and even if we perceive Greek culture as absolutely exceptional, it is certainly not because of the rationalism of its epic. Unfortunately, this opinion is widespread in contemporary scholarship.

Jasper Griffin's influential article "The Epic Cycle and the Uniqueness of Homer" aims to show the differences between the Homeric and Cyclic epics. He claims that with regard to fantastic, miraculous, and romantic elements, there are "austere limits to which the *Iliad* confines them."[10] Griffin contrasts the poem's unique quality with the rest of the epic tradition understood in the way peculiar to Homeric scholarship—as a later distortion of the ideal prototype. He suggests that we find the continuation of Homeric motifs (e.g. the fetching of Anios's daughters[11] or the mention of Odysseus's other children by Hesiod, fr. *Theogony* 1011–1018), the transformation of Homeric phrases (fr. 6 *Nostoi* is modeled upon *Iliad* 9.445), interpolations in the Homeric text (e.g. *Iliad* 20.224), and even a certain degeneracy of taste: Griffin invokes Rohde's opinion that in an early epic the perverse motif of the love for Penthesileia's corpse would be impossible.[12]

9 In this respect, the tale resembles also the Georgian epic of Amirani and his brothers.

10 Griffin 1977:367.

11 They miraculously supply food for the Achaean army at Troy. The same motif of a bowl of flour and a jug of oil, which are never exhausted, appears in 1 Kings 17:7–16, where the miracle is guaranteed by the word of Yahweh given by Elijah. In this case, we are dealing with a pattern similar to Homeric "rationalization" of the fairy tale.

12 Griffin 1977:376. Later, evoking the sacrifice of Polyxena on the tomb of Achilles and Helen's exposing herself to Menelaos, he concludes (378): "In the Cycle both heroism and realism are

Griffin's clever observation about Homer's sparing ascription of offspring to his characters (Helen, Odysseus), justified by the concept of the poems, is juxtaposed with the scholia's rejection of the "surplus children" in the remaining tradition as a product of οἱ νεώτεροι ("later poets").[13] Sometimes the scholar admits the existence of an earlier, pre-Homeric tradition, but he uses it as an attack on Cyclic poetry. For example, he perceives the motif of the transformation of Nemesis pursued by Zeus as derivative of the pre-Homeric motif of the transformations of Thetis in the arms of the lovestruck Peleus, because he finds metamorphoses more appropriate for sea gods and goddesses (see Proteus).[14] Griffin makes this qualitative distinction between post-Homeric and pre-Homeric tradition in order to emphasize the exceptionality and originality of Homer, because his starting point is Wilamowitz's remark "Es ist kein qualitativer Unterschied zwischen Ὁμηρικὸν und κυκλικόν,"[15] to which he refers critically.[16] The key problem here is what we understand by the term "cycle." Is cyclic poetry wholly derivative of Homer or does it continue a living epic tradition? As we have already seen in previous chapters, there is a lot of evidence in favor of the latter possibility, which Griffin completely ignores. Therefore, the claim that the rationalistic spirit of Homeric epics was lost in the works of his followers, whose degenerate taste is revealed in the growing number of miraculous and fantastic elements, cannot be upheld. The question remains: why did the followers of Homer not follow his example in the issue which later generations found so important? There seems to be only one logical answer: the Cyclic poems' predilection for the miraculous, fairy-tale, and romantic stems from epic tradition, rather than from a possible Homeric influence.

For some reason, our version of the *Iliad* and, to a much lesser extent, the *Odyssey* lack these elements which are inherent, it would seem, in archaic narration. We note, however, that fantastic and fairy-tale elements occur in the *Odyssey*, mainly in Odysseus's tales about his life.[17] It may, therefore, be associated with the intended authorial distance. Aristotle had already observed that

---

rejected in favour of an over-heated taste for sadistically coloured scenes; more striking, even more perverse effects are once again what is desired."

13 Griffin 1977:373.

14 Griffin 1977:369.

15 Wilamowitz 1884:375.

16 Nagy (1990b:72n99) shares Griffin's opinion and connects the presence of miraculous and magical elements in the Cycle to their links to local cults, which reflects "the more localized interests of individual city-states or groups of city-states." Consequently, the absence of these elements in the Homeric poems would be explained by their Panhellenic character.

17 In the *Iliad*, similarly, the extraordinary exploits of Bellerophon (the slaying of Chimera, the Solymi, and Amazons) are recounted by Glaukos, not the narrator (6.178–186).

Homer puts into the mouths of his characters all matters of uncertain credibility (fr. 163 Rose = 387 Gigon = schol. T *ad Iliad* 19.108).

This chapter analyzes the function of this kind of tale in the Cycle and in the Homeric poems. It concentrates mainly on the role of magic and magical thinking in the construction of epics and in the psychology of characters. It will enable us to look more closely at the affinity of the Trojan Cycle and other epic cycles. I hope that it will also shed more light on the way the songs of the Trojan Cycle were created. Many of these observations draw on the work of other researchers, however, I thought it useful to collect them, sometimes providing my own comments or adding my own findings. I will also put forward two theses and try to demonstrate their legitimacy.

One thesis concerns the primacy of the fantastic and magic world in Greek epic. Although this world preserved its original position and character in cyclic poems, in Homeric works this epic vision is clouded by a rationalism unique to it, so that we can see only its traces, which remained because of loyalty to tradition. The other thesis suggests that Homer, despite his rationalism, kept the magical and fairy-tale elements of the tales known to him, in accordance with the conservative nature of the technique of oral composition.

As we have seen, the first thesis opposes the popular belief about the secondary nature of the fantastic world in Cyclic epics. Since the nineteenth century, scholars have accused the Cyclic poems of romanticism, which stresses the fantastic and the magical, and of pomposity—all of which was supposed to testify to the fact that these works were epigonic in relation to the *Iliad*, itself devoid of these qualities. Trying to demonstrate that the Homeric epics were secondary to the Cyclic poems, Kullmann rejected such assumptions as unscientific, because they are difficult to verify, and he decided not to judge theses which he gathered under the term *petitiones principii*. It seems that his decision to avoid the problem was wrong; if he had managed to dispel this prejudice, he would have straightened the path of progress for later studies of epic. The well-known rationalism of the *Iliad* does not define epic as such, because it is not the essential trait of that poem, but it is Homer's achievement and, we can imagine, the result of the environment in which his work was born. With even more certainty, we can say that this rationalism is an expression of a tendency in Greek mentality contemporaneous with Homer and manifested in Greek epic. This tendency, however, does not necessarily mean a permanent change that would not allow for the survival and reappearance of ancient mythical ideas. Characteristic here is the construction of the *Odyssey*; on the one hand, though created later than the other Homeric epic, it contains a lot of magical, fantastic, or fairy-tale elements, while on the other, there are many instances showing that it shares the rational point of view of the *Iliad*.[18] This does not mean that its plot relies on the *Iliad;* in this respect the *Odyssey* rather seems to disregard it. The fact that the primacy of the rationalism of the *Iliad* is so widely accepted results only from the fact that this epic is fundamental to European culture. An *a priori* acceptance of this opinion is unjustified also because it is easy to demonstrate the presence of the magical and fantastic in the material which was used to create the *Iliad*. The presence of these elements also points to the existence of an even more primitive version of the epic.

Homer's rationalism seeks to eliminate or at least blur the traces of anything fantastic or magical.[19] Because of the enduring stories in oral epic, the poet cannot completely suppress these elements; instead, he reinterprets them and, above all, provides double (divine and human) motivation for all events and actions.[20] Homer's rationalism is not devoid of metaphysical content and cannot be comprehended in the spirit of Enlightenment or Positivism. Myth, when it is still in the phase of taking shape, has no such limitations: it can be both fantastic and irrational. However, there is never absolute freedom in its creation, but it is tightly restricted; in epic, these restrictions result from the use of story patterns. Scenes are built in the way characteristic of myth, the adventures of various heroes form similar narrative sequences, and there is a similar motivation of events. In myth, the climax is achieved not by the vividness of action or by highlighting the fundamental problem, as in drama, but rather by the accumulation of various supernatural factors in a static (from our point of view) scene, which can take on cosmic monumentality. Such is, for example, the scene of Achilles' battle with Memnon.[21] It evinces traits of the primitive method of suspense building in the dueling scenes, which were probably quite frequent in pre-Homeric epic. In early epic, the result of the duel is not decided by the heroes' performance, which is always superb. Both are protected by magic artifacts given by gods and both have divine armor. Their fight is assisted by divine mothers: the sea goddess Thetis, the mother of Achilles, and Eos, the mother of Memnon. Memnon's duel with Achilles must end in the death of one of the heroes; the poetic trick known from the *Iliad*, when a deity saves one of

18 Burkert (1972:82–84) states that the absence of fantastic, miraculous, and superhuman elements is a feature of "Homer's style" and that *The Sack of Oichalia* had been ascribed to Homer just because of its rational and tragic character. Probably one of the *Thebaid* versions was also attributed to Homer because it focused on the suffering of Adrastos and Amphiaraos.

19 Dowden (1996:53) notes that rationalism is the conscious choice of Homer and rightly concludes that the avoidance of fairy-tale episodes does not necessarily indicate a post-Homeric invention. He goes further, saying that for the audience, familiar with tradition, the absence of the miraculous, fairy-tale aspect is a conscious reference to it.

20 Lesky 1961.

21 Discussed in Ch. 2, above.

the warriors from death, is out of the question. Each goddess pleads for her son's success, though at least one of them, Thetis, knows the outcome of the fight or its tragic outcome for Achilles, even if he wins. Zeus does not make the decision himself, but weighs the *psychai* of both heroes on his scales. The scale with Achilles' *psychê* tips in his favor, and consequently he wins. Memnon's body is snatched from the battlefield by his mother, who takes her son to the end of the earth and, with Zeus's blessing, makes him immortal. Later Thetis snatches the corpse of her son from the funeral pyre and carries him, now immortal, to Leuke (White Island).

One glance is enough to see that such a scene is not possible in the *Iliad*. There, for the first time we recognize a clear separation between the natural and the supernatural. Since then, the insurmountable gulf between the human and divine worlds has existed. Earlier, the barrier between them was often and fairly easily crossed, as is common in the thought of many early peoples. It seems that the differentiation between human and divine worlds was born in the development of civilization. In epic song, the border between the real and metaphysical worlds is not very sharp. Both have a parallel or simultaneous existence, and realization of this fact depends on one's cognitive faculties. Naturally, the receiver of the song is introduced by the narrator into this invisible world and knows what divine actions lie behind deeds of particular people, and even learns divine plans concerning the future of mortal men (e.g. in scenes on Olympus). The audience often shares the knowledge possessed by a character as a result of his meeting a god or goddess, whom he recognizes (e.g. the listener knows what transpires during Achilles' meeting with Athena, when she stops the hero from killing Agamemnon, *Iliad* 1.194–218, or during Achilles' meeting with Thetis, who listens to his complaints, 1.357–430). Sometimes the knowledge of the audience is even greater than that of the characters, when, for example, they meet a god without being aware of the fact, because the god takes the shape of a mortal. It is often only a god's sudden disappearance that reveals his divine character (e.g. Hektor immediately recognizes that it was Athena who deceived him, when he was left alone by Deiphobos during his duel with Achilles, 22.294–296). Sometimes the recognition occurs because the god himself discloses his divine status (e.g. Apollo warns Diomedes and Patroklos against attacking him, 5.440–442, 16.708–710). The most characteristic instance of the boundary between these two worlds is Athena's driving the mist from Diomedes' eyes so that he can see gods active on the battlefield (5.127–132), fight them, and even wound Aphrodite and Ares. However, this is Athena's gift only for the duration of the battle, and not the hero's permanent quality. Human beings cannot notice the interference of gods in human affairs because their cognitive faculties are imperfect.

The possibility of reading divine decisions by people possessing such ability springs from the idea that gods and people coexist in the same space.[22] In epic, heroes, who are also in a sense the heroes of the "time of the beginning," usually cross the boundary of the real world without any problems, but Homer makes it difficult for them, reducing their abilities in this regard to that of ordinary people. Every time they need it, heroes get special "permission" to contact the metaphysical world, but in all other respects they resemble other mortals.[23]

To some extent, such discrepancies in the construction of the epic world represented by tradition and the Homeric school can be explained by confusion in Greek eschatology. Walter Burkert has shown that there are parallels between the plot structure of the *Iliad* and the *Sack of Oichalia*, a poem from the cycle of Herakles; the most striking of these is "the emphasis on the theme of mortality."[24] The *Sack of Oichalia* ends with Herakles arranging for the funeral of the warriors who fought on his side, the *Iliad* with Achilles arranging for the funeral of his friend. This is, according to Nagy, a new tragic epic convention, because the epic story of the hero presupposes his death and immortalization. This is true for Herakles, and this is also true for Achilles.[25] If so, then myths about posthumous immortalization of heroes cannot be a result of the popularization of ecstatic and orgiastic cults of eastern origin. The myth of the

22 The idea of Homer's disregard for the art of divination is a misunderstanding resulting from the misinterpretation of the opinions expressed by the protagonists of Homeric epics. The belief that supernatural beings are interested in human affairs and that they influence people's lives is the result of an anthropocentric vision of the world.

23 Czeremski (2016a:45–46), from the standpoint of the cognitive science of religion, states: "The mythical hero is, at first, a counterintuitive figure, identical or similar to supernatural agents. However, being counterintuitive, he acts in a fundamentally intuitive world, which makes myths only slightly counterintuitive stories. Their minimal degree of counterintuitiveness, in turn, means that myths are optimal units of cultural transmission, which—at least to some extent—explains their popularity." Counterintuitiveness here means a discrepancy between the opinions of a man and his intuitive expectations regarding the reality. The myth that uses the action of a counterintuitive agent is typical of oral culture. In Homeric epics, Czeremski notes a departure from the model of the counterintuitive hero. Epic heroes are no longer counterintuitive, but bizarre (due to the exaggeration of certain features). Czeremski concludes that it happened under the influence of writing. Naturally, this point of view should be taken into account, but the influence of writing could be indirect, i.e. it needn't necessarily have affected the composition of the song. This is confirmed by the fact that epic stories all over the world tend to replace a counterintuitive character by a bizarre one (many examples of this process are provided by Meletinsky 2009). Czeremski (46), citing my research, notes the transfer of the category of the bizarre from persons to artifacts (magic power of warriors is transferred onto their weapons and other military attributes). In the *Iliad*, as I try to demonstrate below, the magic nature of these objects is also suppressed. Therefore, I believe that the replacement of the counterintuitive hero by counterintuitive or bizarre artifacts, which are at his disposal, must have taken place in oral culture long before the times of Homer.

24 Burkert 1972:82–84; Nagy 1999:165.

25 Nagy 1999:165.

apotheosis of a hero can be much earlier than the emergence of heroic cult in archaic Greece.[26]

The scenes of immortalization are out of keeping with the character of the *Iliad*, and therefore the poem does not mention them. Significantly, Homer replaces the scene of Eos carrying the body of her son Memnon to the Isles of the Blessed with the moving of the body of Sarpedon, the leader of Lycians who was killed in a duel with Patroklos, to his native Lycia. Neoanalysts argue that Sarpedon corresponds to Memnon, while Patroklos plays the role of Achilles. On the initiative of Hera, and later Zeus, Apollo bathes Sarpedon's body in the river, anoints it with ambrosia, clothes it in immortal robes, then the brothers Hypnos and Thanatos carry it to Lycia (*Iliad* 16.671–675).[27] Hera explains that they do this in order for the brothers and relatives to bury the dead man and to mark his resting place with a mound and pillar, because τὸ γὰρ γέρας ἐστὶ θανόντων "this is the due of the dead." What a crazy idea—gods work a miracle of transferring a corpse only to give it a burial! The reason is not adequate, even if it was done in order to compensate Zeus for the death of his son. (Sarpedon's comrades could bury his body with honors on the spot; after all, at Troy there was a mound of the Amazon Myrina, *Iliad* 2.814.) But the explanation, to honor the corpse with a funeral, is fully consistent with the general concept of the *Iliad*.[28] Here we have an example of how Homer combines the old and the new: he does not make direct allusions to known events, but since in the construction of the scene he cannot omit an important element, he leaves its setting, while changing its character and purpose.[29] This example also gives us an idea of Homer's rationalism. The solutions he proposes, which deviate from the tradition of fairy-tale epic, do not seem to meet the current criteria for rationalism. As we will see, these new motifs are often no less irrational than the former ones.

26 On the development of the cult of heroes in connection with the creation of the polis system see Seaford 1994.

27 Kullmann (2005:21) points to the family relationship of Hypnos and Thanatos with Eos.

28 It is also in line with the *Iliad*, because the notion of funeral as *geras*, 'that which is due to someone', coincides with one of the main issues of the poem, the proper division and the preservation of *geras*. The taking away of Achilles' *geras* is the cause of his wrath (see Ch. 6, pp. 530–543, below); later Achilles, refusing Hektor the right to be buried, deprives him of his right to "what is due to the dead."

29 Nagy (1999:205) claims that the story of Sarpedon and Apollo is not modeled on the story of Memnon and Eos, but both are different oral versions of one myth. In his opinion, the differences between them corroborate his conclusion. Elsewhere (213), he rightly observes that the place of Memnon's immortalization is the place where he comes from, his homeland. But that's just the proof that the *Iliad* version of the story was based on the *Aethiopis* tradition, because Sarpedon was transferred to his homeland.

Pervasive Hidden Magic in the *Iliad*

Magic objects in other cycles

The author of the *Iliad* eschews the fairy-tale and magical elements, yet they are there, concealed but present.[30] This prompts the conclusion that in earlier versions of the *Iliad* they were just as important as in the entire Trojan Cycle and other Greek epic cycles. Scholars have pointed out many forms in which magic can be found in Homer, although still there is no work which comprehensively examines the presence of magic in the epics. In order to grasp the essence of this issue, I suggest we confine our observations to the functions and significance of magic objects in the Greek epic tradition, keeping in mind that I refer to them only as examples which demonstrate the original role of magic.[31]

The priority of the Argonaut Cycle in relation to Homeric poems is unquestioned. This cycle is referred to in the *Odyssey* as familiar and well-liked (12.69–72, Ἀργὼ πᾶσι μέλουσα 'Argo known to everybody'), and its story is absolutely unthinkable without the element of the miraculous: Lynkeus with his wonderfully keen sight, the flying sons of Boreas, Orpheus enchanting with his music, Iphiklos and Euphemos, who like Achilles could run with amazing speed, a speaking ship, a dragon guarding the golden fleece, fire-breathing bulls, etc.[32] Moreover, the goal of the whole expedition, the golden fleece, is in itself a magic object, and the sorceress Medea helps to steal it, using magic herbs and a magic wand.

30 Considering the vast range of opinions on what magic is, I will refrain from trying to define it, limiting myself to showing some of its aspects which I believe are not controversial.

31 We disregard the issue of various types of behaviors, gestures, and spells that appear in Homeric texts. Often we can only guess at the existence of a magical foundation of these behaviors; they are not presented as explicitly as in the epics of other peoples. For example, Odysseus hid the treasures he received from the Phaeacians and θοῶς δ' ἐπὶ δεσμὸν ἴηλε / ποικίλον, ὅν ποτέ μιν δέδαε φρεσὶ πότνια Κίρκη "cast a cord upon it—a cunning knot, which queenly Circe once had taught him" (*Odyssey* 8.447–448, translation, A. T. Murray). Bradford 1967 notes that rather than conjecture that Kirke had taught him a complicated knot, it would be more logical to assume that she had taught him a magic spell which he placed on the knot. This may be confirmed by the meaning of the adjective ποικίλος (which modifies the word "knot"), in lyric poetry associated with magic (Pippin-Burnett 1983:250–251; Zieliński 2006:187–188).

32 Clearly these elements are counterintuitive: the Boreads (category of person)—endowed with the ability to fly (category of animal), the ship (category of artifact)—endowed with speech (category of person). Here it would be difficult to detect the transfer of the hero's miraculous (counterintuitive) abilities to the artifact, the possession of which would make him extraordinary. This would confirm the thesis about the connection of counterintuitiveness with orality. Though undoubtedly it is so, it should also be noted that apart from counterintuitive features of heroes, there are also bizarre ones, like the exceptional sight of Lynkeus or the unusual speed of Iphiklos and Euphemos.

Magic objects play a still more significant role in the Theban Cycle. Their enormous number is due to the fact that they were all gifts of gods at the wedding of Kadmos and Harmonia. Although sources vary with regard to the number and, sometimes, the names of the donors, these are the most important items:[33]

1. Athena or Aphrodite gave a necklace,[34] described as golden (seeing it, all people cried with delight–διαβεβόησαν) and peplos;
2. Demeter gave καρπὸς σιτοῦ 'the fruit of the grain', undoubtedly a magic source of fertility and abundance; in the Kabeiroi version, Iasion, regarded as Harmonia's father, ascended into heaven, and the fruit of his union with Demeter was Plutos, god of abundance and wealth;
3. Hermes gave a lyre (its magical power is presented in another Theban myth: Amphion, son of Antiope, plays the lyre, and blocks of stones listen to the music and form themselves into a city wall[35]);
4. Electra (Harmonia's mother in the Kabeiroi myth) gave holy utensils used in the Great Mother mysteries, together with sacred cult objects—cymbals, tympana, and "objects for the orgy" (Iasion, after his ascension, was also reported to have a son, Korybas, with Kybele).

In the last case, we can talk about the close relationship between initiation rites and magic rites. They have an identical goal: reaching beyond the human condition by increasing the potential of those who are able to use ritual utensils.

All these objects, except the necklace and peplos, were removed from Thebes to Phrygia in Asia by Dardanos, Kybele, and Korybas. Some of them later appeared in the events connected with the Trojan War. In Thebes, there remained only the necklace and the peplos or chiton, associated with the quarrel of Polyneikes and Eteokles. Their extraordinary nature is manifested by the fact that in return for them Polyneikes gives sole rule in Thebes to Eteokles. However, since these myths have come down to us in many variants, preserved only in fragments and mainly in summaries, we are often clueless as far as the cause of events is concerned. There are essentially two versions of the events. In Hellanicus's account, there is a choice of either rule

33 The list according to Diodorus Siculus 5.49.1.

34 According to Apollodorus (*Bibliotheca* 3.2) the neclace was Kadmos' gift to Harmonia given to him by Hephaistos or Europa (see Gantz 1993:471–472).

35 According to Eumelus, when Amphion played the lyre, animals and stones followed him. In Pherecydes' version, the lyre was a gift from the Muses (Gantz 1993:487). Nowhere, however, is it mentioned that it is the same lyre. In Greek myth the miraculous power of objects is translated into the skills of an individual. Compare the myth of Orpheus.

over Thebes or property, but it is unclear why Polyneikes comes back and demands his share of the rule, if his choice was the necklace and peplos. Gantz compares his reaction with Esau's disappointment; in his opinion, Polyneikes regrets the bargain and wants to renegotiate.[36] In the second account, that of Pherecydes, Eteokles expels his brother by force (in some variants of this one, he is the older brother, which probably means that he has greater right to the throne). If we compare the quarrel of Polyneikes and Eteokles with the similar brotherly quarrel of Atreus and Thyestes, it turns out that the most important objects in the story are those chosen by Polyneikes—not because they were valuable, but because they were magical. In the conflict between Atreus and Thyestes, the right to rule belongs to the person of greater magical power. Such power can be obtained by gaining possession of an object more miraculous than the one owned by the rival; in effect, the owner of the golden fleece becomes the king.[37] Thyestes tricks Atreus, stealing the golden fleece from him, and thus gains the rule. Not for long, however. A greater miracle—the sun rising in the west—returns the power to Atreus. So, by analogy, Polyneikes is not stupid or avaricious; his choice is undoubtedly dictated by the magical power of the chosen items. The possession of such objects may give a right to exercise authority, so Polyneikes does not feel cheated, but tries to cheat his brother. Polyneikes returns to Thebes; the possession of magic artifacts gives him the right to rule over the city. As in the case of the golden fleece, it was probably all about being able to exercise a magical influence over nature in order to ensure its fertility and give wealth to people. Eteokles, however, does not yield his power, so here we have a typically epic conflict (visible also in the Trojan Cycle) between power and deception.[38] In this case, power temporarily wins.[39] The magic objects help Polyneikes to organize an expedition, the Seven against Thebes, against his brother. He uses these objects to bribe Eriphyle to persuade her husband Amphiaraos to take part in the expedition;

36 Gantz 1993:503.

37 The golden fleece secures the right to exercise power in the story of the Argonauts. Animal skin can have magical properties, e.g. the skin of Amalthea, the goat which nourished the newborn Zeus, later covers the god's shield, the aegis, which no missile can penetrate. Popko (1991) finds a pattern for the myth of the golden fleece in the Hittite cult of ram skins suspended from a tree. It seems quite likely, but the question remains whether the term "golden" has only a symbolic meaning, indicating the magical nature of the object. Perhaps we should keep in mind that sheepskin was used to capture gold from streams. There were no gold-bearing rivers in Greece, but there were in Asia Minor.

38 It is present in many allomorphs of the Trojan Cycle. Recall the thesis, put forward by Nagy (1999:42–58), of the rivalry between Achilles and Odysseus, i.e. between strength and deception.

39 The context of the *Seven against Thebes* prompts Gantz (1993:506) to note the presence of both Hellanicus's and Pherecydes's versions of the myth in Aeschylus.

Amphiaraos, who was a seer, was reluctant to join the venture which he knew would bring his death.

Many features of this myth resemble the *Mahābhārata* story of the "earrings of immortality," the celestial gift made of *amrita*, the elixir of immortality. The earrings were greatly desired because they conferred immortality on their possessor. This marvelous artifact appears in three different stories that show an undeniable affinity.

Two of the stories are manifestly older and more important for the plot of the epic. Karna, the main enemy of the Pandavas, and especially of Arjuna, wears *amrita* earrings and a breastplate that are a part of his body. He inherited both from his father, the divine Surya, who appeared in them to his mother Kunti. The seduction was very much facilitated by the promise that both objects would be inherited by the son born of their union (III 291–305 Ed. Crit.). The possession of these earrings makes Karna a great danger to the Pandavas. That is why Indra, Arjuna's father, disguised as a brahmin, wangles the earrings and the breastplate from Karna, who cuts it from his body with a knife. The Asura Naraka gets embodied in Karna, "to kill Arjuna" (III 240, 19 Ed. Crit.). Asuras cannot possess *amrita*, so Joanna Sachse supposes that the incarnation took place after Karna had forfeited his earrings.[40]

According to the other story (III 307, 21 Ed. Bombay), Naraka stole the earrings from the goddess Aditi and concealed them in Pragjyotisha, the capital of the asuras. Vishnu defeated him there and took the earrings. There are further contradictory versions: Aditi, who got back the earrings, gave them to Surya, who in turn gave them to Karna—though Karna was reportedly born with them, and they saved his life, when, as a bastard, he was abandoned in a basket on a river.

Vishnu acts on Indra's request, so there is a recurrent pattern, in which Indra (one of the devas) takes away earrings from Naraka (an asura). Sachse combines these stories with two others, presented in books 1 and 14, in which there appear enviable earrings, although it is not mentioned that they are made of *amrita*.[41]

In the first of these nearly identical stories, Uttanka, a disciple of a brahmin, has to pay for his education by bringing earrings which belong to the king's wife and offering them to the brahmin's wife. On his way to accomplish the task, Uttanka meets an unusual rider on a bull, who demands that the disciple eat the bull's feces. Uttanka complies and it turns out that it was very wise of him, because the rider is Indra, and the feces of the bull Airavata are in fact *amrita*.

40 Sachse 2005:247.
41 Sachse 2005:248.

The brahmin's disciple goes to the palace and, after he performs the required ablutions, is given the earrings by the queen. However, on his way back, he is robbed by Takshaka, who takes the earrings to the abode of the Nagas. To the aid of the brahmin's disciple comes Indra, who opens the ground with a thunderbolt. In the underground kingdom, the man sees Indra on a horse called Agni (Fire). Following the tip of the horseman, Uttanka starts a fire so fierce that the Naga returns the earrings, which Uttanka then hands over to his master's wife.

In the second version, the name of Uttanka's guru is changed. The divine earrings, belonging to King Saudasa's wife, which he has to bring to the guru's wife, are, as before, the fee for the training. In both versions, it is not explained how the queen came into their possession. The meeting with the cannibal king enhances the suspense, but Uttanka manages to obtain the earrings. The queen warns him to take care of the precious gift: "If the earrings touch the ground, they will be stolen by Nagas; if they are the possession of someone who neglects ablutions after a meal, they will fall into the hands of Yakshas; and if their owner falls asleep, they will be taken by devas. Moreover, they are desired also by rishis and rakshasas, who want to get hold of them."[42] Then the story essentially follows the first version. On his way back, a Naga (serpent) steals the earrings, but Indra opens the ground with the thunderbolt. In the underground kingdom, Uttanka finds a horse which turns out to be Agni, starts a fire, takes away the earrings from terrified Nagas, and gives them to his master's wife.

In all these versions, there is Indra, who recovers the jewels; sometimes his actions also involve the horse Agni (symbol of fire) and a demon (Asur Naraka or Naga), who temporarily acquires the earrings. Many recognizable and typical motifs occur: wheedling away or stealing an artifact appears in the Trojan Cycle when Odysseus steals the Palladion.[43] The motif of cutting off Karna's breastplate, which deprives him of magical protection, is comparable to Apollo's disarming Patroklos of the armor which made him invincible.

The stories of the *amrita* earrings show how a miraculous object can lose its magical significance. In Karna's tale, possession of earrings and armor means invincibility, invulnerability, and, in a way, immortality. In the stories of the brahmin, however, there is no special reason which would make the earrings so valuable, except perhaps their beauty, although their desirability is strongly emphasized. This is connected with the motif of the competition between various heroes to take possession of a miraculous object. This motif, encountered in numerous folktales of various peoples, disappeared almost completely in Greek myth.

42 Sachse 2005:248.

43 Compare the loss of Odin's eye in the Germanic myth or Perseus's theft of the Graeae's eye.

Artifacts also lose their magical significance in Greek epic. In the myths of Herakles, there is no explanation why, for example, the girdle of Hippolyta is so valuable. We know only that it is an attribute of the Amazon ruler, but it is not clear whether it has any special power, like Aphrodite's girdle. We also do not know why Herakles has to bring the golden apples of the Hesperides, but learn only of the difficulties in obtaining them.

In the last two stories of the earrings, there is no mention of their being made of *amrita*. In spite of that, Sachse proposes that they should be connected with this artifact because their description is parallel to that of objects made of *amrita*: "They were divine objects, made of celestial jewels, glittering; they protected against poison, fire, hunger, thirst and fear, and they were able to produce gold."[44] Such treasures preserve their protective function. Their connection with gold is not accidental either. In Greek myths, the adjective "golden" often is used to express the exceptional value of certain items: the necklace of Harmonia, for example, was made of gold. Gold had magical power, mainly because its luminous glow was associated with the sun, whose light, according to Greeks, was life-giving. For example, Aeneas's spear cannot pierce Achilles' shield, which is heaven-made and stops the blow with its third of five layers; this layer is of gold, which makes the shield shatterproof.[45] In the *Iliad*, Achilles' armor, which is endowed with magical properties and protects Patroklos in battle, is called ἄμβροτα τεύχεα 'immortal armor' (17.194); by analogy to Sanskrit epic we may assume that it was made of an immortal substance.[46]

44 Sachse 2005:248. In the first story, Uttanka partakes of *amrita* on Indra's order; in the second, before he sets out, he gets *amrita* from Indra, who gives it to him at Krishna's request.

45 *Iliad* 20.268–272: this passage was considered very doubtful already in antiquity (Aristotle *Poetics* 1461a31; athetized by Aristarchus Arn/A, by an unknown scholar Did/T, and in some texts left out Did/T). The reasons for their objections are rational: gold as the middle layer neither fulfilled a decorative function, nor was it practical, because it is not hard enough to make the shield invulnerable (Edwards 1991:323 *ad* 268–272; Leaf 1900–1902:368: "neither useful nor ornamental"). Paipetis and Kostopoulos (2008:183–191) disagree; they calculate that a layer of soft gold could really stop a spearhead, so composite shields like Achilles' could really be used in Homeric times in Greece. Thalmann (1984:190n32) notes that the stopping of the missile by the middle layer shows how deeply rooted in the poet's mind is the use of symmetrical construction in narration. But nobody, so far as I know, has taken into account the deliberate irrationality, i.e. the magic function of gold in the shield's construction. Belief in the magic function of gold does not prevent it from being used in composite shields.

46 Nagy (1999:179) understands it as a synonym of immortal fame, because in 17.125 it is accompanied by the epithet κλυτά 'splendid, magnificent'. Objects made by Hephaistos are described as glittering and imperishable; various compounds with *aphthito-* 'immortal, unfailing' are synonyms of the word "golden." However, the interpretation that their imperishable nature and immortality are the result of the fame which they gain in the epic, even if correct, may refer to a later tradition, whereas originally immortality could have been given by the material out of which these objects were made. Gold, which does not corrode, is very appropriate in this context.

In the Theban epic, there are more magic artifacts. Undoubtedly, the silver table and golden cup of Kadmos had some inherent magic—perhaps they were his wedding gifts. Oedipus curses his sons, Polyneikes and Eteokles, who against his explicit order used these objects to serve him a meal. Why did he forbid his sons to use them and did his prohibition apply also to himself? What are the consequences of eating and drinking out of these dishes? The answer is clear, if we acknowledge their magical function. In the *Thebaid*, there is a variant of the scene: he curses his sons, because they do not serve him a due portion of meat at a sacrifice, his γέρας.[47] In both versions, consumption is prohibited. This situation is possible only if Oedipus is blind. Athenaius mentions that Oedipus delivers a curse, seeing the table and the cup, but Gantz suggests that perhaps he can recognize them by touch.[48] In my opinion, what is important in all versions of the story is that Oedipus learns he used forbidden objects. That they were put in front of him would be nothing in itself; what constitutes the violation of the ban is eating and drinking out of them. Undoubtedly, the sons do it in order to deprive their father of his right to rule. When Oedipus uses forbidden objects to eat and drink, he commits a crime, and when he does not get the right portion of meat, it means he is deprived of the honor (τιμή) due to him as a king.[49]

If there is a possible parallel to Kadmos's cup in the *Iliad*, it is that which Achilles takes out of the chest Thetis gave him before he set out; no man was allowed to drink wine from this cup, nor was it possible to use it for pouring drink offerings to any god except Zeus (16.225–227).[50] Perhaps this cup is not exactly magical (after all, Zeus is not obliged to fulfill the whole request of Achilles), but it is not as far from magic as it might seem, because the taboo which limits the use of an object is connected to the exclusive use of magic items by their rightful owners— consider Achilles' horses, armor, and spear, Nestor's cup, Odysseus's bow, Aias's shield. The *Iliad* does not make any reference to their magical power, but it stresses that their size, heaviness, or hardness (the last one in the case of the bow) makes it impossible for anyone else to use them. This exaggeration is a constant feature of Homer's epic landscape,[51]

47 These are probably two different versions of this story. Aeschylus gives a third version (*Seven against Thebes* 778–790). Having realized that he had committed both incest and patricide, Oedipus doubled the evil (δίδυμα κάκ' ἐτέλεσεν): he jabbed out his eyes κρεισσοτέκνων 'dearer than his children' and cursed his children from the incestuous marriage, so that they would split the property σιδαρονόμῳ διὰ χερί 'with the hand dividing with iron', i.e. the sword.

48 Gantz 1993:503.

49 Compare Nagy 1999:132–133.

50 Achilles has used the cup properly (16.228–248), and yet Zeus grants only one half of his prayer. He lets Patroklos drive the Trojans away from the ships, but does not let him return from the battle (16.249–252).

51 Van Wees 1992:5–23.

but also a relic of earlier notions of the supernatural power of these objects, available only to the chosen ones.

The Trojan Cycle abounds in the magical and miraculous. Sometimes, it is a result of borrowing characters or situations from other cycles (e.g. Lynkeus, who scanned the whole Peloponnese and spotted Castor and Polydeukes hidden in the hollow of a tree, *Kypria* fr. 11). In surviving fragments and summaries, we encounter extraordinary figures: Achilles' "monstrous" enemies, who took on the shape of heroes—snow-white Kyknos (*Kypria*) and black Memnon (*Aethiopis*); Anios's daughters, who fed the Achaean army at Troy (*Kypria* fr. 20); and the lovers Nemesis and Zeus who underwent transformations (*Kypria* fr. 7). There are also magic items: the Palladion, a primitively carved wooden statue of Athena miraculously fallen from heaven, stolen from Troy by Diomedes and Odysseus (*Sack of Ilium* fr. 1); the bow and arrows of Herakles, owned by Philoktetes (*Little Iliad*); and Achilles' spear, which first injured, then healed Telephos (*Kypria*). Jasper Griffin, in order to mark the difference between these cyclic stories and Homer, repeats Aristotle's opinion (fr. 163 Rose = 387 Gigon = schol. T *ad* 19.108) that Homer puts all unbelievable phenomena in the speeches of his characters.[52] The fallacy of this opinion has recently been demonstrated by studies on the use of myth in Homer. The fact that in Homer, each mythic tale is recounted not by the narrator, but by the characters, is the result of the persuasive and paradigmatic use of mythic stories in the oral culture of the Homeric world. But why in the cyclic poems shouldn't incredible stories, such as these about Nemesis and Zeus, be put in the mouth of the characters? It would be a typical narrative pattern, characteristic perhaps of more than just one singer. In addition, it may seem that, for example, the stories of the transformations of sea deities, Thetis or Proteus, are more appropriate than those of Nemesis (sea and water are always perceived as subject to constant change), but the inference about the secondarity nature of the metamorphosis of Nemesis and Zeus is too far-fetched; if Homer could change myths to suit his story, so too could other epic poems, e.g. the *Kypria*, present versions different from the "canonical" ones.

Magic objects in the *Iliad*

In order to study the role of magic objects in the *Iliad*, it is necessary to distinguish between embellishments like the extensions of content typical of oral

52 Griffin 1977:367–368. See also Griffin 1980:48–49. But compare H. Parry 1994:19–20: "Whether true or false, the *Apologos* is great entertainment; and the poet-like skills of imaginative storytelling are an Odyssean virtue. But Homer insists by every means at his disposal that Odysseus's autobiography is part of the hero's true history, measured by the standards both of the *Odyssey* and of Homer's own world. The *Apologos* is for Odysseus and his listeners in a sense true "history" in the making, for Homer and *his* audience true "history" now enshrined in the canonical tale."

narration (e.g. the description of the harness of Achilles' supernatural horses 19.391–395), and the magic objects themselves. Homer does not facilitate this task, because he perceives the latter mainly in aesthetic terms. However, as Lord already noted, in the epic poems of Yugoslavia which he studied, the meaning of the most typical descriptions of weapons, meals, etc. was much deeper than ornamental: it was also emotional, magical, or associated with cult or initiation.[53] In Greek archaic poetry, a beautiful exterior, especially its sheen, reveals divine and spiritual power, which determines the value of a person or an object.

In the *Iliad,* only the objects owned by gods bear a clear mark of magical power: the leather girdle of Aphrodite, worn on the breast or around the waist and evoking lust; the terrifying aegis; the cap of Hades which gives invisibility to Athena; and Hermes' caduceus. I would like to point out that nearly all of these artifacts, which are attributes of individual gods, can be borrowed by other gods when they are needed to complete a mission or carry out a military action. Gods reach for them when they need to ensure success for their deeds: Athena must be invisible, so she puts on Hades' cap (how it got into her hands is not mentioned); Hera needs to seduce Zeus, so she borrows the girdle from Aphrodite.

Scholars have noticed that the heroes' equipment also possesses magical power. This equipment reveals the primacy of the heroes' character over the text of the epic. It must be admitted that such objects are relatively few and usually described rather generally, so only their use gives a clue to their traditionally magical character. The classifications made for research purposes do not explain much because they tend rather to describe the world presented in the epics, without paying much attention to the centuries-long tradition which lies behind them, and which could have been modified and reinterpreted in the course of time. In the main plot of the Cycle there are no artifacts without which the story would lose its meaning or motivation. In the *Iliad*, mentions of such artifacts are often very enigmatic: Areithoos's armor worn by Ereuthalion in Nestor's tale (*Iliad* 7.146), for example, is described as Ares' gift, which in itself does not determine its magical character. But we learn that Ereuthalion's father Lykurgos obtained it by vanquishing Areithoos, not by strength, but by guile.[54] The possession of this armor let Ereuthalion "challenge all the champions, who trembled with fear and dared not fight with him" (*Iliad* 7.150–151). The armor made him invincible, and because he knew its power, he could fight anyone. Nestor, who managed to defeat him, does not tell us how he did it, only that Athena gave him victory (*Iliad* 7.154). These details suggest, however, that behind Nestor's story there is an old pattern, in which someone, who has armor given

53 Lord 1960:88.

54 *Iliad* 7.142 τὸν Λυκόοργος ἔπεφνε δόλῳ, οὔ τι κράτεΐ γε ("he killed Lykurgos by guile, not by might"). Compare the acquisition of the "immortal" armor from Karna by deceit.

him by a god, is invincible and can be vanquished only by deceit, by depriving him of its protection.[55]

It is difficult to judge whether Hektor's mention of Nestor's unusual shield and Diomedes' armor,[56] when he addresses his horses, is based on tradition (*Iliad* 8.191–197):

> ἀλλ' ἐφομαρτεῖτον καὶ σπεύδετον ὄφρα λάβωμεν
> ἀσπίδα Νεστορέην, τῆς νῦν κλέος οὐρανὸν ἵκει
> πᾶσαν χρυσείην ἔμεναι, κανόνας τε καὶ αὐτήν,
> αὐτὰρ ἀπ' ὤμοιιν Διομήδεος ἱπποδάμοιο
> δαιδάλεον θώρηκα, τὸν Ἥφαιστος κάμε τεύχων.
> εἰ τούτω κε λάβοιμεν, ἐελποίμην κεν Ἀχαιοὺς
> αὐτονυχὶ νηῶν ἐπιβησέμεν ὠκειάων.
>
> but step together and make haste that we can take
> the shield of Nestor, whose fame now reaches the heavens,
> for it is all of gold, even the rods,
> and from the shoulders of horse-taming Diomedes
> his ornate armor, which Hephaistos wrought with toil.
> If those are taken, I hope
> to make the Achaeans embark upon their swift ships this very night.

The shield of solid gold and a breastplate made by Hephaistos can be seen as typical artifacts whose unusual character not only distinguished the hero, but also made him invincible. This understanding is underpinned by Hektor's hope that once he gets them into his hands, the Achaeans will have to make their escape. Significantly, there is no mention of killing Achaean heroes; rather it seems that they will flee because they will be deprived of the protection of these powerful objects.

55 Homer changes this pattern, stressing the protective function of the mace which Areithoos used in fighting, and which became useless "in a narrow passage" (στεινωπῷ ἐν ὁδῷ, *Iliad* 7.143). Lykurgos's deceit led him to this place. Kirk (1990:254) recognizes here a folk motif: the man fighting with a mace may be pierced by a spear anywhere, but in folk imagination the way to kill him is to take him to a place where his weapon cannot be used. But both earlier (7.137) and later (7.146) Nestor concentrates on Areithoos's/Ereuthalion's armor.

56 Scholars are reluctant to allow the possibility of the existence of an unpreserved tradition corroborated only by such enigmatic mentions. Kirk (1990:313) suspects the final shape of this passage was given by rhapsodists, while Willcock 1978 points to the main author of this book. In my opinion, we should speak about a traditional way of drawing the image of the hero. If Hektor, or another hero in a similar situation, wants to emphasize the value of his enemies whom he intends to defeat, automatically the singer endows them or their equipment with counterintuitive or weird features.

The most important miraculous objects in the *Iliad* are, however, Achilles' weapons. The usual object of study in this context is the armor wrought by Hephaistos at Thetis's request. Its special element is the shield, whose unusual character can be inferred from its extensive description. However, the description focuses upon its beauty and exquisite craftsmanship. Neither the armor nor the shield fulfills any magical function in the plot of the epic.[57] The situation is different in the case of the armor, spear, and immortal horses given to Achilles by his father Peleus. According to Homer, they were gifts offered by gods on the occasion of the hero's wedding with Thetis.[58] Paton found in this story a typical folk theme, in which the hero gets three magic gifts: armor which cannot be pierced, a spear which flies back to its master, and divine horses.[59] That is why all these three gifts should be seen as functioning together in epic songs about Achilles. Let us analyze these three gifts in turn.

In the *Iliad,* Achilles possesses two sets of magic armor. The second set which Thetis asked Hephaistos to forge for him is usually the focus of attention. The *Iliad*, however, emphasizes its exquisite appearance more than any miraculous or magical power. The shield manifests only one magical feature—impenetrability—but the poet does not exploit this motif too much and does not explain the trait of impenetrability by magic. In the fight with Hektor, when Achilles raises his shield, the spear hits it solidly, but rebounds (*Iliad* 22.289–291).[60] Its miraculous power is revealed again, just as when Aeneas's spear was stopped by the gold layer (*Iliad* 20.268–272). In the latter situation the magical function of the weapon appears, as indubitably gold had protective magic.

But this is Achilles' second set of armor, after the first one was lost by Patroklos. The first, lost armor reveals its miraculous, magical character twice in the *Iliad*. Patroklos's death is the first time. The wounding and killing of the hero were possible only after Apollo disarmed him at the critical moment; the god stood behind Patroklos and struck him in the back with his hand (16.789–807). Patroklos's helmet was knocked from his head, the spear in his hand was

57 Finkelberg (1998:113–115), analyzing the description of Achilles' shield, argues that one cannot claim a magic connection between a thing and its representation, where the representation would be treated as a magical substitute of a real object. In her opinion, "anonymity is sharply at variance with the very idea of magical substitution" (114). According to Finkelberg, the anonymity of images, the fact that they do not refer to any specific thing or person, rules out magical substitution in Homer. The figures on the shield or Hephaistos's handmaidens (automata) should instead be classified as *living artifacts*.

58 Information about gifts for Peleus is dispersed in the *Iliad*. Kullmann (1960:232–234) demonstrates in detail that these are wedding gifts and that Homer was familiar with the story of the wedding.

59 Paton 1912:1–4.

60 Teukros's arrow cannot pierce Sarpedon's armor (12.400), and Aias's spear cannot pierce his shield (12.404–405); Helenos's arrow rebounds from Menelaos's breastplate (13.586–587).

shattered, and his shield fell to the ground. Finally, his breastplate was loosened and fell off, and now Euphorbos could approach him from behind (like Apollo) and strike with his spear in the same spot which Apollo chose, in the back between the shoulders. Retreating, the wounded and disarmed Patroklos was killed by Hektor. It is evident that the hero had been protected by an impenetrable breastplate, which was removed by the god's blow.[61] In *The Nibelungenlied,* Siegfried also goes into battle bathed in the blood of a dragon, which makes him invulnerable. But he gets killed by a blow between the shoulder blades, where there was a single spot untouched by the blood. As we can see, it is the same spot as in Patroklos. Parallel to the story of Siegfried is also the myth about Thetis making Achilles invulnerable by dipping him as a baby in the River Styx.[62] These stories should be considered early, i.e. traditional, and are confirmed by Hesiod's testimonium (fr. 300).[63]

Hektor went to fight with Achilles, wearing the armor which he had ripped off Patroklos's body. This impenetrable armor poses a problem even for Achilles, because it covers the whole body. Finally, Achilles decides to drive his spear into Hektor's throat, where the collarbones meet. Achilles' attack is effective, because the place where he hits Hektor is, as the poet stresses, the only one where the blow can be lethal (*Iliad* 22.320–325):

> ...φρονέων κακὸν Ἕκτορι δίῳ
> εἰσορόων χρόα καλόν, ὅπῃ εἴξειε μάλιστα.
> τοῦ δὲ καὶ ἄλλο τόσον μὲν ἔχε χρόα χάλκεα τεύχεα
> καλά, τὰ Πατρόκλοιο βίην ἐνάριξε κατακτάς·
> φαίνετο δ' ᾗ κληῗδες ἀπ' ὤμων αὐχέν' ἔχουσι
> λαυκανίην, ἵνα τε ψυχῆς ὤκιστος ὄλεθρος

> [Achilles] was considering a mortal blow to divine Hektor,
> seeking the likeliest place on his fair body, which would be most
> open to a blow.
> And the rest of his [Hektor's] body was covered so much by the
> bronze armor,

61 Kakridis 1961:291–292; after him Janko 1992:409; Nagy 1999:173; Kullmann 2005.

62 In some versions she immersed him in a boiling cauldron or put him in a fire at night, as the goddess Demeter did with Demophon (fire burnt out the mortal element), while during the day she rubbed him with ambrosia (Apollodorus *Library* 3.13.6; Frazer 1921b:69 and Appendix 1.311–317).

63 Janko 1992:409–410. Scholars point to another similarity, between Euphorbos's blow and Hagen's cowardly blow from behind. Having stolen Siegfried's armor, Hagen throws a spear, aiming at the spot untouched by dragon's blood, and then—just like Euphorbos—escapes.

> the beautiful armor, which he had ripped off Patroklos's might, when he killed him;
> but where the collarbones, reaching from the shoulders, encircle the neck, a piece of tender neck could be seen,
> where the destruction of life is the quickest.

The poet gives a reason for choosing this spot: it is the best place to inflict a quick death. But it is not very logical. Why should Achilles worry about the speed of his enemy's death? Nowhere in the *Iliad* can we find a single description of prolonged agony caused by a wound—death is always instantaneous after a blow. It cannot be a gesture of chivalric compassion, because Achilles shows no respect for his enemy (quick death would probably mean the effectiveness of Achilles' strike). He is not afraid of an attack, because he knows the final blow is his. Probably most importantly, Hektor does not die at once, because there must be an exchange of words with Achilles. That is why the narrator, having first precisely indicated the spot pierced by the blade, adds that it did not cut the windpipe, and Hektor was able to speak. This explanation, however, is improbable. Achilles must have known the virtue of his own armor and that is why he chose a spot unprotected by the breastplate.[64] Homer could not, I think, choose a different spot for Achilles to wound Hektor, because it would violate the traditional image of Achilles' armor, given him by Peleus, as miraculous and magic.[65]

According to Kakridis,[66] the loss of Achilles' armor and its replacement with a new one are connected with the creation of a monumental work and are Homer's innovation. In the *Aethiopis,* Achilles and Memnon wear armor forged by Hephaistos (such a source for Memnon's armor is indicated by Vergil *Aeneid*

64 See Paton 1912. In the figure of Achilles, there is a combination of the motifs of magic armor and magic skin. Magic skin always has a weak spot which does not protect against the blade of a weapon. For example, the skin of Aias is invulnerable everywhere except his armpit or neck. When he was an infant, Herakles wrapped him in his lion skin. Only the place covered by the quiver failed to fulfill its magic function. Hence, the stories about Aias's problems with suicide (*Scholia in Sophoclem, Ajax* 833, Tzetzes, *Scholia in Lycophronem*, 455–461, *Scholia in Homerum, Iliad* 23.821; Frazer 1921b:60–61). Kyknos has armor invulnerable to metal weapons, but Achilles manages to defeat him, by hitting him in the head with a huge stone or strangling him with the straps of his helmet.

65 Allan (2005:11) also notices the singularity of this situation. He remarks that this is the only instance when the place where the spear enters the body is described before the assault. In this way, the poet suggests that Achilles chooses his aim before casting the weapon. However, the conclusions Allan draws are in keeping with narratology and Homer's rationalism: "As the action pauses, the narrative presents Hector as if from Achilles' perspective: the enemy is perceived as an armoured target, but one that Achilles knows well (since it is his own armour) so that he can quickly locate its weakest point." If we followed this line of reasoning further, we would arrive at the conclusion that Achilles, fighting in this armor, should be afraid of being wounded in the neck, which is absurd, because it does not fit the traditional image of his death.

66 Kakridis 1961:288–297.

8.383–384). Homer keeps this idea for the duel of Achilles and Hektor. The introduction of the motif of dressing Patroklos in Achilles' armor, which leads to its loss, made it necessary to supply a new one for the hero. However, this idea caused confusion in the plot of the Cycle; when Aias and Odysseus quarrel over the armor of the dead Achilles, the doubling of the armor makes their quarrel immaterial—each of them could get one! We could almost conclude that the *Iliad* is an unnecessary element disturbing the logic of the Cycle. If we adopt such a para-Neoanalytic point of view, we should acknowledge that the original and, therefore, traditional armor is the one given to Peleus by the gods at his wedding, which he in turn passed on to his son; this is the armor that Odysseus and Aias quarrel over.

This confusion reveals not so much the incompetence in the transformation of a motif as rather a certain degree of independence in an oral song belonging to a cycle. The modifications introduced in a particular song do not influence the basic plot of the macro-story. The *Iliad* is not an exception; rather, it manifests a typical attitude of the singer towards traditional material.

Therefore, the idea of two sets of armor at Achilles' disposal does not seem to be restricted to the *Iliad*. In the story reported in the *Aethiopis*, Achilles, having killed Memnon, also takes possession of enchanted armor made by Hephaistos. Memnon's mother, the goddess Eos, must have gotten it for her son, the Ethiopian king.[67] As we have seen, Memnon's miraculous armor is necessary to make the duel of the heroes more equal. The conclusion we can draw is that Achilles, going into a fight, must always have had enchanted armor. The confusion with two sets of armor may also have resulted from the need to include in the *Iliad* this cyclic theme present in the *Aethiopis*, because from the point of view of the plot, the Trojan does not really need magic armor. Hektor would, then, be a duplicate of Memnon to a much greater degree than Sarpedon, the leader of Trojan allies killed by Patroklos, is.[68]

Nonetheless, many scholars share Kakridis's opinion[69] that the story of Achilles getting his armor before the Trojan expedition from his father, who received it from the gods at his wedding to Thetis (*Iliad* 17.195–196), is a Homeric

67 Vergil *Aeneid* 1.489 *Eoasque acies et nigri Memnonis arma* 'battle-ranks of the Eastern army and black Memnon's armor'—indubitably a type-scene. A Melian amphora from Rhenea of the mid-7th century, now at the museum in Mykonos, shows a naked man being given armor by a woman. It is thought to represent Achilles and Thetis (Johansen 1967:104–122). West (1995:207) rightly questions whether it is really the scene from the *Iliad* 19.3–13, because it can also represent Achilles' departure for Troy. But why couldn't the artists have intended the figures to be Memnon and Eos?

68 The invulnerability of Sarpedon's armor may be inferred from the futile attacks of Teukros and Aias, 12.400–405.

69 Kakridis 1961:290. Apart from the Neoanalysts, also Janko 1992:333; Edwards 1991:139–141.

innovation. According to them, the scene of Thetis's handing over the armor to her son (19.12–13) in the *Iliad* reflects the original version, in which Achilles gets the armor forged by Hephaistos from his mother before leaving for Troy.[70] We should, however, remember that the motif of a wedding gift is probably no less traditional. The similarity to the wedding of Kadmos and Harmony, during which the young couple receive gifts from the gods, induces us to recognize such circumstances as a typical source of magic objects. In epic, magic objects fall from the heaven, as does the Palladion, or they are gifts from gods, often given at special weddings: of Kadmos and Harmony, and Peleus and Thetis.[71] The priority of Peleus's armor is corroborated, however, mainly by the concept of a magical object passed from father to son, like Odysseus's bow, which Telemachos can use, but the suitors cannot. The problem, whether Achilles got this armor from his father or his mother, is the problem of the multiformity of tradition. Moreover, one does not exclude the other. In many South Slavic songs, a hero gets armor belonging to his male ancestors, but the person who gives it to him is a woman, often related to him.

Of Achilles' magical attributes, there is only one thing which Patroklos cannot take—the spear. The narrator of the *Iliad* explains that it is so heavy only Achilles can use it (16.140–141). For a time, it was believed that the description corresponded to a spear from the Mycenaean period: it was bigger than the later ones (like Aias's pike or Hektor's long spear) and used singly (heroes commonly armed themselves with two spears). According to Van Wees, however, here we are dealing with the epic exaggeration of the capabilities of past heroes, who must be extraordinarily tall and strong, and also must possess weapons proportional to their huge frame.[72] Already the first Unitarians, like Knight (1816), explained that Patroklos didn't take Achilles' wooden spear, because, as it was partially wooden, Hephaistos would not be able to make a new one in his forge.[73] Such a problem would not occur to the author of the *Iliad*. The only sensible explanation is the magical force of the spear, which never misses its aim and always kills: φόνον ἔμμεναι ἡρώεσσιν 'to be death to heroes' (16.144).[74] With this spear, Patroklos would be invincible, and, what is more important to the structure of the *Iliad*, without it Achilles would not be able to defeat Hektor

70 Burgess 2009:16: "Thetis' bestowal of divine armor to her son in the *Iliad* also analeptically alludes to the Phthia armoring episode."

71 Compare the wedding gifts given by Aphrodite to Andromache, when Hektor was taking her from her father Eëtion's house: ἄμπυξ 'diadem, frontlet', κεκρύφαλος 'hair net', πλεκτὴ ἀναδέσμη 'woven band', and κρήδεμνον 'veil' (*Iliad* 22.468–472).

72 Van Wees 1992:17–21.

73 An opinion expressed already in *Scholia Venetiana*.

74 The Aeolic form ἔμμεναι ἡρώεσσιν probably indicates the traditional character of this formula. A similar spear, never missing its aim, belonged to the hunter Kephalos.

later. Homer seems to be so attached to the exceptional nature of this spear that the epithets applied to Achilles' spear, when Patroklos could not take it, are also used to describe Patroklos's own spear which shattered in his hand, when he was dazed by Apollo: μέγα στιβαρόν 'very heavy/huge/strong' (16.141= 802).

The *Iliad* also presents another exceptional feature of this spear: when it misses its aim, it returns to its owner. After a futile throw at Aeneas, the spear is brought back by Poseidon (20.322–324), and after a similarly futile throw at Hektor, it is brought back by Athena (although Athena has just spoken with Hektor and set off to fight in the guise of his brother Deiphobos, she returns the spear to Achilles so that Hektor does not notice it, 20.276–278). The magical power of the artifact is transferred to a divine agent who acts on behalf of the owner of the object. For Homer, the substitution of magical power with the intervention of gods is symptomatic. The scene of Achilles and Hektor's duel fully reveals the character of Homer's rationalism: Achilles can repeat his throw, whereas Hektor cannot, because he intended to take a spear from Deiphobos, but Deiphobos had already fled the battlefield. Homer presents it as a deceit of Athena, who impersonates Deiphobos. The goddess, then, embodies both real human behavior (Deiphobos's flight) and the magical force of Achilles' spear (when she, unnoticed, returns it to him). Hektor not even for a moment suspects his brother of betrayal; he knows immediately that it is Athena's deceit (22.298–299). Here rationalism is confined to laying responsibility for all events on the shoulders of the gods.

The enchanted nature of the spear can be explained by its origin. There are two versions: in the *Iliad,* Cheiron himself cut a stem from a Pelian ash tree, shaped it, and gave it to Peleus (16.140–145), while in the *Kypria,* Cheiron cut off the stem, Athena polished it, and Hephaistos fitted it with a tip.[75] The story of the spear reveals the magic and ritual origin of this motif: the maker of a magic object endows it with his/her own magical power. Peleus or Cheiron, who is a double for Achilles' father and who educates the hero in killing and healing, initiates the process of making Achilles' spear. This spear plays its most important role in the story of Telephos, whom it both wounds and heals, since in the realm of magical consciousness, the damage can be repaired only by the object which caused it. Telephos's spear wound cannot be healed until the rust scraped by Achilles off the blade of his spear proves effective. It cannot be any rust, but only the rust from this particular object.[76]

75 According to the *Little Iliad* (fr. 5), the spear had a golden hoop connecting the head with the shaft. In Pindar *Nemean* 3.33, Peleus himself fells a young ash tree. Janko (1992:333–334) believes this is an innovation of the lyric poet.

76 On such magical healing see Frazer 1921b:188–191n1. Asklepios used the Gorgon's blood as a magic elixir (Apollodorus *Library* 3.10.3). The blood from the veins on the right side could raise

Magical power is present in an object which passes from one generation to another within a single family. Achilles, who is referred to as a descendant of Aiakos (16.140), got the spear from Peleus, and after Achilles' death, it came to Neoptolemos. Similarly, Agamemnon's staff, the σκῆπτρον πατρώϊον ἄφθιτον αἰεί 'ancestral staff, imperishable ever' (*Iliad* 2.41, 186), is not only an emblem of authority, but also has special power because it has a divine origin and has been one family's possession for many generations (*Iliad* 2.101–108):

> ἔστη σκῆπτρον ἔχων τὸ μὲν Ἥφαιστος κάμε τεύχων.
> Ἥφαιστος μὲν δῶκε Διὶ Κρονίωνι ἄνακτι,
> αὐτὰρ ἄρα Ζεὺς δῶκε διακτόρῳ ἀργεϊφόντῃ·
> Ἑρμείας δὲ ἄναξ δῶκεν Πέλοπι πληξίππῳ,
> αὐτὰρ ὃ αὖτε Πέλοψ δῶκ' Ἀτρέϊ ποιμένι λαῶν,
> Ἀτρεὺς δὲ θνῄσκων ἔλιπεν πολύαρνι Θυέστῃ,
> αὐτὰρ ὃ αὖτε Θυέστ' Ἀγαμέμνονι λεῖπε φορῆναι,
> πολλῇσιν νήσοισι καὶ Ἄργεϊ παντὶ ἀνάσσειν.
>
> [Agamemnon] stood, holding the staff, which Hephaistos had
> wrought with toil.
> Hephaistos gave it to Zeus, son of Kronos, the ruler.
> Zeus in turn gave it to the Guide, Slayer of Argos.
> Hermes, the ruler, gave it next to Pelops, driver of horses,
> And this Pelops in turn gave it to Atreus, shepherd of the people,
> And Atreus on his death left it to Thyestes, rich in flocks,
> And this Thyestes in turn left it to Agamemnon to bear
> as a lord of many isles and all Argos.

Made by Hephaistos, the staff comes directly from Zeus and is a sign of his approval for the rule of several generations of the Atreidai. It is passed exclusively from father to son and only they can use it. Similarly, the spear, given its power at its creation by Cheiron (or in another version by Cheiron, Athena, and Hephaistos), retains it for the descendants of Peleus. The material from which a

---

the dead, whereas the blood drawn from the left was lethal. Two phials of this blood were given by Athena to Erichthonios: one contained deadly poison, the other a miraculous cure (Euripides *Ion* 999–1017, Frazer 1921b:16n1). Such logic is also applied to people's contact with gods. Only the god who brought misfortune can remove it. That is why Apollo—who was recognized as the one responsible for sending the plague—was worshiped as Paion (Nilsson 1968, 1:541; Muellner 1996:100–101). In the face of a misfortune, man must find out who has brought it on him and for what offence, and he must also find a way to propitiate the angry deity. On the use of sympathetic and contagious magic in the medicine of primitive tribes, see Turner 1970:Chs. 6 and 7.

magic object is made—gold or ash[77]—is already enchanted, but its magical power is magnified by the *mana* of its divine creator.[78]

Achilles' immortal horses, which—like the Argo—could speak with a human voice and foretell the future (e.g. the death of the hero going into battle, *Iliad* 19.408–418),[79] are Poseidon's wedding gift to Peleus.[80] Miraculously swift, divine horses are a frequent attribute of a hero in epic. In the *Iliad*, such horses belong also to Aeneas and later to Diomedes, after he has taken them away from Aeneas; they have as honorable an origin as Agamemnon's staff. In the *Doloneia*, Odysseus steals Rhesos's horses, which in other versions of this legend have very unusual properties—in one, Rhesos can become invincible if he and his horses drink water from the Skamandros.[81] In the Cycle, such divine and swift horses belong to Memnon. Both Achilles and his enemies possess enchanted animals. Perhaps Memnon's horses are being evoked, when Hektor speaks to his horses as if he were speaking to people, trying to motivate them to a special effort. Extraordinary horses are one of the most significant elements of tradition, despite the fact that heroes very rarely drive chariots or fight from them.[82] Miraculous horses, speaking with a human voice, are a frequent element of the fairy-tale landscape and mythological epic (heroic tale).[83] For example, in the Armenian epic *David of Sassoun*, David has a horse, Qurkik Jalali, which he has

77 Spears were made exclusively of young ash trees, so they are synonymically 'ash trees' αἱ μελίαι / ἡ μελίη. Ash spears also appear regularly in Nordic poetry.

78 That is why I disagree with the distinction made by Edwards (1987:84) that the origin of the object is significant, since Achilles' staff is presented as manmade (the tree is cut, the leaves removed), while Agamemnon get his directly from Zeus.

79 Bierl 2012:159–160: "Comparative research supports the hypothesis that the horses, as chthonic and infernal animals which are endowed with prophetic speech and linked to water, are again linked to shamanic concepts in which the horse serves as the medium for the shaman on his journey to the otherworld."

80 16.867 is wrongly viewed as an interpolation. The *Pindar Scholia* mention that Poseidon's gift was horses, and Hephaistos's, a dagger. But Peleus might have received the dagger or sword earlier, in recognition of his purity. Apollorodorus (*Library* 3.13.33; Frazer 1921b:64–65) tells the story of Peleus's hunt with Akastos, who secretly was his enemy. Akastos hid Peleus's magic sword (which gave him invincibility and success in hunting) in cow's dung. In this way, he exposed the hero to the danger of death from the centaurs, who found him unarmed, but Cheiron saved him and found the sword. In the myth, there is a noticeable relationship between the hero's purity, which is his typical state, and impurity, which temporarily stains him. These personal characteristics are transferred to the object representing the hero. A similar issue of the purity of the hero appears in many other epic stories (moral purity is here related to ritual purity).

81 Bierl (2012) demonstrates a network of links between the story of Rhesos in the *Doloneia* and the rest of the *Iliad*, in which the motif of magic horses plays a significant role.

82 One of the proofs of this is the abundance of epithets which emphasize the heroes' ability to drive a chariot. Some of them certainly belong to an older epic tradition. Homeric heroes rarely use chariots because of the change of tactics and the decreased importance of chariots in war at the beginning of the first millennium BCE.

83 Carpenter 1974:22.

inherited from his father and which he has earned by his own actions. This horse can speak and perform heroic deeds.[84] In the songs of Prince Marko, his horse (*Marko and Philip the Magyar*) and his falcon (*Marko in Captivity in Sarajevo*) can speak with a human voice.[85] The horses of both David and Prince Marko are also exceptionally strong and very brave in battle.[86]

In epic songs, not everyone can use a magic object, only its rightful owner. However, if the rightful owner makes it a gift to someone else, then the right to possess the object passes to the new owner (not necessarily a son). Achilles gets divine gifts from Peleus, then gives the armor and horses to Patroklos;[87] in a similar way, Agamemnon's staff passes from one owner to another. When the Greeks learn that the fall of Troy will not happen without the bow of Herakles, they send Odysseus and Diomedes to Philoktetes.[88] Although Odysseus gets Herakles' bow and arrows by deceit, they are not used by anyone else, because he also convinces Philoktetes to go to Troy. And there Philoktetes kills Paris. Herakles' bow in Philoktetes' hands is set against Apollo's bow in Alexander's. Odysseus's conduct towards Philoktetes is not dictated by pity or friendship but, as we can guess, by the conviction that the bow and arrows in themselves would be useless to the Achaeans, who would not be able to use them. Similarly, the suitors cannot stretch Odysseus's bow. But Telemachos can, as the poet says (*Odyssey* 21.128)—certainly not because he is stronger, but because he is Odysseus's heir. This clearly suggests the bow's magical power, because the suitors are older and stronger than Telemachos; moreover, the boy has never seen the bow before, so Odysseus could not have disclosed the secret of stringing it to him.

Achilles' armor is similarly useless to Odysseus. This is evidenced by the fact that he voluntarily gives it to Neoptolemos, although earlier he quarreled over it with Aias (Apollodorus *Epitome* 5.11 λαβὼν παρ' ἑκόντος Ὀδυσσέως τὴν

84 Although it didn't protect the hero against an ambush in Melik's tent, the horse "leaped away as it sensed deceit"–only the hero disregarded the animal's behavior. The horse takes the baby David to Msir, and then manages to avoid being caught by Melik by jumping over the wall of the town.

85 His miraculous horse Šarac drinks wine with the hero and warns him against dangers, waking him up with his hoof; the horse also predicts his death, by stumbling and shedding tears (*The Death of Marko Kraljević*).

86 These animals reveal counterintuitive traits, because they combine the category of animal with the category of person.

87 Compare the motif of donning armor which belongs to someone else.

88 According to Proclus's summary, Philoktetes is brought by Diomedes only. Other sources mention a joint expedition of Diomedes and Odysseus (Apollodorus *Epitome* 5.8, Quintus Smyrnaeus *Posthomerica* 9.325–479, Hyginus *Fabulae* 103, Euripides *Philoktetes*, TGF fr. 613 N[2]). Only in Sophocles is Odysseus accompanied by Neoptolemos; however, the tragedian seems to be familiar with the version with Diomedes (*Philoktetes* 570–597), for more, see Frazer 1921b:222–223.

τοῦ πατρὸς πανοπλίαν). This motif returns in the *Iliad*: when Hektor puts on the armor stripped from Patroklos, Zeus is indignant that Achilles' enchanted armor went to someone who was not the hero's equal. Zeus's words indicate that the appropriation of Achilles' armor will bring about Hektor's death (17.184–208). It seems that donning the armor of a better warrior may amount to the breaking of a taboo, which brings misfortune, or even punishment, to the unworthy owner.[89]

Here another principle is at play: magic can be overcome with greater magic. Let's consider a situation just before a spear is thrown. The spear has already been prepared with various spells so that it never misses, yet at the last moment a hunter or warrior gives it an additional spell. If he misses, though he is an unerring marksman, what has made his skills and spells fail? He does not blame his emotional tension. He does not find fault with himself. It means that his action must have encountered one stronger than his own. If his opponent was not more skilled, then he must have had more powerful magic.

This principle is visible in the abduction of Helenos. The starting point is characteristic of the Trojan Cycle: the Achaeans cannot capture Troy, which means there is yet another obstacle preventing their success. Kalchas announces that Helenos knows the prophecies that protect the city. Abducted by Odysseus, Helenos reveals that Troy won't fall until three tasks are completed: 1) to bring Pelops's bones to Troy, 2) to persuade Achilles' son Neoptolemos to join the Achaeans, and 3) to steal the Palladion, the holiest Trojan relic. The first and third conditions are, naturally, connected with magic: the bones of the hero are expected to magically support the Achaeans in combat;[90] and theft of the Palladion will deprive the Trojans of its magical assistance. The completion of these tasks increases Achaean magical power and reduces the magical power of the enemy. Kalchas's behavior is also revealing, because he does not try to prove that he is a better seer than the best seer of the enemy. His action is typical of a sorcerer. He realizes that behind the failure to capture Troy, there is magic more powerful than the Achaeans possess. To overcome it, one must know what

89 Hektor comes into possession of Achilles' armor without overcoming him in battle, i.e. without obtaining the right to it. Hektor seems to be aware of this, if we can judge by the irony detectable in his words to Dolon, who demands Achilles' horses and chariot as a reward for the night raid on the Achaeans: "Now be my witness Zeus himself, the loud-thundering lord of Hera, that on those horses no other man of the Trojans shall mount, but it is thou, I declare, that shalt have glory in them continually" (10.329–331; translation, A. T. Murray). Naturally, the chariot and horses would have to be won first, but these words ironically suggest that Dolon does not deserve them.

90 The motif of the bones of a hero as a talisman appears also in the corpse of Laomedon, Priam's father, who was moved from his grave near the Scaean Gate, which had to be widened in order to introduce the wooden horse. This violation of his grave was understood as a prophecy of the ruin of the city (see Robertson 1970).

it is. Such knowledge, in his opinion, must belong to the Trojan prophet, who should be forced to reveal his secrets. So, as we can see, the art of prophecy is connected with the knowledge of magic.

Magic versus Homer's rationalism

Magic objects are used in narrative patterns typical of oral epic. Such is, for example, the motif of bribery, where a magic object is used as inducement. In the Theban myth, there are two cases of bribery involving the necklace of Harmonia: it is offered to Eriphyle, first by Polyneikes, and then by his son Thersandros. Its desirability is not only due to exquisite workmanship, but also its magical power. The same story pattern appears in the Trojan Cycle, when Priam bribes Astyoche to convince Eurypylos, her son with Telephos, to go to Troy, where he is killed by Neoptolemos. Eurypylos thus meets the same fate as Amphiaraos, who is killed during the expedition against Thebes, in which he participates against his will. In both the stories of Thebes and Troy, there is bribery, and the person bribed is the wife or the mother of the hero, who dies as a result of her scheme. The bribed woman acts for the benefit of her brother: Astyoche is a sister of Priam, and Eriphyle a sister of Adrastos, the man who persuades Polyneikes to commit bribery. Moreover, the conflict of fathers is passed down onto their sons: Eurypylos and Neoptolemos continue their father's struggles. The bribe offered to Astyoche is Dionysos's golden grapevine, originally one of the wedding gifts for Harmonia, taken from Samothrace. A grapevine was the cause of Telephos's defeat. He was wounded because a divinity and a hero undertook to stop a warrior who is in a destructive rage. Telephos—by the will of a deity—tripped over a grapevine. Similarly, the cooperation of Apollo and a hero puts an end to the fury of destruction, with which Patroklos and Achilles attack the enemy.[91] Such warriors, able to perform deeds which went beyond normal human limits, are certainly closer to gods than mortals.

This leads us to wonder why Homeric warriors do not wear any amulets protecting them against misfortune and death on the battlefield. Warriors of all

[91] In the *Iliad*, λύσσα is ascribed to Hektor (9.239, 305) and Achilles (21.542). On battle frenzy and similar behavior of warriors in Indo-European culture, see: Lincoln 1975; Nagy 1999:34–38; Singor 1991:46. Griffin (1980:92) claims superiority for Homeric warriors: "We are not dealing with berserkers in the pages of Homer, whatever Mycenaean warriors may have been like in reality. Self-respect, respect for public opinion, the conscious determination to be a good man—these motives drive the hero to risk his life ..." Were these features really foreign to "more primitive" Germanic warriors? The pattern of the cooperation of a god and a man aimed at killing a hero in a frenzy probably originated in the conviction that such a warrior is unstoppable by usual means. A warrior in a trance cannot control himself and pushes on, though he should realize that it will end in his death. 'Wolfish rage' λύσσα is certainly akin to the battle fury of berserks.

epochs have always had such amulets and believed in their power to save. Even today's emancipated man has not given amulets up and uses them whenever he is afraid of death.[92] We may come across their traces in the Homeric poems, but the question remains why they are so well concealed and appear so rarely.[93] In Homeric epic, amulets are replaced with a god's personal aid. Human success is a sign of divine help, whereas failure indicates a lack of divine support. Willcock carried the reasoning further: divine intervention is inferred from the success of an action. However, not all events in Homer match this assumption, so Van der Mije suggested that divine intervention was indicated by an *extraordinary turn of events*.[94] Their extraordinary character may have a rational explanation or not, like the removal of Paris from the battlefield. Van der Mije classifies the return of Achilles' spear by Athena as uncertain from the point of view of its rational explanation.[95]

One can see here a clear distinction between religion and magic in the understanding of the effectiveness of human actions: a person using magic is convinced that by applying the right spell, he can affect the outcome of his undertaking, whereas when the spell is replaced by prayer, man is not only unsure about the outcome, but sees himself as helpless against the will of the gods, whom he can only ask for grace. Of course, it does not mean that a man who uses magic would feel like a master of nature or that a prayer would not contain elements forcing the deity to act in a desired way. All in all, however, Homer's faith is not as far removed from magic as it might seem. The failure of an undertaking means a conflict with an opposite action of a deity, just as in the case of magic it meant a conflict with stronger magic.[96] The success of an undertaking means the assistance of a deity, for which a warrior usually prays.[97]

92 The possession of an amulet may indicate belief in a divinity's protection (like later holy medals, pictures of saints etc.); in the *Iliad*, however, there are no mentions of such objects.

93 Achilles' long hair, which he grows as a votive offering for the river in his native land, fulfills the function of an amulet ensuring safety. Murray (1907:123–124) assumes that all the Achaeans made similar vows before the expedition, as evidenced by the epithet κομόοντες 'long-haired'.

94 Willcock 1970; Van der Mije 1987:246.

95 Van der Mije 1987:246.

96 Sometimes opponents expect support from the same deity, but the deity has reasons to favor only one side (this is the predicament of Athena, who is, after all, the goddess guardian of the city of Troy).

97 Benveniste (1973:346–356) explains the Homeric notion κῦδος (*kydos* 'battle glory') as a magic "talisman of supremacy," which gods can give to one side or the other or to specific warriors. This divine support which deprives the other side of any chance (by stupefying or making helpless, which is typical of enslaving magic) becomes recognizable, thanks to extraordinary signs accompanying the hero's triumph. In this sense, *kydos* is an equivalent of the Slavic *čudo* 'miracle'. Benveniste 1973:355: "The *kydos* thus passes from one to another, from the Achaeans to the Trojans, then Hector to Achilles, as an invisible and magical attribute, surrounded by prodigies and a prodigy itself, an instrument of triumph, which Zeus alone holds forever and which he

If magic does not ensure the success of an undertaking, what about a magic object? Can it fail? All magic objects are described as gifts of gods. The same expression is used in reference to special abilities and heroic excellence, but also simply good or bad luck.[98] Some objects, despite their divine origin, do not protect their owner sufficiently or fail in the last moment. Areithoos's breastplate does not save his life, though it is a gift from Ares (*Iliad* 7.146); a bow and arrows from Apollo fail several times in Teukros's hands (*Iliad* 8.302, 311; 15.463–465); Pandaros misses his aim, shooting a bow that was a gift of Apollo (*Iliad* 2.827). Van der Mije concludes that in these instances a "divine gift" means a special ability given by the patron god of that ability. In *Iliad* 4.105–111, there is even a detailed description of Pandaros making his own bow. Scholars classify Hektor's helmet as a gift of Apollo (*Iliad* 11.353), which despite fulfilling its function, to protect the Trojan against spears, does not seem divine—magic—since later Hektor exchanges his own armor for that of Achilles. The incident with the helmet is presented as a miraculous intervention of Apollo. It seems that in these cases Homer did not feel bound by tradition; these objects do not fulfill practically any function in the song, so he preferred to use them for building suspense and introducing irony.

Assuming that the value of such an object is only symbolic does not seem to fit those times.[99] In Homer, the acquisition of special skills is regarded as a divine gift, or else it is believed that these skills were learned from a god. But the idea of an object being a divine gift cannot be confined to the god's patronage over a certain ability. There was a custom that at the end of his life a man gave the tools which he used in his work as a votive offering to a deity. They were "returned" to the god, to whom they had always belonged; the donor was given them only for a certain time to use. There is nothing contradictory in the fact that they were made by a human hand. The deity gives a command or permission to make an object and after the period of use, it returns to its rightful owner. This, in my opinion, is the reason why the Argo (the whole ship or at least its prow,

concedes for a day to kings or heroes." Girard (2005:161–163) reinterprets it as a constant alternation in the gaining of advantage by those involved in a conflict, as a religious-magical fascination with violence, ennobling the winners and paralyzing the defeated; it should be remembered that this state is never permanent, that the winner is only the "victor of the moment," and the defeated can regain the lost *kydos*.

98 Compare classification according to Van der Mije 1987:259–261.

99 Nikoletseas (2013:23–25) suggests that the need to provide Achilles with armor made by Hephaistos and not let him fight either without it, or using any other, respects the principle of substitution, which originally connected the possession of primary power to a totem (*scala totemica*): "The succedaneum theory may be viewed as a mechanism which creates copies of the original, immaterial totem, the likeness and intensity of which diminishes with each successive replication. ... The totemic law that a totem must be matched with the valor of the recipient is evident here. Only an equally valiant totem can match the valor of Achilles."

which possessed the gift of prophecy) was offered to Hera and placed in her temple. Similarly, Philoktetes, approaching the end of his life in Italy, did not pass Herakles' bow to anyone, but put it in the temple of this god/hero. Thus, there is no contradiction in the fact that Pandaros made his bow himself and that it was Apollo's gift.

The origin of such a way of reasoning is indubitably magical. On the manmade bow there must have been placed magic spells to ensure its proper functioning and protect it against counter-magic. The guarantor of the permanence of the spells was the god whose province was archery.[100] There are no images of Apollo's cooperation in shooting the bow, because it was not the god's role. However, it seems that in one case, the original character of the god's gift has been preserved. The object I have in mind is Teukros's bow, described by the epithet ἀμύμων (*Iliad* 15.463). The adjective ἀμύμων or ἀμώμητος[101] means 'one which cannot be found fault with'—it is praiseworthy, excellent, great. This epithet is often used in reference to heroes, and is connected with the importance of praise and reproach in archaic society. Reproach deprived man of honor and thus excluded him from the community, whereas praise, which confirmed his value, was expected by the warrior as something obvious. Sometimes this epithet is applied to the human *psychê* (θυμός, μῆτις), sometimes to other things, like ἔργα 'works, skills' of girls offered to Achilles; dance; αἶνος—Odysseus's tale; Achilles' grave; οἶκος 'home' as it should be, in Telemachos's opinion.

Commentators find it difficult to explain the use of this epithet for Teukros's bow. Teukros, defending the ships, aims an arrow at Hektor, but Zeus breaks the bowstring, and thus the shot is foiled. Anne Amory Parry is surprised by the epithet "without fault," since all other epithets applied to bows refer to their physical properties.[102] De Jong points out that the epithet adds emphasis to a fatal coincidence.[103] In effect, Zeus deprived Teukros of εὖχος, which is usually understood as 'battle glory, victory, distinction'. Nonetheless τὸ εὖχος is, above all, an object of εὔχεσθαι, 'object of prayer, wish' (Sophocles *Philoktetes* 1202), and also a solemn confirmation of a prayer, a 'vow' (Plato *Epigrammata* 5.3). Before an attack, the warrior would fortify a spear or arrow with a short request for success. It was tantamount to a spell designed to ensure the effectiveness of the attack.[104] In the mind of the one throwing the weapon, such an action may be thwarted only by stronger magic. In this case, a deadly shot is foiled by the intervention

100 Political pacts are also protected by magical sanctions, the guarantor of which is a god, mainly Zeus.

101 This word is connected with the name of the god personifying mockery—Μῶμος.

102 Amory Parry 1973:100.

103 De Jong 1987b:157–159. Her opinion is also shared by Janko 1992:279 *ad* 461–465.

104 The same meaning is in εὖχος ἀρέσθαι 'get the result of what one prays for'; εὖχος δοῦναι, ὀρέξαι, πορεῖν τινι 'to give someone the object of his prayer'.

of Zeus himself, who protects Hektor. He does not change the trajectory of the arrow, but breaks the bow. It requires a very strong magic indeed, because the weapon is protected by Apollo's magic. To break the ἐϋστρεφέα νευρήν 'well-twisted bowstring', Zeus has to destroy the magic protecting the bow from the moment of its creation.[105] The protection of weapons and armor with magic spells fulfills the function of amulets protecting warriors and ensuring the effectiveness of action. The use of the epithet ἀμύμων/ἀμώμητος is also justified here; it finds confirmation in the recent recognition that the primitive character of blame poetry as spells or curses could bring disaster and even death to the object of the attack. 'Invulnerable to reproach' originally meant 'invulnerable to the harmfulness of spells or curses'.[106]

We can say that the magical quality of an object does not determine its efficacy, because magic can be opposed by stronger magic. Every object can be given a magical quality by placing a spell upon it, which ensures its effectiveness. The protection by a spell means the protection by an appropriate god and often by a gift, usually a divine one. In epic poems, such a gift, customarily weaponry or a suit of armor, is connected with the motif of arming the hero for a fight. Pandaros made a bow himself, nonetheless it was still a gift of Apollo. Despite its divine origin, the bow partially fails: Pandaros hits his target, but does not do much harm to Menelaos; nor does Paris seriously injure Diomedes. Moreover, the bows do not save the lives of these two Trojan heroes.

I would like to point out two more issues, both connected with the concept of rationalism in Homer's work. If we return to the idea that Homer's rationalism is a primitive feature of Greek epic, let us first adopt the traditional standpoint which assumes that Greek poets enriched rational tales with more and more fantastical elements. The only approach that would not immediately expose the absurdity of this idea is the proposition put forward by Murray more than a hundred years ago. He based his concept on critical studies of the biblical tradition, which noted in the preserved biblical texts a series of various expurgations aimed at creating a uniform shape of Judaism. Murray tried to apply the same method to the Homeric epics.[107] In his opinion, Homer deliberately blurred the manifestations of excessive cruelty, barbarity, ritual killing, etc. It is not an unreasonable conclusion. We should be aware that the heroic epoch was

105 Perhaps the same primitive trait can be found behind the epithet applied to Archilochus's rejected shield ἔντος ἀμώμητον 'unblemished one' (fr. 5.2 W).

106 Amory Parry (1973) distances herself from understanding this epithet in abstract terms as 'blameless' and postulates a more functional understanding, typical of oral culture: 'beautiful in body', that is, handsome, strong, but not morally good. My understanding is similar, applying the meaning of the epithet to the reality of oral culture: 'blameless, that is invulnerable to a curse', can refer both to a person and to an object.

107 Murray 1907:107–140.

not more humanitarian than any other. But the question is, did Homer purge traditional songs of these horrors or did he compose his song, modifying scenes to avoid them? For example, did he insert the comment that Hektor's body was practically intact because Apollo covered it with a magical coating, in order to avoid a realistic description of Hektor's butchered corpse? And did he intentionally omit mentioning unconventional methods of fighting, because they were not fair play?

Blurring the picture of the awful nature of the real world is parallel to the way how fairy-tale and magical elements are blurred in the epic, so it is worth concentrating on it for a moment. Let us, for example, take a closer look at poison. Herakles dips his arrows in poison, and these arrows cause the death of Paris in the Cycle, because Philoktetes inherits Herakles' bow and arrows. In the *Odyssey*, Mentes tells Telemachos that Odysseus went in search of a poison for his arrows and got it from his [Mentes'] father (1.260–264). When we assume the "expurgatory" tendency we should imagine that Achilles, wounded in the "heel," also dies of poison,[108] which would be very realistic.[109] In the *Iliad*, there is a clear trace of this in the scene of dressing Menelaos's wound, when he was scratched by Pandaros's treacherous arrow. Machaon first sucks out the blood and only then does he apply herbs (4.218 αἷμ' ἐκμυζήσας). Was it possible that at some point there existed a version of Achilles' death which named a poison and left out all the miraculous elements, like immersing the baby in the Styx, dipping him in a boiling cauldron, or holding him over the flames? Naturally, it would be impossible, but not only from the perspective of narrative technique. In archaic and primitive cultures, no fact bears rational explanation only; behind each event there are magical and religious powers supporting one side or the

[108] This version of events is given by the author of the medieval *Excidium Troiae;* see King 1987:203. Rose and Robertson (1970) assume that the story of "Achilles' heel" could be traced to a poisoned arrow.

[109] Apollodorus writes (*Library* 3.12.6) that in case of being injured, Paris was expected to go to his first wife, Oinoe, the only one able to cure his wound. When he was hit by the arrow of Herakles, he was carried up Mount Ida to Oinoe, but the nymph, unable to forgive his unfaithfulness, did not keep her promise. When she came to her senses, she hurried to Troy with medicine for the wound, but Paris was already dead. Oinoe, seeing his corpse, hanged herself. Here the healing of the wound can only mean the possession of an antidote to poison. The motif of the impossibility of giving treatment seems typical and is also present in the story of Achilles' wound: Apollodorus reports that the physician Machaon was killed by Penthesileia, although Proclus's summary of the *Aethiopis* does not mention any victim of the Amazon. Because Machaon, who heals the wound of Philoktetes, plays an important role in the *Little Iliad*, we could conclude that Machaon was killed in the *Aethiopis* solely so that he could not heal Achilles' wound. (Tzetzes *Posthomerica* 571–595, mentioning the healing of Philoktetes by Machaon, follows the version of the *Little Iliad*; not so Quintus Smyrnaeus *Posthomerica* 9.461–468, who says that Podaleirios cured him. But Quintus had to reconcile various cyclic poems in order to work out a chronologically coherent version of events, so his testimony is much less credible.)

other. Since both fighting parties invoke these powers, it is not astonishing that there recurs the image of the scales of victory tipping to one side or the other.

Achilles' death is a good example of scholars' expectations regarding the degree of rationality in the Homeric epics. Jonathan Burgess has proposed a new explanation of this issue, which has been broadly accepted (Burgess 1995). He points out the incompatibility of various traditional explanations of Achilles' death, which occurred as a result of his being injured by Paris's arrow, not in the heel, as it is often reported, but in the ankle.[110] Burgess argues that the version of Achilles' invulnerability resulting from being immersed by his mother Thetis in the Styx, is a post-Homeric tradition, perhaps even as late as the Hellenistic period. His imperfect invulnerability is due to the fact that Thetis, bathing him, held him by the leg just above the foot, near the ankle. The versions in which the baby is immersed in a boiling cauldron or over flames are regarded by Burgess as older, but the aim of this treatment was to give immortality, and not invulnerability, to Achilles. So, originally, wounding the hero in the foot meant his immobilization (important in the case of the hero famous for the speed of his feet), but in the traditional epic, his death must have been later, and normal, like that of any other warrior.[111] This version must have been familiar to the author of the *Iliad*, who refers to it when Diomedes is wounded in the foot by Paris's arrow (11.369–400), because, according to Burgess, here also the injury is meant to immobilize the hero.

For Burgess, the two stories—one about dipping the hero in the river Styx, the other about placing him in boiling water or fire—are not convergent. The bath in the Styx is meant to change the boy's nature and it nearly succeeds. In the other, Thetis "tests" her children to learn if they are immortal (according to some sources Achilles was the youngest child of Peleus and Thetis, and the only one who survived her treatment), but does not change their nature. In effect, her children die, all except Achilles; the boy was saved by his father, who, appalled, interrupted the test. Thetis's actions indicate that she was either *uncomprehending or heartless.*[112]

Burgess's interpretation can hardly be right. Thetis does not "test" her children's mortality by placing them in a boiling cauldron, but tries to make them immortal. A meaningful analogy is the action of Medea, who in order to

[110] Burgess (1995:225) refers to the testimonia which use the word 'ankle' σφυρόν, or *talus*: Apollodorus *Epitome* 5.4; Quintus Smyrnaeus *Posthomerica* 3.62; Stesichorus fr. 43.2.8; *Secundus Mythographus Vaticanus* 205, 3.11.24.

[111] Such a version of events, according to Burgess (1995), is suggested by a scene on a Chalcidian amphora (mid-6th century BCE, Inscription Painter, now lost; Rumpf, pl. 12), which portrays a fight for the body of Achilles, who was struck by two arrows; one is sticking just above the foot, another in the flank.

[112] Burgess 1995:220.

rejuvenate an old ram placed it in a cauldron of boiling water, and then did the same with Pelias. The first attempt was successful, because the ram, cut into pieces, emerged whole and young. The second attempt was a failure—but a deliberate one. This myth seems to be a trace of the symbolic death and rebirth of the shaman, because there is the reintegration of the apparently dismembered body of the neophyte, who gets a new life when he gets a new body.[113] The presence of two motifs in the stories of Thetis—placing the baby in boiling water and in fire—confirms the opinion of scholars that these are the same actions, analogous to Demeter's attempts to immortalize Demophon, and Isis's with Arsinoe's child. Demeter did not breastfeed the baby left in her care, but anointed him with ambrosia and at night put him in the fire "like a firebrand." She did so in order to burn out all mortal parts of the baby.[114] Her attempts were rendered fruitless by Metaneira, mother of the child, who saw what was happening and started crying.

In all these cases the intervention of horrified parents interrupts the magic ritual. Contrary to Burgess's interpretation, it does not mean the saving of the child's life, but the loss of immortality, since the interruption of the procedure results in the hero's *imperfect immortality*. The hero has to experience death, but killing him must be, naturally, very difficult. In the myth the interruption of the ritual renders it only partly, not wholly ineffective, and thus, the imperfection of immortality is a part of the epic hero's nature.

It follows that we cannot make a significant difference between the attempts at giving Achilles immortality and invulnerability. In epic songs, what is important is the outcome of these rituals: imperfect immortality. This imperfect immortality is necessary, because, although the epics aim to show the difficulty of killing the hero, the hero must die. In the case of the invulnerability of his skin, there are two solutions: either there is one location on his body where he can be wounded, and it entails his instantaneous death; or the invulnerability to wounds is somehow bypassed, like strangling Kyknos with straps of his helmet. In the first case, death is usually irrational, because for an ordinary person, a wound in such a spot does not mean immediate death. However, this is what happens when Achilles is wounded in the ankle or Aias in the armpit. We can find parallels in other Indo-European epics: Siegfried, who is not protected by dragon's blood in one small spot on his back; Soslan in the Ossetian epic of the

113 Eliade 2001. The rituals of real or symbolic cannibalism in the cult of Zeus Lykaios must have had a similar character.

114 On this sanctification through fire, see Frazer 1921b:311–317; Edsman 1949:224; Delcourt 1965:66–68, and particularly 331–332.

Narts, who can be killed by crushing his knees;[115] and particularly the Norse hero Baldr, at whom gods can hurl various weapons for fun without harming him, and who dies only from an arrow made of mistletoe.

Burgess also maintains that Thetis does not have the ability to immortalize Achilles, which can be inferred from the death of her other children. Again, strict logic is not advisable. The motif of a test, which older siblings fail, and only the youngest one passes, is very frequent in folktales. This motif describes the initiation, which only the youngest, most inexperienced child can survive.

Excluding the possibility that Homer is relying on a story of Achilles' imperfect invulnerability, Burgess infers that the original story of this hero's death was as rational as a reference to it in the *Iliad*, when Diomedes is wounded in the foot (*Iliad* 11.369–400).[116] Unfortunately, this is the case of substituting our rationalism and logic for the spirit of the pre-archaic and archaic times. All versions of making the newborn Achilles invulnerable and the failed attempts at giving him immortality are equal and not mutually exclusive. There might have existed other versions of Achilles' extraordinary invulnerability, which in the end turns out to be imperfect. In the *Iliad*, Aeneas, speaking about Achilles, says that by his side there is always some god who protects him against destruction, but if a god shared the lots evenly, not so easily would Achilles defeat him, "even if he boasts he is wholly wrought of bronze" (20.102 οὐδ' εἰ παγχάλκεος εὔχεται εἶναι). I think that in the whole *Iliad* it would be difficult to find better evidence of Achilles' magical qualities. Homer is perfectly aware of them. He can even refer to different versions in which the hero is variously protected by magic. Aeneas's allusion is covered with a rationalistic interpretation, like in the scene of Diomedes being wounded. However, there are many parallels in Eurasian epics, in which heroes have a body of metal which makes them invulnerable—though, naturally, only for a time.[117] In Greek myth, there is Talos, made wholly of bronze, whose only weak spot, as his name suggests, is his ankle, like Achilles. Talos is a character of the Argonaut Cycle; it is not a coincidence that the same traits are found in both the hero and the monster.

115 Knees are often regarded as the seat of vitality and life. The toughening of Batraz, a hero of the Narts epic, in a huge hearth, may be seen as an analogy to placing Achilles and Demophon in the fire.

116 The subject of Homer following in this scene the traditional pattern of Achilles' death is developed in Ch. 5.

117 The hero of the Nart epic, Batraz, was born with a red-hot metal body, which was later hardened like a sword. When he fought, Batraz did not even need to use weapons, but crushed enemies with his metal body (though he had a sword whose loss caused his death). In Buryat uligeri, heroes are "silver" or "covered with silver," whereas their enemies, the abaasy, are described as "iron" or "covered with iron" (more in Ch. 6, below). In some epic magic runes, parts of Väinämöinen's body are made of iron or stone, or can be a snake (Meletinsky 2009:122).

This model of portraying heroes can also be found in pseudo-Hesiod's *Shield*, which portrays a battle between the Lapiths and centaurs. The former are described as (183): ἀργύρεοι, χρύσεια περὶ χροῒ τεύχε' ἔχοντες ("silver, with golden armor around their body"). The latter are depicted in a parallel formula, which because of the contrast in the weaponry stresses their wild nature and brutality (188): ἀργύρεοι, χρυσέας ἐλάτας ἐν χερσὶν ἔχοντες ("silver, with golden clubs in their hands"). Both sides of the conflict are equal in nature and described as silver, which by analogy to other epic traditions lets us infer that the image memory of a singer and his audience as well as traditional expression originally referred to the material of which the bodies of the heroes and their enemies were made, even if for the author of the *Shield*, the meaning was already metaphorical rather than literal. The warriors were silver, but their armor and clubs were golden. This *crescendo* in the choice of metal results from the typical gradation in the presentation of the extraordinary nature of epic heroes. The exaggeration used in the portrayal of the Lapiths and centaurs is specific to the epic method of introducing a dramatic struggle by stressing the uniqueness of both sides of the conflict. The centaurs retain a monstrous feature, which is revealed by the choice of the primitive club (this weapon is associated with brutality only in Greek epic). The Lapiths have golden armor, so they fight with spears (recall how Nestor overcame the primitive, magical power of Areithoos, who used to fight with a club). Nonetheless, describing both the Lapiths and centaurs as "silver" indicates that we are dealing with a mirror reflection of the hero and his enemy.

As we can see, in the epic tradition there were various ways to endow Achilles with unusual features, in order to exalt him as a hero comparable to other such figures. The Homeric epic focuses on the human aspect of the hero's fate, but it also takes cognizance of the fairy-tale and magical tradition, which it neither mentions, nor ignores; instead, it tries to give a new interpretation to unusual situations, in which tradition abounds. While the focus on the hero as a human is characteristic of Homer as an oral poet, his new interpretation of traditional material is not very rational.

In subsequent generations, the tendency towards rationalism progresses, shaping historical and philosophical thinking in Greece. For us Homer's poems are in a sense its first noticeable manifestation, but is that really true? For example, did he deliberately mention the name of Iphianassa (universally identified by the ancients with Iphigenia) among names of living persons, although—as Neoanalysts have demonstrated—there is evidence of his familiarity with the myth of Agamemnon's sacrifice of his daughter? Did he really do it in order to suppress the shameful human sacrifice? A possible answer may be provided by the theory of oral epic poetry. The singer threads compositional patterns like beads on a string, one after another, but with modifications. Each modification means the choice of a certain possibility, which may or may not be expected by the audience; this choice naturally affects the development of the plot.

In later chapters, I will discuss the method by which the singer evokes the memories of other versions known to his listeners, but only in order to disregard them. It happens, then, that some themes are abandoned and the expected effects do not follow; this is quite natural, despite an earlier thorough planning of the composition. Therefore, the same song may be subject to constant transformation, when the singer adapts it to his goals and the expectations of his audience. The only problem that remains is whether the version of the *Iliad* passed down to us by Homer is the only one which could have functioned in tradition. Here we touch upon the issue of the multiformity of the *Iliad*. The possibility that multiple versions of the *Iliad* exist, differing in "ideological" purport, has recently been pointed out by Casey Dué, who noticed the presence of a magic object in a fragment of the *Iliad* cited in Aeschines's speech *Against Timarchos*.[118] Unlike in the Alexandrian edition, the important role in this text is played by the golden amphora given to Achilles by his mother, Thetis—the amphora, whose destiny is to be an urn for the ashes of Patroklos and Achilles. Dué rightly draws conclusions about the remarkable consequences of this change to the narrative of the whole poem, because it is a clear allusion to the immortalization of the hero, known from the Cycle.[119] The versions of the *Iliad* and *Odyssey* that have come down to us follow another tradition, in which Achilles dies and leads a not-so-happy existence in Hades, although there are also gaps in these versions, through which a different eschatology of the heroes shines. If in the fourth century there were still other versions of the *Iliad* that did not oppose the immortalization of Achilles, it means that the process of rationalizing the *Iliad* and *Odyssey* was a longterm phenomenon, completed as late as the Hellenistic period.

Fantastic Figures Concealed in the *Iliad*

Cheiron and Memnon

One aspect of the tendency to rationalize the *Iliad* concerns the elimination of fantastic characters or the downplaying of their meaning. Hence, the Kyklops and Skylla emerge in Odysseus's tale, and the Chimera in Glaukos's. Apart from that, in the *Iliad* Herakles' fight with a monster attacking the Trojan coast is mentioned (20.144–148):

118 Dué 2001:33–47.

119 Dué 2001:44–45.

> Ὣς ἄρα φωνήσας ἡγήσατο κυανοχαίτης
> τεῖχος ἐς ἀμφίχυτον Ἡρακλῆος θείοιο
> ὑψηλόν, τό ῥά οἱ Τρῶες καὶ Παλλὰς Ἀθήνη
> ποίεον, ὄφρα τὸ κῆτος ὑπεκπροφυγὼν ἀλέαιτο,
> ὁππότε μιν σεύαιτο ἀπ' ἠϊόνος πεδίον δέ.
>
> Having said this, the Black Haired [Poseidon] led the way
> to the wall of divine Herakles, heaped up
> around [the city], high, which the Trojans and Pallas Athena
> built for him [Herakles] to take refuge from the monster,
> which chased him from the shore and across the plain.

This story, told in the typically Homeric fragmentary and allusive fashion, constitutes a part of the myth of Poseidon and Apollo's service to Priam's father, Laomedon, mentioned elsewhere in the *Iliad*. Though Homer manifests familiarity with many stories, which—in the versions known to us—possess folk-tale and fantastic motifs, the story of Herakles' fight is unique in this respect. His mention of the sea monster shows that the miraculous in itself is not unacceptable for the poet; however, he carefully selects the stories and contexts in his digressions, and chooses only such as he considers suitable for the main topic of the song.

In the *Iliad*, the elimination of a character or his traits unnecessary for the narration or for the assumed world view can be observed again and again. The most important in this context is passing over Memnon's participation in the battles of the *Iliad*, and that is why we will study it in more detail at the end of this section. Other figures are presented in the way which fulfills their intended function: in Book 2 of the *Iliad*, Thersites is deprived of his ancestry and merits; in the *Odyssey*, Odysseus presents only positive traits, while Paris in the *Iliad* has only negative ones. The elimination of fantastic elements might have been the reason why the author did not bring up the myth of Iphigenia and possibly why he introduced Phoinix to replace Cheiron, Achilles' mentor, the figure decisive in shaping the hero's character in the Cycle.

In the *Iliad,* the name of Cheiron appears in three places. He makes a miraculous spear for Peleus, the one which Achilles uses in the fighting; its magical properties are not discounted, but they are not mentioned openly. Cheiron teaches Achilles the art of healing, and Achilles passes his medical knowledge on to Patroklos (11.832 ὃν [sc. Achilles] Χείρων ἐδίδαξε, δικαιότατος Κενταύρων '[he] was taught by Cheiron, the most righteous of all the centaurs'). The centaur also teaches this skill to Asklepios (4.218–219). In his article "The Education of Achilles," Emmet Robbins, after a study of the written and visual sources, convincingly argues that Cheiron, the mentor of Achilles and other heroes, is not an invention of later poets, but a figure very much embedded in the Trojan Cycle; he is known to Homer, but deliberately suppressed in Phoinix's story of Achilles' boyhood and education. [120] Phoinix himself, according to Robbins, was created solely for the rhetorical purpose of the embassy scene.

Gregory Nagy proposes an interesting defense of Phoinix's presence in the embassy to Achilles, despite the frequent use of the dual (we might expect the plural, since there are three ambassadors).[121] His analysis of Book 9 of the *Iliad*, made from the standpoint of oral theory, is based on the traditional, as he sees them, themes of Achilles' quarrel with Odysseus and of the embassy consisting only of Aias and Phoinix. I would like to note that even if Nagy's analysis is correct,[122] it would be a younger tradition, created—as Kullmann[123] points out—by the need of a mentor constantly at Achilles' side (this function is fulfilled in turn, but never simultaneously, by Cheiron, Phoinix, and Patroklos) and by the principle of doubling of events in the Cycle. Phoinix is mentioned in the *Kypria*: he is credited with giving Neoptolemos his name and teaching him the art of war (fr. 13).[124] Kullmann presumes an older epic tradition in the case of Cheiron and a younger one in the case of Phoinix.[125] In the oral epic tradition, Cheiron must have been associated with the earlier stage of Achilles' life, teaching him to hunt and to heal, whereas Phoinix is associated with the later stage, teaching him how to wage war and to fight with an enemy.[126] Of the various skills taught by Cheiron, Homer chooses only the medical art and completely ignores the art of killing, much more important for the warrior, because he wants to draw a consistent picture of the hero's past and to contrast it with his behavior in the stories of the conflict with the king and his friend's death.[127] This is also why there is no mention of giving the hero special, magic food, which I have referred to earlier.[128] What Homer eliminates here, however, is not magic (eating parts of wild animals was expected to transfer their traits onto the consumer), but rather savagery, which emanates from those stories, and which was inappropriate for

120 Robbins 1993.

121 Nagy 1999:49–58.

122 While there may be some traditional evidence for the heroes' rivalry, the suggestion that this scene reveals Achilles' dislike for Odysseus is, in my opinion, unfounded. If Achilles had chosen to ignore Odysseus, addressing the embassy in the dual form, Odysseus would not have taken on responsibility for achieving the success of the mission.

123 Kullmann 1960:224.

124 Phoinix is otherwise connected to Neoptolemos; see Quintus Smyrnaeus *Posthomerica* 4.293, Proclus *Nostoi* 110.

125 Kullmann 1960:371.

126 Compare Robbins 1993:9.

127 See Ch. 6, pp. 558–561, below.

128 See Ch. 1, p. 37, above.

the hero's image. That is why this special food is replaced by the story of Phoinix giving Achilles typical food—wine and meat cut into small pieces, which a child could eat (9.486–491).

There are still major discrepancies as to the time when Cheiron and Phoinix had the juvenile Achilles in their care and the question of the presence of Thetis at Peleus's court. I think that the best answer to these issues is that they are remnants of the process of superseding the centaur Cheiron with the growing rationalism of epic stories. Cheiron's presence in the *Iliad* is the result of the singer's duty to respect tradition.

Memnon—crucial for the macro-story of the Cycle, where he is directly connected with Achilles' death—is not even mentioned in the *Iliad*. In the previous chapter, I have put forward some arguments to support the claim that Memnon was deliberately eliminated from the *Iliad*. The chronology of the Trojan War, according to which Memnon arrived at Troy after the events described in the *Iliad*, is not an argument sufficient to explain his absence. As I have already remarked in Chapter 1, all plots at the end of the war take place in the same time, the time of the completion of the Cycle. The killing of Hektor brings Achilles closer to death, just like the killing of Memnon. Memnon seems to be an element of an older tradition, but the introduction of his double in the form of Hektor makes Memnon's presence in the *Iliad* superfluous. Despite his absence, the plot of the Memnon story affected the shape of the *Iliad*. In the previous chapter, I have shown traces of Homer's familiarity with this story—the role of the Ethiopians. The author of the *Iliad* also shapes dramatic events differently, largely giving up the static accumulation of extraordinary elements in the fights of equally powerful opponents, though traces of the old technique are still perceptible.

In the tradition of the Cycle, Memnon has kept the features of a monster rival of the young hero. Homer's rationalism could be classified as a result of the tendency to suppress monsters, which/who are adversaries of the heroes. Herakles, Theseus, and the Argonauts all have encounters with monsters, whereas in "later" epics, tending towards the chivalric, the monstrous is discarded. Enemies such as Kyknos and Memnon lose their monstrous features in favor of heroic ones and become reflections of the heroes, whose task is to defeat them.[129] The Aetolian Cycle seems to take the middle ground; it starts with a fight with a monster (the Calydonian Boar), but later takes on the character of chivalric epic. No wonder that in the *Iliad* there is a reference to the knightly aspect of this epic—the story of Meleagros.

129 Memnon's unusual beauty may be also a reflection of Achilles' beauty, since Achilles was the most beautiful Achaean at Troy (*Iliad* 2.673–674).

When analyzing Memnon, one cannot avoid the issue of the historicity of the son of Dawn, since scholars frequently try to connect him with a real person. Depending on where they place the Ethiopians, Memnon's prototype is sought among eastern or Egyptian rulers. The choice is also strongly influenced by assumed time frames, which in turn depend on whether the scholar regards the *Aethiopis* as a later and epigonic work, or a song based on early prearchaic, or even Mycenaean oral tradition. These attempts, though often admirably erudite and based on subtle analysis, are unfortunately unconvincing. If the East is taken into consideration, the country is Elam,[130] and if Egypt,[131] the pharaohs of choice are Ramesses II[132] (who ruled in 1279–1213), Ammenemes II (1929–1895) or III (1842–1797),[133] and Amenhotep III (1417–1379). Amenhotep III has been proposed several times, but recently he has received a thorough analysis by Robert Drew Griffith.[134] However, in my opinion, Griffith's arguments indicate that the later Greeks, not without certain justification, could have identified Amenhotep III with Memnon rather than the figure of this pharaoh was reflected in the tradition of the Trojan Cycle. Amenhotep III died a natural death and identified himself with the son of Amun Ra, the Sun god, not the dawn goddess. More convincing seems to be the suggestion put forward by Nagy, who connects Memnon with the myth of the husband and son of Dawn, and compares him to Phaeton and Orion. According to Nagy, this myth is Indo-European in origin, which is confirmed by its similarity to the *Rig-Veda* hymns, in which the goddess Ušas "Dawn" is the wife, bride (1.115.2, 7.75.5 etc.), and mother (7.63.3, 7.78.3) of the Sun god Sūrya.[135] M. Janda's proposal goes in the same direction. This scholar derives the name of Memnon from the hypothetical root *μένμα, whose equivalent is the Sanskrit word *mánma* 'spirit, thought, plan, intention', which in turn is a derivative of the root *-man* 'to think'. In the *Rig-Veda* hymns, this noun refers to the process of thinking, which finds its expression in poetry, whose patron was the god of fire Agni, the same god who was sometimes called Ušas's son.[136] Both mythical and historical attempts at explaining the origin of Memnon are hardly convincing. However, when looking for a historical figure,

130 The king Khumban-numena (ruled in 691–689 BCE) appears in the Babylonian Chronicles as Me-na-nu (1.3.15–26): Śmieszek 1926; Hinz 1972; compare Griffith 1998:221. Their research was based on Hüsing 1917.

131 The possibility of its being Egypt is strongly enforced by the scene of *psychostasia*, the weighing of the souls of heroes, similar to the Egyptian weighing of souls in the Underworld.

132 Helck 1979.

133 Bernal 1987.

134 Smith and Torr 1892:462–466; Gilbert 1939:336–339; Griffith 1998:212–234.

135 Nagy 1973 and 1999:197–205. According to Slatkin (1991:40), the immortalization of Achilles by Thetis replicates the relationship of the goddess Dawn with her mortal son/lover.

136 Janda 2006.

we should keep in mind that epic may reflect the experiences of many generations. The Trojan War may have accumulated the memories of numerous wars and contact with foreign peoples. Nonetheless, in the creation of an epic song, this is of secondary importance.

We really need not expect that the besieged Trojans were aided by an Egyptian or Elamite contingent, but it is probable that the story conveys the memory of a major fight between Achaean and, for example, Egyptian armies. The expedition of the Sea Peoples proved that there were great expeditions comprising many tribes, quite possibly of varied ethnicity. However, in oral culture even real events were very quickly combined with fairy-tale and fantastic elements. For example, the *Little Iliad* narrates the skirmish between Neoptolemos and Eurypylos, sons of Achilles and his enemy, Telephos, respectively. The protagonist of the *Odyssey* states that in addition to Eurypylos, many of the Keteians (Κήτειοι) under his leadership were killed (11.519–521). Eurypylos was of Mysian descent, so the ancients believed that "Keteian" was the name of a Mysian tribe, which they identified with contemporary Eleatians. Paul Kretschmer brilliantly derived their name from Hatti—Hittites.[137] It is impossible to exclude a conflict between the Achaeans and Hittites, but could the memory of the fact have survived until Homer's time? Unlike the Mysians or Lycians, the Hittites had not existed for a long time.

I will return to this issue in a moment, but for now let me remark that studies too hastily tend to combine historical and epic data. When we deal with such distant times, historical reality will always take on fairy-tale features. For example, I believe that the derivation of the name of Keteians from τὸ κῆτος 'sea monster'[138] is rejected too precipitately. For Aristarchus, it is an equivalent of μέγαλοι and therefore a metaphor for 'giants', but this derivation, though possible, is not the only candidate and is unsatisfactory. The name may also mean simply 'sea monsters', like 'Myrmidons' mean 'ant-people' commanded by Neoptolemos. We should bear in mind that epic presents the sea as a place hiding dangers rather than as a source of food to man,[139] so the attempts to explain the name of Keteians as a Mysian or Hittite tribe seem to be a form of rationalizing, whereas in Homeric tradition this name might have suggested a fantastic people and unusual, terrifying creatures.

This is why we should exercise great caution in seeking a model for the Amazons, who appear as Trojan allies at the beginning of the *Aethiopis*. Scholars

137 Kretschmer 1930:8–10.

138 Heubeck 1989:108 *ad* 11.521.

139 Hainsworth 1993:58–59. Householder and Nagy 1972:768: "The original selection of ἰχθυόεις was probably motivated not by a striving for fanciful descriptions of the sea, but rather by the implication of lurking danger."

do not try to identify them with a real tribe, but rather search for similar figures in the myths of other peoples,[140] and have located the Amazons in many regions.[141] More important than this issue is the place taken by the episode with the Amazons in the structure of the *Aethiopis*.[142] It is evident that the *Aethiopis* observes the principle of doubling motifs (*Motivdubletten*), typical of the Cycle and the *Iliad*.[143] Memnon's death is primary in relation to the death of Penthesileia, because it foreshadows that of Achilles. The immortalization of Achilles parallels Memnon's. Apparently, in the set of themes chosen by the *aoidos* to sing in the last combat of Achilles, there must be a parallel to Memnon's *aristeia*. Originally, the *aristeia* and death of the "black Memnon" were paralleled by the those of the "white Kyknos," but the growth of the Cycle excluded this possibility: one could not narrate the beginning and the end of the war in one story. And so the mythical Memnon in his fight with Achilles was given a forerunner in the form of the Amazons, known from other epic cycles.[144]

The historicity of the Ethiopians

That the allies mentioned in the *Iliad* are real barbarian tribes inhabiting the Trojan regions of Anatolia—Thracians, Phrygians, Lycians—whereas in the *Aethiopis* the allied tribes are Ethiopians and Amazons indicates only that Homer adapted the idea of Trojan allies to the principles of rationalism.[145] However,

140 The interpretation of archaeological excavations carried out in Kazakhstan (Davis-Kimball and Behan 2003) seems to be an exception.

141 In Proclus's summary, the Amazon Penthesileia is called "Thracian." It also seems to be a trace of the attempt at making this fabulous tribe more real.

142 Compare Griffith 1998:216.

143 Kullmann 1960:224.

144 West (2003b) eliminates Amazons from the *Aethiopis*, using a similar argument to that of Ethiopians. Homer mentions Amazons only once, as a tribe inimical to Phrygians, who were Trojan allies (*Iliad* 3.189). Priam says that in his young days, when he was an ally in the great army of Phrygians, he saw an Amazon army getting ready for battle. It is not clear, however, if the Amazons were the only tribe fighting against the Phrygians and the events are a generation earlier than the Trojan War. Usually, the Amazons are a way to introduce allusions to other epic tales. Both in this place and when he mentions the tomb of Myrina (*Iliad* 2.814), who according to other sources was an Amazon and the wife of Dardanos, the founder of the family (Eustathius *ad Iliad* 351.21), Homer signals familiarity with Amazon involvement in the Trojan myth, though naturally it does not follow that he knows about Penthesileia's expedition. But it certainly shows the facility with which the myth of the militant Amazons could be incorporated into this epic cycle. Perhaps a distant echo of the Amazon intervention can be discerned in *Iliad* 16.710–713, when Hektor's uncle, Asios (impersonated by Apollo), stops the Trojan leader from escaping, encouraging him to kill Patroklos. According to Neoanalysts, this encounter corresponds to the scene of Achilles' death. Asios was reputed to live in Phrygia on the Sangarios River, where Priam said he saw the army of the Amazons.

145 Kullmann (2005:14–15) remarks that the noticeable difference in the character of the Ethiopians in the *Iliad* and *Aethiopis*, considered incompatible by West, indicates a silent assumption that

his rationality should not be overestimated. Carpenter rightly noted that the Cilician or Lycian engagement in the fights at Troy was not plausible.[146] One could say that the Lycians and Cilicians at Troy are as unreal as the Ethiopians and Amazons. Considering what we know about the history of the Mycenaean period, we can be sure that Troy was not a power which could oblige tribes other than those living in close proximity to deliver contingents of warriors. Priam was not the Great King of the Hittites.[147]

The idea of Trojan allies is very important for the history of the Trojan War. Agamemnon refers to it, saying that Greeks are ten times more numerous than the Trojans and they would have captured the city long ago had it not been for the aid of the allies, who balanced the forces of both sides. Thanks to them, the Trojans could meet the Achaeans in the open field. Logically, one could say that it would be impossible to find room for the allies within the city walls, so the presence of the allies makes epic descriptions of fights in the fields outside Troy possible.

Achilles several times causes the Trojans to flee in panic and take refuge within city walls: in the *Iliad*, when in rage after Patroklos's death he kills many Trojans before he kills Hektor; in the *Kypria*, when he kills Kyknos; and in the *Aethiopis*, when he kills Memnon. In the *Iliad*, it is a means to dramatize his duel with Hektor, who is shown as abandoned by everybody, even his brother Deiphobos.[148] In the *Kypria* and *Aethiopis*, the flight seems much more natural, because the army panics after the death of the leader of the allied armies.[149] The Trojans are left alone and the only thing they can do is to seek refuge within

---

the author of the *Iliad* does not know myths which go beyond the world presented in his epic. It is not true, as Homer deliberately ignores myths he is familiar with—Kullmann (26–27) cites the example of Iphigenia.

146 Carpenter 1974:66–67: "How could there [at Troy] have been Cilicians (who belong around Tarsus on the coast this side of Syria) living at 'Thebe-under-Plakos' within raiding distance of Troy? Yet Hektor's Andromache had been a princess in Thebe and was presumably a Cilician." As far as Lycians are concerned, Carpenter puts his finger on the issue, which posed problems for Homer himself: how can Lycians be Trojan allies, if the Lycian and Mycenaean dynasties are related (the story of Bellerophon)?

147 Hektor, challenging the mettle of the allies, asserts that he has not gathered them to take the command (*Iliad* 17.220–221).

148 Allan (2005) stresses the fact that although Hektor is an illustrious warrior, no one fights for his body. However, Allan does not see the difference between the death of the hero and that of his enemy. The pro-Achaean slant of the epic convention was mentioned in Ch. 2. The fight for the body of Sarpedon may be an exception; perhaps this scene was intended as a foreshadowing of the fight for Patroklos's body. These parallel scenes have different endings: the Achaeans retrieve the body of Patroklos (17.722–761), while after the defeat of the Lycians and Trojans, the body of Sarpedon is miraculously transferred by gods to his homeland (16.666–684).

149 There is a parallel image in the *Iliad*, when after the death of their king Sarpedon, the Lycians cannot withstand Achaean pressure and resort to flight. At this very moment, Hektor realizes that Zeus's scales have turned (the most important parallel to the *Memnois*) and runs away,

the walls of the city. In the *Iliad*, there is also the question of the responsibility for the defeat, and here the blame is placed on Hektor, who not only did not take Poulydamas's strategic advice (18.249–253, 313), but also donned Achilles' armor without gaining a right to it, for which deed he is now punished.[150]

Homer enumerates and places Trojan allies with a fairly good knowledge of the geography of the region. For some Hellenistic scholars, including Strabo, his knowledge was absolute and exemplary; that is why in antiquity there were attempts to prove that Homer was right, even though much information was unverifiable. Homer's knowledge of geography is in essence his knowledge of the peoples inhabiting western Anatolia at the time of the crystallization or creation of the *Iliad* (eighth or the beginning of the seventh century BCE). We should ask, however, what did Greeks at the time of the birth of the Trojan Cycle know about geography? I believe that no matter how tolerantly we might approach this topic, we would conclude that their knowledge was very poor. Greeks of the eleventh through the ninth centuries BCE really did not know about much beyond the eastern coast of the Mediterranean Sea, in contrast to the earlier Mycenaeans, whose traces can be found not only in Anatolia and Egypt, but also in the Iberian peninsula and Britain. The Greek world bounced back slowly from the collapse of the Dark Ages. In such a situation, exaggeration, born either of admiration or fear, comes easily and stories told about the past are more important than personal experience. One effect is exaggeration about the past, as for example, the description of Hundred-Gated Thebes in Egypt (*Iliad* 9.381–384).[151] The knowledge of Egyptian, Syrian, and Palestinian coasts was more often a result of pirates rather than commercial expeditions. It was not until the eighth century that we can observe the revival of trade contacts of some centers, like Euboea, with the Levant. This collapse of the entire region was, it seems, brought about by the so-called expedition of the Sea Peoples

followed by the Trojan warriors (16.656–665). They stop only at the Scaean Gate, where Hektor decides to fight with Patroklos (16.712–713).

150 Compare Allan 2005:10.

151 Drawing on archaeological research, scholars claim that this description can only refer to the 14th century BCE or to the reign of the XXV dynasty (715–663 BCE), which restored the greatness of Thebes. However, Burkert (1976:5–21), followed by West (1995:211), believes that the description was influenced by Ashurbanipal's capture of Thebes in 663 BCE, since the rumor of the fall of the largest city in the world and of great treasures taken as booty must have resounded throughout the entire western world. This idea stems from the late date for the creation of the *Iliad* by Burkert and West, for whom 663 BCE is the *terminus post quem*. It seems to me that the matter of dating can be approached differently. The fame of the magnificence of Thebes could have survived since Mycenaean times. This does not contradict, I think, the undoubtedly correct assumption of these scholars that *Iliad* 9.381 was taken from an earlier epic, in which it referred to Boeotian Thebes.

directed against Syria and Palestine,[152] and then Egypt, where it ended in total disaster. Not even a single memory survived of the former contact between the Mycenaean courts and the Hittite empire. It is probable that the *Odyssey* displays some knowledge of the western Mediterranean basin. In the *Iliad* there are obvious traces of the influence of the Mesopotamian poems, but it does not imply any specific knowledge of these peoples or their history. To paraphrase West's words,[153] for the Greeks of those times, the appearance of Amazon or Ethiopian troops in aid of the Trojans was as possible as the coming of Hittite or Egyptian legions. In a sense, it was even more likely.

For the people of the Dark Ages, geographical realities were usually mixed with transcendence. The boundary marking the end of the real world and the beginning of the fairy-tale one was real, but systematically shifted farther and farther from Greece. We can see how throughout the centuries the location of the land of the Hyperboreans moved further north. Wilamowitz was right when he said that for the primitive Greeks everything which was north of Mt. Olympus was a mythical and divine land (*das Götterland*) of happiness.[154] The Island of Leuke, to which Thetis transferred the body of Achilles, was—as E. Rohde writes—"originally a purely mythical place, an island of pallid ghosts (like Λευκὰς πέτρη [*Odyssey* 24.11] at the entrance to Hades [cf. *Odyssey* 10.515])." Nonetheless, Rohde compares Leuke to Elysium and the Isles of the Blessed, calling it "Sonderelysion."[155] Leuke was believed to be in the Black Sea (Pindar *Nemean* 4.49). According to Alcaeus (fr. 354 L-P), the immortalized Achilles is a king of the Scythians. In a later period, Leuke was identified with the bird island close to the mouth of the Danube, where sailors offered sacrifices to Achilles, Patroklos, and Antilochos. The same tendency is behind the placement of Elysium and the Isles of the Blessed at the ends of the earth near Okeanos.[156] The cycle of the Argonautic expedition, probably earlier than the Trojan one, reveals how fantastic were the Greeks' ideas about this region at the beginning of their expansion to the east. They believed that it was possible to sail across the Black

152 Philistine envoys were sent to the king of Danuna (Danaans?) to coordinate the expedition of the Sea Peoples against Syria and Palestine. See Bachvarova 2016:317-319.

153 West 2003b:6-7.

154 Wilamowitz 1931:252–253: "Aber nach Norden sahen sie [Greeks] nur breite und hohe Gebirge; dass sie einst überschritten hatten, war vergessen." Wilamowitz accepts the notion of the Greek invasion from the north (the Balkans), but this concept has been called into question. It seems more likely that Greeks arrived from the east (Anatolia); see Drews 1988.

155 Rohde 1903:2.365–378. This thesis has been intriguingly developed by Nagy (1973:137–177 and 1999:167–169, 203). Jumping off the White Rock into the sea is one of the methods of achieving immortality in Greek myth, in addition to being struck by Zeus's thunderbolt or suddenly swallowed by the earth.

156 See *Odyssey* 4.563 ἐς Ἠλύσιον πεδίον καὶ πείρατα γαίης 'to the Elysian plain and to the bounds of the earth'.

Sea to Okeanos, since it is possible for the Argonauts to return by Okeanos[157] to Libya or, according to other versions, to Kirke, who lives at the western edge of the earth. In the *Odyssey*, Odysseus goes to her island, Aiaia, which is also located on the western edge of the world.[158] From there he travels to the Land of the Dead located beyond the sea, where it flows into Okeanos. After the visit in the Underworld, the ship leaves the streams of Okeanos and sails to the island of Aiaia, which is now at the eastern margin of the world.[159] Nagy rightly concludes that this change is caused by the hero's sojourn in the Land of the Dead.[160] To return to the world of the living, Odysseus has to repeat the journey of Helios. The *Odyssey* mentions that there are two tribes of Ethiopians, both remote from human dwellings. They live where the Sun begins and ends his trip (1.22–24), in the eastern and western margins of the world.[161] This is the logic of myth consistent with the Argonauts' tradition. Diomedes was believed to be transferred to an island in the Adriatic Sea and immortalized there (Ibykos in *Scholia ad Pindar, Nemean* 10.12; Strabo 6.283–284; compare Rohde 1903, vol. 2:370), although Attic Scholion 894 P places Diomedes with Achilles on the Isles of the Blessed.[162] An unknown place remains mythical until it becomes known; then it becomes real,

157 In *Ehoiai* and Pindar (*Pythian* 4.19–27), they reach Okeanos by taking the Phasis River, then the streams of Okeanos carry them to the southern coast of Libya, where they must drag the ship over dry land to the Mediterranean Sea. Hecataeus thought they had crossed Africa by the Nile (1F11).

158 I do not think that the visit to Kirke is merely a result of the influence of the *Odyssey*. Several Greek geographers attempted to identify the return route of the Argonauts: Timagetus was said to have charted a route along the Danube in order to reach the western Mediterranean basin, which allegedly served as a model for Apollonius of Rhodes (Σ AA 4, 282), while according to the geographer Scymnus (2nd century BCE) the Argonauts returned by sailing one of the Scythian rivers to the "great sea," i.e. most likely, to the Atlantic Ocean, which means they sailed from the west, taking the northern route (Gantz 1993:362). Of course, geographers realized that the Black Sea is an inland sea and there is no other connection with other basins except by rivers. West (1997:407–410) links the family relationship of Kirke and Aiëtes (children of Helios) and the name of her island Aiaia with the Egyptian image of the Sun as a falcon via the Semitic language (Hebrew *'ayyah*).

159 Thalmann (1984:2) identifies a similar journey from one end of the world to another (physical world and the symbolic world of values) in Odysseus's visit, at the beginning and end of his wanderings, to the Kyklopes and Phaeacians—related and yet opposite in every respect.

160 Nagy 1999:206. Thalmann (1984:2) notes that in the Homeric *Odyssey*, the vision of the world and the netherworld (10.508, 11.13, 157–159) is horizontal (Hades is placed beyond Okeanos; Elysium at the "bounds of the Earth" (4.563), just as the Isles of the Blessed in Hesiod *Works and Days* 168–172 are placed "beyond Okeanos"), whereas in Hesiod *Theogony* (720–725) the world is vertical (Hades is below the Earth).

161 It means that the division of Ethiopians into two tribes was not a new idea, an Ionic speculation, as suggested by S. West (1988:75–76). The later Greeks, who knew much more about the world, tried to find explanations for these expressions. For Herodotus, it means the division into India and Africa (7.69–70). The recognition of the Ethiopians as Black peoples is already visible in the *Odyssey* in Menelaos's account of his travels (4.84).

162 Nagy 1999:174.

devoid of fantastic elements, and the boundaries of the legend move farther out. Perhaps this is one of the reasons for Homer's rationalism. On the other hand, we inevitably come closer and closer to the opinion that in the epic tradition, the "fairy-tale" Amazons and Ethiopians were at Troy earlier than the "real" Lycians and Thracians.

The historicity of Troy and the Trojan War

This discussion of the "historicity" of Ethiopians would be irrelevant without at least outlining the issue of the historicity of the Trojan War. It is, of course, a difficult and controversial problem, in which emotions often affect the estimation of the evidence. Recent decades have seen so much new material that one can speak of a decisive breakthrough in the research on the authenticity of Troy and its conflict with the Mycenaeans. The most important in this respect are excavations carried out since 1988 on Hisarlik hill and its vicinity by Manfred Korfmann, but also other related excavations in the whole of Anatolia and in the centers of Mycenaean culture. The decipherment of Hittite and Mycenaean writing has given voice to objects of material culture. Many of these findings were received with excessive skepticism, but the pressure of facts has prompted acceptance. An excellent synthesis of this research, which gives a comprehensive picture of the economic and political reality of Troy, was made by Joachim Latacz in his book *Troy and Homer: Towards a Solution of an Old Mystery*.[163] Let me briefly present conclusions concerning the authenticity of the epic picture of the Trojan War.

The excavations conducted in the nineteenth century by Heinrich Schliemann and Wilhelm Dörpfeld showed that in the place where the Homeric texts suggested one could expect to find Troy and centers of Mycenaean culture, there were ruins of citadels and remnants of palace architecture.[164] However, the question, whether the hill at Hisarlik was the site of a city called Troy, was still without an answer. Today, with a probability bordering on certainty, we can state a few basic facts:

1. the authenticity of Troy and other centers of Mycenaean culture (Mycenae, Thebes, Pylos, Tiryns, etc.). The ruins on Hisarlik bear traces of a city, with which we can link the Greek names Ilion/Ilios and Troia, and their Hittite counterparts Wilus(s)a/Wilusija, and—

[163] Latacz 2004. The English edition includes new data that do not appear in the German original *Troia und Homer* (Stuttgart 2001).

[164] Dörpfeld did not find anything in Ithaca. Schliemann and Dörpfeld also had predecessors, such as Frank Calvert, who conducted excavations at the Hisarlik site in 1863–1869. The choice of this hill was suggested by the location of the Roman city of Troy at its foot.

with less certainty—Taruwisa/Tru(w)isa. The original name of the city has not been discovered yet, but quite probably it came from one of the Luwian dialects. The Mycenaean Greek world should probably be identified with the powerful state of Ahhiyawa;[165] in Hittite diplomatic correspondence its ruler is on an equal footing with the kings of Egypt and Assyria or even the Hittite king of Hattusa (as indicated by the frequent phrase "my brother…");[166]

2. the authenticity of the picture of the Mycenaean world presented in the Homeric Catalogue of Ships. Not only big cities, i.e. the centers of palace culture, correspond to the geography of the Catalogue, but the Linear B tablets also corroborate the existence of smaller cities which did not survive into the archaic period.[167] Archaeology also confirms the balance of power in the Mycenaean world, as presented in the Catalogue. Latacz concludes that this can be explained only if we assume that the Catalogue was created in the Mycenaean period;[168]

165 The link of this name with the Achaeans has been under discussion for a long time. Finkelberg (1988) provides linguistic evidence for the derivation of the Homeric Greek form Ἀχαι(ϝ)οί from the Hittite ethnikon *Ahhiyawa*, which happened due to phonetic transformations between the 14th and 8th centuries BCE.

166 Latacz (2004) believes that this fact undermines the identification of Ahhiyawa with the state of Arzawa in western Anatolia, which in cuneiform texts is referred to either as dependent on or as in conflict with the Great King of the Hittites. Latacz's argument is burdened with a large dose of subjectivity. I have the impression that perhaps he does not appreciate the power of the Luwian element in this period.

167 On one of the tablets found in Thebes in 1993–1995, written in Linear B, below the name *te-qa-i* "in Thebes," there appear two place names, *e-u-re-te-u* and *e-re-o-ni*, interpreted as locatives of the towns Eutresis and Eleon. These toponyms are known only from Homer's Catalogue of Ships, in which they are enumerated among Boeotian cities (2.499–500). Kullmann (2002), however, challenges this evidence, claiming that ancient geographers were able to locate the toponyms mentioned in 2.500: Eleon, Hyle, and Peteon.

168 Latacz 2004:248–249. Similar conclusions were drawn by Simpson and Lazenby 1970:156–167, who having much less data at their disposal, also fixed the creation of the Catalogue of Ships to the Late Helladic Period IIIC. Kullmann (2002) and West (2011:112), however, disagree with the hypothesis of the Mycenean origin of the Catalogue of Ships. Kullmann 2009 suggests that the source that gave rise to the Catalogue of Ships was a list of cities participating in the Olympic Games. This theory is untenable, because there is a fundamental difference between a catalogue born in oral tradition and a list of items/names created in writing. Besides differences in structure and function (Minchin 1996), Zadka (2016) also stresses the question of the completeness of oral enumerations (contextualized and connected to the narrative) and incompleteness of written registers (149), "deprived of these elements, so they need more additional and external information to restore their original form." The catalogue consists of repetitive elements which maintain a common structure and can be freely extended by the performer. This specific structure of the catalogue activates different memorizing strategies from those necessary for memorizing stories (Minchin 2001:Ch. 2). It may seem surprising, but oral culture enables the preservation and transmission of detailed topographical data organized in the form of a "map" (Minchin [1996:12] suggests that a catalogue is a "cognitive map"). The best examples

3. Troy persisted for eighteen centuries and appears to have had a fairly big area of ca. 200,000 m^{2}, with 7000–10,000 inhabitants, and have been built like a typical Anatolian settlement, steadily expanding with the increase of population. Troy was not a military power, but it relied on defense; due to its convenient location on the route from the Black Sea to the Aegean Sea, it was an important trading center. It seems to have been a borderland metropolis open to diverse civilizations, a melting pot of Asian and European cultures.[169] In the twelfth century BCE the town declined (there are notable archaeological traces of two catastrophes), and in the mid-eleventh century it was completely deserted;
4. Troy was in the Hittite influence zone, which was probably beneficial to both sides: on the one hand, the Hittites were not threatened militarily, but could take advantage of Troy's economic and commercial advantages; on the other hand, the Trojans could probably count on Hittite military support. However, at least from the thirteenth century BCE Troy found itself in the Ahhiyawa area of interest, and so in this period it was a zone of clashing Hittite and Achaean influences.

These facts allow us to conclude that the historical evidence behind the Homeric epics makes the historicity of the Trojan War highly probable.

Latacz very cautiously confines his conclusions only to such as can be drawn directly from research. However, for the task of this book, which deals with the reconstruction of the lost pre-Homeric epic, it is more profitable to be more daring and to make assumptions which current studies cannot perhaps confirm yet but as to which we can make a reasonable guess. Let us, therefore, try to map out more broadly the research perspective that emerges from the juxtaposition of the epic-mythical world with historical realities. The reliability of the findings presented above allows us to put forward—naturally with moderation and restraint—further hypotheses. I want to point to four groups of issues important for the formation of the Trojan Cycle.

of these are the Aboriginal tales of wanderings of the Djanggawul siblings, which perfectly reproduce the routes of tribal wanderings in the region of Arnhem Land (Berndt 1952; Szyjewski 2014:122–150; Minchin 2007:14–17). Therefore, the survival of a detailed geographical description of Mycenaean Greece for several centuries without the aid of writing is absolutely possible, though a catalogue is undoubtedly a form susceptible to changes in the course of transmission, e.g. because of the needs of its adaptation to a given performance (compare Sammons 2010:5–7; see also Marks [2012], who draws attention to the links between the structure of a catalogue and the narrative of a song).

169 Latacz 2004:102: "the 'international' character of the city."

The dominant role of Thebes in the Mycenaean world

Mycenaean palace archives concretize for us the political situation in Greece only at the end of the thirteenth century. For the earlier period such concretization is impossible, because palace fires preserved tablets from only the latest period; in Greece, unlike in the Hittite state and in Mesopotamia, tablets were not baked. At that time, Thebes dominated the largest territory among the Mycenaean centers, reaching as far as Euboea.[170]

Hittite diplomatic correspondence seems to point to Thebes as the center of Ahhiyawa authority. A letter written in Hittite cuneiform script is sent from the ruler of Ahhiyawa to the king of Hattusa, most probably Hattusili II (ca. 1265–1240). It is the first document sent from the west to the east to be found that is not by a Hittite king,[171] and it refers to earlier correspondence between these rulers. In the letter, the ruler of Ahhiyawa undermines the claims of the Hittite king to the islands in the northern Aegean Sea, Lesbos, and probably Lemnos, Imbros, and/or Samothrace. The king of Ahhiyawa justifies his own claims to these territories by arguing that one of his ancestors (probably from the fifteenth century) gave his daughter in marriage to the ruler of Assuwa, which at the time presumably included Wilusa, i.e. Ilion. The name of the ancestor referred to by the Ahhiyawa ruler is Kadmos, identical with the name of the hero who founded Thebes, and whose name was perpetuated in the name of the Theban citadel—Kadmea. It is the first confirmation of the authenticity of a hero hidden behind mythical decoration in the history of ancient scholarship. Schliemann might have thought that he had found "Priam's treasure" and looked into Agamemnon's face, but these were of course only his subjective impressions.

The same Hittite ruler, Hattusili II, is also the sender of the document known as the Tawagalawa letter, named after the brother of the Ahhiyawa ruler, the addressee: "Tawagalawa, brother of the king of Ahhiyawa."[172] Linguists recognize this name as the Hittite form of the Greek *Etewo-klewēs, an earlier version of the name Eteokles, also known from Theban myth. It is the name of one of Oedipus's sons, who died in a fratricidal duel with Polyneikes. This suggests the possibility that myth might have preserved authentic names of rulers, in this case Theban ones.

Once the authenticity of the Catalogue of Ships has been demonstrated, the prominence of the Theban contingent becomes more understandable.[173] The

170 Latacz 2004:240–243 after: Godart and Sacconi 1999:545.

171 Latacz (2004:243–244) relates results of Frank Starke's reading of the letter.

172 Güterbock 1990:158; Latacz 2004:123–125.

173 Compare Kirk (1962:154–155), who considers the possibility of the influence "a much later Boeotian school of catalogue poetry which we might infer from the poetry associated with

Catalogue mentions the Boeotians first and lists more cities in Boeotia than in any other region, which corresponds to the hegemony or domination of Thebes, at least in the thirteenth century BCE. This may explain why the gathering of the Achaean fleet took place in Aulis instead of one of the ports in the Peloponnese.

Latacz points out that the myth of the Theban War (two expeditions against Thebes, the second one ending in the capture of the city) may be a trace of competition between the Peloponnese and Boeotia in the Mycenean period.[174] The range of conclusions based on these premises can be significantly broadened: the Catalogue of Ships is a list of contingents participating in the expedition to Troy (possibly earlier to other places, especially to the western coast of Asia Minor, e.g. Miletus), which in the period of Mycenaean domination was adapted to new conditions. Therefore, the Catalogue may hint at previous expeditions led by Thebes and its framework was used in new expeditions under the leadership of Mycenae.

The Trojan expedition must have taken place when Thebes was no longer dominant (the *Iliad* mentions the both sacks of Thebes, *Iliad* 4.376–410, 5.802–807, 6.223, 14.113–125, and the funeral of Oedipus, who lived two generations earlier, 23.279–280, compare Hesiod *Works and Days* 163). The claims of Ahhiyawa, which we identify as Thebes or Greece under Theban hegemony, to the islands near the Troad, and the mention of the political marriage linking Thebes and Troy, may be reflected in the Samothracian Kabeiroi version of the myth connecting the foundation of Troy with Thebes.[175]

Hesiod, as well as from the added list of Boeotian and Aeolic heroines in the eleventh book of the *Odyssey*."

174 Drews (1979 and 1988) maintains that the expeditions against Thebes were organized not by Peloponnesian Argos (an obvious anachronism as far as the position of the city in this period is concerned), but by the Argives of Argos, i.e. by Greek tribes from Thessaly, which attacked the northernmost metropolis of Mycenaean civilization. His thesis is possible, but it does not exclude the possibility of rivalry and armed conflicts between Boeotia and the Peloponnese.

175 In the Kabeiroi myths, Dardanos, the founder of the Trojan dynasty, is a brother of Iasion and Harmonia, who was a wife to Kadmos. The otherness of the Kabeiroi myths is, naturally, related to the otherness of Samothracian cults. One cannot recreate historical reality from myths, but in the light of current research it is quite possible to assume that they do have some sort of a historical background. The letter sent by the ruler of Ahhiyawa to the king of Hattusa (mentioned above) indicates that the islands of the region were a matter of contention between Anatolian and Achaean rulers. The marriage of Kadmos's daughter to the ruler of Assuwa, which provided justification for the claims of the Ahhiyawa ruler, clearly points to Thebes as the capital of the Ahhiyawa state. Dynastic relationships between Troy and the Achaeans cannot be ruled out. Such an inference made by Murray (1907:47) from the fact that in the *Iliad* the Greeks speak with the Trojans without obstacles, seems to be naive, but it is founded on the assumption that the Greek invasion was limited to a small group, who took over the power and mixed with local people (Murray 1907:29–58). Murray opposed the then popular idea of *Völkerwanderung*, which has since been discarded. Murray's point of view is therefore close to the concept of "takeover" proposed by Drews (1988:56), which describes the essence of the Hittite and Hurrian invasion

The Hittitologist Trevor Bryce suggested that the Trojan War was not a single event but that the whole western coast of Asia Minor had been pressed by the expansion of the Achaean states for at least a hundred years.[176] Recent findings confirm this in the sense that Greek colonial expansion in these regions from the mid-eleventh century continued the tendency of the Achaean monarchies after the defeat of the Minoan empire in Crete. The main role was played by Miletus (Millawanda). This city served as a bridgehead for the Achaean expansion, though sometimes it was under Hittite domination and was finally subordinated by them in the second half of the thirteenth century. This situation seems to be reflected in Greek myth, referred to in the *Iliad* (2.648–651, 14.250–251), which mentions an earlier capture of Troy by Herakles—a Theban hero.

The situation of Troy under siege

Current knowledge about Wilusa lets us note a few analogies to the myth on which the Trojan Cycle is based. Hittite diplomatic correspondence confirms the existence of a network of alliances connecting individual states with the Hittite metropolis. Such an alliance was also in force between Wilusa and Hattusa, except the time (times?) when Wilusa was associated with the state of Arzawa (ca. 1375–1316), inimical to the Hittites. This fact substantiates the reality behind the Trojan catalogue: the situation depicted in the *Iliad* never suggests the dominant position of Troy, which would be able to compel its allies to come to its defense.[177] After the Achaeans were deprived of their influence in Miletus, probably because of the Great King of the Hittites Tudhaliya IV (ca. 1220 BCE),[178] their attack on Troy can be linked with

("the term 'takeover' for those occasions when outsiders came neither to plunder nor to extend an imperial network, but rather to establish control over a population"). Of the three names of Trojan rulers preserved in Hittite documents—Kukkumi, Alaksandus, and Walmu—the second one probably constitutes a Luwian or Hittite form of a foreign name (Latacz 2004:117 also on Homeric names of Trojan rulers). According to West (2003:265) Alaksandus is an equivalent of the Greek Aléxandros, which is already confirmed in Linear B in the female form *Aleksandra (*a-re-ka-sa-da-ra* MY 303 = V 659). Presumably, the inhabitants of Troy spoke Luwian (Starke 1997:456–458), although it is possible it was only the language used for communication with foreigners and in diplomacy (Latacz 2004:113–117). Woudhuizen 2017:137: "Against the backdrop of the relevant onomastic data, it seems permissible to suggest that the Trojans spoke a vernacular closely related to Thracian and/or Phrygian. ... There are indications ... that the aforesaid Thracian and/or Phrygian linguistic layer was preceded by a substrat of Old Indo-European type."

176 Bryce 2002:267.

177 In 18.289–292, Hektor alludes to paying the allied troops from Phrygia and Maeonia.

178 In one of the letters, this king demands that one of vassal kings, Šaušgamuwa of Amurru, impose a trade blockade on Ahhiyawa (see Latacz 2004:127).

the decline of Hittite power (around 1175 BCE). The loss of Hittite protection made Troy a relatively easy prey.

When trying to find historical reality behind the Trojan Catalogue, we should remember that, in light of the *Iliad*, we can conclude that Troy sought alliances among Luwian peoples or, more generally, among the peoples of the western part of Asia Minor. Furthermore, from the point of view of the cycle, the crucial support for Troy came from the east, whether it was a contingent of Ethiopians under Memnon, Amazons under Penthesileia, or even (mentioned in the *Odyssey*) Keteians, whom Kretschmer, as we have seen, identifies with Hittites, under Eurypylos. We can suppose that all these eastern contingents may reflect the support for endangered Trojans by one of Hittite states, perhaps even by Hattusa.

The fantastic and fairy-tale character of the epic image

Summing up, let us return to the issue of the miraculous, fantastic, and magic in epic. An epic song does not recreate the historical past, it can only refer to it, very often anachronistically mixing up epochs and perceiving the past in the light of the present. "History is history, and oral epic is oral epic: we shall gain nothing by mistaking the one for the other."[179] These words of Rhys Carpenter should always be kept in mind when we try to judge the reality of the epic world. Carpenter buttresses his opinion with significant examples: the *Song of Roland*, which strikingly differs from the mention of Einhard in the *Vita Karoli Magni*, or the *Nibelungenlied*, where characters appear together, although their historical prototypes could never have met in real life.[180] Let me add a less known example, from Armenian epic. The story is set against the Armenian struggle for liberation from Arabs occupying the country in the eleventh century CE. But why should not the Arabs be supported by a contingent of crusaders commanded by the Pope, who is finally killed (*sic*!) by the Armenian hero, David of Sassoun? There is no sense, however, in going to extremes and denying the reality of all information that epic songs contain. Previously, I have suggested that oral poetry may retain certain structures originating in earlier epochs and, despite indubitable anachronisms, preserve some elements of an earlier world and general historical context. An epic is not a record of the past, but rather its projection based on data retained in the conservative structures of oral tradition.

179 Carpenter 1974:67.

180 Carpenter 1974:38–44 and 65: "In medieval German poetry Ermanrich from the fourth century, Attila from the fifth, and Theodoric from the sixth all appear contemporaneously, to be joined by Siegfried, who may be immeasurably older than any of them."

Since the mythic world to a certain extent corresponds to historical facts, it seems that my opinion presented in the previous chapter may be slightly improved. Certainly, fairy-tale and magical features are primary for the epic world. Undoubtedly, this fairy-tale world is situated on the margin of the known world and even farther, at a place which only imagination can reach. The boundaries of the real world changed, but it would be a mistake to believe that the expansion was in only one direction.

The world of the Mycenaean civilization stretched much farther than its immediate vicinity; it maintained trade and political contact with the distant, powerful Hittite and Egyptian states. From the point of view of the cyclic and Homeric tradition, these regions are unknown. The miraculous nature of the epic world reveals the collapse of civilizations in the Dark Ages. Europe experienced a similar decline after the fall of the Imperium Romanum, which does not mean that the Achaeans of the Mycenaean period were less prone to succumb to the mirage of the fairy-tale and magic than their descendants in later epochs. We can suspect that they weren't, but one thing they knew for certain: to the east of the Troad is the Hittite empire. In later times, the world of the epic shrank perceptibly. In the Cycle, the Trojan allies who arrive from the east, Ethiopians and Amazons, are completely fantastic figures. In this respect, Homer's views are not significantly different: on the edge of Phrygia, Priam fought with the Amazons. For him, as for the author of the *Aethiopis*, east of Phrygia and Lycia stretches the world of fairy tales. At the end of the world, there is the land of happy Ethiopians, who enjoy the visits of gods. The migration of the Sea Peoples and the so-called Dorian invasion possibly connected with it overturned the order of the world and destroyed great civilizations, narrowing the boundaries of the world. Those who survived had to start pushing its magical limits away again.

The Catalogue of Ships in its present form, reflecting the reality of the Mycenaean period, on the one hand demonstrates the durability of the text transmitted orally in Greece,[181] but on the other hand also shows the impossibility of modernizing the image of the world conveyed by epic. It was neither possible to draw a geographical picture of Greece, nor to modify it to reflect changes which took place over the centuries (some cities disappeared without a trace), but it does not mean that in oral cultures there are no methods of preserving important geographical data. Once such data get into the myth, they become fixed, despite the fluidity and multiformity of its transmission.

In our attempt to assess the degree to which Greek oral culture preserved traces of the Mycenaean world we must proceed with moderation. Essentially,

[181] Latacz 2004:218–249.

there are only shreds of information and a very broad structure, which corresponds less to Mycenaean culture itself than to the idea of that culture in the minds of later generations. Most of the data recognized by the historian can be attributed to the reality of the Dark Ages,[182] but nonetheless the hyperbole[183] typical of epic plays an important role.

The duality of the Trojan state

In the *Iliad* there are two related tribes: Trojans and Dardanians, and their names are not synonymous, like the Achaeans/Argives/Danaans. Hektor differentiated the Dardanians from the allies—they are at Troy on a different footing. The question is whether perceiving both tribes as part of one state is a sign of tradition or did the Dardanians have their own powerful city, different from Troy?[184]

The name of the Dardanians is probably confirmed in the Egyptian inscription enumerating the *Drdny* among Hittite allies in the battle of Kadesh.[185] The Hittite text about the expedition of the Hittite Great King Tudhalija I against Arzawa mentions two lands among the defeated supporters of Arzawa, one after another: "the land of Wilusija, the land of Taruisa." These names should probably be equated with Ilion and Troy.[186] Does it mean that these two names reflects the duality of the whole state? In the *Iliad,* Aeneas, the leader of the Dardanians, is ignored by Priam and so the angry hero holds back from fighting (13.459–461). Can we infer from this fact the subjugation of the Dardanians by the Trojans or at least the latter's domination in the period depicted by Homer? It seems that these questions will not be answered for a long time to come, but I feel they should be posed.

182 Finley 1977; Dickinson 1986; Morris 1997.

183 In Ch. 1, I suggested that real persons can become heroes of an epic, but the story told about them will immediately take on traits of the miraculous. The singer cannot tell about current events in a way which opposes convention. Real people and real events can function in the memory of subsequent generations only because they have been placed in the frame of a typical epic tale.

184 Since Dardanos appears as a patronymic (of Priam and Ilos), and Homeric patronymics are derived from the name of the father, or exceptionally the grandfather (see Robert 1923:388–389), there is implied "an earlier, less developed family line, with the patriarch Dardanos originally much closer to the generation involved in the Trojan War" (Gantz 1993:557). Gantz's opinion seems to be rather rash. The Greeks—as is evidenced by a fairly long genealogy of the Trojan house—realized that Troy was an ancient city; according to archaeological data it was founded ca. 3000 BCE. The Egyptian inscription (see n185, below) suggests that the use of this adjective as a patronymic was secondary. The name of a people could have been naturally identified with the mythical eponymous hero, the founder of the dynasty.

185 Gurney 1990:46–47; Bachvarova 2016:429.

186 Latacz 2004:92–100.

Interrelations between Cycles

Similarities between cycles

When dealing with the fantastic and magical foundation of Homer's poems, we noticed the relationship between the Trojan and other cycles of Greek epic. This is not surprising, since it is fairly easy to discover similarities. However, scholars have not attached much importance to them.

The fundamental issue is the thematic and formal scope of oral epic poetry. Pondering the essence of Greek epic as a genre, Richard P. Martin notes that what functioned as epic was not limited to a heroic song.[187] Rather, it was a fairly diverse conglomerate of stories about gods and people comprising, beside various songs attributed to Homer, works of Hesiod completely different in nature from the Homeric ones (like the *Works and Days*, which reports a conflict between brothers, and contains proverbs, maxims, fairy tales, and advice on farming and performing ritual); the *Arimaspea*, which can be read as shamanic tales; and mysterious songs connected with mythic figures of Orpheus and Musaios. Such diversity, accompanied by formal homogeneity, finds its parallels in the epic of other cultures. The inclusion of numerous elements seemingly foreign to the narrative is typical of the epic stories of many African peoples. An example of this may be the Mwindo epic of the Nyanga people, observed by Daniel Biebuyck in the Congo.[188] "Significantly, the sequenced singing and recitation of long narratives (*kárisi*) incorporates these other genres of discourse: proverbs, riddles, and prayers in poetic form, eulogistic recitations, formulae used by diviners and medicine men, personal songs, animal tales, instructions and political advice, all find a place within *Mwindo*."[189] The same is true of the epic of northern Egypt studied by Dwight Reynolds: stories about heroic deeds are combined with the praise of Muhammad (*madih*) and the proverbial advice in lyrical form (*mawwal*).[190] Martin concludes on the basis of the study of epic in many different cultures: "The 'epic' must be taken as total social event including audience interaction, instrumental music, and these framing genres, not just the 'text' we might want to cull from it."[191] Moreover, speaking about Greek epic, Martin observes:

> A straightforward assumption can account for the tight bonds among all these hexameter poems: namely, the existence, from at least the sixth century BCE, of traveling reciters or singers, called "rhapsodes"

[187] Martin 2005:15–18.
[188] Biebuyck and Mateéne 1969.
[189] Martin 2005:16.
[190] Reynolds 1995.
[191] Martin 2005:16.

> ("song-stitchers"), at least some of whom traced their ancestry to the master singer Homer himself. These shapers of the canon in any given generation could define "epic" simply as the substance of their repertoire. They could also explicitly cross-reference, and explain to audiences, the complex ways in which the mythological, heroic, and "folk" lore of their poems fit together. We know, from depictions in Plato's *Ion*, *Republic*, and *Laws* (among other sources) that the rhapsodic repertoire included poetry attributed to Homer and Hesiod, as also Orpheus, Musaeus, and other shadowy earlier poets. In sum, the genre inhered in its performers.[192]

A similar thematic diversity can be found in the songs of Demodokos in the *Odyssey*, the second of which deviates in character from the others, rather resembling older Homeric hymns.[193]

Since in tribes where epic is a living genre, this term applies to such a variety of songs characterized by similar performative circumstances and manner of execution, we can infer that in common consciousness rational elements coexist alongside fantastic and fairy-tale ones. We cannot assume that the audience would expect greater rationality from heroic epic than from other types of epic, especially if, as we have seen, in the other songs of the Trojan Cycle as well as in other cycles, the magical and fantastic layer is clearly visible.

The *Odyssey* reveals numerous similarities to the Argonautic Cycle, because, of course, in this Song of Return the motif of journey is omnipresent. It is impossible to determine precisely the extent of the influence the traditional epic of the Argonauts could have had on the *Odyssey* because most of our information on this cycle comes from Apollonius's Hellenistic epic *Argonautica*, which was itself influenced by the Homeric poem. The Argonauts visit Kirke, sail past the Sirens, manage to negotiate the strait of Skylla and Charybdis, avoid the Clashing Rocks, and finally reach the island of the Phaeacians. There are also other, less significant points, where one can detect the influence of the Argonautic epics on the Trojan Cycle—the invincible, monstrous giant Talos, whose only vulnerable spot was near the ankle, is a parallel to Achilles' invincibility and his heel.[194]

192 Martin 2005:16.

193 From the dance of the young men accompanying the second song of Demodokos, Danielewicz (1990:56–57) deduces that it was a lyrical song, but since the performance of epic songs was also very varied in various cultures, we can regard this song as an epic.

194 Kullmann (2012:20–24) notes more links between the Argonautic tradition and Homeric poems, mainly from the family connections of the heroes in both sagas (the sons of the Argonauts take part in the Trojan War). Poias, the killer of Talos, deserves special attention because Philoktetes (*Odyssey* 3.190) is his son. If I rightly believe that Philoktetes as a hero-protagonist in the Trojan cycle precedes Achilles in the same role, the death of Achilles, shot in the ankle by Paris with an

The route of the Argonauts is charted according to predictions, e.g. of Phineus, Idmon, and even a speaking prow, which was made by the goddess Hera herself from a bough of a holy oak from the sacred forest of Dodona. In the *Iliad*, such is the role of Kalchas (1.71–72):

> καὶ νήεσσ' ἡγήσατ' Ἀχαιῶν Ἴλιον εἴσω
> ἣν διὰ μαντοσύνην, τήν οἱ πόρε Φοῖβος Ἀπόλλων
>
> and brought Achaean ships to Ilion
> using the art of prophecy, which Phoibos Apollo gave to him

Some elements of the Trojan Cycle seem to be related also to other epics. The miraculous equipment of Peleus/Achilles is parallel to the equipment of Herakles. The huge club cut from a wild olive tree was made by the hero himself, but all other things were gifts to Herakles from gods: Hermes gave him a sword, Apollo—a bow and arrows, Hephaistos—a golden breastplate, Athena—a robe, and Poseidon—horses.[195] Similarly equipped for battle are other heroes, like Memnon, so this is a clearly conventional motif. It is inseparably linked with the motif of a young hero donning the armor of another warrior, when he prepares for his initiatory fight. The young hero does this because he does not yet have his own breastplate and because he needs to be equipped with magical attributes that will make him victorious.

The greatest number of similarities links the Trojan Cycle with the Theban Cycle. In the relative chronology of myths, the Trojan War took place after the capture of Thebes in the second expedition of the so-called Epigonoi. This is repeatedly confirmed by the *Iliad*: Diomedes and Sthenelos, leaders of the army from Argos, participated in that expedition, succeeding where their fathers failed (4.406–409); Mekisteus, the father of Euryalos, the third of the Argos leaders (2.559–566), is reported to have defeated all his sons at the funeral games in Oedipus's honor (23.678–679). According to ancient sources, Thersandros, son of Polyneikes, participated in the first expedition to Troy, which turned out to be a mistaken attack on Teuthrania, and was killed by Telephos.[196] Mythological sources suggest more links between these two cycles. In the poem *Returns*,

arrow, would recall the death inflicted by Poias on Talos. Talos is also imperfectly immortal, his metal body having only one tiny vulnerable spot—his ankle.

195 Apollodorus *Library* 2.4.11, except the gift of horses from Poseidon, which are mentioned by Diodorus Siculus 4.13.3.

196 *Kypria*—Proclus's summary; Apollodorus *Epitome* 3.17.

Amphilochos, son of Amphiaraos and brother of Alkmaion, and a seer like his father, supported Kalchas in telling prophecies.[197]

The tradition of the Kabeiroi of Samothrace stresses blood ties between the Theban and Trojan dynasties. Troy was believed to be founded by Dardanos, a descendant of the Theban royal family, who had to flee from Thebes to Samothrace. Iasion and Dardanos were brothers of Harmonia, who was married to Kadmos. Dardanos arrived on a raft at the Troad and founded the eponymous Dardania there (the city or the country). He also built a citadel at Troy and ruled over the whole Troad. It is rather unbelievable that the blood relationships mentioned in the Kabeiroi myths were not reflected in epic songs.[198] The Kabeiroi version may be significant because in historical times the islands of Imbros, Lemnos, and Samothrace were still inhabited by non-Greek tribes, probably related to the Trojans.[199]

The city-founding motif is also parallel. Like Kadmos, Ilos obeyed a prophecy and followed a cow in search of "a place found by a roaming cow," where he established a city. The replication of motifs may be understood as a typical method of creating a mythical reality, but in this case there are more similarities, which reflect the construction of epic cycles.

In both cycles, there is the motif of the doubling of an expedition. The first one ends in a failure, the second one in the taking of a city. In the Theban Cycle, the expedition of the Seven against Thebes ends in failure, whereas the expedition of their sons, the Epigonoi, is successful. The Trojan Cycle introduces a very artificial construction, in which the first expedition is abortive because the Achaeans mistakenly attack Teuthrania instead of Troy. The second expedition ends in the capture of Troy.

The main heroes of the Trojan War, Achilles and Odysseus, initially refrain from joining the expedition to Troy and their reluctance is mirrored in Amphiaraos's unwillingness to join the expedition against Thebes. Amphiaraos, due to his gift of prophecy, knows that he will die if he takes part in it. Similarly, an oracle stops Achilles from joining the expedition against Troy, but because Achilles is still a child, his mother hides him. Amphiaraos, like Odysseus, decides this for himself. All three heroes are made to join the expedition as a result of subterfuge. Considering the failure of the Theban expedition, the necessity of Amphiaraos's participation in the new undertaking is not stressed; nonetheless,

197 This Amphilochos is more often identified as the son of Alkmaion and Manto, daughter of Teiresias.

198 Kalypso mentions the love of Demeter for Iasion, *Odyssey* 5.125–128. Compare *Theogony* 969–974; see Scodel 2002:145.

199 They are Tyrrhenians, probably related to Etruscans. Many clues suggest Asia Minor, perhaps the Troad, as the Etruscan homeland, but there is still no definitive evidence which would confirm the ancient Etruscan and Latin traditions.

Adrastos and Polyneikes must be very much set on his going, if they resort to deception to obtain their aim.

In the Theban Cycle, the motif of deception is doubled. Eriphyle is twice bribed with miraculous objects taken from Thebes. Before the first expedition Polyneikes offers her Harmonia's necklace, and Amphiaraos yields to her decision. (Eriphyle is Adrastos's sister and her marriage to Amphiaraos had a condition that if Amphiaraos and Adrastos quarreled, they would be obliged to accept Eriphyle's arbitration.) Next time Thersandros, son of Polyneikes, bribes her to induce Alkmaion, her son with Amphiaraos, to join the expedition; Eriphyle gets Harmonia's peplos. The motif of bribery is reproduced in the Trojan Cycle, when Astyoche, Priam's sister married to Telephos, who was seriously injured by Achilles in the first Trojan expedition, allows herself to be bribed by Priam with a miraculous vine, a gift of Dionysos. In return, she persuades her son to support Troy. Eurypylos goes to Troy, where he is killed by Neoptolemos, son of Achilles.

At the root of both conflicts are two extraordinary weddings celebrating the marriage of a hero to a goddess, or at least a divine creature—Kadmos to Harmonia and Peleus to Thetis. Thetis, though a goddess, is not one of the Olympians, and the status of Harmony, though divine, is rather obscure. According to one source (Hesiod *Theogony* 935–937, 975), she is a daughter of Ares and Aphrodite, so a full-fledged goddess, though she is never referred to as such; according to another (Kabeiroi version), she is the daughter of Zeus and Electra, who was a daughter of Atlas. Both "lesser goddesses" possess the skill of metamorphosis. Thetis undergoes several transformations when she tries to escape Peleus's embrace; Harmonia and her husband at the end of their life change into snakes. In the case of both couples, there is a motif of two separate worlds, which, when they are combined, bring about war.

Gods are invited to both weddings and they give the newlyweds magic gifts which will have an important role in the wars to come. Harmonia's necklace and peplos, which are Polyneikes's choice, probably originally gave their owner the right to exercise power. Then they were used to assemble the team of warriors for the Theban expedition, and at the same time sealed the fate of Amphiaraos. At the wedding of Peleus and Thetis, the gifts are given to the hero Peleus. However, their importance for the Cycle stems from the use that his son Achilles makes of them in the Trojan War.[200] These gifts are undoubtedly also ominous in nature, but not as ominous as the gift of the goddess Eris; her apple (unlike the other gifts, it was not given to the newlyweds) triggers the events leading to the Trojan War. Recall also that in the Kabeiroi version the magic gifts given to the Theban couple were transferred to Troy.

200 Only the miraculous sword that Peleus received from Hermes was not used.

The previously mentioned quarrel of the lion and the boar,[201] ending in their joint participation in the expedition, seems to be another parallel motif. It is difficult to find similarities in the presentation of the fights in the two wars. Both, however, are shown not as sieges but as fights in the open field. In this respect, it is important to note the principle of the equality of forces, which characterizes at least one of the Theban expeditions. The attackers send seven champions to approach the walls of Thebes, and from each of its seven gates there emerges a champion defender. The war is decided in a series of single combats between heroes. In the Trojan War, such equality of forces is ensured only by the arrival of allied contingents who come in aid of Troy.

Thanks to H. W. Singor, we can go further. Studying the text of the *Iliad*, this scholar noticed an unusual regularity in the presentation of battles at Troy.[202] He reconstructed historically diverse methods of combat and concluded that in the original layer there was an attack of nine heroes (spearmen fighting on foot) against a city whose chief armed force was chariots fighting in formation. The most probable place where these two combat methods could have occurred is, in Singor's opinion, Boeotia, i.e. Thebes: the land of chariots would have been exposed to the attack of Achaean warriors from the northern margins of the Mycenaean world.[203] Singor shares Drews's opinion (Drews 1979; 1988) that the origin of the epic should be linked with Aeolian Thessaly, from which raids against rich regions of central Greece set out.

Singor also notes that in epic the protagonist slaughters three times nine enemies. The formula describing such a feat performed by Patroklos (*Iliad* 16.785–786) finds its parallel in Old Irish epic stories, where Cúchulainn regularly kills three times nine men. If we count the number of all opponents killed by Patroklos, it is twenty-seven. In the case of Trojans killed by Achilles we arrive at the same number. The repetition of the number is significant, because Patroklos acts as Achilles' substitute, so the deeds of the hero-protagonist are repeated. Twenty-seven is also the number of the Achaeans killed by Hektor. Moreover, thirty chariots are driven by warriors; twenty-seven (3 x 9) warriors are killed, and only three survive: Aeneas, Glaukos, and Deiphobos, who play important roles in later events in the Cycle. There are only nine great Achaean heroes who are also chariot-fighters: Achilles, Patroklos, Diomedes, Agamemnon, Menelaos, Idomeneus, Meriones, Nestor, and Antilochos.[204] There

201 See Ch. 2, p. 234–244, above.

202 Singor 1991. Compare Fenik (1986), who shows similarities in the narrative structure between Homer and *Nibelungenlied*.

203 Singor 1991:57.

204 According to Singor (1991:49–50), putting Achaean warriors onto chariots shows the accumulation of various historical layers in the development of this epic tradition. From our point of

are also three lesser warriors who use chariots: Menesthes and Anchialos (*Iliad* 5.609), and Iphinoos (*Iliad* 7.14–16), but they appear only to be slain. Because the nines appear in various configurations of names, Singor concludes that the numerical framework was a constant, but the warriors were not. Many of the nines may be a product of a much later epoch and sometimes they may even be Homer's invention, but—what is really important—the poet needed to adapt his narrative to the earlier structure, probably of Proto-Indo-European provenance.[205] The adherence to this structure inspires admiration for his memory, especially in the case of Hektor's victims scattered from *Iliad* Books 5 to 7. The fact that the numerical framework was so closely respected points to its significance and cannot be treated as a kind of a literary game.

In another article, Singor demonstrates that the Achaean wall in the *Iliad* is derived directly from the Theban Cycle, because it closely reproduces the pattern of the "Seven-gated Thebes."[206] Thanks to this wall, the Achaeans change from the besiegers to the besieged. The war against Boeotian Thebes clearly provides the parallel for that against Troy, described from the perspective of and with a certain sympathy for the besieged. Parts of a "Theban epic" could quite easily have been borrowed or "transported" to yield some material for the siege of the Greeks in their camp before Troy. The poet's source would probably have been an oral epic which preceded the *Thebaid*, just as an oral epic on the Trojan War preceded our *Iliad*.[207] Such recognition of motifs and plot patterns formed in earlier cycles (particularly the Theban one), in the Trojan Cycle has little in common with the search for the most bizarre coincidences with which the Analysts would support their claim that the *Iliad* and its cycle depend on the Theban Cycle.[208]

The shaping of new cycles

These similarities in both cycles can hardly be perceived as an arbitrary repetition of motifs. Both cycles shaped their plot structure with a similar framework or model. This model, however, is not reproduced faithfully in subsequent epics. The Argonautic Expedition, the Calydonian Boar Hunt, the Expedition against Thebes, and the Trojan War—there are clear differences between these songs due to the reworking of the plot. These differences are testimony to both the mechanical and evolutionary ways of constructing songs. The transformation

view, it looks like another example of the technique of making the opposing sides of the conflict similar to each other.

205 Singor 1991:50–60.

206 Singor 1992.

207 Singor 1992:404.

208 Mülder 1910. The best-known argument is the issue of Hektor's tomb in Boeotian Thebes.

of these story patterns on a greater scale must have paralleled that which has been reconstructed for the epic formula.[209] The singer preserves the formulae which he has learned from other singers, but he preserves these old forms only as long as they are useful and sufficient to tell the story in the way he wants to tell it. He does not make changes for change's sake, but he modifies his store of formulae, adapting them to the needs of a new topic or to the expectations of contemporary listeners, so they can understand various levels of his song, from the language to the events. Thus, formulae are subject to various types of mechanical modifications and the obsolete ones are replaced by new ones which are more useful because they communicate more effectively, although they may not be very well fitted into the hexameter.[210]

New songs also follow the pattern of those already in the tradition and modifications which enable the variation of content involve only selected elements. Similarities which result from following one pattern can be observed, for example, in numerous songs of return like the *Odyssey*, or in the *Iliad* and *Aethiopis*, which are based on the same pattern. Moreover, we can assume that the construction of the plot (macro-story) of the whole cycle was also subject to such transformations based on existing patterns. The narrative structure of the cycle transcends the plot of a single song and is respected by this song as a system of references into which it can fit and which gives it significance, i.e. thanks to which it can be understood. Relating the origins of the Theban and Trojan conflicts to the cosmogonic beginning initiated by Zeus's deceitful idea, to an extraordinary wedding linking the human and divine worlds, or to other events of this kind gives the song a deeper context of meanings by placing it in a coherent framework of the past.

One of the most typical and characteristic features of epic is its use of the cosmic scale. It is true also of epic born in cultures very distant from Greece. Martin refers to many African traditions, such as the narration of the *mvet* of the Fang people of Gabon and southern Cameroon. In the *mvet*, the stories of the fights of mortals and immortals constitute only a part of a larger plan covering the etiology of plants and animals, social hierarchy, and world order.[211] The cosmic scale of Indo-European epic has been confirmed in studies conducted by Georges Dumézil,[212] who proved that the proto-Germanic, Celtic,

209 The process of replacing old formulae by new ones, postulated already by M. Parry, was described by later scholars; see in particular Hoekstra 1965.

210 In the *Iliad*, there are formulae which date to before the spread of Linear B, as early as the fourteenth century BCE. Ruijgh (1985 and 1995) and West (1988), using parallels to early Indo-European languages as well as Mycenaean and Homeric Greek, conclude that heroic poetry had been cast in hexameters as early as the 14th century BCE.

211 Martin 2005:17.

212 Dumézil 1968; 1973.

Indian, and Roman traditions are to a large extent historicized and secularized forms of the cosmic myth.

It is a mistake, therefore, to assume that at the origin of a cycle, e.g. the Trojan, there was a song describing the entire war in an embryo form, whose plot was later extended by the incorporation of other songs. If that had been the case, it would amount to the inflation of a simple plot of the proto-song about the abduction of Helen and the capture of Troy. We have already noted that the oral tradition never presents all events, but only selected episodes of a familiar story, and a song built in this way may strike us as not very coherent. Just as there was a tendency to renew songs and introduce new themes, so too was there a tendency to replace one cycle with another. The Trojan Cycle seems to be the youngest of the existing ones and largely based on old patterns. It is not a coincidence that it manifests the greatest similarity to the Theban Cycle, which, I believe, must have preceded it directly, since, in the creation of a new cycle, original ideas were fitted into fixed and useful patterns. Nonetheless, the variety of myths that came down through time shows that the pursuit of novelty did not lead to a complete abandonment of the earlier epic material. That we know only of very few epic songs belonging to other cycles, from the *Sack of Oichalia* (from the circle of myths of Herakles) to the *Thebaid* and *Alcmeonis* (Theban Cycle), and that they always seem to have been less numerous than the songs of the Trojan Cycle, argues that the conquest of Troy was more eagerly attempted in the times of Homer and his successors.

The similarities between plots of various cycles are not, therefore, merely the result of the recurrence of the same themes in various songs as Foley and Arft suggest.[213] The plots of successive songs, fulfilling the same need for the reenactment of myth, are embedded in a common structure, superordinate in relation to individual plot solutions. At their most basic level the plots are inscribed (as was demonstrated in Ch. 1) in a cosmogonic and cosmological frame. However, as various plots fulfill the need for the reenactment of myth, the songs themselves are inscribed in the same plot frame, the shape of which is formed along the lines of those already existing. These plot frames, which we call cycles, did not function parallelly to and independently of one another, but because of their coexistence in the same performative circumstances, they overlapped and in a sense complemented one another.

The "doubling" of the Trojan Cycle

Rhys Carpenter's keen eye spotted a remarkable similarity in the events of the expedition against Troy and the preceding expedition against "false Troy," i.e.

[213] Foley and Arft 2015:84–85.

Teuthrania.[214] Proclus's summary of the *Kypria* presents this sequence of events in such a way that it is possible to speak of doubling all the elements preceding the expeditions: the judgment of Paris, the abduction of Helen, the gathering of allied forces in Aulis, and Kalchas's divination from a serpent devouring sparrows. Identical events precede the expedition which mistakenly landed in Teuthrania. Carpenter does not point it out, but Kalchas's prophecy proves it most clearly: it refers to the length of the war, which, due to an error in navigation, extends for another ten years. The course of the fighting at Teuthrania also closely resembles the fighting at Troy.

Using other sources (Pindar, Pausanias, Quintus of Smyrna, scholia to the *Iliad*), it is possible to reconstruct the order of events in the first expedition. When they land, the Achaeans meet with initial successes. However, after the death of Thersandros, one of the chief Achaean leaders, they are driven back to their ships. Patroklos, who comes to their rescue, gets wounded in a fight over the body of Thersandros, and in effect (probably seeking revenge like in the *Iliad*) Achilles returns to battle, from which, for some reason, he has previously withdrawn. The fight for Thersandros's body has an analogy in the fight for Patroklos's corpse in the *Iliad* and for Achilles' corpse in the *Aethiopis*. The death of an important Achaean warrior such as Thersandros gives an impulse for the Achaean counterattack; in the *Iliad* and *Aethiopis*, it means Achilles' *aristeia*, after the death of Patroklos and Antilochos respectively. Achilles fights with Telephos, the enemy leader, and hurts him badly.

All of this vividly resembles the *Iliad*, but there are even more similarities.[215] As in his fight with Hektor, at Teuthrania Achilles, despite his swiftness, cannot overtake the enemy, but is helped by a deceitful action of the gods. Like Athena, who in the form of Deiphobos persuades the naive Hektor to confront Achilles, Dionysos intervenes and causes Telephos to trip over a vine branch. Achilles treats Patroklos's wounds, then Patroklos tends to Eurypylos's wounds in the *Iliad*; Patroklos is supposed to have learned the art of healing from his friend, who—as the narrator of the *Iliad* points out—learned it from Cheiron. When the Achaeans realize that the city they are laying siege to is not Troy, they decide to return, but then—as after the capture of Troy—a storm breaks out and disperses the armada. As Carpenter notes, in order that the attack on Troy could take

[214] Carpenter 1974:54–56.

[215] According to Kullmann (2012:16), a recently found fragment of Archilochus (*Oxyrhynchus Papyri* vol. 59, Obbink 2005) confirms the hypothesis that the story of the Teuthranian expedition is older than the *Kypria*. The scholar interprets the mention of Telephos in the pseudo-Hesiodic *Catalogue of Women* (fr. 165.8 M-W) in a similar vein.

place, everything must happen again: the assembling of the fleet, Kalchas's prophecy, and the landing at Troy.[216]

As we can see, this is a double use of the same pattern. Carpenter concludes that it was one story told of two different places and believes that the topo graphy of the attack on a city corresponds better to Mysia, where Teuthrania was located, than to Troy.[217] From this, he deduces that the story of the raid against Teuthrania was primary and belongs to an Aeolic epic tradition, which preserves the memory of the Aeolic colonization of these regions in the Dark Ages.[218] The sacking of Troy, then, is a secondary Ionian tradition which reflects the expansion of Ionians even before the commercial expansion of Miletus. The expeditions against Teuthrania and Troy echo the spreading of Aeolians and Ionians along the western shore of Asia Minor and neighboring islands. The organization of these great expeditions recalls the naval raid of the allied tribes of the Sea Peoples, who sailed along the Syrian and Palestinian coast to Egypt, where they were ambushed and conquered by Ramesses III.

Recent archaeological data and documentary texts show that the Mycenaean city-states were interested in the western coast of Asia Minor, where they regularly made large-scale plundering raids, especially in the final period of their culture. The interest of epic in the expansion into the Asian continent can, therefore, be much older than Carpenter estimated. Let us first consider the issue of the doubling of the story of the expedition.

In Carpenter's opinion, the Trojan Cycle must have been the result of pinning together stories of two expeditions, or rather the original story and its replica, poorly adapted to new conditions. This idea was suggested by the correspondence of important motifs in the stories of both expeditions. But these motifs are not identical—they are only similar. The situation resembles the doubling of motifs within the Trojan Cycle. We must answer the following questions:

1. Was the Trojan Cycle created by joining two similar stories that were previously independent? Was it a case of—to borrow a term from metrics—"external expansion"?
2. Or was it a case of the "internal expansion" of the macro-story by the duplication of motifs?

[216] Carpenter 1974:55.

[217] Carpenter 1974:56.

[218] If this story reflects the colonization of Mysian shores by the Aeolians, its dating is a vital issue. Kullmann (2012:19–20) concludes that the early dating of the story of the Teuthranian expedition means that the myth of the Trojan War cannot be traced back to the Mycenaean times (which is assumed by Latacz 2004:277–278), but is a product of the pre-archaic epoch. I will not take up this problem, but focus on the model of creating epic plots.

As for the first question, if we assume some historical reality behind the epic plot, it is very likely that raids on the west coast of Asia Minor were quite frequent, since the influence of the Hittite and Achaean kings collided there. The main role in these territorial disputes was probably played by Miletus (Millawanda). Certainly, neither the expedition against Troy nor against any other coastal city was as important as the *Iliad* presents it. Epic songs do not typically choose as their subject matter events that were crucial historically—the best example being *The Song of Roland* mentioned above.

From Carpenter's point of view, the final shape of the Trojan Cycle is the result of the combination of two epic stories built on the same pattern, one of which was secondary to the other. However, here we have to do with the repetition of the sequence of events which define the whole expedition (i.e. the circumstances of embarking on the expedition and the unlucky return of the dispersed fleet), so it is in fact a repetition of the whole cycle, and not only the pattern of one song. Considering how various cycles develop in relation to one another because they use the same pattern—as we have seen in the Theban and Trojan cycles—we could say that the existence of two cycles of the same pattern is possible. But was it possible that two epic cycles, essentially so different, could make use of the same characters and the same causes for war? The probability that two epic cycles, so similar and yet, at least initially, independent of each other, would come into being approaches zero.

The second case—internal expansion—seems much more likely. Here the principle noticed by Neoanalysts seems to be in force, namely solutions with greater ramifications for the plot of the Trojan story are prior relative to these with the smaller ones (events described in the *Iliad* are supposed to be without meaning for the macro-story). The "Teuthranian Cycle" assumes knowledge of the relationship between Achilles and Patroklos, as well as the story of Achilles' replacement on the battlefield by his friend, which could be found in the *Iliad* or its prototype. The story of Patroklos's death is probably primary in relation to the story of his wounding, although this conclusion seems to contradict the findings of the Neoanalysts about the secondary position of the *Iliad* in relation to the cyclic material of the *Kypria*. Let us, however look at it from a different angle.

The copying of the story of the *Iliad* must be old enough to allow links to be created between various threads in the stories of the sons of Achilles and Telephos. The tale of the bribing of Astyoche, wife of Telephos and mother of Eurypylos, indicates a matching of the plot of the Trojan Cycle to that of the Theban, so either the Theban Cycle was a pattern for the Trojan, or *aoidoi* felt that there was a certain model for a cycle, to which all subsequent episodes had to conform. It is more probable that the "Teuthranian Cycle" was not primary, but secondary to the tradition of the Trojan War, which must already have comprised the *Iliad* or its prototypes. The proof that the theme of the replacement of Achilles with Patroklos is older than the *Iliad* (in the form that has come down to us) is the intricate story of Meleagros told in the poem by Phoinix, with the allusive play on the names Kleopatra-Patroklos, which will be discussed in the next chapter.

In the Teuthranian and Trojan stories, we are dealing with the doubling of the whole cycle pattern: an expedition—a return. This does not mean, however, that all the links of the plot must have been fixed. In other words, the cycle is only a structure into which the song fits. It provides a frame of reference. Songs do not present events one after another, which together make up the whole, known as a cycle. The song reproduces a certain pattern known from other songs within a larger familiar pattern, which is a cycle.

The copying of the plot of the trip to the Asian coast in the Teuthranian story involves the repetition of parallel scenes that somehow did not fit within the framework of the previous Trojan cycle. On the one hand, as we have seen, the multiplication of one pattern in a variable version is a quite natural way for the expansion of the cycle. On the other hand, the repetition of the pattern of substituting Patroklos for Achilles in battle and then the defeat of the enemy leader by Achilles seems no longer possible within the Cycle. The Trojan Cycle must have been closed in the mind of the author composing a separate frame of the Teuthranian expedition for his song. Evidently, the replacement of Achilles by Patroklos was an element of the plot of the Trojan War which was too well known to repeat in the same place, i.e. just before the end of the song.

We arrive, therefore, at the conclusion that while the plot of the Trojan Cycle precedes that of the *Iliad*, the content of the *Iliad*, i.e. the substitution of Patroklos for Achilles in battle must be much earlier than when the Trojan Cycle was fixed in its final shape. The apparent contradiction that the *Iliad* is a model for the *Kypria*, which contains material primary to the *Iliad*, can be eliminated if we assume that before the *Kypria* had been composed, tradition already knew a song (or songs) in which Patroklos was a substitute for Achilles and in which both heroes pursued the path of heroic deeds leading to their death. Only in this sense can we speak of the existence of a proto-*Iliad*. This pattern of the substitution of Achilles could be used many times in the Cycle and may indicate that this sophisticated structure was formed relatively early in the Greek epic tradition. But the situation of Patroklos's death, which causes Achilles to enter the path leading to his own destruction, must be prior in reference to the one in which Patroklos is only wounded, and the subsequent developments do not lead to Achilles' death.

The creation of a cycle

From these considerations a picture emerges of the formation of a cycle in oral epic tradition. We may attempt to sketch its evolutionary model, with the proviso that not all stages must appear in each tradition and, like in the case of Meletinsky's model of the development of epic, the features characteristic of various stages may function side by side. I will concentrate on the development of Greek epic.

The first stage

There are many songs dealing with one hero. It is so, for example, in the stories about Prince Marko or, in the Greek tradition, the stories of Perseus, Theseus, and Herakles. Individual songs depict various episodes from the hero's life and, as a rule, are not related to one another.

The second stage

There is a framework which can embrace various stories about a hero. In the epic of Gilgamesh, for example, the tales have a common frame which unites them, although the song is not very coherent and there are obvious traces of compilation. Nevertheless, they are not mixed up indiscriminately, but arranged in such a way as to show a gradual change in the hero. Gilgamesh, who is initially perceived as a scourge of the city, perhaps also as a source of its misfortunes, becomes its savior and benefactor.[219]

In Greek tradition, among a huge number of stories about Herakles, there are twelve connected by a framework of labors required by Eurystheus. The unsophistication of this construction is demonstrated by the fact that all independent exploits spring from a single cause. Moreover, each subsequent episode is introduced in the same way: Herakles performs a task, and the terrified Eurystheus assigns him a new one. All of these independent stories are bound together by a single motivation—the penalty for the murder of his children—and which, after the magic and solar number of twelve labors is completed, provides an ending to all the episodes. We can assume that in order to capture

[219] The existence of oral versions of the Gilgamesh story other than the written ones is quite possible. The translation of the Sumerian poem *The Death of Bilgamesh* (a Sumerian version of the name Gilgamesh), published in 1999, depicts the death and lavish funeral of the hero. A. George (quoted by Currie 2012:552) notes that "the Akkadian narrative of Enkidu's funeral in [Gilg. SBV] Tablet VIII is reminiscent of Bilgames's funeral in the Sumerian *Death of Bilgames*," which must mean that the Akkadian poet knew the poem about the death of the main character and transformed it creatively. This situation vividly reminds us of Greek tradition, provided we assume that Patroklos's funeral reflects the picture of the traditional funeral of Achilles.

the interest of the listeners, the singer, faced with the demand to present an episode connected with the deeds of this hero, can invent a new plot and fit it into the same plot frame, into which other songs on the same theme have been fitted.

The number of labors, twelve, is also a multiplication of the rule of three deeds (typical of folk tales), which the hero must for some reason undertake. In the *Iliad*, Bellerophon, who must perform three tasks, does not know that they have been assigned to him in the hope of his getting killed, but once he succeeds, he is rewarded in a manner typical of the fairy tale: he gets the hand of a princess and half of the kingdom (6.179–193).

The third stage

In the Greek (and Old Indic—*Mahābhārata*) traditions, there came into being a cycle, in which songs were gathered around a heroic undertaking: hunting for a monster or an expedition. The form of the expedition assumes the structure of a quest: traveling out and returning (in Greek tradition, even if the goal is achieved, the return is usually unfortunate). The hunting/expedition inherently includes the gathering of heroes. The summoning of all known heroes for an expedition organized by a young hero appears also in Slavic songs, especially in those performed by Avdo Međedović, who used it to highlight the mighty deeds of the young hero. Usually, these other heroes are only a background for the protagonist's efforts, but in the Argonautic Cycle, each of them must remove an obstacle encountered during their journey. Thus, they perform the typical function of the fairy-tale hero's magic helpers. In cycles dealing with military expeditions—e.g. the Theban and Trojan ones—the unusual powers of these heroes are revealed in their military performance, but priority is always given to two main heroes: Polyneikes and Tydeus or Achilles and Odysseus, whose relationship is metaphorically depicted as the cooperation of the lion and the boar.

The fourth stage

There is a common formal framework, i.e. the cosmic, divine, primal cause of events, which enables the introduction of songs into the cycle. The will of Zeus and the anger of a deity against a hero (Hera's against Herakles, Apollo's against Achilles, Athena's against the Achaeans, etc.) find their parallel in the foundation of the *Mahābhārata* in the conflict of asuras and devas.

The repetition of the whole pattern of the Trojan expedition with all the accompanying circumstances (the gathering of the fleet in Aulis, Kalchas's prophecy, bringing Achilles, etc.) corresponds to the repetition of the initial situation in the series of Herakles' twelve labors. The song is entered into the cycle in the same way. Or rather we should say that the singer places the plot of his song in a certain permanent structure of events of cosmic magnitude.

Fundamental to the cycle is that the stories should be told in the proper order. This order could have been respected during professional rhapsodic recitations, but also when an epic was performed in private, by someone who is not a recognized master in the art. The latter is suggested by the fact that Achilles and Patroklos take turns when singing the *klea andrôn* (9.189).

A typical, and certainly basic way of telling a myth in order is to tell two stories—one fixed at the beginning of events and the other at the end. The crucial story is the one dealing with the death of the hero, whereas that of his birth is complementary. The *aoidos*'s performance follows the natural order: first the beginning of events, then their end. This can be observed in the *Homeric Hymn* in honor of Apollo, and in the way Demodokos presents the Trojan War. Stories told in an appropriate order give an impression of a certain whole, even if there existed other stories about the same heroes. Thanks to this method of presentation, the tale is sufficient in itself, and yet it does not exclude other stories that can be told immediately following. Such narration of episodes from the cycle does not require any clarification. Moreover, it would also be useful in the *agôn* between *aoidoi*; but perhaps it was the *agôn* itself that gave rise to this way of telling.[220] The singer could present a different myth from his predecessor, or he could choose the same myth, but different episodes; and so the singer might place the beginning in a different spot and provide a different end to the events. The multiplication of these beginnings and ends was achieved by applying the same plot pattern to various heroes (e.g. Philoktetes, Achilles, etc.) or applying it to the same hero's attempts at saving his companions (Achilles). In the latter case, the song of Achilles' death was replaced by new versions of the song anticipating his death, which was imminent just after the events presented by the singer. One such song is the *Iliad*.

The fifth stage

In comparison to Demodokos's performances, in which a single story about the Trojan expedition is told in two separate songs, the *Iliad* displays a significant difference: although it is a story about the end of the Trojan War, it tells it from the perspective of the entire war—its beginning and its end. This strategy is not unique to the *Iliad*; it can be found also in other cyclic epics, so there must have been a tendency to combine two songs of a cycle into one. This tendency in its simplest form is visible in the *Hymn to Apollo*, which despite its clearly

220 On this topic, Derek Collins's observations are extremely valuable (Collins 2004, esp. Ch. 16–19).

dichotomous construction, is now regarded as one whole.[221] It seems that the creation of a monumental work, then, is achieved by merging stories of the cycle into a single song. The methods of generating content are different: from the simple multiplying of obstacles, like in various versions of the *Little Iliad* (where the singer introduced into his poem events known to him from several songs), to more sophisticated methods, like using parallel events, as in the *Aethiopis* and *Iliad* (by doubling the arrival of Trojan allies, Homer's epic seems to copy the solution of the *Aethiopis*). But the *Iliad*—as I will elaborate in Chapter 5—is also a summary fusion of three narrative structures, which I call "the way of the hero."

Quite often one encounters the opinion that the creation of such a monumental poem is possible only due to the spread of writing. However, considering the conditions, particularly the character of the writing materials, the desire to create a monumental composition would have had to spring from some ineffable enthusiasm over the potential of the new medium. Such reasoning is not only unsatisfactory, but also fallible. I believe that what was considered worthy of committing to writing were the poems which had already achieved monumental status much earlier, in the epoch of oral culture. The formation of such great songs embracing the entire cycle, although their plot presented only particular episodes of the macro-story, could only have been possible in specific circumstances, like the great pan-Aeolian and pan-Ionian festivals. In the next chapters, I will try to justify the thesis of the oral basis of such epic song construction as found in the *Iliad*.

221 See Ch. 4, p. 353n34, below.

4
Allusions in the Singer-Audience Relations

The Criteria of Oral Reception

The allusiveness of the text

ONE OF THE MOST important conclusions to be drawn from the preceding speculations is that the *Iliad* could not fundamentally differ from other epic songs in the Trojan Cycle. Moreover, individual songs did not create a chain, in which each story continued the previous one, but each was a complete oral song. Each presented an episode of the cycle from the perspective of the whole cycle. Although the song is an integral entity set in the most important moments of the beginning or end of the Trojan War, it is closely related to the super-text of the overall narrative, so the introduction of a particular episode necessitates the use of a system of allusions which link the song with the plot of the cycle. However, these allusions, going beyond the plot of the song, must assume the listeners' knowledge of events. The epic song did not function independently—all known archaic Greek epic songs belonged to some cycle, and all cycles (κύκλοι = οἰμαί) combined to create the great Cycle encompassing the whole history of gods and people (κλέα ἀνδρῶν καὶ θεῶν 'the glory of men and gods'). The performance of one song brought to life the whole tradition with the metonymical function propounded by John Miles Foley.[1] The creation of a new song was contingent on the existence of other songs in the cycle[2] and new epic cycles followed the pattern of old cycles; the Trojan Cycle is undoubtedly the youngest one. Of the circumstances which allowed the creation of the *Iliad,* the most important is the universality of cycles, which presupposes not only

1 Foley 1991:2–37.

2 Scodel (2002:69) points out that Helen's claim that the gods started the Trojan War so that it could be a subject of a song (*Iliad* 6.356–358), and her statements that Klytaimestra will become an object στυγερή ... ἀοιδή of 'hateful song' (*Odyssey* 24.200), and that gods will create for people ἀοιδήν ... χαρίεσσαν a 'pleasant song' extolling Penelope (*Odyssey* 24.197–198), indicate that the poet knew of the existence of other songs in which these heroines appear and was certain his audience knew them too.

the singer's knowledge of other songs, but first of all the listeners' knowledge of them.

In Greek tradition, the oral performance of songs frequently uses allusions to the macro-story which stretches beyond the boundaries of a given song. The purpose of these allusions is to anchor the narrative in the mythical past well known to the audience. In this chapter, I will present the significance and meaning of these allusions in the context of the singer's influence upon his audience.

Initially, allusions were examined primarily by Unitarians in order to prove the unity of Homer's works and thus to underpin their main thesis. Neoanalysts also were Unitarians, since they claimed that the *Iliad* was a conscious imitation of earlier works, but they regarded the analysis of allusions as something like "drilling holes" through which one could see the reconstructed material on which the song was modeled. However, even more important for them was to show that the *Iliad* was secondary in comparison to its prototypes, more rooted in tradition.

In the 1980s, oralists started to study the way in which allusions set a work in the stream of the common epic narration. Laura M. Slatkin's *The Power of Thetis: Allusion and Interpretation in the Iliad* (1991) opened up new horizons by demonstrating that the function of Thetis in the *Iliad* is much more important than it had been understood. The allusive way that the actions of Achilles' mother are described indicates that the author relied on his audience's knowledge of myths relating to the goddess' past.[3]

Slatkin convincingly points out that the singer refers both to the story of Achilles' death presented in the *Aethiopis* and to the theogonic body of myths known from Hesiod, in which Thetis, in order to counteract a sinister prophecy about her son, is married to a mortal man. Zeus and the other gods treat her with great respect because they are afraid to cross her. Thetis's grief (ἄχος) may lead her to an all-destructive revenge, like that of Demeter in the *Homeric Hymn*. Slatkin presents Homer's ability to transform traditional material and to adapt allusions to bring out the themes of his work.

3 Lang (1983) proposed such an understanding of the story of Thetis supporting Zeus during Hera, Poseidon, and Athena's revolt (149): "This story is presented in seven different passages [of the *Iliad*]; they make up four complementary pairs, appearing in six widely-spaced books (1, 5, 14, 15, 20, and 21). Therefore it is highly unlikely that all these references were invented separately to illuminate particular situations in the *Iliad*." Earlier, Braswell (1971:19) perceived Thetis's support of Zeus during the revolt as Homer's innovation which would give Zeus a reason to help her son. The revolt of the gods, according to him, was also invented in order to give Zeus a stronger motive for taking action. (Scholia could not satisfactorily explain this situation, thus they concluded that this trio would have most firmly resisted the fulfillment of Thetis's request by Zeus.)

Although the scholar assumes that the audience possesses knowledge about events to which Homer only alludes,[4] she does not pursue this train of thought further to see how such allusions could affect the audience and how they correspond to the author's intentions. Homer's work is usually examined from the perspective of the poetic aims which he sought in the organization of his plot, but if we consider that it was an *oral* performance, then perhaps even more relevant is the singer's effect upon his audience. Therefore, it is very important to know what kind of audiences he performed for and what their level of attention, empathy, and understanding was.

The examination of allusions that knit an epic like the *Iliad* to the cycle is intrinsically connected with the birth of this song and its impact as a piece of oral poetry. As Ruth Scodel rightly noticed, even if writing assisted in the creation of the *Iliad*, the poem was nonetheless intended for oral performance. Moreover, even if its text was written down in Homer's times, its copies could be used only as an aid to the singer. There was no readership.[5]

> It is hard even to know what we agree and disagree about until we specify what we are talking about when we talk about tradition. Instead of defining tradition, Homerists tend to reify it. One form of reification ignores audiences completely and looks only at the process of composition. The school of Homeric studies known as Neoanalysis is a particularly clear example of an approach which disregards the relationship between the singer and his audience. Scholars in this school have imagined a Homer who modeled his narrative on earlier texts or, as oral theory has become more orthodox, on earlier oral versions. Yet they have not thought much about how audiences received these parallel versions. While this neglect of the audience does not affect the validity of the arguments, it omits an important dimension essential to understanding the aesthetics of Homeric doubling. The death of Patroklos while he is wearing Achilles' armor imitates the death of Achilles in a

4 Slatkin (1991:xv): "The mythological corpus on which the poet draws, taken together, constitutes an internally logical and coherent system, accessible as such to the audience. The poet inherits as his repertory a system, extensive and flexible, whose components are familiar, in their manifold variant forms, to his listeners. For an audience that knows the mythological range of each character, divine or human—not only through this epic song but through other songs, epic and nonepic—the poet does not spell out the myth in its entirety but locates a character within it through allusion or oblique reference." Slatkin continues: "Allusions form a system of evocation in which each reference produces not a single meaning but a sequence of overlapping significations—as with echoes, in which it is not the original sound but each subsequent iteration that is picked up and relayed" (109–110).

5 Scodel 2002:3. Admittedly, there is no evidence that any oral poet ever used a written text as a memory aid in the performance of an oral text (see Jensen 1980:4).

> way that is thematically important in the *Iliad*. When Thetis responds to her son's grief over Patroklos' death as if she were mourning his death, these details invite even a listener who has not heard a song about Achilles' death to imagine Achilles' death rituals. There is obvious narrative profit for the listener in recognizing the parallel, but it is hard to say whether the poet hopes for listeners who know more than he tells. For example, at the moment when Apollo knocks off Patroklos' armor, it may be an advantage to know that Apollo will also participate in the death of Achilles. However, the narrator has Hektor predict Apollo's role in Achilles' death just before he himself dies (*Iliad* 22.358–360). He thus provides potential narrative pleasure, a small shock of recognition, for the hearer who only at this moment sees this similarity between Achilles' death and his friend's. In contrast, when Diomedes rescues Nestor, the listener who remembers that Antilochus died saving his father might be disappointed by this unpathetic imitation; yet the recollection that Nestor is traditionally rescued makes the story seem right and appropriate. Once the reception of a particular version of a typical story is at issue, it becomes clear that remembering is not an either-or activity.[6]

I have quoted from Scodel's book so extensively because all her objections turn out to be completely groundless when we look at the findings of the Neoanalysts in the context of the singer's impact upon listeners and their expectations for the song. Taking into account listeners' perceptual abilities and their participation in the process of conveying tradition seems essential for understanding what an oral song really is. Until then, oral theory analyzed formulaic language only and resembled Cartesian mechanics of the human body. For many scholars, orality means simply a mechanical repetition of formulae and fixed patterns, which implies the singer's lack of skill and inability to control the material like a real poet. But the orality of the *Iliad* does not result only from the use of traditional diction and traditional song patterns, both of which are very flexible; orality means creating the song as it is being performed, which entails the existence of a narrative strategy related to such a performance. A bad singer can only reproduce a song as he has learned it, but the better the poet, the stronger impact he makes upon his audience, the better he is able to shape his song according to their expectations, and the better he is able to guide his listeners and even to prompt certain reactions from them.

6 Scodel 2002:4.

Impact upon the audience

Our considerations of the reception of epic lead us back to the issue which I believe was the most significant for early ancient literary criticism. For Aristotle, the "Homeric Question" did not exist. He assessed epic in the same way that he assessed tragedy—taking into account how it influenced the audience and how the audience reacted. In his teleological conception, epic is only a preliminary stage for the crowning literary achievement, i.e. tragedy, because it has less impact upon the audience than tragedy, which evokes "pity and fear." Because he is interested in the intensity and economy of an aesthetic and ethical experience, Aristotle discusses the impact of tragedy in a live performance, not the experience of a reader of its text. Comparing tragedy and epic poetry, he could only take into account the rhapsodic performance of epic, i.e. when the recited text finds its way directly to the ear of the listener. Nonetheless, it is doubtful whether Aristotle's notion about performances and about their impact upon hearers was correct or anachronistic.[7]

The Alexandrians perceived Homer as an author of a written text and this attitude generated questions about him.[8] The result in modern times is the Homeric Question, which has flourished for two hundred years. The issue of reception appears already in Parry's first work, his doctoral thesis on the traditional epithet in Homer, although he does not use the term "oral poetry" for the traditionality of epic style which he postulates. Arguing that a fixed epithet fulfills only a metrical role and is only ornamental, he claims that the bard's audience must have been insensitive to the meaning of the epithet and accepted the formula as a single essential idea.

Parry unnecessarily tried to distinguish between what is and isn't a meaningful element, because he shaped his concept of formulae under the influence of structuralism and so he assumed that the only meaningful element is the noun. His main aim was to show the difference between the traditional, formulaic style and that of an individual poet. Although he noticed that an epithet ennobles the phrase (e.g. describing a character as a hero), nonetheless he

7 The interest in the impact of poetry upon the audience is a by-product of Aristotle's polemics with Plato's understanding of *mimêsis*. For Plato, the mimetic aspect of poetry is harmful. Poetry could possibly be useful if it imitated good things, but since poets cannot recognize what is good as well as philosophers do, he postulates that it should be banished from the state. Aristotle, on the other hand, postulating the existence of catharsis, shows the virtues of *mimêsis*. However, while the defense of the role of poetry seems commendable in the face of Plato's authoritarian inclinations, the actual existence of the cathartic effect is very doubtful.

8 Nagy (2010:31) pins down this moment as the "post-Athenocentric period" (4th century BCE); it was then that Homer's action as an author was described with the verb *graphein* 'to write', instead of *poiein*, 'to make' whatever he composes.

claimed that this is its only meaning, in no way connected with context. Many scholars who continued his studies disagreed and denied that the epithet was meaningless. However, it seems that we can safely assume that the formula as a whole carries a meaning, which it may share with other formulae referring to the same person or object, and which it may not. For example, both πολύτλας δῖος Ὀδυσσεύς and πολυμῆτις Ὀδυσσεύς[9] refer to Odysseus and observe the economy of the meter, but they carry various semantic and emotional loads and have various epic associations.

Even when oral studies gained popularity in scholarship, the dependence of the text upon performance was the most controversial issue. Albert Lord proposed that the artistry and monumentality of Homer's poems result from the fact that the text was dictated,[10] so he assumed that a typical performance of a song would never have produced such a masterpiece. This concept was criticized, not because scholars defended traditional performance, but because they did not believe that the current shape of the *Iliad* could be an outcome of chance; after all, a single improvisation entails many errors and inconsistencies,[11] which, in their opinion, don't favor the uniformity and perfection of composition.[12] Lord's approach seemed to mark the return to the Analysts for whom Homer's poems were a random, often faulty conglomeration of ill-assorted elements. Even Parry's son Adam supported the idea that the work was written down by the singer himself. He said that his claim was borne out by the concise nature of the works which was unprecedented in oral artistry and the economy of the artistic means of expression, free from the influence of listeners' reactions.[13] The artistry of the *Iliad* is, I believe, perceived too much according to our standards. The mechanistic diction of oral poetry leads scholars to conclude that the singer was careless about details of his narration which could affect the meaning in a

9 Respectively: "the one who suffered much / the one who can suffer much, divine Odysseus" and "the one who has many secret plans / man of many deceits." Compare Finkelberg 2012.

10 Lord 1953; 1960:148–149, 153. The scholar points out that the singer would have to learn to dictate a song because dictation is something other than a typical performance. Slowing down the performance of a song may be initially annoying, but it gives the singer time to think about the song in more detail.

11 Lord (1960:186–197) in his sample analysis of the *Iliad* tries to demonstrate that its author acts in the same way as a Slavic singer, whose aim is to perform his song to the best of his abilities. Lord believed that such a singer gets "carried away" by his song, often changing his construction plans and emphasizing other matters than he originally intended. Ergo, these are not mistakes, but typical modifications in the plot structure undertaken in order to stress what in a given moment seems more important to the singer. For example, when Athena stops the infuriated Achilles from killing Agamemnon, she promises him to reward his self-possession with gifts "three times as splendid." Later on, the poet evidently forgets about this, and concentrates on the situation and Achilles' demeanor (189–193).

12 For instance, Whitman 1958, Lesky 1967.

13 Parry 1966:214.

longer narrative or deepen contextual value. It seems to me, however, that such a conclusion leads us astray.

James Morrison has demonstrated[14] that deviations from the announced order of narration should be understood as the poet's deliberate attempts to mislead the listener. Quite often, events which have been foretold do not occur at all or happen later than expected, or their course is different. For centuries, these inconsistencies were regarded as the author's mistakes and the Pluralists used them as evidence for the multiple authorship of the epic. However, contrary to the impression of the contemporary reader, the singer does not get lost among a great number of ways in which he can shape his song, but purposefully meanders, perhaps dropping a thread, or adding a new one for the sake of his song, but never taking his eyes off the overall composition—which is possible due to ring composition used in the macro scale. We could say that when the spoken word is concerned, Homer is in his element, perfectly in control of the constraints and—paradoxically—the freedom which stem from the opportunities to multiply the content.

Investigation of the ways in which the singer uses allusions to the epic plot extending beyond his current song will allow us to better estimate Homer's poetic skill. We should consider first the situations in which epic poetry was performed in Greece in the archaic epoch and, insofar as it is possible, earlier.

Singer

The first question is whether every singer is able to control the material of his cyclic song in the same way as the author/authors of the *Iliad* and *Odyssey*, or the fictitious and perhaps idealized singer Demodokos. From Homer's poems, we can infer that *aoidoi* (sg. *aoidos* ἀοιδός) were professional singers, comparable to other artisans (*dêmiourgoi*) like the seer, physician, and spear maker, who, although outsiders, were very useful and therefore readily accepted into society (*Odyssey* 17.382–387). Unlike Demodokos or Phemios, who were singers living in the courts of noblemen, they could travel.[15] Like the Slavic *guslari*, who often traveled from one place to another, especially during fairs or religious

14 Morrison 1992a and 1992b.7,.

15 Perhaps the evidence of this may be found in the story of the singer Thamyris, who during his journey from Oichalia quarreled with the Muses (*Iliad* 2.594–596). Homer's travels can be seen in the Hellenistic *Lives*, which, although unreliable as a biographical source, provide an idea of a typical singer. On the usefulness of this source, see Nagy (2010:29–58), who notes that the *Lives* are a mixture of earlier and later concepts of Homer, and present him as an *aoidos*, rhapsode, and writer. Traveling singers are found in other cultures; here I would like to refer only to the Anglo-Saxon poem *Widsith*. The eponymous Widsith, whose name means "Far Journey," describes his visit to the court of Eomanric, the king of Goths, and other kings, whereas he was based at the court of Eadgils, the prince of the Myrgings (see Chadwick and Chadwick 1932:25).

festivities, this mobility gave Greek singers an opportunity to demonstrate their skills, to listen to other singers, and to expand their repertoire. The benefit was twofold: singers might have new songs to perform and could contribute to the birth of a network of myths, which would finally take the form of a cycle. The allusions in songs to other songs imply that both singers and their audiences had extensive knowledge of such tales.

This universal knowledge of epics is corroborated by amateur performances in the works of Homer. The song of Nausikaa and her companions during a game of ball should be undoubtedly regarded as a choral song, in which the princess has the leading role (*Odyssey* 6.101). Likewise, when Kalypso and Kirke sing at their looms (*Odyssey* 5.61, 10.221), we can assume that it is a lyric song. But when messengers arrive at Achilles' tent, they find him playing the phorminx and singing κλέα ἀνδρῶν 'the fame/famous feats of heroes' (*Iliad* 9.186–194), an epic song or epic lyric (like Stesichorus "lyrical epics" or Sappho fr. 44 L-P) which commemorates the heroic deeds of ancestors.[16] Andrew Dalby rightly notices that Achilles' ability to sing an epic cannot be treated as something exceptional.[17] This is confirmed by comparison with other cultures, in which it was a popular skill: e.g. among Arabic, Japanese, and Celtic warriors, Vikings, and Tibetan students of the early medieval era; also in contemporary cultures of East Africa, including the Fipa.[18]

That is why Dalby rejects both Stephanie West's opinion that all singers in the *Iliad* are amateurs (including Apollo, the Muses, and the two singers on Achilles' shield) and Charles Segal's claim that, unlike the bard's performance, the song of the warrior, i.e. of the amateur, can give pleasure only to the singer himself.[19] There is no reason to think that Achilles was a lousy performer of an epic song. But what about Patroklos? Let us look at his role in the scene in Achilles' tent (*Iliad* 9.186–191):

> τὸν δ' εὗρον φρένα τερπόμενον φόρμιγγι λιγείῃ
> καλῇ δαιδαλέῃ, ἐπὶ δ' ἀργύρεον ζυγὸν ἦεν,
> τὴν ἄρετ' ἐξ ἐνάρων πόλιν Ἠετίωνος ὀλέσσας·
> τῇ ὅ γε θυμὸν ἔτερπεν, ἄειδε δ' ἄρα κλέα ἀνδρῶν.
> Πάτροκλος δέ οἱ οἶος ἐναντίος ἧστο σιωπῇ,
> δέγμενος Αἰακίδην ὁπότε λήξειεν ἀείδων

16 On the meaning of the term κλέος 'glory', see Nagy 1974:244–252; also Nagy 1999:102–103, who compares Hesiod *Theogony* 100, κλέα προτέρων ἀνθρώπων ("the fame of men of the past"), with *Iliad* 9.524–525: οὕτω καὶ τῶν <u>πρόσθεν</u> ἐπευθόμεθα <u>κλέα ἀνδρῶν</u> / <u>ἡρώων</u> … ("We learn this also from the <u>kleos</u> [pl.] *of men of the past, / Who were the heroes…*").

17 As in Hainsworth 1993:37: "A genuine amateur like Akhilleus at 9.186, or King Alfred among the Danes, is rare and the verisimilitude of such representations is called into question."

18 Dalby 1998:197–198 and 207–208; he cites the relevant bibliography.

19 S. West 1988:96; Segal 1992:5.

they found him [Achilles] taking pleasure from the play on the resonant phorminx
beautiful, of elaborate workmanship, with a silver cross-bar;
he chose it as his spoils when he sacked Eëtion's city
and now it gladdened his heart as he sang of famous deeds of the men of the past.
Opposite him sat Patroklos alone and in silence,
Waiting [?] for Aiakos's descendant to finish his song [?].

This translation of the last verse is the most frequent one, although it raises many doubts. The conjunction ὁπότε with the optative, which appears in the subordinate clause, usually expresses a frequent event, and so it should be translated 'whenever, every time'. It indicates that Achilles has stopped his song and resumed it many times. It is in line with Lord's findings—the singer often makes shorter or longer breaks in order to collect his thoughts or to rest his voice.[20] In contrast, Patroklos's action expressed by the participle δέγμενος is open to various interpretations. Aristophanes (*Wasps* 1222) uses this word in the context typical of the singing of a song: 'to take up the song where the predecessor has left off'. It refers to a popular entertainment in which the participants take turns in singing the same song or various songs. Such a passing of the song from one performer to another often happens at a symposium. Nagy finds here an analogy to the continuation of a song by rhapsodes.[21] It means that Patroklos's role is not that of a servant waiting to take the instrument from his master's hands, but that of a fellow singer, who is able to take up a song and continue it where his predecessor has left off.[22] A joint performance of a song does not seem to be unusual.[23] After all, the performer might have become tired, and Achilles and Patroklos sing this song for their own pleasure only, or perhaps

20 Lord 1936. Compare *Odyssey* 8.87 ἦ τοι ὅτε λήξειεν ἀείδων θεῖος ἀοιδός ("whenever the divine singer stopped his song" [Odysseus wiped his tears]).

21 Nagy 1996a:71–72. See Plato *Hipparchos* 228b, Diogenes Laertius 1.57. Chadwick and Chadwick 1932:572 mention that the Saxons had a similar custom for performing. Until the poet Caedmon received a divine gift (Bede *Ecclesiastical History* 4.24), he was unable to perform a song at all, and in the evenings, when men gathered to drink, if there was an occasion for joy, he sat silent when his companions in turn sang with an instrument.

22 Hainsworth 1993:88 *ad* 191: "Patroklos is simply listening to Akhilleus, perhaps with the implication that he would take up the song at the point where Achilles left off."

23 Hainsworth 1993:88: "There are many ways of performing heroic song, including the employment of two singers, but the only one described in Homer is that of the solo singer, *Odyssey* 1.325ff, 8.62ff., 8.499ff., 17.518ff." See Collins 2004:167–175. Turn-taking performances in oral culture are not specific to epic poems; they often happen with other genres of songs. Veselova (2020) describes a couple of Russian folk singers, who performed a *vinogradye* song in this way, i.e. the man continued where his wife had left off and vice versa.

also for the pleasure of other Myrmidon warriors who could have been present, as later Automedon (*Iliad* 9.209) and other companions—ἕταροι—were (9.658).[24]

The question is whether singing in turns means the continuation of a song well known to both performers or whether each of them sings a well-known story in his own way. This question can be linked to the way that rhapsodes performed Homer, taking up where the predecessor left off.[25] In popular modern opinion, this practice of continuing the song reveals the circumstances which allowed the creation of Homer's monumental epics. This belief is based on Aelian *Varia Historia* 13.14:

> Ὅτι τὰ Ὁμήρου ἔπη πρότερον διῃρημένα ᾖδον οἱ παλαιοί. οἷον ἔλεγον Τὴν ἐπὶ ναυσὶ μάχην καὶ Δολώνειάν τινα καὶ Ἀριστείαν Ἀγαμέμνονος καὶ Νεῶν κατάλογον καὶ Πατρόκλειαν καὶ Λύτρα καὶ Ἐπὶ Πατρόκλῳ ἆθλα καὶ Ὁρκίων ἀφάνισιν. ταῦτα ὑπὲρ τῆς Ἰλιάδος. ὑπὲρ δὲ τῆς ἑτέρας Τὰ ἐν Πύλῳ καὶ Τὰ ἐν Λακεδαίμονι καὶ Καλυψοῦς ἄντρον καὶ Τὰ περὶ τὴν σχεδίαν καὶ Ἀλκίνου ἀπολόγους καὶ Κυκλώπειαν καὶ Νέκυιαν καὶ Τὰ τῆς Κίρκης καὶ Νίπτρα καὶ Μνηστήρων φόνον καὶ Τὰ ἐν ἀγρῷ καὶ Τὰ ἐν Λαέρτου. ὀψὲ δὲ Λυκοῦργος ὁ Λακεδαιμόνιος ἀθρόαν πρῶτος ἐς τὴν Ἑλλάδα ἐκόμισε τὴν Ὁμήρου ποίησιν· τὸ δὲ ἀγώγιμον τοῦτο ἐξ Ἰωνίας, ἡνίκα ἀπεδήμησεν, ἤγαγεν. ὕστερον δὲ Πεισίστρατος συναγαγὼν ἀπέφηνε τὴν Ἰλιάδα καὶ Οδύσσειαν.
>
> For the ancients once sang the songs of Homer divided into several parts: for example, the "Fight at the Ships," "Doloneia," "Agamemnon's *Aristeia*," and "Catalogue of the Ships," moreover the "Patrokleis," "Ransom," "Games in Honor of Patroklos," and "Breaking Vows." These were in place of the *Iliad*. The ones in place of the other song were the "Events at Pylos" and "Events in Lacedaemon," "Kalypso's Cave," "Events near Scheria," "Stories told to Alkinoos," the "Kyklopeia," "Nekyia," "Story of Kirke," "Bath (Washing?)," "Killing Suitors," "Events in the Village," and "Events at Laertes' Place." Later, Lykurgos the Lacedaemonian was the first to bring Homer's collected poetry to

24 Servants—δμῳαί—are also mentioned, but the reciter did not have to take their opinion into account.

25 Ford (1992:114–115) also sees in Odysseus's account of his journey the continuation of Demodokos's song about him. His suggestion that it reflects a typical rivalry in the *agôn* in the performance of epic poetry is, I think, overinterpretation. However, the juxtaposition of the Demodokos/Odysseus recitation with the scene in Achilles' tent reveals one striking similarity, i.e. the interrupting of the song by both Demodokos and Achilles. As we can see, such a break may or may not entail the change of performer, which is quite understandable in the light of what is known about such practice among Slavic singers.

> Greece. He brought this collection from Ionia where he traveled. Later, Peisistratos compiled and presented them as the *Iliad* and *Odyssey*.

Herodotus quotes *Iliad* 6.289–292, stressing that it belongs to Διομήδους ἀριστεία—"Diomedes' *Aristeia*," whereas in the traditional division into books Book 5 is called that. It may mean that the oral performance of Homer's song entailed the recitation of segments performed by several rhapsodes[26] in succession, and these segments were independent of the later division into books. Performances in this style might have been responsible for the much later belief that Peisistratos or Solon in Athens or Lykurgos in Sparta collected and wrote down Homer's songs, which had been scattered.[27]

Gregory Nagy in his theory attributing the emergence of Homer's poems to an evolutionary process (*An Evolutionary Model for the Making of Homeric Poetry*) points out that the organization of episodes in Homeric poems is an effect of the growing tendency towards the even weighting of the episodes of which they are composed.[28] A trace of the earlier uneven weighting is visible, according to Nagy, in "the preeminence, let us say, of the Achilles theme in the narrative traditions about the Trojan War—at the expense of themes magnifying the epic deeds of other heroes at Troy."[29] Nagy also demonstrates how the accounts of the "sewing" of Homer's songs together into one rhapsody by rhapsodes (literally 'these who sew together') are an element of a metaphorical image presenting the creation of an oral song (analogous to the metaphorical images of weaving and carpentry), but also reflect the myth of an "instantaneous recovery or even regeneration" of Homer's poems.[30] In reality, the final sequencing of themes in Homer's poems is a result of multiple performances over a long time.[31]

26 All earlier citations of fragments of Homeric verse are identified with names of episodes and not the number of books: Herodotus 2.116; Thukydides 1.9.4 and 1.10.4; Plato *Cratylus* 428c, *Ion* 539b, *Republic* 614b; Aristotle *Poetics* 1454b30, 1455a2, *Rhetoric* 1417a13. For discussion on the division of poems into books, see Jensen 1999.

27 Lykurgos: Plutarch *Lykurgos* 4; Peisistratos: Herodotus 7.6.3, Cicero *De Oratione* 3.137; Hipparchos: Plato *Hipparchos* 228b; Solon: Diogenes Laertius 1.57. On the mythical aspect of perceiving such culturally unique works as scattered and disassembled and then miraculously collected, Nagy 1996b:71–75.

28 Nagy 1996b:77: "The evolution of ancient Greek epic involved a progression from uneven weighting toward even weighting." One can draw a parallel to the custom of singing a song in a preordained sequence in the Apache Changing Woman ritual (Nagy 1996b:79).

29 Nagy 1996b:78.

30 Nagy 1996b:83–89. Testimonia: Scholia *ad* Pindar *Nemean* 2.1d (referring the authority of Dionysios of Argos, fourth/third century BCE), Scholia *ad* Dionysius Thrax, Codex Venetus 489.

31 Nagy 1996b:82: "Once the sequencing of Homeric 'episodes' becomes a tradition in its own right, it stands to reason that any cross-referencing from one episode of the sequence to another will also become a tradition. It is from a diachronic perspective that I find it useful to consider the phenomenon of Homeric cross-references, especially long-distance ones that happen to reach for hundreds or even thousands of lines: it is important to keep in mind that any such

It seems that this conception of how the episodes in the *Iliad* and *Odyssey* were arranged rules out single authorship. Worse still, it makes them only a collection of songs, although the structure of both poems reflects that of a single oral epic. Moreover, individual episodes in the *Iliad* do not possess such a structure, which means that they cannot be perceived as individual songs. Therefore, if particular episodes of the *Iliad* and *Odyssey* were recited by various rhapsodes, it indicates the dispersion of a unified work and not the creation of the whole by collecting variously assorted elements. Undoubtedly, the division of a unified work, like the *Iliad* or the *Odyssey*, is secondary, though the practice of taking turns in performing episodes may reflect the traditional performance of epic songs.

It is not certain whether rhapsodes at the Panathenaia performed only those of Homer's works which are known to us, as Aelian's testimony suggests. After all, "performing Homer" might also have involved performing epic songs from the Trojan Cycle, or even the Theban Cycle, since Homer was credited with the *Kypria* and *Thebaid*, or the epic of Herakles, because the *Sack of Oichalia* was also attributed to him. Like in the case of Demodokos, the singer certainly did not perform only a fragment of a song (since, as I have demonstrated, the *Odyssey* suggests the presentation of complete epics), similarly the rhapsodic performance of Homeric songs, at least in the beginning, might have consisted in singing, in a preordained order, complete songs of the cycle, which present the whole story of the war. It turns out that Nagy's model is even more appropriate for an earlier period, which witnessed the creation of the cycle, and not only a poem of the *Iliad*'s caliber. Ancient testimonies about an actual performance, where successive reciters continued the song, later transformed into the myth about the collection and arrangement of songs carried out by lawmakers or sages (Solon, Lykurgos, and Peisistratos),[32] are misleading because they explain Homer's monumental works according to a principle which was by then already obsolete.

As has been shown in Chapter 1, the performance of songs about the Trojan War might have been governed by the rule of relative chronology, i.e. successive episodes of the cycle might have been presented one after another. We have already seen this early form of establishing chronology in the presentation of Demodokos's songs which focused on the beginning and end of the cyclic plot. The song whose action was situated at the end of the macro-story usually also referred somehow to a song at its beginning (in Demodokos's case, it was

cross-reference that we admire in our two-dimensional text did not just happen one time in one performance—but presumably countless times in countless reperformances within the three-dimensional continuum of a specialized oral tradition."

32 Nagy 1996b:71–75.

the attempt to settle the conflict between claimants to the title of the captor of Troy in favor of Odysseus). Every time it could be a different episode, often modeled on other episodes. However, the proliferation of episodes must have necessitated their arrangement in an orderly sequence, which was later called a cycle. If, as we have already demonstrated, the songs of the cycle showed a given episode in the context of the whole Trojan War, then it follows that they must have retained a certain degree of independence. The presentation of these episodes in sequence must have taken place on special occasions, e.g. during great festivals like the Panathenaia. But the independence of a song depicting a given episode from the perspective of the whole war could have been possible only because the thematic range of the cycle had already been established and familiar, so it seems that the principle of sequential presentation is deeply rooted in Greek tradition.[33] We can speak about continuing this performative custom in the rhapsodic *agôn* at the Panathenaia.

Such a method of arranging material could have been preserved even when the *Iliad* was no longer perceived as one of many poems about Achilles' wrath. It was probably at the Panathenaia that the *Iliad* gained the status of the fundamental song presenting this theme. But because it does not include the scene of the hero's death, pan-Hellenic tradition kept another song which took over this function in the cycle—the *Aethiopis*.

The stage of the thematic disproportion of episodes in the singing of epic is clearly noticeable in Greek tradition. This disproportion is not confined to the domination of the subject of Achilles' wrath. The song about Odysseus's return obliterated other episodes connected with this protagonist, no doubt more important from the perspective of the overall plot of the cycle. These episodes fall into pairs, which must have reflected the earliest method of presenting them.[34] Even if the first episode of Demodokos's song, from the beginning of the war, could be called an 'innovation' introduced by the author of the *Odyssey*, then the episodes recounted in the summaries of the *Kypria* are most certainly traditional. In the *Kypria*, we can find two clearly related Odysseus episodes: 1) Odysseus's pretended madness and Palamedes' exposure of the ruse, and 2) Odysseus's revenge upon Palamedes. In the original presentation of the epic,

33 Nagy 1996b:82–89 argues that we should not make a qualitative distinction between the *aoidos* and the rhapsode.

34 Such an arrangement of the content can also be found in the *Hymn to Apollo*, recognized as the oldest *Homeric Hymn*. Its structure is evidently two-part, though now the prevailing view claims its compositional unity (see Miller 1985; Chappell 2011), with the first part relating the god's birth on the island of Delos, and the second part focusing on his establishing the oracle at Delphi. Here again are narratives which could be placed either at the beginning or at the end of the epic poem dedicated to the exploits of this god.

these stories could have been expressed in two songs, one after another.[35] Another pair of episodes which could be placed at the beginning and at the end of the cycle is 1) leaving Philoktetes on the island of Lemnos, and 2) bringing him to the camp at Troy, where he kills Paris.

Our concept how *aoidoi*/rhapsodes performed songs during important religious festivities should be clarified. They did not present, one singer after another, successive episodes which took place at Troy. Instead, they situated their story at two key points of the cycle: the places which were easily identified as the beginning and the end of all events. This compositional method was conducive to the creation of a framework encompassing a cycle of stories, i.e. the whole mythical history.

Such a performative method reveals the reason why every episode was presented in the context of the whole Trojan War. The same, I believe, holds true for the presentation of songs from other epic cycles. The song is anchored to the story at its beginning or end and shows either the cause of events in the context of their outcome, or the most important event in the life of a god or a hero with reference to the cause. In the heroic myth, the story of the hero's death is brought to the fore, and it is primary, whereas the story of his birth is created secondarily. Originally, the story relating the beginning was created later, and this pattern could also be true of the mature epic tradition. The tale about Paris's defeat at the hands of Philoktetes must have been supplemented by a new story explaining the latter's absence at Troy. Here the author used the narrative model in which the character was at first a member of the expedition but later resigned or somehow got lost. That the problem with the capture of Troy is presented as new reflects the author's use of this model. Paris's bow prevents the Achaeans from gaining victory and appears as a "new" obstacle because it is recounted in the song—and it is immaterial that Paris was there with his bow from the inception of the war. Overcoming such an obstacle requires new forces represented in the song by a young warrior who on account of his age has not participated in the combat yet, so he has to be summoned. This original model has been transformed in the Trojan Cycle in the case of Philoktetes, and also Achilles, who in the Trojan myth is brought "in advance," included when the Achaeans organize the expedition.[36]

35 The fact that Odysseus calls himself Telemachos's father (*Iliad* 2.260, 4.354) does not necessarily indicate the knowledge of the plot of the *Odyssey* or Telemachos's role in it (Aristarchus Arn/A) but acquaintance with the episode describing Odysseus's pretended madness, which was disproved by placing his infant son Telemachos in front of the plow. Telemachos unwittingly decides about Odysseus's participation in the expedition.

36 In spite of his young age, Achilles is necessary at Troy. In Greek epic, the absence of a hero when the community faces an insurmountable problem is usually explained in terms of his wrath, which makes him withdraw from combat. His wrath, as we have seen, is a result of a curse or

This state of things must have influenced the development of Greek epic in the way that I have suggested. I could add that a performative custom of capturing the beginning and end of events could not have been reserved for the presentation of epic songs at great festivals only. They must have been presented in this way also for a smaller audience, as corroborated by Demodokos's recitation of the song about the beginning and end of the Trojan War.

This method of presenting a mythical narrative offers the singer many opportunities for introducing numerous allusions into his song, because it is difficult to present a single episode without relating it to the myth. When singers performed one after another, and their songs were interconnected (that is the later song referred to the preceding one), a competitive spirit inspired the creation of stories. In *Iliad* 9, Achilles and Patroklos did not compete against one another as singers; they could continue an epic narrative well known to both of them. But, unlike amateurs, professionals did compete. In a rhapsodic *agôn*, one singer could show Philoktetes' deeds at Troy, then in reaction to him another singer would present Odysseus and Palamedes, and another one would reply with a story of Achilles. In this context, they could use the same patterns to present their tales and it was very easy and natural to include in their song allusions to other songs.

The insertion of allusions to other songs was an important device which professional singers used to improve their compositions. The singer tried to awaken the curiosity of his audience, balancing what was known to them and what was unknown. Allusions to other songs might have been a result of referring the listeners to the songs of the singer(s) who performed before him. These allusions were introduced not only for the sake of embellishing narration, but also allowed the singer to catch the listeners' attention.

In the *Odyssey*, both *aoidoi* who appear in the story are represented as valued professionals. We have already mentioned Odysseus's praise of Demodokos, but the value attached to singers can be further substantiated by the fact that when Odysseus kills all the suitors, only Phemios, who pleads with him, and Medon, the herald, are spared (22.330–380). Naturally, we can argue that it is self-praise by the author, who displays a kind of professional solidarity with the figures of singers he evokes. However, a more important question here is how a professional singer was evaluated. Let us concentrate on two aspects of such an assessment:

an oracle against the hero. This body of motifs probably came into being because, as the song concentrated on a prolonged war/siege, it was difficult to introduce more and more new characters who would perform heroic deeds, and the pattern of the cycle required a relatively constant number of protagonists.

1. The abundance of songs in his repertoire marks the *aoidos* as someone who collects knowledge. While Homer says that Phemios knows "many feats of gods and heroes" (*Odyssey* 1.337–338),[37] other singers state more generally that a poet possesses knowledge about "all things, wisdom" (Hesiod fr. 320.1 M-W, fr. 306 M-W, *Homeric Hymn to Hermes* 484).[38] Andrew Ford, after Nagy, explains this "omniscience" in the context of Panhellenization. Undoubtedly, the gathering of a great number of singers in one place would further the accumulation and linking of the mythical material. And, as I have already pointed out, the joining of mythical plots and organizing them in cycles must have started much earlier than the development of Homeric poems. What at this point plays an essential role is the scope of an individual singer's knowledge of the past—especially since not all knowledge is equally valuable. The formula applied to the *oimê* on which Demodokos based his first song, τῆς τότ' ἄρα κλέος οὐρανὸν εὐρὺν ἵκανε "whose fame had reached the vast skies those days" (*Odyssey* 8.74),[39] indicates the preference for stories which are familiar rather than those which are obscure (contrary to the preferences of Hellenistic poets). It can be explained by the preferences of the listeners, who demand more famous, better known stories on the one hand, and momentous events on the other. That explains the exaggerations observed earlier in the introductions to songs; their function is to point out the remarkable character of events to be presented.[40] Contending singers try to outdo their rivals with the uniqueness and importance

37 Ford (1992:47–48, 57–79) states the subject of epic is the past understood as the deeds of gods and people. The performance always adheres to the following pattern: an epic song about heroes (*oimê*) is preceded by a prooimion presenting the genealogy and exploits of gods. This maintains the correct chronology: first the affairs of gods, then the deeds of heroes/ancestors. This order of presentation is characteristic of paratactic storytelling. Ford (39) suggests that the prooimion to the third of Demodokos's songs starts with the phrase θεοῦ ἤρχετο "[he] began from the god (goddess?)" (*Odyssey* 8.499). According to him, a prooimion differs from an epic because the singer assumes a different attitude: the epic is impersonal, without any direct address to the audience.

38 Ford 1992:69.

39 In the *Odyssey*, this formula may indicate that a hero and his deeds were a subject of songs: 9.20 when Odysseus uses this formula to tell the Phaeacians about his fame, it sounds like an allusion to Demodokos's song about him (8.74); 19.108 Odysseus addresses Penelope; 15.329 and 17.565 the formula is adapted to describe the pride and violence of the suitors—the epithet εὐρύν 'vast' (sky) is replaced with the unique epithet σιδήρεον 'iron', which may suggest that the suitors are viewed as villains. In the *Iliad*, this formula is applied only to Nestor's unique shield (8.192).

40 Compare *Nibelungenlied* 1.1: "In ancient tales many marvels are told ... now you may hear such marvels told" (translation, Cyril Edwards) or *Beowulf* 1–3: "Lo! the glory of the kings of the people of the Spear-Danes in days of old we have heard tell, how those princes did deeds of valour" (translation, J. R. R. Tolkien).

of the subject-matter of their song.[41] It goes hand in hand with Panhellenization and universalization, because the glorification of deeds of local importance (e.g. an expedition of one hero) must give way to the glorification of acts of a wider scope (an expedition of a group of heroes). Traveling allows singers to learn more local songs, which gives them a wider array of possibilities in the choice of more popular sagas. Homer is also known to adapt local myths, e.g. the episode of Tlepolemos's fight against Sarpedon, which looks like an allusion to the fights between the Dorian Greeks of Rhodes and the Lycians. Innovations introduced into well-known sagas must have been prompted by the audience's desire to learn new details. The singer meets the expectations of his listeners, adding new episodes to an established pattern, as I have shown in Chapter 1.

2. Ford demonstrates that the singer's aim is not originality, but *vividness*.[42] Odysseus remarks that Demodokos tells the story "as if he were there himself or heard from one who was" (*Odyssey* 8.491). Odysseus knows that the singer was not at Troy but he himself, as an eyewitness of the events, confirms the truth of the singer's words.[43] For Homer's audience, it must have been a conventional expression of appraisal. The vividness of the story is evidence of its truthfulness.[44] Demodokos's rendition must have been very suggestive, not confined to a dry presentation of facts in a proper sequence—in fact, it must have resembled Homer's style, so one could argue that the author of

41 A parallel can be found in Avdo Međedović, who frequently makes his songs more solemn and forceful by increasing the importance of the events. Lord (1974:15) demonstrates a striking difference between Avdo's *Wedding of Meho Smailagić* and Šemić's version on which Međedović's was based. In Šemić's version, Meho, the young hero, is sent to the Vizier in Buda to become the new buljukbaša, whereas in Avdo's version, he goes there to obtain the position of the new alaybey. When Lord pointed out the discrepancy to Avdo, the singer answered that to obtain the position of buljukbaša Meho would not have had to go to the Vizier or to Hasan Pasha Tiro, at whose court the action of the song starts—it could have been conferred by Mustajbeg himself. "A buljukbaša commanded a hundred men, but this rank was for thirty thousand. Would that be an *alaybey* or a *buljukbaša*?" Avdo asked. Lord concludes: "Avdo had made the song not only much more meaningful, more magnificent in its scope, but also more accurate!" If we compare Avdo and Homer, it becomes evident that in the case of both singers exaggeration is controlled by reason. However, such a rational attitude cannot be attributed to all singers.

42 Ford 1992:49–56, 130: "The delight in the tale is not the satisfaction of accuracy or communication of some higher truth but the pleasurableness of a convincingly full picture" (53).

43 If the conflict between Odysseus and Achilles was Homer's innovation, these words by Odysseus could be intended to pacify the audience in case this story seemed unknown. They could play the same role if the story about the conflict is traditional but less known.

44 Ford (1992:61) states that this vividness is guaranteed by the assistance of the Muse. According to Finkelberg (1998), the Muse is responsible for the inventiveness of the singer.

> the *Odyssey* tries to "advertise" his own method of shaping the song. However, it's not necessarily a very subjective estimation; it is equally probable that he presents here a traditional model of creating a song which would exert strong influence upon the listeners.

The assessment of the singer's ability must also take other skills into account. Possessing knowledge about the past, he must be flexible and able to adapt his story to the current interests of his audience. Also important is his skill in directing the emotions of his listeners—in other words, his ability to absorb their attention by arousing their curiosity. And so the *aoidos* fulfills a very specific service. He does not really stand apart from his audience; his "piece of meat" at the feast is not a mark of distinction, but a reward for a job done well (*Odyssey* 8.477–481). The support of the Muses and his own knowledge, which he perceives as comparable to that of seers (both know the things that are, the things to come, and things past[45]), indicate that he is aware of the religious and spiritual aspects of epic.[46] This role of the oral poet goes much beyond pragmatic professionalism.[47]

Such an understanding of the poet's role springs, I think, from two sources. As a custodian of social memory, the singer accumulates the knowledge of the whole community, and the presentation of this knowledge has a moral dimension. Comparative Indo-European studies reveal that the poet performed a controlling function over the ruler, since—as a man acting for the common good—he could criticize his actions. This is the context in which we should remember that Agamemnon, departing from home, leaves an *aoidos* to watch over Klytaimestra (*Odyssey* 3.267–271).[48] The observance of moral laws results from the respect

45 About the seer Kalchas: *Iliad* 1.70 ὃς ᾔδη τά τ' ἐόντα τά τ' ἐσσόμενα πρό τ' ἐόντα ("who knew what is, what will be, and what has been"); about the poet: Hesiod *Theogony* 32 ἵνα κλείοιμι τά τ' ἐσσόμενα πρό τ' ἐόντα ("to convey the *kleos* about things that will be and that have been before").

46 Lord (1960:220–221) postulated that we need to see the role of the singer in a deeper religious context of his performance and to identify him with the seer. Ford (1992:15–16, 34–35) agrees that it is necessary to modify contemporary criteria of interpreting Homeric poetry, accepting a deeper religious dimension for epic songs, but he rejects the identification of the *aoidos* with the seer, because in Greek culture these two trades were separate. Nonetheless, such an identification has deep Indo-European roots (Durante 1971–1974 2:167–169, Compton 2006:170–176, 209–210, 237–238).

47 Segal (1994:140) stresses the social function of epic poems, noticing the difference between the *aoidos* and later poets who emphasize the exceptional value of their poetry and creative powers: "The Homeric bard presents himself as more attuned to his audience than to the situation of composition or creation. His chief concern, one could say, is pragmatics, not poetics (which is not to say that he lacks a poetics). His Muses are the repositories of social memory rather than claiming (as Pindar, for example, will do) that he is different from or superior to his audience and thus has a right to speak with a special moral authority on his own account."

48 Compare Svenbro (1976:31), who suggests that a singer was under the pressure of his community and the Muse, who was a kind of a religious representation of social control: "... l'aède

for the divine laws and the fear of divine punishment which, according to the concept of collective responsibility for an individual's bad behavior, would affect the whole community. The punishment of moral offenders is the ruler's province, but someone should also control the rulers, who enjoy impunity, but whose wrongdoing can bring misfortune upon the community. Though the epic songs seem to lack direct praise or criticism, nonetheless they remain the greatest reservoir of social values, and the function of the *aoidos* is not confined to their presentation only (this can be borne out by the lament at the funeral of Hektor, *Iliad* 24.719–721, or Demodokos's second song, which was accompanied by a dance of young men, *Odyssey* 8.262–264, 367–379). Neither is the relationship of *aoidoi* and gods limited to the fact that the Muses transmit to them the content of myths/songs ("teaching" in Homeric diction), which warrants the truth of the song and endows the singer with creative power.[49] The singer Phemios says that a Muse planted mythical motifs in his soul (θεὸς δέ μοι ἐν φρεσὶν οἴμας / παντοίας ἐνέφυσεν, *Odyssey* 22.347–348), which—as we have seen—become the basis for the creation of individual songs. Ford suggests that the whole of the past, which is an aggregate of all *oimai*, is a subject for the divine rather than human contemplation.[50] Here we can find a parallel with the shadow-puppet theatre of Kerala, where the audience of most spectacles are gods and members of the troupe only.[51] Phemios mentions that both gods and people are in his audience (*Odyssey* 22.346): ὅς τε θεοῖσι καὶ ἀνθρώποισι ἀείδω "I who sing for gods and people." Both groups—gods and people—are the subject and audience of the song. Such a communion of people and gods in the performance of a song finds an analogy in the participation of divinities in sacrifices and feasts. The song takes on a religious dimension not only when it is performed at religious ceremonies. Each performance assumes the "presence" of gods.

The audience

The human audience and its expectations for the performance merit closer inspection. In the early stages of archaic culture, audience and performer

dépend de ceux qui sont "plus nombreux" et donc "plus forts," c'est-à-dire de son auditoire auquel il ne saurait s'opposer: s'il ne réussit pas à symboliser les valeure de l'auditoire, il cesse tout simplement d'être aède. … C'est uniquement en acceptant la supériorité de (l'auditoire, la Muse) que l'aède peut chanter. On n'envisagerait donc guère un aède solitaire, sans auditoire, sans Muse. Que ferait-il? Sur son île déserte, l'aède d'Agamemnon meurt." It is unnecessary to accept Page's (1973) suggestion that such an important task was related to the high status of the bard in the Mycenaean epoch, who perhaps functioned also as an important priest maintaining relations with gods. See Scully 1981:esp. 78–83.

49 On the latter aspect, see Finkelberg 1998.

50 Ford 1992:83: "the unity of the whole as an object of divine contemplation."

51 Scodel 2002:9.

are not divided for the performance of a lyric song. One person or a group of several people leads the song, and the rest respond, usually uttering ritual or typical cries, or repeating refrains or quasi-refrains after the "chorus-leader"; compare the depiction of the Muses who act as a chorus and ἀμειβόμεναι ὀπὶ καλῇ "answer with a sweet voice" (*Iliad* 1.604, *Odyssey* 24.24, 60). It is natural that the singing is accompanied with dancing or at least stamping one's feet, clapping hands, etc.,[52] so the song engaged everyone. Assuredly, such a performance involved a large amount of spontaneity and improvisation. Enthusiasm was contagious—the leader of the song infected the whole listening community with it. If such a choral song told a story from the mythical past, the leader of the song could identify himself with the character depicted and evoke strong emotions in people, for whom the scene presented was not so much a reconstruction of a past event as its re-enactment.[53] During the performance of an epic song, however, the participation of the audience seemed to be limited to listening only. But does it mean that the reception was completely passive? Did not the presentation of the mythical past in the song stir emotions, which the listeners could not express? Here arises the question of how much they understood of the 'text' as it was presented.

The assessment of Homer's audience depends on its ability to grasp the exquisite composition of the *Iliad* and *Odyssey*. The virtuosity of these two poems is beyond any of the Balkan songs; no wonder that it prompted some scholars to refuse the Homeric epics the status of oral poetry. In studies on the role of audience in the creation of epic songs, Scodel distinguishes two standpoints: the audience has no influence on the shape of technically perfect works, like those by Homer (so, in her opinion, e.g. Walter J. Ong, Keith Stanley); the audience is competent and becomes a collaborator in the performance of Homeric poems (so, according to her, e.g. Richard Martin).[54] Scodel criticizes both standpoints, arguing that no audience is perfect, no matter how sophisticated and discerning.[55] Moreover, oral poetry needn't be transparent in order to be understood and well received.[56] Not all members of the audience have to understand

52 The Greek song of that epoch could not differ very much from what we know from the research on primitive cultures (Bowra 1962).

53 Nagy 1996a:Ch. 2.

54 Ong 2002:36–56; Stanley 1993:268–279; Martin 1993:227–228. Scodel 2002:6: "An excellent performer must then imply a superb audience, and the Homerist easily slips from reconstructing an ideal experience into assuming that this experience was not only real but universal."

55 Scodel 2002:7.

56 Scodel (2002:7–8) gives an example of the contemporary performance of the Indian Candaini epic, which is performed in two styles: singing (*git*), with the stress on telling the story, and dancing (*naca*). In opposition to *git*, *naca* assumes the audience knows the story. In *git* epic it is not necessary; the thread of the story may be new to the listeners. If the means of expression is

everything. Scodel also remarks that the audience may be critical toward the performer.[57]

Scodel's skepticism is to a large extent directed against the popular identification of Homer's audience with the idealized audience in Alkinoos's palace; I believe that this identification leads to an erroneous reading of passages from the *Odyssey* which describe the behavior of people listening to epic songs.[58] Hearers listen to the first and third of Demodokos's songs in silence and concentration; certainly nobody dances, as they do during the second song. Ford notices the contrast in the reception of Phemios's song about the return of the Achaeans by Penelope, who weeps, and the suitors, who are entertained. Odysseus too sheds tears while listening to Demodokos's song about the fall of Troy, whereas the Phaeacians wonder at his behavior, because they find pleasure in it. According to Ford, Penelope and Odysseus react differently because they take an active part in the story, whereas the suitors and Phaeacians represent a typical listener, who while listening to an epic song, in Hesiod's words (*Theogony* 102–103), αἶψ' ὅ γε δυσφροσυνέων ἐπιλήθεται οὐδέ τι κηδέων / μέμνηται "right away such a man forgets his troubled thoughts, and his cares he no longer remembers."[59]

The image of the performance of an epic song in the *Odyssey* might have been archaized; in Homer's times it might have resembled the competition in the *agôn*.[60] Nevertheless, it cannot be too much divorced from reality, especially in the case of performances for a small group, the possibility of which cannot be ruled out. In other words, undoubtedly the author of the *Odyssey* (and also the *Iliad*) had an opportunity to sing for such an audience and in similar circumstances as Phemios and Demodokos. For the sake of studying performance realities, the Phaeacian community is too idealized; much more can be learned from the scenes taking place in the palace on Ithaca. I believe that the atmosphere in Ithaca must have resembled a Bosnian café (*kafana*), where people drink, do business, chatter, and from time to time turn their ear to the singer's songs.

---

dance, however, the story must be known and clear. *Naca*, I believe, may be parallel to archaic Greek lyric. In lyric, the allusions to myths imply a full and detailed knowledge of mythical motifs presented *in extenso* in epic.

57 Scodel 2002:9.

58 E.g. Ford 1997:413–414; Segal (1994:131) even suggests that in the image of Penelope listening to Odysseus's tale Homer pictured his ideal listener.

59 Translation, Gregory Nagy (2020).

60 Scodel 2002:46. Nagy 1989:6: "Self-references in Archaic Greek poetry may be diachronically valid without being synchronically 'true'. For example, the epic poetry of Homer refers to epic poetry as a medium that was performed in the context of an evening's feast. And yet, we know that the two epic poems of Homer, by virtue of their sheer length alone, defy this context."

Let us have a look how epics were performed in Yugoslavia.[61] They were sung on a variety of occasions, mainly for the adult male population of small towns and villages. "In the country villages," writes Lord,

> where the houses are often widely separated, a gathering may be held at one of the houses during a period of leisure from the work in the fields. Men from all the families assemble and one of their number may sing epic songs. Because of the distances between the houses some of the guests arrive earlier than others, and of course this means that some leave earlier. ... The singer has to contend with an audience that is coming and going, greeting newcomers, saying farewells to early leavers; a newcomer with special news or gossip may interrupt the singing for some time, perhaps even stopping it entirely.[62]

This pattern is also true of towns, but here people gather in cafés and taverns, and there is more commotion. Like in villages, the entertainment is only for men; women (Moslem and Christian alike) are excluded. Such a gathering takes place in the evening. Shopkeepers, farmers from nearby villages, caravan drivers (who come with their merchandise and often spend the night in the tavern, which also provides accommodation) sit, talk, sip coffee or rakia, and listen to songs. In bigger towns like Bijelo Polje, Stolac, Novi Pazar, or Bihać, there are markets attracting a large number of farmers and merchants, who sometimes stay the night and return to their homes in the morning. Many of those men are also singers who travel with their songs from one place to another—and they are a critical audience. These gatherings create great opportunities for singers because the listeners have ready money and may be willing to reward them for their efforts. Singing is not a way to make a living, but the listeners are willing to buy the singer a drink and, if they are satisfied with his performance, are apt to give him a little cash. Sometimes epic songs are sung at weddings, where the confusion is increased by the singing of lyric songs and dancing. The most opportune moment for the epic song is the evening, when the gossiping and games are over and older men are tired and content to listen.

For Moslems in Bosnia the best time for epic songs is the month of Ramadan, when men fast during the day and after sunset meet in cafes to have a good time and listen to singers. The singing may run on until the morning. The singers have an opportunity to perform (or learn) up to thirty songs. The keepers of *kafanas* may even engage a singer a few months in

61 Lord 1960:14–17.
62 Lord 1960:14.

advance, because a well-known singer is likely to bring business to the establishment. A *kafana* keeper may go among the guests to make a collection for the singer.

After the Turkish conquests, the Christian nobility was no longer interested in oral song, but built their literary culture on Western patterns. Muslim nobility continued to support oral epic even as late as the 1930s, when Parry and Lord carried out their investigations there. Drawing on the information collected by Parry, we can find no evidence that beys or aghas performed epic songs themselves, but they often called in singers for special occasions.

Whatever the circumstances of the performances, the variability and instability of the audience are present. The singer must have great concentration in order to sing at all. He should possess dramatic ability and great narrative skill to attract his listeners' attention. Long songs may be totally spoiled by restless audience members. Once the singer starts singing, he may count himself lucky if he is able to sing without an interruption until he is tired. After a break, he may continue unfinished threads of the story and sing the song until its end. However, if the audience is not receptive, he may decide to shorten the song. If he misjudges the span of time he can count on the attention of his listeners, he may be unable to finish it at all, so the length of the song depends not so much on the talent of the singer as on the audience's interest. If different performances of the same epic song by the same man vary in their endings, concludes Lord, it is so because the end is less often sung.[63]

For the sake of the comparison, let us look at the scene in Odysseus's palace from *Odyssey* Book 1. The suitors spend their time playing with pebbles in front of the door and then they enter the megaron for a feast. When the feast is over, they make the singer entertain them, and (1.151–155):

> μνηστῆρης, τοῖσιν μὲν ἐνὶ φρεσὶν ἄλλα μεμήλει,
> μολπή τ' ὀρχηστύς τε· τὰ γάρ τ' ἀναθήματα δαιτός.
> κῆρυξ δ' ἐν χερσὶν κίθαριν περικαλλέα θῆκε
> Φημίῳ, ὅς ῥ' ἤειδε παρὰ μνηστῆρσιν ἀνάγκῃ.
> ἦ τοι ὁ φορμίζων ἀνεβάλλετο καλὸν ἀείδειν
>
> the suitors set their minds
> on song and dancing—which adorn a feast.
> A herald placed a beautiful kithara in the hands of Phemios
> who, forced to sing for the suitors,
> took the instrument and started singing beautifully

63 Lord 1960:17.

The suitors listen very closely to the singer and (1.325–327):

> τοῖσι δ' ἀοιδὸς ἄειδε περικλυτός, οἱ δὲ σιωπῇ
> εἵατ' ἀκούοντες· ὁ δ' Ἀχαιῶν νόστον ἄειδε
> λυγρόν, ὃν ἐκ Τροίης ἐπετείλατο Παλλὰς Ἀθήνη.
>
> The most famous *aoidos* sang for them, and they in silence
> sat and listened; he sang of the return of the Achaeans,
> the fateful one, which Pallas Athena prepared for them when they
> sailed from Troy.

This listening in silence contrasts with their usual vociferousness. Their noisy behavior—clearly inappropriate because it is several times remarked as disturbing other people—is typical of the viciously impudent suitors. This continued silence is believed to be "a remarkable tribute to the power of song and the fascination of Phemios' theme,"[64] but this is, I think, unfounded. The suitors' interest in the song is not necessarily an expression of admiration. They might have been engrossed in the story about the "fateful return of the Achaeans" simply because one of its elements is Odysseus's return—an unwelcome event in their eyes. Stephanie West rightly points out the irony of the situation: the suitors listen with pleasure to a song about the consequences of Athena's wrath, while the goddess herself is sitting among them and planning their downfall.[65] It is worth noticing that the poet does not see anything untoward in Telemachos's conversation with Mentes (who in fact is Athena). They talk in an undertone so that others cannot hear (1.156–157), they are busy for quite a long time, and do not listen to the song. Naturally, this song is not really for Telemachos, who learns about the return of the Achaeans from the Achaeans themselves—Nestor, Menelaos, and finally Odysseus—and then their stories have a happy ending. In this conversation Athena orders Telemachos to go to Pylos and Sparta for news about his father (1.284–285).[66] When an interruption occurs, then, it is not they but Penelope who stops the singer because the song evokes longing for her husband. She suggests a change of topic, which should not inconvenience the singer, who knows many songs (1.337–342):

> Φήμιε, πολλὰ γὰρ ἄλλα βροτῶν θελκτήρια οἶδας
> ἔργ' ἀνδρῶν τε θεῶν τε, τὰ τε κλείουσιν ἀοιδοί·
> τῶν ἕν γέ σφιν ἄειδε παρήμενος, οἱ δὲ σιωπῇ
> οἶνον πινόντων· ταύτης δ' ἀποπαύε' ἀοιδῆς
> λυγρῆς, ἥ τέ μοι αἰὲν ἐνὶ στήθεσσι φίλον κῆρ τείρει

64 S. West 1988:116.

65 S. West 1988:116–117; Dekker 1965:64–66.

66 As if he could not find out the truth about his father from the *aoidos*' story.

> Phemios, you know many other "cures" which soothe the pain
> of mortals,
> about the deeds of men and gods, [deeds] which *aoidoi* celebrate;
> sing one of them, as you sit here, and break off this painful song
> which again and again vexes the heart in my chest

The adverb αἰέν 'constantly, again and again' means that Penelope has had many opportunities to listen to this song, or rather many songs about these returns.[67] In passing, she points out how one should listen to the bard: in silence, drinking wine; this is how Odysseus listens to Demodokos's song in Book 8. The appearance of Penelope provokes the suitors' rudeness and when she leaves, they loudly express their wish to bed her. Telemachos remonstrates with them, telling them to stop shouting and listen to the singer, whom he defends (1.368–371):

> μητρὸς ἐμῆς μνηστῆρες, ὑπέρβιον ὕβριν ἔχοντες,
> νῦν μὲν δαινύμεναι τερπώμεθα, μηδὲ βοητὺς
> ἔστω, ἐπεὶ τό γε καλὸν ἀκουέμεν ἐστὶν ἀοιδοῦ
> τοιοῦδ' οἷος ὅδ' ἐστί, θεοῖσ' ἐναλίγκιος αὐδήν.

> my mother's suitors, insolent and arrogant,
> let us now eat and enjoy ourselves, let the shouting stop,
> because it is a fine thing to listen to an *aoidos*
> such as this one, with a voice like a god.

He addresses the suitors, who reply to him, and nothing indicates that the song will be continued, because the suitors prefer to follow their initial idea. They want something suitable for dancing and probably order the singer to choose another song (1.421–422): οἱ δ' εἰς ὀρχηστύν τε καὶ ἱμερόεσσαν ἀοιδὴν / τρεψάμενοι τέρποντο ("and they took up a dance and a delightful song / and did it with pleasure").

Another time, the shepherd Melanthios enters a feast in the palace, sits opposite Eurymachos, and the suitors call servants to bring him his food, all while Phemios is singing (17.254–263). Soon Eumaios and the beggar Odysseus enter the feast, and Telemachos extends hospitality, sending them bread and meat (17.328–358). The fact that all this may perturb the singer does not bother anyone.

As we can see, the *aoidos* sings and people come and go, talk, stop his song, suggest that he choose another one, and don't care whether it is finished or

67 It may suggest that this is a song favored by the suitors and Phemios responds to this demand.

not.[68] The behavior of the listeners is evidently similar to that observed by Parry and Lord in Yugoslavia. It is not a situation which would enable the creation of Homer's epics. Lord claimed that birth of those poems was possible only in completely different, slightly artificial conditions, i.e. when the singer dictated his song. Lord notes: "The singer is [...] accustomed to the stimulus of an audience, but again an intelligent scribe and a small group of onlookers can provide this stimulus."[69] He adds that the advantage of this kind of audience would be its stability. This is the reason why he rules out the possibility that the poems were composed for a festival. They could, of course, be sung then, but they would never be so long or elaborate because the festival audience is not right for this kind of performance.[70] Lord drew these conclusions, based on his own experiences. But I am not sure if the creation of long epics really demands absolutely ideal conditions.

Invention or Allusion

According to Scodel, there are no singers and no listeners who would know the whole repertoire of the epic tradition.[71] Nonetheless, the listener must perceive the song as traditional. The singer can modify his material, but he has to do it according to existing conventions. The modification does not come from the singer's desire for originality, but from the specific situation he encounters; most often it is the result of the listeners' expectations, e.g. when they ask for a story unknown to the singer. The analysis of Homer's text indicates that, depending on context, he embroiders his narrative with motifs stretching beyond the main story. In their studies of Homer's use of traditional material, Malcolm Willcock and Gregory Nagy have very different interpretations, while Scodel finds the middle ground between them. Willcock claims that Homer modifies traditional material to such an extent (e.g. sketching characters of people) that the characters practically become his inventions.[72]

68 Scodel (2002:39–40) points out that the summary of the events at Troy, which Achilles presents to his mother Thetis (*Iliad* 1.369–392), might have served as an explanation to those people who missed the beginning of the performance because they were distracted or late. She also mentions that the dramatic beginning of the song might have posed reception difficulties for those listeners who did not know the events at Troy well or relationships between the characters in the song.

69 Lord 1953:132.

70 Lord 1960:153: "In some ways it seems to me that a festival would be the least likely circumstance to afford opportunity for a long song. There is too much going on at a festival. The audience is constantly distracted and is constantly moving about. A long song seriously delivered to an appreciative audience can be produced only in peace and quiet."

71 Scodel 2002:61–64.

72 Willcock 1964; 1977. Scodel 2002:25.

The singer adds details in order to make the story paradigmatic, i.e. a point of reference for a situation in the narrative (the best example is the way Achilles uses the story of Niobe, who despite her deep sorrow did not reject food, to convince Priam to eat, 24.601–616). Nagy refutes this, arguing that these contextualized stories were not invented, but chosen from the wealth of tradition ("selection within tradition").[73] Each story must have had its moment of creation but, Nagy says, each innovation takes place within an oral performance and thus remains an element of tradition.[74] Scodel maintains that basing Homer's greatness on the extent of his originality is a wholly inappropriate romantic idea; Nagy justly criticizes this attitude and demythologizes such a concept of the poet.[75] However, considering that the flexibility of an inherited pattern is both typical of oral epic and dependent on the individual skill of the singer, Scodel objects to Nagy's attempt to nullify the role of an individual in the creation of a song. The essential feature of all modifications is their dependence on context (narration and speech).[76]

The state of things as described by Scodel can be supplemented. Bruce Braswell has demonstrated that the inventiveness of Homer is not limited to the use of mythological paradigms observed by Willcock.[77] He points out the common motif of "*do ut des*," i.e. the obligation of the person who is asked or ordered to do something. Such a *demand for compensation* for a good deed or a favor effectively motivates the receiver to act as requested. When Homer needs such a motivation, he invents it. In the Homeric poems there is no place for coincidence, because all acts of people or gods must be explained by a reason; Braswell substantiates Martin West's remark (privately told) by pointing to the typical features of oral performance: telling a story, the singer feels obliged to present the causes for what his characters do, and this is what his audience

73 Nagy 1992; 1996b:132–138; Slatkin 1991:115–122. The opinion that all preserved motifs and themes appearing in stories are part of tradition is also shared by Dué and Ebbot (2010), who provide a broad discussion of the concept of tradition in Homeric studies (Ch. 1).

74 Nagy 1996b:19: "The here-and-now of each new performance is an opportunity for innovation, whether or not any such innovation is explicitly acknowledged in the tradition."

75 Scodel 2002:28: "When Nagy insists that Homer's storytelling is based in tradition and seeks to downplay the role of innovation, he is opposing that romanticization, with good reason. The ability to create appropriate variants for particular uses is one feature of Homer's art and a proof of poetic skill, but it is itself doubtless a traditional procedure. Emphasizing the innovation distorts the standards of the poems themselves."

76 Scodel 2002:29: "Much of what some scholars call 'invented' might better be called 'contextually bound'." Scodel notes also the flip side of introducing "innovations": they bring about "the dissolution of contextual bonds: the bards remove heroes from their original contexts or give one hero an exploit modelled on those of another."

77 Braswell 1971.

expects.[78] This pervasive, slightly naive compulsion to find a reason for everything connects Homer with primitive cultures.[79]

Even if some examples cited by Braswell cannot be viewed as the poet's inventions only (e.g. the motivation of Thetis's request to Zeus to save her son's honor), since such motifs appear in a certain epic/mythological tradition, we can still detect Homer's inventiveness. Naturally, each "new story" or "new version," supplying new particulars, is only a modification of the existing tradition. Moreover, tradition is always used in the way that is justified by the narrative: it is, in Scodel's words, "contextually bound." A new detail changes the context. Let us look at it this way: the singer uses an "innovation" to bring out the aspect that he deems the most important for his song. For example, in his third song, Demodokos is expected to present a sequence of facts known from tradition in such a way as to properly highlight the figure of Odysseus.[80] The epic song, in praise of a hero, is always biased. Therefore, both the *Odyssey* and *Iliad* are biased in the presentation of their heroes: Odysseus in the *Odyssey*, Achilles and perhaps also Odysseus in the *Iliad*. The favoritism in presentation cannot be perceived as an "innovation" of a poet, but as an essential element of tradition. Ironically, this favoritism gives the song its individual character! In this way, the song, moving along the rails of tradition, gains individuality. If neither an individual singer, nor a listener could know the whole tradition, then nobody could say that a given element was not traditional, especially since the Muse was the source of the song and her authority guaranteed its truth, i.e. compliance with tradition.[81]

Odysseus's wish that Demodokos should sing about his role in the capture of Troy (*Odyssey* 8.492–495) indicates that the audience could influence the bias of the song. Certainly, it did not have to be the only reason for the bias, though it might be the most frequent. However, it seems that in the case of Homer's poems it is not the audience's demand, but the intention of the poet, who could take into account the expectations of his listeners. These expectations could

78 Braswell 1971:25: "The source of Homer's casual reasoning lies, then, in the demands of his narrative art. It is a simple art which we may observe when children or unsophisticated people attempt to account for an event by going through each of the causes that led to it step by step."

79 Turner 1970:300: "It might be argued that words such as 'misfortune,' 'accident,' 'bad luck,' 'mischance' are 'erroneous' translations of *malwa* and its synonyms, for there is indeed no concept of 'accident' among the Ndembu, who seek to find a cause for every calamity; far from being 'prelogical,' they are obsessively logical, though on the basis of mystical premises, as Evans-Pritchard 1976:18–32 showed us in his classical study of Azande systems of belief. The Ndembu, like the Azande, consider that calamities and adversities of all kinds are caused by mystical forces generated or evoked and directed by conscious agents." See also Evans-Pritchard 1956:193–194.

80 See Ch. 1, pp. 127 and 131–132, above.

81 Compare Scodel 2002:31.

include the way that the heroes are presented, the rationalization of events, and the suppression of fantastic or magical elements. The sequence of events may be already known, but the presentation of new aspects of the story or a new perspective on the events makes the song new in the ears of the audience.

A song may relate well-known events from a new perspective. This novelty is steeped in tradition. The introduction of a "new" element as an "old" element which has been transformed explains the apparent paradox of the introduction of inventions to the song, whose main function is the transmission of knowledge.[82] In this way, knowledge remains unchallenged, but the song can also be a source of entertainment. This understanding allows us to distance ourselves from bizarre hypotheses like that proposed by Finkelberg, who uses formulae found in Homer and Hesiod to distinguish two methods of influencing the audience: pleasure and enchantment.[83] She claims that enchantment is created by a new song and is different from the pleasure derived from a song which is well known and popular. Therefore, the enchantment is, in her own words, an "incidental effect of song" and comes from the novelty of information. Such an enchantment is, declares Finkelberg, the effect of Phemios's song, which Telemachos describes as the most recent (1.351–352). When Penelope hears it, she calls other songs "charms" θελκτήρια (1.337). The Sirens' song creates similar enchantment, which they believe imparts knowledge, but Kirke believes that it produces bewitchment. However, it should be stressed that: Phemios's song was already known to Penelope (1.341 αἰέν); and Kirke mentions also the pleasure derived from the Sirens' song (12.52 τερπόμενος ὄπ' ἀκούσῃς 'so that you can draw pleasure from listening'). To refute Finkelberg's hypothesis further, let us consider Homer's (*Iliad* 1.603–604) and Pindar's (*Pythian* 1.7–23) image of Apollo enchanting the Olympians with his songs. How could he impart any new knowledge to his divine audience? The Sirens also point to their divine nature, maintaining they know about everything that has happened in the world (*Odyssey* 12.189). It seems that Finkelberg fallaciously assigns too much importance to the gaining of knowledge. In traditional cultures, the transmission of knowledge is important, but it does not mean the discovery of new things, rather the recalling of the knowledge about things already known.[84] It has nothing to do

82 According to Braswell (1971:26), the inconsistencies resulting from these innovations passed unnoticed by the listeners.

83 Finkelberg 1998:88–99. Another mistaken conception is, I believe, the equating of the "the latest song" (*Odyssey* 1.352) with a song about the singer's contemporaries (Edwards 1987:18: "men of his own day"). The kind of epic poetry in which songs perpetuate the glory of heroes, keeping listeners posted on the latest developments, is an illusion.

84 Ong (2002:33–36, 40–42) argues that knowledge, its acquiring, storing, and shaping is fundamentally different in oral and written cultures; however, the subject certainly deserves further analysis.

with stagnation. Novelty perpetually creeps into the songs. They are constantly refashioned or modified, but within the old pattern acceptable for the audience.

This observation leads to the fundamental conclusion that the impetus for epic songs, including the *Iliad* and *Odyssey*, is the singer's desire to capture the attention of his audience. As we have seen, there is no reason to imagine that Homer's listeners differed from those in Serbia, Bosnia, or Montenegro—they had to be induced to concentrate on the song. Parry and Lord's observations indicate that it was in the singer's interest to hold the attention of those gathered, for whom a *kafana* or a neighbor's house was simply a place which offered them an opportunity to meet and talk. If we disregard the idealized picture of listeners in Alkinoos's palace, it turns out that for the Greek *aoidos* also, it could not have been a simple task to entertain his audience. To win and maintain the attention of the listener, the singer has to resort to various devices which embellish and vivify his story. In the case of the *Iliad*, the effect was an exquisite product worth transmitting and—at some point, perhaps quite distant from the moment of its composition—writing down.

Now we have arrived at a thesis important for this book, that the text of Homeric poems is a written record of songs intended exclusively for aural reception; and that its splendid craftsmanship can be explained by the principles and circumstances of a live performance. First, however, we should realize that the reception of the listener fundamentally differs from that of the reader. The listener has contact with the song only while it is being performed. He cannot go back to check on something he has forgotten or perhaps misunderstood, and he cannot stop for a moment to meditate on a particular section. His emotional response and understanding are synchronic with the performance. Moreover, oral compositions have a different tightness than written ones because they must take into account that not all members of the audience listen from the beginning to the end. The listener, without a written copy of the text in his hands, does not know if the end of the song is near or not.

Since the singer does not address any individual listener but a group of people, he has to take into account the preferences, familiarity with other songs, general knowledge, and moral values of his listeners as a group. His strategy for presenting the song is linked to its synchronic reception and so the singer attracts the attention of the recipient in a different way than the writer does. Homer constantly changes the place and time of action, moves between indoor and outdoor scenes, portrays scenes of crowds as well as those with only a few characters, jumps from the human plane to the divine one[85]—never does he allow his listeners to get bored. But the most characteristic feature,

85 Edwards 1987:33–34.

and completely unlike written texts, is his method of building suspense. The singer must assume that the listener already knows the story of Odysseus's return or Achilles' wrath against Agamemnon. Engaging the attention of someone who already knows the outcome of an action and even the sequence of events is much more difficult, and certainly requires other strategies than when the recipient does not know how the story will unfold. Even if he does not know future events, they are revealed for him time after time in numerous and diverse predictions. Usually the poet gradually reveals what is to happen; each successive prediction is longer and more detailed.[86] And yet, the singer is able to keep the listener uncertain whether the prediction will come true and how he will bring it about. One method is to deceive the hearer with misleading or false predictions, which are not the poet's lapses but intentional misdirections aimed at maintaining the attention of his audience.[87] The listener is no longer sure if the predicted event will take place. His expectations are further subverted by the technique of retardation. The audience of the *Iliad* expects certain events to take place soon, in the nearest future, but it turns out that a lot of narrative time passes before they actually occur. In Chapter 2, I have demonstrated that the narration of an epic song in the Trojan Cycle had to start at a critical moment, when the future of the Achaeans is at stake, and it is presented in such a way as if everything was to be decided at this point in time, without regard to many other events which the tradition of the cycle connects with the fall of Troy, like the prediction of Achilles' imminent death or a prompt conquest of Troy.

The elements known from other performances of the song are mingled with new elements. Sometimes the singer may hint at a different course of action, parallel to another story known from tradition. In this way, as S. Douglas Olson has demonstrated, numerous references to the tragedy of the house of Agamemnon scattered in the *Odyssey* propose alternative paths, making the listener uncertain whether the characters in the current song will behave like the characters in those other stories or not.[88] The return of Odysseus turns out to be unlike the return of Agamemnon; Penelope is not another Klytaimestra, Telemachos is not another Orestes, and Odysseus is not another Agamemnon, but the listener is led on to speculate about the outcome of the events in

86 Such are for example the prophecies of Zeus, the most important ones for the narration of the *Iliad*: the god promises Thetis that he will honor Achilles, helping the Trojans and bringing about the destruction of the Greeks (1.517–526); he foretells to Hera Patroklos's defeat by Hektor, who will reach the ships and will remain victorious, at least until Achilles enters the battle (8.473–483); and then he tells what is going to happen and who is going to get killed by whom (15.61–77).

87 See Morrison 1992b.

88 Olson 1990. See also Ahl and Roisman 1996.

Ithaca. In effect, by comparing various people's behavior, he is able to judge the behavior of the characters of the *Odyssey* according to the author's intention.

These methods of sustaining suspense would be inadequate to sustain the uniform attention of the audience, especially in a complex and monumental epic like the *Iliad* with its many scenes of combat, even though they are varied.[89] The singer has to appeal to the feelings of his listeners and to their ability to appraise a situation. Let's consider how Homer affects emotions first. His poems are built with the technique of expansion, by inflating scenes and speeches—quite out of proportion to their significance and content, as some scholars claim. But Mark Edwards noticed that all these amplifications have considerable *emotional effect.*[90] Homer's mastery lies not only in composing decorative descriptions but in using them for emphasis. But when we compare his technique with that of Balkan singers, we conclude that this does not distinguish Homer from other oral poets. Lord claims that Avdo Međedović, the best of the singers he studied, often used extensive descriptions and scene construction for emphasis. Naturally, we cannot compare his talent with Homer's virtuosity, but both use the same method of affecting the audience. Edwards conjectures that the scenes with long speeches by characters might have been presented as a kind of drama,[91] although it would be impossible to render the whole of the song as a kind of realistic theatre or a film, if only because sometimes the realities of the combat are forgotten when the characters start talking (e.g. Glaukos and Diomedes, *Iliad* 6.119–236) or when Achilles steps in and the other Greeks seem to disengage from the fight (20.158–22.369).

The organization of the composition of the *Iliad* indicates that the author could not only evoke emotions in his hearers, but also control them. I don't mean that he suffuses whole scenes with grandeur, but he manipulates the emotions on the level of a linear transmission of a message in an act of oral performance. Homer is here a master of alternating dread with relief. This pattern is well known from Attic tragedy, in which suspense is created by the alternation between dread of an impending disaster and relief—often illusory—that it will not take place. In this way, the attention of the listeners is engaged all

89 Though naturally a great number of those scenes indicates that they were very attractive to the listeners. Battle scenes are especially popular in Javanese shadow puppet theater. It is said that they often wake up dozing spectators (Scodel 2002:35).

90 Edwards 1987:4: "A major part of Homer's technique is expansion, which he uses for emphasis." Austin (1966) made an important contribution by recognizing the relationship between Homer's digressions and the intensification of dramatic impact: "Where the drama is most intense the digressions are the longest and the details the fullest" (306).

91 Edwards 1987:5: "The large proportion of both epics that is presented as direct speech must have been rendered as a kind of drama, and many scenes read almost like a dramatic script (for example, in *Iliad* 6 and 9)."

the time, although it is obvious that the disaster is unavoidable. The audience, aware of impending events, does not listen passively to a story, but gets engaged in it mentally and emotionally.

Foreshadowing future events is incompatible with creating suspense in modern typographic and written literature. The singer uses anticipation to make it easier for his audience to orient themselves in the space of composition; by hinting at the future, he leads the listeners through the stream of words and images, and provides them with a broad perspective from which to understand events. To counteract the effect of the prophecy, he introduces dread and anxiety, thus firing up the interest of the audience. The listener, who does not know how the singer is going to bring the action to a close, is uncertain whether the story will not change its course. Using four methods of affecting the listener—foreshadowing, dread, relief, and irony—the singer repeatedly creates suspense in his song.[92] He keeps the attention of the audience, because he applies these methods in a number of ways. The singer appeals to the emotions. In effect, the hearer gets carried away by the story and empathizes with the characters, their feelings, and intentions. Involved with the fictional reality, he forgets his own world. However, now and then the narrator weaves in references to the listener's world, creating distance from events in the story. The most effective tool here is irony,[93] which helps the listener appraise a given situation from his own experience and his knowledge of other epic songs. Let me give a few examples which will clarify this technique.

Dread and relief

To realize how the alternation of dread and relief affected the audience's emotions it will suffice, I think, to examine one scene—the ransom of Hektor's body by Priam.[94] In fact, it is a sequence of scenes, all of which make up Book 24 of the *Iliad*. Perhaps one could say that one example is not enough, but while analyzing the singer's composition strategies we will keep returning to his methods of using dread and relief.[95]

[92] Rengakos (1999) summarizes the current state of knowledge on the methods of creating suspense in the Homeric poems. His observations will be discussed in the next chapter.

[93] Here I disagree with Ong, who attributes irony to literate cultures (Ong 2002:101).

[94] Here I am indebted to Ilona Chruściak's bachelor's thesis (Chruściak 2008).

[95] I confine discussing emotional reactions to fear in general, because it seems sufficient to demonstrate the singer's method of affecting the audience. However, it would be interesting to observe the evocation of dread and relief in connection with how fear and emotions contrasting with fear are expressed in Homer. Studying the terms used in Homer's poems for dread and fear Zaborowski (2002) describes states of anxiety in Homeric characters; it seems that in the poems there is a strict hierarchy of terms for expressing these emotions but also that sometimes differences between various kinds of fear are even more pronounced than between fear and courage.

Despite Patroklos's burial and funeral games, Achilles' wrath remains unappeased. He cannot sleep, so he gets up and drags Hektor's body around the tomb of his friend. Seeing the dishonor done to the dead man, the gods look down in pity and urge Hermes to steal his body, but Poseidon, Hera, and Athena are opposed to this scheme. On the twelfth day, a quarrel breaks out among the gods. Apollo violently condemns Achilles, whose behavior can bring the gods' justified anger down upon him (24.53 μὴ ἀγαθῷ περ ἐόντι νεμεσσηθέωμέν οἱ ἡμεῖς 'noble though he is, let him not meet with our righteous anger'). The god's words don't augur well for Achilles. The listener knows the terrible effects of Apollo's anger which overtook the Achaeans when they offended his priest at the beginning of the song. The conflict of Apollo and Achilles, which brings about the hero's death, was known to the listener from tradition, and he could learn about it from Achilles himself, who tells about the prophecy repeated to him by his mother, Thetis (21.275–278). It was only natural to expect that Apollo would punish Achilles for the defilement of Hektor's dead body. Apollo's action would be the climax of the story: by bringing about the death of Achilles. Although the god points to the hero's mercilessness, the gods themselves are known not to forgive old offences.[96] The song even mentions the reason for the goddesses' animosity towards the Trojans: they felt disgraced by Paris's judgment (24.28–30). It happened long ago, at the beginning of the events, but despite the passage of time, they are implacable in their anger. The listener can expect that the story has come full circle, as epic demands, and the beginning of the war, defined by Paris's offence, will correspond to some event marking its end. The song of Achilles' wrath points to the death of this hero as an event which demarcates the end of the story.

Meanwhile, the quarrel ends with Zeus's speech, when he mediates between Apollo and χολωσαμένη 'furious' (24.55) Hera. Zeus decides to convince Thetis to prevail upon her son to accept Priam's ransom for Hektor's body (24.74–76):

> ἀλλ' εἴ τις καλέσειε θεῶν Θέτιν ἆσσον ἐμεῖο,
> ὄφρα τί οἱ εἴπω πυκινὸν ἔπος, ὥς κεν Ἀχιλλεὺς
> δώρων ἐκ Πριάμοιο λάχῃ ἀπό θ' Ἕκτορα λύσῃ.
>
> but should one of the gods summon Thetis,
> I could tell her a wise word for Achilles:
> to accept Priam's gifts and give up Hektor.

When Thetis comes to Olympus, Zeus announces his will and, through her, threatens Achilles with his anger (24.113–114): σκύζεσθαί οἱ εἰπὲ θεούς, ἐμὲ δ'

[96] Davies 1981.

ἔξοχα πάντων / ἀθανάτων κεχολῶσθαι ("tell him that gods are angry, and I am angry / more than all the other immortals"). This seems to bode ill for Achilles. The listener knows that the hero's wrath is implacable. His anger towards Agamemnon, which nearly caused the destruction of the Achaeans, has now become unimportant. Now it is Apollo's anger and that of the greatest of gods.[97] But when Thetis passes on Zeus's command, reinforced with a threat, to her son, Achilles simply and matter-of-factly agrees to fulfill the god's will (24.139–140): τῇδ' εἴη ὃς ἄποινα φέροι καὶ νεκρὸν ἄγοιτο, / εἰ δὴ πρόφρονι θυμῷ 'Ολύμπιος αὐτὸς ἀνώγει ("let it be so: who brings the ransom, takes the body, / if this is what the Olympian himself, in his kindness to me, commands"). The listener may be astonished. He certainly remembers that Achilles firmly denied Hektor's wish that the victor not ill-treat his enemy's body, but return it to his companions, keeping only his armor (22.250–259). Achilles brutally refused a similar request of Hektor as he was dying (22.345–355).[98] Now the listener can infer that Achilles' wrath has run out. It seems that the problem has been solved. Gods' threats towards Achilles no longer pose any danger, and so Zeus sends Iris with a message to Priam in Troy that he can safely ransom his son's body.

Future events are presented in detail: Priam shall take the ransom without any companion except for one herald who will drive the wagon, Hermes will escort him to Achilles, and neither Achilles, nor anyone else will kill him (24.144–158). Now the listener knows precisely what's going to happen. And it does happen this way. Suspense has been lost and the poet must build it anew.

When the audience has already been convinced that everything will end well for Priam, the time for rousing doubts comes. The poet makes a powerful contrast by leaving Achilles resigned to his fate and moving the action to Troy where the people are lamenting the loss of their greatest defender. The poet focuses his attention on Priam as he is in despair: Iris gives him Zeus's message and reassures him, then Priam gives orders to get ready to go to the ships. He goes into the palace, meets Hekabe, and tells her about meeting the goddess and her message. Hekabe reacts with pain and violent lamentation. She doesn't believe the enterprise will succeed. She is sure Achilles will not respect Priam; moreover, he will certainly kill him. Then these reproaches against her husband turn into a burst of hatred towards the murderer of her son, but Priam sets her objections aside. He believes the message from Zeus is true because he

97 As he was dying, Patroklos identified Zeus and Apollo as the givers of Hektor's victory (*Iliad* 16.844–845; see Janko 1992:419–420 *ad* 849–850).

98 Kim (2000:130) points out that the issue of Achilles' cruelty is highlighted by a series of unsuccessful requests by Trojan warriors—Tros (20.463–472), Lykaon (21.34–135), and Hektor (22.99–405)—which lays the groundwork for Priam's request. This parallels the requests of three messengers to Achilles who unsuccessfully beg for mercy for the Achaeans, after which finally comes a successful one, by Patroklos, acting on Nestor's advice.

had it directly from a goddess. The poet did not describe earlier how the king could hear the goddess' voice, but since she did not assume a human form, as is usual with a god who intervenes, Priam must have had an epiphany. His final words, that he is ready for death by Achilles' hand, fill the listener with dread (24.224–227):[99]

> εἰ δέ μοι αἶσα
> τεθνάμεναι παρὰ νηυσὶν Ἀχαιῶν χαλκοχιτώνων,
> βούλομαι· αὐτίκα γάρ με κατακτείνειεν Ἀχιλλεὺς
> ἀγκὰς ἑλόντ' ἐμὸν υἱόν, ἐπὴν γόου ἐξ ἔρον εἵην.
>
> if it be my fate
> to die by the ships of Achaeans clad in bronze armor,
> then I accept it; let Achilles kill me there
> after I have taken my son into my arms and satisfied the desire
> to weep.

When the wagon is loaded with ransom, Priam explodes with recriminations against his living sons. It shows he is laboring under great emotional tension, which is revealed again by the request which Priam addresses to Zeus prior to his departure, to confirm his will by a prophetic sign. He prays to Zeus, prompted by Hekabe, who is vexed by worry and uncertainty. And soon over the town, on the right side, there appears an eagle sent by Zeus. The confirmation of the success of the expedition brings relief to the listener, but it is short-lived. Just after the people have rejoiced at a sign of good luck, their joy changes to a funeral lamentation (24.327–328): φίλοι δ' ἅμα πάντες ἕποντο / πόλλ' ὀλοφυρόμενοι, ὡς εἰ θάνατόνδε κιόντα ("all his friends followed him / in a great number, lamenting, as if he were going to his death"). Zeus summons Hermes to fulfill his mission, and the atmosphere of dread is subdued. But when Hermes appears in front of Priam and the herald, both men are badly frightened (24.352–360):

> τὸν δ' ἐξ ἀγχιμόλοιο ἰδὼν ἐφράσσατο κῆρυξ
> Ἑρμείαν, ποτὶ δὲ Πρίαμον φάτο φώνησέν τε·
> "φράζεο, Δαρδανίδη· φραδέος νόου ἔργα τέτυκται.
> ἄνδρ' ὁρόω, τάχα δ' ἄμμε διαρραίσεσθαι ὀΐω.
> ἀλλ' ἄγε δὴ φεύγωμεν ἐφ' ἵππων, ἤ μιν ἔπειτα
> γούνων ἁψάμενοι λιτανεύσομεν, αἴ κ' ἐλεήσῃ."
> ὣς φάτο· σὺν δὲ γέροντι νόος χύτο, δείδιε δ' αἰνῶς,

[99] Chruściak 2008:10: "Priam's attitude is not only dramatic, but also psychologically realistic: divine intervention and confirmation of success do not allay his anxiety and the awareness of the risk he is taking."

ὀρθαὶ δὲ τρίχες ἔσταν ἐπὶ γναμπτοῖσι μέλεσσιν,
στῆ δὲ ταφών.

the herald noticed Hermes nearby,
and told Priam:
"Look, descendant of Dardanos! We have to use our reason.
I can see a man, who, I think, presently will slice us into pieces.
Let us escape in our wagon at once, or in a moment embrace his knees
and beg his compassion, perhaps he will take pity on us."
He said so, and the old man's thoughts twirled in his head, he was in
great fear and he stood dazed.

Homer realistically expresses the fright of his characters, but the listener knows that they have nothing to fear from the god, who was sent to help them. Priam himself seems to have forgotten about the promise of Hermes' help (which he did not mention to his wife), but perhaps he does not expect a man met on the road to be a god. The discrepancy between the ignorance of the characters and the knowledge of the listeners is a device often used by Homer, usually in order to create irony. Here, however, his aim is not to suggest a distance between the audience and the characters. He cannot excite fright in the listeners, so he shows the fright of his characters—and a vivid and realistic description suits his purpose. Like in thrillers, a dramatic scene and fear in the eyes of characters have a frightening effect, although there is no previous build-up of suspense. The poet gives no time to the audience for reflection. Hermes speaks kindly to the old man, but without revealing his divine status. He convinces Priam that he is safe and offers his help. Priam is reassured and even moved by the conversation. The god helps him to get unnoticed into the camp of the Myrmidons and finally reveals his identity.

The climax in Achilles' tent is at the same time an antithesis to previous scenes in the *Iliad* as well as an echo of those scenes, so that the audience cannot avoid seeing the parallels. The poet has prepared for this scene very well, because it is fundamental to his idea of the song. The listener is moved, astonished, and finally feels growing dread. Priam enters Achilles' tent, embraces his knees, kisses his hands, and, evoking the memory of his father Peleus, begs him for Hektor's body. This situation is one in a sequence of events parallel to those from the beginning of the song, a result of ring composition. Now the poet comes back to the events initiating the song—but in reverse order. This compositional device constitutes the frame of the whole song and enables the listener to recognize its main idea. The wrath of Achilles, experienced in solitude; the quarrel of gods on Olympus; Apollo's involvement—first against the Achaeans, then against Achilles; scenes with Thetis, the order of which has been changed—now she talks with Zeus in Olympus, later with her son, and it is Zeus who sends her to Achilles with a request. This sequence of events in the *Iliad* was triggered by the arrival of an old man who came to ransom his child. Now the situation is repeated and the listener cannot help but wonder whether everything will end in the same way. Then, Chryses' demand was rejected by Agamemnon, and this brought on all the misfortunes. So, despite prophecies which clearly announce a happy end, the listener cannot but feel danger. Achilles' anger was fierce beyond measure—Apollo himself was irritated by its vehemence. Achilles, usually gentle and modest, now has surpassed Agamemnon in cruelty. He accepted Zeus's proposal, but will he be able to control himself? Priam behaves unlike Chryses, Apollo's priest, who clothes his request in proud language, threatening the Achaeans with his god's power. Priam's entrance to the tent is not a simple variation of the scene of the embassy's arrival at Achilles' tent. It is night and Achilles is surprised—there are no greetings, he is not kind towards his guest. If in the embassy scene, after a warm reception of his friends, Achilles is so tenacious, why should he relent now, when his pain is much more acute? Priam mentions Achilles' father, who was similar in age (24.486–487). But when Odysseus recalled the image of Peleus (9.251–258), Achilles was unmoved. The dying Hektor also mentioned his enemy's parents, which made Achilles all the more furious (22.337–354):

> τὸν δ' ὀλιγοδρανέων προσέφη κορυθαιόλος Ἕκτωρ·
> "λίσσομ' ὑπὲρ ψυχῆς καὶ γούνων σῶν τε τοκήων,
> μή με ἔα παρὰ νηυσὶ κύνας καταδάψαι Ἀχαιῶν,
> ἀλλὰ σὺ μὲν χαλκόν τε ἅλις χρυσόν τε δέδεξο
> δῶρα, τὰ τοι δώσουσι πατὴρ καὶ πότνια μήτηρ,
> σῶμα δὲ οἴκαδ' ἐμὸν δόμεναι πάλιν, ὄφρα πυρός με
> Τρῶες καὶ Τρώων ἄλοχοι λελάχωσι θανόντα."
> τὸν δ' ἄρ' ὑπόδρα ἰδὼν προσέφη πόδας ὠκὺς Ἀχιλλεύς·
> "μή με, κύον, γούνων γουνάζεο μηδὲ τοκήων.
> αἲ γάρ πως αὐτόν με μένος καὶ θυμὸς ἀνείη
> ὤμ' ἀποταμνόμενον κρέα ἔδμεναι, οἷά μ' ἔοργας,
> ὡς οὐκ ἔσθ' ὃς σῆς γε κύνας κεφαλῆς ἀπαλάλκοι,
> οὐδ' εἴ κεν δεκάκις τε καὶ εἰκοσινήριτ' ἄποινα
> στήσωσ' ἐνθάδ' ἄγοντες, ὑπόσχωνται δὲ καὶ ἄλλα,
> οὐδ' εἴ κέν σ' αὐτὸν χρυσῷ ἐρύσασθαι ἀνώγοι
> Δαρδανίδης Πρίαμος· οὐδ' ὧς σέ γε πότνια μήτηρ
> ἐνθεμένη λεχέεσσι γοήσεται, ὃν τέκεν αὐτή.
> ἀλλὰ κύνες τε καὶ οἰωνοὶ κατὰ πάντα δάσονται."

Weakening, Hektor shook the plume on his helmet and said to him:
"I pray you by your soul and your parents' knees,
do not let Achaean dogs devour me by the ships,
but accept gifts—plenty of bronze and gold,
which my father and mother will offer you,
and send my body to Troy, so that the Trojans and their wives
may give my dead body to fire."
Swift-footed Achilles glared at him from under knitted brows and said:
"Dog, neither embrace my knees, nor [mention] my parents,
because my wrath and soul compel me
to chop you and devour the meat raw for what you have done to me,
there is no one who would drive the dogs away from your head,[100]
even if they came here with ten- or twenty-fold ransom,
and promised more,
even if Priam, the descendant of Dardanos,
offered me your weight in gold, your mother will not
lay you on the bier and lament over the body, which she gave life to,
but dogs and birds will eat you up."

Achilles' answer is as implacable as the one he gave to the embassy. Characteristically, both times he stresses that no amount of treasure would allay his pain and appease his anger.[101] Both Hektor and Achilles expect that Priam will come to Achilles with a ransom. Achilles promises not to accept any ransom, and Hektor's fate is already preordained. The listener who notices the similarities between the scenes worries because he can reasonably expect that Achilles will violently reject Priam's offer. However, Priam's gesture contrasts not only with Chryses' behavior (who expects proper respect due his age and position) but with Agamemnon's hypocrisy in sending the embassy—and it deeply moves Achilles, whose anger and intransigence crumble. The dread because of the similarity of this scene to earlier scenes and speeches is relieved when both characters grieve together over their sorrows (24.507–512):

ὣς φάτο· τῷ δ' ἄρα πατρὸς ὑφ' ἵμερον ὦρσε γόοιο,
ἁψάμενος δ' ἄρα χειρὸς ἀπώσατο ἦκα γέροντα.
τὼ δὲ μνησαμένω, ὃ μὲν Ἕκτορος ἀνδροφόνοιο
κλαῖ' ἁδινὰ προπάροιθε ποδῶν Ἀχιλῆος ἐλυσθείς.
αὐτὰρ Ἀχιλλεὺς κλαῖεν ἑὸν πατέρ', ἄλλοτε δ' αὖτε
Πάτροκλον· τῶν δὲ στοναχὴ κατὰ δώματ' ὀρώρει.

100 κεφαλή 'head' is metonymy for man.

101 Richardson (1993:141 [*ad* 24.344–354]) notes the similar syntax in both of Achilles' speeches.

> said he [Priam], and he [Achilles] was overcome by grief and longing
> for his father,
> so he took the old man's hand and moved him gently away.
> Both began to reminiscence: one, huddled at Achilles' feet, wept
> aloud for Hektor, the slayer of men,
> whereas Achilles wept now for his father, now
> for Patroklos; their lamentations filled the whole house.

There is a moment of relief. Achilles invites Priam to sit down, expresses his admiration for the courage of the Trojan king, and says that misfortunes befall all people, even those who are generally successful, like his father or Priam. In passing, he mentions his own death, which he perceives from the point of view of his unhappy father who in his old age will be left without a protector and heir, just like Priam. The king of Troy thanks Achilles for the invitation to sit down, but the only thing he desires is to see his son and deliver the ransom. These words offend Achilles and the atmosphere of dread returns immediately. Achilles answers, "glaring at him from under knitted brows" (ὑπόδρα ἰδών, 24.559), signaling anger and a threat.[102] The same gesture preceded his furious and pitiless refusal of Hektor's dying request (22.344). Such conventional speech introductions convey the speaker's tone of voice and intentions to the listener (24.559–573):[103]

> τὸν δ' ἄρ' ὑπόδρα ἰδὼν προσέφη πόδας ὠκὺς Ἀχιλλεύς·
> "μηκέτι νῦν μ' ἐρέθιζε, γέρον. νοέω δὲ καὶ αὐτός
> Ἕκτορά τοι λῦσαι· Διόθεν δέ μοι ἄγγελος ἦλθεν
> μήτηρ, ἥ μ' ἔτεκεν, θυγάτηρ ἁλίοιο γέροντος.
> καὶ δὲ σὲ γιγνώσκω, Πρίαμε, φρεσίν, οὐδέ με λήθεις,
> ὅττι θεῶν τις σ' ἦγε θοὰς ἐπὶ νῆας Ἀχαιῶν·
> οὐ γάρ κε τλαίη βροτός ἐλθέμεν, οὐδέ μάλ' ἡβῶν,
> ἐς στρατόν· οὔτε γὰρ ἂν φυλακοὺς λάθοι, οὐδὲ κ' ὀχῆα
> ῥεῖα μετοχλίσσειε θυράων ἡμετεράων.
> τὼ νῦν μή μοι μᾶλλον ἐν ἄλγεσι θυμὸν ὀρίνῃς,
> μή σε, γέρον, οὐδ' αὐτὸν ἐνὶ κλισίῃσιν ἐάσω
> καὶ ἱκέτην περ ἐόντα, Διὸς δ' ἀλίτωμαι ἐφετμάς."
> ὣς ἔφατ'· ἔδδεισεν δ' ὁ γέρων καὶ ἐπείθετο μύθῳ.
> Πηλεΐδης δ' οἴκοιο λέων ὣς ἆλτο θύραζε,
> οὐκ οἶος· ἅμα τῷ γε δύω θεράποντες ἕποντο

102 In Holoka's (1983) opinion, this gesture was used in the hierarchic order by a person of a higher rank to react to improper behavior of a person of a lower rank. That is why he thinks this facial expression in Achilles is peculiar and arrogant. However, it is my conviction that the gesture is primarily about the defense of one's honor and demonstrates the readiness to react to an offence.

103 Foley 1997.

Swift-footed Achilles glared at him from under knitted brows and said
"Vex me no longer, old man. I myself intend
to give up to you the body of Hektor; my mother, who bore me,
a daughter of the old man of the sea, came to me with a message
from Zeus,
and I think, Priam—do not try to conceal it from me—
that one of the gods must have led you to the Achaean ships,
as no mortal, even in the prime of youth,
could sneak into our camp; he could neither pass the guards unseen,
nor could he easily lift the bar on our door.
Therefore feed no more the pain in my heart,
old man, or—though you are a suppliant—
I can lose control and disrespect Zeus's orders."
He said so, and the old man feared and obeyed his warning.
And Peleus's son sprang outside like a lion,
but not alone, as two of his men followed him.

The expression μή μ' ἐρέθιζε should be translated 'do not provoke me', because it is used in order to provoke someone's aggression.[104] The atmosphere of dread returns again, with great force, as Achilles' words are not an empty threat. He can barely contain his anger, completely implacable until recently. Priam is in real danger and reacts to the threat with fear. The poet also stresses this when he again compares Achilles to a lion.[105] This comparison was already used by the narrator during Achilles' fight against Aeneas (20.164–174),[106] by Apollo to describe his fierceness without respect or

104 Agamemnon uses the expression μή μ' ἐρέθιζε to warn Chryses as he is being expelled (1.32). Zeus's mockery is aimed at provoking Hera (*Iliad* 4.5–6) or Hera and Athena (*Iliad* 4.419), but it is better for the goddesses to keep calm, i.e. to ignore the provocation. There is also a simile which depicts Menelaos as a lion tired of being provoked (ἐρεθίζων) by dogs and people who keep it from seizing a cow, throwing spears and firebrands (*Iliad* 17.656–664). The listener may be upset not by the use of this expression in a similar situation at the beginning of the song but because it usually suggests a situation of menace.

105 For Edwards (1987:102) this short simile is only an ornament; however, Minchin (2001:141–142) notes that it not only characterizes Achilles but also makes the listeners worry about Priam's safety: "They [i.e. the lion features which the simile recalls] explain what it is that could cause Priam, or even us, the audience, to fear him. As a consequence, we feel a moment of anxiety on Priam's behalf as the simile is expressed."

106 It is the longest of all the similes comparing a warrior to a lion and, according to Edwards (1991:309 *ad Iliad* 20.164–175), probably the most realistic one. Edwards believes that in this simile, "it is the character of the animal that is important. ... The main point of comparison is the kindled fury of the lion and of the hero."

pity for the enemy (24.41–43), and by Achilles himself, when he disdainfully rejects Hektor's offer of a covenant (22.260–263):

> τὸν δ' ἄρ' ὑπόδρα ἰδὼν προσέφη πόδας ὠκὺς Ἀχιλλεύς·
> "Ἕκτορ, μή μοι, ἄλαστε, συνημοσύνας ἀγόρευε.
> ὡς οὐκ ἔστι λέουσι καὶ ἀνδράσιν ὅρκια πιστά,
> οὐδὲ λύκοι τε καὶ ἄρνες ὁμόφρονα θυμὸν ἔχουσιν
>
> Swift-footed Achilles glared at him from under knitted brows and said
> "Cursed Hektor, do not babble to me about covenants.
> There is no covenant between lions and people,
> and wolves and lambs can never make peace..."

Achilles supervises the preparation of Hektor's body for sending it home. The narrator once more evokes the atmosphere of dread, saying that Achilles deliberately avoided inflaming Priam's suffering, because then, as he well knew, he would have to kill the king of Troy (24.582–586):

> δμῳὰς δ' ἐκκαλέσας λοῦσαι κέλετ' ἀμφί τ' ἀλεῖψαι,
> νόσφιν ἀειράσας, ὡς μὴ Πρίαμος ἴδοι υἱόν,
> μὴ ὃ μὲν ἀχνυμένῃ κραδίῃ χόλον οὐκ ἐρύσαιτο
> παῖδα ἰδών, Ἀχιλῆϊ δ' ὀρινθείη φίλον ἦτορ
> καί ἑ κατακτείνειε, Διὸς δ' ἀλίτηται ἐφετμάς.
>
> he called servants and ordered them to wash and anoint the body,
> but first take it to a place where Priam would not see his son,
> because seeing his child, he might not control the anger
> in his heart and enrage the heart dear to Achilles,
> who would have to kill him against Zeus's orders.

These words reveal how real the danger is and how easy it would be to trigger anger and aggression in the hero, who can kill a man out of irritation in his despair. The poet, who previously escalated the atmosphere of dread, now employs soothing phrases. Achilles persuades his guest to eat with him, but when Priam asks him to let him sleep, the hero agrees, explaining that he cannot allow the old man to use his tent because one of the Achaeans coming to take counsel might see him there (24.650–652). Here the danger is reduced immediately, as soon as it appears. It is quite possible, however, to imagine a plot, in which someone enters Achilles' tent and recognizes the sleeping king of Troy. Priam thus falls asleep, but his rest is broken by Hermes, who comes to announce that he is still in danger of being recognized (24.677–688). Again Priam's reaction is fear (24.689), but the dread cannot be very powerful if the god himself helps him to leave the Achaean camp.

This sequence of scenes lets us draw an important conclusion. From the very beginning the audience is informed about the upcoming events, and each revelation is more detailed than the previous. It would seem that in such conditions spinning a tale is pointless, but Homer, alternating dread and relief, creates such powerful suspense that the listener is not at all sure if the events which have been foreshadowed will really take place; he is even prepared for a sudden plot twist. Because the twist does not come, he is relieved. Homer is a master of dread and relief: in the initial scenes, the feeling of dread is the strongest; then there are longer passages which allay the apprehension of the receiver; at the end, dread is only feigned. Nonetheless, such regular alternation of those two emotions implies the existence of a pattern, which must have been regularly used by the singer to generate suspense. Homer has at his disposal a gamut of methods which he uses to build the atmosphere of dread. He can smoothly pass from one emotion to another. To create tension he uses scenes and speeches that have already appeared in the song. Thus he evokes the mood he wants as the listener recalls the moments which impressed themselves deeply in his memory (e.g. Achilles' reception of the envoys or his brutal refusals of Hektor's requests). The listener subconsciously fears that things will turn out as badly as before, because all the scenes which Homer recalls here (including the rejection of Chryses' demands) ended in misfortune.

Irony

As we have already noted, the poet does not only engage the listener's emotions and arouse his interest in the action, but from time to time allows him to look at the events from a distance. Here irony is an indispensable element of the dialogue with the listener.[107] Irony is not only a manifestation of Homer's standpoint but above all it allows him to influence the reception of his song. He is able to do this by guiding the listener to understand the behavior and points of view of the characters, which he then juxtaposes with the listener's knowledge and morality.[108] The listener enters the world of epic heroes, which he knows well, thanks to many previously heard songs, but he does not observe the heroes passively. The characters in the song behave properly or not; often the thing

[107] Rengakos (1999:310, 323) defines dramatic irony used by Homer as a discrepancy between the knowledge of the listener and the lack of it in the characters of the epic.

[108] The need for the acceptance of the poem's system of values by the original ancient audience was postulated by Adkins (1982).

which seemed right turns out to be wrong, as does the reverse. It is all a part of the singer's play with the hearer. Epic heroes occupy a different world than that of the listeners, in which many things in the heroes' world are impossible. The behavior of gods and heroes often does not conform to the norms of the listeners but there is a kind of behavior common to both. Homer, probably typically of the singers of his time, encourages his audience to judge attitudes and facts which he presents.

While considering the way the poet intends to guide the reception of his song, I believe we should take into account the fact that the song is always performed for a group of people. The singer does not imagine an isolated virtual listener who perfectly understands all layers of his message. Conversely, he adapts his message to the intelligence and perceptive abilities of his listeners, in all probability of various social classes. In those times, such an appeal to the collective mind was nothing exceptional; it was typical of that society, in which common matters were debated in an assembly. In Homeric poems, the frequency of the image of a gathering bears witness to its importance. Kurt Raaflaub rightly points out:

> An assembly is called, often combined with a council meeting, and public debate is arranged in a polis, army, or band of warriors whenever an important issue requires discussion and decision. ... The assembly thus is a traditional institution, deeply embedded in the structures and customs of society.[109]

The silence of the assembly should not lead to the fallacious conclusion that its role is limited to blind obedience to the elders or ruler.[110] By accepting or rejecting the proposals of its leaders, the assembly assumes responsibility for their deeds,[111] so an individual's behavior is always judged by an assembly, which determines whether a deed is good for the community. The leaders try to influence the gathering by persuasion. I believe this is also how the singer carries out his intention to guide the reception of his song. He presents the conduct of his characters as good or bad according to the standards of the group. At the same time, he refrains from strident and one-sided assessments, leaving this

109 Raaflaub 1997:642.

110 Raaflaub 1997:643: "Overall, although it lacks the right of initiative, free speech, and vote—restrictions which are typical of the most ancient societies anyway—the assembly plays a crucial role that should not be underestimated."

111 Raaflaub (1997:644) argues that by approving Paris's conduct the Trojan community has taken responsibility for his wrongdoing (3.205–224; compare 7.345–378). It results in a negative moral judgment of all Trojans; they all become guilty of an immoral deed and starting the war. Similarly, Achilles blames all the Achaeans for their collective support of Agamemnon's conduct (1.410, 16.17–18).

task to the listeners. He does so, I think, not in order to show the ambiguity of human behavior, but to avoid his audience's collective opposition to a one-sided presentation of well-known epic heroes. The *Iliad*, for example, whitewashes Achilles as much as it besmirches Agamemnon. Irony, which Homer often uses, lets his listeners distance themselves from the events and curbs their natural tendency to identify themselves with the protagonists.

The singer employs irony in various ways to activate his listeners' emotions.[112] I do not intend to make an exhaustive study of irony in Homer, but I'd like to concentrate on several important aspects of this issue and illustrate my point by choosing situations in which the poet relies on the listeners' knowledge about events not mentioned in the text of the song.

Words do not always have just one meaning and the listener is sensitive to their double meaning. Most typical is when a character does not realize what he really says. In *Iliad* 3.54–55, the poet very clearly suggests Paris's death in the near future, though the speaker, Hektor, does not realize that what he is saying can really happen: οὐκ ἄν τοι χραίσμῃ κίθαρις τά τε δῶρ' Ἀφροδίτης / ἥ τε κόμη τό τε εἶδος, ὅτ' ἐν κονίῃσι μιγείης ("kithara, Aphrodite's gifts, hair, or looks—they will not protect you / when you mingle with dust [of a battlefield, i.e. when you fall dead]"). Hektor presents here a vision of Alexander's death, which shows the author's knowledge of the future, but also assumes such a knowledge in the listeners. In a traditional community, people superstitiously avoid mentioning words relating to a disaster because they are afraid that gods or demons may hear them and make them come true (e.g. the Polish saying "to utter a word in an evil hour"). Naturally, this is what the listener of Hektor's speech fears. But it is not only a reaction based on superstition; he knows from elsewhere that Paris will die on the battlefield at Troy, so he does not have to deliberate long to conclude that Hektor's words are imprudent and therefore sinister. The ironic effect of these words and the mockery of Paris's beauty, however, work primarily to his disadvantage, as if their aim was to provoke in the external audience a critical attitude towards this hero.

In the *Iliad*, the ignorance of future events manifested by the characters takes various forms. The dying Patroklos foretells Hektor's fate (16.851–854), and the dying Hektor predicts Achilles' death in the near future (22.356–360). In both cases, the heroes take the predictions lightly: Hektor assumes that instead of being killed, he may kill Achilles, and Achilles scornfully treats the prophecy as a futile threat, because he will die only when the gods want it. Such reactions indicate that the singer is playing with the listener, who feels that he has

[112] Lord (1974:13–36) many times points out the use of irony by Avdo Međedović in *The Wedding of Smailagić Meho*. It is one of the ways in which Međedović's version differs from Šemić's song, with which Avdo became acquainted by having it read to him, and then included it in his repertoire.

inside knowledge. However, the effect is not distance from the characters in the story, but the reverse—the actions of heroes from another epoch become close, open to comment and evaluation. The words of Hektor and Achilles must have evoked pity in the listeners and perhaps prompted a general reflection on human ignorance of the future. Superstitious fear is always related to words auguring tragedy; the words of prophets of disaster always come true, so they should not be disregarded.[113]

As we can see, the listener not only empathizes with the characters, but also judges their conduct. His knowledge about future events is not an obstacle; on the contrary, it deepens his intellectual and emotional experience. The awareness necessary to recognize irony is three-fold. The easiest way is to refer to the events and deeds presented in the song; then irony is usually found in the characters' utterances. However, the singer may also rely on the listeners' knowledge of facts from their familiarity with the cycle (macro-story), or, in other cases, he may choose to foreshadow certain events.

Let me give three examples of irony, which an attentive listener can detect in the words of the characters. When Patroklos comes back from the Achaean camp, saddened at the extent of their failure, Achilles feels compassion for him (16.1–5), which, according to Jinyo Kim, springs from the shared feeling of pity for the defeated Greeks.[114] However, Achilles' words do not disclose this attitude (16.7–19):

> τίπτε δεδάκρυσαι Πατρόκλεες, ἠΰτε κούρη
> νηπίη, ἥ θ' ἅμα μητρὶ θέουσ' ἀνελέσθαι ἀνώγει
> εἱανοῦ ἁπτομένη, καί τ' ἐσσυμένην κατερύκει,
> δακρυόεσσα δέ μιν ποτιδέρκεται, ὄφρ' ἀνέληται·
> τῇ ἴκελος Πάτροκλε τέρεν κατὰ δάκρυον εἴβεις.
> ἠέ τι Μυρμιδόνεσσι πιφαύσκεαι, ἢ ἐμοὶ αὐτῷ,
> ἦέ τιν' ἀγγελίην Φθίης ἐξέκλυες οἶος;
> ζώειν μὰν ἔτι φασὶ Μενοίτιον Ἄκτορος υἱόν,
> ζώει δ' Αἰακίδης Πηλεὺς μετὰ Μυρμιδόνεσσι;
> τῶν κε μάλ' ἀμφοτέρων ἀκαχοίμεθα τεθνηώτων.

[113] In ancient times, the prophecies of Patroklos's and Hektor's death were associated with the belief that dying people can foresee the future (Xenophon *Cyropaedia* 8.7.21; Plato *Apology* 39c; Aristotle fr. 10; Artemon of Miletus in MS A and scholia T to the *Iliad*; Cicero *De Divinatione* 1.63; Genesis 49; compare Janko 1992:420 *ad Iliad* 16.852–854). But it should be noted that both Patroklos and Hektor, prophesying death to their enemy, utter an "evil word." In a way they cast a curse upon the enemy with a conviction that it will come true. The reaction of Hektor and Achilles, victims of this verbal assault, is then an attempt at breaking the curse. Nonetheless, in the eyes of the audience, who knows their future, it is a vain attempt.

[114] Kim 2000:60–67, 118.

ἦε σύ γ' Ἀργείων ὀλοφύρεαι, ὡς ὀλέκονται
νηυσὶν ἔπι γλαφυρῇσιν ὑπερβασίης ἕνεκα σφῆς;
ἐξαύδα, μὴ κεῦθε νόῳ, ἵνα εἴδομεν ἄμφω.

Why are you crying, Patroklos, like a silly girl,
who runs after her mother hoping to be taken into her arms,
catches hold of her dress, and hinders her steps,
and looks tearfully up to see if she will pick her up?
You are like her, Patroklos, shedding tears.
Do you have anything to announce to the Myrmidons or me?
Have you had any news from Phthia?
They say Menoitios, the son of Aktor, is still alive.
And Peleus, the son of Aiakos, also lives among Myrmidons?
We would have a reason to grieve if any of them died.
Or are you moaning over the Argives, who are killed
in their hollowed ships because of their own iniquity?
Tell me without hiding anything, so that we both know about it.

Knowing the real reason for his friend's tears, Achilles mentions others, which would really deserve mourning. He presents them in the form of ironic questions, which—they both know—can be answered only in the negative. He is very theatrical about it, addressing not only Patroklos, but also the Myrmidons who are witnessing the scene. The questions are preceded by a very impressive simile. The comparison to a small girl who wants to gain her mother's compassion should make Patroklos realize that Achilles really knows that the tears are a means to coerce him to help the Achaeans. The girl's tearful gaze is not only a perceptive observation of the behavior of a young child, who exaggerates her grief to get what she wants, but it also reveals Achilles' suspicions that Patroklos's grief is pretended and aimed at tricking him.[115] The last request for sincerity is both cynical and bitter. Also ironic are Agamemnon's words about Menelaos's needless care for enemies he wants to save (*Iliad* 6.55) or Nestor's comments about Achilles' concern for the Achaeans (*Iliad* 11.656–657).[116] All these utterances ironically comment on the behavior of the characters. The listener gets to know their points of view and their psyche, but his knowledge is not the result of the singer's suggestion.

[115] Zanker (1994:14–15) suggests that the gibe in this simile helps relieve Achilles' emotions. Compare Gaca (2008) who suggests that Achilles' comparison of Patroklos to a little girl (16.7–11) refers to the situation of conquering a city, when the fleeing mother abandons her child.

[116] Kim 2000: 57–58 and 106–107.

This is the strategy Homer uses when he assumes his audience's knowledge of facts that are not in the *Iliad*, although their knowledge is more extensive than we usually realize. At the beginning of Book 4, the council of the gods ends with a decision to provoke the Trojans to break the truce and return to battle. This mission is entrusted to Athena, who is seen by both armies shooting through the sky like a meteor. Homer, typically (compare *Iliad* 2.271–278), takes this opportunity to introduce conversations of some anonymous soldiers who do not understand the meaning of this sign from the gods (4.81–85):

> ὧδε δέ τις εἴπεσκεν ἰδὼν ἐς πλησίον ἄλλον·
> "ἦ ῥ' αὖτις πόλεμός τε κακὸς καὶ φύλοπις αἰνὴ
> ἔσσεται, ἢ φιλότητα μετ' ἀμφοτέροισι τίθησιν
> Ζεύς, ὅς τ' ἀνθρώπων ταμίης πολέμοιο τέτυκται;"
> ὣς ἄρα τις εἴπεσκεν Ἀχαιῶν τε Τρώων τε.
>
> and this is how many [a warrior] having seen [it] spoke to his neighbor:
> "Which will it be, evil war and terrible turmoil of battle,
> or is Zeus, who allots wars to people,
> going to set friendship between our nations?"
> Thus did many Achaeans and many Trojans speak.

The warriors express their uncertainty about the future just after the listener has learned what the gods have agreed upon. The singer masterfully paints the uncertainty of men in both armies; juxtaposing the knowledge and ignorance of what is to happen, he affects the audience, who cannot but notice the human ignorance of gods' will. The listener is doubly privileged: he identifies the characters' imperfect knowledge of the future with his own uncertainty about tomorrow, but he is also in a situation impossible in everyday life—familiar with future and the will of gods, he can generalize his view of the reality presented in the epic. The singer makes his listeners aware of the common human condition which they share with the characters. However, the singer's aim is not to convey any great truth about people. Human limitations in recognizing gods' will and foreseeing their own future are common knowledge, which the poet can easily refer to and be sure the audience will understand. In a traditional society, knowledge is also traditional: it is a set of often repeated sayings and views, replicated generation by generation, which function as a continuing consensus of all members of the society. Homeric listeners come from a community which recognizes such known and accepted truths. This is how they understand the value of the characters' words.

When Achilles submits to the gods' will in *Iliad* Books 1 and 24, he motivates it with the duty to comply with their authority. In this wild young man, who often is a law unto himself, it may seem astonishing. But here the poet shows a common truth, with which the listeners sympathize. In this way, he gets their approval for his hero, and probably also their empathy. In a traditional society, the truths of the old are also the truths of the young. The truths of common people are also the truths of heroes. Using irony, Homer seeks the approval for his story.

When the singer can count on his audience's knowledge of the cycle, foreshadowing is unnecessary and irony can be more sophisticated. At the beginning of *Iliad* Book 4, the gods, feasting on Olympus, seem to be observing events at Troy, where Aphrodite has rescued Paris and taken him from the battlefield directly to his marital chamber. Zeus uses this opportunity to mock Hera and Athena. Aphrodite's coup induced him to put forward his proposition of making peace between the warring parties (4.5–19). Hera and Athena take offence. Hera reproaches her husband, saying that he wants to humiliate her, wasting all her efforts to organize the expedition against Troy (4.24–29). Zeus seems indignant at her angry outburst (4.30–49):

> τὴν δὲ μέγ' ὀχθήσας προσέφη νεφεληγερέτα Ζεύς·
> "δαιμονίη, τί νύ σε Πρίαμος Πριάμοιό τε παῖδες
> τόσσα κακὰ ῥέζουσιν, ὅ τ' ἀσπερχὲς μενεαίνεις
> Ἰλίου ἐξαλαπάξαι ἐϋκτίμενον πτολίεθρον;
> εἰ δὲ σύ γ' εἰσελθοῦσα πύλας καὶ τείχεα μακρά
> ὠμὸν βεβρώθοις Πρίαμον Πριάμοιό τε παῖδας
> ἄλλους τε Τρῶας, τότε κεν χόλον ἐξακέσαιο;
> ἔρξον ὅπως ἐθέλεις· μὴ τοῦτό γε νεῖκος ὀπίσσω
> σοὶ καὶ ἐμοὶ μέγ' ἔρισμα μετ' ἀμφοτέροισι γένηται.
> ἄλλο δέ τοι ἐρέω, σὺ δ' ἐνὶ φρεσὶ βάλλεο σῇσιν·
> ὁππότε κεν καὶ ἐγὼ μεμαὼς πόλιν ἐξαλαπάξαι
> τὴν ἐθέλω, ὅθι τοι φίλοι ἀνέρες ἐγγεγάασιν,
> μή τι διατρίβειν τὸν ἐμὸν χόλον, ἀλλά μ' ἐᾶσαι·
> καὶ γὰρ ἐγὼ σοὶ δῶκα ἑκών, ἀέκοντί γε θυμῷ.
> αἳ γὰρ ὑπ' ἠελίῳ τε καὶ οὐρανῷ ἀστερόεντι
> ναιετάουσι πόληες ἐπιχθονίων ἀνθρώπων,
> τάων μοι περὶ κῆρι τιέσκετο Ἴλιος ἱρή
> καὶ Πρίαμος καὶ λαὸς ἐϋμμελίω Πριάμοιο.
> οὐ γάρ μοί ποτε βωμὸς ἐδεύετο δαιτὸς ἐΐσης,
> λοιβῆς τε κνίσης τε· τὸ γὰρ λάχομεν γέρας ἡμεῖς."

Cloud-gathering Zeus was greatly angered and said to her:
"Mad woman! What great harm have Priam and his sons done to you
that you are so hotly burning with the desire
to completely destroy the beautifully built city of Priam?
If you could only enter within the gates and great walls,
you would devour Priam raw, and his sons,
and all other Trojans. Would that appease your anger?
Do as you please! Let not this tiff give rise to a quarrel
that would divide you and me.
But I will tell you one thing, and take it to your heart:
whenever I desire to ruin a city,
I will choose the one in which live men that are dear to you;
Do not try to stop my anger; I will have my way.
Because I have yielded to you, although my heart was against it.
Under the sun and starry sky
there are cities of people, who dwell on the earth,
and of these cities sacred Ilion was closest to my heart
and Priam, and his people with a fair spear of ash,
because food was never scarce upon my altar,
nor drink-offering, nor fat, which is our due."

Zeus, reproaching Hera for her hatred for the Trojans, uses questions, as if he did not know the cause. His ignorance is pretended. His previous words to Hera (4.5–6)[117] were sarcastic and provocative. He teases his wife, playing on the fact that she did not give him the reason for her hatred for the Trojans. By not mentioning it himself, he obtains an advantage over her. Moreover, asking the question "What is the great reason for your hatred for them?" he belittles the significance of Paris's judgment. However, his awareness of his spouse's anger indicates a reference to an unspecified past event, when he agreed to Hera's demand: "I have yielded to you, although my heart was against it" (4.43). Hera only says that her efforts to organize the Achaean expedition will now be rendered null and vain, whereas Zeus reveals her real intentions, the destruction of the Trojans. He uses mockery to show the truth, albeit indirectly, and to expose real intentions, although he keeps elegant restraint.

To understand the irony in Zeus's words, the listener must know the reason for Hera's passionate efforts from sources other than the *Iliad*. Karl Reinhardt demonstrates that the scenes in *Iliad* Books 4 and 5 indicate that Homer knew the

[117] αὐτίκ' ἐπειρᾶτο Κρονίδης ἐρεθιζέμεν Ἥρην / κερτομίοις ἐπέεσσι, παραβλήδην ἀγορεύων ("At once the son of Kronos started teasing Hera / with mocking words, and said with malice").

Trojan War was an outcome of Paris's judgment,[118] although the poet alludes to this event only in the last book of the *Iliad* (24.28–30). The fact that the judgment whose consequences were so significant is mentioned only in passing and at the end of the poem has given rise to many doubts, and the verses have been athetized since antiquity. Scholia enumerate many places where it would be more natural to introduce such information, the most suitable being Zeus's question in *Iliad* 4 about the reason for Hera's hatred of the Trojans. In the song, Zeus does not get an answer. But it seems to me that the reason for Hera's enmity is not specified because it was so familiar the author knew his audience would understand the allusion. Instead of mentioning it, he has the interlocutors only make allusions to a well-known event. Thus, the effect of Zeus's ridicule is much more powerful. Zeus does not intend to change destiny; he only teases the goddess, and the listener is well aware of it.[119]

Zeus's speech, with ring composition, returns at the end to the Trojans and shows his friendly attitude to them. The listeners might wonder why the ruler of the gods does not want to save people who are so dear to him. Zeus does not explain why, despite the piety of Priam and other Trojans, he agrees to the destruction of the city. According to the *Kypria*, the capture of the city is a part of "Zeus's plan" (Διὸς βουλή). Zeus does not admit it and in the quarrel with his wife he pretends to compromise—this time he yields, but he reserves his right to destroy what is dear to her.[120] These words ring an ominous tone for the future of the Achaeans, although we don't know their exact meaning.[121] Homer's contemporaries probably also did not know.

118 Reinhardt 1938:16–17.

119 According to Kirk (1985:333 *ad* 4.31–33), Zeus asks Hera about her reason for her hatred of Priam and the Trojans because her anger should be directed against Paris, who dishonored her, choosing Aphrodite.

120 Kirk (1985:333 *ad* 4.31–49) gives another probable reason for Zeus's consent to the capture of Troy: "This may cause the listener to wonder why, nevertheless, he allows the city to fall, even after he has discharged his promise to Thetis. The answer is that this has been made inevitable by Paris's offence against hospitality, which is protected by Zeus ξένιος himself, and by the Trojans' condoning of it by receiving him and Helen." This opinion seems to be borne out by the fact that it is Zeus himself who orders that the Trojans should break the truce. In this way, they take the blame for breaking the oaths, and their guilt for starting the war is renewed. About the nature of Homeric compromise in this scene see Flaig 1994; Elmer 2013:146–150.

121 Lang (1983) surmises that Zeus's quarrels with Hera were a traditional motif which must have been exploited in a number of mythical stories connected with this couple. She also suggests a mutual influence between these myths and the *Iliad*. If so, I think that quarrels between the highest gods could function as a divine initiative for heroic events, i.e. they could be the widest ring in an epic cycle, in which the responsibility for all events would be transferred to gods because all events are a consequence of Zeus's plan (Διὸς βουλή). Such a divine plan as a principle organizing the whole of the epic cycle exists in the Trojan and Theban Cycles and it serves as a cosmological frame, within which the singer places his episode (see Ch. 1 and Ch. 3, above).

Zeus mocks and threatens. He pretends not to know Hera's motives, but his pretended ignorance is exposed by the fact that he bypasses certain matters, which are clear to both the goddess and the audience of the song, whose knowledge of the epic tradition enables them to understand the reasons for her anger. Zeus suggests misfortunes which will fall upon the Achaeans after the war, however, the listeners don't have any basis for conjectures about any future events Zeus may have in mind. Previously there was pretended ignorance concerning the past, but now there is pretended knowledge concerning the future. In one speech, the poet brings the hearer into the world of familiar facts and at the same time misleads him with facts whose significance he cannot guess.[122] Relying on the listeners' knowledge of important facts from the Trojan Cycle seems to be a typical device for the singer and deceiving them as to what is going to happen is another he uses, not at all infrequently. The poet uses irony to tease his audience.

An epic poet is more than accustomed to such a reaction to his story—he even provokes it. Occasionally, by employing the epithet νήπιος 'stupid', he guides the listener to a critical opinion about a character's behavior. The singer may use such signals to lead to the correct evaluation of a situation, when he introduces a new motif, which the listener might not know how to interpret. In such cases, the listener is reduced to the confirmation of the view presented by the poet. This happens, for example, when the singer ridicules Glaukos for swapping his armor (*Iliad* 6.234–236, the listener, not knowing how to react, might admire the gesture as chivalric). In the case of the Trojan Asios, who assaulted the Achaean wall on his chariot (contrary to Poulydamas's advice to attack on foot, 12.60–135), the ridicule is probably connected with the paradigm of inappropriate behavior. The poet wants to tell how to attack the Achaean wall, and to make it more convincing he shows another method, with a critical comment, from which we can learn that anyone who acts differently is in danger of death. The epithet "stupid" always foretells the death of a "stupid" person—the death which he is unable to predict himself.[123] Since the listener also cannot predict it, the epithet makes him privy to what's going to happen. The language of epic may abound in such signals. These signals may be not only words, but also gestures, which are very numerous in the Homeric poems. Steven Lowenstam has demonstrated that even such seemingly meaningless

[122] It seems to me that such an explanation would appeal to the listeners who could not understand why their hometowns suffered various disasters, although they were protected by Hera, the patron goddess of Greeks.

[123] Duckworth 1966:11–12; Lowenstam 1981:39–67, who makes a reference to Kraut 1863.

gestures as slapping one's thighs is a hint that this person is going to die or even that he is ready to die.[124]

Some of the narrator's statements not only indicate his suspicion that the listeners may misunderstand his intentions but, at times, go against their expectations to baffle them, showing things from a new perspective. Thanks to Achilles' withdrawal from battle, the Trojans can for the first time spend the night outside the city walls. A detailed description of their army discloses its power and the danger it poses to the Achaeans. Hidden among these pieces of information is a significant remark about preparing a meal. A meal in archaic Greek culture has more than just a practical side; as an offering, it is a means of coming into contact with gods. The Trojans do what is proper (*Iliad* 8.545–552):

> ἐκ πόλιος δ' ἄξοντο βόας καὶ ἴφια μῆλα
> καρπαλίμως, οἶνον δὲ μελίφρονα οἰνίζοντο
> σῖτόν δ' ἐκ μεγάρων, ἐπὶ δὲ ξύλα πολλὰ λέγοντο·
> ἔρδον δ' ἀθανάτοισι τεληέσσας ἑκατόμβας.
> κνίσην δ' ἐκ πεδίου ἄνεμοι φέρον οὐρανὸν εἴσω,
> ἡδεῖαν, τῆς δ' οὔ τι θεοὶ μάκαρες δατέοντο,
> οὐδ' ἔθελον· μάλα γάρ σφιν ἀπήχθετο Ἴλιος ἱρὴ
> καὶ Πρίαμος καὶ λαὸς ἐϋμμελίω Πριάμοιο.[125]
>
> from the city they drove many oxen and fat rams
> and brought honey-sweet wine and bread from their houses,
> and they gathered much wood.
> They offered hecatombs to the immortals that was their due,
> and the wind carried the smoke from the plain up to heaven,
> [the smoke was] sweet, but the blessed gods did not accept the
> offering,
> neither were they inclined to, because they bitterly hated sacred Ilion
> and Priam, and his people with a fair spear of ash.

Reservations voiced against some verses in this passage refer to the emphasis on the gods against Troy in general, and against Priam in particular, but in oral poetry, such phrasing is not exceptional, especially in view of the final fate of Troy. The religious aspect of the meal is particularly important and here it has an even deeper meaning. That the smoke from the offering has risen up to the

[124] Lowenstam 1981:39–67.

[125] Verses 548 and 550–552 come from Plato *Alcibiades* II 149d; they are not found in manuscripts. Leaf (1900–1902 *ad loc.*) decided they come from a cyclic song, and this is the reason why they are left out in some editions; see also West 1998.

heavens and is pleasant to the gods is a clear sign for the Trojans that their offering has been accepted (compare the ascent of smoke from Abel's offering, which means that God has accepted it, Genesis 4.3–5). It is clearly a favorable sign both for the Trojans as the interior audience, and for the listeners, the exterior audience. However, the singer astonishes his listeners when he adds, "but the blessed gods did not accept the offering." He foreshadows the defeat of the Trojans and reassures his listeners caught between dread and relief that the Trojan menace will eventually pass. Although such foreshadowing and mixing of moods may seem strange, it is typical of Homer. But the poet's prediction has an overtone of irony: it is based on the belief, common to the singer and his audience, that a human assessment of a situation is often faulty. The reading of a sign may be deceptive.

Words regarded as a promise can also be deceptive, because without knowledge of the gods' will, making promises may turn out to be premature. When the listener knows the outcome of events, he can see the confusion in both warnings and hope. When the listener does not know the outcomes, the singer sometimes expresses such discoveries through his characters. Achilles mourns over the dead body of Patroklos (*Iliad* 18.324–330):

> ὢ πόποι ἦ ῥ' ἅλιον ἔπος ἔκβαλον ἤματι κείνῳ
> θαρσύνων ἥρωα Μενοίτιον ἐν μεγάροισι·
> φῆν δέ οἱ εἰς 'Οπόεντα περικλυτὸν υἱὸν ἀπάξειν
> Ἴλιον ἐκπέρσαντα, λαχόντα τε ληΐδος αἶσαν.
> Ἀλλ' οὐ Ζεὺς ἄνδρεσσι νοήματα πάντα τελευτᾷ·
> ἄμφω γὰρ πέπρωται ὁμοίην γαῖαν ἐρεῦσαι
> αὐτοῦ ἐνὶ Τροίῃ
>
> Oh woe, it was really a vain word that "fell out" on that day,
> when I tried to comfort the hero Menoitios in the palace,
> saying that when Ilion has been captured I will bring back to Opoeis
> [his] famous son with his share of the spoil.
> But Zeus does not fulfill all human purposes;
> we are both destined to stain the selfsame earth
> here at Troy.

The "vanity" of the word is akin to the "vanity" of the deed, a deed that is futile. Hera is also afraid of the "vanity" of her efforts, should they be in opposition to Zeus's plans. In ancient cultures, we often come across the conviction of the causative power of words, that once the word is uttered, inevitably it comes true. Achilles here arrives at a certain truth, which the narrator shares. We might say they believe that Zeus does not fulfill human requests and expectations, while Homer declares: "Zeus does not fulfill all human purposes." Zeus does fulfill human purposes, but only some of them. These words refer to the scene just before Patroklos goes into battle, when Achilles prays for Zeus to give his friend glory and let him return alive (16.231–248). Zeus fulfills only half of the request: he covers Patroklos with glory but does not let him survive—and the narrator at once knows that it will be so (16.249–252). Jinyo Kim states that Achilles "recognizes the tragic fulfillment of his own wish" a moment before he says these words, when he complains to his mother that Zeus has granted him his request for the defeat of the Achaeans (18.79–81; see also 1.408–412 and 1.508–510).[126] Achilles' words refer only to the partial fulfillment of his prayer, when he sends Patroklos to battle. In the case of both heroes, Zeus fulfills the request for glory and denies the request to come back alive. Achilles identifies Patroklos's fate with his own. Learning his destiny, he immediately decides to go back to combat.[127]

As we have seen, the observation that human expectations may clash with Zeus's design is important for the author of the song. This observation, which stresses the discrepancy between human and divine abilities, is probably in accord with the beliefs of the singer's listeners, for whom it might simply be a not so trivial truth.

The formula and its effect upon the listener

Here we touch upon an important issue—the listener's sensitivity to the elements of a poem and the extent of his sensitivity. Some elements are fixed features of the epic code which facilitate the understanding of events, while others are so conventional that they hardly attract the attention of listeners. Just like in a spoken language, one cannot emphasize each word. The problem is that the systems of meanings of archaic epic and of a literary work are fundamentally different, a problem which Parry confronted in his studies. Parry, when he defined the formula as a basic structural element of epic poetry, narrowed it to one "essential idea." He decided that in the type of formula he studied most extensively, the noun-epithet formula, the epithet does not carry any meaning and its only function is ornamental. However, the findings of other scholars prompt us to examine Parry's extreme opinion.

[126] Kim 2000:24: "Achilles' 'tragic error', then, is introduced at the very moment he asks his mother to supplicate Zeus" (*Iliad* 1.408–412; 1.508–510). On the tragic aspect of the *Iliad* and the influence of epic upon Attic tragedy, see also Rutherford 1982, for whom the tragic aspect relates to fact that the hero abruptly and clearly realizes that unexpectedly everything he has done and experienced earlier foreshadowed his present defeat, which he is unable to avoid.

[127] On the meaning of Patroklos's death for the composition of the song, see Kim 2000:120.

Although scholars accept the idea that epithets can have contextual meanings, they disagree about their scope and character. Nonetheless, they agree as to several basic conclusions:[128]

1. A generally neutral epithet can in some cases assume a meaning relevant to context, magnifying dramatic tension by stressing a significant element (here, variously, Vivante 1982, Hainsworth 1993, Richardson 1993).
2. If for some reason a given formula cannot be used in a given context, the singer can replace it with its equivalent. He can even try to improvise, using new epithets; here an important role is played by his creativity (Combellack 1976; Edwards 1966 and 1991; Bakker and Fabricotti 1991, Janko 1992).
3. The context of a single formula depends on the singer's and the listeners' knowledge of the meaning of formulae in the whole of epic poetry (Nagy 1976 and 1990a; Foley 1991; Bakker 1995), and in the case of some characters, mainly heroes, the meaning within a given cycle, e.g. *ptoliporthos* 'destroyer of cities', or 'capturer of the city (*sc.* Troy)', or Achilles' epithet—*podarkês* 'swift-footed'.
4. By choosing from among equivalent formulae, e.g. those describing the rising of the dawn, the singer can suggest a certain mood or situation (Kirk 1985). Their choice may foreshadow future events.

All of these interpretative possibilities are connected with a concrete performative situation, which also plays an essential role in reading contextual meaning. Therefore, the singer works to stay in constant contact with his audience, and he does so by three methods: catching their attention by the vividness of events, guiding their moods and assessment of a situation, and, finally, by the clarity of his narration.

The dialogue between the singer and the audience is based on the original layers of form and meaning in which a given formula was shaped. Allusion is only possible in reference to something that is known or predictable. According to Nagy: "A distinctive epithet is like a small theme song that conjures up a thought-association with the traditional essence of an epic figure, thing, or concept."[129] Foley calls it "*traditional referentiality*," because an epic song uses various elements of earlier songs.[130] An element does not serve only its current use but also the multiplicity and multiformity in which it originates.

[128] For more on this topic, see Edwards 1997.

[129] Nagy 1990a:23.

[130] Foley 1991:5–31.

It is a metonymy of the whole contained in epic culture. The context of a given situation is a context of the epic code.[131] The relationship between the function of a formula in the broad context of epic and a similar function of the pattern of an epic story has been noticed by Slatkin:

> But just as an individual formula implies a system of formulaic usage—in each instance expresses not only its individual "essential idea" but a principle of "formularity"—and just as any type-scene involves a recognized pattern, so ... a particular version of a myth is part of a larger whole that invites shaping, focusing, and integrating within a narrative structure, but that, however partially represented, can be invoked in all its dimensions. The epic audience's knowledge of the alternative possibilities allows the poet to build his narrative by deriving meaning not only from what the poem includes but from what it conspicuously excludes.[132]

The conventional treatment of formulae does not necessarily imply that the singer does not use them to emphasize certain elements of action. Foley points out that the audience, accustomed to well-known patterns of type-scenes, notices their different uses.[133] The listeners must have been sensitive to changes of a typical pattern in often repeated utterances, verses, and even fragments of the text. Presenting a scene without its typical elements may sometimes, I believe, be also conventional, i.e. traditional. For example, in the scene when Patroklos puts on Achilles' armor there are no mentions of its brightness, whereas they are numerous in the scene of donning armor by Achilles (*Iliad* 16.130–154; 19.364–398). The way the first of those scenes is presented suggests that Patroklos's enterprise will meet with failure, whereas Achilles will be successful.[134] The listener, familiar with such a conventional hint, is able to read it as a sign foretelling the future. He is also able to assess current events in the light of what will happen later. So, unlike the characters of the story, who are not aware of what the future will bring, the listener—thanks to the narrator—is

131 For example, the verse which introduces Achilles' harsh reply to Priam's refusal to sit down (*Iliad* 24.559): τὸν δ' ἄρ' ὑπόδρα ἰδὼν προσέφη πόδας ὠκὺς Ἀχιλλεύς ("Swift-footed Achilles glared at him from under knitted brows and said"). The listeners' reception was complemented by two associations: the noun-epithet formula, as an indivisible unit of meaning, shows Achilles, with pride, quickness of temper, and arrogance lurking behind his politeness; at the same time, the phrase "glared at him from under knitted brows" shows that it is a typical scene of confrontation, in which an insult is met with an indignant reply. In the world of the traditional song, formulae are a means of identifying people, things, and events.

132 Slatkin 1991:3–4.

133 Foley 1990 and 1991.

134 Example cited after Armstrong 1958.

wiser. This certainly makes him more attentive. His participation in the performance is active, not just passive (so it is similar to the role of the listener in the performance of a lyric song). The singer, introducing smaller or bigger changes in the type-scene, adapts it to the context of the drama he is building. It is so, for example, with the type-scenes of meals, modified in order to suit the context of narration in the *Odyssey*.[135]

The Double Function of Repetitions

Ruth Scodel, discussing the nature of oral tradition, objects to the dogmatic treatment of each performance of a song as a creation.[136] She points out that repetition is an immanent element of oral tradition and we should control our expectations concerning the creativity and inventiveness of the poet:

> While the poets adapted their stories to present circumstances, they never mark innovation as such. Invention within traditionalizing poetry must be invisible. A usable past may need to be reinvented all the time, but if the society knows that its myths are mythic, they will not be very useful. Constant innovation may be necessary, but if the poetry itself does not value invention, modern scholars must be cautious in judging its function.[137]

In this section, we will consider Scodel's point of view, demonstrating in detail how the singer shapes his song in order to get through to his listeners and to arouse their interest. We will take into account not only the mechanics of typical elements in the oral song itself but also the mechanics of these typical elements in its reception. If there is innovation, it is based only on pattern and repetition. We cannot investigate how and to what extent the texts of Homer's poems were repeated verbatim, since he transmitted them orally, but we can examine the function of those fragments which are a faithful or nearly faithful repetition.

I suggest we concentrate for a moment on literal repetitions in the structure of Homeric poems. The contemporary reader may not understand the meaning of repetitions in oral tradition. Usually they bore him or her because they do not push the action forward and he or she skips ahead to another paragraph. Why should they read again the command delivered to someone by Iris, if they have already heard it from Zeus himself? Here we come across differences in

135 Reece 1993:191: "In a practical sense ... the *Odyssey* may be regarded as a sequence of hospitality scenes."

136 Scodel (2002:41) refers to Nagler's standpoint (1974:26): "All is traditional on the generative level, all is original on the level of performance."

137 Scodel 2002:41.

the reception of oral performances and written texts. These differences are most apparent in repetitions and in the extemporaneous creation of song. If we look at fairy tales for children, based on folk tales and written down even as late as at the beginning of the twentieth century, we find that elements of the text are repeated variously and frequently.[138] The protagonist again and again is asked the same questions, to which he or she gives the same answers; a person or object is recalled every time identically, with the same words. Paradoxically, from the point of view of our reading habits, such repetitions attract the attention of the child, make it easier to follow the fairy tale and to see possible differences in the behavior of characters who, for example, unexpectedly give different answers than other characters before them. Very often, the plot or action of the story is wholly based on repetitions. Sometimes, subsequent repetitions are expanded because a further element is added; we could say they grow into a spiral. All elements have to be repeated in the same order, and then at the end a new one is added. Therefore, the audience listens attentively to those chains of repetitions, waiting for a denouement. In this simple narrative form, repetitions familiarize the listener with the story and prepare them for twists in the plot.

Some changes in the expected message are easily detected by the listener because he expects repetitions and follows them attentively. I'd like to point out that a change in the wording is not the only way to intensify the listeners' attention. The singer can use an exact repetition of phrases, or even fragments of the text, to give the listeners the feeling of being in the know and, as a result, to create a distance from the events and vicissitudes of fate, leading to irony.

At the beginning of *Iliad* Book 9, when the warriors debate what to do after defeat on the battlefield, Diomedes sharply opposes Agamemnon's suggestion to abandon the siege of Troy and return home. He starts by recalling Agamemnon's unkind words from Book 4 (4.370–400), when the Greek leader criticized his ἀλκή (*alkê*) 'strength/valor in battle', calling him ἀπτόλεμος (*aptolemos*) 'non-bellligerent, uneager to fight', and ἀνάλκις (*analkis*) 'lacking strength, valor in battle'—a coward, someone unfit for combat (9.35). Diomedes then asks ironically, if Agamemnon proposes flight, because he thinks that the Achaeans are as ἀπτόλεμοι (*aptolemoi*, pl.) and ἀνάλκιδες (*analkides*, pl.) as he suggests (9.41). Diomedes employs this language to impress on the assembly that it is not he, Diomedes, who is cowardly and uneager to fight. In between those two places in his speech he attempts to judge the king and declares that Zeus gave Agamemnon authority but not valor (ἀλκή).

[138] Contemporary writers of stories for children, completely unaware of this fact, do not use repetitions. But their tales are not intended for listening but for reading.

A moment before Agamemnon referred to Zeus's will when he tried to justify his proposition to abandon (at least temporarily) further efforts to capture Troy and to retreat. Zeus's will, incomprehensible though it is, must be complied with, according to Agamemnon, because the destruction of cities is in his power. The king summarizes his conclusion with the formula (9.25) <u>τοῦ γὰρ</u> κράτος ἐστὶ μέγιστον "*because his* power is above all." Diomedes uses the same formula but with a slightly changed beginning (9.39): ἀλκὴν δ' οὔ τοι δῶκεν, <u>ὅ τε</u> κράτος ἐστὶ μέγιστον ("But valor he gave you not, and *this is* the power above all").

The repetition of this formula is not only a typical "filling" for the verse, but a clear allusion to and a polemic with what Agamemnon has just said.[139] Referring to the role of Zeus, Diomedes opposes the king's suggestion, when he says about valor (ἀλκή): "and *this is* the power above all." The change of the formula from τοῦ γάρ to ὅ τε provides emphasis. At the same time, this verbal exchange refers to the conflict in Book 4, though in fact Agamemnon in his rebuke of Diomedes (4.370–400) does not use the expression ἀπτόλεμος or ἀνάλκις. The first mention of ἀλκή appears only at the very end of Diomedes' summary of the events addressed to Sthenelos (4.418): ἀλλ' ἄγε δὴ καὶ νῶϊ μεδώμεθα θούριδος ἀλκῆς ("but let the two of us think of valor"). The reference to it in conflict in Book 9 shows that Diomedes seems constantly to think about his defiled ἀλκή, which is appropriate, since he is portrayed as a young hot-headed warrior, obsessed with the need to prove his mettle in battle and to show his bravery. The repetitions of certain phrases in Diomedes' speech allude to Agamemnon's utterance and are the result of the nature of discourse in oral culture, in which phrases used by one speaker can be given a new meaning by the next. Even if someone convinces listeners with his arguments, the following speaker, by reversing the meaning of his predecessor's words, can sway the listeners to his own point of view. In a dispute, one listens carefully to what the opponent is saying in order to invalidate his arguments, while at the same time seeking applause for one's own opinion.[140]

Agamemnon's speech in *Iliad* Book 9 (9.17–28) is to a large extent a repetition of his speech from Book 2, when he deceptively proposes a similar retreat to the assembly of the Achaeans (2.110–141). But then his intention was to boost the morale of the army by curbing their sudden readiness to return home. Many scholars notice the irony in Agamemnon's words when he is impelled to say in earnest what he deceptively said earlier, when he put the army to the test.

139 This formula appears eight times; it is also applied to an eagle and the Kyklopes. The two-syllable beginning contains τοῦ γάρ, ὅ τε, καὶ εὖ, ὅου, οὗ τε.

140 Martin (1989:47) formulates the rule of "flyting *muthoi*" (more in Ch. 6, p. 552, below). See also Derek Collins (2004: 63–83, 231–235), who describes this type of competitive discourse as 'capping'.

Hainsworth concludes that this repetition is parallel to that of type-scenes and that Agamemnon cannot feel the irony of his repetition.[141] Elaborating on Hainsworth's idea, we could say that the poet several times reuses the traditional image of a despondent Agamemnon, but each time his speech, depending on the context, has a different wording or even a different meaning. However, there is no reason to believe that these places are unrelated to each other, that is, that the differences between them are not perceived by the audience.[142]

The question is whether the audience could feel the irony of the same words repeated by the same person, only in a different context. In oral tradition, the singer is not discomfited by literal or, by our standards, nearly literal repetitions. He must believe that his audience listens to those repetitions patiently and with unabated attention. This can be illustrated by another passage in *Iliad* Book 9. Following Nestor's advice, Agamemnon enumerates the gifts he is ready to give to Achilles in order to convince him to return to the battlefield. He ends his speech with an emotional conclusion (9.158–161):

> δμηθήτω· Ἀΐδης τοι ἀμείλιχος ἠδ' ἀδάμαστος,
> τοὔνεκα καί τε βροτοῖσι θεῶν ἔχθιστος ἁπάντων·

141 Hainsworth 1993:61–62 *ad Iliad* 9.18–28: "It is implausible to suppose that Agamemnon is represented as deliberately using the same words as he had used in the earlier fiasco, nor (in spite of the more appropriate circumstances) does the same result follow; this time the troops stand firm. As far as concerns Agamemnon therefore the repetition must be understood to be accidental. It is difficult, however, for the attentive hearer/reader to ignore the coincidence and accept that the repetition of the verses (presumably as a part of a traditional characterization of a despondent leader or specifically of Agamemnon) is coincidental for the poet too. Yet the fact that it is easy to see irony in Agamemnon's now proposing in earnest what he had previously proposed in deceit should not obscure the points (1) that the text contains no signal that the previous passage is in mind (such a comment would have been appropriate at the beginning of Diomedes' speech at 32ff.), (2) that resounding silences concerning preceding events are more characteristic of the *Iliad* than the exploitation of backward reference, and (3) that the reuse of blocks of verses in widely different contexts is part of the Homeric technique of scene building. It does not follow that a passage cannot recall a previous context, only that such a recall may be read into the text at some risk of over-interpretation and should rest on thematic correspondence rather than verbal repetitions. Agamemnon will propose retreat for the third time at 14.65–81, where it will be Odysseus who leads the objectors. If a despondent Agamemnon is traditional, then for an educated audience the irony is not so much in the present passage as in book 2. bT wish to see in Agamemnon a regal character and defend his dubious actions; here they entertain the idea that this second proposal for retreat is a πεῖρα, like the first; that must be discounted, for lack of any hint in the text."

142 In opposition to Hainsworth, Reichel (1994) points to the functioning of cross-references in the *Iliad* narrative. He evaluates possible cross-references using criteria that determine the nature of these places in the narrative (such as explicitness, direction, scope, point of view, reliability, length). His method leads to the conclusion that a text with such an accumulation of cross-references could have come into being only because oral speech was supported by writing. However, this demonstrates a failure to take into account the peculiarities of oral discourse.

> καί μοι ὑποστήτω ὅσσον βασιλεύτερός εἰμι
> ἠδ' ὅσσον γενεῇ προγενέστερος εὔχομαι εἶναι.
>
> let him humble himself; Hades is unrelenting and implacable,
> and for that reason the most hated by people of all gods;
> let him [Achilles] admit that I am a much greater king
> and I can boast of much better birth.

When Odysseus repeats these words in Achilles' tent, he quite reasonably skips the last section of the king's utterance. Perhaps Hainsworth is right when he claims that for Achilles the previous verse is offensive enough (9.157 = 299):[143] ταῦτά κέ οἱ τελέσαιμι μεταλλήξαντι χόλοιο ("I will give him these [gifts] if he will forgo his anger"). Agamemnon wants to bribe him; there is no sign of remorse on his part. To soften the tone of these words, Odysseus puts forward another motivation with the hope of making Achilles amenable (9.300–306). The audience only learns this information, important for the meaning of the scene and for the action, after the repetition of forty verses, which enumerate Agamemnon's gifts. Such a repetition, like the lengthy and elaborate descriptions used by *guslari* as embellishment, could be attractive for the listeners. More important, however, than the aesthetic admiration for the artistry of the singer was the synchronic admiration for the gifts. We can assume that Homer's audience could assess the value of these gifts, just like Agamemnon's audience, whom he expected to admire his generosity. While this brings down the intellectual level of Homer's assumed virtual audience, it lets the singer surprise them with a punchline, change of subject, or a sudden dramatic leap in the plot.

Having enumerated the gifts offered by Agamemnon, Odysseus goes on to an astonishing conclusion. He does not praise them, he does not say: "Look, they are great, they should restore your honor, everyone will think so," etc. Instead, he says: "But if the son of Atreus is too hateful to your heart, himself and his gifts…" (9.300). It seems that seeing Achilles' reaction to his embassy, Odysseus has to look for other arguments, not included in the original message. James M. Redfield provides an interesting interpretation of this: the catalogue of gifts recited by Odysseus does not sound as magnificent as it does the first time, when "each additional item is further proof of his [Agamemnon's] new good will. When the same list is recited to Achilles, it falls flat, each item flatter than the last; ideally the audience and Achilles realize at the same moment that the gifts will not work, that the embassy must be a failure."[144] We can conclude that repetitions, typical of oral poetics, help shape Homer's narrative, or at least

[143] Hainsworth 1993:79.
[144] Redfield 1994:15–16.

could. The listeners not only notice a significant gap in Odysseus's message, but perhaps they simply get bored, listening again, in a short space of time, to a long list of gifts. Quite possibly the unexpected endings closing those lists might have been added in order to wake up listeners, who might not have been following the song with undivided attention. Homer brilliantly uses the tools at his disposal to make his song directly affect the audience.

A literal repetition of passages is as characteristic of oral creation as the variability of the oral text itself. Adrian Kelly has collected all twenty-two places in the *Iliad* where the same text is repeated by various characters.[145] Those messages, though generally short, are important for the structure of the narration because they usually convey crucial decisions influencing the events in the story. Ordinarily, they are concerned with relaying information and naturally a messenger is obliged to repeat it faithfully. Repeating the same utterances serves the function of fixing some information in the mind of the audience. Kelly observes: "Passages between instruction and relay are usually brief, with a description of the departure, journey, and meeting between the relaying character and the instruction's final object."[146] When they are not brief, the same information is delivered in different words, or, to express it more precisely, with different formulae. Such is the situation in *Iliad* Book 16, when the original utterance and its repetition are slightly more than two hundred verses apart:

> πέμπειν μιν Θάνατόν τε φέρειν καὶ νήδυμον Ὕπνον,
> εἰς ὅ κε δὴ Λυκίης εὐρείης δῆμον ἵκωνται,
> ἔνθά ἑ ταρχύσουσι κασίγνητοί τε ἔται τε
> τύμβῳ τε στήλῃ τε· τὸ γὰρ γέρας ἐστὶ θανόντων.
>
> send Thanatos and sweet Hypnos, to carry him
> to the broad land of Lycia,
> where his brothers and kinsmen will bury him solemnly
> raising a mound and a pillar—because this is the share of the dead.
>
> 16.454–457
>
> πέμπε δέ μιν πομποῖσιν ἅμα κραιπνοῖσι φέρεσθαι,
> Ὕπνῳ καὶ Θανάτῳ διδυμάοσιν, οἵ ῥά μιν ὦκα
> θήσουσ' ἐν Λυκίης εὐρείης πίονι δήμῳ·
> ἔνθά ἑ ταρχύσουσι κασίγνητοί τε ἔται τε
> τύμβῳ τε στήλῃ τε· τὸ γὰρ γέρας ἐστὶ θανόντων.

[145] Kelly 2007a:325–329 calls it "relay instructions."
[146] Kelly 2007a:325.

> he sent for him to be carried by swift messengers,
> the twins, Hypnos and Thanatos, who quickly
> laid him in the fertile, broad land of Lycia,
> where his brothers and kinsmen will bury him solemnly
> raising a mound and a pillar—because this is the share of the dead.
>
> 16.671–675

The last two verses are identical, whereas the earlier ones are not and even differ in number. This suggests that after a longer lapse of time the singer has trouble remembering the exact wording of the message. Similarly, two distant passages—*Iliad* 11.794–803 (Nestor's speech) and 16.36–45 (repetition by Patroklos)—are nearly identical, although they differ in some notable ways. It is doubtful if they result from the poet's attempt to adjust the text to the context and to characterize the speaker.[147] The singer must have performed the song about the wrath of Achilles many times, but after a longer lapse of time it might have been difficult to repeat the text verbatim.[148]

Sometimes the messages relayed are expanded, e.g. by an introduction which tells who has sent the messenger, and/or by remarks at the end, which mainly serve the purpose of making the messenger's mission successful. Now and again the messenger adds something on a personal note; his words convey his emotions and characterize him. Idaios, referring the decision of the Trojan assembly, does not repeat Paris's speech (*Iliad* 7.362–364) faithfully to the Achaeans (7.385–397), but significantly changes the order of the message, first mentioning Paris's readiness to return the stolen treasures and only later his refusal to part with Helen. The first is expanded with a curse damning Paris (7.390 ὡς πρὶν ὤφελλ' ἀπολέσθαι 'would he had perished first!'); to the second one he adds the opinion of the other Trojans (7.393 ἦ μὲν Τρῶές γε κέλονται 'which is what the Trojans demand'). It is a clear signal for the listener that many other Trojans disapproved of Paris's conduct.

147 The change from the third-person singular to the second-person singular necessitates the adaptation of the utterance to the meter. Therefore, verse 16.38, corresponding to 11.796, contains an addition, i.e. the adverb ὦκα 'swiftly', which may color Patroklos's speech with impatience. More important changes, found at 16.40, make Patroklos's utterance more polite, I believe, than Nestor's original simple message in 11.798. Compare 11.798: "καί τοι τεύχεα καλὰ δότω πόλεμον δὲ φέρεσθαι" / "and let him give you his beautiful armor to wear in combat"; with 16.40: "δὸς δέ μοι ὤμοιιν τὰ σὰ τεύχεα θωρηχθῆναι" / "and give me your armor so that I can put it on my shoulders."

148 Perhaps we are dealing with two versions of the same passage in the case of instructions given to Oneiros by Zeus (*Iliad* 2.11–15), and then relayed twice, by Oneiros (2.28–34) and Agamemnon (2.65–70), in a slightly longer form: instead of Τρώεσσι δὲ κήδε' ἐφῆπται 'The Trojans are threatened with a disaster' (2.15), there is Τρώεσσι δὲ κήδε' ἐφῆπται / ἐκ Διός 'The Trojans are threatened with a disaster, with Zeus' approval' (2.32–33).

There is a similar situation in *Iliad* Book 8, when Zeus decides to prevent Hera and Athena from interfering in the battle and sends Iris with a message (8.399–408):

> "βάσκ' ἴθι, Ἶρι ταχεῖα, πάλιν τρέπε μηδ' ἔα ἄντην
> ἔρχεσθ'· οὐ γὰρ καλὰ συνοισόμεθα πτόλεμόνδε.
> ὧδε γὰρ ἐξερέω, τὸ δὲ καὶ τετελεσμένον ἔσται·
> γυιώσω μέν σφωϊν ὑφ' ἅρμασιν ὠκέας ἵππους,
> αὐτὰς δ' ἐκ δίφρου βαλέω κατά θ' ἅρματα ἄξω·
> οὐδέ κεν ἐς δεκάτους περιτελλομένους ἐνιαυτούς
> ἕλκε' ἀπαλθήσεσθον, ἅ κεν μάρπτησι κεραυνός·
> ὄφρ' εἴδῃ Γλαυκῶπις, ὅτ' ἂν ᾧ πατρὶ μάχηται.
> Ἥρῃ δ' οὔ τι τόσον νεμεσίζομαι οὐδὲ χολοῦμαι·
> αἰεὶ γάρ μοι ἔωθεν ἐνικλᾶν, ὅττι νοήσω."
>
> "Go, swift Iris, turn them back
> and don't let them face me, for it will not be nice if we meet in combat.
> This is what I say and this will come true:
> I will maim their swift horses pulling the chariot
> and will hurl them down from it and will break the chariot into pieces.
> Even in the space of nine circling years
> they will not heal the wounds if I hit them with my thunderbolt,
> so that the Owl-Eyed knows what it means to fight against her father.
> But I am not so much indignant and angry with Hera
> because she has always thwarted whatever I intended."

Iris delivers this message, adding a few words at the beginning and end (8.413–424):

> "πῇ μέματον; τί σφῶϊν ἐνὶ φρεσὶ μαίνεται ἦτορ;
> οὐκ ἐάαι Κρονίδης ἐπαμυνέμεν Ἀργείοισιν.
> ὧδε γὰρ ἠπείλησε Κρόνου πάϊς, ᾗ τελέει περ·
> γυιώσειν μέν σφωϊν ὑφ' ἅρμασιν ὠκέας ἵππους,
> αὐτὰς δ' ἐκ δίφρου βαλέειν κατά θ' ἅρματα ἄξω·
> οὐδέ κεν ἐς δεκάτους περιτελλομένους ἐνιαυτοὺς
> ἕλκε' ἀπαλθήσεσθον, ἅ κεν μάρπτησι κεραυνός·
> ὄφρ' εἴδῃς, Γλαυκῶπι, ὅτ' ἂν σῷ πατρὶ μάχηται.
> Ἥρῃ δ' οὔ τι τόσον νεμεσίζεται οὐδὲ χολοῦται·
> αἰεὶ γάρ οἱ ἔωθεν ἐνικλᾶν, ὅττι νοήσῃ.
> ἀλλὰ σὺ γ' αἰνοτάτη, κύον ἀδεές, εἰ ἐτεόν γε
> τολμήσεις Διὸς ἄντα πελώριον ἔγχος ἀεῖραι."

> "Where are you racing off to? Why are the hearts mad in your breasts?
> The son of Kronos does not allow you to help the Argives.
> He expressed a threat, and it may come true:
> He will maim your swift horses pulling the chariot,
> he will hurl you down from it and will break the chariot into pieces.
> Even in the space of nine circling years
> you will not heal the wounds if he hits you with his thunderbolt,
> so that you know, Owl-Eyed, what it means to fight against your father.
> But he is not so much indignant and angry with Hera
> because she has always thwarted whatever he intended.
> But you are worse, you arrogant bitch, if you really
> dare to raise your powerful spear against Zeus."

Both interpolations, at the beginning and at the end of the message, are very emphatic. They reinforce the message in order to make the mission successful.[149] Here they are not meant to present the individual character of Iris, but to impress on the listener the impropriety of the daughter's (i.e. Athena's) rebellion against her father's will. Compare a similar command to refrain from fighting which Iris relays to Poseidon. After he expresses his indignation, the goddess diplomatically induces him to obey Zeus and influences him to change the tone of his speech, pointing out Zeus's rights as an elder brother (*Iliad* 15.200–204). These additions certainly make the action more dramatic, surprise the listener, and provoke him to evaluate the behavior of characters from a moral standpoint.

Such a long and exact repetition, like the enumeration of Agamemnon's gifts, after nearly one hundred verses, must be seen as a manifestation of the singer's great skill. For the author of the *Iliad*, the repetition of the text verbatim is difficult, and contemporary singers must have faced the same problem.[150] A small change at the end of the list, i.e. the replacement of Agamemnon's real

149 Kirk 1990:330 *ad* 8.399–408: "Here she will add her own more trenchant comments, no doubt to ensure that her mission as a whole is successful." Kelly (2007a:322) writes about all of Iris's missions: "Common to all these examples is her facilitation of the desires or instructions of others, yet this does not preclude an individual ability to effect those commands or messages."

150 This skill might not have been recognized by most of the listeners, who might have been bored by a repetition of a long list of gifts. But Minchin (2001:76–80, referring to Radlove's observations of the performance of Kyrgyz epic; compare Chadwick and Chadwick 1940:185) points out that in oral culture, catalogues and other lists are often received with acclaim because they make greater demands upon memory than the narration of events.

intentions with Odysseus's request, must have been surprising. The change characterizes also the person relaying the message and is a hint of the futility of the embassy.

As we have seen, literal repetitions play a double role in the *Iliad*. Apart from contributing to characterization, they fix certain decisions/messages by focusing the attention of the audience.[151] This means that the singer might have assumed his listeners would not be very attentive. Repetitions are employed to this end so many times that we may easily say they were a standard device. Listeners, who were accustomed to it, knew that a repetition spells a turn in action which requires attention. An addition at the end of a repeated passage activates the listeners by presenting a surprise but first of all it characterizes the speaker and hints at the turn the action is going to take. These changes let the audience judge events from a moral standpoint.[152]

Meleagros—Sensitivity to Detail

When we consider the intellectual level of Homer's listeners we cannot but wonder what kind of people they were. Looking at the performances of epic in the *Odyssey*, we see mainly well-born people, but it seems they were not the only audience. Certainly servants could listen to the singer, and also women, from their rooms on the upper floor, like Penelope, who hears Phemios's song (*Odyssey*

[151] Scodel (2002:39–41 and 104) explains the need for the recapitulation of events by Achilles to Thetis, although the hero knows that she is familiar with them (1.365). The scholar maintains that these recapitulations introduce chronological order into the quick pace of events. Perhaps at the beginning of a performance, some of the listeners were not very attentive or simply absent. But even those who listened closely could have had difficulty following the story with so many, often initially unclear, allusions to what had happened: "This early recapitulation, which includes a careful mention of the division of spoils, helped anyone who was actually confused. This clarification, setting events in chronological order, would make everyone confident of understanding the sequence of events correctly. ... If any of this material was new to the audience or differed from a familiar story, repetition not only made it clearer but gave it greater authority—when Achilles tells it, it has already been heard. Like a dhalang, the bard had to manage sometimes contradictory demands, having to maintain standards while pleasing a crowd and to appear aloof while reacting to the audience. ... Homer had a harder task in simultaneously adapting to present needs and maintaining traditionality" (40).

[152] See Ready (2019:96), for whom the messengers' reports are a replication of the performer's communicative situation during performance in oral culture (for the scholar the messenger, like the poet, is a mediator of the message assuming also later recontextualized repetitions of it). Ready notes that "messengers cannot help but perform. On the one hand, then, a speaker performs even when tasked with passing on the words of another. On the other hand, oral texts do not simply circulate in more or less fixed versions. Instead, they come into the hands of performers who decide what to do with them. Both the initial presentation and the subsequent reiteration of an oral text see the speaker assuming responsibility for a display of competence" (96).

1.328–239). Demodokos's second song about Ares and Aphrodite's affair, if it can be ranked as epic, was performed for the whole community of Phaeacians (8.368–369). Furthermore, if we classify Hesiod as an *aoidos*, it would be difficult to assume that his listeners were only wealthy people, especially if we consider his *Works and Days*. The most important question is whether Homer sang for a local audience, i.e. stable and probably familiar with his repertoire, or for people at the pan-Ionian or pan-Hellenic festivals, where naturally the audience would be less familiar or homogeneous.[153] Usually it is claimed that Homer's poems were composed for the latter audience because they do not possess typical features of local epic; instead, they are marked by broad universalism.[154] But this feature is broadly characteristic of Greek archaic epic: epic cycles collect many heroes for a joint performance of a task or they show a hero's travels over most of the known world. The universalism found in the *Iliad* is typical of the whole Trojan Cycle. Here we come across a problem described by Scodel:

> If the implied audience of the epics is not confined to a group for whom the poet had often performed, the categories of narrative material multiply, to include what everyone had heard before, what some individuals had heard but others had not, what nobody in this audience had heard but other Greek audiences had heard, what no Greek audience had heard, and what no audience had ever heard. The poet ... did not always know exactly what stories the audience or most of it had heard before.[155]

Naturally, the poet deals with it, balancing between the tradition in which he and his audience were brought up, and invention, which is demanded by listeners eager for novelty. How the singer can combine the unknown and the known will be discussed in the next chapter. Now let us think to what extent he can refer to tradition, to the known element. It will let us answer the question how familiar the audience of the *Iliad* was with cyclic epic.

Let us consider as an example a story intended to persuade Achilles to go back to battle. Phoinix in a convoluted and obscure way, especially in the beginning, tells the story of Meleagros (*Iliad* 9.524–599). His version of events connected with this hero is different than the version transmitted by mythographers. However, it seems wrong to suppose that Homer did not know that version. Johannes Kakridis, examining the motif of the burning of the log which

153 Scodel (2002:42–64) discusses other aspects of the character of Homer's audience.

154 According to Nagy's model, in the process of the development of Homeric epic, local elements were gradually eliminated. Local epic is limited to the story of the death of a local hero; the storyline goes back towards his birth; see Nagy 1996b:Ch. 2, referring to Blackburn 1989.

155 Scodel 2002:62.

determined the length of Meleagros's life, concludes that because of its commonness in folk culture this strand of the myth is the oldest one.[156] Schadewaldt in turn explains how Homer's innovative version is closely connected with the whole work, so it can't be a separate song adapted by a later poet (*Nachdichter*, in the Pluralist terminology).[157] He also shows that Homer deliberately rejects a well-known version of the myth and develops the tale in such a way as to make Phoinix's story useful for Achilles as a paradigm of action: the parallel with Meleagros should caution Achilles against a mistake. Welcker had already noted that the function of the Meleagros story is not limited to warning Achilles, since the parallelism of both heroes' lives conveys a prophetic message: it foreshadows the tragic fate of Achilles (this idea is present also in Schadewaldt).[158] Significantly, Phoinix does not mention Meleagros's death; he ends his account with saying that Meleagros returned to battle in shining armor and saved the city, but did not get the promised goods. This is exactly what Phoinix wants to convey: don't be stupid, Achilles, take what you are given, because I know you; you will go back to the battlefield anyway, but then you will not get such sumptuous gifts.[159] Such a pragmatic end of a longish sentimental and didactic speech is astonishing, but not when it comes from an old man like Phoinix.[160] Already

156 Kakridis 1949:21–24, 127–148; see Willcock 1964:152, Alden 2000:238. Pausanias 9.31.3, the *Catalogue of Women*, and *Minyades* all present Meleagros's death in a fight with the Kuretes as a result of the support of Apollo, who kills Meleagros either personally or by helping a hero (as he helped Paris in killing Achilles). It is not necessarily an alternative version to the one blaming Meleagros's mother for his death.

157 Schadewaldt 1938:139–142.

158 Welcker 1865–1882:V–VI; Schadewaldt 1938:141–142.

159 Howald (1924:407–408) points out the illogicality of Phoinix's speech; one could hardly suppose that the hero who saved the city would not get his award. Howald maintains that gifts are not mentioned later because their importance dwindles in the face of the danger of death from the curse of Meleagros's mother, which, although not mentioned explicitly, is present in the awareness of the listeners. Alden (2000:29) describes the story as a "negative or dissuasive paradigm."

160 This indicates a huge discrepancy with what Achilles presented as important to himself. Psychologically, to hear such words from the man perhaps dearest to him in his childhood (9.486–489) would be a blow to the young man. Perhaps Homer takes this into account, as Achilles refrains from responding to his guardian and only asks him to choose whose side he is on, and stands firm in his decision not to accept the gifts (9.607–619). Compare Alden 2000:234–236. Alden does not include in his discussion the explanation of the term *atê* offered by Wyatt (1982), i.e. "regret" after the fact rather than "blindness" at the time of acting. Wyatt's position is consistent with anthropological observations (Evans-Pritchard 1956:16–22, 188–196) that the man of an illiterate culture realizes that he has committed a wrong or error by experiencing various misfortunes (in his understanding: the consequences of his deed). This is especially the case when the group blames him for his actions. This is not to say that the man is thoughtless and cannot anticipate that his action may provoke censure from the community. As a rule, therefore, he avoids committing acts perceived as wrong (Evans-Pritchard 1956:182). Young Phoinix (9.458–461; see Alden 2000:221–226), like Hector (22.99–110), anticipated that he might face group disapproval for his act. The anger in his heart has now died and he no longer remembers

in 1924, Howald had noticed that the story of Meleagros functioned not only as a paradigmatic story, but also as a forecast of future events. In the *Iliad*, the change of his wife's name from the traditional Alkyone to Kleopatra was made for the purpose of stressing the similarity of Patroklos's function in sending Achilles to combat (Kleo-patrê is an allusion to Patro-klos/Patro-kleês).[161]

As we can see, the end of the myth contains a predictor of future events (prolepsis), which is contrary to Phoinix's intentions, but clear for the listener who knows that Achilles, like Meleagros, won't listen to the persuasion of his friends. Only Patroklos's death will drive him to the battlefield, just as the final intervention of Kleopatra made her husband, Meleagros, return to combat. The sound and probably also the meaning of the names Patro-klos/Kleo-patra 'glory of fathers/ancestors' are hints for the listener.[162] Phoinix does not prophesy, but the singer draws the audience into the play of anticipations. This story of Meleagros makes sense only because oral composition alludes to events outside the narrative. The poet could not intend Phoinix's tale to become clear only when Achilles enters the battle, several thousand verses later; by that time, such a subtle and single allusion would be completely forgotten, and the whole story would be meaningless during its narration. The numerous unjust critical remarks by scholars who analyze only the obvious meaning of the story and are insensitive to the suggested hidden meaning are proof of this. It also means that we can neither believe in the existence of an archetypal, "virginal," authoritative version of the text, which we could go back to, not even in the first singing of the poem, which would surprise the listener with its innovation. The allusion such as the one expressed by the parallelism of names Patroklos/

the pain in his heart that made him deaf to the pleas of those close to him. In his old age, he is practical and perhaps to some extent regrets his youthful step. So he finds no understanding for the pain of his charge, and suggests accepting an outward manifestation of respect, for the gifts accepted would be a visible sign of respect to the entire Achaean community. Phoinix presents himself as a person who has taught Achilles to fight and to speak in public (9.440–443), but it also implies that he has conveyed to him the system of values that Achilles is faithful to. A man must know why he should compete with others. Now, when Achilles claims that Agamemnon's deed has ruined this system of values (9.316–336), Phoinix denies the essence of his previous teachings, and reconciles himself to the injustice and harm done to Achilles.

161 Howald 1924:411–412. According to him, in the original version, Patroklos, like Kleopatra, tries to induce Achilles to go back to battle. An overview of positions on the correlation of these names in the *Iliad* is provided by Alden 2000:240.

162 Sinos (1975:83) notices the function of this name in the creation of the song and its relationships with hero cult: "And just as the name Ἡρακλέης connotes praise-poetry (or κλέος) in connection with the divinity of regular seasons, so, too, the name Πατροκλέης (1.337, etc.) / Πάτροκλος (1.345, etc.) connotes praise-poetry in connection with the ancestors, who ... were frequently conflated with the worship of heroes in cult"; compare also pp. 90–92. Nagy (1999:104–111) translates the names Kleopatra and Patroklos as "the one who has the glory of the ancestors" and points out the parallelism in the construction of both epic themes: Patroklos (an episode of Achilles' story) and Meleagros (adapted to Achilles' story).

Kleopatra indicates the listener's awareness of future events even during the narration of Phoinix's story. The listener knows what will happen to Patroklos, just as he knows what will happen to Achilles or Paris. From what I have just demonstrated, it is possible to conclude that the *Iliad* as a poem intended for oral presentation is, as a whole, based on a network of allusions which are meant to affect the listener during its performance. The work has preserved its flexibility, since the author could change the traditional content of topics he presented, but thanks to allusions which draw on the audience's knowledge, it has kept its coherence.

The listener is drawn into this game at the very beginning of Meleagros's story. The narration completely omits Atalanta, who was the real reason for Meleagros's clash with his uncles. This fact must have disconcerted the audience. However, with Atalanta out of the way, all attention is focused on Meleagros's wife, who is then the only woman with any influence upon the hero. According to the myth, Atalanta entranced Meleagros, so her presence would certainly distract the listener and weaken the intended parallel. This omission, however, has been compensated for by the powerful dramatization of new action.

Homer's transformation of the story of Meleagros gives us an excellent example of the mythic and narrative flexibility characteristic of oral poetry. It also shows how the singer deceives the listener: from the surprise triggered by the omissions to the emphasis on Kleopatra, whom the singer uses to create a parallel for Patroklos later in the story. In effect, the listener feels he understands the deeper meaning of the events, notices the irony of the futile embassy which is unable to pacify Achilles, and recognizes the irony in Phoinix who delivers his *exemplum*, but does not really know what he is saying.[163] The listener knows that the story does not end in the way Phoinix ends it: Meleagros will die, though Homer complicates the action so much that it is not obvious what kind of death it will be (whereas in other versions the kind of death Meleagros suffers is of primary importance); however, the listener has not got time for this kind of speculation because he is not a reader. Instead, the significant omission of

163 Nagy (1999:105) points out the difference between Achilles' reception of the story about Meleagros and Phoinix's intentions: Meleagros is visited by a succession of people in which each one is closer to him (more *philos*) than the previous (Kakridis 1949:21—"ascending scale of affection"; see more Alden 2000:244–246): first the elders, then priests, his father, sisters, mother, friends, and his wife, who finally manages to convince him. For Achilles, the most important fact is that on the top of this hierarchy is the person closest to him, and this observation is triggered by the association of the names Kleopatra/Patroklos; Phoinix wants to forestall the finality which would follow Achilles' return to battle by saying that his "closest friends" are coming to him and that he should decide to cease his anger now, instead of waiting until the last moment for the visit of the closest person. Aias, in turn, wrongly suspects that the closest person for Achilles is Briseis, who is also a parallel to Kleopatra, Meleagros's wife (107–108). Nagy does not examine the impact of the associations Kleopatra/Patroklos upon the recipient.

this hero's death gives the listener a reason to contemplate Achilles, who is also doomed to die, and to die soon after he goes back into battle.

As we can see, the allusiveness of the Homeric text draws deeply on the epic tradition. For the poet, the point of reference is not so much the facts from the history of the Trojan War, but rather images fixed in the group memory;[164] these images can be evoked in a diversified narrative form due to the reuse of all the structural elements of the song: the formula, the type-scene, and the story pattern. The example of the name of Meleagros's wife shows that the singer can employ allusions to refer to the listeners' knowledge of the story he is telling, that is to the tale of Achilles' wrath, which after the death of Patroklos undergoes metamorphosis. So, generalizing, we could say that it is an allusion to the *Iliad* itself. The singer instinctively goes beyond the song which he is currently performing. His success in engaging the attention and interest of his listeners by affecting their emotions and provoking judgment of the characters' conduct to a large extent depends on the audience's knowledge of the epic tradition and sensitivity to it. In debate with the readily accepted notion of a "canon of facts" (the idea introduced by Kullmann), one could say that the listeners know this or a similar story including some important images, not a collection of facts.

This Homeric all-pervading allusiveness (which, as all the evidence suggests, is not his invention but an element of tradition) opens the way for the creation of material that was not in the tradition. Naturally, the listener does not know everything about the Trojan War, but the more he knows, the more curious he is to learn new details. Homer cleverly exploits this opportunity, introducing references to the past which are certainly his own inventions. The latter is a fair inference because there is no justification for their use outside the *Iliad*, i.e. in the multiform tradition. I will clarify my standpoint, using two examples. Patroklos's *psychê* appears to Achilles in his tent and confesses (*Iliad* 23.77–78): οὐ μὲν γὰρ ζωοί γε φίλων ἀπάνευθεν ἑταίρων / βουλὰς ἑζόμενοι βουλεύσομεν ("because alive we will never take counsel together, sitting apart

[164] Bakker 1993:15: "Rather, epic narrative is typically presented as, in narratological terms, the description of things seen, with the narrator (performer) posing as eyewitness." Bakker continues (1993:18–19): "The purpose of the epic performance, the turning of a performer's mental (private) images into public speech, is that what becomes real for the narrator, due to his involvement with the scenes of his imaginative memory, activates visual images in the minds of the audience as well. … The involvement of the performer with his images is nothing other than the natural counterpart of the audience's involvement with their images, the natural consequence of their being 'drawn' into the reality deployed by the performer." Rubin (1995:46) argues that "imagery is a powerful memory aid, with properties which are especially useful for oral traditions." He shows that such images are a common property of a singer and his audience functioning as 'mental models' and 'mental simulations' (see more Rubin 1995:Ch 6). Rubin further explains (1995:50): "Mental images, like physical images, do not preserve sequences unless a set search path is specified for the images." For more on mental images see Ch. 5, pp. 486–504, below.

from our dear comrades"). This vignette shows the intimacy and closeness of their friendship. Though they were among friends, the emphatic expression *philôn... hetairôn* 'dear comrades' indicates there were some things which only they shared. Likewise, during the meeting of Achilles and Patroklos which we discussed earlier, Achilles appeals for sincerity, which their friendship deserves (16.19). Thus Homer, referring to the past which is beyond the current story, characterizes the strength of feeling between the two friends. Following the same pattern, he describes the relationship between Patroklos and Briseis, who laments his death. The reason for her sadness shows her nobility of character (*Iliad* 19.295–300):

> οὐδὲ μὲν οὐδέ μ' ἔασκες, ὅτ' ἄνδρ' ἐμὸν ὠκὺς Ἀχιλλεὺς
> ἔκτεινεν, πέρσεν δὲ πόλιν θείοιο Μύνητος,
> κλαίειν, ἀλλά μ' ἔφασκες Ἀχιλλῆος θείοιο
> κουριδίην ἄλοχον θήσειν, ἄξειν τ' ἐνὶ νηυσὶν
> ἐς Φθίην, δαίσειν δὲ γάμον μετὰ Μυρμιδόνεσσι.
> τώ σ' ἄμοτον κλαίω τεθνηότα μείλιχον αἰεί.
>
> No, you didn't let me weep when swift Achilles
> killed my husband and sacked the city of godlike Mynes,
> but you promised me that godlike Achilles would make me
> his rightful wife, and would take me in his ships
> to Phthia and make a wedding feast among the Myrmidons.
> Therefore I cannot stop lamenting you, dead, but always kind to me.

The past returns not only in extensive stories but also in short allusive references. This obviously routine and conventional device is often used so cleverly that its impact is probably stronger than if an image from the past was recalled in a longer passage. At first the past seems hidden from the listener; Patroklos appears as an enigmatic character marked by his tragic fate, and only after his death do we get to know details from his past, important in the context of the moment. Kullmann claims that considering the amount of traditional information about this hero, different than the information given in the *Iliad*, Patroklos must belong to the epic tradition.[165] Therefore it is striking that the singer seems to deliberately avoid references to the past known from tradition. The story

165 Kullmann 1960:44–45, 60, 193–194. Sinos (1975:104–106) stresses that the figure of Patroklos cannot be regarded as an invention, a new thread created for the sake of the *Iliad*, because "the close correspondence of name and theme within the framework of the *Iliad* assures us that the Patroklos-Achilles association is traditional and basic to the Achilles epic." According to Sinos, the analogy to Gilgamesh and Enkidu in the Gilgamesh epic points to the ancient character of this motif.

gets adapted to the needs of a given performance, and particularly to how the singer intended to present a traditional story. At the same time, the stories he alludes to in order to justify his own understanding of the narrative matter also undergo reinterpretation to meet the current narrative needs. From this point of view, the creation of the past, which was not necessarily reflected in other songs, is just another level of the adaptation of tradition to the current needs of a performance. He makes use of invention, perhaps for the reason proposed by Finkelberg in the case of Demodokos's first song: having no stories appropriate for a given context, he creates new ones.[166] Certainly the aim of this invention is, like in the case of Odysseus, the praise of the hero. But perhaps the singer uses tradition as a blank book, no matter whether someone has already written in it.

Conclusions

Egbert Bakker's studies show that Homer's text has all the markings of spoken, not written, language. Enjambment is superficial because verses are made up by adding phrases which complement the previous ones.[167] Teachers know well that students can hardly keep their attention focused and concentrate long on text that is read out to them. But these same people are able to concentrate and participate actively in lectures. Very often imperfections like illogicalities, unfinished thoughts, repetitions from groping for the right word, or ellipses and digressions are not an obstacle to understanding the message, provided that the lecturer has experience and skill in distilling the essence. Even interludes or an excessive number of pronouns or particles do not cloud the argument; sometimes they even seem to make it more clear. The main conclusion is: epic narration is possible only because it lets the listener concentrate precisely because it is live speech. The phenomenon of its impact can be explained by the fact that, being live speech, it affects the listener's emotions and continually calls for his approval, which requires his understanding of what is happening. Approval is as necessary as the emotional experience of the action, which is why the singer so often resorts to irony.

Epic narration, built in this way, can be very long. It is immaterial whether a poem like the *Iliad* was sung for several days or several weeks. It was sung as long as there was demand for this kind of entertainment, just as in Norwegian or Danish courts, when the storyteller or singer was asked to spin his tales for long months.[168] The singer is concerned only with how to maintain the listeners'

[166] Finkelberg 1987:130.

[167] Bakker 1988, 1990, 1993, 1997a, and 1997b.

[168] Among numerous examples of minstrels', bards' etc. extensive knowledge of history, Chadwick and Chadwick (1932:581) describe an interesting case of a young man from Iceland (*Haralds Saga*

interest in his song. All attempts at explaining the perfection of Homer's poems by his long work on them are not supported by any oral tradition studies; these attempts remain an uncorroborated hypothesis fed by the difficulty in understanding how one-time creation could result in such perfect characters and refinement of meaning. If we realize that the singer creates his story with the intention of drawing the listener into his narration, it becomes clear that the exquisiteness is a product of narration which serves one purpose: to prompt the emotional reception of the song and gain its approval by the audience. The reception must be linear, parallel to the performance of the text. Heightened suspense and deeper characterization, intended by better singers, must be apparent to the hearer at the moment he hears it. These devices are completely different than in written texts and comprise: 1) allusions which go beyond the current story and which can and should be known to the audience familiar with other songs from a given cycle, and 2) foreshadowing of events, which will soon be presented in detail. Thanks to these devices, all kinds of minor details become clear and stimulate the attention of the listener. These details may include small additions or omissions in repeated passages, hints about the mood of a given scene (e.g. information about the place of an event or about the weather), words which have a different meaning for the speaker and for the audience, who are aware of the future course of events, and finally, surprise, specific to oral narration. The hearer, listening to the narration, receives all those signals as they come and reflects on the fate of the characters; his reflection, however, does not go beyond the approval which results from his understanding of the text.

Harđráđa—Fornmanna Sögur) who stayed at the court of the king of Norway, Harald III (1047–1066), all autumn. He spent this time telling stories and during a twelve-days' long celebration of Christmas he narrated the last story about the king fighting on the Mediterranean Sea, gaining the king's special approval. The man, whose name does not appear in the saga, mentioned that the source of his knowledge was Halldór Snorrason's tales presented in Iceland during annual summer gatherings of all the people. Similarly, in the Celtic tradition (*Book of Druim Snechta*) the Irish king has a court singer, *fili*, called Forgoll, who every evening from the 1st of November to the 1st of May tells him various stories. Even if he had done it only for two hours a day, in total it would have made 362 hours of recitation (Chadwick and Chadwick 1932:586).

5

The Parallelism of Scenes in the Cycle and the *Iliad*

ANY INTERDEPENDENCE of scenes in Homer results from the technique of scene parallelism. The frequency of its use demonstrates that this technique was typical of epic songs. It is, in fact, the typical oral strategy of repeating the same motif in a modified form.

Ways of Modification

In Homer, there are several ways of modifying parallel scenes. The poet uses them often, nearly every time a different one. Let us consider examples from *Iliad* Book 5.

The substitution of characters

In this pattern, the poet uses various characters who fulfill identical functions. Two scenes in *Iliad* Book 5 are constructed with similar expressions and a pattern in which one god, acting as a messenger, saves another (5.388–391):

> καί νύ κεν ἔνθ' ἀπόλοιτο Ἄρης ἆτος πολέμοιο,
> εἰ μὴ μητρυιὴ περικαλλὴς Ἠερίβοια
> Ἑρμέᾳ ἐξήγγειλεν· ὃ δ' ἐξέκλεψεν Ἄρηα
> ἤδη τειρόμενον, χαλεπὸς δέ ἑ δεσμὸς ἐδάμνα.
>
> And Ares, hungry for war, would have breathed his last,
> had not the brothers' stepmother, beautiful Eëriboia
> brought tidings to Hermes, who stole Ares away,
> half-dead as cruel bonds overpowered him.

and an earlier passage (5.352–354):

ἣ δ' ἀλύουσ' ἀπεβήσετο, τείρετο δ' αἰνῶς·
τὴν μὲν ἄρ' Ἶρις ἑλοῦσα ποδήνεμος ἔξαγ' ὁμίλου
ἀχθομένην ὀδύνῃσι, μελαίνετο δὲ χρόα καλόν.

she [Aphrodite] left, frantic, and suffering;
swift like the wind Iris led her away from the crowd
in great pain, and her beautiful skin was blackened by blood.

This function is typical of Hermes, who is a kind of trickster, and fond of stealing anything or anyone, whereas Iris is given this role secondarily. Nonetheless, her action in the plot precedes the information about Hermes' analogous deed. It is rather difficult to imagine that the poet invented such a scene, with a character different than the traditional one, on the fly, during a performance, and then, not much later, presented a typical scene. I think that this may prove that Homer used this pattern many times with both divine messengers, probably also outside the *Iliad*: he had worked out a pattern in which Iris was substituted for Hermes, so that he could make use of these scenes in any order.

Analogy

Analogy is usually used for the juxtaposition of the human and divine planes, e.g. after the struggle with Diomedes, Aeneas has to forfeit his chariot (5.319–327); similarly, when Aphrodite is wounded by Diomedes, she needs to ask her brother Ares for a chariot (5.357–363). Andersen[1] rightly notes, "Homeric gods don't need horses to get to Olympus." The goddess' request arises from the similarity of the situations: like her son, she is also deprived of her chariot. On a battlefield, a divine being should behave like a human warrior.

Reversal

The same character plays a role opposite to the one played before, e.g. Aphrodite, who as a mother had to save Aeneas (5.311–318), now is herself hurt and goes for comfort to her mother Dione (5.370–374). In her request to Dione, Aphrodite points to her right to protect φίλον υἱόν, her "beloved son" (5.377), herself appealing to Dione as her φίλον τέκος, "beloved child" (5.373, 382). The juxtaposition of both facts in one speech emphasizes the reversal of roles.

1 Andersen 1978:60.

Gradation

When two scenes are built on the same pattern, the first one is less important than the second. At the beginning of his *aristeia*, Diomedes, who is on foot, faces two Trojans, Phegeus and Idaios, who attack him from a chariot. Phegeus throws a spear, but misses Diomedes, who then kills him. Idaios is saved by Hephaistos and hidden in a cloud of mist, while the chariot becomes Diomedes' property (5.9–26). This scene is a kind of anticipation of a more important fight later in the same book between Aeneas and Pandaros. Pandaros throws his spear without wounding Diomedes, who kills him, and thus completes his revenge. Aeneas, driving the chariot, tries to protect Pandaros's body, but is wounded and saved by the divine intervention of Aphrodite and Apollo. Aeneas's chariot is taken by Diomedes (5.166–328).

Reduction

This is the inversion of gradation: first a scene is recounted in detail and then it appears in roughly sketched variations. The parallel scenes of saving an Achaean warrior when a Trojan arrow kills one of the horses drawing his chariot are analyzed in the later part of this chapter: there is a lengthy description of Nestor's rescue (Book 8), followed by a sketchy reference to this scene in the struggle between Patroklos and Sarpedon (Book 16).

Contrast

Contrast enables listeners to judge characters and events, as the behavior of Diomedes and Sthenelos illustrates. When Agamemnon rebukes Diomedes, Sthenelos bursts with righteous indignation at the injustice of the king's charges. Diomedes does not repudiate the accusation and even upbraids Sthenelos, saying that the ruler is always right (4.401–418). When it is time to fight Pandaros and Aeneas, Sthenelos turns coward and urges the hero to flee. Diomedes, who kept silent when reprimanded, rejects the proposition and orders Sthenelos to get ready to leave their chariot and catch Aeneas's horses, if he, Diomedes, kills their owner. Refusing to mount their own vehicle and thus eliminating his chance to escape, Diomedes fights on foot (5.241–264, 319–330). It is worth noting that Diomedes is very tolerant of his friend and does not reproach him, perhaps because he believes that the situation is really very dangerous. This scene calls for listeners to judge the conduct of both characters: the one who boasted of his bravery turns coward, while the one who did not protest the accusations proves his courage.

The Song and Tradition

When studying the dialogue between tradition and innovation on the one hand and the use of allusions to activate the listeners' memory on the other, we should consider whether all extratextual references are of the same significance. The question is if each, even trivial, element found in Homer has its equivalent in other epic songs. Of fundamental importance here is to evaluate the reliability of various stories, which should be examined from two perspectives: 1) that of the listeners to the song (whether they consider these stories credible) and 2) our point of view (if we can believe they were based on tradition).

Ruth Scodel has proposed an interesting differentiation:[2]

> At one extreme lie bardic performances, based on information provided by the Muses, potentially meaningful far beyond their immediate contexts, but with the details of content not specific to particular occasions, even if a member of the audience has requested the subject of the song. At the other extreme are the false tales that have in the past deceived Penelope and Eumaeus (*Od.* 14.379–385), invented stories that served only the greed of those who told them. In between are the lying tales of Odysseus and the various paradigmatic and autobiographical tales that fill the two epics, which their narrators have acquired from personal experience or oral tradition and adapted to their immediate needs.

Some tales told in epics are corroborated by tradition, some are not, and some may not agree with tradition, so we face a basic issue: how to differentiate between a real and pretended tradition. Naturally, since we deal with fiction, it is a complex theoretical problem to determine to what extent one piece of fiction can be corroborated by another. To a certain extent, it is enough for a piece to be within the boundaries of the models and meanings established in tradition. For example, any story about Odysseus or Achilles must be based on the already existing patterns and must present them in a way which properly underscores their heroic character. Similarly, the stories of Prince Marko usually concentrate either on his wedding or on his (or his friends') rescue from a dungeon, and the role and behavior of the protagonist are almost always identical.

Scodel maintains that in oral cultures knowledge about the deeds of heroes is conveyed not only in epic songs. She summarizes her analysis of how the singer uses tradition to create his own fiction:[3]

2 Scodel 2002:74.

3 Scodel 2002:76–77. However, Nagy (1974:248 and 1999:271) believes that the only form of conveying *kleos* is epic poetry.

> The epic's distancing of itself from oral tradition does not undercut its rhetoric of traditionality. On the contrary, if no performance actually depends on any other, then *when the audience recognizes repetitions from earlier occasions, the similarities are especially powerful markers of stability and truth* [emphasis mine].

Scodel clearly does not take into account the interdependence of epic songs, only the similarities which may affect the audience's approval of a song. She continues:[4]

> By presenting themselves as disinterested, performers discourage the audience from looking for the details that gave one performance a different message from another. By separating their own narrative from its tradition, they place it all under the sign of traditionality. Since the poet could not be certain exactly what was "traditional" for his audience, he carefully pointed to the traditional and disinterested nature of the whole.

According to Scodel, at the threshold of creation lies the singer's uncertainty as to the scope of his audience's familiarity with tradition. Therefore, he has to adapt his song to what they expect and are accustomed to. This does not explain the phenomenon of the emergence of cycles with their logical and relatively coherent macro-story, which may lack a complementary construction (due to numerous variants of certain elements of the plot), yet which preserves the unity of the narrative warp, which must have been respected in the construction of particular songs.

In Scodel's model of epic tradition, songs can be quite independent, like in the South Slavic tradition, or connected loosely and haphazardly. However, considering the lack of such freedom in the Trojan Cycle, I cannot agree with her model. Let us return to Prince Marko. He cannot appear in any other role than that of a hero of exceptional strength and valor, with a certain appearance, and conforming to a canon of rules which constitute the Serbian chivalric ethos; significant also is his status as vassal to the sultan. However, such elements would not be enough to make Achilles recognizable. His actions must not only agree with his character, but also must be correlated with other tales about the Trojan War. This need for correlation is most apparent in the story of the failed Teuthranian expedition, which repeats the pattern of Achilles' exploits: in a duel, he defeats and wounds Telephos, the leader of Mysians (the variant of killing the leader of the allies is replaced here with wounding him). But the

4 Scodel 2002:89.

order of events propelling Achilles to action is analogous to that known from the *Iliad*: Patroklos goes into battle to save the Achaeans and gets wounded in a fight over the body of Thersandros (Proclus, *Chrestomathia*, *Kypria* 7).[5] The variant of wounding fulfills the same function as that of the hero's death: it rouses Achilles to fight. I believe that because the similarity to the substitution of Achilles by Patroklos in the *Iliad* was too strong, it was necessary to move the action to another locality and to create a double of the whole expedition (see Chapter 3). To sum up: this story could not be inserted *anyhow* into the Trojan Cycle. To enable its inclusion, it was necessary to introduce several changes that would differentiate it from a story already well known. However, the variants employed here did not change the meaning of the macro-story.

Let us look again at the classification of stories in epic songs from the point of view of their reliability and the degree to which they are embedded in tradition. In this context, to regard them as not true to the tradition is to argue that they oppose it for the sake of obtaining short-time aims of characters. It is, however, a very hazy criterion. For example, the characters relate various mythical stories, uncorroborated elsewhere; we know these stories functioned in tradition, but not in the version given in the *Iliad*, e.g. Phoinix's story about Meleagros's refusal to defend his city or Achilles' story about Niobe eating despite her grief (9.529–599, 24.601–616). These "new versions," however, suit the intentions of the character who tells them and the context of the situation very well. They modify myths but preserve their fundamental framework: changes may consist in showing new motivations or introducing a new, often discordant, interpretation of events, yet it is still the same story.[6] We infer that

5 See Robert (1923:1148), who, however, does not notice the link between the wounding of Patroklos and Achilles' attack on Telephos. Patroklos's participation in the fight against Telephos alongside Achilles is attested to by Pindar (*Olympian* 9.71–73). Yet, as Pindar states further on, Achilles later advised his friend never to fight separately again (9.76–79). Since Patroklos did fight separately, he must have acted independently of Achilles. The rescue of Thersandros's body by Patroklos and Diomedes seems to be referred to in Pinthias's painting on a kalyx crater (St. Petersburg 1275; see Gantz 1993:579–580). The bandaging of Patroklos's arm by Achilles is depicted on a tondo of a kylix (Sosias Painter, Berlin, Ch 2278), but Gantz (1993:874n52) does not share the opinion that this painting refers to the situation depicted in the *Kypria*. However, it is very likely that Patroklos was wounded in the fight over Thersandros's body, which prompted an attack by Achilles, who after the battle dressed his friend's wound. In the *Iliad* (11.844–848), Patroklos dresses the wound of Eurypylos, but he learned this skill from Achilles, who in turn got it from Cheiron (11.831–832). The *Iliad* seems to reconfigure the traditional image of Achilles the healer by reversing the situation: the patient becomes the doctor.

6 Nagy (1996b:136–138) argues against understanding these transformations as "arbitrary personal inventions" of the author of the *Iliad*. He is of the opinion that such changes constitute a "selection within tradition" (similarly Muellner 2012:197). Without undermining this position, I think it is important to stress that the potentiality of introducing changes involving reconfiguration and reinterpretation is an inherent feature of oral tradition. Although the

the singer can enrich tradition with new stories, provided those stories do not violate it.

Now there arises the question: can we regard the untrue biographies of Odysseus in the same way as we do the genealogies of secondary and tertiary characters from the *Iliad* and *Odyssey*? It seems that the latter, due to their plausibility and skillful placement in mythological and historical contexts, may become an element of tradition. But there is only one biography of Odysseus and it is too well known, and, unlike the hero's interlocutors in the song, the listener will not be deceived by the invented stories about his deeds and descent.[7] Though not believing a single word, the listener—like Athena listening to one of Odysseus's bogus tales (*Odyssey* 13.287–295)—is full of admiration for his cleverness and vivid imagination. Despite the plausibility and the similar way in which these two kinds of stories are woven into tradition, they are not qualitatively identical.

Odysseus's tales display the singer's ability to create alternative stories, which exhibit a certain potential for functioning in the stream of epic narration. A skillful employment of traditional means (primarily plot and story patterns) allows the singer to fabulate, using characters known from the cycle or somehow related to it, e.g. Idomeneus's son in Odysseus's fake tale (13.259–270). The singer can also draw on stories of his own times and weave them into his narrative about the mythical past. This may be the provenance of Menelaos's and Odysseus's stories about their stay in Egypt (4.351–581; 14.257–286).[8] It seems quite natural, as Yugoslavian and Finnish singers could also turn the events from their times into an epic tale.[9]

The possibility of adding anything to tradition results from the perception of tradition as the "truth" about the past revealed in songs inspired by the Muse; thanks to the Muse, the song becomes true. This does not imply that any and

tradition might have included various versions of particular stories, the performer could always tell a traditional story in a way he needed to at any given moment; he could even introduce versions that had not appeared in tradition. Giving a new version of events does not mean striving for originality, because it is not the story itself that is important, but the intention with which it is recalled.

7 H. Parry 1994:12–13: "Whatever Odysseus' motives for lying in a given context, Homer's audience always know ... what is going on. And indeed, where the imperatives of courtesy do not rule this out, his interlocutors sooner or later are enlightened too: the full truth is only postponed. His tales on Ithaca are, like Hera's lies to Zeus, palpable fabrications, short-term strategies to mislead the victim only as long as is necessary."

8 Carpenter (1974:90–111) shows that these stories are related to the employment of Greek mercenaries by the pharaoh Psamtik and his successors. That is why he believes that those stories could not have emerged before 650 BCE. I think his conclusions go too far, but the homeostasis noted by Ong (2002:46–48) is certainly an intrinsic feature of oral tradition.

9 See Kiparsky 1976:95–98.

every creation is possible, but only that which conforms to existing narrative models. In other words, the criterion of truth is its compliance with tradition—its character and code of meanings.

Not all stories told in an epic can be regarded as "true," i.e. rooted in tradition. But tradition is not a fossilized pattern which cannot be changed or reinterpreted. That is why many stories may fit into it, provided they are probable and comply with traditional rules. Many songs may make use of the same pattern and expand the overall narrative of the cycle, even if they start at the same moment in the story presented in the cycle. The end of the war draws near, a new obstacle appears, and the success of the expedition depends on its removal. If we have the *Aethiopis* and *Aethiopis No. 2*—the *Iliad*—why can't we have various versions of Odysseus's return? Naturally, the general outline of the story would not change.

A song always enters an existing cycle and it fits, not because it takes up a motif already functioning there or presents the deeds of a familiar character, but because it finds points of support in the cosmological frame of the cycle. The frame usually contains two elements: a divine inspiration and the first cause of events, which is also situated on the divine plane. For a singer, placing his song in such a "super-pattern," common to many other songs, must have been an automatic action. He would have accommodated his song to the model of events in a given cycle, initially the model of an expedition and return. Matching the song to this model is automatic because the singer would use common patterns in similar situations in the story: e.g. Achilles always has to fight a new enemy who appears on the battleground and wreaks havoc in the Achaean ranks just before the capture of Troy. The singer's compliance with the rules of this "superstructure" results in the unification of the cycle and consolidation of its content. For example, each new song assumes the same causes for the Trojan War, though it could develop this motif in a number of ways. The cycle was not founded on the "earliest song" (*Urlied*), but on a frame binding subsequent episodes added by *aoidoi*, who met their listeners' desires for new stories about favorite heroes or the war. The subordination of an episode to a cosmological frame means entering a network of connections functioning in collective memory. In other words, the knowledge of the cycle and its most important narrative elements was a common good of the singer and his audience.

If we deny the audience the right to be familiar with cycles, which—as we have seen—came into existence long before the creation of the *Iliad* and *Odyssey*, we deprive people of the possibility of combining facts heard from various sources, which are for the listeners a reality as real as their own life. In this chapter, I will try to prove not only that Homer's poems functioned in the stream of epic tradition (which does not need proof) but also that they assume the listeners' knowledge of many "facts" and scenes remembered from other songs, the memory of which is deliberately stimulated by the singer.

The caution displayed by the singer—resulting, as suggested by Scodel,[10] from his uncertainty as to the degree of his audience's familiarity with the epic tradition referred to in his song—reflects nothing more than his use of traditional patterns, which he does freely, yet in a way that does not change the basic message of the myth. It therefore becomes essential to establish to what extent a given myth has already been shaped in epic tradition and what the audience knows of it. Again we turn to Scodel's pioneering studies. In the chapter "Homeric Exposition," she analyzes the expositions of the *Iliad* and *Odyssey* and shows how knowledge of the Trojan Cycle might have varied among audience members and how such differences could have been used by the singer. Analyzing the introduction of characters later in the poems, she demonstrates what the listener must know to understand the story at all and how detailed knowledge about particular heroes facilitates better understanding of Homer's narrative. Following her reasoning, one can conclude that most important for the *Iliad* is the familiarity with the chief characters in the Trojan conflict and with the story of the abduction of Helen. As far as the *Odyssey* is concerned, the listener is expected to know the main features of the protagonist and some events from his return, but not necessarily all the details of his struggle with the suitors.

According to Scodel, the fact "that a character receives an introduction does not prove that he or she is unfamiliar to the audience."[11] Yet, detailed introductions of characters may suggest that "Homer did not want to rely on his audience's knowing about them." It may mean that the characters who are introduced with a detailed exposition may be less known or invented by the poet. There is, however, one more case that should be taken into account here: the introduction of a character who is known, but in this song plays a different role than the one he played in earlier epic tradition. A suitable example here is Thersites, who is presented differently than other heroes in the *Iliad*, because he has the role of giving rebukes and in this capacity he is an alter ego for Achilles. Thersites is a substitute for Achilles in the conflict with Agamemnon and takes on his shoulders the odium of the whole community—thus fulfilling the function of a scapegoat. Due to this substitution the epic narrative transfers the hero's guilt onto a figure generated specially for the role of a "scum."[12] Other examples are that of Paris, whose character was suggestively "blackened" in

10 Scodel 2002:90–99.

11 Scodel 2002:99.

12 I develop the concept of the substitution of Achilles by Thersites in the book I am currently writing: *Achilles the Loser: Picking a Scapegoat in the Oral Culture Community*.

the *Iliad*, or Odysseus, who was "whitewashed," especially in the *Odyssey*. These alterations in the characters are understandable in view of the epic as a song praising the epic hero.

The *Iliad* also introduces Nestor as a silver-tongued counsellor of the Achaeans, and his wisdom is an outcome of his age and experience (*Iliad* 1.247–252). Does this mean that this hero was not known to listeners? Probably not. One of the devices typical of oral narration is redundancy, which demands that the poet remind his audience, sometimes repeatedly, of a character's traits.[13] Does the appearance of Nestor in the *Odyssey* without any introduction (3.32) and without any description throughout the song mean that thanks to the *Iliad* he is such a well-known figure he needs no introduction? As has been demonstrated in Chapter 1, the *Odyssey* does not refer to the *Iliad* alone, but to the whole Trojan Cycle. A lengthy introduction of Nestor at the quarrel of leaders (*Iliad* 1.247–252) is aimed at stressing the role he will play at the critical moment in the story.[14] His advice is not always successful, which may point to a characteristic element of his traditional image.[15]

Scodel concludes that Homer's epic is constructed in such a way that it does not require "extensive, detailed prior knowledge of the characters and stories for its main plot."[16] Using devices, which in all probability were conventional, like catalogues, expositions, and quasi-focalized introductions, the poet guides his "relatively inexperienced listeners" towards the understanding of an episode. As we can see, Scodel assumes that the *Iliad* is a new song, and its audience has only a sketchy knowledge of the Trojan War. It is astonishing how easily one can yield to the illusion of this concept. Perhaps it is so alluring because it sees Greek epic in terms of the conditions of South Slavic epic, where the singers introduce new and unrelated (at least at first glance) stories e.g. about Prince Marko. But, as I pointed out in Chapter 1, in comparison with the Greek cyclic tradition, the Prince Marko stories deserve at most the name of a *quasi*-cycle. When performances of songs of a similar character are accumulated

13 Ong (2002:38) gives a brave soldier or a beautiful princess as examples.

14 Race (1993:101) demonstrates that in the *Odyssey*, characters are described precisely (and in a way which indicates their role in the whole story) when they are first introduced: "The impressions gained from our first view of each character may be qualified and deepened by subsequent actions and words—Telemachos, for example, is a striking example of one who matures in front of our eyes—but they are never proven wrong."

15 Nestor failed to quench the conflict between Achilles and Agamemnon (1.254–305); the embassy to Achilles failed (9.9–112, 669–692); Antilochos ignored his suggestions at Patroklos's games (23.304–350, 418–447); even the protective wall built on his advice around the Achaean camp could not keep them safe from danger (7.337–343, 374–468).

16 Scodel 2002:122.

in one place and time—as happened in the Greek tradition—the creation of a new plot cannot be limited to the combination of recurring traditional themes.

Such a conception about the audience's knowledge seems unconvincing. Naturally, we can assume that even an absolutely inexperienced audience could understand the song (Scodel's analysis shows it is possible); but since that epic tradition gave birth to such a complex structure as a cycle, the situation assumed by Scodel seems highly unlikely, if not almost impossible because tradition is the common domain of the singer and his audience: when it was so much developed (as shown by the abundance of cyclic stories and the amount of allusions to them in the Homeric poems), the myth of Trojan War must have been known to many people and many Greek communities. Adjusting the song for the reception of a "layman" does not exclude its reception on a much deeper level, which might have been much more complex than Scodel imagines.[17] Her conception can be easily challenged: at the end of the previous chapter, I proved that the author of the *Iliad* assumed at least part of his audience would know that Patroklos would influence Achilles to change his mind at the crucial moment. This means that the singer performed for an audience who was not only familiar with the major facts of the Trojan War, but also knew the tale he was singing. Constructing his song, the singer could rely on this knowledge, and, as he added new strands to the story, he could introduce allusions to the basic plot. These allusions could fill a double function—justifying the additions and vivifying the action.

Let's mention one of many other examples. According to the scholia, Zenodotus's version lacked several important passages, including Achilles' advice to Patroklos to curb his battle fury and restrict himself to driving the Trojans away from the ships (16.93–96):

> "Μή τις ἀπ' Οὐλύμποιο θεῶν αἰειγενετάων
> ἐμβήῃ· μάλα τούς γε φιλεῖ ἑκάεργος Ἀπόλλων·
> ἀλλὰ πάλιν τρωπᾶσθαι, ἐπὴν φάος ἐν νήεσσι
> θήῃς, τοὺς δ' ἔτ' ἐᾶν πεδίον κατὰ δηριάασθαι."

[17] Currie (2016:30), convinced of the widespread presence of allusions in Homeric poems, believes that we should allow for the category of the "ideal listener," who could read all allusions contained in the works intended for oral reception. I sincerely doubt, however, that the oral author in any way envisioned a connoisseur capable of picking up hidden details unavailable for others to perceive. Such is the purpose (clearly realized and even propagated as appropriate since Hellenistic literature) of the use of allusions in the written tradition. The oral poet addresses a group familiar with the tradition, but such a group is unstable by nature. Therefore, the oral author assumes a certain common mental base of the audience, which will make it possible to read the meanings conveyed in his narrative (see Ch. 4) rather than an ideal recipient who will have a perfect understanding of his message. Therefore, the benefit of adopting such a category in research seems questionable. The singer may like to be admired for his artistry, but he expects recognition from the whole community rather than the few initiated.

> "Or one of the ever-living gods from Olympus
> will cross your path: they [Trojans] are beloved by death-sowing
> Apollo;
> so return as soon as you bring the light among the ships
> and let the rest of them fight on the plain."

According to Zenodotus, instead of these lines, there should be only one line: μή σ' ἀπογυμνωθέντα λάβῃ κορυθαίολος Ἕκτωρ ("Or Hektor, shaking the plume on his helmet, will catch you naked"). For Whitman, this version indicates Achilles' knowledge of Patroklos's destiny: Hektor will kill him just because Apollo will beat the armor off his body.[18] Whitman believes, "there are crucial spots in the text of Zenodotus which clearly anticipate or summarize a longer version"[19]—the version which, let us add, Zenodotus's version is conscious of. But this allusion reminds the listener of what he already knows, the manner in which Apollo will treat Patroklos. As far as its function is concerned, we can say that allusions such as this one unify the poem.

The singer uses various methods to evoke reminiscences of important events in the cycle which guarantee a proper understanding and a more emotional experience of the story. This kind of manipulation of the listener's emotions can be seen as typical, if the singer addresses an audience familiar with such songs. In the previous chapter, I presented the basic methods with which the singer influences the listener: the alternation between dread and relief, and multi-layered irony. Now we will observe how the reception of whole scenes is controlled by the recall of events known from other songs of the Trojan Cycle.

The functionality of allusions

A particular element of traditional diction acquires its meaning in repetition, due to its use in tradition.[20] Tradition also brings a vision of a certain whole, in which a given element, even if altered and placed in a different context, can be understood. Formulae, type-scenes, and story patterns constitute a system of meaning comprehensible primarily to those who know an epic tradition. These elements of oral technique are points of reference to other epic songs, both known and unknown to the hearer. It therefore seems improbable that narrative structures, especially structures of such complexity, would not include allusions to other familiar stories within the same cycle. Since the cycle really functioned—which is corroborated by the fact that the understanding of the

18 In this version, Achilles also seems to display awareness of the magical power of his armor.

19 Whitman 1958:84 and 330n66.

20 Foley 1991:7.

Iliad often depends on the familiarity with tradition present in the cycle—we have to accept the idea that the cycle itself must be alluded to in songs to a greater, or even much greater extent than the bare minimum of information allowed by Scodel.[21]

According to Kullmann, allusions can be divided into two groups: those which refer to earlier events than the ones presented in the *Iliad* (*antehomerica*), and those which refer to later events (*posthomerica*).[22] This division may be misleading because it assumes that a fixed sequence of events is followed, whereas in fact episodes are substitutive, that is some events must have happened earlier or later, but basically they happen at the same time: see, for example, the succession of events which leads to Achilles' death or the conquest of Troy, already discussed in Chapter 2 (the protagonist always faces the same problem, and the solution—defeating the enemy—is generally independent of similar exploits presented in other songs). That is why in order to examine the mutual influences between the singer and the audience it seems more appropriate to employ the distinction used in narratology between analepses (stories of events preceding that told in a song) and prolepses (accounts of future events). Even more important is the division of prolepses and analepses into external, those which describe events outside the song, and internal, which predict events later in the story (returning to what was said earlier in the song is less important here, so we will not deal with internal analepses).[23]

It should be noted that the modern novel often uses internal prolepses and analepses, whereas external ones are very rare because the author cannot cross the boundaries of the fiction which he has created, unless he refers to historical facts which the reader should know. In Homer, the situation is the reverse: external prolepses and analepses are even more important than the internal ones.[24]

21 I might add that the region in which *aoidoi* worked was not big—just a dozen or so Ionian *poleis*; considering the numerous pan-Ionian, and even pan-Hellenic festivals present in Greek culture since the 7th century BCE, which certainly must have attracted singers, it is almost impossible that their audience would not have known the songs in the Trojan Cycle quite well. This conclusion assumes the barest minimum; in fact, we should suppose there was a need for the re-enactment and re-creation of the myth during such festivals, which would lead to the deliberate multiplication of stories within a given cycle (see Ch. 1, pp. 153–159, above).

22 Kullmann 1960:5–11.

23 De Jong 1987a:81–90. Perhaps the definitions of these terms are slightly simplified but I believe they are adequate for my purposes.

24 Pigoń (2004:24–25) notes that a prior recipient's knowledge of both mythical and historical stories is typical of ancient narratives, epic, tragedy, or historiography: "Ancient readers of the *Peloponnesian War* usually reached for the work of Thucydides not to learn about the plague in Athens or about the course of Sicilian expedition—*facts* were basically known to them. They expected something else: an interpretation of these facts, a certain vision of historical events, and—last not least—a lively, moving and artistically satisfactory narrative. What was the rule in ancient times, in modern times, especially in the novels of the 19th and 20th centuries, has

Let us concentrate on the meaning of the terms "prolepsis" and "analepsis." I assume that each is not only an utterance revealing the future or past, but any kind of device typical of oral tradition and composition whose aim is to induce the listener to compare what is being presented with his knowledge or expectations of people and events. We will deal also with various allusions, not only predictions.

External analepses presuppose the author's and listeners' knowledge of other epic works. In Homer, some references to other epic songs seem quite obvious:[25] Helen mentions to Hektor that she and Paris will be heroes of songs sung by future generations (*Iliad* 6.357). Speaking to Achilles, Aeneas refers to their mutual knowledge of πρόκλυτ'... ἔπεα, 'formerly-heard tales' presenting the history of their lineage or, perhaps, only parents (*Iliad* 20.204). An equally probable example comes from the *Odyssey* (8.74): Demodokos sings of the quarrel between Achilles and Odysseus, which is part of an οἴμη, "whose fame had reached the vast skies those days." The references to the external mythical and epic space go even further. As I have already pointed out, the *Odyssey* refers to the universal knowledge of the Argonautic Cycle, and allusions in both Homeric poems suggest familiarity with other cycles, e.g. the Theban and Aetolian.

There is a distinct difference in the frequency of internal and external prolepses/analepses in the *Iliad* and *Odyssey*. In the *Iliad*, there are very many events which are foreshadowed, but not subsequently narrated in the song. Their casual mentions undoubtedly testify to the listeners' knowledge of the events to which they refer. The most numerous are, naturally, the predictions of Achilles' death and the fall of Troy, introduced either by the narrator or by the characters themselves (1.352, 416; 9.412–413; 11.794–795; 16.36–37, 710; 17.197; 18.54–60, 95–96, 101, 328–332; 19.328–329, 408–417; 20.337; 21.108–113, 276–278; 22.358–360; 23.80–81, 144–151; 24.540). But the song abounds in allusions to other events from the cycle, indirect but easily recognizable for the audience of oral epic poetry. After the exposition of Achilles' wrath and his withdrawal from combat in Books 1 and 9, in the subsequent Books (2 and 10), the *Iliad* presents Odysseus who mobilizes the army and is engaged in fighting. Haft claims that such a construction of the plot underscores the role of the hero from Ithaca in the later conquest of Troy, stressed further by Odysseus's epithet ὁ πτολίπορθος, 'this city conqueror' (2.278, 10.363).[26] Similarly, the epithet ὁ τλήμων 'the/this

become an exception: the reader must be content with what the narrator chooses to reveal to him; sometimes the narrator himself knows as much as the reader."

25 See Lesky 1963:30.

26 Haft 1990:45 "the sacker of Troy." However, according to Erbse (1982:5), the introduction of this epithet in 2.278, instead of being an allusion to the subterfuge with the Trojan Horse, is only a reference to Kalchas's prophecy about the fall of the city. Seen in this light, the epithet simply

enduring one' in 10.231, 10.498, with the article, or perhaps rather demonstrative pronoun, assumes the knowledge of Odysseus's later adventures. In the *Odyssey*, he is qualified by the epithet πολύτλας 'subjected to many sufferings, submitted to many sufferings'; Odysseus calls himself πολυτλήμων 'who can endure suffering' (18.319). This is, I believe, not so much a proof of the heterogeneity of this passage or its being an interpolation, but of a different oral tradition of this part of the *Iliad*.[27] From the point of view of the author of the *Iliad*, one cannot speak about the end of Troy, pointing only to Achilles' role in its downfall; it is also necessary to mention, at least in short but suggestive allusions, the secondary, though significant role of Odysseus. For the poet, the cycle is a complementary whole, in which elements are arranged in a hierarchical order.

Equally numerous are allusions to the events preceding the beginning of the story told in the song. These include the abduction of Helen, the judgment of Paris, the gathering of the fleet in Aulis and Kalchas's prophecy, and the sack of neighboring cities by Achilles.[28] In comparison with the number of external analepses, the *Iliad* contains many fewer instances of the foreshadowing of events which will take place in the song, either expressed directly, like the revelation of future events by Zeus (15.59–71) or the prophecy of Hektor's death by Patroklos as he dies (16.852–855); or indirectly—most important is perhaps the parallel of Achilles' situation depicted in Phoinix's tale about Meleagros with its suggestion about Patroklos's role in the events to come (9.529–599).

In contrast to the *Iliad*, in the *Odyssey*, internal prolepses dominate. If the song mentions any facts beyond the narrative of the return, it relates them in full, with details (e.g. the conquest of Troy) and, naturally, stresses the special role of Odysseus. However, nearly all prolepses revolve around dramatic events in Ithaca. The function of prolepses is even given to myths related by various characters in order to admonish or instruct someone, e.g. the myth of the

suits the context of the situation. This explanation is not convincing, because Erbse ignores the importance of the pronoun ὁ.

27 Similarly Hölscher (1978:53–54), who believes, however, that Odysseus's epithets like 'much-enduring', 'resourceful', or 'wily' refer to his image as a folk-tale hero, whereas the epithet 'city conqueror' relates to the epic tradition, which finds even a much stronger corroboration in the *Iliad*, where he is called 'Telemachos's father' (60).

28 Burgess (2004b) rightly postulates caution in this respect. He shows how the thesis put forward by Scodel (1977) is unfounded. Inspired by Konstantinos Kavafi's poem *Apistia*, Scodel identified the motif of Apollo's false prophecy of Achilles' happy future, made at the wedding of Peleus and Thetis, as belonging to tradition. Such a version of events can be found in a fragment of Aeschylus's lost tragedy (fr. 350 Radt); Hera's accusation of Apollo of unreliability (*Iliad* 24.63) is perceived by Scodel as a corroborating reference. However, Burgess proves that it disagrees with the Trojan Cycle tradition, which pictures Thetis aware of the tragic end awaiting her son and repeatedly trying to avert it. Aeschylus's modification is an invention made in order to allude to current political events, though both Homer's and Aeschylus's remarks are typical references to a popular and traditional motif of Peleus and Thetis's wedding, attended by deities.

centaurs told by Antinoos, one of the suitors (21.295–304). Antinoos intends to warn Odysseus, who asks for a bow, to watch his step when under the influence of wine, whereas for the listener, the meaning of the myth is quite different: the suitors will be justly punished, like the centaurs, who wanted to abduct a bride from a wedding.[29] Menelaos's and Helen's accounts of events at Troy (4.244–259, 271–289) have a similar function: many details of these stories anticipate the return of Odysseus to Ithaca and his revenge on the suitors.[30] The tale of Agamemnon and Orestes provides Odysseus's return with an alternate conclusion.[31] Olson demonstrates how the poet uses the Oresteia myth to hint repeatedly at future events in Ithaca. Homer plays with the listener's expectations, subtly suggesting various possible results of the final scene at Odysseus's home. A grain of uncertainty remains, and the listener wonders what roles Odysseus and Telemachos will play: the murdered Agamemnon, the vengeful Orestes, or even the murderous Aigisthos, and whether the poet will change the traditional end of the story about Odysseus's return. Practically the only significant external prolepsis is Teiresias's prophecy concerning Odysseus's life after reclaiming the throne (11.119–137). The adventures of a sailor who wanders to a place where people don't know what an oar is, is a popular folktale, so I am not certain if it is a reference to another epic tale.[32]

The question is, how many and what kind of references to events outside the current story are really grounded in tradition? There are meaningful differences between the two poems. The *Odyssey* contains many stories which give a detailed account of Odysseus's participation in the conquest of Troy. Nobody would dare claim that they introduce motifs alien to the tradition of the Trojan Cycle. We should say that in the *Odyssey* allusions to events known from the cyclic tradition are strongly subordinated to the predictions of final events.

In my opinion, those elements of the tradition found in the testimonia which conveniently answer the needs of the plot of the *Iliad* are suspicious, because they simply fill the gaps in the story. I have already pointed out (Chapter 1) the unreliability of the information given in the summary of the *Kypria* about the killing of Protesilaos by Hektor. Considering the multiformity of oral tradition, the discrepancy between the versions in the *Iliad* and by Proclus as to the place where Achilles captured Briseis weighs in favor of the motif being a traditional one (Proclus, *Chrestomathia*, *Kypria* 12). Close by, there is another similar piece

29 See Edmunds 1993:Ch. 6; 1997a:418–420.

30 See Andersen 1977.

31 Olson 1990.

32 See Hansen 1997:442–444. Of all cyclic poems, the *Telegony* seems to be the least reliable in transmitting early epic poetry. Considering numerous signals indicating the relatively late date of its creation, it is not certain whether it conveys any traditional material or is simply a free interpretation of the *Odyssey*.

of information—about Achilles capturing Lykaon and Patroklos selling him on Lemnos (*Kypria* 11). Such pieces of information seem to complement the plot of the *Iliad*, where these events are mentioned briefly (21.34–44; 23.746–747).[33] Proclus's summary may also be seen as evidence of how an event invented for one song enters the macro-story. However, it seems that the episodes from Homeric poems did not permanently enter the macro-story of the cycle.

In the *Iliad*, the sale of Lykaon is presented inconsistently. Lykaon reminds Achilles that the hero sold him for the price of one hundred oxen (21.79), but at the funeral games for Patroklos, Achilles gives as a prize for the fastest runner a mixing bowl of silver, which he got as a ransom for Lykaon (23.744–749). Andersen rightly supposes that in these, as well as in other similar instances, Homer freely creates the past, which has never been definitively established.[34] We can infer that he is as inconsistent in presenting the past which is outside the story as he is in recalling the past from within the story (the facts referred to by characters often did not happen that way in the poem or were never related at all). The singer is not obliged to remember exactly how something was presented earlier and, what is more, he modifies the past according to the intentions of the character who recalls it. Andersen concludes, "there cannot really be *exploration* nor even *exposition* of the past in an oral culture, only *exploitation*."[35] Tradition is not stable and unchanging, but in each performance it undergoes constant remodeling.[36] I think that Andersen follows this line of reasoning too far when he concludes, "the epic poem does not 'refer to' and is not 'based on' tradition" and that "for the audience there are no facts beyond the song," because it suggests that the *Iliad* is outside tradition.[37] The problem here is with the understanding of tradition: it is not a stable database but a multiform entity and the way it is evoked intrinsically implies a modification.

Let us have a look at several such mentions of the past in the *Iliad*. Patroklos says that Sarpedon was the first to scale the Achaean wall (16.558), whereas earlier in the poem Hektor is credited as the man who did so (12.438). Andersen rightly rejects psychological attempts at explaining Patroklos's statement, suggesting that the most natural understanding of that passage is that neither

33 These pieces of information don't fit other pieces in this part of the summary. It is unclear if Troilos's death was in any way connected with the conquest of the cities. Lykaon was presumably taken into captivity by Achilles, who sneaked into Troy. After the sharing of the spoils, there is a fragment relating the death of Palamedes, although it is hard to see its connection with any of the events mentioned earlier.

34 Andersen 1990.

35 Andersen 1990:42.

36 Andersen 1990:43: "Tradition in a sense is there only 'for occasion' and may be said to exist only 'on occasion'."

37 Andersen 1990:44.

the poet, nor his listeners had in their minds a clear version of the attack on the wall.[38] If we stick to the idea of the poet's following the oral pattern, we could say that Patroklos's comment spoken over Sarpedon's body is simply functional. It stresses Sarpedon's role as a leader of Trojan allies, the one most dangerous to the Achaeans, who is killed by Patroklos substituting for Achilles. This passage is not so much about the bragging of a young hero but is a signal for the audience of the importance of his deed. Once this is done, the demands of the epic pattern have been fulfilled.

When Iris comes to rouse Achilles to defend Patroklos's body, she says that Hektor intends to cut off his friend's head and fix it on a stake (18.174–177). Earlier, the narrator also informed us about Hektor's stripping Patroklos of the armor and intending to cut off his head (17.125–126). Yet the impaling never happens. Andersen declares, "we should conclude not that *she* [Iris] presents the situation differently, but rather that *Homer* here presents a slightly different situation." We could say that the difference in these two portrayals of Hektor's intentions is due to the poet's creative freedom. We might look at this problem from a different point of view. The cruelty of the Trojan can be a traditional element in the epic which the poet was free to present in the way he wanted. In the poem, Hektor is not shown as a cruel man, so it may not be in his personality, but—as an enemy leader—he is in a situation in which cruelty is traditional. The cruelty of Priam's son is designed to rouse Achilles to revenge. If it was a traditional element, it must have been used as a method to make the hero go back to battle in other cases when he withdrew from combat.

It has been suggested that such a situation was described in the *Aethiopis*. Neoanalysts assume that Achilles returned to battle after he learned about Antilochos's death, but Burgess contests this version of events, pointing out that it is hypothetical.[39] He also believes that the parallel of friendship between Achilles and Patroklos in the *Iliad* and Achilles and Antilochos in the *Aethiopis* is a groundless assumption.[40] If so, the death of Antilochos could not be such a blow for Achilles as the death of Patroklos. Burgess concludes that the motif of Achilles' revenge, and even the motif of his withdrawal from battle, did not appear in the *Aethiopis* at all.[41] Achilles simply turned against Memnon when he killed one of the more prominent Achaeans.

It seems to me that such conclusions are unjustified. Burgess does not explain what information about Memnon Thetis could have passed to her son other than the prophecy of his death, should he kill the Ethiopian king. It must have been

38 Andersen 1990:30.
39 Burgess 1997:15–16.
40 Burgess 1997:10–13.
41 Burgess 1997:16.

a serious matter if Proclus mentioned it in his brief summary (*Chrestomathia*, *Aethiopis* 2). The *aristeia* of the leader of the Trojan allies, an uninterrupted string of successes which is to be stopped by Achilles, is possible only when the Greek hero keeps away from the combat. Otherwise, epic narrative convention would demand to know why "the best of the Achaeans," although present on the battlefield, is not fighting. It is much more proper to show his absence. If we don't need to assume that Achilles returns to battle stimulated by his friendship with Nestor's son, it is possible that he does so on learning of the cruelty of the Trojan ally. In the *Aethiopis*, it might have been communicated by a god (e.g. Iris, like in the *Iliad*) or one of the protagonists. Maybe that is why in the *Iliad*, it is Antilochos who tells Achilles about his friend's death. Achilles' vengeance might have had a weaker foundation than that in Homer's poem, but the defilement of the heroic Antilochos, who was dear to his heart (we learn this from *Iliad* 23.555[42]), was a reason strong enough to induce him to return to the battlefield. It is also possible to think of another variant of this motif, that Achilles learns about the death of his friend and the enemy's cruelty at the same time.

We will come back to some examples of the multiform past cited by Andersen later. At present, we will confine ourselves to the conclusion that despite the freedom to create the past, the singer must respect the pattern of the song, and since this approach is based on the assignment of certain functions to scenes and their elements, a clear message is sent to the listener who is usually familiar with their purpose. We also note that the facts from outside the story, even those invented by the poet, anchor the song in the space of the cycle. His song becomes a part of an *oimê*—a huge macro-story, analogous to the *Mahābhārata*, comprising many events and episodes built around the Trojan War.

Beside the creative supplementation of the past, about which neither the singer nor his audience could have had detailed knowledge, there are also

42 Antilochos is chosen to tell Achilles the news of Patroklos's death (17.652–655), and then restrains Achilles from taking his own life under the influence of violent grief for his friend (18.32–34). During the chariot race, Antilochos shows distinct characteristics of Achilles' substitute. For example, for the sake of victory and his own glory, he cuts Menelaos up in a narrow stretch, thus putting his life in danger (23.418–437), which may be a symbolic representation of the threat brought to the Achaeans by Achilles defending his glory. Also, the speech of Antilochos, who feels wronged by Achilles' judgment (23.542–553), mirrors the argument of Achilles asserting his rights in his dispute with Agamemnon: Antilochos perceives the lack of reward as a deprivation (1.299, similarly Thersites, 2.240 and Nestor, 9.110); he makes an appeal to the generosity of Achilles, who possesses much wealth (Agamemnon does not show the generosity necessary in a superior, 9.331–335, as Nestor has urged him to do, 9.112); Antilochos suggests that he can give a reward to Eumelos, who came in last, also later and even at a higher value (compare 1.128); he is ready to defend his due reward by force (1.300–303). The character of Antilochos in the *Iliad* is thus probably shaped in a way that relates to a tradition in which he functioned as a substitute for Achilles, much like Patroklos in the *Iliad*. In both cases, the death of the substitute could provide a reason to shake the protagonist out of his idleness.

instances of the deliberate adjustment or modification of facts known from tradition, or even their replacement with "new" facts. We have seen how the story of Meleagros (*Iliad* 9.529–599) must have undergone significant changes, unknown in tradition, but the main facts from his life have been preserved, even if they are overwhelmed by others, invented for the sake of the moment. This is most apparent in Meleagros's death, seemingly absent in the story; but although omitted to maintain the point of the discourse, it is implicit in view of the parallel fates of Meleagros and Achilles which are stressed. In the *Iliad*, the modification of tradition, both creative supplementation and the presentation of a non-traditional version of events, can be found in the scene of Achilles' taking farewell of his parents before leaving for Troy. In Homer, this scene is evoked several times, describing precisely what was said, by whom, and even with what gestures. Odysseus reminds Achilles of the advice given to him at leave-taking by his father Peleus (*Iliad* 9.251–258); similarly, Nestor reminds Patroklos of the advice given to him by his father Menoitios (*Iliad* 11.768–789). These words are trustworthy because they are spoken to the people who participated in the event and do not mind being reminded of their father's warnings.

Achilles' mother Thetis tells Hephaistos that she herself sent her son to the war (18.438–440):

> "Νηυσὶν ἐπιπροέηκα κορωνίσιν Ἴλιον εἴσω
> Τρωσὶ μαχησόμενον· τὸν δ' οὐχ ὑποδέξομαι αὖτις
> οἴκαδε νοστήσαντα δόμον Πηλήϊον εἴσω"
>
> "I sent [Achilles] to Troy with beaked ships
> to fight Trojans. I am not going to see him in my house again,
> coming back to his homeland, to Peleus's house."

Robbins rightly notes that these words suggest Thetis is living with her husband in Phthia on the day of her son's departure and when she speaks to Hephaistos. It is inconsistent with the traditional myth of the Trojan War and with the pattern of the folktale on which this epic story is based—in both, Thetis returns to her submarine world, leaving her husband and child.[43] In contrast to this Homeric version of events, in the same *Iliad*, Thetis lives together with her sisters in the watery palace of her father, which she leaves whenever her son calls her (1.357–359, 17.35–38). As we can see, the singer modifies his story according to his narrative strategy, but he cannot disregard facts well-grounded in tradition. And so he leaves unexplained the discrepancy between Thetis's speech when

43 Robbins 1993:7–8. Compare Ch. 6, pp. 574–575, below.

she mentions her house in Phthia and the fact that in the world depicted in the poem her house is in the depth of the sea.

The range of allusions and their variety in the Homeric epics are impressive and indicate the singer's comprehensive knowledge of the macro-story. The openness of tradition gives him not only a chance of supplementing it with new details and episodes, structurally related to the patterns obligatory in epic, but also the opportunity to develop various strands of his story. Thanks to his skillful and even systematic use of allusions, the poet is able to place his song and his vision of an episode in a broader framework of the cycle.

This placement of the song in the broader epic tradition makes it possible for the singer to build suspense, using the listeners' knowledge of this tradition. Suspense in epic, as Goethe noticed, is created in a different way than in drama. The poet surprises the listener not by unexpected events but by how the familiar outcome of those events is reached.[44] Contemporary studies distinguish a number of suspense-building devices used in Homeric poems.[45] According to Rengakos, they include the following:

1. Retardation, in the form of an interruption (*Unterbrechung*) of narration by the introduction of another motif; the slowing down (*Verlangsamung*) of the pace of narration; and a temporary reversal of the timeline (*Umkehr*).
2. A gradual foreshadowing of events.
3. Dramatic irony due to the contrast between the listener's knowledge and the ignorance of characters in the song (alternatively, between characters possessing and not possessing such knowledge).
4. Deliberate deception of the listener by suggesting a different course of future events than the one that will be followed.

In Rengakos's opinion, the use of surprise in the *Iliad* is limited to suggestions of departing from the traditional course of action. In such instances, the singer resorts to the conventional use of the conditional sentence, i.e. that something would have happened differently if the thing he is going to relate had not happened (καὶ νύ κεν εἰ μή ...). Such a suggested departure from tradition employs a temporary plot twist. Among many significant examples of this technique there are the insidious testing of his troops by Agamemnon (2.142–207),

44 Goethe, in his letter to Schiller of April 22, 1797. describes this phenomenon, respectively, as "Spannung auf das Was" and "Spannung auf das Wie" (after Rengakos 1999:309–310 and 321). In the terminology used by G. E. Duckworth (1966 [1933[1]]), it is "suspense of uncertainty" and "suspense of anticipation."

45 The distinction after Rengakos (1999), who summarizes the latest state of research.

which nearly results in the Achaeans' abandoning the war; the duel of Menelaos and Paris (3.67–120, 245–380, 448–461), which indicates the possibility of an early end of the war; and the action of the third day of the battle (Books 13–15), which pursues, against destiny, Zeus's plan for supporting the Trojans. According to Rengakos, all three kinds of retardation, often used in combination, help to keep the audience's attention.[46] Let me add that, at least in the case of the third kind of retardation, the listener's interest implies his knowledge of tradition. While the poet stimulates the anticipation of the traditional course of events, he also develops the action contrary to expectations.

Anticipation, which consists in a gradual foreshadowing of events, is a technique opposite to that of surprise. A very good example is the way in which Zeus announces more and more precisely the main events of the wrath of Achilles (8.470–477, 11.187–194, 15.56–77).[47] However, anticipation is quite often disrupted by deviations from the course of events which has been forecast. Morrison perceives such deviations as deliberate attempts to deceive the listener by arousing his doubts about the accuracy of his knowledge of what is going to happen; thus, it is also a form of surprise. Unfulfilled or only partially fulfilled predictions concerning secondary events can make the listener uncertain whether the story will end as expected.[48] In the *Iliad*, this uncertainty concerns the degree of Trojan superiority on the battlefield, the moment of Achilles' intervention, and the place of Patroklos's death. Rengakos has noticed a similar method of deceiving the listener in the *Odyssey*.[49] But he also finds a significant difference in the two Homeric poems as far as the use of surprise resulting from the deliberate deception is concerned and, hence, various methods of creating suspense. The *Iliad* suggests "impossible variants" of action, while the *Odyssey* proposes "possible variants" leading to the denouement, all within the boundaries of tradition.[50] In other words, the *Odyssey* refers to other versions of Odysseus's return, which—in Rengakos's opinion—must have functioned in the epic tradition. These include the suggestions that Odysseus would use either subterfuge in dealing with the suitors or resort to hand-to-hand combat; and if the latter, that he would use a bow or a spear to take revenge. Or events might

46 Rengakos 1999:315–319. Rengakos perceives the whole action of the *Iliad* as a retardation in the macro-story of the Trojan War (320), because the song never presents the important events—the death of Achilles and the capture of Troy—that it foreshadows. See also Reichel 1990.

47 Rengakos 1999:322: "Das Prinzip der fortschreitenden Enthüllung bedeutet insofern eine Verstärkung der antizipatorischen Spannung, als sich die Aufmerksamkeit des Rezipienten, ständig in Anspruch genommen durch eine wohldosierte Informationsvergabe, mit zunehmender Intensität auf das Eintreffen des Vorausgesagten richtet."

48 Morrison 1992b.

49 Rengakos 1999:327–335.

50 Rengakos 1999:335–336.

go in another direction: Penelope could recognize her husband before the bow contest, or Odysseus could share the fate of the sons of Atreus.

From these considerations Rengakos draws conclusions which I find unconvincing. According to him, the references to the listener's knowledge of the past in the *Iliad* do not build narrative suspense. The plot of the song is, in his words, "a stiffish adaptation of the motifs of the saga" (in this case the *Aethiopis*), and symbolic references to these motifs can serve only the purpose of entertaining the listener.[51] A representative example for Rengakos is Paris's wounding of Diomedes in the foot (11.375–378), which reminds the listeners about Achilles' death, but since the actual wound is not fatal and does not change Diomedes' life, the scene lacks suspense. Because I disagree with this interpretation, I will consider Morrison's and Rengakos's observations together with an analysis of scenes which many scholars link to the *Aethiopis* and the events it portrays.

I think that the foreshadowing of events in oral performance is necessary to keep the listeners aware of the direction of the narration. The poet's employment of surprise in the *Iliad* is closely related to the listeners' familiarity with the cycle—their knowledge of essential "facts" (and really, memory images) for the *Iliad* as well as their memory of scenes and sequences of events important for the macro-story of the cycle. In other words, the singer builds his scenes parallel to those known from tradition (the reconstructed traditional scene which I will call a priority scene). As I have already demonstrated in the previous chapter, in order to awaken the interest of his listeners, who are not necessarily concentrating on the song, the singer stimulates their emotional response. This response is based on their feeling of dread, which is in turn based on their awareness of the story's unhappy end. At the crucial moment, the singer changes the action and rescues the protagonist from his predicament. The listener sighs with relief: "Safe for now, though this or that character did not save himself from such a scrape." Temporary relief does not eliminate, however, constant anxiety concerning the development of the most important events—the fates of Patroklos and Achilles—which the listeners anticipate with growing dread. Regular reminders of their tragic end, suggested already at their first appearance in the *Iliad*, keep up this feeling. The dread is linked to the constant need to judge the character's conduct according to the listener's moral sense and epic code of behavior, but it also involves confrontation with his knowledge of past and future events in the macro-story. As we have seen, to obtain this aim, the *aoidos* often evokes tragic irony.

I summarize the main points of my position in this matter. Allusions organize the work and ensure its integrity. Internal analepses (e.g. when Achilles

[51] Rengakos 1999:337.

tells his mother what happened in the assembly) and internal prolepses (e.g. foreshadowing what will happen to Patroklos) bind the whole story together. In this way, the author of the *Iliad* makes sure that his listeners can constantly have a clear picture of the events. However, I find that external analepses and external prolepses play an equally important role. The former allow the audience to understand the reasons for what is happening, while the latter are like lanterns showing the aim of the narrative. The poet cannot let his listeners lose sight of either the past or the future in the stream of complicated, digressive narration, because they give meaning to the events. They link the current epic narration to the macro-story of the cycle, known to the audience.

In comparison with the *Iliad*, in the *Odyssey* there is a noticeable drop in the frequency of external prolepses in favor of internal prolepses. The *Odyssey* is shaped mainly by the predictions of events at the end of the song, while the *Iliad* is composed in such a way that allusions to external events make it possible to situate it in the epic tradition, suggesting that the plot of the *Iliad* embraces much more than in fact it does.

On the surface, thanks to references made in the course of the narrative to events taking place in the final scenes of the song, the action of the *Odyssey* appears to be more tightly constructed than the action of the *Iliad*. The problem is that if we perceive the *Iliad* as a poem full of events that need to be elaborated in another poem, it means that we are looking at the action as a linear sequence of events subordinated to the chronological order. Whereas, as it was demonstrated in Chapter 1, adopting such a standpoint leads the researcher of Homer and oral tradition astray.

Uncertainty introduced by deliberately misleading the listener, often by allusions to the fates of Agamemnon, Klytaimestra, and Orestes in the *Odyssey*—which Rengakos has not noticed—invigorates the action; and surprise is important for the poem's dynamics. Allusions are, then, signals which suggest a course of action, but also evoke anxiety about an unexpected turn of events. Above all, however, the *Odyssey* does not choose a plot development which defies destiny because its plot is based on an untypical treatment of the character of Odysseus, who in tradition was not so much a protagonist as a trickster who is a threat to the hero. Thus, despite the fact that the Homeric poem repeats the traditional tale of the hero returning home, the introduction of the trickster Odysseus into this role creates many difficulties, which the author of the *Odyssey* tries to overcome in a number of ways. So, while in the subsequent epic songs Achilles always plays his role, Odysseus steps into someone else's shoes.

Parallel scenes in the *Iliad* and *Aethiopis*

We can observe how scenes, in which allusion is the main construction device, affect the emotions of the listener, as exemplified by scenes borrowed—according to Neoanalysts—from cyclic poems. Neoanalysts assume the priority of cyclic poems over the *Iliad* and the *Odyssey*, but their interpretation has been opposed by Unitarians, e.g. H. Erbse, who defend the priority and independence of plots in the Homeric songs. Oralists also distance themselves from such a simplified interpretation of similarities between scenes in the Homeric poems. They claim that in the *Iliad*, the narration of scenes is autonomous, purposeful, and sufficient.[52] In their opinion, there is no reason to suppose that one song is dependent upon another; all of them (e.g. Homer's works or cyclic poems) developed in a way typical of orality and their likeness results from similar construction, characteristic of oral poetry.[53] Some scholars believe that although Neoanalytic methodology is inappropriate and leads to erroneous conclusions, we should assume that a prototype of the epic exists. [54] How such a prototype would have looked is rather misty.

I think that Neoanalytic arguments should be amended with the findings of oral theory, without resorting to the interpretation of the *Iliad* as a product of a written or mixed oral/written tradition. However, the function of the text shaped in a performative act and intended to be received by listeners needs to be reformulated. According to some research, certain parts of the text absolutely indicate that the poem must have reached a more or less stable form (even given the conditions of oral culture) at some point, which later on underwent transformations.[55] How did such transformations take place in the conditions of orality? How could the narrative, a performative act intended for aural reception, have been modified and for what purpose? I think that the whole problem arises from the misunderstanding of the role of tradition in oral culture. Tradition was re-enacted in a performance, but its presence in the awareness of the whole community, including the performer and his audience, went far beyond the repetition of some structures, conveying a fixed code of meanings. With the accumulation of performances in one place and time, traditional themes could not be used at will or in any configuration. It is true that there is a degree of liberty in the use and transformation of motifs, but this process must always

52 Kelly 2006; 2012.

53 Foley and Arft 2015.

54 Heubeck 1989; 1992; Edwards 1990; Janko 1992; Willcock 1978; 1997; Dowden 1996; Cairns 2001; West 2003b; Burgess 2006; Currie 2012; 2016; Davies 2016.

55 Cairns 2001:36: "That the *Iliad* makes use of material which had already attained a degree of textual fixity (though not necessarily in written form) cannot really be doubted." See also Dowden 1996.

conform to certain rules. These rules do not mean the mechanical repetition of certain phrases and sets of phrases in the construction of the song. Primarily, they serve the cultural need for repeating old and multiplying new stories. The *Iliad* uses traditional structures in a repetitive configuration, giving them a meaning appropriate for the intention of the message sender. In the course of this adaptation of traditional material, the song makes significant references to traditional images functioning in collective memory. In this way, the listener is expected to compare the events presented in the song with the scenes he remembers from tradition.

We can start with a scene particularly important for the Neoanalysts, the scene in which Diomedes saves Nestor (*Iliad* 8.80–171). We will observe how the singer affects his hearers. The Trojan attack causes panic among the Achaeans. A storm is coming from the direction of Mt. Ida and the Achaeans interpret the thunder and lightning as signs of Zeus's support for the Trojans (naturally because this is also the direction of the Trojan attack). The Achaean warriors take flight—all except Nestor, who cannot escape because Paris killed one of the horses drawing his chariot (80–88). It was a third horse, attached beside the regular pair (ἵπποιο παρηορίας). The situation parallels the one we know from Proclus's summary of the *Aethiopis*, which mentions Antilochos's death at the hands of Memnon (see also *Odyssey* 4.188) and then Achilles' killing of Memnon; and from a short description of this event in Pindar (*Pythian* 6.29–39[56]). In the *Aethiopis*, it seems that Nestor is in danger for the same reason: Paris's arrow wounds a horse drawing his chariot. The old man shouts for help and Antilochos dies defending his father. Antilochos is killed by Memnon, who has already defeated many Greek warriors.

Nestor jumps to the ground and starts cutting away the dead horse's traces, when suddenly Hektor is charging at full speed toward his chariot. Nestor's life is in danger and the listeners are afraid for his safety. However, the author tempers the dread (8.90–91): καί νύ κεν ἔνθ' ὁ γέρων ἀπὸ θυμὸν ὄλεσσεν / εἰ μὴ ἄρ' ὀξὺ νόησε βοὴν ἀγαθὸς Διομήδης ("And the old man would have lost his life, / had not the booming-voiced Diomedes noticed him"). The listeners are relieved: Nestor is safe—Diomedes will rescue him. But the narrator has to start building suspense from scratch. Diomedes shouts to Odysseus for help, rebuking him for fleeing from the battlefield. Normally, it would be enough to stop Odysseus,

56 "Long ago, too, powerful Antilochus showed that he had this way of thinking; he died for his father's sake, by awaiting the man-slaying commander of the Ethiopians, Memnon. For the horse kept Nestor's chariot from moving, since it had been wounded by Paris's arrows; and Memnon was aiming his strong spear. The old man of Messene, his mind reeling, shouted to his son; the cry he hurled did not fall to the ground; his god-like son stayed on the spot and paid for his father's rescue with his own life" (translation, Diane Arnson Svarlien, 1990).

who would not risk tarnishing his honor. But the singer surprises his listeners—Odysseus does not stop. The situation is much more dramatic than it seemed a moment ago. Now the dread is growing because circumstances, outlined in such detail, remind the listeners of a similar scene from the *Aethiopis*. They remember that Antilochos paid with his life, shielding his father from the enemy with his body. The listeners are not afraid for Nestor, since they have already been told that he will not suffer, but for Diomedes. Is he going to share Antilochos's fate? After all, Zeus promised the Trojans that they would reach the Achaean ships, so the listeners can expect—or rather fear—that this is the turning point of the battle, the beginning of the Greek defeat. They can expect that this is the fulfillment of Achilles' revenge and, if they know the outline of the story related in the *Aethiopis*, that now the Achaeans will suffer a serious loss, which will draw Achilles into battle. The victim of Hektor's attack may be Diomedes—the only one who has not run away. He is certainly dear to the audience, having gained their approval with his heroic exploits in Book 5, where, with Athena's help, he managed to injure Aphrodite and Ares, and with the humility with which he accepted the reprimand in Book 4.[57]

The ties binding Nestor and Diomedes are not so close as those between Nestor and Antilochos. Therefore, Homer has to build the pathos of the scene differently. Diomedes does not shield the old man with his body, but stops in his tracks and gets ready to fight Hektor. He tells Nestor to leave the chariot to their squires, Sthenelos and Eurymedon. Nestor does as he is told and then mounts Diomedes' chariot, takes the reins, and drives toward Hektor. And Hektor is still going towards them at full speed (8.117)! Even in the middle of the battle, there is enough time for the protagonists to regroup; it seems that the enemy attack is in slow motion. Moreover Paris, whose arrow caused this fight, somehow gets lost. Finally, the warriors clash.

Juxtaposing this scene with the analogous one from the *Aethiopis*, some scholars stress that the heightened pathos of the scene in the *Aethiopis* is typical of post-Homeric epic.[58] When, however, we abandon the assumption that the *Aethiopis* is an epigonic work, it is possible to reverse our interpretation and note that the pathos of the scene in the *Aethiopis* goes hand in hand with its significance, as perceived by Neoanalysts.[59] So one could get the impression that pathos is alien to the *Iliad*.[60] Perhaps the scene in the *Iliad* lacks the naturalness of the scene in which Antilochos protects his father, but it does not lack pathos,

57 The listeners have not been informed plainly yet that Patroklos will be the victim, so they can fear that Diomedes will die.

58 Schadewaldt 1938:97fn2; Erbse 1993:397.

59 Kullmann 1960:30–31; 2005:18–19.

60 Griffin 1977 (see my discussion of this issue in Ch. 3).

though it is of a different kind: a lone hero turns against the attacking enemy and wins, notwithstanding the overwhelming odds against him. This effect has been repeatedly used in war and action films, where—despite its incredibility—during a violent enemy attack there is always time for talking, regrouping, or arming the protagonists.

The dramatic tension of the scene grows, and dread intensifies. The listener is caught up in the whirl of events and then an unusual thing happens. The hero suddenly (like in films) starts performing miracles of bravery: he kills Hektor's charioteer. Hektor is in trouble—we don't know how he managed to control the galloping horses; we have been told that his chariot was going ahead at full speed when Diomedes threw his spear. Hektor looks for and finds a new charioteer (never mind how difficult it is during the Trojan pursuit of the enemy who is fleeing in panic). We understand that now Hektor can start fighting again, but the battle does not turn in the Trojan favor. Suddenly the narrator says something that comes as a complete surprise—Diomedes seems to turn the battle's fortunes (8.130–132):

> Ἔνθά κε λοιγὸς ἔην καὶ ἀμήχανα ἔργα γένοντο,
> καί νύ κε σήκασθεν κατὰ Ἴλιον ἠΰτε ἄρνες,
> εἰ μὴ ἄρ ὀξὺ νόησε πατὴρ ἀνδρῶν τε θεῶν τε·
>
> And then there would have been a defeat and deeds which cannot be prevented,
> and the Trojans would have been driven to Ilion like sheep to their pen,
> had not the father of people and gods been quick to notice [them].

Here Homer shows his bias in favor of the Achaeans. "Our" hero is able to change singlehandedly the battle's outcome and defeat all enemies.

A dramatic change is wrought by a thunderbolt thrown by Zeus, which hits the ground just in front of Diomedes' horses.[61] Nestor is overcome with awe; for him it is a visible sign of Zeus's disfavor, and he sensibly urges Diomedes to get away (8.132–141). The dramatic impact of this scene is again intensified by the reluctance of the hero. Nestor tries to persuade Diomedes to leave the battlefield, but the young man does not appear to be faint-hearted. The listeners are left wondering if the time has come to fulfill Diomedes' destiny,

[61] The circumstances in which Homer places Diomedes are similar to those accompanying the death of Amphiaraos, who is swallowed up by the earth when Zeus's thunderbolt opens a chasm in front of his chariot. This analogy proves not only the use of motifs from the Theban Cycle in the Trojan story, but also shows that it was possible to evoke fear in listeners, who associate Diomedes' situation with the moment of Amphiaraos's spectacular death.

because he is faced with the problem fundamental to every epic hero: to submit to a god's will or to let his natural foolhardiness and lust for battle blind him and to disobey the god.[62]

Fortunately, Nestor manages to dispel Diomedes' fears concerning possible charges of cowardice and they retreat (8.150–158); again the listeners sigh with relief. Nestor first tries to convince the battle-hungry warrior that flight is not dishonorable. It is only a temporary state of affairs and it may change soon: today Zeus supports Hektor, tomorrow he can support Diomedes. Nobody can thwart the will of a god. These rational arguments fail to sway the son of Tydeus, so Nestor changes his tactics and says that Diomedes has already proved his courage enough, so he can disregard Hektor's accusations—neither Trojan men nor women will believe them.[63] And, as if on cue, Hektor starts hurling insults, accusing Diomedes of cowardice (8.160–165). In view of Nestor's arguments, these insults would seem to be irrelevant, but Diomedes is still of two minds whether he should escape or return and fight Hektor (8.166–170). So, in fact, until the last minute we don't know if everything will end well. The action changes kaleidoscopically. One moment, characters are in danger of death, the next they are happily saved. The scales of battle swing this way and that.

In this short scene, there are five situations of danger and five situations of relief—five turns of action:

1. The killing of Nestor's horse and a threat to his life—Diomedes comes to rescue Nestor.
2. An unsuccessful summons for Odysseus's help—Diomedes takes the initiative and with Nestor prepares to attack Hektor.
3. Hektor finds a new charioteer—a conditional sentence suggests the Trojan defeat.
4. Zeus's thunderbolt strikes in front of the two Achaeans, and Diomedes is reluctant to flee—Nestor speaks convincingly and takes the initiative (turning the chariot).
5. In response to Hektor's contemptuous words, Diomedes considers whether to return to the fight—finally thunder, a sign of Zeus's will, makes a convincing impression on him.

62 More on the conceit of the hero which leads to the conflict with a divinity, plus parallel situations from other epics in Ch. 6, below.

63 Homer seems to point to the young warrior's weakness for women: both Nestor and Hektor allude to it. The former mentions Trojan wives, who will not believe in Hektor's words; the latter jeers that he won't carry off any Trojan women.

The narrator turns away from the departing Achaeans, letting us guess that they have managed to escape. Hektor speaks at length, addressing his brothers in arms and then his horses, bragging and expressing his conviction of an imminent victory (8.171–196). Finally, he announces that he will kill Diomedes and strip him of the armor made by Hephaistos, which will cause the Achaeans to set sail on that very night.[64] Hektor's speech irritates Hera, who unsuccessfully tries to rouse Poseidon to support the Achaeans against Zeus's will (8.197–210). Instead of Diomedes, as the listeners were led to fear, Hektor's pride incurs the anger of the deity. However, Homer quickly realizes where this motif might lead him and changes the subject, choosing not to pursue the consequences of Hektor's pride for the moment.

In order to prove that this passage in the *Iliad* is earlier than the scene in the *Aethiopis*, Erbse points out to numerous differences between the two stories.[65] His argument is unconvincing. The points of contact are few, but there are enough of them for an audience familiar with tradition to notice that the stories are linked. This has nothing to do with imitation, a notion completely unintelligible in the sphere of oral culture, but with a reference, which is used in order to evoke certain reactions in the audience. The dramatic tension in the Homeric scene is based on the listeners' familiarity with the story of Antilochos's death. The poet treats the listeners to a seesaw of dread and relief, not quite understandable from the point of view of suspense, but absolutely reasonable from that of the visualization of a text transmitted orally. To create the feeling of dread, the poet does not return to earlier parts of the *Iliad*, but—drawing on the familiarity of his listeners with other stories from the cycle—he goes beyond the plot of his own song. Thus, an oral poet builds tension differently than nineteenth- and twentieth-century novelists. Images from other songs seem to be more important to him than his own plot. The reason behind this is the economy of action: by referring to knowledge derived from tradition and emotions evoked by traditional songs, the oral poet can instantly have a strong influence upon his listeners by controlling their emotions.

The scenes in the *Iliad* have their own meaning and coherence, and they are intended to express pathos, just as in the scenes of the cycle. One cannot brandish the Neoanalytic argument of a greater significance and power of expression in the scenes of the cycle, because for the listener, the pathos of the scenes in the *Iliad* is comparable. The sacrifice of one's life is replaced by the courage to

[64] It indicates that Hektor treats Diomedes as if he were Achilles. The way the episode is narrated stresses the desire to eliminate this hero from the battle (Hephaistos's armor, depriving the Achaeans of their main defender). Hektor's bragging is, then, directed at Diomedes as a substitute for Achilles.

[65] Erbse 1993:394–398.

undertake a fight, despite being left alone on the battlefield and facing an inevitable defeat. For Homer, it is important to stop this unnecessary bravado. This is done by submission to Zeus's will, manifested in meteorological phenomena. Diomedes does not exhibit recklessness, characteristic of the epic hero, which leads him to a conflict with gods and consequently to his death. Diomedes does not cross this threshold even earlier in his *aristeia*, when he fights only those gods whom Athena allows him to fight; when he recognizes Apollo, he gives up fighting after trying to attack the god three times. Despite his quickness of temper, which is typical of his role as a young hero, Diomedes—thanks to Nestor, who provides advice—restrains himself in this moment, always crucial in the "biographies" of young heroes. In this scene, suspense is created by allusion to scenes known from tradition. The poet employs them to repeatedly renew the feeling of dread. Dread does not grow gradually, but returns, alternating with moments of relief.

I think, therefore, that the Neoanalysts' interpretation, with some modifications, deserves support. The aim of Neoanalysis is to demonstrate that the author of the *Iliad* imitated in his work the plot of the cycle. I would suggest that it was not imitation but stimulation of reception through references to the listeners' knowledge of the most important scenes of the cycle. This perspective provokes the question: what is the point of multiplying versions of the model scene? There is not any canonical version of myth.[66] But it should also be noted that myth—evoked in multiple variants, the compositional shape of which depends on the performative context—despite differences, remains recognizable. Its adaptation to the needs of the moment (such as the circumstances of the performance or persuasive goals) changes the narrative, but it is still the same story for both the performer and the audience. Any references to it must therefore take into account its multiform character.

Diomedes—Achilles' alter ego

To be able to continue with our argument, more analysis is required to explain why Diomedes should be perceived as a surrogate for Achilles in the *Iliad*.[67] In Chapter 2, I pointed out that the story pattern in which Achilles kills both the leader of the Trojan allies and Priam's son is repeatedly used in the cycle, and

66 Slatkin (1991:6), in accord with the statement of Lévi-Strauss (1970:12–14), notes: "It is important to stress that no aboriginal prototype of a myth exists that can claim priority over other versions."

67 This is the opinion of Schoeck 1961:75–80; Erbse 1961; Nagy 1999:30–31; Mueller 1984:97–98; Kullmann 1984:312–315; Burgess 1995:239; Nickel 2002:223–225. Many other scholars do not share their point of view.

Achilles' tasks, or some of them, are often fulfilled by his substitutes, most often Patroklos and Neoptolemos. In the *Iliad*, this role is also played by Diomedes.

Diomedes is the most important character in the *Iliad* when Achilles is inactive and before Patroklos enters the picture. His heroic deeds are done when Achilles has withdrawn from battle. We are referring to Books 5–11, which—except for "The Embassy to Achilles" (Book 9) or scenes like the "Parting of Hektor and Andromache" (6.369–502[68])—are a favorite target of Pluralist criticism, because they do not move the action forward. That is why the Pluralists considered these parts to be additions by a later, less talented poet. If we were analyzing a literary work of art, they would be absolutely right—in a literary work, such scenes are redundant. Unitarians like Schadewaldt[69] demonstrated that these scenes are organically linked to the rest of the work, but only the analysis of how they function in an oral poem reveals their real purpose. The description of Diomedes' deeds, extending the narration without changing the fundamental story of the wrath of Achilles, contributes to the monumentality of the *Iliad*. As we will see, the scenes with Diomedes expand the plot and supply facts which are external to the current song, but are important for the story of Achilles. They can be seen as allusions anchoring the *Iliad* in the structure of the cycle.

When Achilles returns to the battlefield, Diomedes practically disappears from view. Diomedes represents the ideal warrior, young and hot-headed, but loyal and obedient. He is a kind of alter ego for Achilles' better side, which cannot surface in the poem.[70] The differences between the characters of both heroes, otherwise so similar, are emphasized in order to show how Achilles could and should behave—only he does not do so for obvious reasons. Such parallelism cannot be coincidental, but does it exhaust Diomedes' functions in the structure of the work?

If we divide Diomedes' actions in the *Iliad* into sections, it is apparent that they correspond to those of Achilles. I mean here Achilles' actions which are presented in the *Iliad* and foreshadowed in allusions—in short, his future. This conclusion would be impossible without Neoanalytical studies, which reveal the fundamental fact: the author of the *Iliad* was familiar with the sequence of events in the *Aethiopis*. The logic of this Homeric discourse becomes visible only

68 Although Hektor's visit in Troy is aimed at stopping Diomedes' attack.

69 Schadewaldt 1938.

70 Drews (1979:129–133) expresses the opinion that Diomedes, a character from the Theban Cycle, of Aetolian descent, was erroneously linked with Argos in Peloponnese. Expeditions against Thebes were, according to Drews, organized by the northern Aeolians (the Thessalians and Aetolians). Diomedes was introduced as Achilles' alter ego; therefore, he is a kind of "value added" to the *Iliad*. The identification of his birthplace with Argos in the Peloponnese enables Homer to present him as Agamemnon's subordinate, which is important for his concept of contrasting Diomedes' loyalty with Achilles' rebelliousness.

when we look at these scenes from the point of view of their impact upon the listener.

At first, Diomedes is shown as the antithesis of Achilles, but later in the story his identification with the protagonist is so strong that he even experiences the "death" of the best of the Achaeans. He takes Achilles' place and fulfills the same functions with all his appearances in the *Iliad*. When the army is getting ready for battle, he humbly accepts Agamemnon's reproaches, who calls him an inferior fighter compared to his heroic father Tydeus (4.368–402). Diomedes goes even further and stresses the value of loyalty and submission to the leader (4.411–418). This is in stark contrast to Achilles' disobedience and lack of restraint during his quarrel with Agamemnon in Book 1, especially as Sthenelos's violent protest (4.403–410) indicates that in the case of Diomedes the king's reproach was as unjust as it was in the case of Achilles.

When the battle begins, Diomedes fulfills his *aristeia*, which is of the highest kind because he can successfully fight gods (5.311–444, 793–867). The only other hero who accomplishes a similar feat is Achilles in the third part of the poem (21.211–384). In the rational *Iliad*, only these two warriors perform such a "miraculous" feat, typical of the epic hero, whose valor enables him to fight gods. It is a trace of the earliest stories about the "heroes of the Beginning Time." This is probably why Hermann Fränkel ascribes Book 5 to a very old cultural layer.[71] Diomedes' *aristeia* provides a contrast to Achilles: such glory can be attained in battle and—here comes a meaningful hint—by those who are loyal. Because Achilles has withdrawn from fighting and does not deserve the status of a hero, he loses his glory in favor of Diomedes, who becomes the leading figure for the Achaeans. Moreover, Diomedes' *aristeia* is presented according to the same pattern as that of Patroklos,[72] who substitutes for Achilles on the battlefield and who fights in his armor and on his behalf. In particular, Diomedes' fight with Pandaros (5.166–296), whose treacherous shot confirmed the Trojan guilt for starting the war, finds a parallel in the later struggle of Achilles and Hektor. Killing Pandaros appears to be a symbolic anticipation of the fate of Hektor (as the death of the main hero on the enemy side) and also of Troy (in terms of moral guilt and group responsibility).[73]

Diomedes' glory is also an offshoot of his ability to deal with the gods. Athena supports Diomedes in his fighting and surrounds him with radiance

71 Fränkel 1975:74n14: "The remarkable and extremely primitive fifth book of the *Iliad*..."

72 Fenik (1968:191–194) observes that both heroes provoke the Trojans, killing the first of them who stand in their way, and then they deal with other leaders; this is followed by a simile describing the destruction they wrought; they continue to spread death until they are stopped—Diomedes by Pandaros's arrow, Patroklos by Sarpedon.

73 Kyriakou (2001:253) points out formulaic similarities between both scenes.

(5.1–7), which clearly anticipates her doing the same for Achilles (18.205–214).[74] Diomedes, with Athena's help, injures Aphrodite and Ares, but he can also exercise self-control and in obedience to divine orders refrain from fighting gods, as he does first in confrontation with Ares, and then with Apollo.

The swapping of armor with Glaukos (6.232–236)—a symbol of chivalry and nobility (as it shows that even on the battlefield both heroes respect the friendship struck up by their grandfathers)—contrasts with the way Achilles treats Hektor's body.[75] This scene also refers to Achilles' loss of his father's armor and acquisition of a new one, made by Hephaistos.

In the rescue of Nestor, Diomedes takes on the role of another young hero, Antilochos, whose death in the story described in the *Aethiopis* makes Achilles attack Memnon and move toward his own death. Diomedes' extraordinary bravery nearly leads to a complete—against destiny—defeat of the Trojans; such a possibility is later suggested by the narrator in reference to the exploits of Patroklos and Achilles. In contrast to Patroklos, Diomedes is able to control his zeal and take Nestor's advice to withdraw from battle.[76]

During the night war council Diomedes again comes into conflict with Agamemnon, accusing the king of cowardice. However, he displays some diplomacy at least, by establishing his right to rebuke the ruler and imploring him not to react with anger (9.32–33). This scene is an obvious reference to the first gathering in Book 1. This time Nestor manages to prevent a quarrel (9.51–77).

After the unsuccessful embassy to Achilles, Diomedes criticizes him and the attempt to appease his anger. He also advises a rest before the next day's battle (9.696–710). If we regard the *Doloneia* as an integral part of the *Iliad*, then Diomedes, accompanied by Odysseus, performs heroic deeds during the foray behind the enemy lines, killing Rhesos, one of the leaders of the Trojan allies.

During the battle described in Book 11, Diomedes acts in concert with Odysseus. Diomedes does not run away in the face of Hektor's attack, but even hits him on the helmet with his spear, making him retreat (11.345–367). Immediately afterwards, Diomedes is injured by Paris's arrow in the heel, which compels him to leave the battlefield (11.369–400).

74 The light enveloping these two heroes precedes their entering the battle. In the description of these battles, the poet uses extended similes; the one he applies to Achilles is longer and clearly presages the rescue of the Achaeans who are defending themselves against the attack of the Trojans (5.5–7; 18.207–214).

75 Diomedes' conduct expresses the highest respect for *philia*, close friendship formed in extending hospitality to a guest. By detaching himself from the common cause of the Achaeans, Achilles violates *philia*; yet in spite of that—as is demonstrated by Elmer 2013—the hero is the embodiment of respect for this form of relationship.

76 Frame (2005:96–115 and 2009:23–102) explains the role of Nestor as "he who brings back to life and light," so he also comes to the rescue of Diomedes.

Diomedes is not Achilles and he is not able to stop the advance of Hektor and other Trojans; he is the first one mentioned by Nestor in his account of the Achaean leaders who are wounded and therefore cannot repel the enemy (11.660). Later Diomedes advises the wounded leaders to go to the first line of fighters and spur them on (14.109–132), which they do (14.379–384). Thanks to Poseidon's help, after Hera puts Zeus to sleep, the Achaeans manage to drive the Trojans away from the ships, but their success is shortlived. Patroklos's report from the battlefield (16.25) reveals that the situation is essentially the same as in Nestor's account. Achilles, speaking about the desperation of the Achaeans, mentions Diomedes in the first place (16.74).

Diomedes' appearance in the scenes most important to Achilles' stay at Troy is not coincidental. He is not only constantly compared to Achilles, but also temporarily fulfills his role. A closer look at the sections of the *Iliad* devoted to Diomedes' actions will let us create a catalogue of the means by which the singer can affect the listener. I hope this will prove that these scenes are neither an addition by a later poet, nor are a kind of preparatory stage for the real scenes in the so-called *Patrokleis* and *Achilleis*. They are all a prelude to the death of Achilles—in the sense that in each of them his death is experienced indirectly. The threat is graduated; we feel it approaching.

Before Diomedes started fighting gods, he participated in several duels with Trojans, the most important being the last, with Aeneas. For Andersen, Apollo's rescue of Aeneas is arranged only to make Aphrodite's situation more pitiable.[77] In this and many other instances, Andersen believes that these scenes function only to heighten the dramatic tension through the magnification of an event or situation which has already been described. Any such scenes found in the poem are, according to him, typical motifs. For Neoanalysts, these repetitions indicate a borrowing from another poem. For their critics, it means that the poet is toying with a motif throughout the epic. In my opinion, however, dramatic tension is not the only means of the poet's influence upon his audience, nor is the role of these motifs limited to the "rehearsal" of particular scenes, nor are they only adaptations of a borrowed motif.

Duplicated scenes differ in certain elements and their placement in the poem is not random—they are arranged in a coherent system, in which the change of an element is not arbitrary; the listener's familiarity with a parallel scene from another poem of the cycle is not meaningless. This system of duplication lets the listener comprehend the poem, but it is a different comprehension than in our experience with literature. For us, understanding means grasping an idea extrapolated from the structure of the whole work. In oral tradition, it

[77] Andersen 1978:59.

means experiencing, simultaneously with the narration, the aim of the narration. The variation of the scenes because of the different characters involved in them, together with the modification of other elements of these scenes, enables the listener to feel the dramatic tension of the story without forgetting the expected outcome of these scenes.

To follow this process in detail, let us return to the scene which precedes Diomedes' *aristeia*, the moment when, just before the battle, Agamemnon reproaches the hero. The king contrasts Diomedes' conduct with the courage of his father Tydeus (4.370–400). To ensure the intelligibility of the scenes which the listener should juxtapose, the poet-singer deliberately inserts certain signals which direct the audience's attention. Agamemnon's story about Tydeus includes signs—noticeable to the sensitive listener—which appear later in Diomedes' actions. Agamemnon brings up the comparison between father and son; this story, albeit in a modified form, returns in Diomedes' *aristeia*, so the listener can compare how the father's deeds are reflected in those of his son. In Agamemnon's story, there is also a motif of human obedience to signs sent by gods.[78] Ominous signs prevent the Myceneans from joining the expedition against Thebes (4.381–382), then obedience to the signs from the gods makes Tydeus spare Maion (4.398). The doubling reinforces the signal for the listeners who have to evaluate Diomedes' actions during his *aristeia*. The narration engages the attention of the listeners on two levels: 1) the direct observation of the verbal conflict and 2) the recognition of meanings connecting this motif with the story of Achilles. First, Sthenelos, son of Kapaneus, who is Diomedes' charioteer, states that they, the generation of sons (*Epigonoi*), surpassed their fathers' deeds, by capturing Thebes (4.405); and they did it in submission to "the portents of the gods (4.408)." Sthenelos points out the unfairness of Agamemnon's reproaches. "The portents of the gods" is an important signal, since it demonstrates that the *Epigonoi* had gained the victory, though they were fewer in number and the walls around Thebes were strengthened, because throughout the war the *Epigonoi* were obedient to gods (4.406–408).

In both cases the "portents" are mentioned very vaguely, without going into details. But they obviously refer to the piety of the conquerors of Thebes and Tydeus in particular. In Agamemnon's story, Tydeus seems to be deliberately whitewashed. Sthenelos, however, reminds the king that the champions of the first expedition perished through their "impiety" (4.409)[79]; Homer, probably

[78] Andersen (1978:33–43) raises the question of the characters' piety.

[79] Austin (1966:300–301) refers to the version of the story of Tydeus presented by Sthenelos as "an apologetic paradigm," but it is primarily a device typical of quarrels in the oral tradition: the reversal of the opponent's argument is perceived as a weak point in his utterance; by attacking it one can undermine the value of the whole utterance, even if the element in question was not

deliberately, passes over the profane cannibalism that took away Tydeus's immortality. But these oppositions do not exhaust the function of divine signs. They are a kind of introduction to the problem of the protagonist's future conduct. At the moment, the protagonist in question—Diomedes—keeps silent.[80] The question of his attitude towards the gods is unanswered and the listeners don't know if he will follow the example of his father (who is presented to him as a paragon of heroism) only to meet an equally tragic fate.[81]

Various elements of this scene come alive later. Athena is as gracious to Diomedes as she was to Tydeus; in his prayer to her, Diomedes refers to her affection for his father. The action of the goddess becomes a source of anxiety when she bestows upon the hero the ambiguous gift of being able to distinguish between gods and men on the battlefield, warning him to refrain from attacking gods other than Aphrodite (5.129–132). This warning, which protects the hero from the folly of fighting gods, is coupled with what practically amounts to an encouragement to wound Aphrodite. Diomedes, with Athena's consent, does so (5.330–339), and it seems to work against him. Dione predicts his death (5.406–411),[82] and soon after Diomedes, forgetful of Athena's words, in the heat of battle attacks Apollo (5.431–439). Diomedes charges him three times (5.436–437) and his life may be in danger. If we assume that the motif of a triple assault upon a god, resulting in death (used also in Patroklos's clash with Apollo), may be linked to the scene of Achilles' death, or that this motif is usually followed

essential, as in the case of Agamemnon. Since in laying the blame Agamemnon used the story of Tydeus, Sthenelos invalidated the accusation by giving another version of the story, in which things are presented differently than the previous speaker suggested. Compare Alden 2000:119–120 and 140 fn. 57.

80 Diomedes does not answer Agamemnon's criticism, but his reaction is practically forced by Agamemnon, see Martin 1989:71.

81 Alden (2000:112–152) points out that all references to the fate of Tydeus coming from the lips of the characters in the poem (similarly like the fate of Lykaon and Bellerophon in Diomedes' confrontation with Glaukos) are parallels to Diomedes' situation in the *Iliad*. The stories about the heroes from the past complement the main narrative, in which Diomedes plays a specific role, and constitute a multiform fulfillment of a single pattern. The hero is entangled by Athena in the conflict of the gods (5.405–406) and, by confronting Aphrodite and Ares, exposes himself to the fate of θεομάχος 'fighting against the gods'. For the wounded gods will eventually wreak their revenge on him. Alden (2000:150) believes that the revenge of these deities actually catches up with Diomedes when he is eliminated from battle by Paris. Diomedes being wounded in his foot provides a parallel, according to Alden, to the fate of Bellerophon, who was lamed by the gods. As a result, Alden (2000:150–151) suggests that the scene of Diomedes' wounding inspired the depiction of Achilles' death in the *Aethiopis*.

82 Andersen 1997 discusses the dependence of the scene of the goddess being injured and her complaining to her divine mother on a similar scene found in the *Epic of Gilgamesh*, which may be its model. He notes that there is a difference in the brutality towards gods in the examples given by Dione, parallel to the brutal treatment of Ishtar by Gilgamesh and Enkidu, and a slight wounding of Aphrodite by Diomedes (34).

by the death of the hero who has fought with a divinity, then Diomedes' fate seems sealed. Diomedes has transgressed Athena's order and he has perhaps disappointed her, just as his father had. The matter of his father's death, though unmentioned, is nonetheless present. An intrinsic element of this scene is the motif of breaking a divine order. Dione calls Diomedes a fool, since he, a mortal, dared to fight against gods (5.406). A parallel scene of Patroklos's last attack upon the Trojans, when he is stopped by Apollo, is introduced by an apostrophe to the hero: "A fool! If only he had done as Peleides told him to (16.687)."

There emerges a pattern, in which a hero who is under divine protection receives a divine commandment, fulfills an *aristeia*, but defies the god/goddess by breaking his/her order, and is punished—either by death or by the loss of his immortality, as it was with Tydeus. In the scene of Achilles' death, there might also be an element of breaking a commandment. Achilles refrains from fighting, mindful of Thetis's prophecy; his return to the battlefield after Antilochos's death may be understood in terms of ignoring her words. In the cycle, Achilles also could have been under Athena's protection. The scene of checking Achilles' anger during his quarrel with Agamemnon has the markings of such a pattern: a goddess appears, prevents him from committing a crime, promises a special reward for listening to her command, and the young hero extols the virtue of obedience to the gods (1.194–214). The *Iliad* does not follow the whole pattern, but since it does not include Achilles' death, it does not have to show the hero's transgression which deserves to be punished by death. The tradition of the cycle links Achilles' death with an offence against Apollo, whose temple was defiled when Achilles killed Troilos in it.[83]

Typical of the Homeric pattern of parallel scenes (those related by content and structure) is the optimistic ending of the first one. Apollo warns Diomedes and the hero withdraws in awe. The god is no longer interested in him, leaves him alone, and carries Aeneas to his temple (5.440–446). In spite of the listeners' fears, everything ends well. But the situation which once ends well, another time can end unhappily. This danger will return in the scenes of Patroklos's and Achilles' struggles. The prophecy concerning the results of the mortals' struggle with the gods will be fulfilled only in Patroklos, but the threat is renewed when Achilles refuses the demand of the river god Skamandros to stop slaughtering Trojans in his waters (21.214–226) and when Apollo himself (who, according to the words of Achilles, is destined to kill him: 21.277–278) makes sinister criticism of the hero's cruelty (24.32–54).

83 This is one of the possible reasons behind Achilles' conflict with Agamemnon. Gantz (1993:591) suggests that the first cause of the conflict was the killing of Tenes on Tenedos (see also Hirschberger 2012:185).

Diomedes' withdrawal from the fight gives an advantage to the Trojans, who are supported by Ares. Now Athena takes the initiative and reproaches Diomedes. She again recalls the image of his valiant father and makes a comparison between him and his son (5.800–813). The goddess promises her help and spurs him on to fight Ares.[84] A goddess must intervene to make the hero overcome his scruples resulting from his piety and obedience to the gods and their signs, which—as is stressed in an earlier part of the poem—he should respect.

Passing over certain topics in silence can also play a role here. Andersen believes that Athena's going back on her promise of immortality to Tydeus is in the poet's memory, although there is no mention of this in the poem. The story of Tydeus's transgression does not suit the "paradigmatic aim," but in the background the memory of his guilt and infamous end lingers. Still, we can wonder if the listeners were not dissatisfied by missing Tydeus's death and if the lack of allusions in itself was not a hint for them.[85] We might also consider

84 Apthorp (2000) argues that 5.808, about Athena's help to Tydeus at the Cadmean games, is an interpolation. The purport of the goddess' words is that Tydeus acted against her orders, whereas Diomedes can be certain of her support in the struggle against the Trojans and Ares. It goes against Agamemnon's claims that Tydeus gained a victory in Thebes thanks to Athena's help (4.390). For Apthorp, however, Agamemnon's remark must have been the reason why this information was later added to Athena's speech.

85 The absence of allusions to the circumstances of Tydeus's death does not mean that the *Iliad* does not refer to a hero's guilt resulting in his death. Muellner (1996:43–44) points to the fact that in Homer's mentality there functions the principle of collective responsibility, which he calls "solidarity in blame"; an example of this is Sthenelos's statement about the "impiety" (*atasthalia*) which was the cause of their fathers' deaths in the attempt to conquer Thebes. "In the *Iliad* formulaic references to *atasthaliai* 'acts of wantonness' consistently point to the responsibility of a whole group, including its leaders, for what it suffers ... Diomedes refuses to respond, but Sthenelos cannot keep from pointing out that 'those men [the Seven] perished by their own *atasthaliai*' (κεῖνοι δὲ σφετέρῃσι ἀτασθαλίῃσιν ὄλοντο [4.409]). He does not mean that the death of the Seven was not his fault, but that they all perished together and deserved it." Indeed, Sthenelos is not talking about Tydeus's individual guilt. But the principle of collective responsibility for individual guilt functions in the *Iliad* from the very beginning (the Achaeans die because of Agamemnon's guilt over Chryses and then Achilles), and there is no reason to assume it worked differently in archaic Greece than in other cultures and religions (e.g. in the Old Testament). According to this principle, a misfortune affecting the entire community implies the guilt of an individual. The story of Tydeus's wicked behavior is a typically mythical exemplification of an offence shared by all heroes. Their guilt is indicated by the failure of the enterprise and, consequently, their death. That there is no mention of individual guilt does not mean that this problem does not exist. Sthenelos speaks generally about the guilt of their fathers, without suggesting the individual guilt of any particular person, because as a descendant of one of the participants of the expedition against Thebes, he wants to emphasize his role in the glorious act of conquering the city. Moreover, it would not be appropriate to point to the shameful behavior of his friend's father: if they all lost the battle and perished, they were all equally guilty. Muellner assumes that the *Odyssey* "refuses to confuse the offending party with the group to which they belong," and suggests that "differentiations of blame are impossible in the *Iliad* but that the *Odyssey* is at pains to legitimate them." According to Muellner, in the *Odyssey* there is a clear distinction between the "blameless," with a right to vengeance, and the

whether such "presentiment" is of any use to the listener. Andersen imagines that in the "undisturbed dissonance" of the image of the pious hero painted by the *Iliad*, without any mention of his death, the listener must have "sensed" Tydeus's wildness, which led him to a crime.[86] This suggests that the lack of the most important fact of Tydeus's story creates anxiety, if the change which occurred in the father will not occur in the son. All of Diomedes' heroic deeds are seen not only from the perspective of Achilles' deeds, but also in the light of a possible reversal of fortune. Perhaps the sensation of danger which surrounds Diomedes is stronger, because the listener is not certain whether the hero won't do something that will make Athena desert him. The story of Diomedes is both modeled upon and anticipates the story of Achilles.[87] Diomedes does not repeat the actions of Achilles in the *Iliad*, but the whole path of this hero in multiform tradition. The singer duplicates the pattern *not* because, unable to leave the trodden path, he has no choice but must depend on mechanical repetition. The author of the *Iliad* always makes a *functional* use of the pattern. The singer casts over the listener a net of threats, which does not disturb his audience, but, conversely, deepens his interest in the story.

A hero's actions always bring danger not only to the people around him, but also to him personally. Acting as an individual, he also represents a community. His character is a combination of social fears and expectations. The rescue he brings to the community means that his action is successful, i.e. it has the approval of the gods. Yet the figure of the hero embodies the ambivalence of deities, or rather the binary nature of human destiny. The hero's conflict with a deity is a projection of possible dangers and failures. That is why this issue is of fundamental importance for the heroic tale. From our point of view, minor remarks about divine support—or the lack thereof—seem to play only an ornamental role, whereas for Homer's audience it was very significant information.

This issue is connected with another matter—Diomedes' appeal to Odysseus for help in rescuing Nestor (8.92–98). Kullmann tries to explain it by claiming that the unsuccessful request stresses Diomedes' loneliness in the face of

"blameworthy," who are punished. In my opinion, this distinction is illusory due to Muellner's failure to respect the mechanism of attributing the right to vengeance to oneself by various protagonists (Odysseus and Telemachos argue that they possess such a right), as well as the arbitrariness of attributing blame in the Homeric world (e.g. what the suitors do is not inappropriate by itself—they do not violate any law which forbids courting the woman whose husband did not return from the war, but in the poem their actions are considered unlawful, and the "evidence" of the offence is their failure to perform the duties of a host, which was the role they assumed). I must postpone a wider discussion for another occasion.

86 Andersen 1978:17.

87 Which is admitted also by Alden 2000:142.

danger, equating it with Antilochos's loneliness in a similar situation.[88] Erbse disagrees with this interpretation, saying that there are at least two more people involved in this action: Sthenelos and Eurymedon, Diomedes' and Nestor's charioteers.[89] But, one could reply, their help does not count; they are there only to take Nestor's chariot back to the camp. Since we have only a summary of the *Aethiopis*, we cannot discount the fact that Odysseus or another character might have appeared in this scene, but his presence was so incidental that Proclus did not mention it. In the *Iliad*, Odysseus refuses to help—is it a coincidence? Odysseus's flight is puzzling because elsewhere in the song he and Diomedes cooperate. This question may be answered using the interpretation of the epic code presented in Chapter 2. If so, we need to apply the principle of referentiality and the concept of the substitution of characters.

Diomedes, who in other cases plays the role of Achilles' alter ego, in this scene is the counterpart of Antilochos. In Book 11, Odysseus calls out for help and Diomedes obeys his summons; having defeated three chariot teams, Diomedes knocks out Hektor with his spear, but then he is eliminated from combat by Paris's arrow, which hits him in the heel, in an obvious anticipation of Achilles' death. Diomedes fights at Odysseus's side as a "second Achilles." We have already noted the importance of the conflict between Achilles and Odysseus in the context of the epic. In tradition, Achilles is in conflict with Odysseus, because both aspire to the title of "the best of the Achaeans," and, consequently, the conqueror of Troy. To reach his aim, Agamemnon needs the quarrel and co-operation of those two heroes (*Odyssey* 8.77–78), the lion and the boar (see Chapter 2). The *Iliad* and the *Odyssey* depict the tension between these two, because the success of one diminishes the glory of the other (in both poems there are hints of their later reconciliation, which is missing in the case of Odysseus's quarrel with Aias). In this critical moment when Diomedes takes the part of Antilochos, Odysseus seems to break his ties with Diomedes. The name "Anti-lochos"—"the one who is against ambush," or "the one who fights without resorting to ambush"—is consistent with Antilochos's character as we know it from the *Iliad*, but also reveals him to be the opposite of Odysseus, who is described as a person who fights using deceit and ambush. Antilochos and Diomedes, who represents him, are in the same opposition to Odysseus as Achilles: it is the opposition of βίη to δόλος (or λόχος). This crack in the relationship between Diomedes and Odysseus is not apparent later in the story. Diomedes is not resentful, and it is not an obstacle in their cooperation.

88 Kullmann 1960:31–32. Lattimore (1951:121) and Wilson (1996:184–185) also believe that the fact that Odysseus turns a deaf ear to Diomedes' request stresses the loneliness of the hero in danger and accentuates his heroism.

89 Erbse 1993:395.

Rescuing Nestor

The decipherment of allusions and finding links between the scene of saving Nestor in the *Iliad* and other scenes in the epic tradition make sense only if we consider their usefulness for the strategy of narration; there immediately arises the question why this scene was placed at this particular point in the story. Since it evokes such a significant event as Antilochos's death, it should play an important role in the structure of Homer's poem. Moreover, if—as I suggest—the author deliberately relies on his listener's familiarity with the traditional image of Antilochos's death, there appears another question: why is he telling it right now? The answer is not obvious, because, on the face of it, this scene seems to have no special significance.

In his commentary on this section, Wilson tries to justify it in the following way:[90]

> The episode of Nestor and his chariot has occupied 50 lines, a treatment that may seem excessively generous. But the importance of the episode lies less in the story of Nestor's difficulties and rescue, than in the reversal that this causes in the fortunes of the battle as a whole. It begins as the Akhaian leaders are in flight (78–9); but with his rescue of Nestor Diomedes seizes the initiative, and his success becomes apparent through his killing of Hektor's charioteer.

But Wilson's argument would carry more weight if this were the beginning of Diomedes' *aristeia*. In fact, it is only a single action and the Achaean initiative at this point seems temporary, if not doubtful. The hint of a possible change of fate in the battle only intensifies the atmosphere of dread. It is not a turning point, but just a moment of temporary relief in the face of the Achaean defeat. What is the importance of Diomedes' success at this particular moment?

If we want to discover the meaning of this scene, we need to look at it from the perspective of the whole of Book 8, which comprises the action of one complete day in the battle. This stretch of narration is framed by formulae marking dawn (8.1) and dusk (8.485–486), and includes Hektor's decision that the Trojans should spend the night on the battlefield. Hektor's speech at the evening council discloses his anticipation that a new day will determine the battle's outcome (8.525–528). In Taplin's opinion, the approaching night marks

[90] Wilson 1996:186.

the end of the first part of the poem, according to his division of the epic into three sections reflecting the units of oral performance.[91]

The action in Book 8 shows the retreat of the Achaeans, who have to seek safety behind the wall surrounding their camp, whereas the victorious Trojans can afford to remain outside the city walls. Homer presents these events in three sequences of parallel events. Each time the human actions are inspired by gods, and the end stresses Hektor's role.

1. Zeus forbids the gods to get involved in the war (1–52);
    - both parties enter the fray (53–65);
    - Zeus puts the fate of both sides on the scales—Achaean defeat (66–79);
    - Nestor is rescued; Diomedes' counterattack is stopped (80–171);
    - Hektor boasts and promises victory (172–197).
2. Hera, irritated by the Achaean defeat, unsuccessfully tries to convince Poseidon to interfere (198–212);
    - Agamemnon gains control over the situation—exhortations and a sign of Zeus's approval (213–252);
    - Achaeans attempt a counterattack (253–334), with the action of Diomedes, who takes the field first (256–259), and Teukros's *aristeia*, which ends when he tries to kill Hektor (273–334);
    - Trojan counterattack and Hektor's victory (316–349).
3. Hera and Athena, exasperated, get themselves ready to interfere, but Zeus turns them back (350–484);
    - dusk falls—the battle stops (485–488);
    - Hektor holds a council of the Trojans (489–529);
    - and he foretells Achaean destruction on the next day (530–541);
    - the Trojans make a night camp (542–565).

The composition of these three sequences of events does not correspond to the linear sequence of events. The story is told three times and each time it starts as if from scratch. The multiform repetition of the same motif of the Achaean defeat reveals redundancy as an important tool of oral poetics, since it serves to

[91] Taplin (1992:15–22) argues that the first section ends precisely at 9.712. However, his is not the only suggested division into three sections dependent on oral performance (compare Schein 1997:349), nor is it consistent with the three-part construction of the poem as I understand it; see Ch. 4, above.

emphasize the importance of a given event. Zeus decides on the Trojan victory and, when the armies enter the field, the Achaeans are forced to run away. An important role in the Trojan action is played by Hektor, who foretells the Achaean defeat, brings it about, and predicts an even greater defeat on the next day.

In this setup, the rescue of Nestor is only a prelude to the greatest—in Homer's view—defeat of the Achaeans at Troy. The beginning of the battle assumes a cosmic scale (8.66–74):

> ὄφρα μὲν ἠὼς ἦν καὶ ἀέξετο ἱερὸν ἦμαρ,
> τόφρα μάλ' ἀμφοτέρων βέλε' ἥπτετο, πῖπτε δὲ λαός.
> Ἦμος δ' Ἠέλιος μέσον οὐρανὸν ἀμφιβεβήκει,
> καὶ τότε δὴ χρύσεια πατὴρ ἐτίταινε τάλαντα·
> ἐν δ' ἐτίθει δύο κῆρε τανηλεγέος θανάτοιο
> Τρώων θ' ἱπποδάμων καὶ Ἀχαιῶν χαλκοχιτώνων,
> ἕλκε δὲ μέσσα λαβών· ῥέπε δ' αἴσιμον ἦμαρ Ἀχαιῶν.
> Αἱ μὲν Ἀχαιῶν κῆρες ἐπὶ χθονὶ πουλυβοτείρῃ
> ἑζέσθην, Τρώων δὲ πρὸς οὐρανὸν εὐρὺν ἄερθεν.
>
> As long as the morning lasted and the holy day grew [until midday],
> the weapons of both parties struck home, and soldiers died.
> But when Helios reached the mid-heaven,
> the father balanced his golden scales.
> He put on them two fates [*kêre*] of long-grieved death:
> one for the horse-taming Trojans and one for the Achaeans in bronze attire.
> He held [the scales] to balance them; the Achaean day of doom sank.
> The Achaean *kêres* sank towards the nourishing earth,
> and the Trojan ones rose to the wide sky.

By mid-day the fate of the battle has changed. It is an absolutely traditional situation, which is corroborated by the use of a fixed formula regularly occurring in such circumstances (compare 11.84–91). This change does not happen unexpectedly, as the poet introduces the image of Zeus weighing the battle's outcome. The listener is privy to the god's plans of supporting the Trojans at the expense of the Achaeans. Now he expects to see the Achaean defeat, especially since the ruler of the gods forbids other gods to help either of the parties and strengthens his prohibition by a threat of severe sanctions. What the listener does not know is how and exactly when this will happen.

The narrator transfers this state of uncertainty to the divine level: Zeus weighs the fates, as if not knowing who is destined to win, although, when Zeus takes the scales into his hands, it always means someone's imminent defeat. Zeus confirms the verdict of the scales with a sign clear to the participants of the battle (11.75–77):

> αὐτὸς δ' ἐξ Ἴδης μεγάλ' ἔκτυπε, δαιόμενον δὲ
> ἧκε σέλας μετὰ λαὸν Ἀχαιῶν· οἳ δὲ ἰδόντες
> θάμβησαν, καὶ πάντας ὑπὸ χλωρὸν δέος εἷλεν.
>
> He [Zeus] himself thundered aloud from Ida, and sent a blinding glare
> towards the Achaean troops. At this sight, they
> were scared and seized with green fear.

It is a signal for the listener that this feared moment of defeat is at hand. However, the principle of misleading the listener means that something certain becomes uncertain and, although the Achaean fate is sealed, the defeat does not come at once.[92] The narrator uses here a very clear sign of the fate awaiting the Achaeans only to introduce the scene in which Nestor's life is in danger. Instead of presenting the extent of the Achaean destruction, the singer concentrates on this situation. Both in this scene and in the Achaean counterattack in the next sequence (8.253–334), the danger to the Achaean army is made less real: the poet introduces the motif of killing the Trojans in such numbers as if the victory were to fall to the Achaeans.

As we have already seen, this method of building pathos is typical of the *Iliad*—audiences prefer to think about defeat from the perspective of the heroic deeds of their countrymen. But it does not answer the question why such an important sign was used to introduce a relatively insignificant scene of the threat to Nestor. Why did the poet choose this figure to exemplify the Achaean defeat? Nestor's old age and infirmity are not particularly stressed, although there is a clear contrast between his old age and the youth of his rescuer. Moreover, in this scene the Trojan danger to the Achaeans is not very convincing.

The Neoanalytic argument that this scene is modeled upon a parallel scene in the *Aethiopis* does not explain why it was placed at this point in the narrative. Willcock's assumption that the poet was familiar with the priority scene (i.e. a scene from the *Aethiopis*, which, according to Neoanalysts, the author of the *Iliad* imitated) is of little significance. After all, whether he himself used to sing of

92 A similar pattern of a postponed fulfillment of fate is also followed in the case of Troy and its defender, Hektor.

Achilles' death or heard it sung by another singer is not very important. The placement of this scene at this point of the story as—in Willcock's[93] words—a "thematic association" would only point to Homer's creative weakness, because, since the association is accidental, it does not contribute anything of value. The scene would be, in fact, a kind of parody, since in the *Iliad*, the protagonists survive unharmed. But even as a parody it would be poor and aimless. Moreover, if this scene in the *Iliad* is linked to that of rescuing Patroklos's body, and if Patroklos at his death also plays the role of Antilochos, then such a double reference certainly introduces compositional chaos. We will entertain a similarly low opinion of Homer's compositional talent if we adopt the standpoint typical of Oralists, who—like Lattimore—consider this scene to be only a variant of a traditional theme.[94] It still does not explain its function in the poem and suggests that the choice of scenes and their order in the *Iliad* are random.

Only when we assume that the singer expects his audience to know the scene to which he makes a reference do we finally get the impression that the introduction of this scene in this place is purposeful. Why? Because in the tradition represented by the *Aethiopis*, the danger to Nestor's life announces the decisive moment of the Achaean defeat, which makes Achilles return to battle and kill Memnon. This, in turn, entails the unavoidable and quick death of Achilles, which results in the capture of Troy. Thanks to *anamnêsis* of this event, the poet awakens in the listeners the expectation of an analogical chain of events. The audience also anticipates events which will result in Achilles' death, which in turn will enable the capture of Troy. Evoking reminiscences and stirring up emotions by stimulating the listeners' expectations and raising the feeling of dread is consistent with the principles of oral aesthetics. The listener can sigh with relief when, contrary to his fears, his favorite heroes, Nestor and Diomedes, come out unharmed, but he can also expect that this scene will trigger a sequence of events which will lead to the death of the greatest hero, i.e. Achilles.

An allusion to the key image in the Trojan tradition awakens in the listeners the feeling that the defeat of "their" Achaeans is close at hand. This similarity, so clearly marked, triggers emotions based on the listeners' fear for the hero. I believe that in oral tradition this seemingly insignificant beginning of the story was for the poet like starting to sing from the high C for the tenor.

93 Willcock (1976:287) has put forward a thesis that the song of Achilles' death was in Homer's repertoire; hence the similarities between the *Iliad* and *Aethiopis*. This opinion is shared by West 2003b.

94 Lattimore 1951:*ad* 8.80–171.

Scene sequences

From the Neoanalytic perspective, in the *Iliad*, the original scene of Antilochos's death is fragmented and appears again in the duel between Patroklos and Sarpedon (16.420–503). This time Sarpedon plays the role of Memnon, while Patroklos has that of Antilochos, who is in danger of dying. Seeing many of his Lycians killed, Sarpedon tries to stop the others who are running away and decides to confront Patroklos himself (16.420–426). Patroklos dismounts from his chariot, and they spring at each other (16.427–431). At this moment, the action is suspended, and the poet relates a conversation between Zeus and Hera, who are observing the duel (16.432–459). Zeus knows the fate of his son Sarpedon and wonders whether he can postpone his death at Patroklos's hands. Hera dissuades him from doing so and suggests that after Sarpedon's death Hypnos and Thanatos carry his body to his homeland to be buried in a noble fashion. The king of gods sheds bloody rain drops (16.460–462), probably a portent of an unusual fight or a misfortune awaiting the Lycian leader. The heroes approach each other and Patroklos kills Sarpedon's charioteer Thrasymelos (16.463–466). Sarpedon throws his spear, but, instead of hitting Patroklos, he strikes a horse, Pedasos.[95] The horses panic, but Automedon, the charioteer, cuts the dead animal loose and regains control over the chariot (16.471–476). Sarpedon throws his spear and misses again. Finally, Patroklos kills the Lycian leader, who, dying, asks Glaukos to make other Lycians fight for his body (16.478–503).

The deliberate doubling of the scene of Nestor's rescue has often been criticized. Why should one scene from the *Aethiopis* be the model for two such different scenes? In Book 8, the poet would have been influenced to emphasize the threat to Nestor's life and Antilochos's self-sacrifice, whereas in Book 16, his imitation would have been dictated by the identification of Patroklos with Antilochos. The only Neoanalytic argument in favor of Homer's decision is the evidence of a mistaken or unsuitable use of some elements of the reconstructed priority scene. Such an argument, as Adrian Kelly rightly notices, is methodologically unsound, "for it assumes what it seeks to prove."[96] An important Neoanalytic argument centers around the trace horse in Patroklos's chariot. Kullman regards this motif as more suitable for the *Aethiopis* (though Pindar does not mention it), because Nestor, rescued by his son, would be able to return to the camp in his own chariot; in Book 8, this motif is insignificant, since Nestor

95 Pedasos was taken as booty by Achilles when he killed Eëtion and yoked the horse to his divine chariot (it is described identically as in the scene of rescuing Nestor—παρήορος 'trace horse', 16.467–470).

96 Kelly 2006:7.

climbs into Diomedes' chariot. In Book 16, the situation has no consequence.[97] Ernst Heitsch, in turn, regards the use of the scene from the *Aethiopis* in Book 16 as primary (though the heroes fight on foot), and in Book 8 as secondary, because the killing of the trace horse is more pertinent in the case of Achilles' immortal horses driven by Patroklos (since only Pedasos can be killed).[98] Kelly, however, does not see any reason why the author of Book 16 should think about the episode from the *Aethiopis* as a model for his scene.[99] He regards them as two independent epic themes: one of the hero, whose horse has been killed, and another of a rescuer of someone whose horse has been killed. If both scenes were derived from a common source, why should Sarpedon take on the role of Memnon? And since in Pindar's narrative, Nestor's horse is struck by Paris, does it mean that Sarpedon, who kills the horse in Patroklos's chariot, would combine both roles, those of Paris and Memnon? Besides, Memnon wins and Sarpedon dies. What would justify such numerous and significant departures from the source?

It seems to me that, despite Kelly's doubts, it is possible to attempt to answer all these questions. In the reconstructed scene in the *Aethiopis*, Nestor is endangered because his horse has been killed. The other horses, harnessed to the shaft and pulling the vehicle, panic. Unfortunately, the function of the third horse is not clear. Normally, it should be controlled by reins, like the other horses, and also pulling the chariot. This would explain the importance of cutting the straps which harness the horse to the rig when rescuing Nestor. Perhaps it was not a pulling horse but an extra, attached to the shaft and walking beside the others. If it had been tied to some other place, it would not have been necessary to dismount from the chariot to cut loose the dying animal. Another possible explanation is that when one horse was injured, in the resulting confusion the harness straps got tangled.[100]

When we take a close look at the scene in the *Patrokleis*,[101] we note that the danger posed by Sarpedon is downplayed. The leader of Lycians wounds one horse, and the other animals panic; Automedon manages to regain control of

97 Kullmann 1960:315.

98 Heitsch 1990:167.

99 Kelly 2006:11.

100 Such is probably the meaning of Pindar's expression (*Pythian* 6.32) Νεστόρειον γὰρ ἵππος ἅρμ' ἐπέδα 'because the horse stopped Nestor's chariot', literally 'tied', as the verb πεδάω means 'fetter the legs, bind up with fetters, shackle', hence 'restrain, impede', so in this case it means to stop the movement by tangling the straps attaching the horse to the chariot. Kelly (2006:16) unconvincingly associates this expression with *Iliad* 23.585 where, according to him, this verb would indicate chariots locked up together by their shafts—which was forbidden and dangerous—in Menelaos's and Antilochos's competition at Patroklos's funeral games.

101 By the *Patrokleis* I do not mean a hypothetical separate song about Patroklos (it is absurd to assume the existence of such a song), but I apply the term used in scholarship only as a kind of

them—but it really doesn't matter, because the heroes fight on the ground. How does it happen that Sarpedon strikes the horse, if Patroklos is standing on the ground, unless he is standing very unfortunately in front of his horses? Even more questionable is how Patroklos could hit Thrasymelos the charioteer, since Sarpedon is not in his chariot.[102] Another astonishing fact is that Sarpedon, having struck a horse, throws his spear again. It is unprecedented that a character throws his spear twice in a row, without waiting for his enemy's reaction. Sarpedon not only throws twice; he also misses twice, which is, I believe, equally unusual. The situation of danger is, then, created by the fact that the character who misses first usually wins the duel.[103] If we assume that the wounding of the horse, which results in confusion and problems with regaining control of the rig, should evoke feelings of severe dread through the memory of a more familiar scene, the problems mentioned above might be the outcome of the automatic use of a pattern. I do not mean a clumsy imitation, but a functional approach to the pattern. Evoking the feeling of dread is more important than the realism of details. The singer suggestively creates serious menace, momentarily magnified by the fact that Sarpedon throws the spear "out of turn," but then quickly removes the threat, saying that he has missed.

Too much realism in the interpretation of these scenes has left its mark on Heitsch's opinion, mentioned above, that the motif of the extra horse would be appropriate only for the *Patrokleis*.[104] However, if we consider the models used in epic poems, then we should recall that the immortality of horses is a regular motif of epic poetry.[105] An immortal horse cannot be killed, captured, or tamed. To increase the dramatic impact, there was developed a scene, in which the rig is equipped with an extra—mortal—horse, whose only purpose is to be killed in order to put a hero in danger. Having cut loose the dying horse, the hero can drive away and save his life. The rescue may be permanent or only temporary, after which the man may face danger again.

In the first reference to the priority scene of Nestor stranded on the battlefield (8.80–171), the situation is described in such a way as to evoke a strong reminiscence of the traditional image embedded in the audience's memory. In its construction, the poet employs many elements of this image:

mental shortcut useful in the discourse relating to the part of the *Iliad* that presents the hero's *aristeia*.

102 In the same book, Patroklos, trying to strike Hektor, instead kills his charioteers, but at least the Trojan is then in his vehicle. Similarly, in Book 8, Diomedes strikes Eniopeus, the driver charging in Hektor's chariot (118–122). In Book 16, Thrasymelos is killed in revenge for killing a horse.

103 Fenik (1968:145–146) finds only one exception to the rule: 21.161–183. Compare Thalmann 1984:46.

104 Heitsch 1990:167.

105 More on this motif in Ch. 6.

Nestor in peril, Paris's shot, the death of the extra horse, a young hero coming to the rescue. The next time (16.420–503), the poet departs from this pattern, making do with sketching only the most characteristic element—the confusion after the horse is wounded. The action also takes a different turn: a Trojan enemy is killed instead of an Achaean warrior. Despite the scarcity of reminiscences and the introduction of other variants, the similarity is nevertheless sufficient to awaken the feeling of dread, as if the singer was certain that the image used previously (in Book 8) had been vividly imprinted in the memory of the audience. The narrator's further effort is therefore directed towards creating the mood of dread by other methods, so that the scene takes on its own distinctive features.

All available allomorphs of the Trojan Cycle depart from this simple pattern. In Book 8 and in the *Aethiopis*, the protagonist is an old man, aided by a young hero. Old age stresses the helplessness in dealing with a disabled rig. In the *Iliad*, however, the old man manages quite well on his own and does not need any help with controlling the horses or slashing the traces. The motif of senile decrepitude, no matter how appropriate it would be to this scene,[106] does not yield helpful conclusions. As we can see, the epic poet does not take into account (or does not emphasize) an outcome of events that we would expect. He also surprises us with the brevity of the moments of dread, which he quickly tones down, but sometimes equally quickly revives. Two versions of the same scene bring two variants of heroism: one time, the hero comes in aid and is killed (the motif of a young hero's self-sacrifice), another time he demonstrates great valor and nearly changes the course of events. In Book 16, the endangered young hero not only escapes death, but heroically attacks and kills an extraordinary enemy. Patroklos's conduct here is comparable to the behavior of Diomedes, who does not escape but faces his enemy. Both kill the driver of the enemy chariot, but only Patroklos kills the main warrior. All of these versions show that it is not enough to rescue a character from a predicament, but it is also necessary to display heroism. This heroism, understood as exceptional valor, is a characteristic feature of the epic hero. His heroism is in the foreground of the epic and should impress itself most forcefully on the listener.

The conclusion that the singer can arbitrarily use a well-known model would be too hasty. Homer uses this model and deceives the listener, who expects the hero to die. Homer's model is not a primary, abstract model but a specific one, which is also used in the *Aethiopis*. In the *Patrokleis*, the attempt to

[106] Kelly (2006:6) believes that in the *Aethiopis*, Nestor could not move, which means that he could not run away from the battlefield.

gain control of the horses seems absurd or irrelevant, but the death of one of the animals serves the purpose of suggestively creating a situation of danger to the hero's life.[107] This is why the singer allows Sarpedon, against tradition, to throw his spear twice—and immediately reduces the atmosphere of dread, saying that the throw will not harm Patroklos. For the singer, this scene is only a means by which to obtain his aim, so he does not worry about inconsistencies. For a moment, the danger has been removed and Patroklos is triumphant, but several hundred lines later, there will appear a new danger, much more serious, which will end in the hero's death.

When this scene is referred to for the first time, in Book 8, it does not end in tragedy. It is not a coincidence, since a gradation of parallel scenes is typical of the author of the *Iliad*. At first, in similar circumstances, a character (or various characters who play the same role) manages to defeat his enemy or to rescue himself, only to meet a tragic end in the last scene. This is not an arbitrary modification of a model scene. Homer can build dramatic tension this way only because he uses a familiar pattern, in which the protagonist dies. That is why his audience is always anxious about the safety of the beloved hero. In both scenes with Diomedes and Patroklos, Homer replaces the motif of the hero's self-sacrifice with other solutions, probably because this motif is crucial for the traditional image of Achilles' death. The hero dies bringing rescue to the whole Achaean community, not just one person.

Let us examine the arrangements of scenes which are similar enough to justify our conclusion about the existence of a common pattern in Homer's mind. We begin with the scenes which are said to provide evidence that the *Iliad* was constructed on the basis of the *Memnois*[108] (a hypothetical part of the *Aethiopis*), in which Antilochos's death convinces Achilles to take up the fight against Memnon. Then comes their duel, a victory for Achilles, after which Eos takes the body of her son and carries it to Ethiopia, his homeland, and makes him immortal. As a consequence of these actions (most probably predicted by an oracle revealed to Achilles by Thetis), Achilles meets his death at the hands of Paris, who is supported by Apollo. These are the events that Homer seems to refer to in several sequences of scenes.

I have already analyzed scenes referring to the beginning of this chain of events. Now I will show that subsequent elements of this chain are evoked in numerous scenes, which—placed side by side—demonstrate the regularity of Homeric modifications. References to the famous rescue of Nestor from the *Aethiopis* appear in three scenes of the *Iliad*:

[107] It is unnecessary to present the hero's attempt to control the horses so the listeners can concentrate on his valor.

[108] I use the term *Memnois* in the same way I use the terms *Patrokleis* and *Achilleis*.

1. Diomedes succeeds in rescuing Nestor (8.80–171), in contrast to the *Aethiopis*, when Antilochos dies in his attempt to save his father.
2. Antilochos kills Sarpedon's companion Atymnios, then nearly dies by the hand of Maris, the victim's brother, only to be saved at the last moment by his own brother, Thrasymedes (16.317–329).
3. Sarpedon kills a horse in Patroklos's rig (just as Paris kills Nestor's horse), but Automedon cuts free the dead horse and saves Patroklos, who also does not share the fate of Antilochos (16.426–505).

The last two scenes, again referring to the heroic death of Antilochos while he shields his father with his body, are found in the *Patrokleis*, much later in the song than the episode of Diomedes rescuing Nestor. Both variants of the priority scene can be presented more briefly and can quite freely depart from the "original" because the original was easily recognizable. Moreover, the listener more quickly feels the atmosphere of dread, because it takes less effort, and fewer words, to recall the image of a familiar scene. The closeness of the last two scenes to one another also has its impact. In all these cases, suspense is relieved because, unlike in the priority scene, its protagonist gets off safe and sound. With the elements of one scene, Homer builds several variations: in the first, a young hero rescues Nestor; in the second, there is a motif of saving one's relative, though here Antilochos is the one saved, not the rescuer; in the third, circumstances are similar to those from the first scene, but this time it is a young hero who is in danger. In the third version, the situation resembles most closely the *Aethiopis*, though if we take into account other elements, the differences are the most striking. The analogy to the *Aethiopis* is underpinned by the names of Antilochos's brother, Θρασυμήδης 'Thrasymedes', and Sarpedon's charioteer Θρασύμηλος 'Thrasymelos', which also tie the last two scenes together.

We must look next at another thematically linked group of scenes. In the first duel between Hektor and Achilles, the latter wants to respond to the attack, but Apollo rescues Hektor, shrouding him in a cloud of thick mist (20.419–454). Achilles then utters a most surprising thing (20.450): νῦν αὖτέ σ' ἐρύσατο Φοῖβος Ἀπόλλων ("now again Phoibos Apollo saved you"). Achilles seems to refer to a situation which has not been pictured earlier and which, as I have already pointed out after Andersen, is an element of spurious tradition. There is a lot of evidence that Hektor is a character only in the *Iliad* and Homer introduces him into the epic tradition by suggesting a situation similar to the one he is describing. But, as Andersen observes, this situation also bears resemblance to Hektor's encounter with Diomedes.[109] Then the Trojan was saved not by Apollo

109 Andersen 1990:35.

himself but by a helmet, which was his gift (11.349–353). Diomedes shouts a reproach at Hektor similar to that uttered by Achilles, drawing on the same formula.[110] The scenes have a similar construction: the leader of the Trojans, eager for revenge, goes on the attack. In Book 11 he rushes forward, killing one Achaean after another and encouraging others to follow his example (11.284–309), but the only significant duel is the one with Odysseus—and it happens in reaction to the death of several Trojan warriors killed by Diomedes.[111] In Book 20, Hektor challenges Achilles after the death of his youngest brother Polydoros. In Book 11, dread is introduced by Diomedes' words foretelling the destruction of the Achaeans (345–348); in Book 20, Hektor boasts that he will kill Achilles and throws his spear first (436–438). In both scenes, after Hektor has been defeated and withdraws from the fight, Achaean warriors hurl at him a similar reproach, in which—apart from insults and Apollo's hand in rescuing him—there is also a promise to make an end of him and bragging that now they are going to kill other Trojans. In the case of Diomedes, however, it is only empty talk because Paris's arrow quickly eliminates him from the battle.

The threat of mortal danger to Hektor is presented in the following sequence of scenes:

1. Hektor escapes death in his encounter with Diomedes (Achilles' alter ego); he is saved not by Apollo himself but by his gift—a helmet. Here there are two surrogates: a "surrogate Achilles" and a "surrogate Apollo" (11.284–367).
2. Hektor avoids death in combat against Achilles; now he is rescued by Apollo himself, but slightly earlier Athena saves Achilles, breathing upon Hektor's spear and turning it aside (20.419–454).
3. In the final duel, Apollo abandons Hektor,[112] and Achilles, aided by Athena, kills him (22.131–369).

The first two scenes delay the Trojan prince's death. The first time, his killer is substituted by another young hero. The second time, the listener can expect that now Hektor will meet his death, because this time he is being attacked by the right hero, Achilles, but, to the listener's astonishment, it does not happen.

110 Andersen believes that in this case Homer cannot allude to any particular situation from the past.

111 The dread of the situation is reduced by the victorious fights of Odysseus and Diomedes (11.310–342), acting in tandem. However, when they come across Hektor, Diomedes quickly concludes that this man is their destruction, desperately hurls a spear, and stuns him, stopping his impetus (11.343–350).

112 The narrator mentions that Apollo supports Hektor for the last time, increasing the strength of his legs, so that Achilles cannot catch up with him (22.202–204).

The third time, when Hektor is abandoned by the god who used to protect him, it is a clear signal that his death is imminent.[113]

Neoanalysis has noted the similarity in the construction of some scenes with Diomedes and the traditional scene of Achilles' death. Diomedes follows closely the path of Achilles: Agamemnon's reproach, which, however, does not lead to a quarrel; the deeds in Diomedes' *aristeia* (which are in part Achilles' future deeds, and in part perhaps also his past ones, not included in the *Iliad*); Diomedes' encounter with Apollo at the moment of his greatest success, which foretells Achilles' death, but also of his substitute, Patroklos; the swapping of armor with Glaukos; Nestor's rescue, where Diomedes is a counterpart of Antilochos; the repetition of the conflict with Agamemnon, which in this case does not lead to a split in the army; finally, the injury, which effectively eliminates Diomedes from fighting in Book 11—his wounding in the heel by Paris's arrow is an analogy to Achilles' death.

These scenes are clearly arranged in sequences. During his first *aristeia* on the first day of battle, Diomedes sheds the blood of many Trojans; this attracts the attention of Aeneas (5.166–168), who goes to Pandaros and tries to persuade him to shoot Diomedes with his bow (5.170–178). Pandaros complains that he has taken his bow in vain because he managed only to wound Menelaos and Diomedes slightly, hitting the latter in the shoulder (5.95–100), and those injuries only made them more furious. Aeneas, however, convinces Pandaros to deal with Diomedes; they agree that Aeneas will drive the chariot and Pandaros will wield the spear (5.230–238). Seeing the enemies charging, Sthenelos advises Diomedes to withdraw and mingle in the Achaean ranks, afraid that his companion might perish in combat against such mighty opponents (5.243–250). Diomedes, however, answers with a boast: he does not know fright and expects to win. Moreover, he tells his driver to abandon their chariot when the duel is over and to snatch the famous horses belonging to Aeneas (5.251–273). The dramatic tension of this scene is created like that of rescuing Nestor: after relating a longish conversation, the narrator returns to the swiftly approaching Trojans (5.274–275). There ensues a fight: Pandaros warns Diomedes, throws a spear, and misses him. Diomedes reciprocates with a deadly throw (5.276–296). Aeneas springs from his chariot and tries to protect the body of his companion (5.297–302), but Diomedes hits him with a stone and Aeneas faints (5.297–310).

113 Kelly (2008:188) shows an analogous progression in the arrangement of scenes in the *Odyssey*, where the suitors three times throw objects at the beggar-Odysseus (17.411–491, 18.349–411, 20.291–319): the selection of them seems to be increasingly humiliating to the hero, but the effectiveness of the attack decreases and at the same time Telemachos's reaction becomes more and more forceful.

Now the narrator characteristically introduces a conditional sentence: the hero would have died if it weren't for someone's aid—this time it is Aeneas's divine mother Aphrodite (5.311–312). Diomedes wounds her and she drops her son, but Apollo catches him and hides him in a dark cloud, making him invisible (5.344–346). Aphrodite flees to Olympus, where her mother Dione, in an attempt to comfort her, utters a threat against Diomedes (5.406–415):

> "νήπιος, οὐδὲ τὸ οἶδε κατὰ φρένα Τυδέος υἱὸς
> ὅττι μάλ' οὐ δηναιὸς ὃς ἀθανάτοισι μάχηται,
> οὐδέ τέ μιν παῖδες ποτὶ γούνασι παππάζουσιν
> ἐλθόντ' ἐκ πολέμοιο καὶ αἰνῆς δηϊοτῆτος.
> τὼ νῦν Τυδεΐδης, εἰ καὶ μάλα καρτερός ἐστι,
> φραζέσθω μή τίς οἱ ἀμείνων σεῖο μάχηται,
> μὴ δὴν Αἰγιάλεια περίφρων Ἀδρηστίνη
> ἐξ ὕπνου γοόωσα φίλους οἰκῆας ἐγείρῃ
> κουρίδιον ποθέουσα πόσιν τὸν ἄριστον Ἀχαιῶν
> ἰφθίμη ἄλοχος Διομήδεος ἱπποδάμοιο."
>
> "Fool that he is, Tydeus's son does not realize
> that nobody who fights the immortals will live long,
> and his children [won't sit] on his lap [and] won't call him daddy,
> when he comes back from the war and dire combat.
> Now Tydeides, strong as you are,
> beware of fighting someone stronger than yourself,
> or Aigialeia, the wise daughter of Adrastos,
> the worthy wife of the horse-taming Diomedes,
> will wake up the household from sleep with her lament,
> wailing for the love of her wedded husband, the best of the
> Achaeans."

In the meantime, the hero tries to get the unconscious enemy. Three times he attacks Aeneas, and three times Apollo pushes back Diomedes' shield. Finally, hearing the god shout that he should not fight gods, Diomedes restrains himself (5.432–444):

> Αἰνείᾳ δ' ἐπόρουσε βοὴν ἀγαθὸς Διομήδης,
> γιγνώσκων ὅ οἱ αὐτὸς ὑπείρεχε χεῖρας Ἀπόλλων·
> ἀλλ' ὅ γ' ἄρ' οὐδὲ θεὸν μέγαν ἅζετο, ἵετο δ' αἰεὶ
> Αἰνείαν κτεῖναι καὶ ἀπὸ κλυτὰ τεύχεα δῦσαι.
> τρὶς μὲν ἔπειτ' ἐπόρουσε κατακτάμεναι μενεαίνων,
> τρὶς δέ οἱ ἐστυφέλιξε φαεινὴν ἀσπίδ' Ἀπόλλων·

ἀλλ' ὅτε δὴ τὸ τέταρτον ἐπέσσυτο δαίμονι ἶσος,
δεινὰ δ' ὁμοκλήσας προσέφη ἑκάεργος Ἀπόλλων·
"φράζεο Τυδείδη καὶ χάζεο, μηδὲ θεοῖσιν
ἶσ' ἔθελε φρονέειν, ἐπεὶ οὔ ποτε φῦλον ὁμοῖον
ἀθανάτων τε θεῶν χαμαὶ ἐρχομένων τ' ἀνθρώπων."
ὣς φάτο, Τυδεΐδης δ' ἀνεχάζετο τυτθὸν ὀπίσσω
μῆνιν ἀλευάμενος ἑκατηβόλου Ἀπόλλωνος.

Sonorous-voiced Diomedes assailed Aeneas,
though he knew that Apollo himself held his arms over him [for protection],
but he was not in awe of the great god and kept on storming,
to kill Aeneas and strip him of his famous armor.
Three times he sprang forward eager to slay Aeneas,
three times Apollo struck mightily his shining shield.
But when he rushed forward for the fourth time like a god,
Apollo the death-sower cried menacingly [at him] and said:
"Take heed, Tydeides, and step back, do not try
to equal yourself with gods since people who walk upon the earth
are not of the race of immortal gods."
Thus he spoke and Tydeides drew back a little,
wanting to avoid the wrath (*mênis*) of Apollo who strikes from afar.

The scene is very elaborate, expanded with several delays, including the shifting of the place of action to Olympus. The hero exhibits courage and initiative, and the danger posed by Pandaros and Aeneas does not seem very serious. However, Dione's words introduce a threat, which becomes real at the moment of Diomedes' confrontation with Apollo. The god is certainly more powerful than Diomedes. Moreover, the listener remembers that Athena allowed the hero to fight only against Aphrodite. Fortunately, relief comes soon. Diomedes withdraws in obedience to the divine warning. The listener knows that Diomedes won't be punished, and a moment later he is proved right: the god leaves the battlefield, taking Aeneas with him.

The listener certainly feels the danger to Diomedes' life is very real because it comes right after Dione's story about ancient heroes who inflicted suffering on the gods. The story ends with a prophetic threat that very soon Diomedes' wife may mourn the death of her husband. His death at Troy is not confirmed by tradition, but the listener cannot be sure of it—he may not have adequate knowledge to realize that Dione's threat is groundless. Moreover, it suggests a sequence of events, which is typical for Achilles, the protagonist of the epic. The hero enters into a conflict with a god, and as a result, he dies. *Mênis*—Apollo's wrath—turns against Achilles, thus sealing the fate of the hero. It is not a coincidence that Dione describes Diomedes as "the best of the Achaeans," the title which belongs to Achilles.

The triple attempt at attacking Apollo may also carry much more significance—as an allusion to the death of Achilles, because the same situation is repeated in Book 16. Patroklos keeps storming Troy, despite being three times repulsed by Apollo, who finally shouts to him very much as he did previously to Diomedes (16.698–711):

> Ἔνθα κεν ὑψίπυλον Τροίην ἕλον υἷες Ἀχαιῶν
> Πατρόκλου ὑπὸ χερσί, περὶ πρὸ γὰρ ἔγχεϊ θῦεν,
> εἰ μὴ Ἀπόλλων Φοῖβος ἐϋδμήτου ἐπὶ πύργου
> ἔστη τῷ ὀλοὰ φρονέων, Τρώεσσι δ' ἀρήγων.
> Τρὶς μὲν ἐπ' ἀγκῶνος βῆ τείχεος ὑψηλοῖο
> Πάτροκλος, τρὶς δ' αὐτὸν ἀπεστυφέλιξεν Ἀπόλλων
> χείρεσσ' ἀθανάτῃσι φαεινὴν ἀσπίδα νύσσων.
> Ἀλλ' ὅτε δὴ τὸ τέταρτον ἐπέσσυτο δαίμονι ἶσος,
> δεινὰ δ' ὁμοκλήσας ἔπεα πτερόεντα προσηύδα·
> "χάζεο διογενὲς Πατρόκλεες· οὔ νύ τοι αἶσα
> σῷ ὑπὸ δουρὶ πόλιν πέρσαι Τρώων ἀγερώχων,
> οὐδ' ὑπ' Ἀχιλλῆος, ὅς περ σέο πολλὸν ἀμείνων."
> Ὣς φάτο, Πάτροκλος δ' ἀνεχάζετο πολλὸν ὀπίσσω
> μῆνιν ἀλευάμενος ἑκατηβόλου Ἀπόλλωνος.
>
> Then the Achaean sons would have seized high-gated Troy
> by the hands of Patroklos, who raged with his spear in the forefront,
> had not Phoibos Apollo taken his stand on a finely built tower
> planning his death and aiding the Trojans.
> Three times Patroklos scaled the battlements of the high wall,
> Three times Apollo pushed him back forcefully.
> But when he rushed forward for the fourth time like a god,
> [the god] cried menacingly [at him] and uttered winged words:
> "Step back, Patroklos of divine race, it is not your lot
> to take the city of gallant Trojans with your spear,
> neither is it Achilles' lot, who is much better than you are."
> Thus he spoke and Patroklos drew back a good distance,
> wanting to avoid the wrath (*mênis*) of Apollo who strikes from afar.

Patroklos also backed off in awe (a good distance—πολλὸν ὀπίσσω, and not, like Diomedes, only a little—τυτθὸν ὀπίσσω), but it did not appease the wrath of Apollo. Diomedes did not die, although he had assaulted the god; for the listener, this is related to his loyalty and obedience to the king and gods. Patroklos died, despite his great deeds and despite backing off in fear of Apollo. Diomedes' conflict with Apollo is an anticipation of the triple attack by Patroklos, whom Apollo pushes back from the walls of Troy. In both cases, the god's cry checks the hero's fourth attempt, but Patroklos reacts differently than Diomedes—he withdraws in fear. The similarity of those scenes, even if given a different ending, is striking. The parallel in itself does not contribute anything to the content of the *Iliad*. If someone, following the deeds of Patroklos, remembers the scene from Diomedes' *aristeia*, the comparison does not bring him any profit: the god's behavior is very ambiguous and there is no clear contrast between the heroes.

The listener does not compare the encounters of both Patroklos and Diomedes with Apollo, because he has no time for that. In both cases, he compares the current situation with that which he knows from the tradition represented by the *Aethiopis* (which depicted the death of Achilles). In the Trojan Cycle, this hero had to be the main victim of Apollo's wrath, so it is not surprising that the dominant theme in the *Iliad* is the complementary wrath of the hero Achilles and the god Apollo. The terrible consequences of their wrath are foretold in the beginning of Book 1. Both scenes of Diomedes' and Patroklos's struggle with Apollo are, then, a prelude to the final encounter of the hero and the god. The poet gradually increases the suspense created by the analogies with the familiar scene of the encounter between Achilles and Apollo. At first, the listener's anxiety is short-lived, and the peaceful ending of the conflict illustrates the difference in Diomedes' and Achilles' characters and conduct. Next time, the listener's fear for Patroklos is linked to the feeling of the imminence of Achilles' death. The dread, which in Diomedes' story seemed distant, in Patroklos's story is close at hand, especially as the continuation of this scene ends in the hero's death.

Here again there is a repetition of Patroklos's triple attack. The fourth attack is stopped by Apollo's intervention, which brings about Patroklos's death (16.784–787):

> τρὶς μὲν ἔπειτ' ἐπόρουσε θοῷ ἀτάλαντος Ἄρηϊ
> σμερδαλέα ἰάχων, τρὶς δ' ἐννέα φῶτας ἔπεφνεν.
> ἀλλ' ὅτε δὴ τὸ τέταρτον ἐπέσσυτο δαιμονι ἶσος,
> ἔνθ' ἄρα τοι Πάτροκλε φάνη βιότοιο τελευτή.

> Three times he sprang forward swiftly like Ares
> with a terrible war-cry, three times did he kill nine men.

> But when he rushed forward for the fourth time like a god,
> then for you, Patroklos, the end of your life drew near.

Both scenes where Diomedes and Patroklos confront Apollo allude to the same situation and the listener recalls Achilles' death. His sadness at the death of Patroklos is increased by the awareness that Achilles will meet his fate in the same way. Possible doubts whether a triple attack upon Apollo constitute a recognizable reference to the last fight of Achilles should be dispelled by the fact that the *Iliad* uses the same set of formulae in the first duel between Achilles and Hektor (20.445–447):

> τρὶς μὲν ἔπειτ' ἐπόρουσε ποδάρκης δῖος Ἀχιλλεὺς
> ἔγχεϊ χαλκείῳ, τρὶς δ' ἠέρα τύψε βαθεῖαν.
> ἀλλ' ὅτε δὴ τὸ τέταρτον ἐπέσσυτο δαιμονι ἶσος
>
> Three times swift-footed divine Achilles sprang forward
> with a spear of bronze, three times did he pierce thick mist.
> But when he rushed forward for the fourth time like a god

There is a series of three scenes, which do not so much foreshadow the death of Achilles as, because of their construction, remind the listener of it. They use the same principle of gradation. The first time, the protagonist of the scene comes out unscathed, but the next time he is killed. When for the third time, the protagonist is Achilles himself, he can come out unharmed, because the author of the *Iliad* does not intend to show his death. There are only three cases of scenes with such a construction; they clearly do not echo one another, but all refer to the priority scene. First the role of Achilles is played by his rival Diomedes, then by his friend Patroklos, who makes himself in his image by donning his armor.

The last scene, in which Achilles himself makes an appearance, is also the second link in the chain of three scenes of the conflict between Achilles and Hektor. From our point of view, the poet seems either to get lost in his allusions or to turn away from them in order to freely model his material on various patterns. However, the overlapping of arrangements of scenes does not obfuscate the picture, which remains clear. The singer, composing these scenes, combines elements of several variants, but leaves unmistakable signals to scenes from outside his song to stimulate the feeling of dread in his listeners.

After the scene of Hektor's duel with Diomedes, presented similarly to his first duel with Achilles, the action takes a strange turn. Diomedes, in keeping with what he has shouted to Hektor as he escapes (just like Achilles in his scene), gets to work murdering other Trojans. He kills Agastrophos, son of Paion (11.338–342), then smites Hektor on the helmet, thus eliminating from combat the hero who was called the scourge (*pêma*) of the Achaeans, and at this very moment Diomedes is struck by Paris's arrow (11.369–379):

> αὐτὰρ Ἀλέξανδρος Ἑλένης πόσις ἠϋκόμοιο
> Τυδεΐδῃ ἔπι τόξα τιταίνετο ποιμένι λαῶν,
> στήλῃ κεκλιμένος ἀνδροκμήτῳ ἐπὶ τύμβῳ
> Ἴλου Δαρδανίδαο, παλαιοῦ δημογέροντος.
> ἤτοι ὃ μὲν θώρηκα Ἀγαστρόφου ἰφθίμοιο
> αἴνυτ' ἀπὸ στήθεσφι παναίολον ἀσπίδα τ' ὤμων
> καὶ κόρυθα βριαρήν· ὃ δὲ τόξου πῆξυν ἄνελκε
> καὶ βάλεν, οὐδ' ἄρα μιν ἅλιον βέλος ἔκφυγε χειρός,
> ταρσὸν δεξιτεροῖο ποδός· διὰ δ' ἀμπερὲς ἰὸς
> ἐν γαίῃ κατέπηκτο· ὃ δὲ μάλα ἡδὺ γελάσσας
> ἐκ λόχου ἀμπήδησε καὶ εὐχόμενος ἔπος ηὔδα·
>
> But Alexander, the husband of Helen of beautiful hair,
> flexed his bow [aiming] at Tydeus's son, the leader of warriors,
> leaning against a stele on the barrow made by the men of old
> for Ilos, son of Dardanos, a ruler of the people in ancient days.
> This one [Diomedes] was busy stripping mighty Agastrophos of his breastplate,
> his shiny shield from his shoulders
> and a heavy helmet; the other one [Alexander] threw a missile from his hand, and not in vain,
> striking him on the flat of his right foot; the arrow pierced it
> and fixed itself in the ground, and he [Paris] rejoicing,
> sprang from his shelter and gloated.

Paris's arrow wounds Diomedes in the foot, which seems a clear reference to Achilles' death.[114] It is highly probable that other details also allude to this event, e.g. shooting at Diomedes from behind cover. Thanks to *anamnêsis*, the singer is able to evoke feelings of dread and anxiety for the hero's life. And right away, as he does in so many other places, the singer reduces the dread, endowing all traditional elements of this scene with his individual interpretation. Paris could also have gloated when he hit Achilles in the priority scene, but now he regrets not having hit Diomedes in his side, which was protected by a shield (11.381).[115]

[114] This opinion is shared by von der Mühll 1952:195–196; Erbse 1961:175–176; Kakridis 1961:293; Fenik 1968:94–95; Heubeck 1974:46; Burgess 1995:239–240; Nickel 2002:224–225.

[115] This is where Homeric warriors are often mortally wounded. It was so because of the shape of the shield, which was stretched and fixed to a frame at the top and bottom, and as a result the middle section was slightly narrower. A warrior, moving to the right or left, protected his body

So he himself admits his attack has been unsuccessful. In his speech, Paris also compares the Trojans' fear of Diomedes to goats' fear of a lion (11.383). As we have already noticed in Chapter 2, Achilles is the hero typically identified with the lion, so Diomedes, as a lion, plays his role.

Diomedes responds with contempt, describing Paris's deed as unmanly because he used a bow and shot from behind cover (so Homer sees such acts as blamable for a hero). He also mentions that the wound is not serious, nothing more than a scratch. In the same speech, Diomedes foretells Paris's death, and his words are characteristic (11.390–392):

> "κωφὸν γὰρ βέλος ἀνδρὸς ἀνάλκιδος οὐτιδανοῖο.
> ἦ τ' ἄλλως ὑπ' ἐμεῖο, καὶ εἴ κ' ὀλίγον περ ἐπαύρῃ,
> ὀξὺ βέλος πέλεται, καὶ ἀκήριον αἶψα τίθησι."
>
> "The missile of a man without strength, a non-entity.
> It won't be so when it is [thrown] from my [hand]; even if it just
> grazes you,
> the missile will be sharp and quick to kill."

Diomedes makes an explicit allusion to the irrational death of Achilles. In normal circumstances, such a small wound in the foot would not be lethal. Homer rationalizes the story and endows it with an ethical dimension, openly criticizing Alexander for what was, in his opinion, an act of cowardice.

According to Neoanalysis, this scene is a copy of Achilles' death. However, at most it is a variant, not a copy, because it lacks Apollo's support for Paris[116] and the wound is not really harmful, its only effect being Diomedes' withdrawal from combat. Nevertheless, it does successfully eliminate the hero from the battlefield. Like in the scenes relating to the heroic self-sacrifice of Antilochos (8.80–171, 16.317–329, 16.420–503), the first time the correspondence is more pronounced: the greatest number of details are used in the first reference to the priority scene. Both in the case of Nestor's rescue and Achilles' death, quite a lot of details are necessary, because the protagonists of those priority scenes, Antilochos and Achilles, are replaced by Diomedes. To notice the substitution,

with a shield, but, when he protected one side, the other was open to attack. If he was not quick enough, it was easy to hit him.

116 Perhaps, however, the role of Apollo in this encounter is alluded to by the patronymic of the Trojan warrior killed a moment earlier by Diomedes: Paionides (also 11.339 and 368). Its sound may be associated with the cult epithet of Apollo the 'healer'—Paion. Here Diomedes would remove the god from this incident, which would match the meaning of the scene, eliminating the deadly effectiveness of Paris's arrow shot. It would not be so much a suggestion that Diomedes eliminates/kills the god, but that without divine support Paris is not a threat to the Achaean hero.

the listener needs more details which will direct him to the appropriate priority scenes. When the proper heroes appear, i.e. Antilochos and Achilles, the author of the *Iliad* does not present priority scenes, but their variants. Moreover, the course of action takes a different turn than the listener expects: Antilochos is rescued by his brother and Hektor escapes Achilles. Only the third recurrence of the scene ends in the way that the story pattern requires.[117]

The scene in which Diomedes "experiences" Achilles' death is the first reference to the traditional image of the death of Achilles. The same image is evoked again by the scene of the death of Patroklos. Both heroes (Patroklos in the *Iliad* and Achilles in tradition) are killed when they chase Trojans who are running away in panic. Both die in the same place: at the Scaean Gate. For the depiction of this event the singer uses elements which were omitted in the scene of Diomedes' wounding. Apollo actively participates in inflicting death. This scene is preceded by showing Patroklos at the peak of his accomplishments, when he attacks the Trojans three times, each time killing nine men. The audience listens with dread, remembering his recent triple assault of Apollo. Now, when for the fourth time Patroklos launches an attack, the god does not warn him but acts (16.787–793):

> ἔνθ' ἄρα τοι Πάτροκλε φάνη βιότοιο τελευτή·
> ἤντετο γάρ τοι Φοῖβος ἐνὶ κρατερῇ ὑσμίνῃ
> δεινός· ὃ μὲν τὸν ἰόντα κατὰ κλόνον οὐκ ἐνόησεν,
> ἠέρι γὰρ πολλῇ κεκαλυμμένος ἀντεβόλησε·
> στῆ δ' ὄπιθεν, πλῆξεν δὲ μετάφρενον εὐρέε τ' ὤμω
> χειρὶ καταπρηνεῖ, στρεφεδίνηθεν δέ οἱ ὄσσε.
> Τοῦ δ' ἀπὸ μὲν κρατὸς κυνέην βάλε Φοῖβος Ἀπόλλων

> then for you, Patroklos, the end of your life drew near
> as in the midst of a fierce struggle Phoibos,
> the terrible, met you, and this one [Patroklos] in the turmoil of the battle did not recognize him
> because he advanced enfolded in thick mist;
> he stood behind [Patroklos] and struck him between the shoulder blades

117 Erbse (1961:175–176) and (to a lesser degree) Fenik (1968:94–95, 234) call into question this reference, indicating that Diomedes was also wounded earlier, by Pandaros's arrow (5.95–100). So, they claim, this one is only a type-scene. I think that in the pattern of the scene sequence, in which the danger is warded off the first time, but the next one ends badly for the character, Diomedes' earlier injury, which was not serious, must have affected the expectations of his later injury in Book 11. This time the fight ends badly for the hero, though it is not his death but only a substitute of death (i.e. withdrawal from fighting), and so the scene is only a link in the chain of events relating to Achilles' death.

with the flat of his hand, and Patroklos's eyes whirled.
Phoibos Apollo knocked a helmet from his head

Then other parts of the armor fall to the ground, and finally Euphorbos sneaks from behind and smites the armorless and dazed hero between the shoulders, in the same place where Apollo has struck him (16.806–808). Euphorbos withdraws into the Trojan ranks. Only then does Hektor throw his spear and hit Patroklos in the side (16.818–821). Patroklos collapses onto the ground, but before he dies, he foretells Hektor's death (16.844–857).

The death of Patroklos is, then, the finale of three sequences: one built around the "rescue of Nestor," the sequence with Hektor's duel and his triple charge at Apollo,[118] and the sequence leading to the death of Achilles. It is the culmination of the tragedy and suspense which have been built on reminders of and allusions to facts which the listener knows.[119] The singer constantly deceives his audience: he suggests a scenario which does not happen, and the situation finds another solution. However, he regularly, in various ways, comes back to the motif uppermost in their minds. And yet what he presents is not really the essence of his poem. In other words, the key scene of the poem, the death of Patroklos, is not the essence of the message. Allusions to scenes known from tradition allow the poet to play with dread and relief in earlier scenes and also, equally important, to prepare for the dramatic suspense of the climax.

In the *Patrokleis*, the triple assault on Apollo creates a menacing situation, but the hero's withdrawal brings relief—only momentary, as it turns out. Having decided to show the scene of his death, the poet again evokes dread, using the motif of a triple attack. Now, without unnecessary retardation, he goes on to the description of death. The reference to Achilles' death does not

118 This sequence finds its continuation in the two duels between Achilles and Hektor.

119 Renehan (1987:109) believes that the death of Patroklos cannot be regarded as fully heroic because the mortally wounded hero tries to escape. Kyriakou (2001:257) notices, however, that his retreat is a consequence of his dizziness caused by Apollo's blow (16.788–815). Kyriakou's idea could be developed further. Contrary to Renehan's view, Patroklos's death contains elements of heroism, which is indicated by the sequence of the preceding events: 1) military successes of the hero, both in terms of quantity (3 × 9 enemies killed) and quality (as a result of a blow Kebriones' eyes fall out of his head); 2) a "treacherous" attack by Euphorbos, from the back; 3) the mortal wound was inflicted in the stomach, and not in the back, as it would have been if Patroklos had been running away. Patroklos's withdrawal after Euphorbos's spear stroke, a direct outcome of Apollo's intervention, repeats the motif of his stepping back from Apollo at the walls of Troy (16.710–711). The aim here is not to show a lack of heroism in Patroklos's death, but to highlight a sharp contrast between human potential and the power of the deity: Apollo strikes Patroklos with an open hand (Janko 1992:412: "with the flat of the hand"), which in my opinion means that the hand is not squeezed into a fist, as would be natural in combat, and that the god does not have any weapon. The same formula is applied to illustrate the ease with which Poseidon undermines human actions when he stops the Phaeacian ship (*Odyssey* 13.164).

serve the purpose of increasing the atmosphere of dread, nor does it testify to the poet's inability to find an original denouement. The allusions to the tradition of Achilles' death enable the identification of Patroklos with his friend, who sends him to battle. The audience listens to the story of Patroklos's death, but they can imagine Achilles' death, or rather they are aware that this kind of death awaits the protagonist, who at the moment is absent from the story. The poet never intended to show his death, not because he wanted to avoid such a sad subject, because he constantly touches it. Already in Chapter 1, the death of Achilles was defined as a point towards which the action of the song moves without ever achieving it. Now it is possible to explain the design of the poet. In the course of narration, this scene is evoked many times under many guises, but it is fully experienced only as the death of Patroklos, who functions as the second Achilles.

In the ring composition of the work, the death of Patroklos falls on the middle of the third day of the battle. It is also the ninth day of the real action of the *Iliad* and the twenty-fifth day of all those mentioned in the epic (See Chapter 1). If the expected end of the song (the day of Achilles' death after the return to battle following Hektor's funeral) falls, respectively, on the seventeenth day according to the first numbering (real action) and the fiftieth according to the second (number of days mentioned), then the moment of Patroklos's death marks precisely the middle of the whole narrative. Wilamowitz, respecting the principles of a literary work of art, assumed that the *Iliad* in its original form must have ended in the description of the protagonist's death, the death foretold so many times.[120] However, a work of oral literature like the *Iliad* is governed by different rules of construction: *that which is the most important is in the middle*. Naturally, it could not be done by placing the death of the protagonist in the middle of the song, and that is why instead of his death, the poem presents the death of his doublet. In ring composition, the action describes a circle and as it nears the end, it refers in reverse order to the events from the beginning, at the same time inverting the meanings. The middle point, which is Patroklos's death, is the climax of the story, and at the same time it foreshadows, and in a way also makes real the events which are beyond the narration of the song.[121]

[120] Wilamowitz 1916:77–79, 513.

[121] An analogous situation is described by Thalmann (1984:13–14) in his analysis of the ring construction of *Theogony* 137–158. After the birth of Kronos, there is a digression about the Kyklopes and Hecatoncheires. It is an important signal of future events, i.e. the overthrow of Kronos by Zeus, who secured their help in this undertaking, and the clearest allusion to this event can be found in the very middle of this passage (v. 141). "Hesiod thus hints at the real significance of Kronos's overthrow of Ouranos by letting us glimpse the ultimate consequences of that act—not merely Kronos's own punishment, but what is far more important, the ultimate supremacy of Zeus." Thalmann (17–18) finds a similar situation in another passage with ring composition,

The idea that the scene of Achilles' death was the pattern for Patroklos's death has raised many objections—mainly because of numerous additional elements which do not have a counterpart in the reconstructed scene in the *Aethiopis* (especially the role of Euphorbos). The opponents conclude that it was a free composition of a new scene built with traditional elements. But I would suggest we look at Euphorbos's role and other puzzling elements from another point of view. The poet tries to evoke in his listeners the memory of scenes known from tradition, but each time he attempts to depart from the prototypes. In the scenes which are the most faithful to the original, he uses different characters; where the characters are the same, the scenes are less faithful. In the most important scene, the identification of Patroklos with Achilles is the most powerful; nonetheless, the poet tries to make Patroklos different, though not radically different than his model. The allusion cannot be too obvious. Patroklos is not only a copy of Achilles; he is also an individual character in his own right. The changes in the structure of the scene show his independence, which the poet stresses as soon as the hero enters the scene as the second Achilles. When Patroklos appears in the latter's armor on the battlefield, his disguise fails. At first, the Trojans seem to labor under the delusion that he is Achilles (16.280–282), but Glaukos, answering Sarpedon's question about the identity of the warrior (423–425), discloses his knowledge that it is really Patroklos (543).[122]

In order to show my standpoint more clearly, I will present in more detail my interpretation of the scene of Patroklos's death. Until recently, the most popular proposition was the purely Neoanalytic one put forward by Mühlestein, according to which Euphorbos, a seemingly redundant character, was introduced

this time from the *Iliad*. Lines 16.364–393 describe Patroklos's attack, the crossing of a trench by his chariot, and the chariots of Hektor and other Trojans as they retreat. In the very middle of this construction (16.373–376), we are told where this is all heading: to the dispersal of the Trojans and their tumultuous flight back to the city. Another, but of much greater significance, analogy to placing the death of the hero in the middle of the described events may be the fact that Odysseus's visit to the Underworld takes the central position among the events told by the hero to the Phaecians (7th out of 13); it is unique and has no counterpart, while all the others are arranged in doublets (see Scully 1987:403–404); not according to the principle of ring composition, however, but by repeating an analogous series of events with clearly marked opposites. Thus, the hero's "journey" is doubled, but, as Scully (1987:413–415) observes, Odysseus is now a different man: aware of the purpose of his journey, using the experience he has acquired, determined, responsible for others and generally someone who (p. 415): "has gained a knowledge both of his own humanity and of the nature of man."

122 Janko (1992:310–311) claims "the earlier songs probably used the theme of armor as disguise, protecting its wearer by scaring the enemy, as Nestor proposes to Patroklos. But this idea is not developed." There were important reasons for that: it would be against the heroic ethos, because the warrior's glory depends on his being recognized; moreover, it would be to Hektor's discredit if he killed Patroklos under the impression that he was killing Achilles.

as a doublet for Paris.[123] This scene, then, would be a twofold imitation: of the scene of Achilles' death, when Euphorbos strikes Patroklos, and that of Antilochos's death, when Hektor deals the blow (in the *Aethiopis*, Antilochos's death was the cause of the main event, the death of Achilles). Patroklos, then, appears in a twin role as both Achilles and Antilochos. The weakness of this concept is not only that one character would appear in two roles, but also that in the second case, the imitation would refer to a less significant scene, since it is Hektor who deals the mortal blow. In favor of this concept is the parallel between the images of Euphorbos and Paris. Euphorbos is shown as a man who excels all Trojans in casting the spear, in horsemanship, and in speed of foot (16.806–815). In Mühlestein's opinion, this description hints at Paris's defeat of his brothers at the games when he returns incognito from his exile on Mount Ida. Euphorbos's name, which according to the scholar means "rich in pasture,"[124] also would be a reference to Paris's young years spent as a shepherd. Moreover, Euphorbos dies by the hand of Menelaos, i.e. Paris's rival. In the scene of his death, Homer stresses the beauty of his hair, now stained with blood (17.50–52). The tenuous nature of this popular thesis has been demonstrated by Nickel. He points out that Euphorbos does not correspond very well to Paris: his weapon is a spear, not a bow; he is not presented as Aphrodite's favorite; the allusion to Paris's victory in funeral games is also very thin.[125] Nickel proposes a different, at first sight fanciful reading of this character—namely, that Euphorbos represents

[123] Mühlestein 1972. Other scholars supporting his view include Van Thiel 1982:416; Burkert 1987:47; Edwards 1991:18; Janko 1992:410, 414; Baldick 1994:81; Dowden 1996:47–61; Scodel 2002:96; West 2003b:5.

[124] This opinion is supposedly backed by the derivation of the names 1) of Patroklos's father, Menoitios, from οἶτον ἔμενε 'the one who waits for death', and 2) of Patroklos, from πατρὸς ἔκλυε 'the one who has heard his father'—in both cases as references to Antilochos, who having heard his father calling, provokes death by shielding him with his own body. The arbitrariness of these etymologies is obvious; compare Kelly 2006:7–8. As far as Patroklos is concerned, Nagy's etymology 'the one who has the glory of the ancestors', mentioned in the previous chapter, is much better substantiated (Nagy 1999:111–115).

[125] Nickel (2002:218–221) underscores the argument that the sources for the image of the shepherd Paris and related events, i.e. Hekabe's dream, the abandonment of Paris, his life as shepherd, and the defeat of his brothers in funeral games commemorating him, are late (the earliest ones date to the fifth century BCE) and therefore untrustworthy, since they may be a post-Homeric elaboration. The same argument is put forward by Kelly (2006) and approved by Allan (2005). However, in my opinion, this argument is given too much weight and treated as a proof. It is known that tragedians drew on topics from cyclic poems. No mention about Paris's youth in the summary of the *Kypria* is easily explainable. Pieces of information about his young days could have appeared in other songs of the Trojan Cycle in the form of digressions and not necessarily as episodes. In Proclus's summary of the *Kypria*, there would be no place for such a trifle. After the wedding of Peleus and Thetis, there must be a scene of Paris's judgment. Who he is and how he happened to be there could have been mentioned only parenthetically.

Achilles.[126] Euphorbos not only fulfills the prediction of Achilles' death, but he also imitates the manner in which it happens—Achilles chooses to die by deliberately entering a course of events marked by fate. Nickel notices an interesting parallel in the scene of Achilles' taking aim with his spear at Hektor wearing his, i.e. Achilles', armor—here Achilles in a way kills himself, since he is aware of the inevitable consequence of this deed, his own imminent death.[127] A very similar situation arises when Euphorbos strikes Patroklos, who has been disarmed by Apollo. Euphorbos's characterization also matches Achilles' model better.

Allan also opposes the identification of Euphorbos and Paris. He points out that by accentuating Achilles' quasi-suicide we run the risk of ignoring Patroklos's responsibility for his own death, which he brought upon himself by his disobedience of Achilles' orders when he chased the enemy to the walls of Troy (16.684–687).[128] In Allan's opinion, the importance of Euphorbos lies in questioning Hektor's military wisdom (so he functions like his admonishing adviser Poulydamas). Because of Euphorbos, Hektor is portrayed not as Patroklos's killer, but as someone who stripped him of Achilles' divine armor. His action gains the disapproval of Zeus, since he obtained it οὐ κατὰ κόσμον 'in an inappropriate way', because Patroklos was not its rightful owner.[129] Hektor appropriates something he does not deserve. Homer seems to suggest that Hektor's death is his own fault. His fault is not the killing of Patroklos, but taking Achilles' armor. According to Allan, each character in this scene plays his own important role in the narrative; Euphorbos absolutely cannot be classified as redundant. To treat him as a doublet of another character is to neglect his particular meaning and role.[130]

The differences between Patroklos's death in the *Iliad* and what we know about Achilles' death indicate that the former does not imitate the latter but it is a freely created scene, in which some common elements are used in order to create a parallel situation.[131] There are two significant differences: Patroklos is killed with a spear (whereas Achilles is killed with an arrow, or arrows,

126 Another doublet for Achilles is also, according to Rabel (1990b), one of the minor Trojan warriors, Hippothoos (17.288–303). Nickel (2002:225–228) accepts this proposition and adds one more doublet for Achilles—Euchenor, killed by Paris (13.663–670). However, this concept meets with Allan's criticism): "The argument is certainly neat, but it seems to me that the parallels between Euphorbos and Achilles are exaggerated and that the persistent interpretation of the scene in terms of doublets obscures the agency and motivation of the character involved" (2005:3).

127 Nickel 2002:230–231.

128 Allan 2005:4.

129 Allan 2005:8.

130 Allan 2005:12.

131 Allan 2005:16: "The poet has constructed a powerful and uncanny end of Patroclus, and has done so using a unique combination of typical elements."

from Paris's bow), and immediately before Hektor's mortal blow, Patroklos is wounded by Euphorbos. Allan does not rule out the possibility that Homer might have copied another scene or alluded to it, "encouraging an audience to think of those future events," but he thinks it unlikely.[132]

If we take into account the model of scene sequences, we draw different conclusions than these scholars. All these scenes are not just incidental variations of a traditional scene, but are linked by the necessity of going beyond the plot of the song. In the *Aethiopis*, priority scenes of the self-sacrifice of Antilochos, who is saving his father, and the death of Achilles after killing Memnon, are in a logical cause-and-effect relationship (a highly probable motive of revenge); in the *Iliad*, the references to these scenes preserve this logical relationship. What is important in the use the author of the *Iliad* makes of them is not that they are a matrix, which can be reproduced in the creation of new scenes, but that the poet deliberately avoids or stresses similarities, drawing his listeners into an intriguing game based on a constant seesaw of emotions. Because the singer cannot be sure of the listeners' undivided attention, he must constantly stimulate their interest. Such an approach to priority scenes makes it possible to use them over and over; any element of these scenes can be used to create an atmosphere of dread. But it also means that, in the Homeric text, priority scenes undergo fragmentation. Often one of their elements is considered sufficient on its own to achieve its effect in the singer's performative strategy. What we are dealing with is only references to priority scenes fixed in tradition, and not their duplication. Effectiveness is of crucial importance here, which is why the number of elements of the priority scene used in a new one is variable: usually, the first time, the singer needs to use a greater number of elements in order to make the suggestion clear, whereas later fewer elements may be enough to achieve the same effect.

This system has not been recognized because literary studies do not take into account the phenomenon of substitution. Substitution has been deeply rooted in human culture since the very beginning and has largely determined its character. It is recognized as a fundamental factor in the formation of human culture by anthropology, ethnology, and religious studies. Ironically, it is sadly underappreciated by literary studies, whereas I believe that it is a key to the understanding of oral culture. Even if Homeric scholars notice one character playing the role of another, regardless of the action of the story, they rarely, if ever, try to find out the aim of this device. If we do not understand the overall purpose of substitution, it does not matter if in a particular instance it strikes us as meaningful or not, because the question is: what is its point at all? The

132 Allan 2005:13–15.

issue of substitution is very complex, but in the field that really interests us, we can say that it is an attempt at reconciling the conflicting expectations of the listeners, who want a reenactment of the heroic myth, but also want to satisfy their curiosity and to get new information about events and heroes.

The significance of a story is not limited to knowledge of its content, but lies in the emotional experience. Substitution allows the listeners to experience the same traditional message in a new, intriguing set of events and a new configuration of characters. Just as one sacrifice (e.g. of an animal) can be substituted for another (e.g. human), so does the Homeric story of Diomedes or Patroklos go beyond the presentation of the achievements of these heroes at a given moment.[133] The *aristeias* of Diomedes and Patroklos are replicas of the pattern of Achilles' *aristeia*. They lead to the representation of the death of the hero, crucial for the mythic story, and each of these *aristeias* gives the listeners the emotional experience of the hero's death. It is neither an abstract image of the death of a hero, any hero, nor a specific image showing this hero dying in this way and another hero dying in another, as we might be inclined to think. In an oral story, some basic elements should be included so that the substitution can be recognized. However, Homer does not conduct his narration in such a way that one can get to know various fates of the warriors at Troy: the recurrence of themes[134] would entail a plot, in which Diomedes managed to survive and Patroklos did not. By introducing these characters, Homer makes the listener think about them as doublets for Achilles.[135] One could say that every step they take brings them closer to Achilles' death. The element of the traditional image (i.e. of the priority scene) chosen for the creation of tension in one scene returns in later scenes, usually with a different cast of characters. Each time, however, these actualizations are arranged in recognizable three-element sequences. It is possible for successive elements of various priority scenes to overlap, and we may get the impression of a double substitution of characters. It is quite possible that in one scene there may appear references to two priority scenes.

Such linking of elements of various priority scenes can be also found in Hektor's defeat by Diomedes and then Diomedes' wounding by Paris (11.310–367,

[133] Let us note that in the *Iliad* there are no references to the achievements of these two heroes in the earlier stages of the Trojan War, which many seem strange. In my understanding, it confirms the fact that in this song they function only as substitutes for Achilles, and so their epic biographies were shortened to the "here and now" of the action in the *Iliad*.

[134] Foley and Arft 2015:83–84.

[135] Kelly (2008:191–193) argues that the false tales of Odysseus in the *Odyssey* indicate the facility of creating stories based on similar themes. Their use of a "Cretan identity" linked to the events of the Trojan War, however, indicates the easiness of substituting the "right" hero by new characters, "plausible" to the tradition, although, let us note, the substitution does not confuse the external audience who recognize the falsity of these stories.

368–400), which refer to Achilles' struggle with Memnon and his death at the hands of Paris and Apollo.[136] In effect, we get a sort of summary of events respecting the logical sequence of priority scenes: Achilles defeats Memnon and then dies himself. But we must remember that the fate of the substitute affects the emotional reception of the later scenes with Achilles.

When in the analogous scene of the first duel between Achilles and Hektor (20.419–454), Achilles wins, the listeners could have feared that now the hero would suffer the calamity which Diomedes managed to avoid. Their fear would be justified because the danger once avoided strikes a second time. Yet it does not happen because, despite similarities, both scenes depart from their model in one important respect: the Trojan leader is not killed. Finally, when Hektor meets a tragic end, it would be natural to expect that Achilles will be the next one to die. But the listener is no longer anxious for Achilles, because, though his fate is sealed, it is delayed by his withdrawal from the battlefield with his enemy's body.

I believe that the differences in the presentation of Achilles' and Patroklos's deaths are explicable and do not interfere with the idea of Homer's deliberate references to the traditional scene. Naturally, by "references" I do not mean a literary imitation, but reliance on the listener's familiarity with this image in the creation of suspense. Making references to images known from tradition is not accidental or random; on the contrary, they appear in coordinated sequences of scenes, which are variations of the same pattern(s). The order of variations is also regular: first come elaborated scenes, which are closer to their prototypes, but do not imply their tragic consequences, while the last scenes in the sequence have only one or two points of similarity to the prototypes, but these references are essential for re-enacting the heroic myth. The first one to appear in the sequence is always the scene where the hero avoids the danger.

136 Burgess (1995:239–240) argues that the wounding of Diomedes' foot cannot refer to Achilles' "imperfect invulnerability" but rather to the immobilization of "swift-footed" Achilles with an arrow, which made him an easy target for another blow (Burgess suggests another arrow from Paris's bow). This concept does not, however, undermine the scholar's belief that the scene of Patroklos's death reflects that of Achilles. For more extensive criticism of Burgess's standpoint, see Ch. 3, p. 299–303, above. Compare Christensen (2015:37): "The contextual demands of the performance of the *Iliad*—one in which audience and poet alike were engaged in the creation of songs built against and rivaling earlier songs and competing traditions—prompted a playful appropriation of, and perhaps a critical reception of, its own mythopoetic inheritance. In short, as part of the aesthetics of composition in performance, elements like the foot wound may have received critical attention from the performer as a part of his and his audiences' reaction to an archaic symbol embedded in myth, an attempt to analyze and assimilate elements that were no longer harmonious with their views on the world. In addition, as a feature of competition with contemporaneous oral traditions, Homeric poetry actively forcefully appropriates and manipulates vital scenes to assert its own dominance."

This is possible because allusions to priority scenes produce dread. A dialogue with tradition gives the singer the opportunity to surprise the audience. The links between the scenes of Sarpedon's, Patroklos's, and Hektor's deaths were noticed also by Thalmann, in whose opinion the repetition of the pattern of the hero's death would have suggested to the audience the death of Achilles.[137]

The singer chooses certain elements of tradition to suggest analogies to a familiar image, and at the same time he uses other elements of tradition to make his scene unique and to stress differences between his scene and those which the listeners remember from other poems. This technique of using references requires the existence of a recognizable image of Achilles' death in the minds of the singer and his audience. Since the scenes constructed by Homer based on the priority scene differ significantly from one another, there arises the question of what the priority scene was like.

The discrepancies between the images of Achilles' death (even if some of them are considered to be later versions, e.g. his death in the sanctuary of Apollo Thymbraios) prove that even in the post-Homeric period there was not only one, fixed image of the death of this hero. Homer tries to evoke this image in the memory of his audience, though it is not certain if this model had ever been applied to the death of Achilles.[138] The version presented in the *Iliad* cannot be treated as a poetic invention since its structure indicates that it belongs to tradition. An analogy to Patroklos's death can be found in Siegfried's death in *The Song of the Nibelungs*, which points to the Indo-European provenance of this motif.[139]

Most probably, there were several versions of the death of Achilles, just as—according to many scholars, e.g. Rengakos—there were several versions of Odysseus's return, the evidence of which Rengakos finds in the *Odyssey*. Achilles' invulnerable armor and his imperfect invulnerability are two equally traditional motifs. The death of Patroklos includes references to both. The first reference is his being disarmed by Apollo, the second his being wounded between the

137 Thalmann 1984:45–49: "This fate looms over the final third of the *Iliad* not only because of explicit prophesies and symbolic anticipation but also by virtue of the pattern of the action. There is good reason to believe that the significant deaths that form a sequence through the later books, by the motifs they express and the circumstances that surround them, would have evoked in the listeners' minds Achilles' own death as they had heard it told in other poems, just as narrative patterns elsewhere in the *Iliad* allude to events of the Trojan story that precede and follow those that form its plot" (49).

138 In the same scene, we come across another echo of Indo-European epic. Singor (1991:45) finds a parallel to 16.785–786 in a Celtic epic: "It is CúChulainn who regularly slays his enemies in groups of three times nine together—one is reminded of Patroclus 'three times hurling himself forward and three times slaying nine men'."

139 Janko 1992:310–312, 409–414.

shoulders by Euphorbos (as in the death of the invulnerable Siegfried, who was wounded in this spot).[140]

The references to both versions are a result of the overlapping of tendencies in the telling of epic stories, which must have occurred, considering the masses of stories told at pan-Aeolian and pan-Ionian festivals. In Homer, this accumulation of performances results in a certain merging of various versions of the story. On the one hand, in Homer there is a strong tendency to rationalize the course of events. The evidence of this is Diomedes' foot wound, which turns out to be harmless, and also Achilles' fatal wound (21.166–167). On the other hand, from under this world of rational explanations, there gleams the irrationality of fairy-tale epic tradition. This irrational world of tradition is revealed by Diomedes' statement about the quickness of Paris's death even if he is only scratched by Diomedes (11.390–392); the loss of the divine armor by Patroklos; and his wound between the shoulders, which in the case of all other warriors in the *Iliad* is fatal. Rational thinking neutralizes the logic of the magical and the fairy-tale elements, and makes their co-existence possible. The invulnerability of the armor and the body may coexist in the death of Patroklos (Achilles' doublet), because they have been invalidated by Homer's rationalism. The singer does not mention the magical power of Achilles' armor, but he does not ignore it, which is visible in Apollo's act of stripping Patroklos of the armor and in the fact that Hektor, who is wearing it, is killed by Achilles with a spear stroke above the collarbone. Similarly, Homer does not mention Achilles' (and Patroklos's as his substitute) immunity to wounds. He goes even further and negates it, showing the wounding of Achilles. What is more, he stresses the hero's lack of immunity, when Agenor, collecting his courage, comments upon the fact of Achilles' susceptibility to injuries and his mortality (21.568–570): Καὶ γάρ θην τούτῳ τρωτὸς χρὼς ὀξέϊ χαλκῷ, / ἐν δὲ ἴα ψυχή, θνητὸν δέ ἕ φασ' ἄνθρωποι / ἔμμεναι ("He too has skin vulnerable to sharp bronze, / he too has only one soul and people say he is mortal"). As we have seen, the similarity between the deaths of Patroklos and Siegfried is based on the motif of the magical invulnerability. But in his rational approach, Homer also contests this image: Euphorbos's blow is unsuccessful, i.e. it is not mortal. The failure of the blow is not attributed to Patroklos's miraculous immunity to injuries, but explained by its harmlessness: Euphorbos's stroke is only indirectly responsible for Patroklos's death, because Hektor deals the mortal blow.

[140] Siegfried has invulnerable skin except for one spot on his back where he is dealt a treacherous blow by Hagen, which may suggest the possibility of the existence of a similar motif of Patroklos's invulnerable skin in tradition. Euphorbos's blow from the back in a cowardly manner corresponds to Hagen's underhanded method of killing Siegfried: both men act from ambush, both personify cowardice and both strike in the same spot.

Hektor hits Patroklos in the side (16.821–822), in the spot where Paris wishes he had hit Diomedes (11.381). Paris's wounding of Diomedes in the foot with an arrow, a clear evocation of a traditional motif, is as unsuccessful as Euphorbos's blow. Departing from traditional motifs, Homer opts for rational explanations, but rationalization may be purely superficial, because it is absolutely immaterial if a wound in the foot or a stroke with a spear between the shoulder blades may be fatal or not. According to our criteria, Homer seems to overturn tradition, but he does not: he recalls a traditional image in order to create an atmosphere of dread and then replaces it with a new, more rational solution.

Homer does not renounce tradition; quite the opposite, he actively recalls it in images evoking fairy-tale epic solutions and then he counters it with the rationalistic message of his poems. Fairy-tale epic must have been still vivid in the minds of his listeners (which is corroborated by the presence of fairy-tale epic motifs in cyclic poems), though in Homer's time there must have existed a strong tendency to replace elements of the miraculous with rational interpretation. However, no historical epic ever abandoned the miraculous. On the one hand, Homeric poems demonstrate a strong toning down of the irrational. On the other, the irrational must have been so vivid in his listeners' minds that he deliberately uses it in order to counter it with a rational or quasi-rational explanation.

Levels of the reception of the plot

In the course of the story, when selecting variants of traditional scenes and even juxtaposing variants of such scenes, the author of the *Iliad* does not *refer* to tradition, but *moves within it*. He remains within the boundaries of epic tradition, even when he presents solutions which are novel—if we consider the rationalizing tendency to be a novelty. These variants do not mean only the use of traditional patterns, which enable an oral artist to conduct narration. These variants function as allusions to the images contained in tradition, either by bringing the listener closer to or by distancing him from priority scenes, which constitute a message of a higher level. The action that is currently taking place is important and involves the audience emotionally, but still it remains in close contact with the event which is the most important in Trojan history—the death of Achilles. The audience knows what must ultimately happen—that element is traditional.[141] The awareness of the hero's death creates strong suspense: the singer

[141] We can find more examples of such knowledge in other oral cultures. The audience usually knows the plot by heart; sometimes the storyteller makes a radical summary of it, recalling it in the minds of the audience rather than literally recreating it. The Huichol Indians (Myerhoff 1976:18–20) are accustomed to telling their myths in a way that boils down to formulas such as "he went there and did it", wherein "there" and "it" are well-known to everyone. Myerhoff cites

engages his audience in an intensive reception of the story. These casual profits, however, are not the essence of maintaining tradition during performance. They enable the singer to keep listeners' attention from flagging, but the meaning of this strategy is much deeper. Maintaining the link between the current plot and the images rooted in tradition answers the need to convey a myth, i.e. the priority story in the tradition of the Trojan War. To a certain extent, what is narrated in the *Iliad* is an anticipation of future events—the listeners are not allowed to forget where the story is going. What is being told now and what is to come (i.e. what they have heard in the past) are kept in tension with each other. This relationship is so strong that what is being told now is only a *substitute* for what is to come, that is, what is known and expected by the community familiar with its epic tradition.

The action is constantly perceived on two levels: the current plot and the traditional plot, which is seen as a "future" in relation to the events being narrated. The existence of two levels of reception in oral culture should not be surprising—it can be found almost everywhere. I have already mentioned the function of myth and all other kinds of stories in Homeric poems; they all have a double bottom: they seem to say one thing, while in fact they communicate something else. These Homeric tales are used for persuasive purposes and are adapted to the requirements of the moment. We have seen, for example, that in the story of the inappropriate behavior of the centaurs at the wedding of Peirithoos, king of the Lapiths (*Odyssey* 21.295–304), there is a discrepancy between the intentions of the storyteller Antinoos and the completely different meaning of the story suggested to the exterior audience. We can look at this issue in a wider perspective: in oral culture, utterances usually take the form of a riddle. Stories such as fairy tales, parables, and myths are meant to make their recipient aware of something: they warn, encourage, explain, etc.[142] What is important is not familiarizing the recipient with a story, but its paradigmatic use. So, as we can see, in oral culture, the reception of a story on two levels is not unusual. The same can be said about the function of

J. E. Grimes's opinion: "The ordinary style for telling Huichol myths presupposes a good deal of background information on the part of the audience. For example, in one story the characters are not named until about half way through. Furthermore it is not considered necessary to go into detail about all of the actions involved in the story" (19) Myerhoff adds further: "The sensitivity of the Huichol narrator to the understanding of his audience is clearly one criterion of his artistry and success. This sensitivity is exemplified by the marked difference in styles of myths designed to be told for children, who do not command the lore and symbolism familiar to their parents" (19–20).

142 See van Dijk (1997:79–80), where αἶνος is defined as "spoken words with a hidden meaning." For more on using *ainos*, see Alden 2000:30–37.

substitution in the creation of a story. But let's try to find out what it means for Homer's listeners.

I have described the allusions in the *Odyssey* as internal because they aim at preparing for the most important event for Odysseus's return, i.e. the killing of the suitors, which constitutes a part of the poem. External allusions are there to show the value of the hero. Both Telemachos and the listener are gradually prepared for the fact that nobody but Odysseus would be able to perform such an astounding deed as the killing of the suitors. External allusions reach outside the poem, linking it to facts known from tradition, but, more important, they set up the conflict on Ithaca: Helen's story about Odysseus's spying foray (4.240–258) is a parallel to his entering his own palace disguised as a beggar.

At first sight, allusions in the *Iliad* seem to be of a different character, because they all point to an event which is beyond the plot—the death of Achilles. And yet, paradoxically, his death, and all that it leads to, are present in the poem. Homer carefully prepares certain heroes for their role as Achilles' doubles: he makes them experience all that the hero is to experience, but he alters conditions and modifies the sequence of events. The listener does not get a description of Achilles' death in the *Iliad*, but he experiences it when Patroklos dies and earlier, when Diomedes is wounded in the foot in Book 11. The dreadful finale is gradually prepared by various versions of the single story.

According to Neoanalysis, the identification of Achilles and Patroklos is referred to in the scenes of the duels between Patroklos and Sarpedon, and between Achilles and Hektor. The problem with such identifications is, I believe, that when scenes are analyzed in isolation, the conclusions are bound to be faulty. Allan, for example, argues that Patroklos's death represents a quite different variant of a hero's death, with only a few points in common with that of Achilles.[143] Georg Schoeck, in the Neoanalytic vein, points out that all scenes in the *Iliad* follow the same pattern, e.g. Aias always protects retreating warriors with his shield, like in the traditional scene when he defends Achilles' body—the scene, by the way, which is a pattern for the scene of defending Patroklos's body in the *Iliad* (17.102–361, 626–752). But the only explanation that occurs to Schoeck is the secondary nature of Homer, who, in his attempt to create a poem of monumental proportions, expands the plot with all possible variants of one story. Schoeck compares this strategy to the fugue in which the theme is developed through variants. In Schoeck's eyes, the *Iliad* combines virtuosity with the inability to escape a vicious circle of familiar motifs and formulae.[144]

143 Allan 2005.

144 Schoeck 1961:109–120.

The verification of Homer's dependence on other songs is possible only with a larger perspective. The complementary character of the Homeric scenes described above indicates that they cannot be analyzed separately and out of context, because they form dovetailed sequences, in which each scene influences the understanding and reception of the next one. When the author refers to the traditional images of Achilles' death and the circumstances directly leading to it in the presentation of Diomedes' battle struggles, he assumes that he will come back to them many times. Presenting the fate of one hero (Diomedes), he introduces tension that will work also for the other heroes (Patroklos and Achilles). This is why in the first scenes based on a common pattern, the characters always remain unscathed: they either escape death or win, but gradually the tragic epilogue comes closer and closer. For the listeners of the *Iliad*, a happy end to scenes suggesting a misfortune must have been surprising. The optimistic outcome would be remembered and therefore the audience could be surprised again with a tragic end and the death of the hero (e.g. in the case of Patroklos), although such an ending is typical, embedded in tradition.

The composition of the *Iliad* is based on a triple repetition of a story pattern, in which a young hero enters combat and is victorious, but at the peak of his success, he confronts a deity and dies. The last part of this sequence is basic for understanding the meaning of this multiplication. The image alludes to a well-known scene of the death of Achilles, the hero and protagonist of the Trojan War. The audience realizes the threat hanging over Diomedes, and their fear for him gives way to unexpected relief when he manages to squeeze out of a tight corner. When the situation is repeated in Patroklos's encounter with Apollo, the listeners, who remember Diomedes' lucky escape, hope for another miracle, but they are disappointed. This time the character with whom they identify themselves dies. The danger returns for the third time, when Achilles himself enters combat and in a critical moment encounters the same god. It would seem that this event has no consequences—but no, it has, only they are delayed. The listeners know that the hero will die shortly, although his death is not told in this epic. Diomedes' *aristeia* has no consequences; Patroklos's ends in the traditional way, with the death of the hero; Achilles' death is left unsaid. It is not shown directly but it is emotionally experienced by the audience listening to the *Iliad*.

We can see that the composition of the *Iliad* employs the same method of the simple addition of structures which were used, as we have observed, in the *Little Iliad* or *Aethiopis* (see Chapter 2). It consists of a triple repetition of the same pattern—let's call it "the way of the hero." These structures do not even overlap, they just follow one another. The original pattern is, however, repeated each time in a modified form. This is exactly the three-part composition noticeable in the linear arrangement of content. As we can see, it poorly corresponds to Taplin's concept of linking the three-part construction of the song to its performance practice.[145] There is a significant quantitative difference: Patroklos's "way" is definitely shorter than the "ways" of Diomedes and Achilles, but it is there that the story is reflected in full. Its finale, the lofty death of the hero, focuses the attention of the listeners. This is the aim of the entire narrative.

Flexibility and traditionality

Not only is Diomedes' role a kind of jigsaw puzzle of Achilles' life, the *Iliad* as a whole is a great jigsaw puzzle—but well-ordered and logical. The main principle of its organization is the retardation of the main action. Again and again the listener fully experiences the current event, at the same time getting a foretaste of the ending as the poet slowly reveals subsequent pieces of the puzzle. Similarity of events may prompt us to arrange the pieces in two- or three-element sequences, in which each element is repeated in a slightly modified shape.

The question is why and what for? Usually, the similarities have been explained by a (better or worse) imitation of a pattern. In the analysis above, I have shown the reason for this strategy: it allows the poet to carry on a dialogue with the listener. The dialogue fulfills a twofold function. By evoking memories of the key events in the hero's life, the poet introduces alternately the atmosphere of dread and relief; fear for the life of the hero changes into relief, or into sorrow, when he meets a tragic end. The allusive nature of scenes prepares the listeners for the most important point in Achilles' story, i.e. his death, though Homer never intends to depict it in his song. Subsequent returns of this motif allow the listener to experience the events and also those which are certain to happen, but will not be presented in the epic.

[145] The structure of the *Iliad* is quite complex: if we take into account that the starting point of epic narration is a conflict resulting from a crisis and coming to the surface in the scene of an assembly, we note that quarrels in the assembly do not immediately result in the hero's rush to the battlefield to do mighty deeds. Diomedes' part (one of three "thirds" in the tripartite division of the *Iliad*) opens with Achilles' quarrel, and Patroklos's "third" with the scene of the assembly in which Diomedes enters into a quarrel (at the beginning of Book 9). We can also observe the overlapping of subsequent narrative structures of "the hero's way": Diomedes' fate should be fulfilled at the end of his *aristeia*, whereas he is shot in the foot and eliminated from combat in Book 11 (which belongs to Patroklos's "third"). Book 8, which should end the exploits of this hero, includes only a scene in which his life is in danger: the danger to Diomedes' life, and not to Nestor's, is more important in this scene. Only Achilles' "third"—note that it also begins with a delay (after he gets new armor, 19.40–22.400)—seems to be more separate. But here likewise is a modification: despite the crisis caused by the death of the "best of the Myrmidons" (i.e. Patroklos, as Achilles calls him, 18.10), this "third," untypically, does not start in a quarrel, but brings reconciliation.

The success of such a poetic plan depends on two factors: the recipient must be a listener, not a reader, and he must be familiar with the basic myth of Achilles' death. This is the traditional epic song of Achilles' death, which can function in various versions.[146] Despite their variations, the songs in the cycle do not lose sight of the most important facts and meanings; that is why, for example, the heroes, whose later lives are subjects of other songs, cannot die in the *Iliad*. Homer reveals the tragic fate of Achilles slowly, apparently singing about someone else, but the listener compares what he is told with what he knows. The poet alternately engages his hearer in a dramatic account of events, then lets him regain his distance so that he can look at what is happening from the perspective of inside knowledge and judge everything himself. The frequency of leaving the estimation of events to the audience is proof that the work is oral, designed for a live performance before an audience; the singer not only enchants the listener with the vividness of narration, transferring him into another space and time, but also keeps the singer-listener contact alive so that the listener can immediately react to the story. The immediacy of reaction is important: the singer does not intend the listener to turn over the story in his mind before reaching a decision, but to react to the linear presentation. This is what the listeners of oral poetry do; I don't mean that they argue with the singer, but they usually show that they know what is happening, where the action is heading, what the real meaning of a given utterance is, etc. Their reaction may be in the form of applause, nodding the head, clicking the tongue, exchanging a few words with a neighbor to confirm their understanding or guess, etc. To grasp the story, one does not need sophistication or depth of thought. The singer appeals to reason and refers to traditional opinions and the knowledge of other songs.

Having already analyzed irony in the previous chapter, now I want to refer to two kinds in order to show how the singer uses allusions to two types of facts from outside the story—unfamiliar and familiar to the audience. In the case of the former, the important factor is whether the attitude of the group is suitable

146 In tradition, some things must remain intact. It would be unbelievable or simply untrue to deny the absolute meaning of the story, by claiming, for instance, that it was the centaurs who defeated the Lapiths or that Achilles survived the siege of Troy. This may seem peculiar but the same situation can be affirmed in the process of the formation of modern myths. In the myth of the Roswell incident, various components of the narrative have appeared to explain what really happened, but in no version of the myth could the spaceship not have been destroyed (Ziegler 1997:38–40). Without the crash, the story makes no sense because it would be inconsistent with the cognitive context of the group of believers: "The continuing credibility of tales that group members avowedly believe to be true (i.e. legends and myths) depends on the tales' remaining consonant with changing subcultural concepts" (Ziegler 1997:39). At the same time, some variants incongruent with the other versions are repudiated, that is, they are usually not repeated by others.

to judge the meaning of past events which were not necessarily reflected in tradition. For example, Diomedes in his *aristeia* first killed Abas and Polyeidos (5.148–151), sons of Eurydamas, the reader of dreams, and then Xanthos and Thoon, the only sons of Phainops (5.152–158). They were not a familiar element of the saga. Homer comments on the death of Abas and Polyeidos by saying that their father did not explain their dreams when they were setting out for the war. After Diomedes has killed Phainops's sons, the poet describes the despair of their father, who has lost his heirs. In the conclusion, Homer uses the past tense (5.156–158):

> ...πατέρι δὲ γόον καὶ κήδεα λυγρά
> λεῖπ'· ἐπεὶ οὐ ζώοντε μάχης ἐκνοστήσαντε
> δέξατο· χηρωσταὶ δὲ διὰ κτῆσιν δατέοντο.

> And he [Diomedes] left lament and painful grief to their father,
> Because he did not welcome his sons at home alive
> returning from the war; distant relatives divided his wealth among themselves.

The short final statement creates distance from the events and lets the listeners judge them from their own experience: "well, such things happen...." The listeners do not puzzle over those ephemeral characters and do not get lost, overwhelmed by the number of Diomedes' victims, but reflect on the irony of fate in their lives.

A clear example of the second kind of irony—allusions to facts familiar to the audience—are Agamemnon's words to Kalchas (1.106): μάντι κακῶν οὐ πώ ποτέ μοι τὸ κρήγυον εἶπας ("prophet of disaster, you have never foretold anything but evil to me ..."). These words have been understood by modern scholars as Homer's poor opinion of seers, but this opinion is groundless, prompted by a quite anachronistic prejudice against divination. In the *Iliad* itself, there is evidence that Kalchas's prophecies were not always inauspicious; it will suffice to mention the auspicious prophecy of the fall of Troy mentioned by Odysseus (2.300–332). Agamemnon's words quoted above indicate the king's annoyance with an unfavorable prediction. Kullmann, however, rightly remarks that it is not enough to justify the words "you have never." For him, it is an obvious allusion to events from outside the story of the *Iliad*, i.e. to the sacrifice of Iphigenia.[147] The scholar notices the motive for Agamemnon's excessive irritation, but for him that's all there is to it.

147 Kullmann 1960:198, 2005:26; see also Taplin 1992:86, Dowden 1996:53, Nelson 2022:72–76.

If we assume that Agamemnon is really thinking about the sacrifice of Iphigenia, which was a result of Kalchas's prophecy, then this allusion not only refers to his memories, but it must also take into account the reaction triggered by the king's emotional words, because otherwise it would be pointless. The army present at this conflict knows what the king is referring to and is ready to agree with him, and Homer's audience must also have grasped the allusion. The singer would have expected them to understand the king's words and his angry charge. The king's point is strengthened because the external audience is treated on a par with the warriors at the assembly, whom the king wanted to influence. However, in the next chapter, I will demonstrate that a later part of Agamemnon's speech shatters the general approval, because by mentioning his wife, Klytaimestra, he alludes to his future downfall, which he will bring upon himself.

Homer's *Iliad* is not a series of free variations on traditional themes, but a dialogue with tradition.[148] Thanks to modifications which have been introduced, without revoking or changing tradition, the poet is able to come up with an absolutely new song, which his society is certain to accept and which helps its members to experience and understand their tradition better. Tradition is in flux; it continuously changes its shape. It can be complemented with new events and facts, and this flexibility makes it difficult to distinguish between when the singer recalls memories of significant events and when he only simulates the existence of such an epic reality.

We can get a better idea of Homer's subtlety of method by looking at the scenes evoking the immortalization of Memnon by Eos. Memnon dies at the hands of Achilles and after death is taken from the battlefield by his divine mother. Like in other cases presented before, Homer splits this scene into several, which use fragments of the original: Sarpedon, killed by Patroklos (who functions as Achilles' double), is taken from the battlefield and carried to his homeland by Hypnos and Thanatos (16.667–684); Aeneas is twice saved by gods and taken away from the battlefield, where he fights Diomedes (Achilles' alter ego), and then Achilles himself.

[148] Alden (2000:18–21) shows the interdependence of side stories (paranarratives, see Ch. 1, fn. 62) and the main narrative. The scholar shows how individual paranarratives allow listeners to see various aspects of the main plot and enable a fuller understanding of certain issues by bringing them closer, as if through a lens. Far from depreciating this position, which allows us to analyze the mechanism of repetition of plot elements within the *Iliad* and the *Odyssey*, I would like to point out that this compositional principle works on a much larger scale: the poet's choice as to why a given episode should take a given shape are determined not only by its link with the main narrative of the poem but also with the images already functioning in tradition and determining the shape of the Trojan myth. This means that just as the side stories are shaped in relation to the main narrative, the main narrative is shaped by the poet in relation to tradition. The oral poet proceeds here in the same way, that is, by creating successive stories that duplicate in a reconfigured form the content of the traditional story.

Aeneas is rescued first by Aphrodite and Apollo (5.311–446), then by Poseidon (20.290–340). The first time, when his divine mother carries him from the battlefield, is a clear allusion to the priority scene of Memnon and Eos, although Aphrodite's rescue is perversely unsuccessful against Diomedes' attack. The second time, the link is less obvious, because Poseidon saves the hero; earlier, however, Apollo motivates Aeneas for a fight against Achilles, claiming that *his mother* is more powerful than Thetis (20.105–107).[149] Homer does not create his own themes using a common pattern so much as he deliberately obscures the original image by inverting the order of situations, etc. But he cannot depart very far from the original version of the event, which is familiar to the listeners, because he would not be able to create a proper sequence of dread and relief. That is why there are several variants of a given scene, each one stressing a different element of the traditional story, but at the same time using other elements.

These scenes are, then, allusions to recognizable images rooted in tradition and foreshadow disasters known to the listeners from other songs. These disasters are not part of the events in the song, but nonetheless, due to allusions, they are always present in it. The experience of the alternation of dread and relief depends upon the comparisons which the listener is expected to make with corresponding scenes from the traditional tale of Achilles' death. These scenes play the same role as prolepses concerning the fate of Achilles and Troy. Likewise, the deaths of Patroklos, Sarpedon, and Hektor described in the *Iliad*, analogous to the deaths of Antilochos, Achilles, Memnon, and Paris, foreshadow the end of the war. There are no full equivalences; variation is the ruling principle, hence the deaths of both Sarpedon and Hektor correspond to the death of Memnon. The *Iliad* uses the pattern of Achilles killing the leader of the Trojan allies and Priam's son which is exploited in the Trojan Cycle. Finally, Achilles dies by the hand of another of Priam's sons. The identification of characters between songs cannot be too close or else it will distort the basic pattern of the story. In the tradition of multiformity, fundamental events remain unchangeable. For example, the story of Antilochos is an immanent part of the story of the fight against Memnon and so it can be used only as an allusion. In the *Iliad*, Diomedes, not Antilochos, is Achilles' substitute, because in the cyclic tradition, Antilochos dies rescuing his father, and this is his proper history. In the *Iliad*, Patroklos is the substitute of Achilles who dies and thus triggers the course of events ending in Achilles' death. Diomedes functions as the substitute who provokes the memory of significant events, but he himself gets away unscathed.

[149] The listener gets conflicting signals that the outcome of the fight has been and hasn't been determined in advance (20.23–30, 41–53, 97–111, 129–131, 133–143, 158–176).

The multiformity of traditional scenes in the *Iliad* parallels the variability of uses of the *Oresteia* myth in the narration of the *Odyssey*. The variability of scenes functioning as allusions leaves the listener uncertain if the course of events will confirm his expectations; but, just like the frequent prolepses, it strengthens his conviction that everything will end in the way it should. The fate of heroes is known beforehand. That is why the listener can experience current events and simultaneously look at their development from the perspective of their outcome. Thus, on the one hand, he can feel emotions evoked by what is happening just now and, on the other, he is able to judge the whole situation. Like a spectator watching a tragedy, who knows right from the start the outcome of events, the listener also feels apprehension at the inevitable tragic end but does not know how the poet is going to reach it. He experiences the present moment, but he also knows the future; thus, he feels empathy towards the characters and realizes their imperfect (in comparison with his own) knowledge of the future.

Conclusions

The singer's habit of alluding to a particular scene known to his listeners seems to contradict Foley, who links specific referentiality to the individual style of written literature.[150] This kind of referentiality is, nonetheless, an element of tradition. The singer's memory is based on sequences of associations.[151] It is connected, however, with the suggestiveness of the image in the collective mind. Its lifespan and impact are incomparably stronger in oral culture. Aural text is received through visualization.[152] The image fixed in collective memory to a certain extent restricts the freedom of an oral text. Once an image is rooted in memory, it persists despite the versions advanced by other songs. It is also a point of reference for the whole community, which has accepted it. As David Rubin has shown, in oral tradition, imagery is spatial (and therefore not sequential), organized and specific.[153] The system of recalling images embedded in the long-term memory of the audience during a performance,

150 Foley 1999a:13–34.

151 Minchin (2001:Ch. 1) shows that the creative modification of typical scenes is determined by the knowledge of certain scripts for routine activities or sequences of events. Sabynin (1995), in turn, shows how an oral singer automatically connects elements with each other: if he said A, he must say B, and in consequence C, D, etc. even if this may sometimes seem like a nonsensical or odd continuation (for instance: "He left the city, he left the village"). Not so far from this are the thoughts of Beye (1964) who found that battle scenes were composed according to a repeatable pattern (A, B, C parts) where some contents appear always in the same sequence.

152 Havelock 1969:188 and Rubin 1995:60–61; though what they have in mind is primarily the facility with which performers can memorize "easy to imagine words and ideas."

153 Rubin 1995:49–63.

outlined here, seems to fully correspond to this description. Individual scenes reconfigured by the singer according to specific rules trigger the listeners' active reception by stimulating their memory. The scenes relating to the death of Antilochos contain, first of all, the image of the killing either of a chariot horse or of a person the hero has to protect (*Iliad* 8.80–90), or of the hero himself, acting at that moment as a protagonist (16.467–477). The image has a specific character: a concrete thing rather than an abstract situation is evoked. The fact that it is used in different places in the narrative indicates that it does not have a sequential character. Instead, the image has a spatial character, since it can be used in various locations, provided they are crucial for the narrative.[154] Scenes used in this way also have an organized character, as they fit into the logic of the story, making the audience expect that events will have consequences analogical to the ones in the primary scene. The same is true of the scenes evoking the image of Achilles' death, where the recognizable elements would be the fight of the hero with Apollo and the hero's being slightly, yet fatally wounded by Paris. Each time, therefore, the traditional image thus evoked activates the same sequence of events in the minds of the listeners. The singer does not feel obliged to fulfill these expectations of his audience; he simply introduces a situation of danger. However, the feared consequences may be fulfilled later in the course of the narrative, in other circumstances. Either way, therefore, the danger introduced by the *anamnêsis* finds its fatal end. Deceiving the listener does not mean turning upside down his reception of the story. If the evoked image is not followed by the expected consequences, it only means a retardation of the traditional plot.

The character of narration, adapted to the singer/listener interactions, brings the *Iliad* closer to film than a work of literature.[155] Though this comparison, giving an idea of how content is conveyed in a sequence of images, is quite

[154] Minchin (2007:18–32) shows how the spatial imagery works in the *Iliad*: "The setting is not only a backdrop for the action ... the setting *cues* the words to be spoken or the actions that arise. What we notice ..., by contrast with some works of literary fiction, is the poet's emphasis on location" (22). She goes on: "These recurrent fixed locations appear to be a feature of a developed spatial memory system that assists the singer in a positive way, in *organizing the sequence* of his song and *in cueing content* of each scene" (27). Minchin (2007:23–24) notes an economy in using landmarks: "Such economy has a practical rationale: it would not be possible for a poet in performance *both* to retain more than a limited number of features at any one time in active memory, along with the material of his song, *and* to be (relatively) consistent in his references to them as he located and recounted events on the plain."

[155] This metaphor has been used by Rubin (1995:41–46, 60) as well as Minchin (2001:25), who concurs: "We must conceive of epic song ... as a movie which runs in the cinema of the mind: the mind of the poet and of the audience." See also S. Richardson 1990:197.

appropriate[156], it does not reflect the specific interaction between the performer and the listener in the oral tradition, where the listener is aware of the aim of the story and the narrative paths. To me, the *Iliad* resembles a Passion Play, where the listener constantly experiences afresh the protagonist's moments of glory, suffering, and death. What happens to other characters is perceived in the context of the fate of the main hero. The idea of referring to a traditional image in order to produce appropriate tension in oral narration springs from the understanding of *what* a given song is within this tradition. The *Iliad* is one of many songs about the capture of Troy—and each of them recreates the same situation, but the multiformity of the story involves repetition with thematic variations. At first sight, the episodes seem to be completely new, with different heroes, but they all constitute a continuous polymorphic re-enactment of one mythical truth. As it has already been remarked in the first chapter, this polymorphism, the use of episodes which reproduce "the same story," is most probably the result of the rivalry of singers at a festival—it is as if each of them was telling the same "holy story" in his own way. The *Iliad* cannot be an exception—like other songs, it sings the death of the hero, who "saved" the Achaeans and thus enabled them to take Troy. The *Iliad* does not refer to the *Aethiopis*. The *Aethiopis* is merely the only work known to us which actually tells the death of Achilles. Perhaps the *Aethiopis* emphasized this event because it also presented the posthumous immortalization of this hero—then his death would be only a prologue to the theme of apotheosis. In other cases, the creation of "new" episodes will always make use of allusions to the image of this death, as in the plot of the *Kypria*, where the death of Patroklos is replaced with his wounding, which is followed by a sequence of events with Achilles, similar to the one in the *Iliad*.

It would seem, therefore, that the story narrated in the *Iliad* is one of many versions of the events that precede the fundamental developments in the story of the Trojan War. But in fact, it is an alternative way of telling these events. In particular, it allows them to be experienced emotionally, even though the

156 Bonifazi's (2007) analysis of using some markers in Homeric discourse allows to see how the oral poet passes in his narrative from one image to another: "Discourse markers usually occur in sentence initial position, whereas propositional adverbs usually occur in mid sentence position. The procedural meaning of the ancient Greek words considered here rests primarily on the visual discontinuities existing between different sections of the epic narration. In particular, they work as 'road signs' of the discourse, prompting specific cognitive activities related to visual imagery: shifting between different kinds of shots, (long shots, mid shots, and close-ups), shifting between less and more detailed depictions (zooming in), and shifting between ordinary moments and special instants of the narration (flashes). By means of these markers the mind's eye of the performer and of the audience, who both re-see the mythical events, is helped in visualizing the next focus of the visual field" (59–60).

experience will be triggered by another plot. Like in Passion Plays, it is therefore important to re-enact the death—perceived as a sacrifice for the common good—and the apotheosis of the protagonist, but unlike in the Christian play, which presents only the death and resurrection of Jesus, the hero can be replaced by his substitutes. The substitutes cannot fully replace Achilles, but they do activate religious, ethical, and aesthetic experiences associated with the myth of this hero. The *Iliad*'s listeners emotionally experienced Achilles' death even though it was not described in the song.[157] Like in the case of the death and the resurrection of Jesus in the Christian paschal tradition, the story strikes a different tone, depending on which of the two events is stressed. It means that an epic story may, like the *Iliad*, focus on the death of a hero (important here are not only the images of his death, but also of the funeral along with the ritual mourning)[158] or on his apotheosis.[159] The Christian experiencing the passion and death of Jesus focuses only on this aspect of the holy story, even though he knows that Jesus will soon be resurrected. The knowledge about the

[157] Kelly (2012:249), taking up the topic of the mourning of Achilles by Thetis before his death, and disagreeing with the Neoanalytical arguments from the standpoint of oral theory, claims, "It is typical of Thetis' character throughout the *Iliad* that she is constantly in mourning for Achilles' coming death." This observation prompts Kelly (2012) to conclude that the author of the *Iliad* followed a pattern of narration which makes the song self-sufficient and independent of other songs ("There is nothing inexplicable or poorly motivated here, and nothing which would be better motivated in another text/poem/story than it is in the *Iliad*" [255].). Kelly continues: "There is no compelling reason to conclude that Homer is drawing on anything other than traditional, typical resources in his construction of of the episode, nor that he is particularly alluding to an episode from another text/poem/story instead of trying to create significance within his own narrative" (263). But the problem is how we understand tradition. Kelly understands it as an abstract pattern which can be filled with any data. He equals this pattern with the basic *Gestalt* (Nagler 1974), which can be transformed in subsequent realizations. He juxtaposes the behavior of Thetis in Book 18 with the behavior of other (mainly female) characters in the Homeric poems and infers that the original theme is the one of distraught women's attempt to separate themselves from others and of expressing anxiety for their menfolk, whose life is in danger, in the "prospective lamentations," in the circle of other women. Kelly suggests that the primary behavior is the ritual one, whereas in fact it is not so. Kelly's argumentation is frequently open to doubts, but here I will focus only on the issue at hand: the repetitive lamentations of Thetis are due to the fact that in various songs about Achilles she plays the same role of *mater dolorosa*, always being close to her son, whose death is inevitable and imminent. This may be at odds with the original myth in which the mermaid abandoned her child (see Ch. 6, p. 574–575, below), but the image of the bond between mother and son developed in epic songs, in which the mother repeatedly gives prophecies to her son to warn him against danger, indicates that this is not a new idea of the author of the *Iliad*. Perhaps Thetis and Achilles, who takes on the role of the hero-protagonist of the Trojan Cycle, replaced another mythical couple, carrying out a pattern in which the goddess laments the premature death of her son, comparable to the story of a goddess mourning the death of her lover (e.g. Aphrodite and Adonis).

[158] In the *Iliad*, Patroklos's funeral is a substitute for Achilles'. However, not only is Patroklos ritually mourned, but Achilles too—although he is still alive. This was first noticed by Kakridis 1949:695.

[159] Of course, we can think of such parallels as Adonis's rituals as well.

resurrection does not reduce his emotional involvement in the experience of Jesus's death.

We have seen that in his narrative, the author of the *Iliad* resorts to a special tactic: although he fulfills what is expected by his audience, he tries to do everything not to tell the final events that constitute the real end. This makes his whole story a mere retardation of what is to come. The death of Achilles is reached by a very convoluted path. Subsequent events seem to diverge from the main theme, but in reality, the main theme is still in the listeners' mind. There are numerous variants of the "holy story," which seemingly distort it and make it void, but in fact they resemble and confirm it. In telling his story, the author of the *Iliad* seems to be like a drunk man in a narrow alley, staggering and bumping against the walls, but still heading in the right direction. Perhaps this comparison will not find favor with the reader, but I believe that such an interpretation of Homer's narrative strategy confirms Lord's position. As we remember, he suggested that the oral author of the *Iliad* constantly juggled various ways of presenting traditional themes, giving up one in favor of another, letting himself be carried away by the current of his narrative.[160] The disagreement to this interpretation voiced by many Homer scholars results from the assumption that such a technique implies randomness in conducting the narration, while the *Iliad* seems to be an ordered and well-planned work. And yet the rotation of narrative elements observed by Lord, i.e. discarding some solutions and switching to others, does not mean any randomness or chaos. It is so because the singer knows what he is aiming at and all the deviations from the right course pave the way for the traditional story on the one hand, and its partial reconstruction on the other.

Contrary to our expectations, the story is not important in itself; rather, the importance lies in the process of telling it. The singer does not recollect the past or put it into the limelight, but uses it to tell the story, which he does for as long as possible. The audience does not know how or when the song will reach its expected end. The listener gets involved emotionally and intellectually, entangled in a net of connections between the plot and the tradition, with which he is familiar, but also the tradition which is suggested to him. The singer evokes some images from the memory of his audience and manipulates them. Also, in many cases he hints at the memory of situations and events which quite probably (sometimes almost certainly) were unknown to the listeners. In a stream of narration, the audience is not able to separate real memories from fake ones. They are victims of a very strong suggestion.

[160] Lord 1960:186–197.

Using various ways of affecting the audience, the author of the *Iliad* harnesses the plot of individual episodes to the accomplishment of the fundamental goal of the heroic story, while meeting the listeners' expectations of the epic story of Achilles. But these expectations are fulfilled only partially. Listeners are perpetually misled. Their expectations are fueled and then suddenly disappointed; the events they are certain are coming are constantly postponed. Instead of the expected depiction of Achilles' death, the listeners receive a triple repetition of the entire narrative pattern of the "hero's way." As a result, something that in terms of plot is not achieved, is achieved in the awareness of the audience. The multiplication of one sequence of events intensifies the dread.

In oral culture, the repetition of a message makes it more powerful and stresses its importance. Oral tradition is by nature redundant and needs many repetitions to achieve its communicative purpose. This observation by Ong [161] shows the interformularity of the Homeric poems postulated by Bakker in a broader perspective. Bakker demonstrates that in the course of a narrative, a formular utterance is repeated in various contexts. When the listener hears it a second time he compares its meaning derived from its use in the previous context or contexts, if it has already been used many times.[162] This shows that in an oral message even repetitions, both exact and only similar in sound and wording, gain new meanings in a different context. One should add, however, that in the listener's mind successive meanings overlap and the significance of the entire message (like a whole epic song) is revealed to the listener, so to speak, aggregatively. Certain themes appear repeatedly in the course of the narrative, but almost every time in a modified form. Since this is a completely different message from that of the written culture, it is often wrongly inferred that the poet is ambivalent in his treatment of meanings, even the ones relevant to him.[163] Meanwhile, in oral communication, some readings of the narrative do not exclude others; they may even contrast with one another, but the listener is guided so he/she can properly respond to the narrated events and attitudes of the characters. A given behavior is not unambiguous by its very nature;

[161] Ong 2002:38–40, though Ong does not fully capture the significance of the problem.

[162] Bakker 2013:Ch. 4 and 5, 163–168.

[163] For example, the plague strikes the Achaeans as a result of Chryses' prayer/contract, but also his words act as a curse that must be fulfilled (the Achaeans do not accept his good word, so they get a bad one from the man using the causative words ἀρητήρ, which can be a blessing but also a curse, 1.11, 18–19, 42). Nor can it be said that Apollo does not defend broken moral principles, punishing the Achaeans like Yahweh (1.43–53, compare 24.30–54). All these reasons, even if not explicitly expressed (however, see Ready 2019: Ch. 1 and 2 on the listeners' filling in the "intertextual gap" between the knowledge conveyed in the performance and the listeners' prior knowledge), are equivalent in the oral narrative and together comprise the message transmitted to the listener. Compare the way in which various versions of Achilles' invulnerability discussed in Ch. 3, above, are equivalent and alluded to in the narrative of the *Iliad*.

only the context allows the audience to learn its meaning and judge it accordingly.[164] The ultimate value and meaning of the depicted events are revealed to the listener step by step in successive multiform contextualizations of a given theme. Thus, the listener remains sensitive not only to the repetition of sound, but also to the repetition of images conveyed in the narrative.

This theory explains also the duality of the reception of this story, which may seem strange to today's readers: that the listener could experience the death of Patroklos and at the same time the death of the hero-protagonist—Achilles. But we must remember two things. First, tracing the message at two levels of meaning is neither unknown in epic nor unique or confined to only this part of the song. I will try to demonstrate this duality in the next chapter. Second, the listener expects, as we imagine it, a cult story, i.e. one in which all elements turn to the original source. In ritual, the idea of substitution is ubiquitous—and the same is true of myth. Myth does not have to be closely related to ritual, but is based on analogical principles. The idea of substitution is one of them.

164 To use a vivid example from the story of Uttanka, the brahmin's disciple discussed in Chapter 3: eating animal feces is the gravest offense that can be committed by a brahmin, who is obligated to maintain purity founded first and foremost in guarding oneself against impurity. However, once he committed the offence, it turned out that he had done the right thing. Likewise, the deeds of Homeric heroes show their value only after a lapse of time, and they are often labelled only by the narrator or the progress of the narrative. This is the case, for example, with Achilles' decision to send Patroklos into battle, Hector's decision to stay on the battlefield, or even with Paris's abduction of Helen. In themselves they are neither bad nor good, in the narrative they are qualified only by their consequences.

6
The Relationship between *Êthopoiia* and the System of External Allusions in Homer

IN EARLIER CHAPTERS, we discovered how traditional plot patterns help to increase the number of songs in oral epic and how the repetition of familiar patterns in numerous variations promotes the creation of suspense. We have also seen that the singer expects his listeners to be sensitive to detail and to be able to apply their knowledge of tradition to the current story.

As we approach the end of the book, it seems proper to demonstrate how the construction of the song is adapted to aural reception and to what extent the quality we perceive as Homeric artistry is a result of his deliberate attempt to affect his listeners. Because of the length of the *Iliad*, I will concentrate on its most important figure—Achilles. In previous chapters, I have already shown that in the presentation of characters the singer is at liberty to change their personalities and interpret their deeds known from tradition to their advantage or disadvantage. The *Odyssey* seems to be nearly one-dimensional in its constant praise of Odysseus, whereas the *Iliad* seems to be ambivalent and sometimes even critical in the presentation of its protagonist. We begin our analysis with the conflict between Achilles and Agamemnon, which is also the starting point for the song.

Protagonists in the Homeric epics receive no detailed characterization, and yet their characters are consistently and clearly defined. Since antiquity, the interpreters of the *Iliad* have looked askance at Achilles' behavior, whereas Agamemnon has enjoyed much more indulgence. Agamemnon is responsible for the whole army and the success of the expedition, and his authority is guaranteed by Zeus. Achilles, when he is offended by Agamemnon, asks Zeus for the destruction of the army he is a part of.[1] For centuries, Achilles has been the

1 New studies, which modify this system of values (Zanker 1994 and Latacz 1995), point out the contrast between Achilles' and Agamemnon's conduct resulting from the injustice of the latter. Erbse (2001:243) mocks such a black-and-white image of these two characters and notices blunders in the behavior of both leaders, although Achilles' is decidedly more serious. Erbse believes that each of Agamemnon's actions is excusable, based on his analysis of the quarrel between the

exemplar of how young people should not behave. Scholars have stressed his impulsiveness and obstinacy. But the list of his vices is longer: impetuosity, hot-headedness, youthful stupidity, undue pride, aristocratic egotism (i.e. putting self-interest over the common good), ignoring the rules of social coexistence, excessive nonconformity, unwillingness to forgive, and vengefulness.[2] We have to bear in mind that such a judgment of Achilles' behavior is determined by the tendency, dating back to antiquity, to glorify self-control. Current scholars seem to favor the opinion that the ambiguity of the main characters, not only in Homer but in epic in general, suggests a lack of moral judgment by the poet; the songs only tell a story, without clearly condemning negative behavior. Andrew Ford explains it as the way the singer affects the listener in oral poetry: "Understanding this pleasure permits us to define epic as the *presentation* of the past, without moralizing; it was a pleasure simply to represent the past 'as it was' and still is for the Muses without pointing to the presence of the performance."[3] I can agree neither with Ford's interpretation of the behavior of the protagonist of the *Iliad* nor with Ford's understanding of the function of epic narration. I believe that what is really important in oral tradition is neither the story itself, which can appear in various forms, nor its performance, but the meaning which the singer endows it with during the performance.

The Reason for the Quarrel

In Greek epic, the quarrel is given various, sometimes very sophisticated motivations. The Greek leaders' fight for primacy undoubtedly reflects the realities of the life of Greek warriors.[4] In Demodokos's song, Odysseus and Achilles quarrel about who will capture the city (*Odyssey* 8.75–77), just as Alcaeus's friends quarrel at a feast over who will defeat Pittakos, a quarrel which the poet

leaders in Book 1. Since I have undertaken a linear analysis similar to Erbse's, I will often refer to his study.

2 For example, Lohmann (1970:279n118), who points out that Achilles is impulsive and likely to reject opinions which he cannot agree with.

3 Ford 1992:18, see also 52.

4 I do not want to enter into a discussion about whether this scene reflects historical reality; it is enough to assume that it is understandable to the primary audience because of the similarity of the situations to those in their own experience. So it is more than just an acceptance of a certain reality by the audience because of its constant presence in epic tradition. Elmer (2013:63–67) draws attention to a system of norms embodied in traditional elements of narration (formulae, type-scenes etc.) and the intentional significance ("tension and dynamism," p. 66) which the *Iliad* acquires due to the departure from these norms. I would like to add that a breach of norms which results in conflict needn't have been a distinctive feature of the *Iliad*, but it must have been an element of many songs which started with a crisis leading to a quarrel and so it would also be a constant element of oral epic.

tries to calm down (fr. 70 L-P). In the *Iliad*, the division of the spoils naturally provokes a quarrel. Because of its potential for conflict, the division is guarded by many time-honored rules, which must be observed. When Achilles describes the situation to his mother, he says that the division of spoils was made properly (*Iliad* 1.368): τὰ μὲν εὖ δάσσαντο μετὰ σφίσιν υἷες Ἀχαιῶν ("Achaean sons divided them [spoils] *fairly* among themselves"). The spoils should be shared according to the warrior's status and merits, but nobody can be left without at least a modest part (like in the division of a sacrifice). Spoils are considered a kind of common property and, though they are probably divided by the main leader (9.368), he represents all warriors. Achilles several times stresses this point: he got his spoils from all the Achaeans, not from Agamemnon (1.162, 392). The spoils express the appreciation of the community, so in a way they are a measure of the value of the warrior. To be able to choose one's own spoils is considered the greatest privilege (9.138–280). Achilles was granted this privilege after the capture of Eëtion's city (9.187). The fundamental rule was that once the division of spoils was made, it was final. Otherwise, it would be possible to question the shares, and would unavoidably lead to conflicts, so one had to accept what he was given. In the *Iliad*, the problem arises when Agamemnon wants to change the way that the spoils have been distributed.

The reason for the Trojan War is Helen. The object of the quarrel in the *Iliad* is also a woman, Briseis; this is what Aias reproves Achilles for when the envoy is leaving the hero's tent: he is implacable in anger "because of one girl" (εἵνεκα κούρης / οἴης, 9.637–638), while they offer him seven. Aias treats a woman like a thing, an item, clearly in opposition to Achilles, who only a moment earlier, seems to be frank in admitting his feelings for Briseis and stressing his right to indulge in them (9.342–343). Achilles, however, also shares Aias's masculine point of view and claims that the reason for his refusal is that Agamemnon offended him. By agreeing with Aias (9.645), he withdraws his demands, which makes his earlier assertion of feelings for the captive woman serve only to emphasize the magnitude of his loss. It is parallel to Agamemnon's previous deceitful inflation of Chryseis's value, when he insisted she was more precious to him than his lawful wife (1.112–115). Achilles remarks that since the Achaeans are fighting for the wife of one of the Atreidai, he is also entitled to his woman, but he has voluntarily forfeited this right, giving up Briseis without a fight (9.334–341). Achilles' words and deeds are Agamemnon's in reverse: unlike the chief leader, he has no lawful wife whom Briseis would replace, but, like Agamemnon, he does not resist when he has to give up his captive woman, though he does not say he is doing it for the sake of the army. Achilles tries to save his honor at the expense of his feelings. Unlike Agamemnon, he seems to be sincere in his feelings for Briseis, and the decision to surrender her involves a real loss; it is not only a gesture calculated to bring him the appreciation of the warriors.[5]

The real cause of the quarrel is neither the division of spoils, nor a woman,[6] whom another man wants for himself (Agamemnon, getting ready to send Briseis back to Achilles, stresses that he has never taken her to bed, 9.131–133), although both reasons lie behind the conflict between the leaders. The essence of the conflict is the competition for the most important role in Achaean society. In Achilles' eyes, it is tantamount to being "the best of the Achaeans" by earning merit in combat; in Agamemnon's eyes, it means emphasizing his dominant position in the army. Both men aspire to the same role from different positions. The quarrel reveals that they cannot share the same portion of respect to reach a common aim, which is what Nestor suggests in his conciliatory speech (1.275–281)—because they both aspire to the same title/role of "the best of the Achaeans," though each of them understands it differently (merits versus authority). This differentiation in the understanding of the traditional role may be Homer's innovation, but an innovation nested in tradition: in the Odysseus/Achilles rivalry, there are two ways to reach the same aim (the title of "the best of the Achaeans")—power and deceit. The rivalry between Odysseus and Achilles, though taking place on different levels, is backed by real achievements—their actions show that they deserve the title. Depending on the perspective adopted in a song, the title falls to Achilles (in the *Iliad*), or Odysseus (in the *Odyssey*). Within tradition there are various ways of achieving the status of "the best of the Achaeans," yet the social need that enabled the constitution of this role is the individual's willingness to sacrifice oneself in order to save the community in a moment of danger. In the confrontation between Achilles and Agamemnon, the latter is not able to buttress his claim to the title with any *real* actions—so he *pretends* to be doing the correct thing (as the analysis below will demonstrate, this is the purpose for his return of Chryseis), but it is done only for the sake of appearances.

The real reason for the quarrel turns out to be the dishonor of one of the parties. Achilles, deceived and humiliated, is forced to defend his honor, but having rejected violent revenge, he compensates with a verbal reproach of Agamemnon and a secret vengeance aided by supernatural powers. The system

5 The fact that Achilles himself agrees with Aias (9.645), which may be a bit confusing as far as his intentions are concerned, does not indicate the lack of an emotional bond with Briseis and her objectification, but rather shows that he appreciates the value and strength of the ties of brotherhood linking him with the fighting Achaeans. Nonetheless, male solidarity regains its value due to the downplaying of the place of women in the calculations of men.

6 That is why I cannot agree with Gotschall (2008), for whom the essence of Homeric poems boils down to the scarcity of women, for whom men have to fight.

of values, which Achilles respects absolutely, demands revenge for wrongs and some kind of compensation for the loss of honor, so Achilles' demand is comparable to that of Agamemnon when he had to give back Chryseis.[7] What both of them want for themselves is also an imperative dictated by society, in which the status of its members is inseparably connected to the protection of their honor.

Achilles' Deceit

Let us follow Achilles' quarrel with Agamemnon from the middle, exactly from the place whose interpretation many scholars find troublesome. In his second speech, Agamemnon addresses Achilles, using astonishing words (1.131–132): μὴ δὴ οὕτως, ἀγαθός περ ἐών, θεοείκελ' Ἀχιλλεῦ, / κλέπτε νόῳ, ἐπεὶ οὐ παρελεύσεαι οὐδέ με πείσεις ("Do not thus, mighty though you are, godlike Achilles, / seek to deceive me with your wit; for you will not get by me nor persuade me").[8] Literally: "Do not act this way [with me]; mighty though you are, godlike Achilles, do not think you can rob me, because you will neither surpass[9] me, nor trick me." This statement seems astonishing because in none of the texts which have come down to us is Achilles the kind of man who would resort to deceit or subterfuge. What does the king of Mycenae mean addressing thus a man who has never, in any story of the cycle, been deceitful and who has never been characterized as tricky? To speak like this, Agamemnon must really feel that Achilles is using underhanded methods against him. That Agamemnon is mistaken is obvious from the whole poem, in which Achilles several times demonstrates his dislike and even abhorrence of guile. It also ironically reflects on Agamemnon, who is blind to the young hero's nobility.

7 Here again a similar demand for compensation as a token of respect means something else in the case of Agamemnon and Achilles.

8 Translation, A. T. Murray (1924).

9 In Homer, παρέρχομαι 'overtake, pass', is used both literally, in the context of running—ποσὶν μή τίς με παρέλθῃ 'not to let anyone surpass me in running' (*Odyssey* 8.230; compare *Iliad* 23.345 about a chariot race), and also figuratively—κερδαλέος κ' εἴη καὶ ἐπίκλοπος, ὅς σε παρέλθοι / ἐν πάντεσσι δόλοισι, 'deceitful and larcenous would be he who would surpass you in all manner of guile' (*Odyssey* 13.291–292). Both passages refer to Odysseus and they complement one another in characterizing him: it is possible that someone may overtake him in running, but as far as deceit is concerned, Odysseus is unsurpassed. The *Odyssey* stresses the opposition between *biê*, represented by Achilles, and *mêtis/dolos*, represented by Odysseus. This polarization is important for achieving the status of *aristos Achaiôn* and is also present in Agamemnon's speech: Achilles will be better at running, but he will not be better at deceit. Agamemnon is in opposition to Achilles and as a master of deceit aspires to the role of *aristos Achaiôn*. This title is always the reason that Homeric characters quarrel.

Is Agamemnon justified in his assumption? For Griffin, Agamemnon's remark "is not a logical thing to say, unless it is Achilles' all too formidable prowess which has already made Agamemnon uneasy about him."[10] This conclusion is drawn from the words of the chief Achaean leader, which suggest that Achilles had been hostile to him in the past. Later in the quarrel, Agamemnon says (1.176–177): ἔχθιστος δέ μοί ἐσσι διοτρεφέων βασιλήων. / αἰεὶ γάρ τοι ἔρις τε φίλη πόλεμοί τε μάχαι τε ("Of all the kings fed by the god you are the most hateful to me, / since quarrels, wars, and fights are always dear to you"). Griffin supposes that the listeners know of an earlier clash between these characters, which Agamemnon alludes to. It might seem that Agamemnon is promoting peace, but this is a verbal attack, typical among Homeric characters. Van Wees points out that in the mentality of heroic society, like that of criminal groups, there is a tendency to aggression and hierarchical rivalry.[11] The members of both organizations attach the greatest importance to their standing within the group, and they perceive the worth of their words and deeds as indisputable. For a hero, a rebuke is tantamount to an attempt to lower his value. He cannot allow this to happen, because often even a slight concession is discreditable, whereas in the eyes of society he must always be above reproach. That is why even a trivial critical remark is quickly followed by a violent quarrel and a total condemnation of the opponent, who is presented as a completely worthless individual: this is how Idomeneus refers to Aias, son of Oileus (23.483–484), or Zeus to Ares (1.890–891), etc. Agamemnon's total criticism of Kalchas, who supposedly has never given him any favorable prophecy (1.106–108), may be brought about by his memories of other bad predictions, but it also indicates that in anger Agamemnon forgets the instances when the seer's prophecies were good for him. We learn from Odysseus's speech during the second gathering of the army that Kalchas did make prophecies favorable to Agamemnon (2.300–330). However, the logic of quarrel makes Agamemnon condemn Kalchas and forget about his good services.

Griffin's supposition cannot be correct.[12] It is affected by the conviction of animosity between the two heroes which is commonly held by scholars. I will try to verify this belief later, but for the time being let us assume that Agamemnon's accusation of Achilles' intended deceit does not have any logical explanation. It

[10] Griffin 2004:163. Pulleyn (2000:163) understands this passage similarly: "One may infer that Agamemnon resents Achilleus' excellence, and tells us as much in this Freudian slip."

[11] Van Wees 1992:61–62.

[12] Kirk (1985:67) proposes an explanation of Agamemnon's charge, which is, however, vague and unconvincing. He suggests that Agamemnon feels that Achilles prevaricates when he says he cannot fulfill the king's expectations: "He openly accuses Akhilleus of deceit—by which he presumably means that the result of his supposedly close reasoning is intolerable, and the reasoning itself therefore specious."

is not the only unclear passage in the *Iliad*—the poem is teeming with them—but it is not a real problem; much more serious is the habit of arbitrarily imposing meaning on various passages juxtaposed in various configurations. This habit—which I believe leads to misunderstanding and erroneous conclusions—is the effect of approaching the Homeric epics like a reader: the text is treated selectively. Even if the context is correct, scattered pieces of information may build an image quite different from that intended by the poet. Naturally, it is not easy to guess the intentions of the singer; some scholars decline to attempt to discover them. However, it seems to me that the task of a classical scholar is to try to recreate the original understanding of a poem at the time of its creation, taking into account the mentality of the people of those times. The reading of the Homeric text must reckon with its oral origin. The scholar should judge and interpret the events in the song from the point of view of an aural recipient.[13]

Principles of Aural Reception

We must return to the issue of the reception of an oral work. First and foremost, for the listener, the plot is linear. The modern reader of Homer is limited in his perception of the text, which he discovers through painstaking analysis and comparison of passages from elsewhere in the song. However, for Homer's contemporaries, meaning must have been revealed as the poet sang.[14] The listener cannot go back to check what is in the text, if he does not understand or forgets something. He is also unaware how much text is still before him, i.e. he does not know when the story will end. Moreover, he cannot in a fit of impatience look at the ending to satisfy his curiosity, or—like today's typical reader (and, regrettably, often the scholar)—skim the text.[15] Linear reception is not easy, especially when the listener must keep his attention focused on the performer because, unlike the reader, he cannot shut the book to reflect or to rest, and then resume reading. Breaks are not for the listener but for the tired performer, whom the audience can only encourage to continue his story.

The listener is helped by the system of allusions and the omnipresent ring composition. Allusions fulfill two functions: they predict (and sometimes mislead the listener about) future events in the story; and refer to the

13 Erbse (2001) in his study of events which constitute the quarrel of the leaders does not consider the difference between reading and aural reception. On the basis of this scene, Griffin (2004:156–159) suggests that the narration of the *Iliad* might have been attractive to the audience because of the expansive portrayal of the characters' feelings. However, the scholar's vivisection of narration, typical of literary criticism, does not show how oral presentation could have affected the poem's reception by the primary audience.

14 Compare Thalmann 1984:28–29.

15 Rubin 1995:65–66.

macro-story of the cycle, known to the singer and to his audience. The listener finds justification for a fact or phrase in the epic code, which lets him interpret a scene or speech. By the principle of referentiality, which applies to significant events in the cycle, the listener associates the action of the song with familiar events from the cycle; this strategy directly affects his involvement in the poem because *anamnêsis* evokes strong feelings of dread and relief—and also of irony, which releases the tension from this piling up of emotions. An allusion may consist of a single phrase, a scene, or even a whole sequence of scenes. Ring composition, returning in reverse order to issues and images presented before, enables the listener to distil the essence of the matter. Both the system of allusions and ring composition shape the stream of linear narration and allow the listener not to get lost, especially in longer stretches of narration. They also allow him to judge a speech or evaluate characters' behavior. That is why even digressions—so often used in the paratactic style, because they can expand and develop narration at any point in the story—usually underpin the main narration: the story of Meleagros (*Iliad* 9.529–599) offers a parallel to Achilles' destiny in the *Iliad*, or Demodokos's song about Aphrodite and Ares' affair (*Odyssey* 8.266–366) is a parallel to Odysseus's destiny on Ithaca.

Achilles and Agamemnon's quarrel is introduced as a subject of the song already at the beginning of *Iliad* Book 1, in the invocation. After the episode with Chryses, whose prayer to Apollo triggers the disasters in the Achaean camp, the poet relates these events in great detail. While the brief presentation of the Chryses episode is rendered as an account of past events, the clash between Achilles and Agamemnon is shown as if happening now. This device, typical of oral poetry, enables the audience to visualize events. Plato (*Republic* 392c–394b) criticizes Homer for inserting Chryses' and Agamemnon's speeches in the Chryses episode, since he believes that they introduce an emotional element superfluous for judging events.[16] But, whether Plato likes it or not, this is exactly what these speeches are meant to do: they intensify the emotions of the audience by enabling them to visualize the action.[17] The emotional power of

16 See Griffin 2004:157–158.

17 Plato's opinion was influenced by contemporary rhapsodic performance of epic, which must have relied on acting techniques like voice modulation and gesture. All that was almost absent in aoidic performance. The rhapsode Ion from Plato's dialogue (*Ion* 535b–e) mentions that pretended tears or joy evoke a similar emotional reaction in the audience. However, Ford (1997:413–414) points out the singularity of Odysseus's and Penelope's reaction to the *aoidos* (*Odyssey* 8.83–92; 1.336–344); they were moved to tears, but it was because the story told in the song referred in a way to their lives. Lord (1960:34) says that to attract the attention of the audience, the *guslar* must possess dramatic talent and narrative skill. But both the *guslar* and *aoidos* have their hands busy playing the instrument, so they cannot gesture much, if at all. Sometimes an emotional response can be prompted by a change of melody, but this is not very effective. The methods of performance by the rhapsode and the *aoidos* are different because they aim to affect

the speeches increases the listeners' empathy and affects their emotional and rational opinions of the characters' conduct.

In oral epic, there are typical characters who share similar characteristics. In the earlier stages of the development of this genre, the psyche of epic heroes was identical with the psyche of other characters in the song. All heroes shared the same character traits, ethos, ways of thinking, and behavior. According to Eleazar Meletinsky, the epic of the Turkic-Mongolian peoples of Siberia is just at this stage of development. He claims that the individuation of characters is absent to the extent that we can practically speak about "one heroic character."[18] In Greek cycles, there is a certain degree of individualization, but it is not well established. In spite of individual traits, many characters also have typical traits, which make them alike in certain respects. Moreover, they fulfill similar functions, which make them interchangeable, i.e. one character can appear in circumstances similar to another or, in other versions of the same song, can even replace him. *Êthopoiia*—character creation—depends on the skill of the singer, who can endow his characters with clear traits and use their conversation to build emotional tension. All this is done in order to arouse the interest of the listener.[19] If, as Odysseus says, the singer describes the situation as if he himself had been at Troy or had heard about the events there from an eyewitness (*Odyssey* 8.491), it means that his listeners are also transferred to another reality and can see everything with their own eyes, though their bodies do not leave their world and they only look at the singer who monotonously chants his story.[20] And here, undoubtedly, the author of the *Iliad* is unparalleled.

their audiences in different ways; reception by these audiences is also different. The *aoidos* does not intend to arouse emotions and empathy in his audience, and so they react less impulsively and rely more on imagination, which must follow the action. The art of the rhapsode was developed to arouse emotions in the listener.

18 Meletinsky 2009:335: "The psyche of epic heroes ... is absolutely uniform and very simple. Its uniformity and simplicity explains why the epic song is more concerned with the hero's deeds than his feelings. On a side note, in olonkho [Yakut heroic epic tale] monologues are scarce. They are often very emotional but they lack the emotional dynamics and practically do not contribute anything to the image of the hero created by the simple description of his deeds."

19 Martin (1989:89–101), drawing on a wide range of comparative material, demonstrates that the differentiation of the speeches of characters is expected by the audience of an oral performance because a competitive society judges "what a hero says and does and, most important, how he does it" (90). Martin stresses that words and deeds "are evaluated precisely *for style*" (91). The issue of who is a better speaker is important in traditional oral cultures, and in poetry it certainly influences the individualization of characters. Martin (1989:104–105): "It might be argued that we are veering away from the study of style and into 'characterization' or narrative when we examine what Nestor says about speech, rather than how he makes his speeches. But the line between style and other aspects of the poetry is difficult to draw exactly because Homeric ideology would conflate the two: style is the man."

20 The notion which we express with a single word, "imagination," the contemporaries of Homer could only describe as a process. The invocation to the Muses in Book 2 of the *Iliad*, just before

In songs, emotional suspense is created by the linear narration. The singer cannot resort to such literary devices as a sudden twist in the plot, i.e. nothing can happen out of the blue. It would seem that long speeches might tire the listener, but they do not. He gets to know not only the opinions of characters, but also their intentions, and it gives him a thrill, especially as the words and intentions of characters are usually revealed in the conflict.[21] Homer does not rummage deeply in the past of his characters in search of something that would influence their deeds. However, he provides psychological foundations of their decisions and actions: he brings in their past known from other epic songs through external allusions and suggests what could have influenced the characters to speak or behave as they did.

The Quarrel between Achilles and Agamemnon

Now that we know the ropes of the oral technique, we can return to the beginning of the *Iliad* and try to imagine how Homer's contemporaries might have understood it. Like many other oral epic songs, the story starts with a gathering and introduces the motif of a quarrel, which triggers the action.

Even before the real action starts, the listener learns about the conflict between the protagonists, about the effects of the conflict, and its divine inspiration—the role of the god Apollo and the fulfillment of Zeus's will. Next, the summary of the Chryses episode familiarizes the listener with Agamemnon's guilt, which casts a shadow over this character in the context of the quarrel. Chryses arrives at the camp and addresses the Achaeans as custom requires: he behaves as a suppliant, submits his request to the Greeks, and particularly to the Atreidai, the leaders of the expedition, and brings a handsome ransom for his daughter. Chryses comes with the symbols of priesthood and power, a gold scepter adorned with *stemmata*, ribbons or strands of dyed wool. His attire and attitude are those of a priest making a sacrifice, which indicates his relationship to the deity he serves. He ends his request with a peculiar warning, suggesting that to comply with his plea means honoring the "striking from afar" Apollo; in

---

the Catalogue of Ships, shows precisely how they understood it (2.484–493). Muses, as immortal beings, can see things distant in time and space, and as the daughters of Mnemosyne, they are also custodians of memory; they communicate what they see to the singer, who can visualize everything in detail. Endowed by the Muses with the skill to pass on their message, he can make other people visualize the scene which he describes. So, in effect, his listeners also can travel in time and space and be eyewitnesses to past events. It was difficult to explain this happening otherwise than by a direct intervention of a deity. Ford (1992:49–56) stresses that the visualization of the image, its vividness, is the poet's most important task.

21 A more extensive study of intentions and motivation of characters was conducted by Zanker 1994.

other words, not to comply will bring about the anger of the "bringing a lot of death" god (*Iliad* 1.21).[22]

The ransoming of captives does not seem to be unique; in the *Iliad*, it is mentioned several times. The priest, behaving as custom requires and deliberately stressing his position, which was not without importance in a highly hierarchical society, is favorably received by the Greeks (1.22). But Agamemnon, surprisingly, refuses the request. Chryses does not know what has happened to his daughter, but he rightly believes she is alive. She was taken by Agamemnon, who has no intention of returning her. He sends the priest away, saying that he will respect neither Chryses' age (he addresses him as "old man"), nor his position, and he is not afraid of the priest's relationship with the god. Agamemnon even says (1.28): "Your staff and god's wreath will not protect you." Agamemnon utters these words in public and does not give any reason for his refusal except that he will do as he pleases. He not only refuses, but also deliberately torments the old man, describing the pitiable future of his daughter, who will grow old in her captor's house as a slave and concubine. There is no evidence that the Achaean leader cares for her at all. Quite probably his behavior springs from his irritation with Chryses' display of dignity and power. However, the Achaeans do not find any fault with the priest's conduct and neither does Agamemnon, whose arrogance and pride are roused by the father begging for his daughter's return. Agamemnon opposes the voice of the army, emphasizing the fact that he is a man who can force through a decision, even if everyone else is against it. From his point of view, his decision is unassailable, since he is the commander. But this time, standing against the opinion of all other men, he commits a foul deed; the gathering considered the return of the daughter as right and proper.[23] The warriors cannot be motivated by greed because the girl belongs to Agamemnon. And he, in turn, is not prompted by the desire to hold on to something valuable but by a much more important reason: to display his position.[24]

22 Apollo's epithet ἑκηβόλος refers to the archer god striking from a distance. Apollo's arrows mean death by disease—not disease affecting individuals, but many people, i.e. the plague. That is why the epithet stresses a great number of arrows shot. The image of the angry god punishing the Achaeans parallels the story of Niobe related by Achilles: Apollo and Artemis killed all her children, six sons and six daughters (24.603–609). The plague is silent, but causes high mortality rates.

23 Muellner 1996:98: "There could not be a clearer indication that both the process of exchange and the value of the terms offered meet with social approval, as Mauss's theoretical principles would require."

24 Van Wees (1992:64–165) rightly criticizes the notion put forward by Adkins (1960:33) that Homeric characters are motivated only by material gain. Van Wees argues that very often much more important for them is to secure a position in their society, to see that hierarchy is respected, and to defend their honor. Sometimes, like for example in this case, material value is

The priest leaves the camp and when he is alone, he curses the Achaeans; the god eagerly wreaks vengeance. The narrator makes the listener privy to the facts which the Achaeans are ignorant of. From the invocation, the audience already knows the reason for the quarrel: Apollo's revenge for dishonoring his priest by the son of Atreus (1.11–12). The first step leading to the fateful quarrel is the calling of the assembly by Achilles. Like all deeds of this kind, it must be inspired by a divinity. The commentators, however, are often mystified by the fact that the idea which brought such evil consequences to the Achaeans was suggested by Hera (1.55–56): τῷ γὰρ ἐπὶ φρεσὶ θῆκε θεὰ λευκώλενος Ἥρη· / κήδετο γὰρ Δαναῶν, ὅτι ῥα θνήσκοντας ὁρᾶτο ("white-armed Hera gave him [Achilles] this thought, / because she felt sorry for the Achaeans, when she saw them dying").

Critics' doubts reflect the issue of divine intervention.[25] At first sight, it seems that characters blindly follow gods' commands. Is Achilles only a tool in the hands of the goddess? No, he calls the assembly, fully aware of the purpose it has to serve: he presents the problem and suggests a possible solution. Later, when Athena descends from heaven to prevent him from revenging himself upon Agamemnon, Achilles obeys her because one should obey divine orders. One could conclude that the author assumes the hero does not understand the consequences of his deed. Nothing could be more wrong. Before Athena tries to stop him, Achilles debates whether he should kill Agamemnon or not. There is a reason which holds him back from immediate retaliation, and he is aware of it.[26]

In an oral text, a reference to the divine impulse exempts the poet from the obligation of explaining the reasons for characters' behavior (as yet, he is unable to provide such explanations). Nonetheless, it is a clear signal for the listener how to understand their decisions.[27] Achilles' deed, combined with Hera's inspiration, shows the hero's concern for the Achaeans' fate. The poet refers to the audience's knowledge that in this conflict Hera is on the side of the Achaeans. This conclusion is corroborated by a similar statement in the invocation: Apollo is named as the god who incited the quarrel between the heroes. Later, there is no confirmation of this fact. But the poet points to this god and

insignificant. Zieliński (2019b) argues that Agamemnon seeks to assert his dominance over the Achaeans.

25 Erbse (2001:242 and 244) claims that these passages indicate that man never makes decisions himself but his actions are ruled by gods; this would mean that the fact that the assembly was called by Achilles is immaterial.

26 Athena does issue an order, but also puts forward a proposition favorable to Achilles. Symptomatic is the use of the formula αἴ κε πίθεαι 'if you could be convinced' (1.207).

27 In a primitive society there is no notion of chance. Behind every event, and especially a calamity, there is a reason, which is anchored in the actions of gods or magical (deliberate or not) actions of other agents (Evans Pritchard 1976:18–32; 1956:16–22, Turner 1970:300).

his enmity towards the Achaeans, particularly towards Achilles, because in epic tradition the conflict with Apollo leads to the death and apotheosis of this hero.

The *Iliad* presents four assemblies. Two of them, the first and the last, are called by Achilles (1.54, 19.40–41), the other two by Agamemnon (2.72, 9.9–12), so it is generally assumed that not only the chief leader but also other *basileis* could call assemblies.[28] In the *Odyssey*, the assembly on Ithaca is called by Telemachos (*Odyssey* 2.6–7), even though he is not yet of age.[29] To learn that it was Achilles' decision must have been significant for the audience. The hero is introduced as a person who will come in conflict with Agamemnon. The listener, aware of Agamemnon's guilt, will understand this as a sign of Achilles' worry about the destiny of the army—and this is corroborated by Hera's inspiration. One could ask why the chief leader did not show concern for his soldiers by calling the assembly. For the present, the listener has no time to ponder this question, but it must exist in the singer's mind, and he will repeatedly suggest it to the listener.

The problem of guilt seems to be the main one for the morality of that time.[30] A calamity which falls on the whole community and which has no rational explanation is perceived to be the result of someone's crime against a god. The crime may be a neglected sacrifice or overlooking a god at a sacrifice, but it may also consist in doing a deed which offends a god. All this provokes the god's anger, which, on the principle of collective responsibility, is directed at the whole community. Here the main responsibility lies on the ruler, because maintaining good relations with gods, i.e. making proper sacrifices on behalf of the community and inflicting punishments for crimes committed within the community, are his province.[31] The reason for the plague is usually attributed to his error or *hybris*.[32] Unlike the listeners in the *Iliad*, who are told right at the

28 According to Mueller (1984:32), Achilles, and not one of the older warriors, calls the assembly, because he is worried that after ten years of fighting he has not gained the glory which would justify the fact of bringing him to the war. The plague only feeds his frustration. I believe that such a psychological interpretation is unfounded. One argument that presents itself immediately is how could the listeners infer it? No suggestion points this way. The first mention of the predicted short life of Achilles appears only in 1.352. How could the listener assume earlier that the issue of choosing one's fate is the main topic of this song?

29 Note the motif of a young hero calling an assembly which initiates the plot.

30 The opinion that the characters in the *Iliad* have the feeling of guilt is expressed in Zanker 1994:59–64.

31 Hitch (2009:67, 72–92) points out that in the *Iliad* only Agamemnon or someone at his behest presides over a sacrifice in the Achaean camp. According to her, it is the only way in which his authority is shown in the epic. For more on the priestly functions of the king, see West 1997:15–16.

32 It may seem surprising, because in modern opinion there is a fundamental difference between an error—which is done unconsciously—and an intentional act of *hybris*, but to the ancients they were equal, because both brought about misfortune (Evans-Pritchard 1956:17–18). A calamity was a punishment sent by a deity, whether the offence was intended or not. In both cases, the

start the causes of the plague, the community usually has no such knowledge and so it searches for the reasons. A seer is consulted because he can recognize which god/goddess is angry, what offended him/her, and what kind of compensation is needed. In the *Iliad*, the guilt for the calamity is imputed to the chief leader, Agamemnon. The situation is, then, analogous to the beginning of the Trojan War, when Artemis, offended by Agamemnon, sent contrary winds, which detained the expedition. In the *Iliad*, the seer, disclosing the reason for the god's wrath, points to the leader as the culprit. In Aulis, as we know from the Trojan Cycle, the victim of Agamemnon's guilt is his daughter Iphigenia, killed ritually as a "substitute sacrifice" for Agamemnon.[33]

Achilles, giving the reason for calling the assembly, tells Agamemnon that in his opinion they will have to head for home and forego the capture of Troy (1.59–61). Achilles' suggestion, considering the losses the Achaeans have suffered from the war and plague, has to be taken into account, but it is bad advice, the opposite of *euboulia*, which aims to show how to capture Troy. This is a traditional pattern for an epic story. The action starts at the moment of crisis—despite Achaean efforts, Troy cannot be taken. Someone or something stands in the way, either a man or a magic artifact. The obstacle has to be removed: the man must be killed, the artifact acquired. Or the community has to acquire a hero or a magic object to restore the balance of power and to overcome the obstacle.[34] Bad advice, arguing that the army should return home, probably stresses the seriousness of the situation.

In the *Iliad*, three of the four assemblies described start with bad advice (1.59, 2.140, 9.27), a proposal to flee, and the action begins as if anew.[35] In Books 2 and 9, the proposal comes from Agamemnon, who opens the assembly (also in Book 14, at the gathering of wounded leaders); the first time, he deceitfully puts his army to the test; the second time, he frankly suggests return, prompted by fear and cowardice. Thersites' exhortation to return home springs from his proper understanding of the perversity of Agamemnon's proposition (2.110–141), but he is severely chastised by Odysseus; this is a typically oral variation of a motif. The proposal to return, expressed by the chief leader, is rejected by the protagonist—Diomedes (9.95–112) and then Odysseus (14.83–102)—who

offender was equally guilty, equally unclean, and—as an abomination to the community—equally deserving of rejection.

33 Nelson 2022:60–64, 76–77.

34 It was discussed in detail in Chs. 2 and 3.

35 In my opinion, the assemblies in Books 1 and 9 open two parts of the triad, in that the assemblies which reveal the crisis threatening the community start a repetitive story-pattern of the epic, the pattern which I call "the way of the hero." The first and second instances of this pattern overlap; see Ch. 5, p. 492–493, above. The assembly in Book 2 is a variation and supplementation of the gathering in Book 1, which did not accommodate all the important elements of the introductory scene.

urges the army to continue fighting, preventing a general panic and retreat. The scene of Achilles' proposal to return does not fit into this pattern. Though his is a bad piece of advice, nobody opposes it. It does not really matter because Achilles does not insist on following it, and Agamemnon does not pay any attention, because it is presented not as a genuine piece of advice, but as a danger which should be averted.[36] The disgraceful proposal of return is a conventional element of a certain epic pattern, which the singer can modify at will, but which he cannot leave out.[37]

The proposition of an ignoble return gains here another meaning. Achilles takes on his shoulders the concern for the good of the army, and Agamemnon does not, although he should. Achilles' explanation is matter of fact and crisp (1.59–67), and—contrary to what the listeners know—shows his lack of knowledge about the reason for the misfortunes, although he does know which god is responsible for them. The listener, accustomed to the fact that he is privy to heavenly events, but the characters in the story are not, unless they are informed by divine messengers, may have been surprised. But in this case, it is only an apparent problem, because we can assume that Apollo was universally recognized as the bringer of the plague (*loimos*). What is important is that the reason for his anger and a way to propitiate him are unknown. Achilles suggests two hypothetical causes: a broken vow and a missed hecatomb.

Since no ordinary man can know what to do, Achilles advises that they should consult a specialist. Unmentioned by name, Kalchas, who the narrator says is the expert, rises to his feet (1.69–71):

> ...οἰωνοπόλων ὄχ' ἄριστος
> ὃς ᾔδη τά τ' ἐόντα τά τ' ἐσσόμενα πρό τ' ἐόντα,
> καὶ νήεσσ' ἡγήσατ' Ἀχαιῶν Ἴλιον εἴσω

> ...the best of bird-diviners,
> he knew what is, what will be, and what was before,
> and led the Achaean ships to Ilion.

Before Kalchas tells the characters in the story what the listeners of the song already know, he wants a guarantee of security from Achilles. The seer, without mentioning any names, suggests that Agamemnon himself will be cross with him for what he is going to say (1.78–79): ἦ γὰρ ὀΐομαι ἄνδρα χολωσέμεν,

36 Achilles does not propose to return but to make an appropriate sacrificial offering.

37 Perhaps such a proposal, made by the protagonist of an epic song, whose task it is to bring rescue to a threatened community, had not previously appeared in the tradition. After all, it is in the interest of the young hero to oppose such a way out. That is why, in the *Iliad*, Achilles does not make this proposal sincerely.

ὅς μέγα πάντων / Ἀργείων κρατέει καί οἱ πείθονται Ἀχαιοί ("Because I think I will anger the man who rules / over the Argives and whom the Achaeans obey").

It is sometimes claimed that Achilles keeps a diplomatic silence about Agamemnon's guilt,[38] but this presupposes that he must have associated the Chryses episode with the plague. It is difficult to decide if Achilles really knows the cause of Apollo's anger, though the plague naturally points to this god.[39] With Agamemnon, it might be another story. The calling of the assembly by Achilles could have alarmed him. At the public disclosure of what Achilles suspects and what others perhaps also suspect, Agamemnon erupts with anger. From Proclus's summary of earlier events, we know that Kalchas not only found a way to appease Artemis's anger, but he also managed to discover which divinity was responsible for the winds keeping the fleet in Aulis. Since Agamemnon explains that he wants to retain Chryseis and does not try to discredit Kalchas's prophecy, he, like the other Achaeans, also realizes which god is spreading the plague and why. He does not call the assembly because he feels guilty or is afraid to be pointed out as guilty. He does not care about the army at all and plays the role of a good ruler only later, when his guilt has been announced publicly.[40] So Agamemnon, feeling the danger, really has reasons to be worried.

A moment earlier Achilles says reassuringly that as long as he lives, nothing is going to happen to Kalchas, using words which seem quite inopportune (1.90–91): οὐδ' ἢν Ἀγαμέμνονα εἴπῃς, / ὃς νῦν πολλὸν ἄριστος Ἀχαιῶν εὔχεται εἶναι ("even if you give the name of Agamemnon,[41] / who now considers himself to be the best of the Achaeans"). Achilles is free with his tongue, not out of stupidity but because he knows his value and fears no one.[42] In this speech, we can detect

38 See, for example, Pulleyn 2000:143.

39 Agamemnon's use of the term ἑκήβολος 'death-sower' instead of 'Apollo' (1.110) seems to corroborate this opinion.

40 In the scene of Achilles and Agamemnon's reconciliation, Agamemnon takes the blame upon himself and explains himself by saying he was momentarily blinded (19.85–91). This does not mean he is remorseful or feels responsible for what has happened. Van Wees (1992:134) claims: "One can take the view that an angry man has the right to refuse any amount of compensation, and that those who provoked him remain responsible for the consequences of his anger."

41 Kalchas, like a typical soothsayer, speaks in riddles. He does not refer to Agamemnon by name, as if leaving the question of identity open. But who else could it be, if there is only one person who rules over "all the Achaeans"? Kalchas not only asks for a guarantee of immunity, but he also suggests that Achilles is the only person to whom he is ready to disclose what he knows (1.76): τοὶ γὰρ ἐγὼν ἐρέω· σὺ δὲ σύνθεο ("I will tell you and you try to understand what I mean"). Achilles, mentioning Agamemnon, cleverly suggests that he has guessed whom the seer has in mind. The question is, does Kalchas want him to solve the riddle or the problem? If the guilty person is Agamemnon, Achilles seems to be the only warrior who could put things right by confronting the leader. The seer does not intend to accuse Agamemnon openly and start a quarrel with the king. He leaves the matter in Achilles' hands.

42 Zanker (1994:75) considers Achilles' promise to protect the seer as proper conduct, obeying the rules of the community and contrasting the dishonorable way in which Agamemnon treated the priest.

a slight mockery of Agamemnon's claims to the title of *aristos Achaiôn*, which Agamemnon must have publicly used at some earlier time, certainly before the beginning of the *Iliad*. Achilles reveals his claim to be recognized as *aristos Achaiôn* in a bitter coda to insults hurled at Agamemnon, when he foretells Achaean failures (1.243–244): σὺ δ' ἔνδοθι θυμὸν ἀμύξεις / χωόμενος ὅ τ' ἄριστον Ἀχαιῶν οὐδὲν ἔτισας ("you will claw at your heart in anger that you have failed to honor the best of the Achaeans"). Though the title is his, in his answer to Kalchas Achilles does not seek to confront Agamemnon. It is a subtle verbal game in which Achilles does not seem to question Agamemnon's opinion about himself, although in fact he completely deprecates it. Were Agamemnon indeed "the best of the Achaeans," there would be nobody who could offer Kalchas protection against him. The appearance of this phrase in this context corroborates the interpretation that Agamemnon's aim in sending Chryses away was to confirm his dominant position among the Achaeans. Agamemnon reaches for the title which he does not deserve. For him, power is not enough, he must also be "the best of the Achaeans."[43]

Homer does not want to paint a portrait of an incompetent ruler, but one who uses his power for wrong ends. Verbal rivalry indicates the uncertainty and impermanence of one's position in the group—one needs constantly to reaffirm it. Agamemnon fails to do this by word or deed, so he tries to secure his position in an irregular way at the expense of others. It is evident in his brutal treatment of Chryses against the will of the army and in his usurpation of the title of "the best of the Achaeans." However, being "the best" entails not only prestige, but also, or perhaps even above all, a religious and cultural responsibility of the hero, who is expected to come to the rescue when the community is in danger. It is necessary to *prove* that one can fulfill this role; an empty declaration is not nearly enough. Throughout the story this will be demonstrated again and again. Of these two heroes, only Achilles seems to understand what the role of "the best of the Achaeans" requires. His ironic words addressed to Agamemnon summarize the confusion of ideas in the Achaean camp created by Agamemnon's excessive ambition.[44]

Achilles, opening the assembly, proposes that the Achaeans should ask a seer or a priest or an interpreter of dreams how to appease Apollo's anger. Achilles does not turn to Kalchas personally, but only presents a list of ways the

43 Martin (1989:113–119) shows that Agamemnon in his speeches reveals himself as somebody who ineptly tries to demonstrate his advantage over other heroes, but in fact he loses every time—even Diomedes' silence after Agamemnon's reproach defeats Agamemnon's inappropriately addressed and articulated rebuke.

44 The issue of violating hierarchy and social norms is not new. This is a problem that has grown; it had its first disastrous consequences after Agamemnon expelled Chryses and culminated when he deprived Achilles of his honor.

angry god might be satisfied. Kalchas comes forward of his own accord and does not explain how he obtained the knowledge that he now divulges. The listeners know that the seer is telling the truth because they have been told all this by the singer, but the Achaeans don't know it. The only warranty of the truth of his words is his professional competence mentioned by the narrator and his credit for earlier services. This may all be known to the Achaeans, but Agamemnon starts his speech by denying Kalchas any credit. In spite of that, Agamemnon does not reject Kalchas's explanation of the causes for the plague, but accepts it as a fact, or rather as a possibility. There is no attempt to clarify the situation. The listener does not need it because he already knows the reason and Kalchas's words confirm his knowledge. Agamemnon does not refute the explanation but blames the seer that it is to his disadvantage. The leader's guilt is established and the only thing for him to do is to try to extricate himself from the situation. The conviction of Agamemnon's guilt has been imposed on both him and the audience.

Pulleyn believes that Achilles' speech diplomatically[45] avoids the possibility that Apollo's wrath could be a result of Agamemnon's deed, but the assumption that Achilles attributes guilt to Agamemnon is, I believe, groundless. If Achilles mentioned this possibility, it would be tantamount to a charge against Agamemnon. Then the conflict would revolve around the blame for arousing the god's anger. Agamemnon would have to contest the validity of the charge by presenting Achilles as untrustworthy. Therefore, the accusation comes from Kalchas, whose reliability is strongly stressed by the author. Thanks to a well-organized narrative, the audience accepts the allegation against Agamemnon as true. That is why Agamemnon can later suspect a plot hatched by Achilles and Kalchas; according to the leader, the seer is Achilles' voice, whose task is to justify the accusation against him.

The author intends that Achilles' action should be free from such insinuations or suspicions. That's why it is shown as honest and done in the interest of the common good. Such is the traditional role of this hero in epic songs:[46] he lays down his life for all Achaeans and opens the way for the sack of Troy. Calling the assembly is the first step towards propitiating Apollo, and, as Kim[47] points out, Achilles deserves credit for that. Agamemnon constantly puts himself in the role belonging to Achilles: he usurps the right to the title of "the best of the Achaeans" and he declares that he does not want his army to perish, that he intends to save it. That is why he magnanimously gives in and promises to return Chryseis to her

45 See n38 above.

46 Compare Muellner 1996:107: "By blaming Agamemnon for another grievous mistake about a person's value—in this case, failing to respect and recognize Achilles' own value as 'the best of the Achaeans'—Achilles is identifying the outrage done to him with the outrage done to Chryses."

47 Kim 2000:77.

father. In fact, the salvation of the army depends not on him, but on Achilles, as will become evident later, when the Achaeans experience the bitterness of defeat. In the first assembly, Agamemnon, who did not call it, "steals" from Achilles the "healing" of the army by an action which is aimed at stopping the anger of the god. However, for Achilles, resolving the issue is more important than taking credit for it. Perhaps his words (1.90–91) are not directed against Agamemnon, but they must irritate the leader nonetheless, since he listens to them tensely.[48]

Kalchas's diagnosis traps Agamemnon, who must defend himself. At first, the defense is violent, which corresponds to the weight of the accusation, but after a while Agamemnon changes his tone and with great cunning presents himself as a savior (1.101–120):

> ἤτοι ὅ γ' ὣς εἰπὼν κατ' ἄρ' ἕζετο· τοῖσι δ' ἀνέστη
> ἥρως Ἀτρεΐδης εὐρὺ κρείων Ἀγαμέμνων
> ἀχνύμενος· μένεος δὲ μέγα φρένες ἀμφιμέλαιναι
> πίμπλαντ', ὄσσε δέ οἱ πυρὶ λαμπετόωντι ἐΐκτην·
> Κάλχαντα πρώτιστα κάκ' ὀσσόμενος προσέειπε·
> μάντι κακῶν οὐ πώ ποτέ μοι τὸ κρήγυον εἶπας·
> αἰεί τοι τὰ κάκ' ἐστὶ φίλα φρεσὶ μαντεύεσθαι,
> ἐσθλὸν δ' οὐτέ τί πω εἶπας ἔπος οὔτ' ἐτέλεσσας·
> καὶ νῦν ἐν Δαναοῖσι θεοπροπέων ἀγορεύεις
> ὡς δὴ τοῦδ' ἕνεκά σφιν ἑκηβόλος ἄλγεα τεύχει,
> οὕνεκ' ἐγὼ κούρης Χρυσηΐδος ἀγλά' ἄποινα
> οὐκ ἔθελον δέξασθαι, ἐπεὶ πολὺ βούλομαι αὐτὴν
> οἴκοι ἔχειν· καὶ γάρ ῥα Κλυταιμνήστρης προβέβουλα
> κουριδίης ἀλόχου, ἐπεὶ οὔ ἑθέν ἐστι χερείων,
> οὐ δέμας οὐδὲ φυήν, οὔτ' ἂρ φρένας οὔτέ τι ἔργα.
> ἀλλὰ καὶ ὣς ἐθέλω δόμεναι πάλιν εἰ τό γ' ἄμεινον·
> βούλομ' ἐγὼ λαὸν σῶν ἔμμεναι ἢ ἀπολέσθαι·
> αὐτὰρ ἐμοὶ γέρας αὐτίχ' ἑτοιμάσατ' ὄφρα μὴ οἶος
> Ἀργείων ἀγέραστος ἔω, ἐπεὶ οὐδὲ ἔοικε·
> λεύσσετε γὰρ τό γε πάντες ὅ μοι γέρας ἔρχεται ἄλλῃ.

48 Perhaps by calling an assembly and requesting seers to explain the situation Achilles takes over Agamemnon's prerogatives, which might have irritated the leader. If consulting the soothsayer was Agamemnon's prerogative (Hittite sources *ANET* 394–395 indicate that demanding explanations from various seers was in the competence of Hatti kings; see West 1997:47–48), analogous to the exclusive right to make public sacrifices, it would be another instance of the modification of a plot element: Agamemnon infringes on Achilles' domain by usurping the right to the title of "the best of the Achaeans," while Achilles violates Agamemnon's authority when he summons the assembly and consults the seer on a matter concerning the whole army. By employing such symmetrical actions, the author of the *Iliad* gives his listeners a chance of judging the juxtaposed heroes by comparing the meaning of their analogous behaviors.

Having said this, [Kalchas] sat down.[49] And [in reaction] to these words stood up
the hero Atreides, mighty ruling Agamemnon
with a gloomy face, and his thoughts (*phrenes*) turned black and filled with anger,
But his eyes were like glowing fire.
First, he looked at Kalchas with an evil eye and said:
"Prophet of misery, you've never said a thing that would benefit me.
You always announce these unfortunate things for me as the intention of the gods,
a noble word you have never uttered nor brought to pass.
So now you have publicly proclaimed among the Danaans as the voice of the god
that the reason the Bringing-a-lot-of-death apparently is giving us pain
is that in exchange for the girl, daughter of Chryses, I refused to accept
a fine ransom. [Well, I refused] because I want very much
to keep her at home because she surpasses even Klytaimestra,
my wife wedded as a virgin, because she's [Chryseis] no worse than she is
neither in stature, nor in height, nor in reason, nor in skill.
But still, I'm ready to return her if this is better.
It is my intention to save, not to destroy the army.
So ready me a portion of the loot [*geras*] so that
I alone of all the Achaeans am not without a portion [*geras*], because that would be unseemly.
You all see that my portion [*geras*] goes elsewhere.

The seer's accusation makes Agamemnon erupt with fury, which the narrator paints very vividly (1.101–105). Agamemnon starts his speech with a violent attack upon Kalchas. He claims that the seer has never foretold him "anything but evil"—he has never done any good for the army or served the common cause. However, Agamemnon's words—apparently addressed to the

49 In this simple sentence, which enumerates only two actions performed by Kalchas ("he said and sat down"). Homer places as many as three particles reinforcing the meaning. The simplicity of the description of what Kalchas did must correspond to the seer's intentions: he does not intend to interpret what he said or draw consequences from it. He said what he was asked to say and the rest is up to others. The particles presumably suggest the impression he made on those listening to his speech.

soothsayer, and in fact meant to affect the whole army—are contrary to what the narrator says about Kalchas.[50] Agamemnon is furious with him because he always foretells disasters and has never deserved any credit, but is insolent enough to utter such dishonorable words "among the Danaans." Then the Mycenaean ruler excuses his conduct towards Chryses. What is astonishing is that he does not try to refute the charge, but distances himself from admitting its truth (1.109–110).[51] Finally, he accepts the prophecy, but not because it is right; he behaves as if he has decided to follow the advice that he believes is the best for everyone (1.116). Agamemnon does not try to establish his innocence, but he does not admit he is culpable or deny that his guilt brought about the calamities.[52] He concedes that it was egotism which pushed him to do what he did. However, now he gives another motivation for his deed: he did not cast out Chryses to show he can do as he pleases, but because he is very much pleased with the priest's daughter. Considering how worthless the girl was to him when he spoke about her to her father, it is hardly believable that now he is telling the truth.[53] All the more so because he goes too far, excusing his egotism by saying Chryseis is closer to him than his wife, Klytaimestra. This statement raises the question, which must have occurred also to the surprised and perhaps even indignant audience, how the king could make such a comparison between a slave and his royal wife (1.112–115).

The question is whether the listeners knew the future lot of Agamemnon from other songs of the cycle. The chief leader is indignant with the seer, who "never" favors him and "always" prophesies him evil. It is a typical heated argument when charges go too far.[54] Under the influence of emotions, we are apt to forget our opponent's good points and concentrate on the wrong he has done to us. The expressions "you always" and "you never" are explicable as an emotional outburst, even if they are not true, considering Kalchas's services to

50 Pulleyn (2000:151) believes that Kalchas's prophecy, being consistent with what really happened, corroborates the seer's reliability: "This must reinforce our impression of him as a seer because he shares Homer's (all-seeing) perspective on events."

51 Pulleyn (2000:159) reads this utterance as sarcastic.

52 Agamemnon does not argue with the accusation, because it would be pointless. After all, the warriors witnessed what he did and they all know that inappropriate conduct can bring about calamities affecting the community. Instead, Agamemnon tries to suggest that this is only one of the possible causes of the misfortune and, to keep on the safe side (although he does not confirm the correctness of this interpretation), he agrees to do what is expected of him.

53 Erbse (2001:242) takes everything Agamemnon says on trust because he does not juxtapose these two speeches. That is why he says: "Es handelt sich um ein besonders wertvolles Ehrengeschenk, das er vom Gesamtheer erhalten hat, ähnlich wie Achilleus die Briseis." But there is nothing in the text to suggest that what is at issue here is the exceptional value of the gift.

54 Van Wees 1992:96–97. Scodel 2002:106: "Angry speakers use hyperbole of this kind," but she does not go further to infer that Agamemnon's words may be an allusion to the events at Aulis.

the expedition mentioned by the narrator. Nevertheless, when Agamemnon resorts to "always" and "never," he must refer to at least one situation, in which Kalchas's predictions were bad for him.

The allusion to earlier predictions may be deliberate. If the audience draws on their knowledge about Agamemnon's death, carried out or at least inspired by his wife Klytaimestra, they might be able to anticipate the charges later put forward against him. Agamemnon shows himself guilty in the current situation from the perspective of the guilt which will cause his death. The mention of Klytaimestra is not astonishing if we assume that the attack on Kalchas is grounded in the sacrifice of Iphigenia.[55] The memory of the sacrifice of Iphigenia entails the memory of her mother, who, according to many ancient sources, could not forgive Agamemnon and for whom this crime was the main reason which propelled her to murder her husband. Here the mythical story is used to draw a psychological portrait of Agamemnon, who takes it out on Kalchas, his associate in crime, and then expresses his animosity towards his wife, who could not forgive him for his heinous deed. Speaking to the assembly, Agamemnon gives excuses for the decision to keep Chryseis and to reject the old priest's request to ransom his daughter, and at the same time is thinking about his old crime, which he aggravated by his marital infidelity (Aeschylus *Agamemnon* 1439–1440). He will pay for it later with his death. The whole scene, from the moment when Kalchas speaks before the assembly to that when Agamemnon mentions his wife's name, appears to be an allusion to Agamemnon's life before and after the Trojan War.[56]

Kullmann, using Neoanalytic argumentation, sees in this passage an allusion to the fate of Iphigenia and challenges the authority of scholia, which claim that Homer did not know such a character.[57] Scodel takes the middle ground. Trying to determine which characters Homeric listeners could be familiar with, she concludes, "The audience ... probably should not remember the story, at

55 Few scholars see the possibility of Homer taking into account the myth of Iphigenia. Clark 1998 notes differences in the scenes of Chryses' supplication of Agamemnon and Priam's supplication of Achilles, but according to him, they do not remove the intended parallelism of these scenes. Clark sees a significant difference between these scenes in the fact that Chryses in his request to the Achaeans deliberately refrains from using the obvious argument of reminding the supplicated that they too have someone very dear in their family. The decision not to remind Agamemnon of his daughter is an attempt to avoid bringing up the memory of Iphigenia. According to Clark, this fact indicates that Homer not only knows but also alludes to the myth of Iphigenia.

56 Frame (2009:205n103) cites an analogical situation: "It is worth stepping back for a moment to appreciate the unusual concentration of allusions in *Iliad* 8 to Nestor's past and future all in the same episode: his race against the Epeian twins in the past; his *nóstos* with Diomedes in the future; the death of his son Antilochus before the end of the war; his split with Odysseus on Tenedos after the war. All these different moments are present in the episode."

57 Kullmann 1960:198, 201, 267–268; 2005:26.

least in detail." This opinion is based on her analysis of Agamemnon's situation. The mention of the sacrifice of his daughter could create too much sympathy for him, but, because it would make Agamemnon a "relatively innocent victim" of a god's decree:[58]

> His behavior now could seem grotesque: a man who has been forced to kill a daughter should not have been cruel to a man trying to ransom his daughter, a man who has caused disaster to his army by a foolish boast that angered Artemis should have known better than to antagonize a priest of Apollo, and a man who has had to kill his own child should be better able to evaluate his loss of a prize.

Scodel notices the parallelism of those two stories, but she does not see any reason for the introduction of this allusion, and so she assumes that the allusion is possible, but not necessary for the audience to become involved in the story.

I disagree with this line of reasoning. There is a noticeable scheme in the presentation of the episode. Agamemnon's *hybris* provokes divine anger. The king agrees to part with a girl (first, a daughter, then a slave). It seems that either this is a traditional way to introduce Agamemnon, or it is a reference to an episode which is so familiar that Iphigenia does not have to be mentioned by name, or even more, she does not have to be mentioned at all. The *Iliad* repeats with modification the situation known from the *Kypria*: there a seer demands the sacrifice of Agamemnon's daughter, here the same seer suggests that Agamemnon should return his captive woman.[59] The loss of the slave is certainly less painful than the loss of the daughter, which is consistent with the Neoanalytical point of view that in comparison with the episodes of the *Kypria*, those of the *Iliad* are less important and less moving. But Homer's virtuosity is unparalleled: the exaggerated magnitude of the loss of Chryseis stresses Agamemnon's *hybris* instead of showing him as a victim of divine wrath.

Scodel's reasoning presupposes a certain psychological continuity and consistency in Agamemnon's character (e.g. he should remember the destiny of his daughter, the anger of a deity, etc.). It means that in the minds of the audience there is a coherent psychological image of the chief leader.[60] However,

58 Scodel 2002:106. She similarly views Kalchas's exposition with references to the past: "The poet, then, does not rely on prior knowledge of Calchas but tells the audience everything necessary for understanding his role. The poet does, however, surround this figure with vague references to past events that he does not narrate" (106).

59 See the same opinion of Nelson 2022:77–79.

60 Trying to psychologize, one can say that people often make the same mistakes; Nelson (2022:76): "The king, it seems, has not learned from his previous transgression. Indeed, Achilles' claim that Agamemnon does not know how to look to the past or the future (*Iliad* 1.343) could be taken as an implicit gesture to his failure to learn from past mistakes."

Scodel does not allow for the fact that songs may have various aims. Earlier, I demonstrated that the psychological images of Odysseus, Paris, and, to a certain extent, Achilles, all lack coherence.[61] Why should Agamemnon be any different? In the cycle, Odysseus often uses subterfuge against his companions (Palamedes, Aias, Diomedes, Philoktetes), but we can't find any trace of it in the *Odyssey*. Agamemnon's traditional image can be modified by the author of the *Iliad*. If Agamemnon's portrait is traditional (even if it implies a certain inconsistency of image),[62] the audience may assume his guilt in rousing divine anger. In both cases, Agamemnon surrenders a girl for the sake of the expedition and Achilles plays an important role: in Aulis he is deceived, at Troy he is offended because he is deprived of his war-prize. Achilles also loses potential wives twice: Iphigenia is decoyed there under the pretext of her marriage to him, while Briseis, as she laments over Patroklos's body, mentions his promise that Achilles would marry her (19.297–299), even though she was a slave.[63]

These parallels would only point to a variable treatment of the subject, if it were not for Agamemnon's improper equating of Chryseis with his wife Klytaimestra. He praises Chryseis and Klytaimestra only to make an impression; in fact, both are equally worthless to him, so why should we expect that his daughter, whom he sacrificed in order to sail to Troy, was dear to his heart? In this subtle way, Homer shows Agamemnon to be an egoist who does not care for anyone except himself, and it is an element of his overall picture of the leader who is not concerned about his army, but only about his position.

Later, when Agamemnon mentions three daughters living in his house (9.145), the name of one, Iphianassa, echoes the name of Iphigenia and there may be a deliberate allusion to affect the listener. The daughters are presented as possible candidates for Achilles' wife. The association with Iphigenia makes the audience remember the previous situation when Achilles was offered Agamemnon's daughter as a bride. The allusion shows the emptiness and perversity of Agamemnon's promises when he is sending an embassy to Achilles. And, like with the multiple evocations of Achilles' death in its clearest form—the death of Patroklos—the similarity is deliberately muted. An allusion is all the listeners need to recall a particular memory and to interpret the message correctly. Closer analogies would interfere with the understanding of the current situation.

61 See Ch. 2, below.

62 In tradition, Agamemnon repeatedly incurs the wrath of a deity, but the image of the hero himself may be inconsistent, i.e. his role in these events may be interpreted variously by singers, although I doubt if he would ever have been portrayed as an "innocent victim" (Scodel 2002:106) of divine whim. Nelson (2022:64–65, 87) suggests that, in tradition, Agamemnon may have shown anger and despair as his daughter was being led to her death.

63 For discussion on the situation of Briseis, see Dué 2002:67–81.

Kalchas's delay in answering what or who is behind the anger of the deity can intrigue the listeners, or even cause their apprehension, because his allusion to the violence of a great lord (in whom it is not difficult to see Agamemnon) suggests that the prophet can expect to be treated like Chryses or maybe even worse. Astonishment is caused not by Agamemnon's outrage but by the way that he expresses his anger. The allusions to Iphigenia and Klytaimestra situate his speech in the perspective of the distant past and the distant future—a terrible past and a sinister future.

Having made his excuses, Agamemnon plays the role of a magnanimous ruler and declares that he will return the captive woman for the good of all. He does not want to be a cause of affliction for the army but its savior, but then demands compensation from the army he has so obviously rescued (1.117–120). The way that Agamemnon makes his excuses lets us infer that he has always been aware of his responsibility for the destruction of people. He tells his warriors that Chryseis is closer to him than his wife, going over the top to publicly demonstrate his attachment to the captive woman in order to prepare the ground for his grand gesture. However, for the listener who knows Agamemnon's past and future, these words unintentionally reveal the real thoughts of the Mycenaean ruler. Agamemnon realizes or at least assumes that reproaches are circulating in the army because he formulates his good will in a way that Zenodotus deemed stupid and postulated the need to athetize the line (1.117):[64] βούλομ' ἐγὼ λαὸν σῶν ἔμμεναι ἢ ἀπολέσθαι ("As for me, my intention is to save, not to destroy the army"). Zenodotus seems to be right: what leader would want to destroy his army? But this is not the point. Agamemnon, who has been identified as the one responsible for the destruction of the army, presents himself in the opposite role: as its healer and rescuer.

The very idea that he might want to destroy the army and his people means that Agamemnon is aware of the deplorable results of his deed and of the seriousness of the charge. His words express the need to reverse the situation: to remove the accusation of bringing about the failure of the Achaeans. Demanding compensation, Agamemnon feels that he is in control of the situation, and this consolatory thought pushes him to counterattack. Not expecting resistance from his subordinates, he demands that they recognize his dominant position, thus cleverly distancing himself from the responsibility for the whole situation. But by demanding compensation, he contradicts his earlier words: Chryseis could not be as valuable to him as he suggested; she is no better than

64 Scholia quote Zenodotus's argumentation: ὡς τῆς διανοίας εὐήθους οὔσης ("because the very thought is absurd"). Aristarchus argued this line should be preserved because he regarded it as fitting the character. The antithetic nature of Agamemnon's expression, typical of an oral speech, was already unclear for those scholars.

a "head," since she can be satisfactorily exchanged for another "head," i.e. another captive woman (1.116–120).

The quarrel has not started yet, but the listener already feels the tension. So far there has been only one awkward expression used by Achilles, which roused the chief leader's and also the listener's attention. Agamemnon's demand for compensation is not exceptional and it does not indicate his exorbitant greediness. Agamemnon skillfully casts himself in the role of the injured party, exaggerating his loss, but also pointing to something much more important: the unfairness of the division of spoils. The rule is simple: the best warriors get the best morsels at a feast and the best prizes after the capture of a city, but nobody can be deprived of his share, be without his *geras*. Even the least important soldier must get something, even if it is of little value; nor can he go hungry, be deprived of his piece of meat at a meal.[65] Giving up Chryseis, Agamemnon shows himself as the only one without his part of the spoils (*agerastos*). It is very improbable that after sacking a city the chief leader would get only one slave as his prize,[66] but this is how Agamemnon presents the situation. And the situation is really unacceptable, because it puts him outside the pale of society, depriving him of the token of respect not only as the chief leader but also as a member of the community. Agamemnon presents himself simply as one of the warriors: it is not right that anyone should be in such a predicament. His demand, in fact, means that he expects the Achaeans to show him respect by offering him a valuable prize. This would re-establish his position and would free him from blame.

As I have said, his demand is not reprehensible.[67] Agamemnon depends on appearances, but it would not be easy to make this a reproach against him. However, Agamemnon's demand causes Achilles' discomfiture, because now there is no way to meet it. Achilles answers with a slight mockery, calling him φιλοκτεανώτατε πάντων, "the greatest spoils lover of all" (1.122). Achilles' use of the word "all" is probably deliberate, in opposition to Agamemnon's image

65 As I understand *geras*, it is not a mark of respect due only to kings or aristocrats (as suggested by Benveniste 1973:334–345), but a better part of the loot granted at the distribution, though usually it does fall to the members of the elite.

66 Thersites in his attack on the king (2.226–228), clearly states that it is not true.

67 In the mentality of the characters of the *Iliad* there exists the principle of polarization. A reproach means the taking away of respect. The opposite is not the withdrawal of the reproach but showing respect by deed and/or word, i.e. praise (on linking praise to the acceptance of the group, see Elmer 2013:21–47). This is connected with the wider issue of how the logic of events is perceived: the absence of a negative action means that there is a positive action. That is why Apollo, who punishes the Achaeans with plague, becomes a healer ("Paian") when the plague ceases. Conversely, the undertaking of a positive action means the withdrawal of the negative action, like here: showing respect cancels reproach.

of himself as a poor wronged man: "so that I alone of all the Argives am not without *geras*."[68]

Achilles' irony is not a trivial thing, but a reaction to what he hears from Agamemnon. In order to save his skin, Agamemnon magnifies the worth of Chryseis, saying that he holds her dearer than his wife, he gives to her the highest possible value a woman can have. Chryseis is his *geras*, but she also turns out to be the most valuable of his possessions.[69] Agamemnon resorts to exaggeration for a reason: his grand gesture is going to save the army. Agamemnon is showing himself to be an epic hero, whose job is to save the community from danger. However, the essence of the epic hero's role is not the ability to do deeds but his readiness for self-sacrifice.

Walter Burkert has demonstrated the mechanism of finding deliverance from danger by getting rid of some possessions.[70] The forsaking of the most precious thing reveals determination in seeking rescue. It means that Agamemnon knows that the role of the "best of the Achaeans" involves the readiness for self-sacrifice. But he chooses the least painful way: the sacrifice of a precious possession, like Polykrates of Samos, who threw his ring into the sea.[71] However, Agamemnon is insincere: he lies to magnify the value of his sacrifice. Despite the semblance of the generosity (loss of a slave, animals for a hecatomb), he escapes with a cheap gesture. Pretending to save the community, he tries to save only himself. Achilles' first words indicate that he is well aware of what Agamemnon is up to. Since the role of the epic hero is in fact Achilles', then Agamemnon not only assumes someone else's title, but also publicly signals a deed that would prove his right to it. However, his self-sacrifice is feigned. At this point, Achilles only mentions that Agamemnon is resorting to a trick imitating a truly heroic deed.

68 Agamemnon goes over the top claiming that the loss of Chryseis makes him *agerastos*, and this exaggeration provokes Achilles' reaction.

69 Compare Muellner 1996:98–99: "Now there is ample reason to believe that a hero's wife in the Homeric hierarchy of value is the most costly and valuable of all exchangeable goods, in that she represents in her person the hero's own accumulated worth and prestige. So Agamemnon's avowal that he prefers Chryseis to his wife amounts to a peremptory statement that she is not exchangeable for anything at all, including his wife. No little irony resides in Clytemnestra's corresponding preference of someone else to him, which makes her the negative ideal of a Homeric wife (*Odyssey* 24.199–202), but Agamemnon is unconscious of that irony, so that the face value of his statements in terms of the conventions of the Homeric society is worth bringing to mind. Agamemnon has taken leave of his social obligations and, on the basis of his own desire, valued this girl as an incommensurable piece of property. In doing so, he has made a grievous and obvious mistake about what she is (or is not) exchangeable for."

70 Burkert 1996:Ch. 2.

71 Herodotus 3.40–43. Fearing the gods, who do not like to see people too prosperous, Polykrates decided to protect himself against a reversal of fortune and to get rid of his ring, most probably a signet ring, which was used for sealing his property (see Seaford 1994:220–232). As such, it was the most precious of his possessions, because it allowed him to protect and thus to increase his wealth.

The loss of one's most valuable thing will resurface again, this time in relation to Achilles. First, he loses a woman who was very dear to him (unlike Chryseis was to Agamemnon) and whom he says he loved (9.335, 342–343). The loss of the woman is not at issue here, but the loss of honor (*timê*) symbolized by the taking of Briseis. Talking with the ambassadors, Achilles states that by losing honor he became a nobody, someone who does not belong to the group (τιν' ἀτίμητον μετανάστην, 9.648).[72] His rejection of the proposed gifts is justified by the fact that the only precious thing which has been left to him and which cannot be exchanged for anything else is his life (9.401–416).[73] The most precious thing is not exchangeable, which is in stark contradiction to Agamemnon's demand to get compensation for Chryseis. After Patroklos's death, Achilles sacrifices his life to avenge his friend. His own life becomes valueless when he realizes that it means nothing to him after the loss of his friend. He cannot resign himself to this death in any way; neither revenge nor mourning—though extreme—can quench the feeling of loss.

Achilles is not starting a quarrel yet; he reasonably argues that all spoils have been divided and there is no common store from which the army can reward the king. He also points out that in these circumstances to demand compensation would violate a custom (1.126): λαοὺς δ' οὐκ ἐπέοικε παλίλλογα ταῦτ' ἐπαγείρειν ("it would be unseemly[74] [to make] the army heap up all things again)." Achilles means that once things have been apportioned, they cannot be reapportioned (strictly speaking, they could be reapportioned, but it would wrong the army). The compensation for Agamemnon may be done only from a common store. Achilles appeals to Agamemnon's reason, promising the gratitude of the warriors, who will appreciate this gesture. Achilles, thinking rationally, stresses that it would be best to solve the problem in the future. He logically assumes that after the fall of Troy, the grateful army will reward Agamemnon amply for the sacrifice the chief leader says he is making for the sake of the community.[75]

72 Achilles says that Agamemnon treated him as a nameless person (μετανάστης), someone who wanders around the world having no home, because he has been expelled. He, Achilles, has also lost his home and the respect of his community, and therefore is nobody, being a stranger to the people he meets as he wanders.

73 Compare Muellner 1996:Ch. 2, esp. p. 34.

74 He may be teasing Agamemnon, answering with these words to his "so that I alone of all the Argives am not without *geras*" (1.119). Achilles may be slightly amused and smilingly expresses his astonishment, but this also reflects another rule concerning the division of spoils. Such vying, in which parties refer to tradition and common wisdom, is a typical way of conducting a dispute in oral cultures. The reasons of both parties are of equal importance: neither this, nor that course of action is good (see Zieliński 2019b:247–248).

75 According to Erbse (2001:242–243), Achilles' proposal is improper and offensive to the leader because it is a kind of proposal that can be put forward by a superior promising a warrior a greater share of future spoils if he shows bravery in action. Erbse cites the example of

Agamemnon understands things differently. His reaction—"don't try to trick me"—indicates that he is sure he has got wise to Achilles' sneaky scheme. In his eyes, recent events are all part of Achilles' plan: he called the assembly and perhaps plotted with Kalchas to belittle his, Agamemnon's, position. And a sure sign of this is their tricky attempt to deprive him of his possessions. Agamemnon cannot allow this. He has uncovered a plot against himself and now he starts making threats (1.135–139). He is the only one who can take whatever he wants from any of the Achaeans. He answers Achilles by trying to get this message across: "If there is a problem with compensating me for my loss, I will simply take whatever I want from whomever I want." So far, it is only bluster—he does not want to go ahead with it. Instead, he makes his army a good offer (1.140–147); this gesture should restore his dominance, which seemed secure when he was casting Chryses out of the camp. Agamemnon's offer boils down to the following: "Though I can take whatever I want from you, I prefer to give you something so that you know how good I am." To appease the anger of the god, he suggests a special expedition headed by one of the Achaean leaders. He ends his speech by making this offer to Achilles himself. A hecatomb also means large meals. It may seem very appealing to leaders and even to Achilles, especially as Agamemnon, proposing this "bribe," plays on his ambition, calling him πάντων ἐπαγλότατ' ἀνδρῶν—with an ambiguous meaning: "the most redoubtable, fiercest of all men" or "the most admirable, most marvelous of all men" (1.146).[76] In the singer's presentation of the scene, Agamemnon mocks Achilles, just as Achilles mocked him earlier.

Agamemnon, who makes such a promise to Teukros (8.287–291). From this one case, the scholar makes a rule with far-reaching consequences, whereas in the *Iliad*, the promise of a very valuable prize is several times presented as the result of an agreement proposed by the subordinate: Othryoneus is promised by Priam the hand of Cassandra if he manages to drive the Achaeans away from Troy (13.363–369), and Dolon gets Hektor's guarantee that he will be given Achilles' chariot and horses as his share of spoils if he makes a successful spying expedition (10.315–333). The status of both warriors is low: the former could not afford to pay the bride-price, the latter is a herald's son. Soon after Achilles makes his proposal to Agamemnon, he himself receives a similar one from Athena, who offers him triple gifts for restraining himself from killing the chief leader (1.210–214). Achilles accepts this proposal, not because Athena is his superior but because one should obey gods (see Martin 1989:48–49). I do not share Erbse's view also for another reason. The dispute Achilles entered with Agamemnon is a kind of game. If the proposal had been wrong, it would have meant Achilles' immediate loss—this is how Agamemnon would interpret it. Collins (2005:56–57, 231–232) shows how the violation of the principle of discourse in oral cultures leads to the failure of rivals entering a verbal dispute. The point is that Achilles, by referring to a custom, makes a rightful accusation that the leader's behavior is unacceptable. Moreover, the inequality of status suggested by Erbse also does matter in a dispute—dispute destroys hierarchy, as René Girard (2005:Ch. 2) rightly points out.

76 This expression appears only once more in a formula addressed to Achilles (18.170), in which Iris tells him to defend Patroklos's body. Muellner (1996:105) translates this phrase as "most hostile of all men" and opines that this epithet marks Agamemnon's "turning to the language of insult":

How could the listener realize the character of Agamemnon's suspicions of Achilles, if he could not go back in the story to analyze everything in detail, as we have? The key to understanding lies in the traditional character of the subject matter or at least in the traditional pattern of the song and in the frequent foreshadowing of events. The traditionality of the motif of a leader who suspects he is being tricked and fears that people whom he trusted are plotting against him is corroborated by the action in some tragedies. Both Oedipus in *Oedipus the King* and Creon in *Antigone* come to believe that someone is deliberately deceiving them. Both "get wise" to their interlocutors: Oedipus suspects a conspiracy between Teiresias and Creon (*Oedipus the King* 345–349, 378–400), whereas Creon, talking to a sentry, concludes that he has uncovered bribery committed by unknown conspirators who are rebelling against his authority (*Antigone* 288–313); later, he assumes that Teiresias is in league with them (1033–1039). Both Oedipus and Creon become overconfident and succumb to anger. Both believe that they have exposed sinister designs and undertake actions to frustrate them. In the *Iliad*, there is the same issue of the guilt of a ruler, who either does not see it or tries not to see it. The king's suspicions that the whole situation is a trap indicate his attempts to avoid responsibility.

All this does not bring the quarrel any closer, although because of foreshadowing it looms ahead. But it is not the result of an already existing difficulty and dislike between characters. The problem starts the moment that Agamemnon suddenly thinks he has got wise to Achilles' scheme and puts his cards on the table. His uncovering the plot against himself makes Agamemnon the master of the situation and prompts him to counterattack; he utters a threat against Achilles but, cleverly enough, also mentions other important leaders, Aias and Odysseus (1.138). In this way, Agamemnon makes Achilles equal to the others, both compliant and helpless: neither Aias nor Odysseus reacts to his words.[77] Now Agamemnon, certain of his ground, cuts off the debate, which would probably concentrate on his guilt, seemingly in order to discuss more important matters. His manner is that of a man saying, "Enough of that, let us go on to more pressing issues." In fact, he tries to quench legitimate reproaches and

"It is possible for him to do so because the essential outlines of the conflict between them have already been defined." In my opinion, Agamemnon, far from formulating an explicit reproach, has simply clapped back at Achilles for *his* epithet, which also bordered on reproach. Tension is mounting, but so far both heroes pretend there is no quarrel. A conflict between leaders is a kind of social institution; formally initiated, it has far-reaching consequences, which Agamemnon is trying to avoid. The ambiguity of the epithet is also stressed by Martin 1989:116–117.

77 Zeus uses similar threats towards the Olympians to make them realize that his power is unshakable. For more on the parallel behavior of Agamemnon and Zeus, see Muellner 1996:110–116.

introduces diversion in the form of the proposal of an embassy to Chryses to return Chryseis and to propitiate Apollo.[78]

Achilles' reaction contrasts with the silence of the other leaders. Though Agamemnon does not say anything specific about taking away their part of the spoils, Achilles is offended by the very possibility of depriving him of this sign of respect, because he feels that his service to the community puts him above the ruler. He is indignant that Agamemnon dares to threaten him. As far as threats are concerned, it is he, Achilles, who can make threats, for example, that he will quit. And how are they going to manage without him?

We can see the standpoints of both characters change. Agamemnon, who appeared on the scene as a conceited egotist, avoids blame and turns things to his advantage. He adopts the role of a just ruler, ready to put the good of the community over his own and to return Chryseis to her father. Achilles goes in the other direction. Calling the assembly, he was motivated by his concern for the army; but when Agamemnon threatens him with taking away his honor, which he has worked hard to deserve, Achilles suddenly changes his standpoint and distances himself from the common cause. He says that the Trojans have never offended him nor robbed him—which Agamemnon threatens him with—so he has no reason to fight them, especially under such a leader. He has been laboring for someone who cannot appreciate it. Therefore, his participation in this war is superfluous and he decides to withdraw from fighting. Achilles' speech is marked with the bitterness of ingratitude, but also with rigorous logic. He constantly tries to explain something to the leader, who, however, does not understand anything. Achilles seems to expect an attempt at keeping him; he

78 Erbse (2001:243) calls it "a reasonable proposition," which could lead to "a peaceful patching up of a difference of opinions." From this point of view, both the rejection of the proposition by Achilles and his motivation for doing so are absurd: they make Achilles' withdrawal from alliance commitments, which he voluntarily accepted, regardless of the realities of the war and Agamemnon's conduct, completely unjustified. His criticism of the king's qualifications as a commander is also unjustified and aimed only at gaining a response from the army, which he is calling to revolt. But the army is not on his side. According to Erbse, Achilles' insubordination and conceit irritated Agamemnon, who was forced to threaten him in order to save his authority, "which for obvious reasons is of great importance to him" (2001:247). Achilles should have offered him his slave, hoping that the king, moved by the loyalty of his subordinate, would return her to him. Erbse concludes (2001:247): "Unfortunately, Achilles is not ready to do it." Instead, the army shows its wisdom, remaining deaf to his call to disobedience. The conclusion which arises from this argument is that the irresponsibility of Achilles' behavior, postulated by Erbse, consists in a failure to understand the soldier's duty, in disregarding military hierarchy and disobeying orders. Therefore, this hero cannot be right in the dispute. It is difficult to agree with this standpoint. Loyalty and obedience may be of paramount value nowadays, though even of that I would not be too certain. Agamemnon's reasons for protecting his authority are not so obvious. Erbse imposes on the Homeric world his contemporary understanding of correct relations within the army and, moreover, does not take into account the dynamics of the dispute based on the need for competition.

hopes Agamemnon will come to his senses and will restore his honor for the good of the community.[79]

Both men's speeches reflect the changes in their behavior. Agamemnon, who earlier stressed his egotistical "I," in his last speech uses the first-person plural (μεταφρασόμεσθα, ἐρύσσομεν, ἀγείρομεν, θείομεν, βήσομεν—"let us think," "let us launch [a ship]," "let us gather [rowers]," "let us put on board creatures for sacrifice," "let us embark [on it Chryseis]," 1.140–144).[80] Achilles, opening the assembly, used the first-person plural, because he spoke on behalf of everybody (ἄμμε ... ἀπονοστήσειν, φύγοιμεν, ἐρείομεν "we should ... return," "we would escape [death]," "let us ask," 1.59–62);[81] now he emphasizes the pronoun "I." The young hero shows that he, too, can be egotistical, if he chooses, and he is also probably irritated by Agamemnon's insincere concern for the army. The threat to go home is an answer to the threat of taking away his *geras*. It is equivalent to posing the question: "Can you manage without me?"

In Achilles' subsequent speeches, the first lines contain epithets for Agamemnon which are neologisms. According to Adam Parry, they reflect the hero's youthful intelligence,[82] but because they always appear in the initial lines of speeches addressed to the chief leader, it seems that Achilles groped for

79 The sincerity of Achilles' intentions is underlined by a certain dreamy quality associated with his youth and almost romantic sadness. In this very emotional context, the description of his native Phthia and of the space separating it from the battlefield at Troy indicates a moment of weakness. Achilles' daydreaming unintentionally reveals his longing for his homeland (1.154–157): οὐ γάρ πώποτ' ἐμὰς βοῦς ἤλασαν οὐδὲ μὲν ἵππους, / οὐδέ ποτ' ἐν Φθίῃ ἐριβώλακι βωτιανείρῃ / καρπὸν ἐδηλήσαντ', ἐπεὶ ἦ μάλα πολλὰ μεταξὺ / οὔρεά τε σκιόεντα θάλασσά τε ἠχήεσσα ("they never drove off my cattle or horses, / and never in deep-soiled Phthia, nurturer of men, / did they destroy crops, since between these countries [Troy and Phthia] there are many / shadowy mountains and a roaring sea").

80 Kirk (1985:68) claims that the hortatory character of these appeals to achieve a common goal is insincere, because they are aimed at obfuscating Agamemnon's earlier egocentrism.

81 The first-person plural pointing to his identification with the Achaeans comes back in Achilles' speeches only after he kills Hektor, whose body he lets other warriors mutilate. Both the deed and the words suggest that it was a joint killing (22.391–394).

82 Parry (1956a) concludes this from the use of neologisms which are compound adjectives. Parry argues that Achilles' position contradicts the values of the Homeric world and to express it, he must break with the traditional formulaic language which conveyed these values. Many scholars who have analyzed the language of Achilles are critical of this thesis: see Reeve 1973; Claus 1975; Nimis 1986; Martin 1989. Not only does the language of Achilles not break with traditional formulaic diction, but also his conduct defends traditional values, which Agamemnon violates to gain advantage over others. Elmer (2013:80) presents a very incisive approach: "In fact, the root of Achilles' problem and the cause of his alienation are not that he is struggling to say something that cannot be said but that he is committed to a transparent relation between language and reality in a world in which that relation has been broken. [...] Achilles is struggling to maintain a language transparent enough to be serviceable to the community and to hold together language and reality in spite of the cleavage between the two that has emerged. When he sees others

appropriate words to describe Agamemnon's behavior and reveal his real intentions, without offending the ruler. Now Achilles addresses him (1.149): ὤ μοι ἀναιδείην ἐπιειμένε, κερδαλεόφρον ("Oh, clothed in shamelessness, thinking of profit—guileful/cunning)." These words sound like an insult, but they are rather a warning against the violation of traditional values. Ἀναιδείη (*anaideiê*)—'lacking shame'—means acting against the code of behavior of a given community. Generally, it refers to living according to rules accepted in a society (in this case, a warrior community) and principally based on respecting honor and honorable behavior. Respecting *aidôs* means respecting bans which function in the community and are sanctioned by tradition.[83] The meaning Achilles gives to the epithet is different than our rather inadequate translations: Agamemnon is being warned that he is doing things that custom forbids. With the second epithet ('thinking of profit'), Achilles suggests that Agamemnon is not guided by the common good, as he declares he is, but by his own profit.[84] The young hero refuses to be deceived; Agamemnon can pull the wool over other people's eyes, but not his. Achilles accuses the leader of greed and deceit, as if, thinking of Agamemnon's subterfuge, he wants to say: "Look, now, who is trying to steal from other people?"

Agamemnon seizes on the hero's last words and tells him to be off, indicating that nobody needs him, that he is dispensable. And this is a real offence. Up to this point, the matter could have been settled amicably. Now Achilles learns that everything he did for the common good was worthless. He has a reason to feel deeply discouraged and resentful (1.188, Πηλεΐωνι δ' ἄχος γένετ', "grief came upon the son of Peleus"); in one moment, all his sacrifices have become meaningless. But Agamemnon does not stop here: earlier, the taking away of Achilles' *geras* was only a threat; now it has become the king's decision. To avoid misunderstandings, he explains how Achilles should understand it (1.184–187):

> ...ἐγὼ δέ κ' ἄγω Βρισηίδα καλλιπάρῃον
> αὐτὸς ἰὼν κλισίηνδε, τὸ σὸν γέρας, ὄφρ' εὖ εἰδῇς
> ὅσσον φέρτερός εἰμι σέθεν, στυγέῃ δὲ καὶ ἄλλος
> ἶσον ἐμοὶ φάσθαι καὶ ὁμοιωθήμεναι ἄντην

violating their commitments or misrepresenting social realities by strategic concealment, he stakes out a position that requires him to speak his mind fully and to abide by what he has said."

83 See Cairns 1993b; 2011:790–791. This code is binding on all members of the group, whether they are high or low in the hierarchy.

84 This term seems to suggest strongly that the material value of objects was of secondary importance. Achilles shows such an attitude is reprehensible. Nonetheless, it is not an attack on the system of values; on the contrary, Achilles expresses the universal belief that the lust for possessions becomes a problem when it is satisfied at the expense of other people.

> ... I myself shall come to your tent and take fair-faced Briseis,
> your *geras*, so that you understand well
> how much mightier I am than you and so that another may fear
> to claim he is my peer and to set himself against me

This expression is meant to scold Achilles and to make him realize that Agamemnon is more powerful, but it is also a warning for the other leaders. The chief leader decides to mete punishment out to Achilles to scotch possible rivalry. The idea of being his equal is perceived by Agamemnon as an attempt at stealing his position. The comparison of the mentality of both Achaean leaders to the mentality of gang members seems to be very appropriate: the boss of the gang must be ruthless and get rid of his rivals, because he is always in danger of getting ousted by someone who is more ruthless and who feels he is better suited for leadership. Agamemnon fears that the whole incident has been engineered by Achilles in order to usurp his position. To let anyone take anything from him would be a clear signal that he is weak and he would lose the respect of the army. Sooner or later, one of the warriors would conclude that he should take over because Agamemnon can't cope.[85]

Agamemnon switches responsibility for the quarrel to his opponent. Saying that Achilles is "the most hateful [one]" (1.176) to him, Agamemnon suggests that the young hero is guided by personal motives: when he attacked him, Achilles did not think about the good of the army, but was motivated by his hatred. Saying that quarrels, wars, and fighting are always dear to Achilles (1.177), Agamemnon lays blame for the whole situation on his quarrelsome character. Before the eyes of the assembly, Agamemnon paints the picture of a quarreler who is motivated by self-interest. He cunningly turns the tables: the injury done to the community is no longer important; what counts is the verbal fight started by Achilles, which he, Agamemnon, must win. Defending his position, the chief leader improvidently gets rid of Achilles. He alters the reality to suit his purpose: he says that Apollo himself is taking Chryseis from him, which means that it is the decision of a divinity, something that he cannot be blamed for. But he is going to take Briseis from Achilles, and in this way puts himself in the position of a god towards Achilles.[86]

One thing leads to another and finally, but quite late, the disagreement becomes a violent quarrel. Modern scholars often claim that the quarrel arises out of the mutual aversion of both leaders. According to them, the aversion

85 Karkowski (2014:15–25) also views this scene as an attempt at a coup; what he does not notice, however, is that it is not in fact Achilles' intent, but only Agamemnon's perception.

86 See Muellner 1996:108–109.

becomes evident if we read the initial speeches of the opponents as spiced with mocking irony.

Achilles' words explaining what is and what isn't done are quite daring and his whole speech may be understood as bitter or sarcastic, but his language also reveals a degree of amusement with which the hero receives Agamemnon's speech. A trace of irony can even be detected in the way he proposes fleeing back home, which he perhaps does not really mean. But even if he does, then irony results from his inability to understand why Agamemnon has not lifted a finger to save the dying Achaeans. An ironical overtone may be also heard in Achilles' assertion to Kalchas that he will protect him even against Agamemnon. His declaration states openly what the seer has left unsaid. This irony contrasts Agamemnon's image with what Achilles sees as reality. Agamemnon's image of himself is in opposition to his behavior. The mockery of the chief leader does not, however, exceed a certain acceptable limit; probably other leaders could also take similar liberties, although Achilles' audacity surpasses that of everyone else and seems to border on impudence.

Agamemnon's expression ἀγαθός περ ἐών "mighty though you are" (1.131) in response to Achilles' κύδιστε "the most famous" or "most lucky" (1.122) indicates pretended politeness. At a certain point, Agamemnon breaks from these stinging mutual civilities and proceeds to utter threats, and Achilles retaliates. If there really were any dislike or mutual hatred between the leaders, Achilles would certainly harp on the subject of Agamemnon's guilt, the mention of which would certainly be distasteful to the king, who tries to wriggle out of the responsibility. Meanwhile, Achilles does not dwell on the possibility of divine wrath resulting from the offence to Apollo's priest,[87] or mention other possible causes, like an unfulfilled oath or hecatomb; when Agamemnon changes the topic, Achilles readily follows. When Agamemnon demands compensation, he gives thought to the possibility of its fulfillment. And when the chief leader threatens several Achaeans with depriving them of their *geras* and tries to soothe ruffled feelings with the proposal to send a mission to propitiate the god, Achilles concentrates only on this.

The subject of Agamemnon's guilt comes back later, when Thersites brings it up, but the author attempts to mark this as improper. It seems that Thersites does not have the same right as Achilles to hold a similar opinion. He cannot compete for the title of "the best of the Achaeans" (*aristos Achaiôn*), since he is assigned the role of "the worst of the Achaeans" (*aischistos Achaiôn*).[88] However, Thersites does what should have been done at the first assembly: he calls on

87 Kirk 1985:60: "He [Achilles] omits [it] perhaps deliberately."

88 See Nagy 1999:259–264.

the army to rebel against the leader, arguing that he should be driven away. But Thersites cannot replace Agamemnon as the chief leader; he can do it only as an act of tomfoolery (2.215–216): ἀλλ' ὅτι οἱ εἴσαιτο γελοίιον Ἀργείοισιν / ἔμμεναι, "to hold him [Agamemnon] to ridicule among the Achaeans." Achilles always refrains from pointing to Agamemnon's guilt. He only refers to the impropriety of Agamemnon's words, which inflict undeserved harm upon him: first, when Achilles called the assembly to find a way to save the army, he was accused of bad intentions; then his service and sacrifices for the common good were slighted and he was offended by being deprived of his property. Probably at first, he teased Agamemnon, which could have irritated the leader, but it did not play a significant role in the quarrel. Unlike Thersites, Achilles does not accuse his adversary of the intention or rather of an attempt to destroy the army.

Agamemnon's speeches are a blend of boasts and threats, though uncertainty and ineptitude are also there.[89] Agamemnon turns out to be a skillful and flexible politician, changing his tone several times during one speech; he is also an extreme hypocrite guided only by his own interests and struggling at all costs to maintain his position. In his statements, he is very theatrical, because he directs his words not so much at his adversaries, Achilles and Kalchas, as at the silent crowd of the Achaeans. Unable to pass blame for the plague decimating the army onto someone else, he tries to put the responsibility for the conflict on Achilles' shoulders. Agamemnon's words at the end of his speech quoted above fully expose his true intentions: to make his privileged position so secure that nobody would be able to even dream of overthrowing him (1.185–187). When Agamemnon describes Achilles as "the most hateful" (1.176) person, a possible reference to some earlier conflicts between them is less important than the fact that by doing so he wants to present Achilles to everyone who is listening (the interior audience) as the one who likes to argue and fight. He seems to say that Achilles cannot be right because he is impetuous. To conclude that there is animosity between these characters is unfounded. Although the cycle mentions an earlier dispute between them resulting from a belated invitation of Achilles to a feast (on Lemnos, before landing at Troy), this motif is so frequently used in the construction of a cyclic song that we cannot attach too much importance to it. Even if Homer refers here to the knowledge of this dispute among his audience, we cannot infer from it that their quarrels were frequent.

Agamemnon fails miserably to follow the rules of the dispute and only stirs it up more. Both participants of the quarrel invoke the custom in the form of an admonition that something "would not be seemly" (1.119, 126). Achilles'

89 Griffin (2004:163) similarly sums up Agamemnon's utterances within the whole poem: "An alternation of bluster and bullying with uncertainty and sudden collapses."

statement undermined the legitimacy of the ruler's demand, and Agamemnon, unable to respond in the same way, changes tactics, resorting to a threat. He observes the principle of symmetry only to the extent that he responds to Achilles' irony with ironic remarks addressed to the hero. Achilles answers a threat with a threat. Apparently, Agamemnon also loses in this confrontation, because he reaches for an even stronger weapon: insults. On reflection, Achilles repays insult with insult.

On hearing Agamemnon's affronts, Achilles finds himself in a fix: his achievements to date have been annihilated and his loss of honor is exacerbated by his commander's decision to take away some of his loot, regardless of his rank and merit, thus putting him in the position of someone who is unable to defend his possessions. Agamemnon, who was under a similar threat, extricated himself by shifting it to Achilles. The mechanism observed in organized crime groups operates also here. A boss, whose position has been threatened, must severely punish the culprit, even if the object of the quarrel may be insignificant in relation to his wealth. The punishment is a measure designed to make a point, because his subordinates must know he is not a man whom one can rob with impunity. This is the reason for Agamemnon's unmasking of the conspiracy. Depriving him of one captive woman would not significantly diminish his wealth, but it is a dangerous signal for others. Feeling this, he immediately demands compensation, because this step would secure his position. When Achilles points out the impropriety of the chief leader's demand, he straightway lays himself open to the suspicion that his real aim is to rob Agamemnon in order to shake his position. Agamemnon surmises that Achilles wants to replace him and reacts violently. One consequence of their quarrel is that Achilles loses his *geras*—which mirrors the situation Agamemnon was threatened with. By publicly depriving Achilles of his share of the spoils, Agamemnon demonstrates his authority and puts the hero in a situation in which he cannot defend his property.

In the eyes of the community, Achilles loses his honor not so much because he proves to be weaker than Agamemnon—in this respect his status would not differ from that of the other Achaeans—but because he would be the one from whom something was taken away and did not oppose it. In such a situation, men of honor have only one way out: revenge.

The principle of necessary revenge for the harm done is found even now in some parts of Greece.[90] It is remarkable, then, that Achilles, instead of retaliating right away, ponders *whether* he should kill Agamemnon (1.188–194). To restrain his anger—a step he contemplates—means to accept the role of someone worse than Agamemnon. It seems that he has scruples concerning

90 Athanassakis 1992: 161–162.

the murder of a countryman. Still, it is astonishing because both in the *Iliad* and in Greek mythology there are numerous instances of crimes of revenge committed on fellow citizens, and even on one's own family; to give just one example—Patroklos is said to have killed a friend in a quarrel (23.84–90).[91] Such killers always had to flee from their homeland, but it is not the fear of exile that makes Achilles hesitate. The real obstacle is the immorality of such a deed. When Athena appears, she does not advise him to give up revenge, but to express it in a different way: hurling insults at someone also deprives him of his honor, because it is a public revelation of his misdeeds. Even now, though in a fit of anger, Achilles does not reproach Agamemnon for bringing the plague upon the Achaeans. He explains his decision to refrain from killing him by the dishonorable nature of all Achaeans who suffer Agamemnon's behavior (1.231): ἐπεὶ οὐτιδανοῖσιν ἀνάσσεις "since you rule over people without value," i.e. without honor. Achilles lays blame on the Achaeans and Agamemnon alike, and in this way the injury to his honor is less serious, and he does not go so far as shedding blood. However, the vengeance by blame misses its target, exactly like in the second assembly, when Thersites tries to ridicule Agamemnon (2.225–242), because the army does not condemn the leader. By accepting his wrongdoing, the community brings down punishment upon themselves. They really turn out to be people "without value," deserving a penalty: they committed ὑπερβασίη 'transgression' (16.18), crossing the border of decency. An unjustified wrong done to a member of the group requires collective responsibility; here the wrath of the god is replaced by the wrath of the hero.

Later Achilles continually feels like a man who has lost his value in the eyes of the whole community. And their regard is of great importance—it is a measure of honor. Although he isolates himself from the group, the hero does not deny its value: he does not think that these people are unworthy and that he does not want to have anything to do with them. Achilles' revenge affects the entire Achaean community, but it does not mean that he hates them. He has not become a misanthrope; he still has respect for people. Keeping clear of the battlefield, he ponders how the army could restore his dignity.

In the assembly, facing Achaean warriors, the hero in a fit of anger accuses the chief leader of baseness, cowardice, and greed. Now Achilles undergoes a real change; since others do not need him, he ceases to care for them. It is no longer his war, but an individual issue between him and Agamemnon. Since his honor has been harmed, no sacrifice is too great to restore it. He changes from a man who thought only about others and devoted himself to their good to one

91 Zieliński 2013:110–113; 2021:70–71.

who thinks only about himself and does not care about the fate of others. This makes him decide to withdraw from fighting. Now Achilles carries out what he previously meant only as a bluff. Agamemnon's attitude made him bring his threat into effect. Achilles thus acts in a way similar to Agamemnon, who first only threatened to deprive the hero of his *geras*, and then, in reaction to Achilles' behavior, decided to take this step.

Analysis of the quarrel shows that the author intended to show Achilles as a man who was wrongly hurt. If such damage cannot be redressed by personal vengeance, it requires divine revenge. Like an ordinary human harmed by a stronger man, Achilles prays for vengeance that would restore justice.[92] But an epic hero cannot be thus perceived; that is why Thetis, when passing his request to Zeus, mentions a previous service, expecting the god to reciprocate it (1.503–505; compare 1.393–412). Achilles cannot manifest his helplessness. For him, it is essential to show that his and Agamemnon's positions are equal.

When we consider the quarrel of Achilles and Agamemnon, we can see that it did not have to lead to such extreme consequences. In fact, a bit of good will on either side could have stopped this argument. Unfortunately, the characters do not have a common ground; they completely misunderstand each other and do not try to figure out why everything suddenly ends in a disaster. I have already analyzed the reasoning of Agamemnon, who right at the start suspected Achilles of ill will, hypocrisy, and intrigue. Whatever Achilles says, Agamemnon interprets it as a perverse pretense of nobility, which covers an attempt at his humiliation. Agamemnon easily attributes perversity and hypocrisy to his opponent because he is like that himself—it is corroborated by his speeches, in which he pretends to care for the army. Agamemnon thinks he recognizes an insidious attempt at depriving him of his property. It is not important how much Chryseis means to him. Taking her away—like taking away any other thing from him, no matter how trivial—reduces his rank in the eyes of his subordinates. Agamemnon, like a gang boss, cannot afford magnanimity.

The position Achilles aspires to within the group threatens the position of the leader. Homer outlines a special case in this simple pattern: here a young hero does not intend to replace the leader; he simply does not accept certain manifestations of his authority. As a result, the *status quo* of the group is breached, although the hierarchy remains unchanged. Achilles' step creates tension, which may at any moment turn into an open conflict. Nestor's mediation is belated and ineffective—both heroes stick to their guns. Agamemnon faults Achilles for not submitting to him, and Achilles does not intend to—but he raises moral arguments to justify his standpoint. It is indecent for Agamemnon

92 A similar attitude can be observed in Archilochus, Aesop, and Hesiod.

to take the property belonging to someone else. Everything Achilles possesses has been deserved because he earned it in arduous struggles and at the risk of his own life. Despite his services, he neither got much nor did he demand much. This self-praise is followed by his criticism of Agamemnon, who is greedy and takes what he does not deserve. He is always the first to take (and to take a lot) and the last to fight. Achilles breaks convention by not acknowledging Agamemnon's authority, which is something Nestor criticizes. Agamemnon violates custom by demanding the redistribution of the loot, which would mean depriving warriors of the prizes they have earned. As we have seen, Agamemnon may feel additionally justified because he believes that Achilles is deceiving him in order to downgrade his position. He is, however, wrong and therefore he had no right to act as he did.

Achilles' Character

Achilles is triply offended by Agamemnon: instead of getting credit for his service, he learns that he is dispensable; he is found guilty of the quarrel; and, finally, Agamemnon announces that he will take Achilles' slave away from him, and thus, depriving him of *geras*, deprives him of honor. For a man wronged by the chief leader, there is only one path left, if he wants to remain a man of honor: revenge. Achilles is powerful enough to repay insults with violence. However, as we remember, when the crucial moment comes, the narrator shows Achilles' hesitation (1.188–192):

> ... ἐν δέ οἱ ἦτορ
> στήθεσσιν λασίοισι διάνδιχα μερμήριξεν,
> ἢ ὅ γε φάσγανον ὀξὺ ἐρυσσάμενος παρὰ μηροῦ
> τοὺς μὲν ἀναστήσειεν, ὁ δ' Ἀτρεΐδην ἐναρίζοι,
> ἦε χόλον παύσειεν ἐρητύσειέ τε θυμόν.

> ... And his heart
> in his hairy breast was torn,
> whether to draw a sharp sword at his side
> to disperse people and kill the son of Atreus,
> or to forego his anger and calm his heart.

It is difficult to determine the character of Achilles, who is a rather ambiguous figure.[93] The author does not use direct characterization, but does this mean

[93] Redfield (1994:17) provides a good characterization of this hero.

that Homer did not imagine the personality of his characters? Even a reader who is not very well-informed will deny this.

How does the singer portray his characters? He disseminates information about them, both their appearance and character,[94] throughout the work. The singer concentrates the listener's interest on a few character traits of Achilles and Agamemnon, who are contrasted as far as these features are concerned. The narrator's attention focuses on three aspects, all of which are interrelated: egotism and concern for the fate of the group; greed and modesty of needs; cruelty and pity. In the author's understanding, or, more broadly, in the mentality of those times, these features were constituents of an epic hero's character and perhaps they were the essential traits for assessing a man in real life. We must take into account how epic heroes, Achilles and Agamemnon in particular, are characterized in the Trojan Cycle and how the author of this song characterizes them. We will study their traits one by one, finishing our analysis with an attempt to answer the question of why Homer outlined these two heroes in the way he did and, perhaps, find the reasons for their differentiation.

Egotism and concern for the fate of the group

The proof of Achilles' concern for the army can be found in Odysseus's argument in *Iliad* Book 9, when he wants to bring about the hero's return to the battlefield. Odysseus changes the purport of Agamemnon's offer, not mentioning the demand that Achilles recognize the chief leader's superiority. Agamemnon had made rich gifts conditional on fulfilling this demand (9.160–161): καί μοι ὑποστήτω ὅσσον βασιλεύτερός εἰμι / ἠδ' ὅσσον γενεῇ προγενέστερος εὔχομαι εἶναι ("[he] will admit that I am a much greater ruler than he, / and that I descend from a nobler family").[95]

94 Usually in epic poetry, the description of a hero's physical appearance reveals his character. In the epic of the South Slavs, such description is usually provided by one of the characters; it is conventional, but it is also so traditional that the listener usually knows who this person is. For example, this is how Prince Marko is regularly presented: "A knight sitteth in the wide meadow. / He hath planted his spear in the unploughed earth. / And hath tethered his horse to the spear-shaft. / And hard by there lieth a wine-skin: / He drinketh not as men use to drink. / But from a copper basin of twelve okas. / He drinketh half, and half he giveth to the horse. / His horse is not as other horses. / But brindled like as beeves; / The knight is not as other knights. / But on his shoulders is a cloak of wolf-skin, / On his head is a cap of wolf-skin / Bound on with a brown head-cloth; / In his teeth he holdeth something black. / That for size is as a lamb of half a year" (translation, D. H. Low). This description is repeatedly applied to Prince Marko, but also to every other hero of Serbian epic poetry. In this song, Vuca the General does not recognize Marko, but he answers his daughter-in-law: "I have his fellows in the dungeon, / And him also I shall take presently" (translation, D. H. Low).

95 Most translations of this verse suggest that Agamemnon, aware of the fact that Achilles is the son of a goddess, stresses the difference in their ages, with the idea that this should oblige

Agamemnon's admission of guilt resulting from a temporary clouding of judgment does not look sincere. Worse yet, he perceives the aim of the embassy which should appease the offended adversary differently than Nestor, who encouraged him to take this step. Nestor describes Agamemnon's conduct towards Achilles in the following way (9.110–111): ἄνδρα φέριστον, ὃν ἀθάνατοί περ ἔτισαν / ἠτίμησας ("the best man, whom the immortals honored, you dishonored"). Despite all the seriousness of the situation, the chief leader assesses Achilles' value much lower (1.116–117): ἀντί νυ πολλῶν / λαῶν ἐστὶν ἀνὴρ ὅν τε Ζεὺς κῆρι φιλήσῃ ("worth many soldiers is the man whom Zeus loves in his heart")—as if Achilles could be exchanged for a contingent of soldiers.[96] Even in such a critical situation, Agamemnon really cares only about having his superiority recognized.

Nestor advises Agamemnon to make amends for the insult with gifts and kind words, such that could appease Achilles' anger (9.113): δώροισίν τ' ἀγανοῖσιν ἔπεσσί τε μειλιχίοισι. Agamemnon, however, takes only one half of the advice: the list of gifts is perhaps too long,[97] but there isn't even a single soft word.[98] This acceptance of only half of Nestor's "good advice" determines the failure of the embassy.

Achilles to respect his higher position. But why should older age be of such importance for their culture and for Agamemnon in particular? Such a translation also involves a change in meaning of γενεῇ from 'family, descent' to 'age, number of years'. Typical of aristocratic mentality is laying emphasis on the greatness of one's family while slighting the position of others. In the eyes of Agamemnon, the fact that Achilles' mother is a goddess may be of little importance or, conversely, it may be the reason why it is so important for him that Achilles acknowledge his superiority; Nestor saw special value in Achilles' descent from a goddess (1.278–281). It seems that Agamemnon does not allow the thought that Achilles, or anyone else, could be better than he. Translating this phrase "I am more advanced in ancestry," Martin (1989:98) also chooses this interpretation, though in a footnote he mentions the ambiguity of the original.

96 Similarly, he also did not value Chryseis as a person, since she could be replaced by any other prize.

97 The problem of the exaggeration of Agamemnon's generosity is taken up by Donlan (1993) and Sammons (2008).

98 Griffin (1995:89) has not noticed Agamemnon's error: "Agamemnon produces the gifts but no softening words: that is left to Phoenix." Griffin assesses the situation from the point of view of the economy of narration. My interpretation is supported by Wilson (1996:221), who comments on Nestor's words (9.164–165)—δῶρα μὲν οὐκέτ' ὀνοστὰ διδοῖς Ἀχιλῆϊ ἄνακτι / ἀλλ' ἄγετε κλητοὺς ὀτρύνομεν ("you gave worthy gifts for the ruler Achilles / come, now, let us send chosen messengers")—in the following way: "The μέν after δῶρα has no corresponding δέ. There may be nothing at all in this; the unbalanced μέν, the so-called μέν *solitarium*, is common enough in Homer. But Nestor is perhaps intending to say, 'Gifts you have offered; *would that your words have been equally generous' and then balanced at such criticism of Agamemnon at the moment* [my emphasis]—though Taplin (1992:69–70) plausibly suggests that μέν could be balanced by the ἀλλ' of 165—'You offer gifts; I will attend to the practical details.' " It is amazing to me that the need to address Achilles in a way that might win him over and make him forget the insult can be described as "practical details." Even if Nestor has to accept Agamemnon's standpoint, such

When the deputies, full of anxiety, arrive at Achilles' tent, they are—undoubtedly to the surprise of the exterior audience—very hospitably received by the hero. The scene of preparing the meal is presented with all possible details, and Achilles' most important subordinates, Patroklos and Automedon, participate in these activities, not to mention the hero himself, who personally cuts the meat. According to Wilson, all this stresses the significance of the occasion for the listeners and for the participants of the meeting alike.[99] A detailed presentation of these activities also, or rather primarily, shows that Achilles behaves properly, respects customs, and has good manners: he courteously greets his guests, treats them to the best meat (loin/sirloin), and does not ask the reason for their visit while they eat.[100] And yet, at the end, he is accused by Aias of behavior contrary to the customs and principles of their community.[101] Aias, then, seems to point out that his friend performs superficial gestures, even if his cordiality flows from a sincere heart, whereas they would expect him to forget his own grudges and support his comrades in a difficult situation.[102] This is a fairly frequent instance in Homer of a discrepancy between word and gesture, because the words of Achilles are at odds with the role of a perfect host.[103]

Before the messengers start out, the narrator reports that Nestor consults for a long time with Odysseus, but he does not familiarize the audience with the

---

messages, seeking to influence the aggrieved party to desist from revenge, are usually based on an attempt to abandon the idea that one is always right and to at least partially acknowledge the opponent may be also right, i.e. above all, to admit error and express regret for the harm done.

99 Wilson 1996:226 *ad* 9.206–217: "The preparations for the meal are given at remarkable length; compare the much shorter account at 24.621–626 (where 625–626 closely resemble 216–217 here) of Akhilleus' preparations for his meal with Priam. By the proliferation of detail here, Homer conveys the importance of the occasion, not only for his listeners but also for the participants."

100 The meal scene, presented in such detail, also fulfills another function. Like the enumeration of gifts, it delays the delivery of the message, which stimulates the audience's anxiety about the hero's response. This expectant mood is heightened by the silence accompanying the preparation of the meal. And thus suspense increases.

101 Mueller 1984:48: "The words of the plain soldier are particularly valuable because they show how much Achilleus' behaviour breaks established norms."

102 Just as words without deeds are worthless, a gesture of hospitality is meaningful when the guest is not only given food, but also help, when his request is answered—real hospitality in the *Odyssey* entails giving support to Odysseus and Telemachos to the extent that is possible for the host.

103 A deliberate discrepancy between a verbal and non-verbal message is observed by Chruściak (2018:123–146). Martin (1989:211–212), demonstrating modifications of formulae and their atypical use in Achilles' speeches, notes also the peculiarity of expressions in the initial part of the hero's reply to Odysseus (9.308–311). Martin attributes this to the fact that "Achilles' depiction as a perfect host requires that he utter something like the host's formula 'speak what is on your mind and I will fulfill it'; ... At the same time, the narrative requires that Achilles speak his refusal at this point, and do so vehemently .... It is this conglomeration of motives, inherent in the conception of Achilles as a hero in the *Iliad*, that produces the expanded, seemingly incoherent opening to Achilles' great reply."

content of this conference (9.180–181). The listener, however, gets the idea that there is a surprise in the offing, because both heroes are preparing something special that can determine the outcome of the difficult mission.

Although Nestor appointed Phoinix to take the lead, and Aias signals Phoinix to start speaking (9.168, 223–224), Odysseus, probably as the most eloquent speaker, usurps the leading role and takes the initiative. We can assume that he chooses an approach which in his opinion may best placate Achilles. Concentrating on the difficult position of the army, Odysseus appeals to Achilles' pity.[104] He seems to know perfectly well how seriously the hero is hurt, how obstinate he is in his intransigence, and what arguments *will certainly not* impress him. Therefore, his choice falls on the only argument which in his opinion may ensure the success of the embassy. Odysseus takes the risk of speaking first, although he could save his speech for the end, which would be much more convenient for him. He does not wait, perhaps fearing that one of his companions might inadvertently irk their host. Meanwhile, he wants to induce Achilles to forget about himself and react like the man he was before the quarrel. Only a man who used to care for fellow warriors may yield to compassion, give up his anger, and return to the battlefield.[105] After thanking Achilles courteously for a kind reception,[106] Odysseus presents the inevitable fate of the Achaeans if Achilles won't support them (9.230–231): ἐν δοιῇ δὲ σαωσέμεν ἢ ἀπολέσθαι / νῆας ἐϋσσέλμους, εἰ μὴ σύ γε δύσεαι ἀλκήν ("[we are] in doubt if we can save ourselves and the benched ships / from destruction, if you will not clothe yourself in valor").

Agamemnon referred to the same fundamental choice in his speech when he was blamed for bringing plague upon the Achaeans (1.117). This time the responsibility for the life or death of all warriors is placed on Achilles' shoulders. It is his duty to do whatever he can to save the army. Achilles has already announced his return home, but Odysseus is trying to make him realize it is the wrong decision. He tells him to put himself in the place of the army, and then he will see that it is an unacceptable choice. More precisely, Achilles, opening the

104 Van Wees 1992:133–135.

105 It is often pointed out that Odysseus's speech, built on the principle of ring composition, is rhetorically the best of the messengers' speeches. Kennedy 1980:9–14; compare Hainsworth 1993:92–94.

106 Hainsworth 1993:93: "He begins with a modest, low-key exordium, complimenting Achilleus' gracious entertainment (225–8)." According to the principles of the theory of rhetoric, Odysseus starts with a *captatio benevolentiae*, but the question is why he mentions the feast given by Agamemnon. Probably he intends to present the chief leader as someone who cares for the warriors, so he cannot be evil to the core. Otherwise, his words might imply that he deems Achilles' hospitality unnecessary, which, instead of mollifying Achilles, would irritate him and would work against the purpose of the embassy.

assembly, spoke like a simple soldier; now he is put in the position of a leader responsible for the fate of his people, whom he can save. The fact that the possibility of return is not mentioned makes it a shameful choice; Odysseus thus puts Achilles in psychological check so that he cannot stick to his earlier decision to sail home.

Next Odysseus presents the extent of the threat posed by the Trojans, emphasizing Hektor's boasts that he will destroy the Achaeans (9.232–246). Then he makes an appeal to Achilles to save the Achaeans (9.247–248), supporting it with the argument that Achilles will not have a second chance to do so, and with an appeal to the hero to recall his father's words and restrain his anger. The central part of the speech, in terms of its structure, is the enumeration of Agamemnon's gifts. The ring composition is marked with two relatively short statements that allow both Achilles and the external audience to capture the most important elements in his speech. The essential message seems irrelevant to Achilles—"if Agamemnon and his gifts are hateful to you ... " (9.300)—which makes Odysseus come back to his initial arguments: first, he asks Achilles to take pity on the Achaeans, tempting him with a vision of fame and honor for killing Hektor (9.301–303); second, he teases him with the Trojan's boasts and flatters his self-love, suggesting that he is Hektor's most worthy opponent (9.304–306). Displaying compassion for his people and gaining honor and fame are tantamount to standing up to fight and kill Hektor.

In response, Achilles does not assume his previous attitude of a leader taking care of his army, because Agamemnon's selfishness has forced him to think about his own honor. At the assembly, Agamemnon played the role of a good leader for the sake of the gathered warriors, but he reveals his egotism in front of the elders, when he sends the embassy. Achilles knows this well, though he was not present. Because the young hero—perhaps alerted by the extravagance of the gifts—notices that the offer of reconciliation comes too easily, he cannot again become the old Achilles from before the quarrel. In his opinion, Agamemnon has not suffered enough; Achilles *simply knows* that the leader is not concerned with the fate of the army, but only his pride. It is still a struggle between these two heroes to abase the other one. Achilles cannot be bought:[107]

[107] Claus (1975:20–24) draws attention to the heroes' reflection on their value. Heroic conduct, involving risking one's life in battle, is compensated with prizes offered by the community, in essence, by receiving a greater share of common goods. But this risk is not only a subject of economic calculation. Although material compensation is not worth the lives of Achilles and Sarpedon, both heroes voluntarily and gratuitously undertake the risk, treating gifts as a symbol of their status. By depriving Achilles of his *geras* and insulting him, Agamemnon (p. 23) "has transformed the gifts from their proper status as a mere symbol of Achilleus' *aretê* into a practical measure of it." In the scene of the embassy (pp. 23–24), "Achilleus recognizes that despite the reversal of situations and the value now placed upon his participation in battle his worth

he rejects the gifts, because Agamemnon has not admitted his error and has neither apologized nor asked for his help.[108]

It transpires that not only Achaean leaders, but also Homeric scholars turn a blind eye to Agamemnon's egotism, but are ready to condemn Achilles' egotism, faulting him for youthful stupidity.[109] The point of Odysseus's speech is not to explain to an irresponsible boy the importance of taking care of the army, but to remind the hero that not so long ago it was what drove him. Achilles recognizes Odysseus's intention and it is the first thing he refers to in his reply (9.321–329):

> οὐδέ τί μοι περίκειται, ἐπεὶ πάθον ἄλγεα θυμῷ
> αἰεὶ ἐμὴν ψυχὴν παραβαλλόμενος πολεμίζειν.
> ὡς δ' ὄρνις ἀπτῆσι νεοσσοῖσι προφέρῃσι
> μάστακ' ἐπεί κε λάβῃσι, κακῶς δ' ἄρα οἱ πέλει αὐτῇ,
> ὣς καὶ ἐγὼ πολλὰς μὲν ἀΰπνους νύκτας ἴαυον,
> ἤματα δ' αἱματόεντα διέπρησσον πολεμίζων
> ἀνδράσι μαρνάμενος ὀάρων ἕνεκα σφετεράων.
> δώδεκα δὴ σὺν νηυσὶ πόλεις ἀλάπαξ' ἀνθρώπων,
> πεζὸς δ' ἕνδεκά φημι κατὰ Τροίην ἐρίβωλον.
>
> It did not bring me a profit when I endured suffering in my heart
> endlessly risking my life in combat.
> Like a mother bird, who brings food for her chicks who can't fly
> as soon as she catches something, and with her own self it goes ill,
> so did I spend many sleepless nights
> and I passed my days in bloody fights,

continues to be regarded by Agamemnon and the others as something that can be calculated and obtained by an adequate enumeration of gifts, when he knows himself that his efforts and willingness to die can only be a gesture offered freely, out of *charis*, ultimately unanswerable except by other gestures. Simply put, he must be paid, but he cannot be bought."

108 Redfield (1994:16) draws attention to the false generosity of Agamemnon; he offers great gifts, the cities which his daughter would bring as her dowry, but it would make Achilles dependent on him as his son-in-law. That is why Achilles "lays such stress in his reply on his own property and on the fact that he has a father of his own in his own country." Although Odysseus does not quote the last part of Agamemnon's message, Achilles guesses his real intention. As in the case of quarrel, now in offering gifts, Agamemnon's aim is to humiliate and subjugate his opponent. What he has not achieved by threat, he tries to achieve by bribery. "If you cannot beat them, buy them," a Chinese proverb says. Naturally, Agamemnon would not have to ask forgiveness; it would be enough if he admitted his words were inappropriate and unjust to Achilles. Compare Griffin 1980:74; Schein 1984:104–106.

109 For example, Hainsworth 1993:94: "Unfortunately for Odysseus, Akhilleus is about to be depicted as an unreasonable young man to whom glory now means nothing and who will seize on the very point that Odysseus was careful to omit, the real attitude of Agamemnon."

battling husbands for their wives;
setting off on ships, I took twelve cities,
and eleven I captured on foot near Troy of fertile fields.

Achilles' care for the army implies complete dedication, exposing himself to hardships and death, all in order to provide the Achaeans with loot, giving profit to the warriors, while neglecting his own interest. Thanks to Achilles, they could live and get rich, but his work was not rewarded. From his point of view, the chief leader unfairly divided precious spoils won by Achilles. Agamemnon "gave out little and kept most for himself": διὰ παῦρα δασάσκετο, πολλὰ δ' ἔχεσκεν (9.333).

Achilles here portrays Agamemnon's greed more plainly than he did earlier. Then, he contrasted the chief leader's greed with his own modesty and contentment with little (1.166–168). What Achilles used to satisfy himself with was disproportionate to his battle effort—he even suggests that he did not want more because he was so battle-tired that the only thing he desired was to return to his tent and to rest. Offended, he argues that Agamemnon, instead of taking part in battle, takes a part of the prize from "whoever contradicts him" (1.228).[110] In his reply to Odysseus, Achilles accuses the chief commander of cheating all the warriors. They allowed it, satisfying themselves with the part of the spoil that was accorded to them, whereas he, Achilles, was the only one who dared to break with the *status quo*. For the hero, it is important that the leader did not deprive anyone but him of a part of his prize (9.335–336).[111] Achilles confines himself to showing Agamemnon's baseness but does not call for rebellion, as Thersites does. He does not care about the support of the warriors and does not undermine the value of what they got. He only wants to show them the harm that has been inflicted on him.

Achilles does not boast of his courage; his actions were in his opinion only necessary for the common good. They were almost unselfish, the payment being—according to him—symbolic. In this respect, he is completely unlike Agamemnon, who treats war as a source of profits and a means of building power. In Achilles' view, Agamemnon did nothing for the common good. As we can see, Achilles does not stress his bravery, but his effort. His courage, which

110 Insatiable greed is a charge that later Thersites throws at Agamemnon. And he draws a very serious conclusion (2.233–234): οὐ μὲν ἔοικεν / ἀρχὸν ἐόντα κακῶν ἐπιβασκέμεν υἷας Ἀχαιῶν ("it is not right / for our leader to bring disaster upon Achaean sons"). Thersites accuses Agamemnon of wronging the army, despite his earlier declaration.

111 Thus Achilles is the only *agerastos* 'deprived of his part of the spoils'. Agamemnon, presenting himself at the assembly as someone in such a situation, judged it unacceptable, contrary to custom (1.119).

can be deduced from his achievements, is emphasized by the cowardice of Agamemnon, who avoids fighting.

Odysseus's approach to Achilles is quite crude: he teases him with Hektor's boasts, though he also resorts to flattery by presenting him as the only warrior whom Hektor considers worthy of himself (9.305–306). In a verbal contest between characters, which Richard Martin calls "flyting *muthoi*," the rebuking of the addressee is typically accompanied by the presentation of various "heroic alternatives." Martin mentions this strategy, which "depends on the juxtaposition of praiseworthy foil with blameworthy addressee:" you are not the bravest warrior, even this and this enemy are better than you are.[112] Glaukos resorts to this "foil technique" to urge Hektor to fight for the body of Sarpedon: brave was the dead Sarpedon, brave is Achilles, though now absent on the battlefield; even Aias, second to Achilles, is better than you are, he taunts (17.140–168).

Achilles is not dumb and he cannot be fooled. An attempt at provoking him by ruffling his self-love, which drove him to secure fame by defeating his rivals, proves unsuccessful, though, it must be admitted, Odysseus never says simply: "Nobody but you can beat him."[113] Odysseus is only afraid that the gods can grant Hektor's prayers and desires. He never asks honestly for help. Achilles notices it and, addressing his answer to Odysseus, says that he has already had an encounter with Hektor and nearly killed him (9.354–355), and that he is not interested in fighting him again (9.356). Achilles intelligently notices Odysseus's omission of his decision to return (9.359–361):

> ὄψεαι, αἴ κ' ἐθέλῃσθα καὶ αἴ κέν τοι τὰ μεμήλῃ,
> ἦρι μάλ' Ἑλλήσποντον ἐπ' ἰχθυόεντα πλεούσας
> νῆας ἐμάς, ἐν δ' ἄνδρας ἐρεσσέμεναι μεμαῶτας
>
> You will see, if you want and if you care about it,
> at the break of dawn, my ships sailing out onto the Hellespont
> teeming with fish,
> my men eagerly pressing oars

Is it possible that Achilles suspects that Odysseus wishes him to leave? Perhaps he also secretly competes for the title of "the best of the Achaeans."[114] These words prompt the conclusion that Achilles notices a false note in Odysseus. The contempt expressed by Achilles at the beginning of his speech for a man

[112] Martin 1989:74.

[113] Perhaps he does this deliberately, as discussed in more detail below, downplaying Achilles' contribution to saving the army so as not to ascribe to him the role of the epic hero ("the best of the Achaeans") that he wishes to reserve for himself.

[114] On the rivalry of Achilles and Odysseus, see Nagy 1999:42–58.

who thinks one thing and speaks another applies to both Agamemnon and Odysseus. Agamemnon's offer is not sincere, but equally meant to deceive is the way Odysseus tries to conceal this fact. More importantly, however, instead of pleading with Achilles as the only one who can save the army, thus choosing him for the role of the epic hero, Odysseus merely states that without his support it will be difficult for the Achaeans to deal with the threat, in this way placing him in the role of a mere helper (9.229–230, 243–247). Rather than persuading Achilles to return, Odysseus seeks to coerce him into doing it. In this way, he hopes to achieve the desired result, despite a lack of "flattering" words in Agamemnon's offer. Perhaps he chooses such a strategy expecting that there is no chance that arguments relating to the concern for the fate of the army will change Achilles' decision. So maybe Odysseus does his best to fulfill his mission by setting an emotional trap for Achilles and thus bringing him back to battle. But he also may have a secret plan, in which he does not care at all for the success of his mission; conversely, his main aim may be to get rid of Achilles by sending him home. He rushes to speak so that no one tries to supplicate the hero on his own behalf (and thus be disloyal to Agamemnon's intentions), which might in effect convince Achilles to return to the common cause. Achilles may therefore feel that in fact Odysseus does not care at all about his return to battle in the role of hero, which the king of Ithaca wants to keep for himself. Achilles feels blackmailed into being ashamed of his decision to leave the Achaeans, but he avoids this trap.[115] Looking directly into Odysseus's eyes, he repeats firmly his decision to return, as if there was nothing inglorious about it; on the contrary, he states that all his people will accept it gladly.

Odysseus tries to corner Achilles by referring to social norms. Achilles' declaration that "and now I don't want to fight divine Hektor" (9.356) suggests that he is above the principle of competition—a situation that is unthinkable in the social system of his times, since the inability to compete means the inability to secure a desirable position within the community. However, Achilles is alienated from the community, and therefore its rules cease to apply to him. The loss of respect has turned him to a nobody, someone who does not deserve to be a part of a social group; and since he is a nobody, there is no shame in leaving the ranks of Achaean warriors and sailing home. Achilles dissociates himself from the group, suggesting that having once been deprived of honor,

[115] The combination of these two arguments, i.e. the appeal to Achilles' commitment to the common good and to his desire to prove himself better than Hektor, clearly indicates that Odysseus is trying to trap Achilles. By letting himself to be carried away by his emotions and reacting angrily to Hektor's boasts, Achilles would show that he is in fact driven not by altruism but by selfishness stemming from his desire to secure the title of "the bravest one." Instead, by ignoring Odysseus's provocation, Achilles demonstrates that his devotion to the Achaean cause is sincere and pure.

he cannot be deprived of it again. He says that since the basic principles ruling hierarchical society have been violated, everything has become meaningless—there are no rules which one should obey (9.316–319).[116] Odysseus's emotional blackmail is unsuccessful. Achilles does not intend to dissociate himself from his past, which Odysseus recalled to him, but as a counterargument he draws a picture of his future: he will sail home, enjoy his wealth, and accept nothing from Agamemnon, even should the king offer him infinitely more gifts.

In his answer to Odysseus, Achilles employs the word βασιλεύτερος, 'more royal' (9.392) to describe a man suitable for Agamemnon's son-in-law. His paratactic, ironic use of this epithet is a reference to the final part of Agamemnon's speech (9.160), which Achilles could not know, of course,[117] because Odysseus has omitted this part of the message. These words in Achilles' mouth signal that he knows Agamemnon's intentions and the real meaning of his gifts, and he has seen through his trap.[118]

At the first assembly, Agamemnon attributed to Achilles his own propensity for deception and erroneously thought he had caught him scheming; now Achilles has seen through the insidiousness of Odysseus, who, in turn, has underestimated his intelligence. Odysseus cannot influence him, not because his speech is "too cold,"[119] but because he resorts to deception, which puts off and even irritates the honest Achilles.[120] Therefore, the only one who gains something is Aias (9.636–642), because he is honest and bases his request on the bond of the brotherhood of arms (*philotês*).[121]

[116] Compare Hammer 1997.

[117] In 1.186, in Achilles' presence, Agamemnon states: "I am better than you are" (φέρτερός εἰμι σέθεν).

[118] Whitman (1958:182) was the first to notice that Achilles seems to realize Odysseus's omission of the ending of Agamemnon's message. Compare Taplin 1992:150n4. Achilles' speech is also an interesting example of reformulating someone's statement to one's own advantage (I have pointed out earlier, in Ch. 4, this method of constructing statements specific to a verbal dueling); in this case, it is the statement of someone who is absent at the moment. For Homer's audience, aware of this technique, the recalling of the key word uttered by Agamemnon must have been noticeable. This device produces the impression that Achilles is talking not to the deputies but directly to Agamemnon.

[119] Griffin 1995:103: "It is an able performance, but vehemence and personal passion of Achilles' reply make it look, by comparison, thin and impersonal, the speech of a mouthpiece."

[120] Muellner (1996:142) differently interprets Odysseus's failure. Instead of winning Achilles over as a *philos*, Odysseus reproaches him for a lack of *philophrosúnê*, 'solidarity': "No wonder Odysseus's speech in book 9 backfires: it exacerbates Achilles' *mênis* instead of arousing his *philotês*."

[121] Compare Lloyd-Jones 1971:18–19. In Ch. 4, I pointed out that Phoinix wants to tempt Achilles with gain. Despite the emotional quality of his speech, its purpose is very practical: he makes it clear that the hero can draw a lot of benefits from the present situation; if he fails do it now, he won't have another opportunity (9.600–605). Phoinix seems not to notice that what is at stake is Achilles' life, not riches.

The situation is similar to the embassy sent to Philoktetes: there too Odysseus cannot succeed by deceit, and the honesty of Diomedes or Neoptolemos (to some extent) induces Philoktetes to give way.[122] If we assume that this situation reflects the traditional model, then in the Homeric scene there is a significant modification: Aias's sincerity does not make Achilles return to the battlefield, although it changes his attitude enough to make it possible, because the hero withdraws his decision to sail home (9.650–655).

Achilles' character traits are contrasted with Agamemnon's.[123] Achilles is portrayed as a man who has always cared for his companions and for the whole army, and who is not acquisitive. Excessive greed is the main charge against Agamemnon made by Achilles at the first assembly and by Thersites at the second one. In poetry, it is a conventional reproach, but at the same time the most severe. Achilles' charges are not groundless; neither is his opinion about himself. The narrator confirms everything with a number of minor allusions, which he uses sparingly, but throughout the whole song.

Greediness and modesty of needs

At the first assembly, Achilles points out that whenever they capture a Trojan city, his prize is always incomparably smaller than that of Agamemnon (1.163) and does not reflect his contribution to military action (1.165–166). His effort is not taken into account at the division of the spoils (1.166–168):

> ... ἀτὰρ ἤν ποτε δασμὸς ἵκηται,
> σοὶ τὸ γέρας πολὺ μεῖζον, ἐγὼ δ' ὀλίγον τε φίλον τε
> ἔρχομ' ἔχων ἐπὶ νῆας...

> ... when it comes to the division of the loot,
> you take a much greater share [*geras*], whereas I carry a smaller but pleasure-giving [my own] part to my ships...

[122] Diomedes: Proclus *Chrestomathia*, the *Little Iliad* 2, probably also in Euripides' *Philoktetes* (Dion of Prusa, *Oration* 59); Neoptolemos: Sophocles, *Philoktetes* 1393–1408.

[123] Felson (2002:38–40) notes contrasted images of a caring father (Odysseus 2.260, 4.354; Peleus 9.394–397) and a bad one, i.e. Agamemnon, to whom Peleus entrusted his son. Achilles, in turn, unable to fulfill his filial duty of taking care of the elderly parent—θρέπτρα ("the return made by children for their rearing" 4.478, 17.302)—expresses his regret and a quite natural desire to repay Peleus for the hardships of bringing him up (the reciprocated "provision of food, nourishment"), an unreal desire because he realizes the shortness of his life. A side-effect of this is his compassion for Priam as an elderly father deprived of the care of prematurely deceased sons (24.527–542).

Achilles' contentment with little, contrasted with Agamemnon's avarice, is confirmed by the following small but significant details: the phorminx, which he chose as his prize after sacking Eëtion's city; and the cremation of Eëtion in his armor. The right to choose one's own prize from the spoils was a distinction. The choice of such a tasteful trifle clearly shows him as ungreedy person. The provenance of the instrument is mentioned when, on entering Achilles' tent, the envoys find him singing about the heroes of the past (9.185–188). This stands in stark contrast to Agamemnon's exaggerated list of gifts and is a signal that great treasures are not a real temptation to this humble man. This minor fact foreshadows and justifies Achilles' reaction to the terms of agreement offered to him.

Achilles' treatment of Eëtion's body (6.416–419) reflects respect for a worthy opponent. From Eëtion's treasures Achilles chooses a piece of iron which served Eëtion as a discus (23.825–828). The primitive nature of this lump of iron suggests heroism (synonymous with great strength; it certainly was much more difficult to throw a rough lump than a properly shaped discus). Eëtion fits the traditional portrait of the heroes of the past, who were depicted as using clubs in battle and stronger than Homeric heroes.

The reproach of greediness is the fundamental accusation in reproach poetry, so making Achilles free of this vice is a significant element of his praise. It may seem that the fact that Achilles took a high ransom for Eëtion's widow (6.425–427), whom he got as his *geras*, darkens this bright picture. However, accepting ransom indicates not so much Achilles' avarice as his lack of cruelty. Unlike Agamemnon, he obeys custom and does not stress his power and position by rejecting the ransom. The bright picture of Achilles in the *Iliad* does not necessarily coincide with the image that emerged from epic tradition; it could be just as dissonant as the image of Odysseus in the *Odyssey* and in other parts of the cycle. The image of a generous and modest Achilles could have been created as a contrast to a closefisted and avaricious Agamemnon.

Cruelty and pity

Jinyo Kim, in her extraordinary book *The Pity of Achilles: Oral Style and the Unity of the Iliad*, presents the issue of pity as essential not only for the ideology but also for the composition of the whole song. In our study of the dichotomy of Achilles' and Agamemnon's behavior, let us refer to some of her findings.

The warrior should be merciless to his enemies, but full of pity for his companions, which means he should do all he can to save them. The warrior also feels pity at the sight of his slain companions and this grief evokes a desire for revenge. Kim argues that the tripartite structure of the *Iliad* is determined by the role of pity:

1. In the first section, Achilles' pity for the army equals Hera's for the Achaeans, but after his withdrawal from the struggle, his pity dramatically changes into merciless abandonment (Books 1–8).
2. The second section starts with the display of Achilles' pitilessness in the scene of the Achaean embassy and ends with the painful loss of his friend; the loss was an effect of a rush of pity for the Achaeans, which made him send Patroklos into the battle to help the army. Of a series of pleas directed to Achilles in this part, the hero answers only the last one. However, it should be noted that with each plea addressed to him, Achilles' stance changes in favor of the Achaeans (Books 9–16).
3. In the third section, Achilles' pitilessness is directed against the Trojans. He rejects numerous Trojan pleas.[124] Unexpectedly, his intransigent wrath turns to pity for Priam (Books 17–24).

Achilles' sudden pity for the enemy is, I feel, insufficiently explained by Kim. In her opinion, it is an effect of the transformation of the concept of φιλότης 'friendship—feeling which connects you with the group'. Withdrawing from battle, Achilles reconsiders his point of view: the Achaeans are not close to him because they are his comrades, but because they are mortal, like him;[125] Priam also becomes close because of his suffering and his mortality.[126] The broadening of the meaning of φιλότης shows that Achilles begins to understand and accept his own mortality.

Kim makes an unfounded assumption that mercilessness is the only acceptable attitude towards the enemy. Therefore, she believes that the cruelty of Agamemnon, who is a merciless fighter, is approved of in the *Iliad*, while the opposite conduct is branded as incorrect, and therefore Menelaos is rightly reprimanded by his brother for pitying the enemy.[127] Kim notes that equating the Trojans with the Achaeans, because they are all mortal, conflicts with tradition and should be regarded as Homer's innovation. In her eyes, this novelty is a deeply humanistic concept, which the author associates with the behavior of the young hero, whereas Agamemnon represents traditional values.

From our modern point of view, this breach in traditional morality seems extremely valuable. However, the question is whether Homer's contemporaries would perceive Achilles' behavior similarly. It seems to me that approval of

[124] Kim (2000:131–140) points out that the youth and shortness of life of the begging warriors emphasized in their pleas are references to the fate of Achilles.

[125] Kim 2000:146.

[126] Kim 2000:150.

[127] Kim 2000:57–58.

Agamemnon's conduct, even temporary, would be contrary to the message of the poem. Kim notes only that Achilles' pity for Priam contrasts with Hektor's lack of pity towards his father and mother: Priam begs his son to have pity for his white hair and refrain from fighting Achilles, which Hektor does not do (22.37–78, 79–89). What she does not notice, however, is that Achilles' behavior contrasts with that of Agamemnon, who rejected Chryses' requests. How could the listener, for whom Agamemnon's pitilessness for the defeated enemy seems quite natural, accept Achilles' behavior towards Priam? Especially since Agamemnon's conduct, both towards Chryses and Achilles, is not accepted by the Achaeans.

The image of Achilles is developed both from the epic tradition and his past created by the author of the song. In the traditional image, a prophecy predicting the death of a merciless warrior makes him withdraw from fighting; later, the return to the battlefield brings about his death and gives him the status of a hero. Homer changes Achilles' past and character: he is not only modest and temperate in the matter of spoils, but, even before the action of the song, he is merciful to his friends and his enemies alike. The last trait is corroborated by the story of Lykaon; at a previous encounter Achilles did not kill him, but only took him captive and sold him on Lemnos (21.34–119). Ransomed, Lykaon returns to battle, but now Achilles has no mercy for the Trojans: he murders Lykaon, defenseless and begging for mercy, and throws his body into the river for the fish to eat (21.64–127). In his behavior, Achilles makes a full circle; once again, when he returns to battle, he has pity for his people and for his enemies, but only after he has felt it for Priam.

The signals the listener gets about Agamemnon are completely different. His past is confirmed only by the present, by the action of the *Iliad*. Achilles and Thersites criticize him for excessive greed, supposedly characteristic of him earlier and now confirmed by the stealing of Briseis. On the first day of fighting, after the gods have left the battlefield, the account of the Achaean chain of successes is interrupted by a significant scene in which Adrastos begs Menelaos to spare his life (6.37–50). Menelaos—the narrator says—is inclined to grant his request. However, at this moment Agamemnon appears and reproaches his brother for showing compassion to enemies who did not respect his home, an allusion to Paris, whose despicable behavior Agamemnon extends to all Trojans. He urges the soldiers to have no pity for Trojans, even for children in the womb. He refuses them the right to a proper burial or mourning (6.55–60). Under the influence of his brother, Menelaos pushes away the hand of the supplicant. Agamemnon kills the man (6.61–63)[128] and scornfully places his foot on his chest

[128] Kirk (1990:161–162) remarks that Agamemnon's cruelty and savage violence are emphasized by the rhetoric of his statements. Menelaos accepts the words of his brother as αἴσιμα 'sign of destiny'. Kirk warns against taking this word in moral terms ('justified'); killing enemies belongs,

(6.64–65). Nestor, coming in with support for Agamemnon, calls the Greeks to forget about loot and to kill as many enemies as possible (6.66–71). In spite of these appeals, several dozen lines later Diomedes does not fight Glaukos, and, in obedience to the laws of hospitality, proposes an exchange of armor (6.119–236).

During his *aristeia,* Agamemnon is constantly shown as cruel and pitiless toward the defeated enemy, often mutilating their corpses. First he kills Isos and Antiphos, sons of Priam; the narrator points out that they were once captured by Achilles, but he let them go, taking ransom instead (11.101–121). Agamemnon's cruelty is underlined by a moving comparison to a lion which kills fawns, ripping their hearts from their chests (11.113–121). The narrator mentions that Agamemnon recognized Priam's sons at once, because they had been in the camp as Achilles' captives, yet the king was not deterred from inflicting death on them. He takes no pity on Antimachos's sons when they beg for his mercy, because their father, bribed by Paris, opposed the return of Helen and voted for killing Menelaos and Odysseus, ambassadors to Troy (11.122–142). Nor does Agamemnon spare the sons of Antenor, who saved Menelaos's life, when he opposed the murder of envoys (11.221–263). Then Agamemnon murders the surrendering warriors, whom Menelaos intended to save. Menelaos was motivated by pity, not by a desire for ransom, which is a reference to Achilles, in contrast to Agamemnon's conduct. Agamemnon's ironic speech reproaching his brother for showing pity indicates his lack of understanding of such impulses. Yet, I believe, the listener might not have found his mercilessness natural or understandable. He also could have felt pity for defeated enemies, especially when the reason for sparing them was deeper than a desire for ransom, like in the case of Antenor's sons.

This issue is related to the problem of assessing Homer's attitude to the Trojans. An opinion repeated in scholia bT that Homer was pro-Achaean is sometimes dismissed by modern scholars. They argue that though the Achaeans are usually represented as the winners of duels, and even when they are defeated, their heroic successes are more often shown than those of the victorious Trojans, there are many instances of the poet's kindness towards the Trojans, especially towards Hektor and Aeneas.[129] Research on the formulae defining the Trojans made William Sale draw a conclusion about the traditionality of the Hellenic image and Homer's inventiveness. Formulae containing an epithet describing

in his opinion, to "the normal consequences of defeat." Such a situation on the battlefield is undoubtedly ordinary, but its presentation in the *Iliad* may point to a deliberate poetic device. Menelaos, however, does not withdraw from his merciful reaction because he recognizes the soundness of Agamemnon's words; the narrator leaves us with the impression that Menelaos gives in because he recognizes that this is what is "apportioned or destined."

129 Allan (2012:68) points out that the pro-Achaean slant must have suited the Panhellenic audience, but all the same the work cannot be described as anti-Trojan.

the Trojans are scarce, but in various utterances there is a recurring term, in the nominative, referring to them: ὑπερφίαλοι 'audacious, boisterous, wicked'—the same one that is also used for the suitors in the *Odyssey*.[130] We can, however, assume a certain epic traditionality in the balancing of the troubles for each side of the conflict, noticeable in the repeated expression that the Trojan War brought suffering to both the Achaeans and the Trojans (e.g. 3.126–128).[131] Thus, the concept of the mercy of the singer of the *Iliad* meets the expectations of the listeners, who were not as barbaric as it might seem.

The *Odyssey*, as a song in praise of Odysseus, interprets his past in his favor, passing over the events which would present him in unfavorable light; in the plot of the poem everything confirms his glory. It is not so with the image of Achilles in the *Iliad*. It is dynamic: at some points, Achilles' behavior contradicts his glorious past, which is seen not through the prism of his heroic deeds but certain character traits, like modesty of needs and pity for his people and defeated enemies. His withdrawal from and then return to the battlefield are used to present Achilles' maturation. In the heat of battle, he returns to his traditional role as a cruel hero. Yet even then, his attitude to his enemies is changed: he has no pity for Lykaon, but he addresses him as φίλε 'my friend' (21.106).[132] When Achilles finally becomes his old self again, he contradicts, first and foremost, the traditional image of the hero who gains apotheosis and glory in his death. Only his mortality, to which he is reconciled, matters.

Such an unconventional representation of this hero is possible due to the juxtaposition of the behavior and character of Achilles and Agamemnon.[133] For the listener, all these motifs become fully understandable with the completion of the ring composition, in which Achilles, despite his anger, is moved by Priam, because he comes to him personally to ask for the body of his son. Priam's

130 Sale 1989:378–379: "The traditional poets shared the Achaean attitude towards the Trojans and handed on to Homer a set of formulae that he could not employ as R[egular] F[ormulae] because he looked upon the Trojans with much greater favor than they did."

131 Nagy (1999:69–90) describes the ambivalence of the term ἄχος 'grief', applied to both fighting parties, present in the tradition of the *Iliad*.

132 Kim (2000:156) interprets this as a signal of Achilles' identification with the victim because they were both destined to die. It is certainly possible, but it seems to me that the term φίλε qualifies Lykaon as someone who is not a stranger. It would be, again, the evocation of the past, in which a captive was treated more like a guest, a stranger accepted into the close circle of friends and acquaintances. These ties would not be formal, like in the case of a guest, but rather based on emotions. By this form of address, Achilles shows to Lykaon that he recognizes him but, despite earlier friendly relationships, he must kill him.

133 The change in Achilles' behavior, when compared to his past conduct mentioned in the song, has been noted also by Zanker (1994: 8–9, 49–51, 74–76); Zanker points out that other heroes (Diomedes, Agamemnon, Nestor) also undergo such a change. It is explicable by the escalation of cruelty resulting from the frustration accumulating in the Achaeans due to the prolonged war.

behavior is the opposite of Agamemnon's in Book 9, whereas Achilles' behavior is the opposite of Agamemnon's conduct towards Chryses in Book 1.[134]

Achilles as an Epic Hero

In the *Iliad*, the polarized conduct of the protagonists prompts us to ask about its origins. The theme of the quarrel, frequent in Greek epic, introduces the problem of rivalry or even hostility between the characters connected by the bonds of ethnicity and a common goal. One character takes on the role of an antagonist whose deeds lead to disasters for the community. Agamemnon commits *hybris*, which causes the escalation of Achaean suffering, when they are decimated by the plague and then defeated by the Trojans. Achilles defends the traditional code of behavior in the group, i.e. *aidôs*. Agamemnon's conduct evokes his anger, *mênis*, analogous to the anger of gods.[135] Like the wrath of gods, the wrath of Achilles is directed against the whole community—since the group has not opposed the individual who broke the established order, the rule of collective responsibility applies.

Taking away someone's *geras* means the negation of his value; that is why it deprives him of due respect. If the act is unjust, it destabilizes the life of the community because it destroys criteria for ranking, which are adopted to distribute loot and determine the hierarchy within the group. This is Achilles' conclusion in his response to Odysseus's embassy speech (9.316–319):

> ... ἐπεὶ οὐκ ἄρα τις χάρις ἦεν
> μάρνασθαι δηΐοισιν ἐπ' ἀνδράσι νωλεμὲς αἰεί.
> ἴση μοῖρα μένοντι καὶ εἰ μάλα τις πολεμίζοι·
> ἐν δὲ ἰῇ τιμῇ ἠμὲν κακὸς ἠδὲ καὶ ἐσθλός.

> ... since there was no reward
> for ceaseless battle, without respite, against our foemen.
> He who fights his best and he who stays away [in the camp] earn the same share of the spoils:
> alike in honor (*timê*) are the coward and the brave.

134 For more on the extraordinary behavior of Achilles towards Priam, see Zieliński 2021a:79–82.

135 Muellner (1996:133) defines *mênis* as a "highly specialized social term denoting the cosmic sanction against tabu behavior." His penetrating and multilevel analysis lets him reconstruct the complexity of the meaning of this word within its poetic context. Muellner shows the relationship between anger and the need to keep social order based on the principle of group distribution and reciprocal exchange (especially Ch. 2). See Pulleyn (2000:116), more generally: "The word is most often used to describe the angry response of gods towards those whose transgressions threaten the settled order (e.g. V 444)."

On the scale of values, the expression "the coward and the brave" (κακὸς καὶ ἐσθλός) equals our polarization: "good and bad." Agamemnon's conduct has shattered criteria fundamental for evaluation. The capability of distinguishing good from bad is the basic duty and privilege of man,[136] so Achilles' wrath defends the traditional order of things.

William Sale also notices the traditional crisis of values in this passage.[137] However, he perceives the hero's complaint only as a stylistic device, which deepens the depiction of Achilles' character and which was introduced by the author of Books 9 and 19, added to the original *Achilleis*. Sale refers to the conception of the Pluralists, who interpreted the scene of the embassy to Achilles as one of the latest strata of the *Iliad*, loosely connected (only by Book 19) to the rest of the poem. For Sale, as for the Pluralists, Achilles' expectation (in Books 11 and 16) that the Achaeans would beg for his return and compensate him for forsaking his wrath is irreconcilable with the rejection of the requests and gifts offered him by the embassy in Book 9.[138] Without going into an unnecessary polemic against this position now, I will only point out that this is not necessarily so. Recall the hero's words which are a source of this confusion. When sending Patroklos to Nestor for information about the battle, Achilles says (11.609–610): νῦν ὀΐω περὶ γούνατ' ἐμὰ στήσεσθαι Ἀχαιοὺς / λισσομένους· χρειὼ γὰρ ἱκάνεται οὐκέτ' ἀνεκτός ("I think now the Achaeans will soon kneel at my knees / with pleas, because they are in unbearable need").
Agreeing for Patroklos to go to battle, Achilles expects that in the end it will bring him honor (*timê*), fame (*kydos*), the return of Briseis, and other gifts as compensation for the offence he has suffered (16.84–86):

> ὡς ἄν μοι τιμὴν μεγάλην καὶ κῦδος ἄρηαι
> πρὸς πάντων Δαναῶν, ἀτὰρ οἳ περικαλλέα κούρην
> ἂψ ἀπονάσσωσιν, ποτὶ δ' ἀγλαὰ δῶρα πόρωσιν.
>
> so that you may win me great honor (*timê*) and fame (*kudos*)
> among the Achaeans, so that they will give me back the beautiful girl
> and bring me fine gifts besides.

136 Semonides accuses some types of women of confusing these values (τὸ κακόν, τὸ ἐσθλόν) in order to addle their husband: the woman who comes from a vixen (7.10–11)—"Nothing of what is bad escapes her notice, not even of what is good, since she often calls the latter bad and the former good." Or they are unable to differentiate between what is good and what is bad, which indicates bottomless stupidity: the woman who comes from the earth (7.22–23)—"For such a woman knows neither what is bad nor what is good" (translation, D. E. Gerber).

137 Sale 1964:86–87.

138 A similar opinion is expressed by Page 1959:305–307; Kirk 1962:214; van Thiel 1982:87; and Hainsworth 1993:289–290.

One could say that Achilles, staying at Troy despite his threats of sailing back home, does not imagine he can go back to the battlefield unless the Achaeans beg him to and offer him gifts. In oral poetry, there are circumstances which demand a consistent set of elements, which means that every time a given situation comes around, those elements are repeated. This technique makes the story understandable to the listeners, so the singer has no other option: taking up a theme, he must include all its traditional components. Whenever the singer returns to Achilles in the narrative, he returns to the starting point, the hero's expectation of compensation for the harm he has suffered.[139] However, we can see that Achilles' position is justified because the offer of gifts mentioned by the envoys in Book 9 was not meant to restore his honor; on the contrary, it was intended to finally subdue Achilles to Agamemnon. Achilles, therefore, may simply want a fair presentation of this offer, with a clear statement that it is he, and he alone, who can rescue the army.

The disruption of the traditional social order, however, lies at the root of Achilles' anger (*mênis*) and cannot be considered as an addition and later development of a simple motif of taking away the hero's slave. In Chapter 2, I pointed out that the traditional motif is the one of Achilles' withdrawal from battle under the influence of the oracle given to him by his divine mother. Since this is the pattern repeated in the cycle, it follows that the withdrawal from the fighting because of Agamemnon's insult is the *Iliad*'s innovation. If we talk about the original *Achilleis* (not a prototype of the *Iliad*, but a traditional multiform song of Achilles), it would contain this pattern of the protagonist withdrawing from battle out of fear for his own life, but the end is supposed eventually to come on the battlefield after killing the enemy—usually the leader of Trojan allies. All traditional stories of Achilles either depict the hero's death (like the *Aethiopis*) or foreshadow it as a necessary event (like the *Iliad*). What the *Iliad* changes is Achilles' motivation for his withdrawal from battle.

The *Iliad* overturns the traditional role and destiny of the hero by presenting the possibility that he may reject the heroic struggle and try to avoid death at an early age. Dale Sinos points out that the origin of an epic hero such as Achilles can be traced to the Greek iconic image of the hero.[140] Schroeder's and Van Windekens's hypothesis that the related words *Hera* and *hero* (Ἥρα/ἥρως) come from the IE root *iēr- meaning, according to Pötscher's etymology, "year," imposes the interpretation that they were the original married couple of deities symbolizing youth and maturity for marriage.[141] With time, the goddess Hera,

[139] On the consistency of this passage with the necessity of remunerating a hero for his service, see Claus 1975:26–28.

[140] Sinos 1975:26–27.

[141] After Pötscher 1961:304.

without losing her character as the guardian of marriage, obtained a higher status, thanks to her identification as the wife of the main god Zeus, while the hero was downgraded to the role of an ancestor/protective spirit, identifiable with the warriors of the mythical period. According to Sinos, Hesiod ranks cult heroes among the generation of the silver age. Sinos stresses the relationship, indicated by Pötscher, between the words *Hera/hero* and ὥρα, meaning "season, ripeness, timeliness, being seasonal."[142] In Sinos's opinion, this etymology links the hero with the vegetative cult (the concept which Pötscher rejected), but he perceives the hero's maturity as an analogy to the time of sowing or growth, as evidenced by the frequent epic metaphors comparing heroes to grown plant shoots, especially Achilles (e.g. ἔρνεϊ ἶσος 'like a young shoot', *Iliad* 18.56, 437; also Telemachos, *Odyssey* 14.175).[143] Although in Hesiod the heroes of the Trojan War belong to the fourth generation (*Works and Days* 164–166), Achilles shares all the traits attributed to the heroes of the silver generation:[144] a long childhood (the humans of the silver generation spent the first hundred years like foolish and carefree children—Hesiod, *Works and Days* 130–134—there is a parallel motif of upbringing/nutrition by a goddess), short youth, *hybris*, death in conflict with gods, a happy life after death and religious worship (*timê*).

Douglas Q. Adams also links the etymologies of *Hera/hero* to the root *iēr-, but—unlike the scholars mentioned above—not in the sense of 'year'.[145] Moreover, Adams rejects previous attempts to derive the word *hero* from the assumed **herwa* related to the Latin *servāre* 'watch over, protect' or Avestan *haurvaiti* 'protects', rightly pointing out that the notion of protection is important for nineteenth- and twentieth-century conceptions of a hero, but that does not necessarily correspond to early Greeks' ideas on the subject.[146] Without determining its origin, Adams notes that the word *hero*, if taken from the alternative hypothetical form **s/ieE-r-ou*, is parallel to *Anér- (*Ae/on-r*), in Proto-Indo-European meaning 'man, hero' (originally 'one imbued with élan vital')—represented by the Greek ἀνήρ 'man, hero', Sanskrit *nā* (*nár*) 'man, male, Hero', and Avestan *nā* (*nar-*) 'man, male'. A similar relationship exists in the case of words formed from the root **wīró*, meaning 'man', such as Latin *vir* or Sanskrit *vīrá-*, which are derivatives of **weiH-*, seen in Latin *vīs* (f.) 'power, strength', pl. *vīrēs* 'physical forces, male sexual organs', Greek ἴς (ī-) 'strength, force', or Sanskrit *váyas-* 'energy, vigor, vigorous age, youth'.[147] Adams concludes that

142 Sinos 1975:11–12. Compare Davidson 1980:199.

143 Sinos 1975:27–37.

144 Nagy (1999:151–173) points out analogies between the silver generation and the fourth generation of heroes.

145 Adams 1987.

146 Adams 1987:171–172.

147 Adams 1987:173–175.

whatever the original root of the Greek *Hera/hero* (**seE-* or **ieE-*), it must have carried the meaning of 'strength, vitality, and youth' (related to *Hebe*, 'youth', personified as the goddess of youth). Other analogies to Proto-Indo-European forms derived from **iē-* (earlier **ieE-*), let us identify the verbal noun *yeE-r̥* 'deed', which might have given rise to adjectival derivatives meaning 'doing deeds, potent, capable', or agent nouns meaning 'characterized by capability', or the verb 'to do, make'.[148]

These two etymologies and interpretations are not mutually exclusive. The maturity that enables marriage is connected with youth and with features associated with youth, i.e. vitality, strength, and the readiness and ability to commit heroic deeds. All these elements correspond to the characteristics of both the cult and epic hero in Greek tradition. The perception of epic heroes as relics of gods who have lost their divine status (e.g. the hero as Hera's husband) does not seem correct in the light of modern research. The epic hero has his own genealogy, though sometimes gods can be shown as epic heroes, and epic heroes can become gods. In Meletinsky's evolutionary theory, in the original folk tale, the central figure is "a man," devoid of individual traits.[149] With the passage of time, he is replaced by the culture hero, identified with an idealized ancestor; the culture hero embodies the collective power of his tribe and symbolizes its unity against hostile external forces, especially foreign tribes. The next stage, according to Meletinsky, is the heroic tale, in which the hero performs extraordinary deeds, such as fighting monsters, winning a "distant fiancée," or avenging himself on his father's murderers, but he does all this for personal reasons and not in the interest of the community.[150] The next step is epic, which presents a historical background, gradually eliminating fairy-tale and mythological elements. This kind of song marks the transition from mythological to historical epic. Unlike the protagonist of earlier fairy and mythological tales, who was motivated by a personal reason (e.g. revenge), the epic hero is primarily guided by the good of the community to which he belongs (not only the house or family, but also more broadly—the tribe or ethnic community). This change is connected with a sort of universalization, typical of epic, which assumes a much broader perspective than that of the tribe, where the key issue is the continuation of the family line (we can compare it with the phenomenon of pan-Hellenism and pan-Indism mentioned in Chapter 1).

148 Adams 1987:175–177.
149 Meletinsky 2009:73–74.
150 Meletinsky 2009:75–91.

There is a noticeable similarity between the Homeric heroes and those of the Caucasian Nart epics.[151] The Narts are an extremely powerful people from the distant past, who out of pride (*hybris*) often entered into conflict with the gods, thus choosing a glorious death: they behave like the heroes of the Greek Silver Age.[152] Hesiod (*Works and Days* 138–142) says that Zeus "hid," i.e. destroyed this generation because they did not worship the gods. Similarly, a fragment of a papyrus roll (*Oxyrinchus* 3829) indicates godlessness in the generation of heroes as the original cause of the Trojan War; this is the issue Zeus discusses with Themis when he is planning to bring about their destruction (Proclus, *Chrestomathia*, *Kypria* 1).[153] The Nart generation in the Caucasian epics is, then, comparable to the heroic generation in Greek epic. The bravest Nart, Batraz, having avenged the death of his father, in undying battle frenzy "turns first against the Narts, and then against gods."[154] This is an obvious parallel to Achilles' wrath, unrestrained even after avenging his friend and threatening the order protected by the gods (24.53–54). In Diomedes' *aristeia*, which is a reference to Achilles' heroic fight, the gods fear that the hero can turn against them, even against Zeus himself: Aphrodite says, "the Danaans are at war with the immortals" (5.380); Apollo, "he would fight even Zeus himself" (5.457); Ares, "so that he would not vent his pride on us, immortal gods" (5.882).

Achilles' childhood, presented in the cycle, is similar to that of the heroes of the Silver Age and finds its counterpart in many other epic traditions. The heroes of the Silver Age always, from childhood, or even from the moment of their birth, demonstrate extraordinary physical force, which borders on cruelty, as well as carelessness and foolishness. This is true in the case of David of Sassoun, the protagonist of the Armenian national epic, and his son Mher the Younger, and the Narts, as well as Amirani, a hero of the Georgian epic.[155] At first, the strength of an extraordinary child is directed against his peers, whom he physically abuses, usually because the group has rejected, insulted, or ridiculed him. This demonstration of the boy's strength may give him a purpose

151 The name of this fabulous tribe is most likely derived from the old Iranian *nara* meaning 'daredevil, warrior, hero'. Meletinsky (2009:162) considers this etymology as the most probable one. Thus, this etymology of the name of the tribe has Indo-European parallels in Greek ἀνήρ, Sanskrit *nā* (*nár*) 'man, husband, hero', and the Roman name *Nero*.

152 In Meletinsky's opinion (2009:163), these conflicts between gods and heroes preserve traces of resistance to the spread of Christianity. However, it seems that he is wrong.

153 It coincides with the beginning of the *Kypria* in Proclus's summary, where such a conference is enigmatically mentioned. Finkelberg (2015:136) argues that the motif of the destruction of heroes is present in Hesiodic and the Cyclic traditions, but not in Homeric. For Finkelberg, it is one of the arguments for treating Homeric works as breaking with the oral tradition ("meta-epic").

154 Meletinsky 2009:197.

155 Meletinsky 2009:216.

for his further efforts: the boys beaten by Amirani say, "instead of beating us, you'd better find out what has happened with Iamani's eye" or "you'd better free Camcumi chained by Baqbaq-Devi," etc. Likewise, an old woman, whose field of millet was destroyed by David of Sassoun, tells him to attend to a more important matter, the recovery of Cowasar, his father's mountain, on which he had rebuilt the temple of Maruta, the Virgin Mary. The young hero is often engaged in trifles and deserves a rebuke: David, returning from a hunt, meets an old woman who reprimands him and sends him against Kobadin, who persecutes the Armenians by collecting taxes from them.

In the Trojan Cycle, Achilles has since childhood been distinguished by extraordinary strength, evident in his hunting skills during his education with Cheiron. Another of his teachers, Phoinix, mentions in the *Iliad* (9.490–492) that the hero's childhood clumsiness caused him a lot of problems. I believe that it is the same motif of childhood foolishness, which in Greek epic appears in a much milder form. In the *Iliad*, Patroklos's eagerness to fight in Achilles' stead is called νήπιος 'childish, stupid', because he seems to be unaware that the consequence of his behavior is death (16.686). The same childish stupidity and uncontrolled aggressiveness were responsible for young Patroklos's killing of another child over a game (23.86–88).

Heroes' extraordinary courage and strength make them fall into pride, which leads them to challenge God/Christ/gods (depending on the version), which provokes a divine reaction, and the hero ends up chained to a rock or knocked down to hell.[156] The unrelenting wrath of the hero would be, then, an offshoot of his conceit, which pushes him to fight against forces far beyond his reach. His actions threaten the world or its order established by gods, and that is why they bring about the hero's death. Among the Greeks, however, the same punishing divinity causes the posthumous glorification of the hero both in cult and in the epic picture of his happy existence after death. Apollo is challenged to fight neither by Achilles, nor by his substitutes (Patroklos, Diomedes), because it is more important for the singer to point to the impassable gap separating the world of people and gods—that is why the heroes lose their strength, becoming more like ordinary people, and the gods, their power unthreatened, move away from people. Diomedes, Patroklos, and Achilles retreat before Apollo, aware of his power. The singer, however, knows stories in which gods suffered from the power of human heroes: Dione mentions this fact (5.383–404), but she threatens Diomedes with an inexorable and untimely death for attacking gods (5.406–409).[157]

156 This is the case of the Georgian hero Amirani and Abkhazian Abrskil; see Meletinsky 2009:207–209.

157 Despite many transformations, this pattern is discernible also in the Prince Marko cycle. Marko's cruelty is enormous, both to enemies and to all those who do not show him due respect (e.g. he

Achilles, like all protagonists of an epic song, is presented as ready for marriage. The motif of his marriage is marked in the cycle by the preparations for his supposed marriage to Iphigenia. The *Iliad* also suggests possible marriages for Achilles—when Agamemnon again offers him the hand of his daughter (9.141–146),[158] and when Briseis mentions Patroklos's promise of her marriage to Achilles (19.297–299).[159] Achilles, however, will never marry: he is destined to die prematurely. Such a death links him with cult heroes and heroes of the Silver Age, like Adonis or Phaeton, but it is also often a feature of epic heroes. The *Iliad* stresses the shortness of life cut off at its prime in the case of Trojan heroes killed by Achilles. Kim notes that the Trojans begging Achilles to spare them refer in their pleas to Achilles' life, which is several times described as "short-lived" μινυνθάδιος.[160] Tros says he is as young as Achilles (20.463–472, ὁμηλικίη). Lykaon supplicates for his life, saying that his mother bore him for a short span of life (μινυνθάδιον, 21.83–84), using a formula analogous to the one with which Achilles complains to his mother (1.352). Hektor does not intend to beg Achilles to spare his life (22.123–124), but only to give his body to his family (22.338–339), however, at the moment of his death, his "youth and manhood," which desert him—λιποῦσ' ἀνδροτῆτα καὶ ἥβην (22.363)—are mentioned by the narrator; earlier, too, there are indications that his life will be short (μινυνθάδιος, 15.612).[161]

A young hero usually has to fight a monster or an enemy warrior. In accordance with the principle described earlier, the enemies become similar to the hero

mutilated Rosanda, the sister of Leka-Kapetan, who rejected his courtship, and the smith Novak, who forged a better saber for his enemy Musa than for him). Sometimes Marko's cruelty is difficult to understand, for example when he kills an Arab girl who is in love with him and helps him escape from prison. His cruelty prevails even over the rightness and nobility of his conduct. Despite his killing the vizier for breaking the wing of his falcon, the Sultan does not punish Marko, but rewards him because Marko is so brave ("Any Turk may become Vizier, / but there is no knight of prowess like unto Marko"). This motivation, however, is insufficient, because the narrator adds: "Now the Sultan gave not Marko the ducats. / hat he should drink red wine, / But that he should get him out of his sight, / (For of Marko's anger he was sore adread.)" (translation, D. H. Low). Marko, in his anger, does not threaten God (He is the only one Marko is afraid of), but the Sultan, in whose service he is. When Marko's death comes, however, it is not from the hand of man, but from the hand of God. The prince accepts his coming death and prepares for it: he kills his wonderful horse Šarac, destroys his weapon, writes a will, and lies down by the roadside.

158 This issue returns in the response Achilles gives to the envoys (9.388–400).

159 The possibility of marrying a captive woman is provided for in Deuteronomy 21.10–14, where she is even granted certain rights: she can mourn her murdered family for a month and if her husband is not pleased with her, he can send her away like an unwanted wife (he can no longer sell her because by becoming a wife she ceases to be a slave).

160 Kim 2000:131–140.

161 For Rabel (1990b:129–130), the application of this epithet to the Trojan warrior Hippothoos (17.302) is the main argument for treating this character as Achilles' doublet (apart from the fact that they both die far from their homeland and their death is a cause of their parents' suffering).

that deprives them of life and they lose their monstrous features. They start looking like him, then they take on his character traits. Pitilessness is undoubtedly a heroic feature; in the Homeric image of Achilles, it is heightened to such an extent that the gods are unable to control it. Excessive pitilessness is also found in his rivals. The ruthlessness of Achilles justifies the warnings of Hektor's family, who ask him not to fight the Greek hero. Achilles' mercilessness corresponds to that of Hektor, revealed by his indifference to the requests of his father, mother, and wife.[162]

Achilles' unchecked cruelty, directed not only against his enemies, but also against his companions, results from the nature of his anger, *mênis*, which it accompanies in many cultures.[163] It emanates from the power of the whole tribe, although in the epic plot the hero's cruelty is often targeted against his own people. Such is the case, for example, of Sosruko, the central character of the Nart epic. Sosruko wins the dance contest with the other Narts, who did not let him participate in the khasa, then he kills them (one of them is pushed into the ground so that only his head sticks out) and makes their women sew a coat for him from the dead men's moustaches and scalps.[164] Achilles' cruelty undoubtedly belongs to his traditional image as a hero. A fiery halo which appears above his head when he, although unarmed, goes to fight for Patroklos's body and gives a terrifying shout (18.205–214), signifies the traditional power of his wrath. His earlier gentleness must be a novelty introduced by the *Iliad*. From the perspective of Achilles' supposed gentleness, his later boundless cruelty towards his companions (refusing to fight, he condemns his brethren to death) and towards his enemies (he murders them mercilessly and maltreats Hektor's corpse) seems to be an exception to his normal behavior, though it is an element of his traditional image.

Homer thus creates a dramatic image of the hero, who only now achieves heroic status, although such an escalation of cruelty characterized him in every song of which he was a protagonist. Homer uses the traditional image of the hero, at the same time questioning the value of such heroism. By accepting his death, Achilles accepts his fully human condition. Thanks to this brilliant strategy of contrasting the new image of the hero with his traditional role, the story, although told in the traditional fashion, reveals the hero's anti-heroic

162 Compare Kim 2000:142.

163 Thalmann (1984:82–83) believes that Achilles in his anger crosses the boundary allowed to humans and brings upon himself the anger of a god. People have been given endurance—*tlêmosunê*—which allows them to bear the suffering and death of loved ones (24.46–49). It may be well to recall the remark of Davies 1981:62 that unlike people, the gods of the *Iliad* cannot afford to forgive and desist from vengeance. The name of the Armenian heroes, the invincible Sassouns, is derived from the word *sasun* 'rage' (Meletinsky 2009:241).

164 Meletinsky 2009:178–179.

dimension. Similarly, as we have seen, Homer uses the traditional motif of Achilles' withdrawal from battle under the influence of the prophecy given to him by Thetis. In both cases, many scholars have been deceived, treating these traditional motifs as Homer's inventions. By scattering throughout the song little hints, the author of the *Iliad* sketches a completely untraditional picture of Achilles—a noble youth devoted to a common cause; at the same time, Homer subjects the hero's traditional conduct, in which he reveals his merciless power, to criticism for its morality. Nevertheless, Homer defends his protagonist, showing that he was forced to act as he did by the unworthy conduct of another man.

In his traditional image, Achilles must have been bold, cruel, and ruthless—heroic, in a word, like all the other protagonists of epic poems, from Sosruko or Batraz in the epic about the Narts to David of Sassoun or Prince Marko. In his song, the singer refers to tradition, using a variety of allusions, which allow the public to read the proper message of the scenes. In the case of Achilles, Homer seems to mislead his audience because he carefully uses allusions suggesting that before the action of the song, in the tradition, his protagonist was different: gentle, merciful, good-natured. The singer alters not only the hero's time at Troy, but even his childhood, in which an act of cruelty, the killing of another child—presumably a typical element of the image of a hero in this tradition—is transferred onto Achilles' substitute Patroklos. The change which Achilles experiences in the poem, becoming unforgiving and merciless to enemies and friends alike, refers to his traditional image; in effect, the poem shows his typical representation. However, this image is disturbed by the way the hero distances himself from his heroic nature.

Homer's portrayal of the past of his hero-protagonist inspires respect and amazement. He hardly refers at all to Achilles' heroic achievements from outside of his song, which must have been known to an audience familiar with other songs about this hero. Neither the elimination of allied leaders, such as Kyknos, nor the killing of other sons of Priam, is recalled in detail. It seems as if the singer, when using the pattern of a song of Achilles, could evoke the hero's deeds that form the basis of the pattern only once.[165] This is surprising, because by mentioning earlier mighty deeds, the singer could get more appreciation for the hero. Such deeds are often used as self-praise by a hero aiming to cancel his adversary's reproach.[166] By giving up on this, Homer can show the actions of his hero from a different perspective, a perspective in which heroism takes a back seat.

[165] This confirms my earlier conclusion that oral tradition does not know historical thinking.

[166] For example, Beowulf's boasting speech mentioning his earlier achievements, which invalidated the accusations made by Unferth, son of Ecglaf (*Beowulf* 529–606), or Arjuna's speech to Yudhishthira (*Mahābhārata* 8.49.73–8.49.90) fulfilling the same function.

Perhaps this "gentleness" of Achilles was not wholly invented by Homer. In this respect, he could also have based it on some tradition. Sinos points out the deficiencies in the image of Achilles which are completed by Patroklos: gentleness, humanitarianism, prudence. In his opinion, it is not so much the fact that Achilles lacks these qualities, but rather he is not allowed to manifest them because of his role as "the best of the Achaeans," imposed upon him in the epic. Sinos notes that both in the *Iliad* and in the fragmentary remnants of the cycle we can encounter evidence of the conflict between Achilles' peaceful nature and his tasks as a warrior: Achilles' disguise as a girl on Skyros in order to avoid participation in the war, his learning to play the lyre from Cheiron, and some of the hero's statements in the *Iliad*, in which he mentions his and Patroklos's joint plans for the future (23.77–78), or when he informs Agamemnon about his lack of hostility towards the Trojans (1.152–153).[167] According to Sinos, Achilles in the tradition was characterized by gentleness and other similar traits, which he could not show in the *Iliad* because of the specific role that Homer intended for him. However, such an interpretation of events is unconvincing, since the rivalry for the title of "the best of the Achaeans" must be considered a traditional epic theme.

The matter seems to be turned on its head: the traditional has been considered secondary. But I believe we can assume that the ambiguity of the hero's image in epic songs is traditional. My analysis of the character of the Homeric Achilles points to the stress which the *Iliad* places on the peaceful nature of the protagonist as a part of the past to which there is no return; this is obvious, if we consider the aims of the song's author, whose main task is to praise the protagonist. A biased depiction of heroes in epic is the dominant feature of the song. The *Iliad* presents Achilles' nobleness, whitewashing his image in allusions to his past deeds, just as the *Odyssey* whitewashes Odysseus's actions. In Homer's *Iliad*, the changes in the protagonist deepen his personality, making him more than just a heartless killing machine, and emphasize the tragic dimension of the hero, because in contact with human baseness and the brutality of the world, he loses his innocence. Moreover, it enables a dynamic development of the protagonist, who in the end gives up his life, having come to the understanding that—despite his uncommon magnificence—his lot is similar to that of other people. However, at the apex of anger and accumulated hatred towards the enemy, the hero is capable of a gesture of pity.

This split in the traditional image of Achilles stems from the equally traditional concept of his withdrawal from fighting, motivated by fear for his life.

[167] Sinos 1975:100–101, 138–139. Sinos treats the mentions of the past in the *Iliad* as references to facts known from tradition. He does not allow for the possibility of the poet inventing new facts within tradition, i.e. of adapting traditional stories to the needs of the present narration.

Such unheroic behavior preceding a heroic act must have influenced the effort to understand the causes and consequences of this state of affairs and, as a result, a proliferation of plot variants. Undoubtedly, the attention of people who listened to songs that belong to this trend was drawn to the tragic fate of Achilles, whose uniqueness was perceived in the light of his imminent and irrevocable death—death which he brought upon himself, killing the person he should not kill. His tragic dimension is manifested above all by his awareness of the consequences of his deed, of killing a monstrous warrior, such as Memnon or Hektor.[168] However, in this event he does so for reasons more important than the concern for saving his own life: one of them is revenge for killing his friend (this is the motivation in the case of the deaths of Antilochos and Patroklos). In tradition, Achilles never opposes his mother, but by being obedient to her and withdrawing from battle, he resists his fate. Considering that the young hero's task is to do a mighty deed, then such behavior means that he may never fulfill his heroic mission. The withdrawal of Achilles from battle gives the poet several ways to continue the plot: he has the opportunity to place before the hero the choice of his fate.[169] But the choice is illusory, because Achilles as a hero can never choose a fate other than heroic fame.

The emphasis on the tragic does not seem to be a feature of Homer's style that distinguishes him from the rest of the epic tradition, as Burkert believed.[170] The tragic aspect of Achilles' life is a part of the epic representation of this hero, so Homer fits in the tradition, although he gives it an original and distinctive dimension.

Sometimes scholars perceive Achilles as a new figure in the Trojan epic, since he is missing at the climax (or what seems to be the climax) of the story, at the capture of Troy, as if all the roles were already dealt out and there was no room for a new character.[171] However, acquaintance with the rules of creation of oral epic allows us to reject such assumptions. A typical starting point for an oral song is a crisis resulting from an extraordinarily prolonged siege of a city. The capture requires an unusual deed. Overcoming the obstacle is a task for an epic hero and conquering the city is only a consequence, which may or may not be presented in an oral song.

In the image of Achilles, all typical features of the epic hero are clearly manifested: a young hero performs a deed which brings enormous benefit to the

168 In only one version of the battle with Tenes does Achilles kill his enemy unconsciously, but it is undoubtedly a late version (Plutarch *Quaestiones Graecae* 28).

169 Offering a protagonist an alternative—either immortal fame but a short life, or a long life but without glory—is a common folk motif (Carpenter 1974:21–22).

170 Burkert 1972:83–85.

171 For example, Howald 1924:410. This issue has already been discussed in the previous chapter.

whole community. It is evident that the epic hero has lost the features of a culture hero, whose actions benefitted the next generations of humanity, often limited to his tribe. A culture hero gives humanity all the skills necessary for survival: cattle breeding, fishing, plant cultivation, handicrafts, and, above all, the use of fire.[172] Nonetheless, Achilles preserves some of his features. As a culture hero, he frees the earth from monsters and rescues his tribe from disease, pestilence, and other calamities. One of Achilles' tasks that keep recurring is to kill warriors with monstrous features.[173] In pre-Homeric epic, there is a change: monsters look like the heroes who fight with them—they become beautiful young men of great strength and have miraculous artifacts at their disposal, just like the heroes. The armor of Hephaistos, worn by Memnon, may be a symbol of this likeness. It is analogous to Achilles' miraculous armor, which is a gift given by Hephaistos to his father Peleus; a variant of this is the armor forged for Achilles by Hephaistos in the *Iliad*. From this perspective, Achilles' victorious duels with the leaders of the Trojan allies seem to be his primary deeds. The coda to these feats is his death at the hands of Priam's son, Paris/Alexander. Killing other sons of Priam, including Hektor, simply doubles Achilles' fundamental deeds, i.e. defeating monsters. In the development of epic poetry, additional elements have become a priority.

Achilles represents a newer type of the epic hero—an idealized warrior. Odysseus, who resorts to trickery and descends to the land of the dead, has preserved more traces of the culture hero, though he also is a new hero-warrior.[174] This type of hero is no longer seen as the first man or the founder of the tribe; he is a descendant of a patriarchal family. The biography of such a hero usually contains the following elements: a miraculous birth, heroic adolescence, invulnerability (often this feature is discovered at some later stage), name-giving, receiving his father's armor, and winning or choosing horses or a

172 Meletinsky 2009:89–90.

173 A similar evolution can be observed in the poems of the Turkish-Mongolian peoples of Siberia. There are stories about heroes who defeat monsters, generally known as mangadhays or abaasy. In the Yakut epic (olonkho), abaasy possess some features of warriors, still preserving their monstrous features (often their ugliness is revealed by disability—they are one-eyed, one-armed, etc.). In contrast to heroes, who are usually referred to as "silver," the abaasy are referred to as "iron" (a similar distinction can be found in Buryat uligeri). See Meletinsky 2009:271–272. Compare Ch. 3, above.

174 Such an evolution can likewise be noticed in the Nart epic, in which Sosruko (Soslan), who steals fire from a giant, is gradually replaced by Batraz, a noble hero who performs heroic deeds. Batraz is clearly more appreciated in the Ossetian version of the epic. He defends his tribe against giants, who are the mythological image of hostile foreign tribes. See Meletinsky 2009:194: "The figure of Batraz ... was probably born in the last stage of Alanian military democracy, when patriarchal order triumphed. ... He is already a typical epic hero, idealised warrior, and in comparison with Soslan, marks a new phase and a higher form of heroism."

horse—usually a miraculous animal (it often speaks with human voice). All these elements are connected with the story of the marriage of Peleus and Thetis. Both Achilles' parents have superhuman traits, which makes him different from all other heroes at Troy.[175] According to Carpenter, numerous *Märchen* (fairy-tale) elements accumulated in the figure of this hero are responsible for his uniqueness in the Trojan War epic and also for his isolation (the motif of isolation recurs frequently in the cycle). Folk etymology linked the name 'Peleus' with the mountain 'Pelion'.[176] With such parentage, mountain for father and sea for mother, the swift-footed Achilles may originally have been a swift-running river elevated to the rank of local hero or divinity.[177] If at least a part of these identifications is correct, it throws a different light on the words which Patroklos, full of sorrow, addresses to Achilles (16.33–35):

> νηλεές, οὐκ ἄρα σοί γε πατὴρ ἦν ἱππότα Πηλεύς,
> οὐδὲ Θέτις μήτηρ· γλαυκὴ δέ σε τίκτε θάλασσα
> πέτραι τ' ἠλίβατοι, ὅτι τοι νόος ἐστὶν ἀπηνής.
>
> O, pitiless one! Neither the horseman Peleus was your father,
> nor Thetis your mother, but the grey sea bore you
> and rocks unpassable, since your heart is so hard.

The motif of the birth from a stone is one of the most typical for a heroic childhood.[178]

In the case of Achilles, the theme of a miraculous birth is associated with the worldwide motif of the Swan Maiden. The male character captures a girl who periodically transforms herself from a human to a swan (sometimes to a wild animal, fish, or other sea animal, like a seal or mermaid); he hides her animal skin so that she cannot find it, and the girl becomes his wife and bears him a child, or children. After some time, as a result of an insult (often related to her former existence) by her husband, or because an accidental discovery of the skin awakens longing for the past, she leaves her family and returns to her former life. Frazer finds this pattern in the story of Peleus and Thetis's wedding.[179] A remarkable similarity can be found in a contemporary Cretan

175 Carpenter 1974:71–73; Janko 1992:320, 335.

176 Carpenter 1974:73.

177 Carpenter 1974:73.

178 Sosruko and Syrdon, the protagonists of the Nart epic, were born from stone; likewise the Iranian god Mitra and his son; Melanesian culture hero Qat; and in one of the Khakassian poems, the hero Ak-khan finds a child born from a white, shiny stone lying on the bottom of the sea. See Meletinsky 2009:34, 164, 171–175, 317.

179 Frazer 1921b:383–388, who refers to earlier findings of W. Mannhardt.

folk tale, recognized by Mannhardt and Frazer as independent of the story of Peleus and Thetis: in the tale, a man falls in love with one of the sea nymphs, manages to capture her, although she keeps changing her form, and, on the advice of an old woman, marries her. However, the girl's muteness disturbs his marital happiness. Again following the old woman's advice, he kindles fire in the furnace and threatens to throw their child into it if his wife does not speak to him. His wife, however, only curses him, takes the child into her arms, and runs away. Unable to join other nymphs, because she has become a mother, she lives near their cave at a stream, where she appears two or three times a year with a child in her arms.

Peleus wins Thetis in a similar way, keeping her in his embrace until she returns to her proper form. Sophocles calls their marriage "silent" (ἀφθόγγους γάμους, *Troilos* fragment 618.1). Thetis also leaves Peleus after his scream of terror interrupted her attempts to make Achilles immortal by immersing him in a fire or cauldron of boiling water.[180] Some testimonia suggest that Peleus reproached his wife, who felt offended.[181] The *Iliad* does not mention this story, but Thetis is depicted living with her father Nereus and sisters in the depth of the sea (1.357, 18.35–69, 24.83–84), and Peleus as an old man lives a sad, solitary life in his house (18.434–435). As a result, Achilles grew up outside his home, which is a popular motif in the biographies of many epic heroes. The centaur-monster Cheiron, who brings him up, gives him a name, although the explanation of this name by later Greek sources as "lipless" seems preposterous.[182]

It is worthwhile to compare epic poems of the Turkish-Mongolian peoples of Siberia, especially the poems about the epic hero's formation (particularly Yakut epic). Hunting an animal is the first heroic act of a hero and only later is he given a name.[183] Achilles' education with Cheiron is presented as the time of learning how to hunt and kill animals.[184] Similarly, the naming of Odysseus by his grandfather Autolykos involves a boar hunt, during which the hero receives a scar on his thigh (*Odyssey* 19.399–466). As I have observed in Chapter 2, epic poetry traditionally linked the figure of Odysseus with the wild boar, and this link works not only with this hero, but also with Tydeus. Perhaps there is a connection between giving the name "Odysseus" to the boy and his killing a

180 According to Meletinsky (2009:433), the connection with the element of water and tempering Achilles in fire or water links the tales of his birth and heroic childhood with archaic epics of peoples of the Caucasus (the Narts emerge from water, and this motif also appears in the epic of Amirani).

181 Scholia on Apollonius of Rhodes 4.816; scholia on Aristophanes *Clouds* 1068.

182 Apollodorus *Library* 3.13.6.

183 Meletinsky 2009:327.

184 Pindar *Nemean* 3.43–52; see Ch. 1, pp. 37 and 305, above.

boar, which initiates his path as a hero. This motif, however, is suppressed and generalized in Greek epic: many heroes were educated by Cheiron.

The heroes of the Yakut olonkho and Altai poems rarely resort to magic; they perform heroic deeds through their extraordinary strength and courage. Such strength sometimes leads to pride and rebellion against a god. According to Meletinsky, "the hyperbolization of strength leads to the hero becoming more and more like a giant"[185]—often the proportions and strength of Homeric heroes are exaggerated. Frequently they are immune to iron and cannot be wounded, which simply means invincibility for the heroes, whereas in their enemies, these features reveal the existence of the "outer soul," which must to be found and destroyed so that they can be fully defeated.[186] Such are Achilles and his foes, like Kyknos or Memnon.[187] A similar combination of the loss of parents and immunity to wounds obtained by bathing in the blood of a slain dragon can be found in the myth of Siegfried, a Germanic hero, who—like Achilles—after a heroic life meets untimely death.[188]

A hero never abandons the task he has undertaken and never leaves the chosen path of fame. Often, a wife or sister tries to turn him back because of danger lurking ahead, but the hero is willing to sacrifice his life in a heroic fight. Stopped by a divine "letter" before an expedition against his enemies, one of Khan-Mergen's sons explains: "If gods have predestined us to die, we will die anyway. If the horse is not made of gold, why shouldn't it die? Why shouldn't a man die if he is not immortal? Are we going to live many days if we hide? Let us die if it is gods' will."[189]

Here we have a motif similar to the one in the story of Achilles, where his mother discourages him from fighting by revealing the prophecy about his death. In the Greek cycle, the warning succeeds in stopping the hero from going to the war; as we have seen, this course of events gives an opportunity to show a tragic dimension of his fate from the confrontation of the youth and vitality of the hero with his inevitable death. This is probably related to the concept of compensating the heroes for the toil of battle and their death with a posthumous apotheosis and happy afterlife. Achilles' withdrawal from battle does not interfere with manifestations of superhuman courage and boasting of not being afraid of anyone. Similarly, Karaaty-Pergen says about himself: "There is not one person on the face of the earth that I am afraid of ..." He does not differ from

185 Meletinsky 2009:342.

186 Meletinsky 2009:343.

187 The Nart epic seems to picture how enemies become similar in this respect to heroes. Meletinsky 2009:171: "A rare tale about the death of Sirdon's son tells that the Narts long tried to shoot the boy, who was 'immune to wounds'. Only Soslan, who arrived later, was able to kill Sirdon's son."

188 Reichert 1985:75–82; Ehrismann 1987.

189 Meletinsky 2009:344.

the rest of the heroes of Turkish-Mongol epics who often reveal the need to prove that they are the best and the strongest in the world, but usually they are reproached and even punished for such boastfulness.[190] This corresponds to the rivalry of Homeric heroes for the title "the best of the Achaeans." In epic, even a hero who has been criticized is admired for his strength, courage, and beauty.

In Karelian-Finnish *runos* and stories of the North Caucasus, epic idealization lies mainly in the fact that sons of Kaleva and the Narts belong to a special, extinct species of semi-mythical beings. These characters were created on the basis of myths and legends about purported giants, distant ancestors, and predecessors of people.[191] In the epic of Siberian Turks, heroism is considered an individual trait of a given person, not a natural quality characteristic of a whole bunch of demi-mythic beings. The Turkish hero has a purely human nature, and an especially emphasized and celebrated aspect of his heroism is his personal courage and strength.[192]

Greek epic seems to possess both attitudes toward heroism. Heroes belong to a different generation of people—demigods—who, in keeping with their divine status, after death are transferred to the Isles of the Blessed. Although they are endowed with extraordinary strength, they are thoroughly human. Like ordinary people, they face an impassable wall which separates them from gods. Probably here we have to do with the tendency of "humanizing" heroes in Greek epic, and Achilles' recognition of his human condition in the *Iliad* is a manifestation of this tendency. Hence the discrepancy between the eschatology of the heroes in the cycle and Hesiod on the one hand, and in Homer on the other. In Homer, the heroes enter Hades like other people. Achilles says to Odysseus, who arrives the land of the dead (*Odyssey* 11.489–491):

> βουλοίμην κ' ἐπάρουρος ἐὼν θητευέμεν ἄλλῳ,
> ἀνδρὶ παρ' ἀκλήρῳ, ᾧ μὴ βίοτος πολὺς εἴη,
> ἢ πᾶσιν νεκύεσσι καταφθιμένοισιν ἀνάσσειν.
>
> I would rather serve as a hireling for another man,
> a poor one, whose livelihood is small,
> than rule over all the corpses of the dead.

Achilles' wrath is caused not only by the loss of respect or unjust distribution of τιμή, but also by his participation in death, which he rebels against. In a way, this is also an element of tradition, because it is linked to the wrath of Thetis

190 Meletinsky 2009:345.

191 Meletinsky 2009:146–152, 196–203.

192 Meletinksy 2009:355–356.

(concealed in the *Iliad*), which springs from the fact of Achilles' mortality.[193] In the *Iliad*, Achilles' return to battle is not just an impulsive decision precipitated by the loss of his friend, but it is also his voluntary act of embracing death and his acceptance of mortality (see 18.98, 115–116; 22.365–366).

This change in the eschatology and the condition of the epic hero is the basis for the tragedy of Achilles' fate. An inspiration for the figure of Achilles must have come from the Sumerian-Akkadian *Epic of Gilgamesh*, in which there is the motif of the protagonist's fear of death and his search for immortality. Gilgamesh's rejection of death results from his awareness of the nature of his heroism, which justifies his demand for divine status. Anxiety and depression are also an expression of his despair after the death of his friend Enkidu; here an important role is played by his observation of the body's decay, which makes the hero realize the fragility of human life.

These parallels with the fate of the Homeric Achilles and Patroklos have been noted by many scholars. The approach adopted in this book gives us grounds for arguing that the reinterpretation of the epic hero's attitude, which gives him a tragic dimension, could have emerged long before the *Iliad* took its final shape.[194] My observation is corroborated by the fact that this new image of the protagonist is used as a pattern for constructing epic songs, when the hero abstains from battle under the influence of a prophecy. The aim of this device is mainly to exaggerate the obstacle which the hero has to overcome and which blocks the ambitions of the community. This exaggerated obstacle is of a different kind than before; it does not concern the adversary, but the hero himself and the risk he runs when taking up the challenge. Contrary to the Middle Eastern model, after unwillingly performing the deed, the Greek hero Achilles really dies.[195] In this way, his dilemmas, which make him similar to Gilgamesh, are justified.[196]

193 Slatkin 1991:100–103; Kim 2000:165–166.

194 I disregard here the similarities in the construction of the monumental epic songs, i.e. using similar stylistic devices to widen and consolidate the plot, such as repetitions (duplication of motifs); retardation; the doubling of action due to foreshadowing, dreams, and divine intervention; speeches; detailed descriptions and the presentation of the internal world of characters. In the *Epic of Gilgamesh*, the transformation of loose Sumerian epic tales into a coherent epic most probably was done due to Akkadian redaction.

195 Naturally, we do not know exactly how the *Epic of Gilgamesh* originally ended. Scholars usually agree that the last part of the poem is the protagonist's conversation with the spirit of Enkidu, after he has lost his chance to gain immortality (XII tablet). If we do not count this tablet as part of the Akkadian epic, it could have ended with Gilgamesh bragging about building the walls of Uruk.

196 Gilgamesh was two-thirds god and one-third human. As Meletinsky 2009:395 rightly observes, "this formula only emphasizes the human nature of Gilgamesh," because it helps to express his tragic fate.

Achilles attains his role as an epic hero by making a sacrifice for a common cause. As a hero, he not only risks his life for the sake of others, but he actually sacrifices it. His sacrifice means the fulfillment of the most important condition for the conquest of Troy. It involves a ritual sacrifice of a member of the community in order to appease the anger or envy of a deity. In this light, Achilles would be a scapegoat, a role occasionally undertaken voluntarily, which might possibly have been a source of hero worship in his case, but this issue requires a deeper analysis, beyond the scope of this study.

The Aim of the *Iliad*

Finally, we have reached the stage when we can properly answer some fundamental questions: What is the action of the *Iliad* leading up to? What is the aim of creating an unconventional—gentle and altruistic—past for Achilles, which gets rejected when he enters the path of vengeance and mercilessness? What is the poet's intention behind disturbing the traditional image of the epic hero, in which the rescue of the community, and even his self-sacrifice, lose their supreme importance, so characteristic of traditional epic songs?

The key to understanding the story is its ring composition. The meaning of the episode of the Trojan War shown in the *Iliad* is revealed by the juxtaposition of the scenes in *Iliad* Books 1 and 24, and especially the question of proper behavior towards a stranger who comes with a request. In both cases, an elderly father comes to ransom his child. The *Iliad* refers to the most fundamental values of culture, based on family relationships. The mothers of the heroes, Thetis and Hekabe, despair and mourn for their sons, not only when they are dead but also when the men are still alive, though destined to die. Despite their old age, the fathers are forced to act: they try to get their children back—one alive and one dead. To do so, they follow the rules of their civilized world: they bring a generous ransom and find the right words and gestures to express their request. This exchange, which we could view as the beginning of international law, is the only form of contact between the parties of the conflict. Those who approach with a request and those who are approached remain strangers, but they can settle a private matter, even if their communities are intent on killing one other. In Book 1, although Chryses has not only fulfilled all the formal requirements, but also declared himself to be a neutral party, which he stresses by wishing victory and a happy return home to the Achaeans; but his request is brutally rejected by Agamemnon. The Greek leader has no reason to do so except to satisfy the desire to impose his will on the army and to demonstrate his power. The insult to the priest rouses the deity to react—and many lives are lost in the plague. Agamemnon's selfish step is followed by another, which brings more suffering to the Achaeans: when Achilles, offended by Agamemnon, abandons the Greek cause, the specter of defeat and destruction looms over the army. All the unhappy events which follow are a consequence of Agamemnon's disgraceful and selfish action, motivated by greed for power. For the first time in the history of mankind, we come across the awareness of power which for rulers becomes an end in itself and is exercised even against the interests of their community.

Similar events happen at the end of the *Iliad*. The structure of ring composition is not only about returning to events in reverse order, but also about giving them antithetical meanings. While Agamemnon has every reason to consent to the old man's request (especially as Apollo sees to it that the moral code is obeyed), he does not do so. He commits *hybris*. Unlike him, Achilles has hardly any reason to listen to Priam's request: the Trojans are his enemies, and the suppliant is the father of his most hated enemy. Despite all this, Achilles agrees to return the body of Priam's son, even though he rejected an identical request from the dying Hektor. Achilles yields to the request of Zeus, which means that he realizes that this is a morally correct act. The primary reason why he grants Priam's request is different: he is moved by the old man's humble supplication. The king of Troy presents himself as the most humiliated man in the world and Achilles takes pity on him, but not because he draws satisfaction from his humiliation. No—the proof of that is the way he accepts the suppliant.

Achilles was able to cope with the loss of the closest friend much less than anyone else could. Revenge should relieve pain: in a clan system, it is usually enough to kill *anyone* from the enemy clan to revenge the death of a member of one's own clan. Achilles kills very many Trojans, but even the death of the perpetrator of his misfortune does not bring solace. The abuse of the corpse of a defeated enemy is not unusual or inappropriate, but the hero goes over the top even in that, trying to drown his pain. He cannot eat and cannot sleep. Richard Seaford rightly points out that Achilles is unable to end the mourning, the point of which is to enable us to accept the death of a loved one within a limited time.[197] The consent to release the corpse certainly means that he has come to terms with both his loss and his fate. This reconciliation with life is perhaps more important than his acceptance of death—which he had to accept earlier, when he decided to choose the path of heroism.

But even more important is another aspect of this scene. Achilles not only agrees to Priam's request but also shows him respect, of which the old man has just deprived himself by imploring and kissing the hands of the murderer of his children. Showing respect to the enemy means Achilles' return to his old self, to

[197] Seaford 1994:164–177, Parker 1983:59–64.

what he was when he honored Eëtion by placing him on the funeral pyre in his armor (6.416–419). Restoring honor to the enemy who has lost it is certainly a much more spectacular deed. But Achilles does not stop there: he invites Priam to a meal. That this must have been a really overwhelming situation is revealed by the horrifying moment when the king tries to excuse himself, and Achilles' speech, in which he modifies the myth of Niobe to persuade the old man to accept the invitation. In the end, Achilles and Priam eat together, admiring each other.

For the primary audience, this scene must have caused a kind of cultural shock.[198] Sharing meals with an enemy is something that is not done. Eating together means establishing close ties of friendship—*philia*. *Philoi*, members of one's close circle, eat together. One can welcome a stranger as a guest, but then he and his descendants become as if *philoi*, 'one of one's own group'. One cannot be a *philos* to the enemy. Homer here seems to violate a basic principle of his epoch expressed concisely by Archilochus: ἐπ]ίσταμαί τοι φιλ[έο]ν[τα φ[ι]λεῖν, / τὸ]ν δ' ἐχθρὸν ἐχθαίρειν, "I know how to treat a friend as a friend, and an enemy as an enemy" (fragment 23.8–9 W). Homer creates an unacceptable confusion of ideas, which seems to contradict the whole heritage of humanity at that time. The audience of the *Iliad* did not perceive this as an assault on their values, I suppose. They came to the understanding of this deeply humanistic idea, accompanying Achilles on his way to verify the values respected in his world. Agamemnon's breach of rules was necessary to enable Achilles and Priam to sit together at a meal. Homer was the first one to propose the idea that it is possible to treat an enemy with friendliness, like a member of one's own community. In the *Iliad*, enemies are already transformed from the more traditional monsters into people who deserve respect, and even love—*philia*. Achilles, unable to come to terms with the loss of his *philos*, wreaks cruel revenge, thus manifesting the greatest devotion to his *philos*, whose death does not remain unavenged. Yet the same Achilles makes a *philos* of his greatest enemy. It is much more than pity for the defeated enemy. Is it possible to imagine greater magnanimity?

This is how—I believe—Homer wanted us to understand the story of Achilles. And that is why he told it at all. What is important is not the story in itself, but its message.

198 See Zieliński 2021a:81–82.

The End

IN THE PREVIOUS CHAPTERS, I have tried to show that the *Iliad* is not a new creation separate from the tradition in which it grew. Its pattern is analogous to many other songs in the Trojan Cycle, just as the structure of the entire cycle is modeled on other, already existing cycles. Nevertheless, I do not intend to join the chorus of voices seeing Homer's orality simply as a duplication of traditional patterns. On the contrary, I believe that a singer, within a familiar pattern, has complete freedom in creating his song. This approach requires us to assess the relationship of a particular song to tradition.

Wherever we notice something which we might judge as Homer's innovation from what we perceive as tradition, we are, in fact, dealing with modification, with a conscious reconfiguration of elements. Modification is an immanent part of oral tradition and means the adjustment of traditional material to contextual needs—a traditional plot may take a different shape when performative circumstances are changed. In effect, this process may bring about the creation of new plots, although similar to those already existing in oral tradition. Thus, in thinking of the *Iliad* as part of tradition, we cannot assume that each element of the song already existed in tradition and we cannot take for granted that what is unique for Homer is unique only because songs which incorporated this "uniqueness" have not come down to us. It is not so. The change understood as modification *is* tradition. Changes within tradition do not result from mnemonic problems,[1] from the difficulty of recreating the traditional story accurately. Tradition is multiform due to deliberate transformations introduced by individual singers adapting traditional material to changing needs. In oral tradition, neither the story itself nor its presentation, the act of singing/telling it, is as important as the intentions of the teller, i.e. the meaning with which he tries to endow a traditional story. To do so, he modifies the story, employing a reconfiguration of traditional elements according to current needs. The changes that are accepted by the audience can be permanent. Adaptation is not a product of the performative circumstances exerting pressure on the performer, because they also embrace the way the storyteller reinterprets the

1 Even if they happen, they do not substantially affect the shape of tradition.

story. The singer tells his story according to how he understands it and how he wants his audience to understand it.

The essence of the oral poet's intentionality can only be described by taking into account the specific conditions of story transmission in oral culture and the ways in which the singer exploits the cognitive capacities of his listeners. Both singers and their audiences are familiar with a considerable number of stories, which makes the way they present them and recognize their meanings a common heritage of both.[2] The singer does not remember the text verbatim but as a sequence of events or images, which he sees in his "mind's eye" and which he describes for his audience. The process of recalling them from memory is combined with reviving them in imagination, which may result in the production of a new version of events. The same images are also embedded in the memory of the audience, who in turn are able to recognize them in new versions of the plot. Memory images are therefore not the same as narrative scripts, which the poet uses in an expanded or reduced form. The knowledge of scripts allows the audience to follow the development of the plot, to expect the sequence of events, and to understand their meaning. Minchin points out that the feeling that these scripts are natural springs from the fact that they mirror the common experiences of the people of those times, which are often, though not always, the experiences of the contemporary reader.[3] They are based on a cause-and-effect chain, understood in a way which is typical of Homeric times, assuming a direct correspondence between human decisions and divine actions.[4] Using narrative scripts and memory images, the poet enters into a dialogue with tradition on the one hand, and his audience on the other.

The singer tells his story, actualizing new images floating before his eyes with the help of the conventional language of formulae. He seems to fall into ruts cut by generations of his predecessors; when his song fits into the framework of a cycle, its protagonist always possesses a particular set of traits and plays a predefined role in the macro-story. The outline of the macro-story, spread between the organization of the expedition inspired by the evil will of the gods and the return of the heroes, is also schematic. But the variety of Greek myths shows how much space remains for imagination. A few simple strategies, such as duplicating scenes and characters or introducing their modified parallels, enable the creation of completely original stories, in which the similarity to

2 Rubin 1995:125: "Oral traditions are productive systems, not isolated lists."

3 Minchin 2001:Ch. 1.

4 One could add that in Homeric narrative, deviations from these "natural" scripts play an important role. They are ubiquitous: for some reason, even ritual actions such as supplication can deviate from the norm, e.g. Chryses gives up the ritual gestures of humiliation expected of supplicants, trying to convince the Achaeans by the use of appropriate language to return his daughter.

their structural skeletons is almost completely blurred. Provided that the poet does not change the basic meaning of the myth, he can transform it in every performance by enriching familiar stories with innumerable details and reproducing the core of the myth in plots created for his current audience. He has a lot of freedom, but—the core of the myth being known both to the singer and his audience—he is also under control, which does not let him plunge into some kind of Lucian-like fantasy. The creation of songs and their performances always have a common goal: to tell a heroic myth, but any version reflects the singer's intentions and the expectations of the audience.

The analysis of the *Iliad* which I have presented shows that this constraint does not trammel on the singer's freedom; on the contrary, he uses his listeners' knowledge of the myth to increase both their interest and the dramatic impact of action. He does not refer to any verbal material but to images in their memory. These images are so rooted in listeners' minds that sometimes a slight allusion is enough to recall events known from tradition. However, the singer does not confine himself to single allusions scattered throughout the text, but brings the right memories to his audience. At appropriate moments important for the narrative, he not only relies on their familiarity with the "scenario" of a type-scene imprinted in their memory by numerous previous performances, but he also enlivens that memory, which is crucial for the plot of the entire cycle. In various configurations of allusions, Homer refers mainly to two scenes: Memnon's killing of Antilochos and Achilles' death, thanks to Paris and Apollo.[5]

For the audience of an oral performance, tradition is stable. In the listeners' minds, the images once created persist no less than in that of the singer. He remembers a sequence of images and creates a new song as a sequence of the same images. The most important images known from tradition remain in the minds of the listeners and the poet tries to stimulate this memory on important occasions. These images are recalled in various versions, yet they remain recognizable to the listeners. The composition of the *Iliad* shows that the reconfiguration of traditional elements of narration may result in the reinterpretation of the characters' attitude and endowing them with traits which they may not have possessed in other songs. To a certain extent, the poet can alter the past of his hero by distancing him from events described in other songs, and use this modification to give the hero's actions a new meaning. This is the way in which Homer suggests Achilles' past, which affects the interpretation of his behavior in the *Iliad*. Much more vital, however, is recalling images which function in the

5 Frame (2009:196–209) shows that there are also references to the myth of divine twins. These allusions are, however, of a slightly different kind, although they also place both Homeric poems within the epic tradition of the Trojan War, because they revolve around the return of the heroes from Troy.

cycle, using a system of allusions which allow the singer to incorporate his song into the cycle and which ensure the desired emotional reception. Strategies for developing such *anamnêsis* are extremely sophisticated, but it is not astonishing since the singer is also unusual.

The *Iliad* displays a masterful level of reinterpretation through the reconfiguration of elements of traditional narratives. Its novelty lies not so much in inventing the plot, since there are many indications that this song had already existed before Homer (one of them being the poet's reliance on listeners' familiarity with it—see Chapter 4), as in subordinating the song to his own concept of the protagonist, Achilles (but also other characters, like Agamemnon, Odysseus, Paris, or Diomedes). Homer tells the familiar story in his own way, perhaps transforming greatly what he himself heard earlier. The monumentality of his work is a matter of secondary importance, most probably resulting from the expectation of long epic narration (see Chapter 1). The *Iliad* observes all the canons of oral poetics and in no way constitutes a formal novelty. Homer's storytelling gift is incomparable to anything else in the literature that has come down to us. He is a great storyteller, conscious of the aim of his narrative.

The Neoanalysts have looked at two parallel sequences of events in the *Iliad* and the *Aethiopis*. In the *Iliad*, there is the death of Patroklos at the hands of Hektor, and Hektor's by Achilles, which heralds Achilles' own death by Paris. In the *Aethiopis*, there are three killings: Antilochos by Memnon, Memnon by Achilles, and, finally, Achilles by Paris. In the repetitive structure of the story, the Neoanalysts noted that the *Iliad*, copying certain "facts" known from tradition, makes them meaningless. Such is, for example, the case of the doubling of Thetis's prediction of her son's fate. Thetis predicts Achilles' death twice: once it is to happen after Hektor's death (*Iliad* 18.95–96), and once after Memnon's death (Proclus, *Chrestomathia*, *Aethiopis* 2). If the first event—situated according to the Neoanalysts chronologically earlier—should lead to the death of the protagonist, it would make no sense to repeat the same sequence of events at a chronologically later moment. Whereas in the second case (when the goddess warns Achilles against killing Memnon) the sequence of events leads directly to the death of Achilles, so in this case the prediction is justified. This convinced them about the priority of the *Aethiopis* material.

This book, however, tries to demonstrate how not only formulaic language and particular themes constitute the material of oral tradition, but also whole sequences of events. In oral tradition one sequence of events is used to introduce one particular theme. Thetis always predicts the death of her son following his killing of an outstanding warrior. Nor is it significant that in the *Iliad*, Achilles' death does not happen, that it remains in the sphere of predictions. As the capture of Troy is delayed by the necessity of removing more and more obstacles, each of which essentially constitutes a separate plot for a song, similarly delayed is Achilles' death. When, where, and under what circumstances it will occur is relatively fixed: at the end of the war, at the Scaean gates of Troy, as a result of Paris and Apollo's cooperation. But there is no historical order of events here. After Hektor's death, it is not necessary for Memnon to die first so that Achilles can die after him, etc.

The *Iliad* is contained in a certain pattern of events. The basic pattern is defined by Minton as a sequence: crisis-combat-disaster.[6] Such a reduced form of the pattern can, however, be applied to every epic song in the Greek tradition. Songs of the Trojan Cycle have their own special pattern that differentiates them from those belonging to other epic cycles; in its simplest version, it probably appears in the Philoktetes theme: his absence from the battlefield, his arrival there because of trickery, and his victory over Paris thanks to the bow of Herakles, which opens the way to the capture of Troy. This sequence of events was also used in other songs, where other heroes of the Trojan Cycle were protagonists. Absence from the battlefield, although with a different motivation, also appears in the cases of Odysseus, where it is caused by his reluctance to participate in the expedition, and Achilles, who gets hidden from the heroes by his mother. This motif is further developed in the story of Achilles, who is always prevented from fighting by his mother's prophecy (the motif of prophecy probably replaced that of a curse stopping heroes from acting, dominant in earlier cycles—see Ch. 2). In brief, again and again we deal with the same thing: there is no hero who could solve a crisis. Typically, the assembled warriors/heroes realize that they cannot do so, and the situation can be mended only by someone from the outside. The absence of the hero who could solve the crisis creates the need to bring him or to convince him to fight. This is due to the transformation of the original scheme of the epic song, in which the act of liberating the community from a disaster has to be done by a young hero—one who has only just entered adulthood, and the performance of this heroic deed constitutes his initiation. The *Iliad* skillfully expands this topic: initially, the cause of the crisis is the plague; later, when the plague is under control, the real problem, which brings many heavy blows from the enemy, is the withdrawal of the hero, who has been offended at an assembly.

There are various methods for bringing the hero to the battlefield: in the case of Philoktetes or Achilles on Skyros, the thing that does the trick is Odysseus's subterfuge; when it comes to Odysseus, it is Palamedes' discovery of his deception. Breaking Achilles out of his anger or fear of death (these elements

6 Minton 1960:295–297.

may be related, as in Homer) can take various forms: in the *Iliad*, it is the death of a friend (a motif repeated in the *Aethiopis*).[7]

Both Achilles and Philoktetes appear on the battlefield to kill the most important Achaean enemy. Song after song, Achilles kills one son of Priam and then another, but is unable to kill Paris, because this is reserved for Philoktetes. With time, Achilles' deeds began to be perceived as more important than the key deed performed by Philoktetes. This is the result of the perspective of the epic song: the deed it describes is always highlighted as the most important for the fate of the war. Achilles became "more fashionable" because his actions could be multiplied without end. This is connected with the depreciation of not only Philoktetes, but also Paris, whose conduct began to be criticized for moral reasons. Perhaps, originally, Achilles appeared in order to defeat the leader of the Trojan allies, such as Kyknos or Memnon. However, for the epic song, this one deed would be insufficient, which is why, like Philoktetes, it was linked to the need to kill a son of Priam. The necessity of having these two acts done together gives the singer great opportunities to shape the dramatic tension of events. He can increase or decrease tension, substitute the protagonist in some ventures, etc. But the essence of Achilles' motif is his death after overcoming the biggest obstacle blocking access to the city. It expresses the idea of his self-sacrifice and justifies our perception of him as a scapegoat.

The obstacle which prevents the capture of Troy can assume the form of unusual, invincible warriors. The leaders of Trojan allies still retain traces of the original monster; in their case, however, the monster defeated by the hero in the original myth is already transformed into a mirror reflection of the hero (see Chapter 3). They are eliminated, one by one, by Achilles or other warriors who function as his substitutes, like Patroklos or Neoptolemos. There can also be other obstacles, often even more magical in character. The capture of Helenos, the magician who protects the enemy, and the theft of the Palladion protecting the city are carried out by Odysseus, though in the second case, Odysseus cooperates with Diomedes. A theft as a heroic deed is typical of the culture hero in a very early stage of the development of epic (compare Prometheus or Väinamöinen). In this respect, Odysseus resembles such heroes who rely more on tricks and magic than force and courage. But the co-operation of Odysseus and Diomedes represents another motif, also dating back to an early stage of the development of Greek epic, the co-operation between a lion and a boar; most probably, it was adapted to the Trojan Cycle from the Theban (see Chapter 2).

7 Perhaps also in the Teuthranian expedition, when Achilles enters combat after Patroklos gets wounded.

Typical of epic songs in this cycle is not a description of the seizure of Troy but the presentation of events which precede it and the removal of the last obstacle preventing its fall. After a lapse of time, the events usually left unmentioned find their way into a song. What is really important is the prospect of destroying the city, a disaster that is usually only predicted; it is destined to happen when the Achaean situation changes for the better because of an exploit of the hero who is the protagonist of a song.

In such a situation, one could hardly expect that anything would be fixed permanently. And it would probably have been like this also in the case of the *Iliad* and the Trojan Cycle, had these poems not been written down. Recording songs in writing, even if done randomly, could have had a slowly stabilizing effect upon the plot of the cycle.[8]

If we assume the existence of other versions of the song about the wrath of Achilles, let us try to consider what they could have looked like and in what respects Homer's song could have differed from the song he had learned from another singer. In what way is his creativity manifested?

If we look at the account of events initiating the action, which the resentful Achilles gives to Thetis (*Iliad* 1.366–392), we notice significant differences in comparison with the events narrated earlier. After relating, in the right chronological order, the circumstances of gaining spoils (Chryseis included) by the Achaeans, Achilles faithfully presents Chryses' visit to the camp. Somehow, he is aware that Chryses has cursed the Achaeans, praying to Apollo for help. This, however, is not a problem—the singer does not have to watch carefully that the characters say only what they are expected to know. After all, Achilles simply gives a summary of events. Yet when he describes the decimation of the army by the plague as a result of divine anger, he relates something that seems to deviate from our version of events (1.382–388):

> ἧκε δ' ἐπ' Ἀργείοισι κακὸν βέλος· οἳ δέ νυ λαοὶ
> θνῆσκον ἐπασσύτεροι, τὰ δ' ἐπῴχετο κῆλα θεοῖο
> πάντῃ ἀνὰ στρατὸν εὐρὺν Ἀχαιῶν· ἄμμι δὲ μάντις
> εὖ εἰδὼς ἀγόρευε θεοπροπίας ἑκάτοιο.
> αὐτίκ' ἐγὼ πρῶτος κελόμην θεὸν ἱλάσκεσθαι·
> Ἀτρεΐωνα δ' ἔπειτα χόλος λάβεν, αἶψα δ' ἀναστὰς
> ἠπείλησεν μῦθον ὃ δὴ τετελεσμένος ἐστί·
>
> He sent towards the Argives an evil missile, and soldiers
> kept dying one by one, the god's arrows were

8 See Holmberg 1998:472–473.

> everywhere in the Achaean camp; and a seer
> with knowledge disclosed publicly the oracle of the Bringing-a-lot-of death.
> I immediately, as the first one, insisted we should propitiate the god,
> but Atreus's son, seized by anger, rose
> and made a threat, which he now has fulfilled.

The quarrel at the assembly is presented differently. First, the seer reveals Apollo's oracle, and then Achilles summons the Achaeans to propitiate the god. In fact, Achilles did not propound anything like this; by demanding the seer's answer, he only pointed out that in order to take appropriate measures it is necessary to know the god's motives. We can, of course, argue that it is a kind of shortcut and probably the singer wanted to suggest that this was how this matter appeared to the protagonist. However, if we take Achilles' account literally, we are dealing with an alternate version of events. Now the logic of events seems much simpler: since in reply to the seer's words Achilles called for making amends in order to stop the divine anger, the amends must have involved the return of Chryses' daughter, even if he did not say so explicitly. Naturally, this could immediately evoke Agamemnon's outrage and desire to retaliate.

Then Achilles relates the events faithfully: his Briseis was taken by heralds, who came on behalf of Agamemnon. However, on several earlier occasions Agamemnon said that he would take her personally (1.137, 161, 185); moreover, Thersites also mentions that Agamemnon had done it himself (2.240): ἑλὼν γὰρ ἔχει γέρας αὐτὸς ἀπούρας, "for he *himself* has taken away his *geras* and is keeping it."[9] Taking Briseis personally means that—unlike the Agamemnon of the *Iliad*—he is not afraid of Achilles. The Homeric Achilles does not admit even to himself that he could yield to the chief leader. In the case of the taking of Briseis by Agamemnon personally, Achilles' position would have to be much lower. He could be the son of a goddess, a warrior with invulnerable skin, possessor of magic armor, the bravest of the Achaeans, but his attitude towards Agamemnon could be like that of Aias or Odysseus.

Significant for Homer is Achilles' awareness of his own relevance. By stressing it, he emphasizes the importance of the hero's honor, which he defends against every injustice. This idea alone would be a great challenge to the world which always used to fall to its knees before rulers. The Homeric Achilles is disappointed because he thought he had earned his greatness and expected due recognition, but Agamemnon tells him that all this is an illusion. His only greatness consists of the lucky circumstance that he is the son of a goddess. Nobody

9 This version of events can be found painted on a red-figure vase by Makron (LIMC, "Agamemnon," np. 52* [Paris, Louvre G 146]); see Lowenstam 1997:39–44, Burgess 2001:59.

stands up for him; the entire army, although aware of his achievements, submits to the will of the stronger one, the chief leader. Agamemnon is guilty against him as he was guilty against Chryses. Both victims seek divine justice. Achilles becomes the first in a series of lonely heroes confronted with the heartlessness of the world, like Don Quixote or Hamlet. And like many of them, he fights without taking up the fight. He puts away his sword, with which he could have taken revenge upon Agamemnon.

Homer variously signals that Achilles deserves the honor which he has been deprived of. The hero himself places the source of his honor in his military deeds, but the singer shows him as merciful, polite, modest, obedient to gods, sincere in friendship, and honest. The insult he suffered, however, makes him deny his real character. The epic hero is required to perform heroic deeds, while Achilles' withdrawal from battle sentences everyone to destruction. The death of Patroklos turns everything upside down. Then Achilles, already disappointed with others and with the world, becomes disappointed in his own greatness. Because of his pride, he has lost someone he loved the most. Here Homer presents an astonishing man who in order to protect his dignity risks all his past and future. And instead of gaining something, he incurs an even heavier loss. Nothing matters any more. Achilles makes peace with Agamemnon and the Achaeans, and returns to battle, overwhelmed with only one vision—revenge. And here is the third appearance of Homer's genius: revenge, once completed, does not bring relief. In a fit of perversion, Achilles outrages Hektor's body, but it does not bring him any satisfaction either. This is because he has nothing to live for.

Achilles' life regains its value after the recurrence of pity, and not because of his reconciliation to fate. Reconciled to fate, he agrees to comply with the demand of gods and returns the body of his enemy, but his real change happens only after the meeting with the unfortunate father of Hektor. Earlier, accepting his own death, Achilles for the first time experienced the misery of the human condition, so far unfamiliar to the semi-divine hero. Now, feeling pity for the enemy, he experiences the true taste of humanity. He is alive again, but Homer leaves us convinced that it is not for long, that he will die soon.

The drama of the Homeric Achilles is not the choice between a long life at home and glory after an early death in combat. Perhaps it was important in another song about Achilles, perhaps even about his wrath. But here more important matters are at issue. Much more important.

Bibliography

Aarne, Antti, and Stith Thompson. 1961. *The Types of the Folktale: A Classification and Bibliography*. Helsinki.

Abramowiczówna, Zofia. 1965. "Najnowsze kierunki w badaniach homeryckich." *Eos* 55:192–201.

Abush, T. 1999. "The Epic of Gilgamesh and the Homeric Epics." In *Mythologies: Methodological Approaches to Intercultural Influences, Proceedings of the Second Annual Symposium of the Assyrian and Babylonian Intellectual Heritage Project*, ed. Robert Whiting, 1–6. Paris.

Adams, Douglas Q. 1987. "Ἥρως and Ἥρᾱ: Of Men and Heroes in Greek and Indo-European." *Glotta* 65:171–178.

Adkins, A. W. H. 1960. *Merit and Responsibility: A Study in Greek Values*. Oxford.

———. 1972. "Homeric Gods and the Values of Homeric Society." *The Journal of Hellenic Studies* 92:1–19.

———. 1982. "Values, Goals, and Emotions in the *Iliad*." *Classical Philology* 77:292–326.

———. 1997. "Homeric Ethics." In Morris and Powell 1997:694–714.

Ahl, Frederick, and Hanna M. Roisman. 1996. *The Odyssey Re-Formed*. Ithaca.

Ahrensdorf, Peter. 2014. *Homer on the Gods and Human Virtue: Creating the Foundations of Classical Civilization*. Cambridge.

Albracht, Franz. 2005. *Battle and Battle Description in Homer: A Contribution to the History of War*. Ed. and trans. P. Jones, Malcolm M. Willcock, and G. Wright. London. Orig. pub. as *Kampf und Kampfschilderung bei Homer*. Naumburg, 1895-1896.

Alden, Maureen. 2000. *Homer Beside Himself: Para-Narratives in the Iliad*. Oxford.

———. 2017. *Para-Narratives in the Odyssey: Stories in the Frame*. Oxford.

Allan, William. 2005. "Arms and the Man: Euphorbus, Hector, and the Death of Patroclus." *Classical Quarterly* 55:1–16.

———. 2008. "Performing the Will of Zeus: The Διὸς βουλή and the Scope of Early Greek Epic." In Revermann and Wilson 2008:204–216.

———. 2012. *Homer: The Iliad*. London.

Allen, Nick J. 1993. "Arjuna and Odysseus: A Comparative Approach." *South Asia Library Group Newsletter* 40:39–43.

Allen, Thomas W. 1908. "The Epic Cycle." *Classical Quarterly* 2:64–74, 81–88.

Amory Parry, Anne. 1966. "The Gates of Horn and Ivory." *Yale Classical Studies* 20:1–58.

———. 1971. "Homer as Artist." *Classical Quarterly* 65:1–15.

———. 1973. *Blameless Aegisthus: A Study of AMYMΩN and other Homeric Epithets.* Mnemosyne Supplement 26. Leiden.

Andersen, Øivind. 1977. "Odysseus and the Wooden Horse." *Symbolae Osloenses* 52:5–18.

———. 1978. *Die Diomedesgestalt in der Ilias. Symbolae Osloenses* Supplement 25.

———. 1990. "The Making of the Past in the *Iliad*." *Harvard Studies in Classical Philology* 93:25–45.

———. 1997. "Diomedes, Aphrodite, and Dione: Background and Function of a Scene in Homer's *Iliad*." *Classica et Mediaevalia* 48:25–36.

Andersen, Øivind, and Matthew W. Dickie, eds. 1995. *Homer's World: Fiction, Tradition, Reality*. Bergen.

Anderson, Michael John. 1997. *The Fall of Troy in Early Greek Poetry and Art*. Oxford.

Apthorp, Michael J. 2000. "Did Athene Help Tydeus to Win the Cadmean Games (*Iliad* 5.808)?" *Zeitschrift für Papyrologie und Epigraphik* 131:1–9.

Arafat, Karim W. 1990. *Classical Zeus: A Study in Art and Literature*. Oxford.

Arend, Walter. 1933. *Die typischen Scenen bei Homer*. Berlin.

Arft, Justin. 2017. "Structure as *Sēma*: Structural and Liminal Middles in the Odyssey." *Yearbook of Ancient Greek Epic* 1:5–45.

Armstrong, James I. 1958. "The Arming Motif in the *Iliad*." *American Journal of Philology* 79:337–354.

Assmann, Jan. 2008. "Communicative and Cultural Memory." In *Cultural Memory Studies*, ed. A. Erll, A. Nünning, and S. Young, 109–118. Berlin.

Athanassakis, Apostolos N. 1992. "Cattle and Honour in Homer and Hesiod." *Ramus* 21:156–185.

Austin, Norman. 1966. "The Function of Digressions in the *Iliad*." *Greek, Roman, and Byzantine Studies* 7:295–312.

———. 1972. "Name Magic in the *Odyssey*." *Classical Antiquity* 5:1–19.

———. 1975. *Archery at the Dark of the Moon: Poetic Problems in Homer's Odyssey*. Berkeley.

———. 1983. "Odysseus and the Cyclops: Who is Who." In Rubino and Shelmerdine 1983:4–37.

———. 1994. *Helen of Troy and her Shameless Phantom*. Ithaca.

Bachvarova, Mary R. 2016. *From Hittite to Homer. The Anatolian Background of Ancient Greek Epic*. Cambridge.

Baehrens, W. A. 1920. "Zur Entstehung der *Ilias*." *Philologus* 76:1–59.

Bakker, Egbert J. 1988. *Linguistics and Formulas in Homer*. Amsterdam.

———. 1990. "Homeric Discourse and Enjambement: A Cognitive Approach." *Transactions of the American Philological Association* 120:1–21.

———. 1993. "Discourse and Performance: Involvement, Visualisation and 'Presence' in Homeric Poetry." *Classical Antiquity* 12:1–29.

———. 1995. "Noun-Epithet Formulas, Milman Parry, and the Grammar of Poetry." In Crielaard 1995:97–125.

———. 1997a. *Poetry in Speech: Orality and Homeric Discourse*. Ithaca.

———. 1997b. "The Study of Homeric Discourse." In Morris and Powell 1997:284–304.

———. 2002. "*Khrónos*, *Kléos*, and Ideology from Herodotus to Homer." In Reichel and Rengakos 2002:11–30.

———. 2003. "Homer as an Oral Tradition." *Oral Tradition* 18:52–54.

———. 2013. *The Meaning of Meat and the Structure of the Odyssey*. Cambridge.

Bakker, Egbert J., and Florence Fabricotti. 1991. "Peripheral and Nuclear Semantics in Homeric Diction: An Investigation of Dative Expressions of 'Spear'." *Mnemosyne* 44:63–84.

Bakker, Egbert J., and A. Kahane, eds. 1997. *Written Voices, Spoken Signs: Tradition, Performance, and the Epic Text*. Center for Hellenic Studies Colloquia 1. Cambridge, MA.

Baldick, Julian. 1994. *Homer and the Indo-Europeans: Comparing Mythologies*. London.

Ballabriga, Alain. 1997. "Survie et descendance d'Enée: le mythe grec archaïque." *Quaderni Urbinati di Cultura Classica* n.s. 55:22–39.

Bannert, Herbert. 1981. "Phoinix' Jugend und der Zorn des Meleagros." *Wiener Studien Zeitschrift für Klassische Philologie und Patristik* 15:69–94.

Barker, Elton T. E., and Joel P. Christensen. 2019. *Homer's Thebes: Epic Rivalries and the Appropriation of Mythical Pasts*. Hellenic Studies 84. Washington, DC. http://nrs.harvard.edu/urn3:hul.ebook:CHS_BarkerE_ChristensenJ.Homers_Thebes.2019

Bartol, Krystyna. 1999. *Liryka grecka, t. I, Jamb i elegia*. Warsaw.

Bassett, Samuel E. 1923. "The Proems of the *Iliad* and the *Odyssey*." *American Journal of Philology* 44:339–348.

———. 1933. "Achilles' Treatment of Hector's Body." *Transactions and Proceedings of the American Philological Association* 64:41–65.

Baudouin, Charles. 1952. *Le triomphe du héros: Étude psychanalytique sur le mythe du héros et les grandes épopées*. Paris.

Bäumlein, Wilhelm. 1856. "Grote's Ansicht über die Composition der *Iliad*." *Philologus* 11:405–430.

Beck, Götz. 1964. *Die Stellung des 24. Buches der Iliad in der alten Epentradition*. Tübingen.

Bednarek, Bogusław. 2001. *Epos europejski*. Wrocław.

Beekes, Robert S. P. 1969. "ἔτος and ἐνιαυτός in Homeric formulae." *Glotta* 47:138–143.

Bennet, John. 1997. "Homer and the Bronze Age." In Morris and Powell 1997:511–534.

Benveniste, Émile. 1973. *Indo-European Language and Society*. Trans. E. Palmer. 2 vols. London.

Bernal, Martin. 1987. *Black Athena: The Afroasiatic Roots of Classical Civilization*. 2 vols. London.

Berndt, Ronald M. 1952. *Djanggawul: An Aboriginal Religious Cult of North-Eastern Arnhem Land*. London.

Bertolín Cebrián, Reyes. 2006. *Singing the Dead: A Model for Epic Evolution*. Frankfurt.

Bethe, Erich. 1927. *Homer: Dichtung und Sage*. Vol. 3, *Die Sage vom troischen Kriege*. Leipzig.

Bettarini, Luca. 2003. "Λῆμνον ἀμιχθαλόεσσαν (*Il.* 24, 753)." *Quaderni Urbinati di Cultura Classica*, n.s. 74:69–88.

Beye, Charles R. 1964. "Homeric Battle Narrative and Catalogues." *Harvard Studies in Classical Philology* 68:345–373.

Biebuyck, D., and K. Mateéne, trans. and eds. 1969. *The Mwindo Epic from the Banyanga (Congo Republic)*. Berkeley.

Bierl, Anton. 2012. "Orality, Fluid Textualization and Interweaving Themes: Some Remarks on the *Doloneia*; Magical Horses from Night to Light and Death to Life." In Montanari, Rengakos, and Tsagalis 2012:133–174.

Blackburn, Stuart H. 1989. "Patterns of Development for Indian Oral Epic." In *Oral Epics in India*, ed. S. H. Blackburn, P. J. Claus, J. B. Flueckiger, and S. S. Wadley, 15–32. Berkeley.

Blondell, Ruby. 2010. "'Bitch that I Am': Self-Blame and Self-Assertion in the *Iliad*." *Transactions of the American Philological Association* 140:1–32.

Boardman, John. 1973. "Heroic Haircuts." *Classical Quarterly* 23:196–197.

Boedeker, Deborah Dickmann. 1974. *Aphrodite's Entry into Greek Epic*. Leiden.

Bolling, George M. 1906. "The Etymology of ΟΔΥΣΣΕΥΣ." *American Journal of Philology* 27:65–67.

Bonifazi, Anna. 2007. "Memory and Visualization in Homeric Discourse Markers." In Mackay 2007:35–64.

Bowden, Hugh. 1993. "Hoplites and Homer: Warfare, Hero Cult, and the Ideology of the Polis." In *War and Society in the Greek World*, ed. John Rich and Graham Shipley, 45–63. London.

Bowra, Cecil M. 1952. *Heroic Poetry*. London.

———. 1962. *Primitive Song*. London.

———. 1972. *Homer*. London.

Bradford, Ernle. 1967. *Wędrówki z Homerem*. Trans. Edda Werfel. Warsaw.
Braswell, Bruce K. 1971. "Mythological Innovation in the *Iliad*." *Classical Quarterly* 21:16–26.
———. 1982. "The Song of Ares and Aphrodite: Theme and Relevance to *Odyssey* 8." *Hermes* 110:129–137.
Bravo, Benedetto. 2001. "Un frammento della Piccola Iliade (*P.Oxy*. 2510), lo stile narrativo tardo-arcaico, I racconti su Achille immortale." *Quaderni Urbinati di Cultura Classica*, n.s. 67:49–114.
Breed, Brian W. 1999. "Odysseus Back Home and Back from the Death." In Carlisle and Levaniouk 1999:137–161.
Brillante, Carlo. 1990. "History and the Historical Interpretation of Myth." In Edmunds 1990:93–138.
———. 1992. "Omero e la tradizione epica: riflessioni su uno studio recente." *Quaderni Urbinati di Cultura Classica*, n.s. 40:135–148.
Broeniman, Clifford. 1996. "Demodocus, Odysseus, and the Trojan War." *Classical World* 90:3–13.
Brown, Christopher. 1997. "Iambos." In *A Companion to the Greek Lyric Poets*, ed. D. E. Gerber, 11–88. Leiden.
Bryce, Trevor. 2002. *Life and Society in the Hittite World*. Oxford.
Burgess, Jonathan S. 1995. "Achilles' Heel: The Death of Achilles in Ancient Myth." *Classical Antiquity* 14:217–243.
———. 1996. "The Non-Homeric *Cypria*." *Transactions of the American Philological Association* 126:77–99.
———. 1997. "Beyond Neo-Analysis: Problems with the Vengeance Theory." *American Journal of Philology* 118:1–19.
———. 2001. *The Tradition of the Trojan War in Homer and the Epic Cycle*. Baltimore.
———. 2002. "Kyprias, The 'Kypria', and Multiformity." *Phoenix* 56:234–254.
———. 2004a. "Early Images of Achilles and Memnon?" *Quaderni Urbinati di Cultura Classica* n.s. 76:33–51.
———. 2004b. "Untrustworthy Apollo and the Destiny of Achilles: *Iliad* 24.55–63." *Harvard Studies in Classical Philology* 102:21–40.
———. 2004c. "Performance and the Epic Cycle." *Classical Journal* 100:1–23.
———. 2005. "The Epic Cycle and Fragments." In Foley 2005:344–352.
———. 2006. "Neoanalysis, Orality, and Intertextuality: An Examination of Homeric Motif Transference." *Oral Tradition* 21:148–189.
———. 2009. *The Death and Afterlife of Achilles*. Baltimore.
———. 2015. "Coming Adrift: The Limits of Reconstruction of the Cyclic Poems." In Fantuzzi and Tsagalis 2015:43–58.
Burkert, Walter. 1960. "Das Lied von Ares und Aphrodite. Zum Verhältnis von *Odyssee* und *Ilias*." *Rheinishes Museum* 103:130–144.

———. 1972. "Die Leistung eines Kreophyles. Kreophyleer, Homeriden und die archaische Heraklesepik." *Museum Helveticum* 29:74–85.

———. 1976. "Das hunderttorige Theben und die Datierung der *Ilias*." *Wiener Studien Zeitschrift für Klassische Philologie und Patristik* 10:5–21.

———. 1984. *Die orientalisierende Epoche in der griechischen Religion und Literatur.* Heidelberg.

———. 1987. "The Making of Homer in the Sixth Century BC: Rhapsodes versus Stesichorus." In *Papers on the Amasis Painter and His World*, 43–62. Malibu.

———. 1992. *The Orientalizing Revolution. Near Eastern Influence on Greek Culture in the Early Archaic Age.* Trans. M. E. Pinder and W. Burkert. Cambridge, MA.

———. 1996. *Creation of the Sacred: Tracks of Biology in Early Religions.* Cambridge, MA.

———. 2002. "Die Waffen und die Jungen: Homerisch OPLOTEROI." In Reichel and Rengakos 2002:31–34.

Bynum, David E. 1974. *Four Generations of Oral Literary Studies at Harvard University.* 1974. https://mpc.chs.harvard.edu/about/bynum.html

Cairns, Douglas L. 1993a. "Affronts and Quarrels in the *Iliad*." *Papers of the Leeds International Latin Seminar* 7:155–167.

———. 1993b. *Aidos: The Psychology and Ethics of Honour and Shame in Ancient Greek Literature.* Oxford.

———, ed. 2001. *Oxford Readings in Homer's* Iliad. Oxford.

———. 2011. "Shame." In Finkelberg 2011:790–792.

Camerotto, Alberto. 2003. "Le storie e i canti degli eroi." *Quaderni Urbinati di Cultura Classica*, n.s. 74:9–31.

Campbell, Joseph. 1949. *The Hero with a Thousand Faces.* Princeton.

Cantilena, Mario. 1982. *Ricerche sulla dizione epica I: Per uno studio della formularità degli Inni Omerici.* Rome.

———. 1992. "L'ultimo libro di Albert Lord." *Quaderni Urbinati di Cultura Classica*, n.s. 40:129–133.

Carlisle, Miriam. 1999. "Homeric Fictions: Pseudo-Words in Homer." In Carlisle and Levaniouk 1999:55–91.

———, and Olga Levaniouk, eds. 1999. *Nine Essays on Homer.* Lanham, MD.

Carpenter, Rhys. 1974. *Folk Tale, Fiction and Saga in the Homeric Epics.* Orig. pub. 1946. Berkeley.

Carter, Jane, and Sarah Morris, eds. 1995. *The Ages of Homer: A Tribute to Emily Townsend Vermeule.* Austin.

Caskey, J. L. 1964. "Archaeology and the Trojan War." *The Journal of Hellenic Studies* 84:9–11.

Catenacci, Carmine. 1993. "Il finale dell'*Odissea* e la recensio pisistratide dei poemi omerici." *Quaderni Urbinati di Cultura Classica* n.s. 44:7–22.

Chadwick, Hector M., and Nora K. Chadwick. 1932–1940. *The Growth of Literature.* 3 vols. Cambridge.

Chadwick, Nora K., and Victor Zhirmunsky. 1969. *Oral Epics of Central Asia.* Cambridge.

Chantraine, Pierre. 1968–1977. *Dictionnaire étymologique de la langue grecque.* 4 vols. Paris.

Chappell, Mike. 2011. *The Homeric Hymn to Apollo: The Question of Unity.* In *The Homeric Hymns: Interpretative Essays*, ed. Andrew Faulkner, 59–81. Oxford.

Christensen, Joel. 2015. "Diomedes' Foot Wound and Homeric Reception of Myth." In *Diachrony*, ed. José González, 17–41. Leiden.

Chruściak, Ilona. 2008. *Alternacja grozy i ulgi w scenie wykupienia zwłok Hektora przez Priama* [The alternation of dread and relief in the scene of ransoming the body of Hector by Priam]. Bachelor's thesis. Archive of the Institute of Classical, Mediterranean and Oriental Studies at the University of Wrocław. Wrocław.

———. 2018. *Funkcja gestu w oralnej kompozycji Iliady.* [The role of Gesture in the Oral Composition of the *Iliad*]. PhD dissertation. Archive of the Institute of Classical, Mediterranean and Oriental Studies at the University of Wrocław. Wrocław.

Clark, Matthew. 1997. *Out of Line: Homeric Composition Beyond the Hexameter.* Lanham, MD.

———. 1998. "Chryses' Supplication: Speech Act and Mythological Allusion." *Classical Antiquity* 17:5–24.

———. 2004. "Formulas, Metre and Type-scenes." In Fowler 2004:117–138.

Clark, M. E., and W. D. E. Coulson. 1978. "Memnon and Sarpedon." *Museum Helveticum* 35:65–73.

Clarke, Michael. 1995. "Between Lions and Men: Images of the Hero in the *Iliad.*" *Greek, Roman, and Byzantine Studies* 36:137–159.

———. 2004. "Manhood and Heroism." In Fowler 2004:74–90.

Claus, David B. 1975. "*Aidôs* in the Language of Achilles." *Transactions of the American Philological Association* 105:13–28.

Clay, Jenny Strauss. 1983. *The Wrath of Athena: Gods and Men in the* Odyssey. Princeton.

Collins, Derek. 2004. *Master of the Game: Competition and Performance in Greek Poetry.* Hellenic Studies 7. Washington, DC. http://nrs.harvard.edu/urn-3:hul.ebook:CHS_CollinsD.Master_of_the_Game.2004

Collins, Leslie. 1988. *Studies in Characterization in the* Iliad. Beiträge zur klassischen Philologie 189. Frankfurt.

Combellack. F. M. 1976. "Homer the Innovator." *Classical Philology* 71:44–55.

Compton, Todd M. 2006. *Victim of the Muses: Poet as a Scapegoat, Warrior, and Hero in Greco-Roman and Indo-European Myth and History*. Hellenic Studies 11. Washington, DC. http://nrs.harvard.edu/urn-3:hul.ebook:CHS_Compton.Victim_of_the_Muses.2006

Cook, Erwin F. 1999. "'Active' and 'Passive' Heroics in the *Odyssey*." *Classical World* 93:147–167.

———. 2009. "On the 'Importance' of *Iliad* Book 8." *Classical Philology* 104:133–161.

———. 2014. "Structure as Interpretation in the Homeric Odyssey." In *Defining Greek Narrative*, ed. D. Cairns and R. Scodel, 75–100. Edinburgh.

Cornford, Francis M. 1927. "The Origin of the Olympic Games." In Harrison 1927:225–238.

Crielaard, J. P., ed. 1995. *Homeric Questions*. Amsterdam.

Currie, Bruno. 2005. *Pindar and the Cult of Heroes*. Oxford.

———. 2012. "The *Iliad, Gilgamesh*, and Neoanalysis." In Montanari, Rengakos, and Tsagalis 2012:543–580.

———. 2016. *Homer's Allusive Art*. Oxford.

Curschmann, Michael. 1967. "Oral Poetry in Mediaeval English, French, and German Literature: Some Notes on Recent Research." *Speculum* 42:36–52.

Curtius, Georg. 1848. "Homerische studien." *Philologus* 3:1–21.

Czeremski, Maciej. 2009. *Struktura mitów. W stronę metonimii* [*The Structure of Myths—Towards Metonymy*]. Kraków.

———. 2016a. "Bohaterowie optymalnie niemożliwi. Geneza, struktura i funkcje mitycznej kontrintuicyjności [Optimally Impossible Heroes. Genesis, Structure and Functions of the Mythical Contrintuitiveness]." *Rocznik Lubuski* 42:29–49.

———. 2016b. "Stabilność 'literatury oralnej' a kognitywne uwarunkowania genezy światopoglądu społeczności tradycyjnych [The Stability of 'Oral Literature' and the Cognitive Determinants of the Genesis of Traditional Societies' Worldview]." *Quaestiones Oralitatis* 2:153–181.

———. 2016c. "Podmiot i przedmiot w procesach mitologizacji [El sujeto y el objeto en los precesos de mitificación]." In *Mitologizacja człowieka w kulturze i literaturze iberyjskiej i polskiej*, ed. W. Charchalis, B. Trocha, 25–35. Zielona Góra.

Čolaković, Zlatan. 2006. "The Singer Above Tales: Homer, Međedović and Traditional Epics." *Seminari romani di cultura greca* 9:161–187.

———. 2019. "Avdo Međedović's Post-Traditional Epics and their Relevance to Homeric Studies." *Journal of Hellenic Studies* 139:1–48.

Dalby, Andrew. 1998. "Homer's Enemies: Lyric and Epic in the Seventh Century." In *Archaic Greece: New Approaches and New Evidence*, ed. Nick Fisher and Hans van Wees, 195–212. London.

———. 2006. *Rediscovering Homer: Inside the Origins of the Epic*. New York.

Danek, Georg. 1988. *Studien zur Dolonie*. Vienna.

———. 1998a. *Epos und Zitat: Studien zu den Quellen der Odyssee*. Wiener Studien Beiheft 22. Vienna.

———. 1998b. "Darstellung verdeckter Handlung bei Homer und in der südslawischen Heldenlied-Tradition." *Wiener Studien* 111:67–88.

———. 2002. "Traditional Referentiality and Homeric Intertextuality." In *Omero tremila anni dopo*, ed. F. Montanari and P. Ascheri, 3–19. Rome.

———. 2010. "The Homeric Epics as Palimpsests." In *In the Second Degree: Paratextual Literature in Ancient Near Eastern and Ancient Mediterranean Culture and its Reflections in Medieval Literature*, ed. P. S. Alexander, A. Lange and R. J. Pillinger, 123–136. Leiden.

———. 2012. "Homer und Avdo Međedović als 'post-traditional singers'?" In *Homer, gedeuted durch ein grosses Lexikon (Akten des Hamburger Kolloquiums vom 6.-8. Oktober 2010 zum Abschluss des Lexikons des frühgriechischen Epos)*, ed. M. Meier-Brügger, 27–44. Berlin.

———. 2016. "Modes of Intertextuality in Homer and Bosnian Epic." In *Omero: Quaestiones Disputatae*, ed. F. Gallo, 123–145. Ambrosiana Graecolatina 5. Milan.

Danek, Georg, and Stefan Hagel. 1995. "Homer-Singen." *Wiener Humanistische Blätter* 37:5–20.

Danielewicz, Jerzy. 1990. "Towards an Understanding of the Chorus: Homer on Early Forms of Lyric Poetry." *Eos* 78:55–62.

Danka, Ignacy R. 1971. "Pierwotny Apollo, Pajan, Helios." *Meander* 26:153–167.

Davidson, Olga Merck. 1980. "Indo-European Dimensions of Herakles in the *Iliad*." *Arethusa* 13:197–202.

Davies, Malcolm. 1981. "The Judgement of Paris and *Iliad* Book XXIV." *The Journal of Hellenic Studies* 101:56–62.

———. 1988. *Epicorum Graecorum Fragmenta*. Göttingen.

———. 1989a. *The Epic Cycle*. Bristol.

———. 1989b. "The Date of the Epic Cycle." *Glotta* 67:89–100.

———. 2003. "The Judgements of Paris and Solomon." *Classical Quarterly* 53:32–43.

———. 2016. *The Aethiopis: Neo-Neoanalysis Reanalyzed.* Hellenic Studies 71. Washington, DC. http://nrs.harvard.edu/urn-3:hul.ebook:CHS_DaviesM.The_Aethiopis.2016

Davis-Kimball, Jeannine, and Mona Behan. 2003. *Warrior Women: An Archaeologist's Search for History's Hidden Heroines*. New York.

De Jong, Irene J. F. 1985a. "Eurykleia and Odysseus' Scar: *Odyssey* 19.393–466." *Classical Quarterly* 35:517–518.

———. 1985b. "*Iliad* I.366–392: A Mirror Story." *Arethusa* 18:5–22.
———. 1987a. *Narrators and Focalizers: The Presentation of the Story in the* Iliad. Amsterdam.
———. 1987b. "Paris/Alexandros in the *Iliad*." *Mnemosyne* 40:124–127.
———. 1994. "Between Word and Deed: Hidden Thoughts in the *Odyssey*." In *Modern Critical Theory and Classical Literature*, ed. Irene J. F. de Jong and J. P. Sullivan, 27–50. Leiden.
———. 1997. "Homer and Narratology." In Morris and Powell 1997:305–325.
———. 1999. "Auerbach and Homer." In Kazazis and Rengakos 1999:154–164.
———. 2002. "Developments in Narrative Technique in the *Odyssey*." In Reichel and Rengakos 2002:77–91.
———. 2005. "Convention versus Realism in the Homeric Epics." *Mnemosyne* 58:1–22.
Dekker, Annie F. 1965. *Ironie in de Odyssee*. Leiden.
Delcourt, Marie. 1965. *Pyrros et Pyrra: Recherches sur la valeur du feu dans les légendes héllenique*s. Paris.
De Vries, Jan. 1933. "The Problem of Loki." *Folklore Fellows Communications* 110:269–272.
———. 1954. *Betrachtungen zum Märchen, besonders in seinem Verhältnis zu Heldensage und Mythos*. Folklore Fellows Communications 150. Helsinki.
Dickie, Matthew W. 1995. "The Geography of Homer's World." In Andersen and Dickie 1995:29–56.
Dickinson, Oliver T. P. K. 1986. "Homer, the Poet of the Dark Age." *Greece and Rome* 33:20–37.
Dickson, Keith. 1992. "Kalkhas and Nestor: Two Narrative Strategies in *Iliad* 1." *Arethusa* 25:327–358.
Dietrich, Jessica. 1999. "*Thebaid's* Feminine Ending." *Ramus* 28:41–53.
Dihle, Albrecht. 1970. *Homer-Probleme*. Opladen.
Dimock, G. E., Jr. 1956. "The Name of Odysseus." *The Hudson Review* 9:52–70.
Dodds, Eric R. 1951. *The Greeks and the Irrational*. Berkeley.
Doherty, Lillian E. 1991. "The Internal and Implied Audiences of *Odyssey* 11." *Arethusa* 24:145–176.
Donlan, Walter. 1993. "Duelling with Gifts in the *Iliad*: As the Audience Saw It." *Colby Quarterly* 29:155–172.
Dowden, Kenneth. 1996. "Homer's Sense of Text." *The Journal of Hellenic Studies* 116:47–61.
———. 2004. "The Epic Tradition in Greece." In Fowler 2004:188–205.
Drews, Robert. 1969. "Aethiopian Memnon: African or Asiatic?" *Rheinisches Museum* 112:191–192.
———. 1979. "Argos and Argives in the *Iliad*." *Classical Philology* 74:111–135.

———. 1988. *The Coming of the Greeks: Indo-European Conquests in the Aegean and the Near East*. Princeton.

Dubois, Thomas A. 1995. *Finnish Folk and the Kalevala*. New York.

Duckworth, George E. 1931. "ΠΡΟΑΝΑΦΩΝΗΣΙΣ in the Scholia to Homer." *American Journal of Philology* 52:320–338.

———. 1966. *Foreshadowing and Suspense in the Epics of Homer, Apollonius and Vergil*. New York. Orig. pub. Princeton, 1933.

———. 1936. "Foreshadowing and Suspense in the Posthomerica of Quintus of Smyrna." *American Journal of Philology* 57:58–86.

Dué, Casey. 2001. "Achilles' Golden Amphora in Aischines' *Against Timarchus* and the Afterlife of Oral Tradition." *Classical Philology* 96:33–47.

———. 2002. *Homeric Variations on a Lament by Briseis*. Lanham, MD.

———. 2005. "Homer's Post-classical Legacy." In Foley 2005:397–414. Oxford.

Dué, Casey, and Mary Ebbott. 2010. *Iliad 10 and the Poetics of Ambush: A Multitext Edition with Essays and Commentary*. Cambridge, MA.

Dumézil, Georges. 1948. *Loki*. Paris.

———. 1968. *Mythe et épopée, tome 1: L'idéologie des trois fonctions dans les épopées des peuples indo-européens*. Paris.

———. 1973. *The Destiny of a King*. Trans. A. Hiltebeitel. Chicago.

———. 1988. *Mitra-Varuna: An Essay on Two Indo-European Representations of Sovereignty*. New York.

Dumézil, Georges, and Didier Eribon. 1996. *Z Georgesem Dumézilem rozmawia Didier Eribon, Na tropie Indoeuropejczyków. Mity i epopeje*. Transl. K. Kocjan. Warsaw.

Durante, M. 1958. "Ἔπεα πτερόεντα: La parola come cammino in immagini greche e vediche." *Rendiconti della Classe di Scienze morali, storiche e filologiche dell' Academia dei Linzei* 13:3–14.

———. 1971–1974. *Sulla preistoria della tradizione poetica greca*. 2 vols. Incunabula Greca 50, 64. Rome.

———. 1976. "Eridità micenee in Omero." In *La civiltà micenea. Guida storica e critica*, ed. G. Maddoli, 153–170. Universale Laterza 387.

Easterling, Patricia E. 1984. "The Tragic Homer." *Bulletin of the Institute of Classical Studies* 31:1–8.

Ebbott, Mary. 1999. "The Wrath of Helen: Self-Blame and Nemesis in the *Iliad*." In Carlisle and Levaniouk 1999:3–33.

Edmunds, Lowell, ed. 1990. *Approaches to Greek Myth*. Baltimore.

———. 1993. *Myth in Homer: A Handbook*. Highland Park, NJ.

———. 1997a. "Myth in Homer." In Morris and Powell 1997:415–441.

———. 1997b. "The Seal of Theognis." In *Poet, Public, and Performance in Ancient Greece*, ed. Lowell Edmunds and R. W. Wallace, 29–48. Baltimore.

———. 2005. "Epic and Myth." In Foley 2005:31–44.

Edsman, Carl M. 1949. *Ignis Divinis*. Lund.

Edwards, Anthony T. 1984. "Aristos Achaiōn: Heroic Death and Dramatic Structure in the *Iliad*." *Quaderni Urbinati di Cultura Classica* n.s. 17:61–80.

———.1985a. *Achilles in the* Odyssey. Beiträge zur Klassischen Philologie 171. Königstein.

———. 1985b. "Achilles in the Underworld: *Iliad, Odyssey* and *Aethiopis*." *Greek, Roman, and Byzantine Studies* 26:215–227.

Edwards, Cyril, trans. and comm. 2010. *The* Nibelungenlied: *The Lay of the Nibelungs*. Oxford World's Classics. New York.

Edwards, Mark W. 1966. "Some Features of Homeric Craftsmanship." *Transactions of the American Philological Association* 97:115–179.

———. 1968. "Some Stylistic Notes on *Iliad* XVIII." *American Journal of Philology* 89:257–283.

———. 1969. "On Some 'Answering' Expressions in Homer." *Classical Philology* 64:81–87.

———. 1970. "Homeric Speech Introductions." *Harvard Studies in Classical Philology* 74:1–36.

———. 1975. "Type-scenes and Homeric Hospitality." *Transactions of the American Philological Association* 105:51–72.

———. 1980a. "Convention and Individuality in *Iliad* 1." *Harvard Studies in Classical Philology* 84:1–28.

———. 1980b. "The Structure of Homeric Catalogues." *Transactions of the American Philological Association* 110:81–105.

———. 1986. "Homer and Oral Tradition: The Formula, Part I." *Oral Tradition* 1:171–230.

———. 1987. *Homer: Poet of the* Iliad. Baltimore.

———. 1988. "Homer and Oral Tradition: The Formula, Part II." *Oral Tradition* 3:11–60.

———. 1990. "Neoanalysis and Beyond." *Classical Antiquity* 9:311–325.

———. 1991. *The* Iliad*: A Commentary*. Vol. V, *Books 17–20*. Cambridge.

———. 1992. "Homer and Oral Tradition: The Type-scene." *Oral Tradition* 7:283–330.

———. 1997. "Homeric Style and Oral Poetics." In Morris and Powell 1997:261–283.

———. 2003. "Homer and the Oral Tradition." *Oral Tradition* 18:65–67.

Ehrismann, Otfrid. 1987. *Nibelungen Lied: Epoche-Werk-Wirkung*. Munich.

Eichholz, David E. 1953. "The Propitiation of Achilles." *American Journal of Philology* 75:137–148.

Eliade, Mircea. 1993. *Kowale i alchemicy*. Transl. A. Leder. Warsaw.

———. 2001. *Szamanizm i archaiczne techniki ekstazy.* Transl. K. Kocjan. Warsaw.

Elmer, David F. 2010. "*Kita* and *Kosmos*: The Poetics of Ornamentation in Bosniac and Homeric Epic." *Journal of Homeric Folklore* 123:276–303.

———. 2013. *The Poetics of Consent: Collective Decision Making and the* Iliad. Baltimore.

Emlyn-Jones, Chris J. 1967. "ἔτος and ἐνιαυτός in Homeric Formulae." *Glotta* 45:156–161.

Erbse, Hartmut. 1961. "Betrachtungen über das 5. Buch der *Ilias*." *Rheinisches Museum* 104:156–189.

———. 1969–1975. *Scholia Graeca in Homeri Iliadem (Scholia Vetera).* 4 vols. Berlin.

———. 1982. "*Ilias* und '*Patroklie*'." *Hermes* 110:1–15.

———. 1993. "Nestor und Antilochos bei Homer und Arktinos." *Hermes* 121:385–403.

———. 2001. "Achills Erziehung: Versagen und späte Einsicht." *Rheinisches Museum* 144:241–250.

Evans-Pritchard, Edward E. 1956. *Nuer Religion.* Oxford.

———. 1976. *Witchcraft, Oracles and Magic among the Azande.* Oxford.

Fantuzzi, Marco. 1980. "Oralità, scrittura, auralita: Gli studi sulle tecniche della communicazione nella Grecia antica (1960–1980)." *Lingua e Stile* 15:593–612.

Fantuzzi, Marco, and Christos C. Tsagalis. 2015. *The Greek Epic Cycle and its Ancient Reception: A Companion.* Cambridge.

Faraone, Christopher A. 1992. *Talismans and Trojan Horses.* Oxford.

Felson, Nancy. 2002. "'Threptra' and Invisible Hands: The Father–Son relationship in *Iliad* 24." *Arethusa* 35:35–50.

Fenik, Bernard C. 1964. Iliad *X and the Rhesus: The Myth.* Brussels.

———. 1968. *Typical Battle Scenes in the* Iliad. *Hermes* Einzelschrift 21. Wiesbaden.

———. 1974. *Studies in the* Odyssey. *Hermes* Einzelschrift 30. Wiesbaden.

———, ed. 1978a. *Homer: Tradition and Invention.* Leiden.

———. 1978b. "Stylization and Variety." In Fenik 1978a:68–90.

———. 1986. *Homer and the Nibelungenlied: Comparative Studies in Epic Style.* Cambridge, MA.

Figueira, Thomas J., and Gregory Nagy, eds. 1985. *Theognis of Megara: Poetry and the Polis.* Baltimore.

Finkelberg, Margalit. 1986. "Is κλέος ἄφθιτον a Homeric Formula?" *Classical Quarterly* 36: 1–5.

———. 1987. "The First Song of Demodocus." *Mnemosyne* 40:128–132.

———. 1988. "From Ahhiyawa to Ἀχαιοί." *Glotta* 66:127–134.

———. 1989. "Formulaic and Nonformulaic Elements in Homer." *Classical Philology* 84:179–187.

———. 1998. *The Birth of Literary Fiction in Ancient Greece*. Oxford.
———. 2000. "The *Cypria*, the *Iliad*, and the Problem of Multiformity in Oral and Written Tradition." *Classical Philology* 95:1–11.
———. 2003. "Neoanalysis and Oral Tradition in Homeric Studies." *Oral Tradition* 18:68–69.
———. 2004. "Oral Theory and the Limits of the Formulaic Diction." *Oral Tradition* 19:236–252.
———, ed. 2011. *The Homer Encyclopedia*. Chichester.
———. 2012. "Oral Formulaic Theory and the Individual Poet." In Montanari, Rengakos, and Tsagalis 2012:73–82.
———. 2015. "Meta-Cyclic Epic and Homeric poetry." In Fantuzzi and Tsagalis 2015:126–138.
Finley, Moses I. 1964. "The Trojan War." *The Journal of Hellenic Studies* 84:1–9.
———. 1977. *The World of Odysseus*. New York.
Finnegan, Ruth. 1976. "What Is Oral Literature Anyway? Comments in the Light of Some African and Other Comparative Material." In Stolz and Shannon 1976:127–166.
———. 1977. *Oral Poetry: Its Nature, Significance and Social Context*. Cambridge.
Fisher, Nick. 1976. "Hybris and Dishonour: 1." *Greece and Rome* 23:177–193.
Flaig, Egon. 1994. "Das Konsensprizip im homerischen Olymp. Überlegungen zum göttlichen Entscheidungsprozess *Ilias* 4.1–72." *Hermes* 122 (1):13–31.
Floyd, Edwin D. 1980. "*Kleos aphthiton*: An Indo-European Perspective on Early Greek Poetry." *Glotta* 58:136–157.
Foley, John M., ed. 1981. *Oral Traditional Literature: A Festschrift for Albert Bates Lord*. Columbus, OH.
———. 1988. *The Theory of Oral Composition: History and Methodology*. Bloomington.
———. 1990. *Traditional Oral Epic: The Odyssey, Beowulf, and the Serbo-Croatian Return Song*. Berkeley.
———. 1991. *Immanent Art: From Structure to Meaning in Traditional Oral Epic*. Bloomington.
———. 1994. "Sixteen Moments of Silence in Homer." *Quaderni Urbinati di Cultura Classica* n.s. 33:7–26.
———. 1995. *The Singer of Tales in Performance*. Bloomington.
———. 1996. "Guslar and *Aoidos*: Traditional Register in South Slavic and Homeric Epic." *Transactions of the American Philological Association* 126:11–41.
———. 1997. "Oral Tradition and Its Implications." In Morris and Powell 1997:146–173.
———. 1998. "Individual Poet and Epic Tradition: Homer as Legendary Singer." *Arethusa* 31:149–178.
———. 1999a. *Homer's Traditional Art*. University Park, PA.

———. 1999b. "Epic Cycles and Epic Traditions." In Kazazis and Rengakos 1999:99–108.

———. 2002. "What South Slavic Oral Epic Can—and Cannot—Tell Us about Homer." In Reichel and Rengakos 2002:53–62.

———. 2004. "Epic as Genre." In Fowler 2004:171–187.

———, ed. 2005. *A Companion to Ancient Epic*. Malden.

———. 2007. "'Reading' Homer through Oral Tradition." *College Literature* 34:1–28.

———. 2011a. "Oral-Derived Text." In Finkelberg 2011:ii.603.

———. 2011b. "Oral Dictated Texts." In Finkelberg 2011:ii.603–604.

———. 2011c. "Oral Traditions." In Finkelberg 2011:607–610.

Foley, John M., and Justin Arft. 2015. "The Epic Cycle and Oral Tradition." In Fantuzzi and Tsagalis 2015:78–95.

Fontenrose, Joseph. 1960. "The Cult and Myth of Pyrros at Delphi." *University of California Publications in Classical Archaeology* 4:191–266.

Ford, Andrew. 1985. "The Politics of Authorship in Ancient Greece." In Figueira and Nagy 1985:82–95.

———. 1992. *The Poetry of the Past*. Ithaca.

———. 1997. "Epic as Genre." In Morris and Powell 1997:396–414.

Fowler, R., ed. 2004. *The Cambridge Companion to Homer*. Cambridge.

Frame, Douglas. 2005. *The Myth of Return in Early Greek Epic*. Washington, DC. Orig. pub. New Haven, 1978. http://nrs.harvard.edu/urn-3:hul.ebook:CHS_Frame.The_Myth_of_Return_in_Early_Greek_Epic.1978

———. 2009. *Hippota Nestor*. Hellenic Studies 37. Washington, DC. http://nrs.harvard.edu/urn-3:hul.ebook:CHS_Frame.Hippota_Nestor.2009

Frangoulidis, Stavros A. 1993. "Polyphemus' Prayer to Poseidon: Hom. *Od.* 9, 528–535." *Quaderni Urbinati di Cultura Classica* n.s. 43:45–49.

Fränkel, Hermann. 1939. "Der Charakter in der Sprache der frühgriechischen Dichtung (Homer, Semonides, Pindar)." *American Journal of Philology* 60:475–479.

———. 1960. *Wege und Formen frühgriechischen Denken*. Munich.

———. 1975. *Early Greek Poetry and Philosophy: A History of Greek Epic, Lyric, and Prose to the Middle of the Fifth Century*. Trans. M. Hadas and J. Wills. Oxford.

Franko, George Fredrik. 2005/2006. "The Trojan Horse at the Close of the *Iliad*." *Classical Journal* 101:121–123.

Frazer, James G. 1893. "The Youth of Achilles." *Classical Review* 7:292–310.

———. 1912. *The Golden Bough: A Study in Magic and Religion*. Part III. *The Dying God*. Orig. pub. 1911. London.

———. 1921. *Apollodorus: The Library*. 2 vols. Cambridge, MA.

Frisk, Hjalmar. 1960–1970. *Griechisches etymologisches Wörterbuch.* 3 vols. Heidelberg.

Gaca, Kathy L. 2008. "Reinterpreting the Homeric Simile of *Iliad* 16.7-11: The Girl and her Mother in Ancient Greek Warfare." *American Journal of Philology* 129:145–71.

Gantz, Timothy. 1993. *Early Greek Myth: A Guide to Literary and Artistic Sources.* Baltimore.

Garner, Richard. 1990. *From Homer to Tragedy: The Art of Allusion in Greek Poetry.* London.

———. 1992. "Mules, Mysteries, and Song in Pindar's 'Olympia' 6." *Classical Antiquity* 11:45–67.

Geddes, A. G. 1984. "Who's Who in 'Homeric' Society?" *Classical Quarterly* 34:17–36.

Gentili, Bruno. 1990. *Poetry and Its Public in Ancient Greece: From Homer to the Fifth Century.* Trans. Thomas Cole. London.

Gil, Luis. 1999. "Ex Aegypto lux: *Il.* 22, 25–32." *Quaderni Urbinati di Cultura Classica* n.s. 61:35–42.

Gilbert, Pierre J. J. 1939. "Homère et l'Égypte." *Chronique d'Égypte* 14:47-61.

Girard, René. 2005. *Violence and the Sacred.* Trans. Patrick Gregory. Baltimore.

Glenn, Justin. 1971. "The Polyphemus Folktale and Homer's Kyklopeia." *Transactions of the American Philological Association* 102:133–181.

Godart, Louis, and Anna Sacconi. 1999. "La Géographie des États mycéniens." *Comptes Rendus des Séances de l'Académie des Inscriptions et Belles-Lettres* 143:527–546.

Goldhill, Simon. 1988. "Reading Differences: The *Odyssey* and Juxtaposition." *Ramus* 17:1–30.

González, José M. 2013. *The Epic Rhapsode and his Craft: Homeric Performance in a Diachronic Perspective.* Hellenic Studies 47. Washington, DC. http://nrs.harvard.edu/urn-3:hul.ebook:CHS_GonzalezJ.The_Epic_Rhapsode_and_his_Craft.2013

Goody, Jack. 1977. *The Domestication of the Savage Mind.* Cambridge.

———. 1986. *The Logic of Writing and the Organisation of Society.* Cambridge.

———. 2010. *Myth, Ritual and the Oral.* Cambridge.

Gottschall, Jonathan. 2008. *The Rape of Troy: Evolution, Violence, and the World of Homer.* Cambridge.

Graver, Margaret. 1995. "Dog-Helen and Homeric Insult." *Classical Antiquity* 14:41–61.

Graziosi, Barbara. 2002. *Inventing Homer: The Early Reception of Epic.* Cambridge.

Graziosi, Barbara, and Johannes Haubold. 2005. *Homer: The Resonance of Epic.* London

———, eds. 2010. *Homer.* Iliad. *Book VI.* Cambridge.

Gresseth, Gerald K. 1979. "The *Odyssey* and the *Nalopākhyāna*." *Transactions of the American Philological Association* 109:63–85.

Griffin, Jasper. 1977. "The Epic Cycle and the Uniqueness of Homer." *The Journal of Hellenic Studies* 97:39–53.

———. 1980. *Homer on Life and Death.* Oxford.

———. 1995. *Homer. Iliad IX.* Oxford.

———. 1999. *Homer.* Trans. Robert A. Sucharski. Warsaw. Orig. pub. Oxford, 1980.

———. 2004. "The Speeches." In Fowler 2004:156–167.

Griffin, Jasper, and Martin Hammond. 1982. "Critical Appreciations VI: Homer, *Iliad* 1.1–52." *Greece and Rome* 29:126–142.

Griffith, Drew R. 1998. "The Origin of Memnon." *Classical Antiquity* 17:212–227.

Griffiths, Alan. 1985. "Patroklos the Ram." *Bulletin of the Institute for Classical Studies* 32:49–50.

———. 1989. "Patroklos the Ram (Again)." *Bulletin of the Institute for Classical Studies* 36:139.

Grintzer, Pavel A. 1974. *Drevneindijskij epos. Genezis i tipologiâ.* Moscow.

Groten, F.J.Jr. 1968. "Homer's Helen." *Greece & Rome* 15:33–39.

Gurney, Oliver R. 1990. *The Hittites.* London.

Güterbock, Hans G. 1990. "Wer war Tawagalawa?" *Orientalia* 59:157–165.

Haft, Adele J. 1990. "'The City-Sacker Odysseus' in *Iliad* 2 and 10." *Transactions of the American Philological Association* 120:37–56.

———. 1992. "τὰ δὴ νῦν πάντα τελεῖται: Prophecy and Recollection in the Assemblies of *Iliad* 2 and Odyssey 2." *Arethusa* 25:223–240.

Hainsworth, John B. 1964. "Structure and Content in Epic Formulae: The Question of the Unique Expression." *Classical Quarterly* 14:155–164.

———. 1968. *The Flexibility of the Homeric Formula.* Oxford.

———. 1970. "Criticism of an Oral Homer." *The Journal of Hellenic Studies* 90:90–98.

———. 1978. "Good and Bad Formulae." In Fenik 1978a:41–50.

———. 1980. "Elementos Antiguos y Modernos en la Prosodia Homérica." *Classical Review* 30:292.

———. 1993. *The* Iliad*: A Commentary.* Vol. III. *Books 9–12.* Cambridge.

Hammer, Dean. 1997. "'Who Shall Readily Obey?' Authority and Politics in the *Iliad.*" *Phoenix* 51:1–24.

Hampl, Franz. 1975. "Die *Ilias* ist kein Geschichtsbuch." In *Geschichte als kritische Wissenschaft*, ed. F. Hampl, vol. 2, 51–99. Darmstadt.

Hannah, Robert. 2015. "Ancient Greek Calendars." In *Handbook of Archaeoastronomy and Ethnoastronomy*, ed. Clive L. N. Ruggles, 1563–1571. New York.

Hansen, William. 1972. *The Conference Sequence: Patterned Narration and Narrative Inconsistency in the* Odyssey. Berkeley.

———. 1983. "Greek Mythology and the Study of the Ancient Greek Oral Story." *Journal of Folklore Research* 20:101–112.

———. 1990. "Odysseus and the Oar: A Folkloric Approach." In Edmunds 1990:241–272.

———. 1997. "Homer and the Folktale." In Morris and Powell 1997:442–462.

———. 2002. *Ariadne's Thread: A Guide to International Tales Found in Classical Literature*. Ithaca.

Harrison, Jane E. 1922. *Prolegomena to the Study of Greek Religion*. Cambridge.

———. 1927. *Themis: A Study of the Social Origins of Greek Religion*. Cambridge.

Hatto, A. T., and John B. Hainsworth, eds. 1980-1989. *Traditions of Heroic and Epic Poetry*. 2 vols. London.

Havelock, Eric A. 1969. *Preface to Plato*. Cambridge, MA.

———. 1982. *The Literate Revolution in Greece and Its Cultural Consequences*. Princeton.

Heiden, Bruce. 1997. "The *Iliad* and Its Context: Introduction." *Arethusa* 30:145–150.

———. 2008. *Homer's Cosmic Fabrication: Choice and Design in the* Iliad. New York.

Heitsch, Ernst. 1990. "Homerische Dreigespanne." In Kullmann and Reichel 1990:153–174.

———. 2008. "Neoanalytische Antikritik: Zum Verhältnis '*Ilias*—*Aethiopis*'." *Rheinisches Museum* 151:1–12.

Helck, Wolfgang. 1979. "Memnon." In *Der Kleine Pauly*, Vol. 3, 1189–1191. Munich.

Held, George F. 1987. "Phoenix, Agamemnon and Achilleus: Parables and Paradeigmata." *Classical Quarterly* 37:249–261.

Hellwig, Brigitte. 1964. *Raum und Zeit im Homerischen Epos*. Hildesheim.

Henriksson, Göran, and Mary Blomberg. 1993. "Archaeoastronomical Light on the Priestly Role of the King in Crete." In *Religion and Power in the Ancient Greek World: Proceedings of the Uppsala Symposium 1993*, ed. P. Hellström and B. Alroth, 27–39. Uppsala.

———. 1996. "Evidence for Minoan Astronomical Observations from the Peak Sanctuaries on Petsophas and Traostalos." *Opuscula Atheniensia* 21:99–114.

———. 2012. "The Trojan War Dated by Two Solar Eclipses." *Mediterranean Archaeology and Archaeometry* 12: 63–76.

———. 2015. "Minoan Astronomy." In *Handbook of Archaeoastronomy and Ethnoastronomy*, ed. Clive L. N. Ruggles, 1431-1441. New York.

Heubeck, Alfred. 1974. *Die homerische Frage*. Darmstadt.

———. 1978. "Homeric Studies Today: Results and Prospects." In Fenik 1978a:1–17.

———. 1988. "General Introduction." In Heubeck, West, and Hainsworth 1988–1992:vol. 1, 3–23.

———. 1989. "Books IX–XII." In Heubeck, West, and Hainsworth 1988–1992:vol. 2, 3–145.

———. 1992. "Books XXIII–XXIV." In Heubeck, West, and Hainsworth 1988–1992:vol. 3, 313–417.

Heubeck, Alfred, Stephanie West, and J. B. Hainsworth, eds. 1988–1992. *A Commentary on Homer's Odyssey.* 3 vols. Oxford.

Hinz, Walther. 1972. *The Lost World of Elam*. Trans. J. Barnes. London.

Hirschberger, Martina. 2012. "The Fate of Achilles in the *Iliad*." In Montanari, Rengakos, and Tsagalis 2012:185–196.

Hitch, Sarah. 2009. *King of Sacrifice: Ritual and Royal Authority in the* Iliad. Washington, DC. Hellenic Studies 25. https://chs.harvard.edu/book/hitch-sarah-king-of-sacrifice-ritual-and-royal-authority-in-the-iliad/

Hoekstra, Arie. 1965. *Homeric Modifications of Formulaic Prototypes*. Amsterdam.

———. 1981. *Epic Verse before Homer: Three Studies*. Amsterdam.

Hoffmann, C. A. J. 1848. "Lachmann's betrachtungen über Homers *Ilias*." *Philologus* 3:193–222.

Hofmeister, Timothy P. 1995. "'Rest in Violence': Composition and Characterization in *Iliad* 16.155–277." *Classical Antiquity* 14:289–316.

Holmberg, Ingrid E. 1998. "The Creation of the Ancient Greek Epic Cycle." *Oral Tradition* 13:456–478.

———. 2003. "Hephaistos and Spiders' Webs." *Phoenix* 57:1–17.

Holoka, James P. 1979. "Homer, Oral Poetry Theory, and Comparative Literature: Major Trends and Controversies in Twentieth-Century Criticism." In Latacz 1979:458–481.

———. 1983. "'Looking Darkly' (ΥΠΟΔΡΑ ΙΔΩΝ): Reflections on Status and Decorum in Homer." *Transactions of the American Philological Association* 113:1–16.

———. 2002. "Homer and Simone Weil: The *Iliad sub specie violentiae*." In Reichel and Rengakos 2002:63–75.

Hölscher, Uvo. 1978. "The Transformation from Folk-tale to Epic." In Fenik 1978a:51–67.

Horn, Fabian. 2021. "The Death of Achilles in the *Iliad*. Motif Transference and Poetic Technique." *Mnemosyne* 74:1–28.

Householder, F., and Gregory Nagy. 1972. "Greek." *Current Trends in Linguistics* 9:735–816.

Howald, Ernst. 1924. "Meleager und Achill." *Rheinisches Museum* 73:402–425.

Hüsing, Georg. 1917. "Der elamische Gott Memnon." In *Orientalistische Studien Fritz Hommel zum sechzigsten Geburstag am 31. Juli 1914 gewidmet von Freunden, Kollegen und Schülern*, vol 1, 35–68. Leipzig.

Huxley, George L. 1967. "A Problem in the *Kypria*." *Greek, Roman, and Byzantine Studies* 8:25–27.

———. 1969. *Greek Epic Poetry: From Eumelos to Panyassis*. Cambridge, MA.

Jachmann, Günther. 1958. *Der homerische Schiffskatalog und die* Ilias. Wissenschaftliche Abhandlungen der Arbeitsgemeinschaft für Foschung des Landes Nordrhein-Westfalen 5. Cologne-Opladen.

Jahn, Thomas. 1987. *Zum Wortfeld 'Seele-Geist' in der Sprache Homers*. Munich.

Jamison, Stephanie W. 1994. "*Draupadī* on the Walls of Troy: *Iliad* 3 from an Indic Perspective." *Classical Antiquity* 13:5–16.

———. 1999. "Penelope and the Pigs: Indic Perspectives on the *Odyssey*." *Classical Antiquity* 18:227–272.

Janda, Michael. 2006. "Memnon, Eos und die Aithiopen: Zu Herkunft und Transformationen eines Sagenstoffes." *Gymnasium* 113:519–528.

Janko, Richard. 1990a. *Homer, Hesiod and the Hymns: Diachronic Development in Epic Diction*. Cambridge.

———. 1990b. "The *Iliad* and its Editors: Dictation and Redaction." *Classical Antiquity* 9:326–334.

———. 1992. *The* Iliad*: A Commentary*. Vol. IV. *Books 13–16*. Cambridge.

———. 1998. "The Homeric Poems as Oral Dictated Texts." *Classical Quarterly* 48:135–167.

Jenkins, T. E. 1999. "*Homēros ekainopoiēse*: Theseus, Aithra, and Variation in Homeric Myth-Making." In Carlisle and Levaniouk 1999:207–226.

Jensen, Minna Skafte. 1980. *The Homeric Question and Oral-Formulaic Theory*. Copenhagen.

———. 1982. "A. B. Lord's Concept of Transitional Texts in Relation to the Homeric Epics." In *The Epic: Oral and Written*, ed. L. Honko, J. Handoo, and J. M. Foley, 94–114. Mysore.

———. 1999. "Dividing Homer: When and How were the *Iliad* and the *Odyssey* Divided into Songs?" *Symbolae Osloenses* 74:5–91.

———. 2005. "Performance." In Foley 2005:45–54.

———. 2011. *Writing Homer*. Copenhagen.

Johansen, Knud F. 1967. *The* Iliad *in Early Greek Art*. Munksgaard.

Jones, Peter V. 1988. "The κλέος of Telemachus: *Odyssey* 1.95." *American Journal of Philology* 109:496–506.

———. 1995. "Poetic Invention: The Fighting around Troy in the First Nine Years of the Trojan War." In Andersen and Dickie 1995:101–111.

Jones, Alexander. 2015. "Greek Mathematical Astronomy." In *Handbook of Archaeoastronomy and Ethnoastronomy*, ed. Clive L.N. Ruggles, 1583–1588. New York.

Kahane, Ahuvia. 1997. "Quantifying Epic." In Morris and Powell 1997:326–342.

Kakridis, Johannes Th. 1949. *Homeric Researches*. Lund.
———. 1961. "Achilleus Rüstung." *Hermes* 89:288–297.
———. 1971. *Homer Revisited*. Lund.
Kalinka, Ernst. 1943. *Agamemnon in der Ilias*. Vienna.
Karkowski, Czesław. 2007. *Ze wszystkich śmiertelnych najokrutniejsi. Iliada dziś*. Wrocław.
———. 2014. *Iliada na nowo opowiedziana*. New York.
Katz, Joshua T. 2005. "The Indo-European Context." In Foley 2005:20–30.
Katzung, Peter Gerhard. 1960. *Die Diapeira in der Iliashandlung*. Frankfurt.
Kazazis, John N., and Antonios Rengakos, eds. 1999. *Euphrosyne: Studies in Ancient Epic and Its Legacy in Honor of Dimitris N. Marnitis*. Stuttgart.
Kelly, Adrian. 2006. "Neoanalysis and the Nestorbedrängnis: A Test Case." *Hermes* 134:1–25.
———. 2007a. *A Referential Commentary and Lexicon to Homer*: Iliad *VIII*. Oxford.
———. 2007b. "How to End an Oral-Derived Epic Poem." *Transactions of the American Philological Association* 137:371–402.
———. 2008. "Performance and Rivalry: Homer, Odysseus, and Hesiod." In Revermann and Wilson 2008:177–203.
———. 2012. "The Mourning of Thetis: 'Allusion' and the Future in the *Iliad*." In Montanari, Rengakos, and Tsagalis 2012:221–265.
Kennedy, George A. 1980. *Classical Rhetoric and Its Christian and Secular Tradition from Ancient to Modern Times*. London.
Kim, Jinyo. 2000. *The Pity of Achilles: Oral Style and the Unity of the* Iliad. Lanham, MD.
King, Katherine. 1987. *Achilles: Paradigms of the War Hero from Homer to the Middle Ages*. Berkeley.
Kiparsky, Paul. 1976. "Oral Poetry: Some Linguistic and Typological Considerations." In Stolz and Shannon 1976:73–106.
Kirk, Geoffrey S. 1962. *The Songs of Homer*. Cambridge.
———. 1964. "The Character of the Tradition." *The Journal of Hellenic Studies* 84:12–17.
———. 1966. "Formular Language and Oral Quality." *Yale Classical Studies* 20:153–174.
———. 1970. *Myth: Its Meaning and Functions in Ancient and Other Cultures*. Cambridge.
———. 1976. *Homer and the Oral Tradition*. Cambridge.
———. 1985. *The* Iliad: *A Commentary*. Vol. I. *Books 1–4*. Cambridge.
———. 1990. *The* Iliad: *A Commentary*. Vol. II. *Books 5–8*. Cambridge.

Knight, Richardus P. 1816. *Prolegomena ad Homerum sive de carminum homericorum origine auctore et aetate itemque de priscae linguae progressu et praecoci maturitate maturitate*. Leipzig.

Knox, Mary. 1979. "Polyphemos and His Near-Eastern Relations." *The Journal of Hellenic Studies* 99:164–165.

Köhnken, Adolf. 1976. "Die Narbe des Odysseus: Ein Beitrag zur homerisch-epischen Erzähltechnik." *Antike und Abendland* 22:101–114.

Kopff, E. Christian. 1981. "Virgil and the Cyclic Epics." *Aufstieg und Niedergang der römischen Welt* 2 31: 919–947.

———. 1983. "The Structure of the *Amazonia* (*Aethiopis*)." In *The Greek Renaissance of the Eighth Century B.C.: Tradition and Innovation*, ed. R. Hägg, 57–67. Stockholm.

Kouklanakis, Andrea. 1999. "Thersites, Odysseus, and the Social Order." In Carlisle and Levaniouk 1999:35–53.

Kraut, C. B. 1863. *Die epische Prolepsis, nachgewiesen in der Ilias, ein Beitrag zur Kenntniss des epischen Stils*. Tübingen.

Kretschmer, Paul. 1930. *Kleinasiatische Forschungen*. Band I. Ferdinand Sommer and Hans Ehelolf, eds. Weimar.

Krischer, Tilman. 1971. *Formale Konventionen der homerischen Epic*. Zetemata 56. Munich.

Kullmann, Wolfgang. 1960. *Die Quellen der* Ilias *(Troischer Sagenkreis)*. Hermes Einzelschrift 14. Wiesbaden.

———. 1968. "Vergangenheit und Zukunft in der *Ilias*." *Poetica* 2:15–37.

———. 1981. "Zur Methode der Neoanalyse in der Homerforschung." *Wiener Studien Zeitschrift für Klassische Philologie und Patristik* 15:5–42.

———. 1984. "Oral Poetry Theory and Neoanalysis in Homeric Research." *Greek, Roman, and Byzantine Studies* 25:307–323.

———. 1985. "Gods and Men in the *Iliad* and the *Odyssey*." *Harvard Studies in Classical Philology* 89:1–23.

———. 1986. "Friedrich Gottlieb Welcker über Homer und den epischen Kyklos." In *Friedrich Gottlieb Welcker: Werk und Wirkung*, ed. W. M. Calder III, Adolf Köhnken, Wolfgang Kullmann, and G. Pflug, 105–130. Hermes Einzelschriften 49. Stuttgart.

———. 1991. "Ergebnisse der motivgeschichtlichen Forschung zu Homer (Neoanalyse)." In *Zweihundert Jahre Homer-Forschung*, ed. Joachim Latacz, 425–455. Stuttgart.

———. 2002. "Homer und das Troia der späten Bronzezeit." In *Realität, Imagination und Theorie: Kleine Schriften zu Epos und Tragodie in der Antike*, ed. Wolfgang Kullmann and Antonios Rengakos, 97–138. Stuttgart.

———. 2005. "*Ilias* und *Aithiopis*." *Hermes*:9–28.

———. 2009. "Poesie, Mythos und Realität im Schiffskatalog der *Ilias*." *Hermes* 137:1–20.

———. 2012. "Neoanalysis between Orality and Literacy: Some Remarks Concerning the Development of Greek Myths Including the Legend of the Capture of Troy." In Montanari, Rengakos, and Tsagalis 2012:13–25.

———. 2015. "Motif and Source Research: Neoanalysis, Homer, and Cyclic Epic." In Fantuzzi and Tsagalis 2015:108–125.

Kullmann, Wolfgang, and Michael Reichel, eds. 1990. *Der Übergang von der Mündlichkeit zur Literatur bei den Griechen*. Scripta Oralia 30. Tübingen.

Kumaniecki, Kazimierz, and Jerzy Mańkowski. 1974. *Homer*. Warsaw.

Kumpf, M. M. 1984. *Four Indices of Homeric Hapax Legomena*. Hildesheim.

Kyriakou, Poulheria. 2001. "Warrior Vaunts in the *Iliad*." *Rheinisches Museum* 144:250–277.

Lanata, Guiliana. 1963. *Poetica pre-platonica: Testimoniaze e frammenti*. Florence.

Lang, Mabel L. 1983. "Reverberation and Mythology in the *Iliad*." In Rubino and Shelmerdine 1983:140–164.

Latacz, Joachim. 1979. "Homer: Tradition und Neuerung." In Latacz 1979:1–44.

———, ed. 1979. *Homer: Tradition und Neuerung*. Darmstadt.

———. 1989. *Homer: Der erste Dichter des Abendlands*. Munich.

———. 1995. *Achilleus: Die Wandlung eines europäischen Helden*. Stuttgart.

———. 1997. "Epischer Zyklus (ἐπικὸς κύκλος)." In *Der Neue Pauly*, ed. H. Cancik and H. Schneider, vol. 3, cols. 1154–1156. Stuttgart.

———. 2004. *Troy and Homer: Towards a Solution of an Old Mystery*. Oxford.

Lateiner, Donald. 2004. "The *Iliad*: An Unpredictable Classic." In Fowler 2004:11–30.

Lattimore, Richmond, trans. 1951. *The* Iliad *of Homer*. Chicago.

———, trans. 1967. *The* Odyssey *of Homer*. New York.

———. 1969. "Nausikaa's Suitors." *Classical Studies Presented to Ben Edwin Perry*, 88–102. Urbana, IL.

Leaf, Walter. 1900–1902. *The* Iliad. 2 vols. London.

Lengauer, Włodzimierz. 1999. *Starożytna Grecja okresu archaicznego i klasycznego*. Warsaw.

Lesky, Albin. 1961. *Göttliche und menschliche Motivation im homerischen Epos*. Sitzungsberichte der Heidelberger Akademie der Wissenschaften, philosophische-historische Klasse. Heidelberg.

———. 1963. *Geschichte der griechischen Literatur*. Bern.

———. 1966. "Aithiopika." In *Gesammelte Schriften*, ed. Walther Kraus, 410–421. Bern.

———. 1967. "Oral Poetry als Voraussetzung der homerischen Epen." In *Homeros, Sonderausgabe der Paulyschen Realencyclopädie der Klassischen Altertumswissenschaft*, Supplement-Band IX, 7–18. Stuttgart.

Lévi-Strauss, Claude. 1958. *Anthropologie structurale*. Paris.

———. 1970. *The Raw and the Cooked*. Trans. J. and D. Weightman. London.

Levy, Gertrude R. 1953. *The Sword from the Rock: An Investigation into the Origins of Epic Literature and the Development of the Hero*. London.

Liapis, Vayos. 2006. "Intertextuality as Irony: Heracles in Epic and in Sophocles." *Greece and Rome* 53:48–59.

Lincoln, Bruce. 1975. "Homeric λύσσα: Wolfish Rage." *Indogermanische Forschungen* 80:98–105.

Lloyd-Jones, Hugh. 1971. *The Justice of Zeus*. Berkeley.

Lohmann, Dieter. 1970. *Die Komposition der Reden in der* Ilias. Untersuchungen zur antiken Literatur und Geschichte 6. Berlin.

Lord, Albert B. 1936. "Homer and Huso I: The Singer's Rests in Greek and Southslavic Heroic Song." *Transactions of the American Philological Association* 67:106–113.

———. 1938. "Homer and Huso II: Narrative Inconsistencies in Homer and Oral Poetry." *Transactions of the American Philological Association* 69:439–445.

———. 1951. "Composition by Theme in Homer and Southslavic Epos." *Transactions of the American Philological Association* 82:71–80.

———. 1953. "Homer's Originality: Oral Dictated Texts." *Transactions of the American Philological Association* 84:124–134.

———. 1960. *The Singer of Tales*. Cambridge, MA.

———. 1962. "Homer and Other Epic Poetry." In *A Companion to Homer*, ed. A. J. B. Wace and F. H. Stubbings, 179–214. London.

———. 1968. "Homer as an Oral Poet." *Harvard Studies in Classical Philology* 72:1–46.

———. trans. 1974. *The Wedding of Smailagić Meho, by Avdo Medjedović*. Serbo-Croatian Heroic Songs 3. Cambridge, MA.

———. 1976. *The Traditional Song*. In Stolz and Shannon 1976:1–29.

———. 1978. "The Ancient Greek Heritage in Modern Balkan Epic." *Slavjanskie kul'tury i Balkany* [Sofia] 2:337–355.

———. 1981. "Memory, Fixity, and Genre in Oral Traditional Poetries." In Foley 1981:451–461.

———. 1986. "Preface." In *Oral Tradition and Literacy: Changing Visions of the World*, ed. Richard A. Whitaker and Edgard R. Sienaert, ix–xii. Durban.

———. 1991. *Epic Singers and Oral Tradition*. Ithaca.

———. 1995. *The Singer Resumes the Tale*. Ithaca.

Louden, Bruce. 1999. *The* Odyssey: *Structure, Narration and Meaning*. Baltimore.

Lowenstam, Steven. 1981. *The Death of Patroklos: A Study in Typology*. Beiträge zur Klassischen Philologie 133. Königstein/Ts.

———. 1997. "Talking Vases: The Relationship between the Homeric Poems and Archaic Representations of Epic Myth." *Transactions of the American Philological Association* 127:21–76.

———. 2008. *As Witnessed by Images: The Trojan War Tradition in Greek and Etruscan Art*. Baltimore.

Luce, John V. 1975. *Homer and the Heroic Age*. London.

———. 2003. "The Case for Historical Significance in Homer's Landmarks at Troia." In *Troia and the Troad: Scientific Approaches*, ed. G. A. Wagner, E. Pernicka, and H. P. Uerpmann, 9–30. Berlin.

MacDowell, Douglas. 1976. "'*Hybris*' in Athens." *Greece and Rome* 23:14–31.

Mackay, E. A., ed. 2007. *Orality and Literacy in Ancient Greece*. Vol. 7, *Orality, Literacy, Memory in the Ancient Greek and Roman World.* Mnemosyne, Supplements 298. Leiden.

Mackie, Hilary S. 1996. *Talking Trojan: Speech and Community in the* Iliad. Lanham, MD.

———. 1997. "Achilles' Teachers: Chiron and Phoenix in the *Iliad*." *Greece and Rome* 44:1–10.

MacLachlan, Bonnie. 1992. "Feasting with Ethiopians: Life on the Fringe." *Quaderni Urbinati di Cultura Classica* n.s. 40:15–33.

Macleod, Colin. 1983. "Homer on Poetry and the Poetry of Homer." In *Collected Essays*, ed. Oliver Taplin, 1–15. Oxford.

Maiullari, Franco. 2003. "La mosca, un parodistico simbolo del doppio in Omero (ovvero, la mosca e Tersite)." *Quaderni Urbinati di Cultura Classica* n.s. 74:33–68.

Marg, Walter. 1956. "Das erste Lied des Demodokos." In *Navicula Chiloniensis: Studia philologa Felici Jacoby Professori Chiloniensi Emerito Octogenario Oblata*, 16–29. Leiden.

Marks, Jim. 2002. "The Junction between the *Kypria* and the *Iliad*." *Phoenix* 56:1–24.

———. 2003. "Alternative Odysseys: The Case of Thoas and Odysseus." *Transactions of the American Philological Association* 133:209–226.

———. 2005. "The Ongoing *Neikos*: Thersites, Odysseus, and Achilleus." *American Journal of Philology* 126:1–31.

———. 2012. "Ἀρχοὺς αὖ νεῶν ἐρέω: A Programmatic Function of the Iliadic Catalogue of Ships." In Montanari, Rengakos, and Tsagalis 2012:101–112.

Marquardt, Patricia A. 1992. "Clytemnestra: A Felicitous Spelling in the *Odyssey*." *Arethusa* 25:241–254.

Martin, Richard P. 1989. *The Language of Heroes: Speech and Performance in the* Iliad. Ithaca.

———. 1993. "Telemachus and the Last Hero Song." *Colby Quarterly* 29:222–240.

———. 1997. "Similes and Performance." In Bakker and Kahane 1997:138–166.

———. 2001. "Rhapsodizing Orpheus." *Kernos* 14:23–33.

———. 2005. "Epic as Genre." In Foley 2005:9–19.

Mayer, Kenneth. 1996. "Helen and the ΔΙΟΣ ΒΟΥΛΗ." *American Journal of Philology* 117:1–15.

Mehmel, Friedrich. 1954. "Homer und die Griechen." *Antike und Abendland* 4:16–41.

Meister, Karl. 1921. *Homerische Kunstsprache*. Leipzig.

Meletinsky, Eleazar. 2009. *Pochodzenie eposu bohaterskiego. Wczesne formy i archaiczne zabytki*. Trans. P. Rojek. Cracow.

Merkelbach, Reinhold. 1960. "Aiante." *Glotta* 38:268–270

Merry, William W., and James Riddell. 1886. *Homer's* Odyssey *Books I–XII*. Oxford.

Meuli, Karl. 1935. "Scythica." *Hermes* 70:121–176.

Miller, Andrew M. 1985. *From Delos to Delphi: A Literary Study of the Homeric Hymn to Apollo*. Leiden.

Miller, Dean A. 2000. *The Epic Hero*. Baltimore.

Minchin, Elizabeth. 1986. "The Interpretation of a Theme in Oral Epic: '*Iliad*' 24.559-70." *Greece and Rome* 33:11–19.

———. 1996. "The Performance of Lists and Catalogues in the Homeric Epics." In *Voice Into Text: Orality and Literacy in Ancient Greece*, ed. I. Worthington, 3–20. Leiden.

———. 2001. *Homer and the Resources of Memory: Some Applications of Cognitive Theory to the* Iliad *and the* Odyssey. Oxford.

———. 2007. "Spatial Memory and the Composition of the *Iliad*." In Mackay 2007:9–35.

———. 2012. "Memory and Memories: Personal, Social, and Cultural Memory in the Poems of Homer." In Montanari, Rengakos, and Tsagalis 2012:83–99.

Minton, William W. 1960. "Homer's Invocations of the Muses: Traditional Patterns." *Transactions of the American Philological Association* 91:292–309.

———. 1965. "The Fallacy of the Structural Formula." *Transactions of the American Philological Association* 96:241–253.

Mondi, Robert. 1990. "Greek Mythic Thought in the Light of the Near East." In Edmunds 1990:142–198.

Monro, David B. 1884. "The Poems of the Epic Cycle." *The Journal of Hellenic Studies* 5:1–41.

Montanari, Franco. 2012. "Introduction: The Homeric Question Today." In Montanari, Rengakos, and Tsagalis 2012:1–10.

Montanari, Franco, Antonios Rengakos, and Christos C. Tsagalis, eds. 2012. *Homeric Contexts: Neoanalysis and the Interpretation of Oral Poetry*. Berlin.

Moore, M. B. 1982. "The Death of Pedasos." *American Journal of Archaeology* 86:578–581.

Morris, Ian. 1986. "The Use and Abuse of Homer." *Classical Antiquity* 5:81–138.

———. 1997. "Homer and the Iron Age." In Morris and Powell 1997:535–559.

Morris, Ian, and B. Powell, eds. 1997. *A New Companion to Homer*. Leiden.

Morris, Sarah P. 1989. "A Tale of Two Cities: The Miniature Frescoes from Thera and the Origins of Greek Poetry." *American Journal of Archaeology* 93:511–535.

———. 1995. "The Sacrifice of Astyanax: Near Eastern Contributions to the Siege of Troy." In Carter and Morris 1995:221–246.

———. 1997. "Homer and the Near East." In I. Morris and Powell 1997:599–623.

Morrison, James V. 1992a. "Alternatives to the Epic Tradition: Homer's Challenges in the *Iliad*." *Transactions of the American Philological Association* 122:61–71.

———. 1992b. *Homeric Misdirection: False Predictions in the* Iliad. Ann Arbor.

Mühlestein, Hugo. 1972. "Euphorbos und der Tod Patroklos." *Studi micenei ed egeo-anatolici* 15:79–90.

Mueller, Martin. 1984. *The* Iliad. London.

Muellner, Leonard C. 1996. *The Anger of Achilles: Mēnis in Early Greek Epic*. Ithaca.

———. 2012. "Grieving Achilles." In Montanari, Rengakos, and Tsagalis 2012:197–220.

Mülder, Dietrich. 1910. *Die Ilias und ihre Quellen*. Berlin.

Murnaghan, Sheila. 1997. "Equal Honor and Future Glory: The Plan of Zeus in the *Iliad*." *Classical Closure*, ed. D. H. Roberts, F. M. Dunn, and F. Fowler, 23–42. Princeton.

Murray, Gilbert. 1907. *The Rise of the Greek Epic*. Oxford.

Musurillo, Herbert. 1961. *Symbol and Myth in Ancient Poetry*. Westport, CT.

Myerhoff Barbara. 1976. *Peyote Hunt: The Sacred Journey of the Huichol Indians*. Ithaca.

Nagler, Michael N. 1974. *Spontaneity and Tradition: A Study in the Oral Art of Homer*. Berkeley.

———. 1988. "Toward a Semantics of Ancient Conflict: *Eris* in the *Iliad*." *Classical World* 82:81–90.

Nagy, Gregory. 1973. "Phaeton, Sappho's Phaon, and the White Rock of Leukas." *Harvard Studies in Classical Philology* 77:137–178.

———. 1974. *Comparative Studies in Greek and Indic Meter*. Cambridge, MA.

———. 1976. "Formula and Meter." In Stolz and Shannon 1976:239–260.

———. 1981. "An Evolutionary Model for the Text Fixation of Homeric Epos." In Foley 1981:390-393.

———. 1985. “Theognis and Megara: A Poet’s Vision of His City.” In Figueira and Nagy 1985:31–34.
———. 1986. “Ancient Greek Epic and Praise Poetry: Some Typological Considerations.” In *Oral Tradition in Literature: Interpretation in Context*, ed. John M. Foley, 89–102. Columbia, MO.
———. 1989. “Early Greek Views of Poets and Poetry.” In *The Cambridge History of Literary Criticism*. Vol. 1, *Classical Criticism*, ed. G. Kennedy, 1–77. Cambridge.
———. 1990a. *Greek Mythology and Poetics*. Ithaca.
———. 1990b. *Pindar’s Homer: The Lyric Possession of an Epic Past*. Baltimore.
———. 1992. “Homeric Questions.” *Transactions of the American Philological Association* 122:17–60.
———. 1995. “An Evolutionary Model for the Making of Homeric Poetry: Comparative Perspectives.” In Carter and Morris 1995:163–179.
———. 1996a. *Poetry as Performance: Homer and Beyond*. Cambridge.
———. 1996b. *Homeric Questions*. Austin.
———. 1999. *The Best of the Achaeans: Concepts of the Hero in Archaic Greek Poetry*. Baltimore. Orig. pub. 1979.
———. 2001. “Homeric Poetry and Problems of Multiformity: The ‘Panathenaic Bottleneck’.” *Classical Philology* 96:109–119.
———. 2002. “The Language of Heroes as Mantic Poetry: *Hypokrisis* in Homer.” In Reichel and Rengakos 2002:141–149.
———. 2003a. *Homeric Responses*. Austin.
———. 2003b. “Oral Poetics and Homeric Poetry.” *Oral Tradition* 18:73–75.
———. 2004. *Homer’s Text and Language*. Urbana.
———. 2005. “The Epic Hero.” In Foley 2005:71–89.
———. 2008. *Homer the Classic*. Hellenic Studies 36. Washington, DC. http://nrs.harvard.edu/urn-3:hul.ebook:CHS_Nagy.Homer_the_Classic.2008
———. 2010. *Homer the Preclassic*. Berkeley.
———. 2012. “Signs of Hero Cult in Homeric Poetry.” In Montanari, Rengakos, and Tsagalis 2012:27–71.
———. 2013. *The Ancient Hero in 24 Hours*. Cambridge, MA.
———. 2015. “Oral Traditions, Written Texts, and Questions of Authorship.” In Fantuzzi and Tsagalis 2015:59–77.
Nakassis, Dimitri. 2004. “Gemination at the Horizons: East and West in the Mythical Geography of Archaic Greek Epic.” *Transactions of the American Philological Association* 134:215–233.
Neils Jenifer, ed.1992. *Goddess and Polis: The Panathenaic Festival in Ancient Athens*. Princeton.
Nelson, Thomas J. 2021. “Intertextual *Agōnes* in Archaic Greek Epic: Penelope vs. *Catalogue of Women*.” *Yearbook of Ancient Greek Epic* 5:25–57.

———. 2022. “Iphigenia in the *Iliad* and the Architecture of Homeric Allusion.” *Transactions of the American Philological Association* 152:55–101.

Newton, Rick M. 1984. “The Rebirth of Odysseus.” *Greek, Roman, and Byzantine Studies* 25:5–20.

Nickel, Roberto. 1997. *Paris in the Epic Tradition: A Study in Homeric Techniques of Characterization*. PhD diss., University of Toronto.

———. 2002. “Euphorbus and the Death of Achilles.” *Phoenix* 56:215–233.

———. 2003. “The Wrath of Demeter: Story-Pattern in the ‘Hymn to Demeter’.” *Quaderni Urbinati di Cultura Classica* n.s. 73:59–82.

Nilsson, M. P. 1968–1974. *Geschichte der griechischen Religion*. 2 vols. Handbuch der Altertumswissenschaft 5.2. Munich.

Nimis, Steve. 1986. “The Language of Achilles: Construction vs. Representation.” *Classical World* 79:217–225.

Notopoulos, James A. 1949. “Parataxis in Homer.” *Transactions of the American Philological Association* 80:1–23.

———. 1950. “The Generic and Oral Composition in Homer.” *Transactions of the American Philological Association* 81:28–36.

———. 1951. “Continuity and Interconnection in Homeric Oral Composition.” *Transactions of the American Philological Association* 82:81–101.

———. 1952. “Homer and Cretan Heroic Poetry: A Study in Comparative Oral Poetry.” *American Journal of Philology* 73:225–250.

———. 1957. “Homer and Geometric Art: A Comparative Study in the Formulaic Technique of Composition.” *Athena* 61:65–93.

———. 1962. “The Homeric Hymns as Oral Poetry: The Study of the Post-Homeric Oral Tradition.” *American Journal of Philology* 83:337–368.

———. 1964. “Studies in Early Greek Oral Poetry.” *Harvard Studies in Classical Philology* 68:1–77.

Obbink, Dirk. 2005. “4708. Archilochus. Elegies (more on VI 854 and XXX 2507).” *The Oxyrhynchus Papyri* 69:18–42.

Oinas, F., ed. 1978. *Heroic Epic and Saga*. Bloomington.

Olshausen, Eckart. 1991. *Einführung in die historische Geographie der alten Welt*. Darmstadt.

Olson, S. Douglas. 1989. “The Stories of Helen and Menelaus (Odyssey 4.240–89) and the Return of Odysseus.” *American Journal of Philology* 110:387–394.

———. 1990. “The Stories of Agamemnon in Homer’s *Odyssey*.” *Transactions of the American Philological Association* 120:57–71.

Ong, Walter Jackson. 2002. *Orality and Literacy: The Technologizing of the Word*. New York.

Ossendrijver, Mathieu. 2015. "Babylonian Mathematical Astronomy." In *Handbook of Archaeoastronomy and Ethnoastronomy*, ed. Clive L. N. Ruggles, 1863–1870. New York.

O'Sullivan, James. 1981. "The Sign of the Bed: *Odyssey* 23.173ff." *Greek, Roman, and Byzantine Studies* 25:21–25.

Ovenden, Michael William. 1965. "The Origin of the Constellations." *Philosophical Journal* 3:1–18.

Page, Denys L. 1955a. *Sappho and Alcaeus*. Oxford.

———. 1955b. *The Homeric* Odyssey. Oxford.

———. 1959. *History and the Homeric* Iliad. Sather Classical Lectures 31. Berkeley.

———. 1964. "Homer and the Trojan War." *Journal of Hellenic Studies* 84:17–20.

———. 1973. *Folktales in Homer's* Odyssey. Cambridge, MA.

Pagliaro, Antonino. 1951. "La terminologia poetica di Omero e l'origine dell'epica." *Ricerche Linguistiche* 2:1–46.

Paipetis, S. A., and V. Kostopoulos. 2008. "Defensive Weapons in Homer." In *Science and Technology in Homeric Epics*, ed. S. A. Paipetis, 181–204. New York.

Parker, Robert. 1983. *Miasma: Pollution and Purification in early Greek Religion*. Oxford.

Parry, Adam. 1956a. "The Language of Achilles." *Transactions of the American Philological Association* 87:1–7.

———. 1956b. "Language and Characterization in Homer." *Harvard Studies in Classical Philology* 76:1–22.

———. 1966. "Have We Homer's *Iliad*?" *Yale Classical Studies* 20:175–216.

Parry, Hugh. 1994. "The *Apologos* of Odysseus: Lies, All Lies?" *Phoenix* 48:1–20.

Parry, Milman. 1971. *The Making of Homeric Verse: The Collected Papers of Milman Parry*. Ed. Adam Parry. Oxford.

Paton, William R. 1912. "The Armour of Achilles." *Classical Review* 26:1–4.

Patzek, Barbara. 1992. *Homer und Mykene: Mündliche Dichtung und Geschichtsschreibung*. Munich.

———. 1996. "Homer und der Orient." In *Vom Halys zum Eufrat: Thomas Beran zu Ehren*, ed. U. Magen and M. Rashad, 215–225. Münster.

Patzer, Harald. 1972. *Dichterische Kunst und poetisches Handwerk im homerischen Epos*. Wiesbaden.

Pavese, Carlo O. 1998. "The Rhapsodic Epic Poems as Oral and Independent Poems." *Harvard Studies in Classical Philology* 98:63–90.

Pelliccia, H. 2003. "Two Points about Rhapsodes." In *Homer, the Bible, and Beyond: Literary and Religious Canons in the Ancient World*, ed. M. Finkelberg and G. G. Stroumsa, 98–116. Leiden.

Penglase, Charles. 1994. *Greek Myths and Mesopotamia: Parallels and Influence in the Homeric Hymns and Hesiod*. London.

Peradotto, John. 1997. "Modern Theoretical Approaches to Homer." In Morris and Powell 1997:380–395.

Pestalozzi, Heinrich. 1945. *Die Achilleis als Quelle der Ilias*. Zurich.

Petersmann, Hubert. 1981. "Homer und das Märchen." *Wiener Studien Zeitschrift für Klassische Philologie und Patristik* 15:43–68.

Petropoulou, Angeliki. 1988. "The Interment of Patroklos." *American Journal of Philology* 109:482–495.

Petrosyan, A. Y. 2002. *The Indo-European and Ancient Near Eastern Sources of the Armenian Epic: Myth and History*. Washington, DC.

Pigoń, Jakub. 2004. *Ze studiów nad technikami narracyjnymi Tacyta. Wypowiedzi proleptyczne*. [Tacitus' Proleptic Statements. A Contribution to the Study of the Narrative Techniques in the *Histories* and the *Annals*]. Wrocław. Classica Wratislaviensia 23.

Pinney, Gloria F. 1983. "Achilles Lord of Scythia." In *Ancient Greek Art and Iconography*, ed. W. G. Moon, 127–146. Madison, WI.

Pippin-Burnett, Anne. 1983. *Three Archaic Poets: Archilochus, Alcaeus, Sappho*. London.

Pizzocaro, Massimo. 1999. "Il canto nuovo di Femio: Le origini dell' epos storico." *Quaderni Urbinati di Cultura Classica* n.s. 61:7–33.

Podbielski, Henryk. 2005. "Homer." In *Literatura Grecji Starożytnej, t. I: Epika—Liryka—Dramat*, ed. H. Podbielski. Lublin.

Pontani, Filippomaria. 2007–2020. *Scholia Graeca in Odysseam*. 4 vols. Rome.

Pope, M. 1985. "A Nonce-Word in the *Iliad*." *Classical Quarterly* 35:1–8.

Popko, Maciej. 1971. "Orientalna geneza *Teogonii*." *Meander* 26:463–473.

———. 1991. "Kult świętego runa w hetyckiej Anatolii." *Meander* 3:225–230.

Porucznik, Joanna. 2013. *Anonimowy periplus Morza Czarnego*. Wrocław.

Pötscher, Walter. 1961. "Hera und Heros." *Rheinisches Museum* 104:302–355.

Propp, Vladimir. 1955. *Russkij geroičeskij epos*. Leningrad.

———. 2009. *Morphology of the Folktake*. Trans. L. Scott. Austin.

Pucci, Pietro. 1987. *Odysseus Polutropos: Intertextual Readings in the* Odyssey *and the* Iliad. Ithaca.

Puelma, Mario. 1972. "Sänger und König: Zum Verständnis von Hesiods Tierfabel." *Museum Helveticum* 29:86–109.

Pulleyn, Simon. 2000. *Homer:* Iliad, *Book One*. Ed. with an Introduction, Translation, and Commentary. Oxford.

Putilov, B. 2001. "O prozaizmach i besformul'nych stichach u Kirshy Danilova." *Russkij Fol'klor* 31:68–76.

Raaflaub, Kurt A. 1997. "Homeric Society." In Morris and Powell 1997:624–648.

———. 2005. "Epic and History." In Foley 2005:55–70.

Rabel, Robert J. 1988. "Chryses and the Opening of the *Iliad.*" *American Journal of Philology* 109:473–481.

———. 1990a. "Apollo as a Model for Achilles in the *Iliad.*" *American Journal of Philology* 111:429–440.

———. 1990b. "Hippothous and the Death of Achilles." *The Classical Journal* 86:126–130.

———. 1991. "The Theme of Need in *Iliad* 9–11." *Phoenix* 45:83–295.

Race, William H. 1993. "First Appearances in the *Odyssey.*" *Transactions of the American Philological Association* 123:79–107.

Ready, Jonathan L. 2019. *Orality, Textuality, and the Homeric Epics: An Interdisciplinary Study of Oral Texts, Dictated Texts, and Wild Texts.* Oxford.

Redfield, James M. 1979. "The Proem of the *Iliad*: Homer's Art." *Classical Philology* 74:95–110.

———. 1994. *Nature and Culture in the* Iliad*: The Tragedy of Hector.* Chicago.

Reece, Steve. 1993. *The Stranger's Welcome: Oral Theory and the Aesthetics of the Homeric Hospitality Scene.* Ann Arbor.

Reeve, M. D. 1973. "The Language of Achilles." *Classical Quarterly* 23:193–195.

Reichel, Michael. 1990. "Retardationstechniken in der *Ilias.*" In Kullmann and Reichel 1990:125–151.

———. 1994. *Fernbeziehungen in der* Ilias. Script-Oralia 62. Tübingen.

Reichel, Michael, and Antonios Rengakos, eds. 2002. *Epea Pteroenta: Beiträge zur Homerforschung.* Stuttgart.

Reichert, Hermann. 1985. *Nibelungenlied und Nibelungensage.* Vienna/Cologne.

Reinhardt, Karl. 1938. *Das Parisurteil.* Frankfurt.

———. 1961. *Die Ilias und ihr Dichter.* Göttingen.

Renehan, Robert. 1987. "The *Heldentod* in Homer: One Heroic Ideal." *Classical Philology* 82:99–116.

Rengakos, Antonios. 1999. "Spannungsstrategien in den homerischen Epen." In Kazazis and Rengakos 1999:309–338.

———. 2002. "Narrativität, Intertextualität, Selbstreferentialität: Die neue Deutung der *Odyssee.*" In Reichel and Rengakos 2002:173–192.

———. 2015. "Narrative Techniques in the Epic Cycle." In Fantuzzi and Tsagalis 2015:154–163.

Revermann, M., and P. Wilson, eds. 2008. *Performance, Iconography, Reception: Studies in Honour of Oliver Taplin.* Oxford.

Reynolds, Dwight F. 1995. *Heroic Poets, Poetic Heroes: The Ethnography of Performance in an Arabic Oral Tradition.* Ithaca.

Richardson, Nicholas J. 1987. "The Individuality of Homer's Language." In *Homer: Beyond Oral Poetry: Recent Trends in Homeric Interpretation*, ed. J. M. Bremer, Irene J. F. de Jong, and J. Kalff, 165–184. Amsterdam.

———. 1993. *The* Iliad*: A Commentary*. Vol. VI, *Books 21-24*. Cambridge.

Richardson, Scott. 1990. *The Homeric Narrator*. Nashville.

Robbins, Emmet. 1993. "The Education of Achilles." *Quaderni Urbinati di Cultura Classica* n.s. 45:7–20.

Robert, Carl. 1923. *Die Griechische Heldensage, Drittes Buch: Die Grossen Helden epen, 2. Abteilung, Erste Hälfte: Der Troische Kreis bis zu Illions Zerstörung*. Berlin.

Robertson, Martin. 1970. "Laomedon's Corpse, Laomedon's Tomb." *Greek, Roman, and Byzantine Studies* 11:23–26.

———. 1990. "Troilos and Polyxene: Notes on a Changing Legend." In *EUMOUSIA*, ed. J.-P. Descœudres, 63–70. Sydney.

Robertson, Noel. 1992. *Festivals and Legends: The Formation of Greek Cities in the Light of Public Ritual*. Toronto.

Rohde, Erwin. 1903. *Psyche: Seelencult und Unsterblichkeitsglaube der Griechen*. Tübingen.

Roisman, Hanna M. 1990. "*Kerdion* in the *Iliad*: Profit and Trickiness." *Transactions of the American Philological Association* 120:23–35.

———. 2005a. "Nestor the Good Counsellor." *Classical Quarterly* 55:17–38.

———. 2005b. "Old Men and Chirping Cicadas in the *Teichoskopia*." In *Approaches to Homer: Ancient and Modern*, ed. R. J. Rabel, 105–118. Swansea.

———. 2006. "Helen in the *Iliad*; *Causa Belli* and Victim of War: From Silent Weaver to Public Speaker." *American Journal of Philology* 127:1–36.

———. 2007. "Right Rhetoric in Homer." In *A Companion to Greek Rhetoric*, ed. I. Worthington, 429–445. Hoboken.

Romm, James S. 1992. *The Edges of the Earth in Ancient Thought*. Princeton.

Rose, G. P. 1969a. "The Unfriendly Phaeacians." *Transactions of the American Philological Association* 100:387–406.

———. 1969b. *The Song of Ares and Aphrodite: Recurrent Motifs in Homer's* Odyssey. Berkeley.

———. 1979. "Odysseus' Barking Heart." *Transactions of the American Philological Association* 109:215–230.

Rose, H. J., and C. M. Robertson. 1970. "Achilles." In *The Oxford Classical Dictionary*. Oxford.

Rosner, Judith A. 1976. "The Speech of Phoenix: *Iliad* 9.434-605." *Phoenix* 30:314–327.

Rubin, David C. 1995. *Memory in Oral Traditions: The Cognitive Psychology of Epic, Ballads, and Counting-out Rhymes*. Oxford.

Rubino, C. A., and C. W. Shelmerdine, eds. 1983. *Approaches to Homer*. Austin.

Ruijgh, Cornelis J. 1985. "Le mycénien et Homère." In *Linear B: A 1984 Survey*, ed. A. Morpurgo-Davies and Y. Duhoux, 143–190. Louvain-la-Neuve.

———. 1995. "D'Homère aux origines proto-mycéniennes de la tradition épique: Analyse dialectologique du langage homérique, avec un excursus sur la création de l'alphabet grec." In *Homeric Questions*, ed. J. P. Crielaard, 1–96. Amsterdam.

Russo, Joseph. 1966. "The Structural Formula in Homeric Verse." *Yale Classical Studies* 20:219–240.

———. 1967. "Homeric Modifications of Formulaic Prototypes." *American Journal of Philology* 88:340–346.

———. 1968. "Homer against His Tradition." *Arion* 7:275–295.

———. 1976. "Is "Oral" or "Aural" Composition the Cause of Homer's Formulaic Style?" In Stolz and Shannon 1976:35–37.

———. 1997. "The Formula." In Morris and Powell 1997:238–260.

Rutherford, Richard B. 1982. "Tragic Form and Feeling in the *Iliad*." *The Journal of Hellenic Studies* 102:145–160.

———. 1993. "From the *Iliad* to the *Odyssey*." *Bulletin of the Institute for Classical Studies* 38:37–54.

Ryan, G. J. 1965. "Helen in Homer." *Classical Journal* 61:115–117.

Rzach, A. 1922. "Kyklos." *Real Encyclopädie*, vol. 11. 2, cols. 2347–2435. Stuttgart.

Sabynin, A. 1995. "Diskrietno-ritmitcheskije konstrukcji kak kharakternyj priznak ustojtchivosti bylinnogo tieksta." *Russkij Fol'klor* 28:217–229.

Sachse, Joanna. 2004. "Samochwalstwo i obelgi na polu bitwy w *Mahabharacie*." *Classica Wratislaviensia* 24:218–222.

———. 2005. "Szkice o *Mahabharacie*: historia pewnych kolczyków." *Classica Wratislaviensia* 26:246–249.

Sale, William M. 1964. "Achilles and Heroic Values." *Arion* 3:86–100.

———. 1987. "The Formularity of the Place Phrases of the *Iliad*." *Transactions of the American Philological Association* 117:21–50.

———. 1989. "The Trojans, Statistics, and Milman Parry." *Greek, Roman, and Byzantine Studies* 30:341–410.

———. 1993a. "Homer and Roland: The Shared Formular Technique, Part I." *Oral Tradition* 8:87–142.

———. 1993b. "Homer and Roland: The Shared Formular Technique, Part II." *Oral Tradition* 8:381–412.

Sammons, Benjamin. 2008. "Gift, List & Story in *Iliad* 9. 115–61." *Classical Journal* 103:353–379.

———. 2014. "The Quarrel of Agamemnon & Menelaus." *Mnemosyne* 67:1–27.

Sammons, N. 2010. *The Art and Rhetoric of the Homeric Catalogue*. Oxford.

Saussy, Haun. 2016. *The Ethnography of Rhythm: Orality and its Technologies*. New York.

Scaife, Allen Ross. 1995. "The *Kypria* and Its Early Reception." *Classical Antiquity* 14:164–197.

Schadewaldt, Wolfgang. 1935. "Homerische Szenen I: Hektor und Andromache." *Antike und Abendland* 11:149–170.

———. 1936. "Homerische Szenen: Die Entscheidung des Achilleus." *Antike und Abendland* 12:173–201.

———. 1938. *Iliasstudien*. Leipzig.

———. 1951. *Von Homers Welt und Werk: Aufsätze und Auslegungen zur homerischen Frage*. Stuttgart.

Schaefer, Ursula. 1997. "The Medial Approach: A Paradigm Shift in the Philologies?" In Bakker and Kahane 1997:215–231.

Schein, Seth L. 1980. "On Achilles' Speech to Odysseus, *Iliad* 9.308–429." *Eranos* 78:125–131.

———. 1984. *The Mortal Hero: An Introduction to Homer's* Iliad. Berkeley.

———. 1997. "The *Iliad*: Structure and Interpretation." In Morris and Powell 1997:345–359.

———. 2002. "The Horses of Achilles in Book 17 of the *Iliad*." In Reichel and Rengakos 2002:193–205.

Scheliha, R. 1943. *Patroklos*. Basel.

Schlunk, Robin R. 1976. "The Theme of the Suppliant-Exile in the *Iliad*." *American Journal of Philology* 97:199–209.

Schmid, W. 1925. "Der homerische Schiffskatalog und seine Bedeutung für die Datierung der *Ilias*." *Philologus* 80:67–88.

Schoeck, Georg. 1961. *Ilias und Aithiopis: Kyklische Motive in homerischer Brechung*. Zurich.

Schofield, Malcolm. 1986. "*Euboulia* in the *Iliad*." *Classical Quarterly* 36:6–31.

Scodel, Ruth. 1977. "Apollo's Perfidy: *Iliad* Ω 59–62." *Harvard Studies in Classical Philology* 81:55–57.

———. 1998. "Bardic Performance and Oral Tradition in Homer." *American Journal of Philology* 119:171–194.

———. 2002: *Listening to Homer: Tradition, Narrative, and Audience*. Ann Arbor.

———. 2004. "The Story-teller and His Audience." In Fowler 2004:45–55.

Scott, Littleton C. 1970. "Some Possible Indo-European Themes in the '*Iliad*'." In *Myth and Law among the Indo-Europeans: Studies in Indo-European Comparative Mythology*, ed. Jaan Puhvel, 229–246. Berkeley.

Scully, Stephen. 1981. "The Bard as a Custodian of Homeric Society: *Odyssey* 3.263–272." *Quaderni Urbinati di Cultura Classica* n.s. 8:67–83.

———. 1987. "Doubling in the tale of Odysseus." *Classical World* 80:401–417.

Seaford, Richard. 1994. *Reciprocity and Ritual: Homer and Tragedy in the Developing City-State*. Oxford.

Segal, Charles P. 1968. "The Embassy and the Duals of *Iliad* 9.182–98." *Greek, Roman, and Byzantine Studies* 9:97–114.

———. 1992. "Bard and Audience in Homer." In *Homer's Ancient Readers: The Hermeneutics of Greek Epic's Earliest Exegetes*, ed. R. Lamberton and J. J. Keaney, 3–29. Princeton.

———. 1994. *Singers, Heroes, and Gods in the* Odyssey. Ithaca.

Severyns, Albert. 1928. *Le Cycle épique dans l'école d'Aristarch*. Liège.

Shapiro, Harvey A. 1989. *Art and Cult under the Tyrants in Athens*. Mainz.

Shipp, G. P. 1972. *Studies in the Language of Homer*. Cambridge.

Shive, David M. 1987. *Naming Achilles*. Oxford.

Silk, Michael S. 1974. *Interaction in Poetic Imagery with Special Reference to Early Greek Poetry*. Cambridge.

———. 1987. *Homer. The* Iliad. Cambridge.

Simpson, R. H., and J. F. Lazenby. 1970. *The Catalogue of Ships in Homer's* Iliad. Oxford.

Singor, H. W. 1991. "Nine against Troy: On Epic ΦΑΛΑΝΓΕΣ, ΠΡΟΜΑΧΟΙ, and an Old Structure in the Story of the '*Iliad*'." *Mnemosyne* 44:17–62.

———. 1992. "The Achaean Wall and the Seven Gates of Thebes." *Hermes* 120:401–411.

Sinos, Dale S. 1975. *The Entry of Achilles into Greek Epic*. PhD diss., The Johns Hopkins University. Baltimore.

Slatkin, Laura M. 1991. *The Power of Thetis: Allusion and Interpretation in the* Iliad. Berkeley.

Smith, Cecil, and Cecil Torr. 1892. "Egypt and Mycenaean Antiquities." *Classical Review* 6:462-466.

Smith, D. J. 1977. "The Singer or the Song? A Reassessment of Lord's 'Oral Theory'." *Man* 12:141–153.

Smith, Peter M. 1981. "*Aineiadai* as Patrons of *Iliad* XX and the Homeric Hymn to Aphrodite." *Harvard Studies in Classical Philology* 85:17–58.

Snodgrass, Anthony McElrea. 1974. "An Historical Homeric Society?" *The Journal of Hellenic Studies* 94:114–125.

Soliński, Jędrzej. 2019. "Zakres wariacji w konstrukcji pieśni w ruskiej tradycji epickiej (byliny). Zarys problemu [Range of Variations in the Structure of the Russian Oral Epic Song (The Bylina). The Sketch of a problem]." In *Epos od Homera do Martina*, ed. B. Błaszkiewicz, J. Godlewicz-Adamiec, 153–162. Gdańsk.

Stählin, Friedrich. 1923. "Der geometrische Stil in der *Ilias*." *Philologus* 78:280–301.

Stanford, William B. 1939. "Ambiguity in Homer." In *Ambiguity in Greek Literature: Studies in Theory and Practice*, 97–114. Oxford.

———. 1952. "The Homeric Etymology of the Name Odysseus." *Classical Philology* 47:209–213.

———, ed. 1965. *The* Odyssey *of Homer*. 2 vols. London.

Stanley, Keith. 1993. *The Shield of Homer: Narrative Structure in the* Iliad. Princeton.

Starke, Frank. 1997. "Troia im Kontext des historisch-politischen und sprachlichen Umfeldes Kleinasiens im 2. Jahrtausend." *Studia Troica* 7:447–487.

Steinrück, Martin. 1922. "Der Bericht des Proteus." *Quaderni Urbinati di Cultura Classica* n.s. 42:47–60.

Stolz, B. A., and R. S. Shannon III, eds. 1976. *Oral Literature and the Formula*. Ann Arbor, MI.

Suerbaum, Werner. 1968. "Die Ich-Erzählungen des Odysseus: Überlegungen zur epischen Technik der *Odyssee*." *Poetica* 2:150–177.

Suter, Ann. 1993. "Paris and Dionysos: Iambos in the *Iliad*." *Arethusa* 26:1–18.

Svenbro, Jesper. 1976. *La parole et le marbre: Aux origines de la poétique Grecque*. Lund.

Szyjewski, Andrzej. 2014. *Mitologia australijska jako nośnik tożsamości* [Australian Mythology as a Bearer of Identity]. Kraków.

———. 2016. "Zmiany relacji mit—rytuał w australijskich ceremoniach ognia [Variability in Myth-Ritual Content in the Australian Aboriginal Fire Ceremonies]." *Quaestiones Oralitatis* 2.11: 183–216.

Śmieszek, Antoni J. 1926. *Geneza podania greckiego o Memnonie, królu Etjopów (De origine Graece fabulae quae fertur de Memnone rege Aethiopum)*. Cracow.

Taplin, Oliver. 1992. *Homeric Soundings: The Shaping of the* Iliad. Oxford.

Tedlock, Dennis. 1977. "Toward an Oral Poetics." *New Literary History* 8:507–519.

Teffeteller, Annette. 2003. "Homeric Excuses." *Classical Quarterly* 53:15–31.

Teodorsson, Sven-Tage. 2006. "Eastern Literacy, Greek Alphabet, and Homer." *Mnemosyne* 59:161–187.

Thalmann, William G. 1984. *Conventions of Form and Thought in Early Greek Epic Poetry*. Baltimore.

Thomas, Rosalind. 1989. *Oral Tradition and Written Record in Classical Athens*. Cambridge.

———. 1992. *Literacy and Orality in Ancient Greece*. Cambridge.

Tichy, Eva. 1981. "Hom. ἀνδροτῆτα und die Vorgeschichte des daktylischen Hexameters." *Glotta* 59:28–67.

Torres-Guerra, José. 1995. "Die homerische *Thebais* und die *Amphiaraos-Ausfahrt*." *Eranos* 93:39–45.

Touchefeu-Meynier, Odette. 1984. "Astyanax I." *Lexicon Iconographicum Mythologiae Classicae* 2:929–937.

Tracy, Stephen V. 1997. "The Structures of the *Odyssey*." In Morris and Powell 1997:360–379.

Turner, Victor. 1970. *The Forest of Symbols: Aspects of Ndembu Ritual*. Ithaca.

Trzcionkowski, Lech. 2005. "Historyczne aspekty eposu homeryckiego." *Literatura Grecji Starożytnej, t. I: Epika—Liryka—Dramat*. Lublin.

Tsagalis, Christos C. 2004. "The Poetics of Sorrow: Thetis' Lament in *Iliad* 18, 52–64." *Quaderni Urbinati di Cultura Classica* n.s. 76:9–32.

———. 2008. *The Oral Palimpsest: Exploring Intertextuality in the Homeric Epics*. Hellenic Studies 29. Washington, DC. http://nrs.harvard.edu/urn-3:hul.ebook:CHS_TsagalisC.The_Oral_Palimpsest.2008

———. 2011. "Towards an Oral, Intertextual Neoanalysis." *Journal of Classical Studies* 3:209–244.

Tsopanakis, Agapitos. 1992. "Lestrigoni." *Quaderni Urbinati di Cultura Classica* n.s. 40:7–13.

Turner, Victor. 1970. *The Forest of Symbols: Aspects of Ndembu Ritual*. Ithaca.

Usher, Mark D. 2003. "The Reception of Homer as Oral Poetry." *Oral Tradition* 18:79–81.

Van Dijk, J. 1997. *Αἶνοι, Λόγοι, Μῦθοι: Fables in Contexts in Archaic. Classical and Hellenistic Greek Literature*. *Mnemosyne* Supplementum 166. Leiden.

van der Mije, S. R. 1987. "Achilles' God-Given Strength (*Iliad* A 178 and Gifts from the Gods in Homer)." *Mnemosyne* 40:243–267.

van Groningen, Bernard A. 1935. "Eléments inorganiques dans la composition de l'Iliade et de l'Odyssée." *Revue des Études Homériques* 5:3–24.

van Otterlo, Willem A. A. 1948. *De Ringcompositie als Opbouwprincipe in de Gedichten von Homerus*. Amsterdam.

Vansina, Jan. 1985. *Oral Tradition as History*. London.

van Thiel, Helmut. 1982. *Iliaden und Ilias*. Basel.

Van Wees, Hans. 1986. "Leaders of Men? Military Organisation in the *Iliad*." *Classical Quarterly* 36:285–303.

———. 1992. *Status Warriors: War, Violence and Society in Homer and History*. Amsterdam.

———. 1994a. "The Homeric Way of War: The *Iliad* and the Hoplite Phalanx (I)." *Greece and Rome* 41:1–18.

———. 1994b. "The Homeric Way of War: The *Iliad* and the Hoplite Phalanx (II)." *Greece and Rome* 41:131–155.

———. 1997. "Homeric Warfare." In Morris and Powell 1997:668–693.

Veselova, Inna. Forthcoming. "Transforming Reality: Personal Names in Ritual Speech. The Vinogradye or "Song of Praise" from the Russian North."

Vidal-Naquet, Pierre. 1968. "The Black Hunter and the Origin of the Athenian *Ephebeia*." *Proceedings of the Cambridge Philological Society* 14:49–64.

———. 1998. *The Black Hunter: Forms of Thought and Forms of Society in the Greek World.* Baltimore.

Vinogradov, J. G. 1969. "Cyclic Poetry in Olbia." *Vestnik Drevnei Istorii* 3.109:142–148.

Visser, Edzard. 1988. "Formulae or Single Words? Towards a New Theory on Homeric Verse-Making." *Würzburger Jahrbuch für Altertumswissenschaft* 14:21–37.

Vivante, Paolo. 1980. "Men's Epithets in Homer: An Essay in Poetic Syntax." *Glotta* 58:157–172.

———. 1982. *The Epithets in Homer: A Study in Poetic Values.* New Haven.

Volk, Katharina. 2002. "ΚΛΕΟΣ ΑΦΘΙΤΟΝ Revisited." *Classical Philology* 97:61–68.

von der Mühll, Peter. 1940. "*Odyssee*." *Paulys Realencyclopädie der classischen Altertumswissenschaft*, Suppl. VII, 696–767.

———. 1952. *Kritisches Hypomnema zur Ilias.* Basel.

———. 1954. "Zur Frage, wie sich die Kyprien zur *Odyssee* verhalten." *Westöstliche Abhandlungen Festschrift Rudolf Tschudi.* Wiesbaden.

———. 1995. "Homers *Ilias*: Einleitung." *Museum Helveticum* 52:193–201.

Wachter, Rudolf. 1998. "'Oral Poetry' in ungewohntem Kontext: Hinweise auf mündliche Dichtungstechnik in den pompejanischen Wandinschriften." *Zeitschrift für Papyrologie und Epigraphik* 121:73–89.

Wace, A. J B., and F. H. Stubbings, eds. 1962. *A Companion to Homer.* London.

Wackernagel, Jacob. 1969. "Zum homerischen dual." In *Kleine Schriften,* Vol. 1, 538-546. Göttingen. Orig. pub. 1877, in *Zeitschrift für vergleichende Sprachforschung* 23:302–310.

———. 1970. *Sprachliche Untersuchungen zu Homer.* Gottingen. Orig. pub. 1916.

Wade-Gery, Henry T. 1952. *The Poet of the Iliad.* Cambridge.

Watkins, Calvert. 1995. *How to Kill a Dragon: Aspects of Indo-European Poetics.* New York.

Webster, Thomas B. L. 1964. *From Mycenae to Homer.* New York.

Welcker, Friedrich Gottlieb. 1865–1882. *Der epische Cyclus: oder die homerischen Dichter.* Hildesheim. Repr. 1981.

West, Martin L., ed. 1966. *Hesiod,* Theogony. Oxford.

———. 1969. "The Achaean Wall." *Classical Review* 19:255–260.

———. 1973. "Greek Poetry 2000–700 B.C." *Classical Quarterly* 23:179–192.

———. 1974. *Studies on Greek Elegy and Iambus.* Berlin.

———. 1981. "The Singing of Homer and the Modes of Early Greek Music." *The Journal of Hellenic Studies* 101:113–129.

———. 1988. "The Rise of the Greek Epic." *The Journal of Hellenic Studies* 108:151–172.

———. 1995. "The Date of the *Iliad*." *Museum Helveticum* 52:203–219.

———. 1996. “The Epic Cycle.” *Oxford Classical Dictionary*, ed. S. Hornblower, A. Spawforth, 531. Oxford.

———. 1997. *The East Face of Helicon: West Asiatic Elements in Greek Poetry and Myth*. Oxford.

———. 1998. *Homeri Ilias*. Stuttgart.

———. 2000. “*Iliad* and *Aethiopis* on the Stage: Aeschylus and Son.” *Classical Quarterly* 50:338–352.

———. 2001. *Studies in the Text and Transmission of the* Iliad. Munich.

———, ed. and trans. 2003a. *Greek Epic Fragments from the Seventh to the Fifth Centuries BC*. Cambridge, MA.

———. 2003b. “*Iliad* and *Aethiopis*.” *Classical Quarterly* 53:1–14.

———. 2011. *Making of the* Iliad*: Disquisition and Analytical Commentary*. Oxford.

———. 2013. *The Epic Cycle: A Commentary on the Lost Troy Epics*. Oxford.

West, Stephanie. 1988. “Books I–IV.” In Heubeck, West, and Hainsworth:vol. 1, 51–247.

Whallon, William. 1961. “The Homeric Epithets.” *Yale Classical Studies* 17:97–142.

———. 1966. “The Shield of Ajax.” *Yale Classical Studies* 22:7–36.

———. 1969. *Formula, Character, and Context: Studies in Homeric, Old English, and Old Testament Poetry*. Cambridge, MA.

———. 1979. “Is Hector *Androphonos*?” In *Arktouros: Hellenic Studies presented to Bernard M. W. Knox on the Occasion of his 65th Birthday*, ed. Glen W. Bowersock, Walter Burkert, and Michael C. J. Putnam, 19–24. Berlin.

Whitman, Cedric H. 1958. *Homer and the Heroic Tradition*. Cambridge, MA.

Wieniewski, Ignacy. 1928. *O zapowiadaniu przyszłych zdarzeń u Homera*. Kraków.

Wilamowitz-Moellendorff, Ulrich. 1884. *Philologische Untersuchungen. Siebentes Heft: Homerische Untersuchungen*. Berlin.

———. 1916. *Die Ilias und Homer*. Berlin.

———. 1931. *Der Glaube der Hellenen*. Vol. I. Berlin.

Willcock, Malcolm M. 1964. “Mythological Paradeigma in the *Iliad*.” *Classical Quarterly* 14:141–154.

———. 1970. “Some Aspects of the Gods in the *Iliad*.” *Bulletin of the Institute of Classical Studies* 17:1–10.

———. 1976. *A Companion to the* Iliad*. Based on the Translation by Richmond Lattimore*. Chicago.

———. 1977. “Ad Hoc Invention in the *Iliad*.” *Harvard Studies in Classical Philology* 18:41–53.

———. 1978. *The Iliad: Books I–XII*. London.

———. 1984. *The Iliad: Books XIII–XXIV*. London.

———. 1997. “Neoanalysis.” In Morris and Powell 1997:174–189.

———. 2002. “Menelaos in the *Iliad*.” In Reichel and Rengakos 2002:221–229.

Wilson, Christopher H., trans. and ed. 1996. *Homer,* Iliad. *Books VIII and IX.* Warminster.

Winiarczyk, Marek. 1997. "Mit w Grecji antycznej." *Meander* 52:417–435.

Woudhuizen, Frederik Ch. 2017. "The Language of the Trojans." *Homere et l'Anatolie* 3:127–140.

Waytt, W. F. 1982. "Homeric ἌΤΗ." *The American Journal of Philology* 103:247–276.

Yates, Frances A. 1966. *The Art of Memory.* Chicago.

Zaborowski, Robert. 2002. *La crainte et le courage dans l'Iliade et l'Odyssée.* Warsaw.

Zadka, Małgorzata. 2016. "Lists and Registers in Written and Oral Tradition." *Quaestiones Oralitatis* 2.1:141–152.

Zanker, Graham. 1994. *The Heart of Achilles: Characterization and Personal Ethics in the* Iliad. Ann Arbor.

Zarker, John W. 1965. "King Eëtion and Thebe as Symbols in the *Iliad.*" *Classical Journal* 61:110–114.

Zawielski, Friedrich S. 1981. *Czas i jego pomiary.* Warsaw.

Ziegler, Ch. A. 1997. "Analysis of the Roswell Myth: A Traditional Folk Motif Clothed in Modern Garb." In *Ufo Crash at Roswell: The Genesis of a Modern Myth*, ed. B. Saler, Ch. A. Ziegler, Ch. B. Moore, 30–73. Washington, DC.

Zieliński, Karol. 2004. "Removing the Hunch or Thersites Re-appreciated." *Eos* 91:195–218.

———. 2006. *Słońce w rozpaczy. Liryka miłosna Safony w aspekcie oralności* [*Sun in despair. Sappho's love lyrics in the aspect of orality*]. Wrocław.

———. 2010. "Śunahśepha The 'Dog's Member' and Hermes 'The Dog Strangler', or Dog as *Pharmakos* in the Iambic Code." *Eos* 97:193–231.

———. 2013. "Alienacja i wykluczenie jednostki ze społeczeństwa w greckiej epice archaicznej." In *Świat starożytny. Państwo i społeczeństwo*, ed. R. Kulesza, M. Stępień, E. Szabat, M. Daszuta, 106–116. Warsaw.

———. 2015a. "Skąd Demodok znał historię historię Odysa? Problematyka prawdy i fikcji w eposie oralnym [Whence Demodocus Knew Odysseus' Story—the Question of Truth and Fiction in the Oral Epic]." *Quaestiones Oralitatis* I 1:33–49.

———. 2015b. "Zmiany znaczenia komunikatu w przejściu od kultury oralnej do piśmienniczej w warunkach Grecji archaicznej." In *Historia idei komunikacji,* ed. M. Wendland, 271–304. Poznań.

———. 2016a. "Potwór jako zwierciadło herosa epickiego [Monster as the Mirror of the Epic Hero]." *Rocznik Lubuski* 42:167–188.

———. 2016b. "Wzorzec herosa w kulturze greckiej przy przejściu od tradycji oralnej do piśmienniczej [El modelo del héroe en la cultura griega durante la transición de la tradición oral a la escrita]." In *Mitologizacja człowieka w kulturze i literaturze iberyjskiej i polskiej*, ed. Wojciech Charchalis and Bogdan Trocha, 51–68. Zielona Góra.

———. 2019a. "Women as Victims of War in Homer's Oral Poetics." *Humanities* 8:1–16.

———. 2019b. "Selecting a Scapegoat. The Problem of Guilt and Group Domination in the Dispute between Achilles and Agamemnon." *Anodos—Studies of the Ancient World* 14:245–252.

———. 2020. "Odysseus-Trickster and the Issue of Compatibility of the Image of the Hero with Its Function in the Traditions of the Oral Epic." *Studia Religiologica* 53:187–208.

———. 2021a. "The Flexibility of Traditional Norms in the Perspective of Changes in Oral Narratives. The Case of Homer." In *Worldview in Narrative and Non-narrative Expression: the Cognitive, Anthropological and Literary Perspective*, ed. Maciej Czeremski and Karol Zieliński, 59–87. Wiesbaden.

———. 2021b. "Motyw winy Heleny w tradycji epickiej i w dyskursie Iliady." [The motif of Helen's Guilt in Epic Tradition and in the Discourse of the Iliad] *Collectanea Philologica* 24:5–31.

Index of Passages and Scholia

Index of Subjects